The Eight Guideposts to Economic Thinking

These eight guideposts provide the foundation for the economic way of thinking (they are discussed in Chapter 1). To do well in this course you will need to understand and be able to apply these ideas to a wide range of issues.

1. The Use of Scarce Resources Is Costly; Trade-offs Must Always Be Made.
2. Individuals Choose Purposefully — They Try to Get the Most From Their Limited Resources.
3. Incentives Matter — Choice Is Influenced in a Predictable Way by Changes in Incentives.
4. Individuals Make Decisions at the Margin.
5. Although Information Can Help Us Make Better Choices, Its Acquisition Is Costly.
6. Beware of the Secondary Effects: Economic Actions Often Generate Indirect As Well As Direct Effects.
7. The Value of a Good or Service Is Subjective.
8. The Test of a Theory Is Its Ability to Predict.

Special Topics

These Special Topics covered in the "Applying the Basics" section use the basic concepts to analyze important current-day topics.

1. Government Spending and Taxation
2. The Internet: How Is It Changing the Economy?
3. The Economics of Social Security
4. The Stock Market: Its Function, Performance, and Potential as an Investment Opportunity
5. The Crisis of 2008: Causes and Lessons for the Future
6. Lessons from the Great Depression
7. Lessons from the Japanese Experience
8. The Federal Budget and the National Debt
9. The Economics of Health Care
10. School Choice: Can It Improve the Quality of Education in America?
11. Earnings Differences Between Men and Women
12. Do Labor Unions Increase the Wages of Workers?
13. Are We Running Out of Resources?
14. Difficult Environmental Cases and the Role of Government

Keys to Economic Prosperity

These keys to the economic prosperity of a nation are highlighted throughout the text.

1. **Human Ingenuity.** Economic goods are the result of human ingenuity and action; thus, the size of the economic pie is variable, not fixed. [Economics Chapter 2; Macroeconomics Chapter 2; Microeconomics Chapter 2]

2. **Private Ownership.** Private ownership provides people with a strong incentive to take care of things and develop resources in ways that are highly valued by others. [Economics Chapter 2; Macroeconomics Chapter 2; Microeconomics Chapter 2]

3. **Gains from Trade.** Trade makes it possible for individuals to generate more output through specialization and division of labor, large-scale production processes, and the dissemination of improved products and production methods. [Economics Chapter 2; Macroeconomics Chapter 2; Microeconomics Chapter 2]

4. **Invisible Hand Principle.** Market prices coordinate the actions of self-interested individuals and direct them toward activities that promote the general welfare. [Economics Chapter 3; Macroeconomics Chapter 3; Microeconomics Chapter 3]

5. **Profits and Losses.** Profits direct producers toward activities that increase the value of resources; losses impose a penalty on those who reduce the value of resources. [Economics Chapter 3; Macroeconomics Chapter 3; Microeconomics Chapter 3]

6. **Competition.** Competition motivates businesses to produce efficiently, cater to the views of consumers, and search for innovative improvements. [Economics Chapter 22; Microeconomics Chapter 10]

7. **Entrepreneurship.** The entrepreneurial discovery and development of improved products and production processes is a central element of economic progress. [Economics Chapter 23; Microeconomics Chapter 11]

8. **Productivity and Earnings.** In a market economy, productivity and earnings are closely linked. In order to earn a large income, one must provide large benefits to others. [Economics Chapter 26; Microeconomics Chapter 14]

9. **Innovation and the Capital Market.** If the potential gains from innovative ideas and human ingenuity are going to be fully realized, it must be relatively easy for individuals to try their innovative and potentially ingenious ideas, but difficult to continue if the idea is a bad one. [Economics Chapter 27; Microeconomics Chapter 15]

10. **Price Stability.** Maintenance of price stability is the essence of sound monetary policy; price stability provides the foundation for both economic stability and the efficient operation of markets. [Economics Chapter 15; Macroeconomics Chapter 15]

11. **International Trade.** When people are permitted to engage freely in international trade, they are able to achieve higher income levels and living standards than would otherwise be possible. [Economics Chapter 18; Macroeconomics Chapter 18; Microeconomics Chapter 17]

12. **Role of Government.** Governments promote economic progress when they protect individuals and their property, enforce contracts impartially, provide access to money of stable value, avoid high taxes and excessive regulation, and foster competitive markets and free international trade. [Economics Chapter 16; Macroeconomics Chapter 16]

Macroeconomics

Global Economic Watch Edition

13th edition

Gwartney | Stroup | Sobel | Macpherson

CENGAGE
Learning™

Australia • Brazil • Japan • Korea • Mexico • Singapore • Spain • United Kingdom • United States

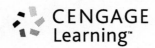

Macroeconomics: Global Economic Watch Edition, 13th edition

Executive Editors:
 Maureen Staudt
 Michael Stranz

Senior Project Development Manager:
 Linda deStefano

Marketing Specialist:
 Courtney Sheldon

Senior Production/Manufacturing Manager:
 Donna M. Brown

PreMedia Manager:
 Joel Brennecke

Sr. Rights Acquisition Account Manager:
 Todd Osborne

Cover Image:
Getty Images*

*Unless otherwise noted, all cover images used by Custom Solutions, a part of Cengage Learning, have been supplied courtesy of Getty Images with the exception of the Earthview cover image, which has been supplied by the National Aeronautics and Space Administration (NASA).

Macroeconomics: Private and Public Choice, 13th Edition
James D. Gwartney | Richard L. Stroup
Russell S. Sobel | David Macpherson

© 2011, 2008 Cengage Learning. All rights reserved.

Global Economic Watch: Impact on Economics, 1st Edition
Global Economics Crisis Resource Center

© 2010 Cengage Learning. All rights reserved.

For product information and technology assistance, contact us at
Cengage Learning Customer & Sales Support, 1-800-354-9706

For permission to use material from this text or product,
submit all requests online at **cengage.com/permissions**
Further permissions questions can be emailed to
permissionrequest@cengage.com

This book contains select works from existing Cengage Learning resources and was produced by Cengage Learning Custom Solutions for collegiate use. As such those adopting and/or contributing to this work are responsible for editorial content accuracy, continuity and completeness.

Compilation © 2010. Cengage Learning.

ISBN-13: 978-1-111-06752-6

ISBN-10: 1-111-06752-X

Cengage Learning
5191 Natorp Boulevard
Mason, Ohio 45040
USA

Cengage Learning is a leading provider of customized learning solutions with office locations around the globe, including Singapore, the United Kingdom, Australia, Mexico, Brazil, and Japan. Locate your local office at:
international.cengage.com/region.

Cengage Learning products are represented in Canada by Nelson Education, Ltd.
For your lifelong learning solutions, visit **www.cengage.com/custom.**
Visit our corporate website at **www.cengage.com.**

Printed in the United States of America

Brief Custom Contents

Macroeconomics
Global Economic Watch Edition
13e
Gwartney | Stroup | Sobel | Macpherson

Macroeconomics
Private and Public Choice
13e
Gwartney | Stroup | Sobel | Macpherson

with

Global Economic Crisis: Impact on Economics
(located after Index)

Preface

This is an exciting time for the study of economics. Most of our lives have been affected by the financial crisis of 2008. Why did this crisis occur? How will it affect our economic future? Has the political response saved us from economic catastrophe, or has it made matters worse? What can we learn from previous experience with economic difficulties? These are vitally important questions that are on the minds of our students. This text addresses all of them and provides both economic analysis and empirical evidence that will enhance understanding of these critical issues.

Some argue that the Crisis of 2008 was the result of capitalist instability, greed of Wall Street bankers, and regulators who were asleep on the job. Others argue that the crisis was the result of government policies that undermined sound lending practices, manipulated interest rates, and promoted excessive debt. Who is right? Of course, the precise answer to such complex questions is debatable, but economic analysis provides considerable insight.

Throughout the life of this text, our goal has been to use the tools of economics to explain how the real world works and to do so in a clear and understandable manner. Recent economic developments have enhanced the importance of this strategy. Perhaps more than ever before, students are seeking to understand the world in which they live and the critical issues we confront. Indeed, this is a teachable moment for economics instructors. This thought was constantly on our minds, as we revised this edition and focused the core principles of economics on the central issues of our day.

Organization of the Text and Instructor Flexibility

The organization of *Economics: Private and Public Choice* is designed to provide instructors with maximum flexibility. Those using the full-length text for a two-semester course can cover either microeconomics or macroeconomics first. As in recent editions, the text is divided into core chapters and a concluding special topics section. The twenty-eight core chapters cover all of the material taught in most principles courses, and they are presented in the usual manner. Examples and data from the real world are used to reinforce the analysis. In addition, Beyond the Basics includes fourteen relatively short special topic applications on high-profile topics like Social Security, the Economics of Health Care, and the Crisis of 2008. Also included in this section are Applications that address questions such as "Is discrimination responsible for the earnings differences between men and women?" and "Are we running out of resources?." These features are sure to grab the interest of students and are short enough for coverage during a single class period. Our own teaching experience indicates that these applications will enrich an economics course. They will also make it easier for instructors to "pick and choose" and thereby tailor the text readings to fit their own preferences and objectives.

Those teaching a microeconomics course and like to stress the importance of public choice will probably want to cover the first six chapters before beginning the core microeconomics section. Other instructors will prefer to cover only the first four chapters and then move immediately to the core microeconomics material. The book is designed for both of these options.

Those teaching macroeconomics integrating public choice will probably want to cover Chapters 5 and 6 prior to the core macroeconomics material. Others may want to move directly from Chapter 4 (or Chapter 3) to the core macro. The macroeconomics chapters have been written such that there will be no problems with either option.

The text is accompanied by a robust set of online learning tools designed to support your classroom work and an Aplia component that includes real-time, interactive tutorials, online experiments, and automatically graded problem sets. Likewise, the book's dynamic PowerPoint presentation—considered by many to be the best in the principles market—has been further enhanced with multimedia to facilitate your teaching.

Changes in this Edition

Substantial changes in both conditions and policies have occurred in recent years. These changes are reflected fully in this edition. The core macroeconomic material has been reorganized in a manner that will make it easier to understand current issues and controversies. Economists are not of one mind with regard to fiscal policy, and a chapter has been added to provide more comprehensive treatment of this issue.

Chapter 11 presents the Keynesian view of fiscal policy and considers its historical development and evolutionary change during recent decades. Following in the Keynesian tradition, Chapter 11 highlights the importance of aggregate demand and the potential use of fiscal policy to maintain full employment equilibrium.

Chapter 12 presents alternative perspectives that highlight the importance of incentives and secondary effects. This chapter contains new sections on the impact of fiscal policy during a severe recession, fiscal stimulus and the speed of recovery, tax cuts versus spending increases, and the paradoxes of saving and spending. Taken together, these two fiscal policy chapters provide a balanced comprehensive analysis of the modern debate about the potential and limitations of fiscal policy.

Chapter 13 on Money and Banking has been updated to reflect recent changes in how the Federal Reserve controls the money supply. The impact of the Fed's power to pay interest to commercial banks on their excess and required reserves is analyzed. A new section on Recent Fed Policy, the Monetary Base, and the Money Supply has also been incorporated into the Money and Banking chapter.

Chapter 14 on Monetary Policy has been substantially revised. New sections on time lags and economic stability, measurement of shifts in monetary policy, the Taylor rule, and monetary policy and the Crisis of 2008 are now included in this chapter.

Chapter 15 on Stabilization Policy has also been substantially revised. This chapter includes a new section on what we have learned about macro policy, which highlights both points of agreement and areas of continuing debate.

The last two chapters of the core macro focus on economic growth. They highlight the importance of trade, entrepreneurship and innovation, and investment as sources of growth. Building on the work of Douglass North, Joseph Schumpeter, William Baumol, and Daron Acemoglu, these chapters focus on the institutional foundations of growth and prosperity. While one new chapter has been added, the overall length of the core macro is largely unchanged.

Three timely new features have been added to the Special Topic part of the text, while two others were omitted. The three new special topics are (1) The Crisis of 2008: Causes and Lessons for the Future, (2) Lessons From the Great Depression, and (3) Lessons From the Japanese Experience. The special topic on The Federal Budget and the National Debt was substantially revised and updated to reflect recent changes in this area. This package of applications provides instructors with powerful materials with which to address the current economic difficulties and their future implications.

Additional Text Features

Economics: Private and Public Choice retains several features that make the presentation of economics both more interesting and understandable:

✗ **Keys to Economic Prosperity.** Students often fail to appreciate the organizational and institutional factors that are the foundation for economic progress. In order to help remedy this situation, we have incorporated a "Keys to Economic Prosperity" feature that highlights the importance of factors like gains from trade, secure property rights, competition, and free trade as sources of economic prosperity. In all, twelve key factors that underlie modern economic prosperity are highlighted at appropriate places throughout the text and are also listed on the inside of the front cover.

✗ **Economics at the Movies.** Both the macro and micro edition again contain box features throughout the text called "Economics at the Movies." The boxes describe various scenes from popular movies that reflect economic concepts. A number of instructors, including the authors, now use clips from popular movies to stimulate student interest and drive home the importance of these concepts. The instructor's manual provides more ideas about how this can be done effectively.

✗ **Applications in Economics.** "Applications in Economics" boxes apply economic theory to real-world issues and controversies. These features illustrate the importance and power of the principles covered in the text.

✗ **Measures of Economic Activity.** The "Measures of Economic Activity" boxes explain how important economic indicators such as the unemployment rate and the index of leading indicators are assembled and what they mean.

✗ **Outstanding Economists.** Boxes throughout the text highlight the lives of major economists and focus on how their work has contributed to the development of economics.

✗ **Myths of Economics.** These boxed articles dispel commonly held fallacies of economic reasoning. Because Students they are tomorrow's leaders, we believe that they should be aware of common economic misperceptions that tend to hamper a nation's economic progress.

✗ **Chapter Focus Questions and Closing Key Point Summaries.** Each chapter begins with four or five questions that summarize the focus of the chapter. At the end of each chapter, the Key Points section provides the student with a concise statement of the material covered in the chapter (the chapter learning objectives). These two features help students better integrate the material into the broader economic picture.

✗ **Critical Analysis Questions.** Each chapter concludes with a set of discussion questions and problems designed to test the student's ability to analyze economic issues and to apply economic theory to real-world events. Appendix B at the end of the text contains suggested answers for approximately half of these questions.

Supplementary Materials

For the Student

Coursebooks The Coursebooks for this edition were prepared by our coauthor Russell Sobel and are now available not in two but three versions, covering all three courses: economics, microeconomics, and macroeconomics. The Coursebooks are more than study guides. Each includes numerous multiple-choice, true/false, and discussion questions to help students self-test their knowledge of each chapter. Answers and short explanations for most questions are provided in the back of the Coursebooks. Each chapter also contains problem and project exercises designed to improve the student's knowledge of the mechanics. Like the textbook, the Coursebooks are designed to help students develop the economic way of thinking.

Support Web Site (http://www.cengage.com/economics/gwartney) Valuable resources can be found on the text's online support site. Students will find interactive flash cards, online practice quizzes, and more.

For the Instructor

We are sure that many of the features incorporated in this textbook will help you become a better teacher and make your classes more interesting to students. Personally, we have incorporated the Keys to Economic Prosperity series, movie clips, ABC Video clips, clips by John Stossel, homework assignments, and online quiz questions into our own classes with great success. The full set of supplements that accompany the book includes the following:

Aplia Aplia (www.aplia.com) has joined forces with South-Western, the leading publisher for principles of economics and finance, to create the Aplia Integrated Textbook Solution. More students are currently using an Aplia product for principles of economics than those who are using all other Web-based learning programs combined. Because the homework in Aplia is automatically graded, you can assign homework more frequently to ensure your students are putting forth full effort and getting the most out of your class.

ABC News Videos This supplement consists of high-interest clips from current news events as well as historic raw footage going back forty years. Perfect for discussion starters or to enrich your lectures and spark interest in the material in the text, these brief videos provide students with a new lens through which to view the past and present, one that will greatly enhance their knowledge and understanding of significant events and open up new dimensions in learning. Clips are drawn from such programs as *World News Tonight, Good Morning America, This Week, PrimeTime Live, 20/20,* and *Nightline,* as well as numerous ABC News specials and material from the Associated Press Television News and British Movietone News collections. Your South-Western Publishing representative will be happy to provide a complete listing of the videos and policies addressed.

Stossel in the Classroom Videos Most instructors are looking for ways to get their students engaged and excited while developing their critical thinking skills. Thousands of teachers across the country have experienced the benefits of using John Stossel's engaging videos from ABC 20/20. A team of instructors, including authors of this text, worked with ABC and Stossel to put together thirty-one short video clips designed especially for use in college-level economics. The DVDs also contain an *Instructor's Manual* with discussion questions, testing material, related activities, and other ideas about how to use the clips most effectively. http://stosselintheclassroom.org/

Tomlinson Learning Path Videos The Tomlinson videos are an online multimedia video lecture series that provide students with instructional assistance 24/7. Students can watch these segments over and over as they prepare for class, review topics, and study for exams. Lecture notes and quizzes for each segment are also available. Professors may require students to view the videos before class to leave the class time free for activities or further explanation. www.cengage.com/economics/tomlinson

JoinIn Turning Point® CD JoinIn is a response system that allows you to transform your classroom and assess your students' progress with instant in-class quizzes and polls. Our exclusive agreement to offer TurningPoint® software lets you pose book-specific questions and display students' answers seamlessly within the Microsoft PowerPoint slides of your own lecture, in conjunction with the "clicker" hardware of your choice. Enhance how your students interact with you, your lecture, and each other. For college and university adopters only. Contact your local South-Western representative to learn more.

Contemporary Issues in Economics We are proud to introduce Cengage's collection, *Contemporary Issues in Economics* as a resource for in-depth coverage of key economic topics. This collection includes readings on major issues pertaining to education, health care, Social Security, unemployment, inflation, and international trade. Our collection examines issues that interest students, while building on core economic principles. By delving deeply into timely interesting issues, students begin to see fundamental economic concepts as important in understanding issues that affect them personally as well as in understanding today's headlines. To view the readings and obtain more information about how to enhance your course with this material, visit **www.textchoice.com/econ_issues**.

WebTutor™ Toolbox for WebCT, Blackboard, and eCollege WebTutor will allow you to jumpstart your course whether you want to simply Web-enable your class or put an entire course online. Using a WebTutor cartridge, it's easy to add, edit, reorganize, or delete content customized for *Economics: Private and Public Choice*. The content includes quizzing, flash cards, and more. To find out more about WebTutor, contact your local South-Western representative. (Other platform choices are available upon request.)

Test Banks The Test Banks for the thirteenth edition were prepared by the author team with the assistance of Joe Calhoun and David Gwartney. The authors have worked hard to update and improve the Test Banks for this edition. The two Test Banks contain approximately 7,000 questions—multiple-choice and short answer. Within each chapter, the questions correspond to the major subheadings of the text. The first ten questions of each chapter are suitable for use as a comprehensive quiz covering the material of the chapter. The multiple-choice questions from the Coursebook and Online practice quizzes are also included in special sections of the Test Bank. Instructors who would like to motivate their students to study the Coursebook and Online practice quizzes can easily use these questions and incorporate them into their quizzes and exams.

Computerized Test Banks (ExamView®) The computerized Test Banks for this edition have been enhanced significantly. ExamView contains all of the questions in the printed Test Bank so that you create and customize tests in minutes. You can easily edit and import your own questions and graphics and edit and maneuver existing questions. You can also use ExamView to test and grade online.

PowerPoint We believe that our PowerPoint presentation, prepared by Joe Connors, is the best you will find in the principles market. The presentation includes chapter-by-chapter lecture notes with fully animated, hyperlinked slides of the textbook's exhibits. Its dynamic graphs and accompanying captions make it easy for instructors to present (and students to follow) sequential changes. The graphs are also used to highlight various relationships among economic variables. In order to facilitate classroom discussion and interaction, questions are strategically interspersed throughout the chapters to help students develop the economic way of thinking. Instructions explaining how professors can easily add, delete, and modify slides in order to customize the presentation to their liking are included. If instructors want to make the PowerPoint presentation available to students, they can place it on their Web site (or the site for their course).

Instructor's Manual and Instructor's Resource CD The *Instructor's Manual* was prepared by our coauthor David Macpherson. It contains special sections for Advanced Placement instructors prepared by James Chasey and Francis McMann, two of the nation's leading A/P instructors. Information on how to use and modify the PowerPoint material is found at the beginning of the *Instructor's Manual*. Also included at the front of the manual is information about Examview, the computerized testing software that accompanies the book. The manual is divided by chapters, and each chapter is divided into three parts. The first part consists of a detailed chapter outline in lecture-note form. It is designed to help instructors organize their notes to match the thirteenth edition of the book. Instructors can easily prepare detailed, personalized notes by revising the computerized version of the lecture notes on the *Instructor's Resource CD*. The second part of each chapter contains teaching tips, sources of supplementary materials, and other helpful information. Part 3 of each chapter consists of in-class economic games and experiments. Contributed in part by

Professor Charles Stull of Kalamazoo College, the games are highly popular with many instructors. We hope you will try them.

The *Instructor's Resource CD* contains the key supplements designed to aid instructors, including the content from the *Instructor's Manual*, Test Banks, and PowerPoint lecture and exhibit slides for overhead use.

Support Web Site for Instructors (www.cengage.com/economics/gwartney) This password-protected Web site includes some of the same essential resources that can be found on the *Instructor's Resource CD,* including instructor's manuals and test banks in Microsoft Word, and the PowerPoint lecture and exhibit slides. To access the site to download these supplements, register online at **http://www.cengage.com/economics/ gwartney.**

A Note to Instructors

As we try to improve the book from one edition to the next, we rely heavily on our experiences as teachers. But our experience using the book is minuscule compared with that of the hundreds of instructors who use it nationwide. If you encounter problems or have suggestions for improving the book, we urge you to let us know by writing to us in care of Cengage South-Western, 5191 Natorp Blvd., Mason, OH 45040. Such letters are invaluable, and we are glad to receive both praise and suggestions for improvement. Many such suggestions have found their way into this new book.

A Note to Students

This textbook contains several features we think will help you "maximize" (a good economic term) the returns of your study efforts. Here are some of the things that will help you and a few tips for making the most of them:

✗ Each chapter begins with a series of focus questions that communicate the central issues of the chapter. Before you read the chapter, briefly think about the focus questions, why they are important, and how they relate to the material in prior chapters.

✗ The textbook is organized in the form of an outline. The headings within the text (in blue) are the major points of the outline. Minor headings are subpoints under the major headings. In addition, important subpoints within sections are often set off and numbered. Bold italicized type is used to highlight material that is particularly important. Sometimes "Thumbnail Sketches" are included to recap material and help the reader keep the important points mentally organized. Careful use of the headings, highlighted material, and the Thumbnail Sketches will help you master the material.

✗ A "Key Points" summary appears at the end of each chapter. Use the summary as a checklist to determine whether you understand the major points of the chapter.

✗ A review of the exhibits and illustrative pictures will also provide you with a summary of the key points of each chapter. The accompanying captions briefly describe the economic phenomena illustrated by the exhibits.

✗ The key terms introduced in each chapter are defined in the margins. As you study the chapter, go over the marginal definition of each key term as it is introduced. Later, you may also find it useful to review the marginal definitions. If you have forgotten the meaning of a term introduced earlier, consult the glossary at the end of the book.

✗ The boxed features go into more depth on various topics without disrupting the flow of the text. In general, the topics of the boxed features have been chosen because they are a good application of the theory described in the book or because students tend to be interested in them. The boxed features will supplement the text and enhance your understanding of important economic concepts.

✗ The critical analysis questions at the end of each chapter are intended to test your understanding of the economic way of thinking. Answering these questions and solving these problems will greatly enhance your knowledge of the material. Answers to approximately half of these questions are provided in Appendix B.

If you need more practice, be sure to obtain a Coursebook and solve the questions and problems for each chapter. The Coursebook also contains the answers to the multiple-choice questions and a brief explanation of why an answer is correct (and other choices incorrect). In most cases, if you master the concepts of the test items in the Coursebook, you will do well on the quizzes and examinations of your instructor. For extra help, in addition to the Coursebook, visit the book's student support Web site **http://www.cengage .com/economics/gwartney** for online quizzes and other tutorials.

Acknowledgments

A project of this type is a team effort. Through the years, numerous people have assisted us in various ways. We are very much indebted to the excellent team of professionals at South-Western, including Steve Scoble, senior acquisitions editor, for his help and support of our efforts; Susan Smart, senior developmental editor, for her commitment to the development of the project and keeping it on schedule; Jana Lewis, content project manager, for orchestrating the copyediting, proofreading, and indexing; Deanna Ettinger, photo rights editor, who helped us locate and obtain permissions for the many photos and movie stills; and John Carey, senior marketing manager, who worked hard to inform the marketplace about the advantages of the book.

As with previous editions, the contributions of Amy Gwartney were invaluable. She edited several chapters prior to their submission to the publisher and proofed every page of the text. Joab Corey and Joe Connors provided us with valuable suggestions for improvement of the text and assisted with supplementary materials.

We would also like to express our appreciation to Chuck Skipton of the University of Tampa and Joe Connors of Florida State University for their contribution to what we believe is the very best set of PowerPoint slides accompanying an introductory economics text. We also appreciate the contributions of Joseph Calhoun, Lynn MacDonald, Dirk Mateer, and David Gwartney to the Test Bank, online quizzes, and other supplementary materials. James Chasey and Francis McMann provided valuable suggestions and handled the parts of the *Instructor's Manual* designed for those teaching the Advance Placement macroeconomics and microeconomics courses. Robert Lawson of Auburn University assisted us with the preparation of several exhibits. The text still bears an imprint of the contributions of Woody Studenmund of Occidental College and Gary Galles of Pepperdine University, who assisted us in numerous ways with past editions.

Many instructors made important contributions to the thirteenth edition by providing us with insightful critical reviews. The following reviewers helped us improve this edition immensely, and we thank them for their comments:

Pete Calcagno, College of Charleston; Joseph Calhoun, Florida State University; Cathy Carey, Bowling Green University; Lee Coppock, University of Virginia; Tawni Ferrerini, Northern Michigan University; Burton Folsom, Hillsdale College; Robert Higgs, Independent Institute; Randall Holcombe, Florida State University; and Ivan Pongracic, Hillsdale College.

We have often revised material in light of suggestions made by reviewers, users, friends, and even a few competitors. In this regard, we would like to express our appreciation to the following people for their reviews and helpful suggestions for recent editions:

Steve Abid, Grand Rapids Community College; Douglas Agbetsiafa, Indiana University, South Bend; James C.W. Ahiakpor, California State University, Hayward; Ali T. Akarca, University of Illinois at Chicago; Stephen A. Baker, Capital University; Bharati Basu, Central Michigan University; Alana Bhatia, University of Colorado at Boulder; Charles A. Booth, University of Alabama at Birmingham; Donald Boudreaux, George Mason University; George Bowling, St. Charles Community College; Robert Brittingham, Christian Brothers University; Ford J. Brown, University of Minnesota—Morris; Dennis Brennen, Harper College; James Bryan, Manhattanville College; Darcy R. Carr, Coastal Carolina University; Kathy Clark, Edison College; Mike Cohick, Collin County Community College; David S. Collins, Virginia Highlands Community College; Jim F. Couch, University of North Alabama; Steven R. Cunningham, University of Connecticut; George W. Dollar, Clearwater Christian College; Jeff Edwards, Collin County Community College; Christina Esquivel, Navarro College; Robert C. Eyler, Sonoma State University; James R. Fain, Oklahoma State University; Kathryn Finn, Western Washington University; Andrew W. Foshee, McNeese State University; Mark xvi   *Acknowledgments*

Funk, University of Arkansas; Gary Galles, Pepperdine University; Marsha Goldfarb, University of Maryland, Baltimore County; Richard Gosselin, Houston Community College; David Harris, Northwood University; Barry Haworth, University of Louisville; Ronald Helgens, Golden Gate University; Robert E. Herman, Nassau Community College/ SUNY; William D. Hermann, Golden Gate University, San Francisco; Brad Hobbs, Florida Gulf Coast University; Rey Hernandez, Metropolitan State College of Denver; Jim Hubert, Seattle Central Community College; Katherine Huger, Charleston Southern University; Woodrow W. Hughes, Jr., Converse College; Tom Jeitschko, Michigan State University, East Lansing; Rob H. Kamery, Christian Brothers University; Derek Kellenberg, Georgia Institute of Technology; Robert Kling, Colorado State University; Frederic R. Kolb, University of Wisconsin, Eau Claire; Barbara Kouskoulas, Lawrence Technological University; David W. Kreutzer, James Madison University; Cory Krupp, Duke University; Jean Kujawa, Lourdes College; George Kuljurgis, Oakland University; Randy W. LaHote, Washtenaw Community College; Tsung Hui Lai, Liberty University; John Larrivee, Mount St. Mary's University; Robert Lawson, Auburn University; Don R. Leet, California State University, Fresno; George P. Lephardt, Milwaukee School of Engineering; Joe LeVesque, Northwood University; Andrew Light, Liberty University; Edward J. López, San Jose State University; G. Dirk Mateer, Penn State University; John McArthur, Wofford College; Ed Mills, Kendell College; David M. Mitchell, Oklahoma State University; Hadley Mitchell, Taylor University; Glen A. Moots, Northwood University; Debasri Mukherjee, Western Michigan University; Todd Myers, Grossmont College; John R. Neal, Lake Sumter Community College; Jennifer Offenberg, Loyola Marymount University; Lloyd Orr, Indiana University, Bloomington; Judd W. Patton, Bellevue College; James Payne, Florida State University; Claudiney Pereira, Tulane University; Jennifer Platania, Elon University; Robert Reinke, University of South Dakota; Robert C. Rencher, Jr., Liberty University; Dan Rickman, Oklahoma State University; Karin L. Russell, Keiser College; Allen Sanderson, University of Chicago; Lewis F. Schlossinger, Community College of Aurora; Thomas W. Secrest, USC Coastal Carolina; Tim Shaugnessey, Louisiana State University, Shreveport; Ben S. Shippen, Jr., Mercer University; Gerald Simons, Grand Valley State University; Charles D. Skipton, University of Tampa; Ken Somppi, Southern Union State Community College; William A. Steiden, Jefferson Community College; Edward Stringham, San Jose State University; Marcia Snyder, College of Charleston; Richard D.C. Trainer, Warsaw School of Economics; Bich Tran, San Jacinto College; Scott Ward, East Texas Baptist University; Tom Lee Waterston, Northwood University; Christopher Westley, Jacksonville State University; David Wharton, Washington College; Jim Wharton, Northwood University; Mark Wheeler, Western Michigan University; Janice Yee, Wartburg College; Edward Wolpert, University of Central Florida; and Anthony Zambelli, Cuyamaca College.

About the Authors

James D. Gwartney holds the Gus A. Stavros Eminent Scholar Chair at Florida State University, where he directs the Stavros Center for the Advancement of Free Enterprise and Economic Education. His writings have been widely published in both professional journals and popular media. He is the coauthor of *Common Sense Economics: What Everyone Should Know About Wealth and Prosperity* (St. Martin's Press, 2005), a primer on economics and personal finance. His current research focuses on the measurement and determination of factors that influence cross-country differences in income levels and growth rates. In this regard, he is the coauthor (with Robert Lawson) of the annual report, *Economic Freedom of the World,* which provides information on the institutions and policies of 141 countries. This data set, published by a worldwide network of institutes in seventy-nine countries, is widely used by scholars investigating topics ranging from economic growth to peaceful relations among nations. He served as chief economist of the Joint Economic Committee of the U.S. Congress during 1999 to 2000. In 2004 he was the recipient of the Adam Smith Award of the Association of Private Enterprise Education for his contribution to the advancement of free market ideals. He is a past president of the Southern Economic Association and the Association for Private Enterprise Education. His PhD in economics is from the University of Washington.

Richard L. Stroup is an adjunct professor of economics at North Carolina State University and a senior fellow of the Property and Environment Research Center (PERC) in Bozeman, MT. He is an emeritus economics professor from Montana State University, where he was head of the Department of Agricultural Economics and Economics from 2003 to 2006. From 1982 to 1984, he was director of the Office of Policy Analysis at the U.S. Department of the Interior, on assignment from MSU. Stroup is a widely published author and speaker on economics, including natural resources and environmental issues, and he has written many articles for professional journals and popular media outlets. His most recent books include *Eco-nomics* (2003), a book on economics and the environment and *Common Sense Economics: What Everyone Should Know About Wealth and Prosperity* (2005), written with James D. Gwartney and Dwight Lee. He held the Hayek Chair in Economics at the University of Graz in Austria, in the fall of 2005.

Russell S. Sobel is a professor of economics and holder of the James Clark Coffman Distinguished Chair in Entrepreneurial Studies at West Virginia University. He received his PhD in economics from Florida State University in 1994. He has published over 150 books and articles and has received national recognition for his works on entrepreneurship and FEMA reform. Sobel was the founding director of the West Virginia University Entrepreneurship Center, and he serves on the advisory boards of four major professional and academic organizations. He has received numerous awards for both his teaching and research. He regularly teaches courses in both principles of economics and public economics and gives lectures at economic education outreach programs.

David A. Macpherson is the E.M. Stevens Distinguished Professor of Economics at Trinity University. Previously, he was director of the Pepper Institute on Aging and Public Policy and the Rod and Hope Brim Eminent Scholar of Economics at Florida State University, where he has received two university-wide awards for teaching excellence. Professor Macpherson is the author of many articles in leading labor economics and industrial relations journals, including the *Journal of Labor Economics, Journal of Human Resources,* and *Industrial and Labor Relations Review.* He is also coauthor of *Contemporary*

Labor Economics, 9ᵗʰ edition. In addition, he is coauthor of the annual *Union Membership and Earnings Data Book: Compilations from the Current Population Survey.* His specialty is applied labor economics. His current research interests include pensions, discrimination, labor unions, and the minimum wage. He received his undergraduate degree and PhD from the Pennsylvania State University.

Brief Contents

Table of Contents

RELATIONSHIP BETWEEN MAIN EDITION AND THE MACRO/MICRO EDITIONS

Chapters

Macro	Micro	Full Length Book Macro—first Version	Full Length Book Micro—first Version	
1	1	1	1	The Economic Approach
2	2	2	2	Some Tools of the Economist
3	3	3	3	Supply, Demand, and the Market Process
4	4	4	4	Supply and Demand: Applications and Extensions
5	5	5	5	Difficult Cases for the Market and the Role of Government
6	6	6	6	The Economics of Collective Decision Making
7		7	17	Taking the Nation's Economic Pulse
8		8	18	Economic Fluctuations, Unemployment, and Inflation
9		9	19	An Introduction to Basic Macroeconomic Markets
10		10	20	Dynamic Change, Economic Fluctuations, and the AD-AS Model
11		11	21	Fiscal Policy, Historical Perspective and The Keynesian View
12		12	22	Fiscal Policy, Incentives, and Secondary Effects
13		13	23	Money and the Banking System
14		14	24	Modern Macroeconomics and Monetary Policy
15		15	25	Stabilization Policy, Output, and Employment
16		16	26	Creating an Environment for Growth and Prosperity
17		17	27	Institutions, Policies, and Cross-Country Differences in Income and Growth
18	16	18	16	Gaining from International Trade
19		19	28	International Finance and the Foreign Exchange Market
	7	20	7	Consumer Demand and Elasticity
	8	21	8	Costs and the Supply of Goods
	9	22	9	Price Takers and the Competitive Process
	10	23	10	Price-Searcher Markets with Low Entry Barriers
	11	24	11	Price-Searcher Markets with High Entry Barriers
	12	25	12	The Supply of and Demand for Productive Resources
	13	26	13	Earnings, Productivity, and the Job Market
	14	27	14	Investment, the Capital Market, and the Wealth of Nations
	15	28	15	Income Inequality and Poverty

Special Topics

Macro	Micro	Full Length Book Macro—first Version	Full Length Book Micro—first Version	
1	1	1	1	Government Spending and Taxation
2	2	2	2	The Internet: How Is It Changing the Economy?
3	3	3	3	The Economics of Social Security
4	4	4	4	The Stock Market: Its Function, Performance, and Potential as an Investment
5	5	5	5	The Crisis of 2008: Causes and Lessons for the Future
6	6	6	6	Lessons From the Great Depression
7		7	13	Lessons From the Japanese Experience
8		8	14	The Federal Budget and the National Debt
	7	9	7	The Economics of Health Care
	8	10	8	School Choice: Can It Improve the Quality of Education?
	9	11	9	Is Discrimination Responsible for the Earnings: Difference between Men and Women?
	10	12	10	Do Labor Unions Increase the Wages of Workers?
	11	13	11	Are We Running Out of Resources?
	12	14	12	Difficult Environmental Cases and the Role of Government

MACROECONOMICS

PRIVATE AND PUBLIC CHOICE

13th edition

The Economic Way of Thinking

Life is a series of choices

Economics is about how people choose. The choices we make influence our lives and those of others. Your future will be influenced by the choices you make with regard to education, job opportunities, savings, and investment. Furthermore, changes in technology, demographics, communications, and transportation are constantly altering the attractiveness of various options and the opportunities available to us. The economic way of thinking is all about how incentives alter the choices people make. It can help you make better choices and enhance your understanding of our dynamic world.

CHAPTER **1**

The Economic Approach

Economist, n.—A scoundrel whose faulty vision sees things as they really are, not as they ought to be.

Daniel K. Benjamin,
after Ambrose Bierce

CHAPTER FOCUS

- What is scarcity, and why is it important even in relatively wealthy economies?

- How does scarcity differ from poverty? Why does scarcity necessitate rationing and cause competition?

- What is the economic way of thinking? What is different about the way economists look at choices and human decision making?

- What is the difference between positive and normative economics?

Welcome to the world of economics. Lately there has been a lot about the economy in the news. The recent financial crisis and recession have affected us all. There is a strong interest among the general public in understanding the causes of the current crisis and what might be done about it. Clearly, knowledge of basic economics is more important now than ever. You will soon see that economics is about much more than just financial markets and economic policy. In fact, a field trip to the fruits and vegetables section at your local grocery store could well be filled with more economics lessons than a trip to the New York Stock Exchange.

In a nutshell, economics is the study of human behavior, with a particular focus on human decision making. In economics you will learn a new and powerful way of thinking that might lead you to question some of your current views and to look at things in a different way. As the satirical definition of an economist in the chapter-opening quote suggests, economic analysis provides valuable insights about how the world really works. These insights, however, often conflict with commonly held beliefs about the way things "ought" to work.

You may have heard some of the following statements: Without a large government stimulus, the economy will fall into another Great Depression. The current financial crisis was caused by greed on Wall Street. Gas prices are so high that the government should regulate them. Americans would be better off if we did not buy so many things from foreigners. A higher minimum wage will help the poor. Health care should be freely available to everyone. Are these statements true? This course will provide you with knowledge that will enhance your understanding of issues like these and numerous others. It may even alter the way you think about them.

You will also develop new insights into how and why people (including yourself) make choices. This course will better enable you to argue political and economic issues with your friends at parties. It may even help you impress your date. On a more serious note, though, the better the decisions you make in your lifetime, the better off you will be. The same goes for a society as a whole. Who knows—you may become so good at economics you discover how to improve the lives of many people around the world, in addition to your own. You could even become the next great economist of our time.

Paramount/The Kobal Collection

ECONOMICS *At The Movies*

Ferris Bueller's Day Off (1986)

In one scene in *Ferris Bueller's Day Off*, Ben Stein plays an economics teacher lecturing about macroeconomics. His students are bored and falling asleep. Although some parts of economics might not be as fun as others, it's a misconception that economics is boring. On the contrary, economics will enlighten you about how people make decisions and the way the world works. It will also help you make better decisions yourself, which will make you better off.

Our "Economics at the Movies" features have been inspired by G. Dirk Mateer, the author of *Economics in the Movies*. (Mason, OH: Thomson South-Western Publishing, 2005).

OUTSTANDING ECONOMIST

The Importance of Adam Smith, the Father of Economic Science

Economics is a relatively young science. The foundation of economics was laid in 1776, when Adam Smith (1723–1790) published *An Inquiry into the Nature and Causes of the Wealth of Nations*. Smith presented what was at that time a revolutionary view. He argued that the wealth of a nation does not lie in gold and silver, but rather in the goods and services produced and consumed by people. According to Smith, coordination, order, and efficiency would result without the planning and direction of a central authority.

Adam Smith was a lecturer at the University of Glasgow, in his native Scotland. Before economics, morals and ethics were actually his concern. His first book was *The Theory of Moral Sentiments*. For Smith, self-interest and sympathy for others were complementary. However, he did not believe that charity alone would provide the essentials for a good life. He stressed that free exchange and competitive markets would harness self-interest as a creative force. Smith believed that individuals *pursuing their own interests* would be directed by the "invisible hand" of market prices toward the production of those goods that were most advantageous to society.

Ideas have consequences. Smith's ideas greatly influenced not only Europeans but also those who mapped out the structure of the U.S. government. Smith's notion of the "invisible hand" of the market has since become accepted as crucial to the prosperity of nations.[1]

[1]For an excellent biographical sketch of Adam Smith, see David Henderson, ed., *The Fortune Encyclopedia of Economics* (New York: Warner Books, 1993), 836–838. The entire text of this useful encyclopedia is now available online, free of charge, at http://www.econlib.org.

The origins of economics date back to Adam Smith, a Scottish moral philosopher, who expressed the first economic ideas in his breakthrough book, *An Inquiry into the Nature and Causes of the Wealth of Nations*, published in 1776. As the title of his book suggests, Smith sought to explain why people in some nations were wealthier than those in others. This very question is still a central issue in economics. It is so important that throughout this book we will use a special "Keys to Economic Prosperity" symbol ⚷ in the margin to highlight sections that focus on this topic. A listing of the major keys to prosperity is presented inside the front cover of the book. These keys and accompanying discussions will help you understand what factors enable economies, and their citizens, to grow wealthier and prosper. ∎

[Economics is] the science which studies human behavior as a relationship between ends and scarce means which have alternative uses.

—Lionel Robbins[1]

What Is Economics About?

While economics is about the choices *individuals* make, we often group together to form collective organizations, such as corporations, labor unions, nonprofit clubs, and governments. Individual choices, however, still underlie and direct the decisions made within

[1]Lionel Robbins, *An Essay on the Nature and Significance of Economic Science* (London: Macmillan, 1932), 15.

these organizations. Thus, even when we study collective organizations like governments, we will still focus our analysis on the choices and decisions made by individuals within those organizations. We begin our journey into economics by discussing the constraints we face as individuals that force us to make choices.

Scarcity Means Having to Make Choices

Would you like some new clothes, a nicer car, and a larger apartment? How about better grades and more time to watch television, go skiing, and travel? Do you dream of driving your brand-new Porsche into the driveway of your oceanfront house? As individuals, our desire for goods is virtually unlimited. We may want all of these things. Unfortunately, both as individuals and as a society we face a constraint called **scarcity** that prevents us from being able to completely fulfill our desires.

Scarcity is present whenever there is less of a good or resource freely available from nature than people would like. There are some things that are not scarce—seawater comes to mind; nature has provided as much of it as people want. But almost everything else you can think of—even your time—is scarce. In economics, the word *scarce* has a very specific meaning that differs slightly from the way it is commonly used. Even if large amounts of a good have been produced, it is still scarce as long as there is not as much of it *freely available from nature* as we would all like. For example, even though goods like apples and automobiles are relatively abundant in the United States, they are still scarce because we would like to have more of them than nature has freely provided. In economics, we generally wish to determine only if a good is scarce or not, and refrain from using the term to refer to the relative availability or abundance of a good or resource.

The unlimited nature of our desires, coupled with the limited nature of the goods and resources available to satisfy these desires, requires that we make choices. Should I spend the next hour studying or watching TV? Should I spend my last $20 on a new CD or on a shirt? Should this factory be used to produce clothing or furniture? **Choice**, the act of selecting among alternatives, is the logical consequence of scarcity. When we make choices, we constantly face trade-offs between meeting one desire or another. To meet one need, we must let another go unmet. The basic ideas of *scarcity* and *choice*, along with the *trade-offs* we face, provide the foundation for economic analysis.

Resources are the ingredients, or inputs, people use to produce goods and services. Our ability to produce goods and services is limited precisely because of the limited nature of our resources.

EXHIBIT 1 lists a number of scarce goods and the limited resources that might be used to produce them. There are three general categories of resources. First, there are *human resources*—the productive knowledge, skill, and strength of human beings. Second, there

Scarcity

Fundamental concept of economics that indicates that there is less of a good freely available from nature than people would like.

Choice

The act of selecting among alternatives.

Resource

An input used to produce economic goods. Land, labor, skills, natural resources, and capital are examples. Throughout history, people have struggled to transform available, but limited, resources into things they would like to have—economic goods.

Scarce Goods	Limited Resources
Food (bread, milk, meat, eggs, vegetables, coffee, etc.)	Land (various degrees of fertility)
Clothing (shirts, pants, blouses, shoes, socks, coats, sweaters, etc.)	Natural resources (rivers, trees, minerals, oceans, etc.)
Household goods (tables, chairs, rugs, beds, dressers, television sets, etc.)	Machines and other human-made physical resources
Education	Nonhuman animal resources
National defense	Technology (physical and scientific "recipes" of history)
Leisure time	Human resources (the knowledge, skill, and talent of individual human beings)
Entertainment	
Clean air	
Pleasant environment (trees, lakes, rivers, open spaces, etc.)	
Pleasant working conditions	

EXHIBIT 1
A General Listing of Scarce Goods and Limited Resources

History is a record of our struggle to transform available, but limited, resources into goods that we would like to have.

Capital

Human-made resources (such as tools, equipment, and structures) used to produce other goods and services. They enhance our ability to produce in the future.

are *physical resources*—things like tools, machines, and buildings that enhance our ability to produce goods. Economists often use the term **capital** when referring to these human-made resources. Third, there are *natural resources*—things like land, mineral deposits, oceans, and rivers. The ingenuity of humans is often required to make these natural resources useful in production. For example, until recently, the yew tree was considered a "trash tree," having no economic value. Then, scientists discovered that the tree produces taxol, a substance that could be used to fight cancer. Human knowledge and ingenuity made yew trees a valuable resource. As you can see, natural resources are important, but knowing how to use them productively is just as important. As economist Thomas Sowell points out, cavemen had the same natural resources at their disposal that we do today. The huge difference between their standard of living and ours reflects the difference in the knowledge they could bring to bear on those resources versus what we can.[2] Over time, human ingenuity, discovery, improved knowledge, and better technology have enabled us to produce more goods and services from the available resources. Nonetheless, we will never be able to produce enough goods to fulfill human desires entirely. Because scarcity can't be eliminated, people will always face choices. This is what economics is about.

Scarcity and Poverty Are Not the Same

Think for a moment about what life was like in 1750. People all over the world struggled fifty, sixty, and seventy hours a week to obtain the basic necessities of life—food, clothing, and shelter. Manual labor was the major source of income. Animals provided the means of transportation. Tools and machines were primitive by today's standards. As the English philosopher Thomas Hobbes stated in the seventeenth century, life was "solitary, poor, nasty, brutish, and short."[3]

Throughout much of South America, Africa, and Asia, economic conditions today continue to make life difficult. In North America, Western Europe, Oceania, and some parts of Asia, however, economic progress has substantially reduced physical hardship and human drudgery. In these regions, the typical family is more likely to worry about financing its summer vacation than obtaining food and shelter. As anyone who has watched the TV reality show *Survivor* knows, we take for granted many of the items that modern technological advances have allowed us to produce at unbelievably low prices. Contestants on *Survivor* struggle with even basic things like starting a fire, finding shelter, and catching

The degree to which modern technology and knowledge allow us to fulfill our desires and ease the grip of scarcity is often taken for granted—as the castaways on the CBS reality series Survivor *quickly find out when they have to struggle to meet even basic needs, such as food, shelter, and cleaning their bodies and clothes.*

Bill Inoshita/CBS Photo Archive/Getty Images

[2]Thomas Sowell, *Knowledge and Decisions* (New York: Basic Books, 1980), 47.
[3]Thomas Hobbes, *Leviathan* (1651), Part I, Chapter 13.

fish. They are thrilled when they win ordinary items like shampoo, rice, and toilet paper. During one episode, a contestant eagerly paid over $125 for a small chocolate bar and spoonful of peanut butter at an auction—and she considered it a great bargain!

It is important to note, however, that scarcity and poverty are not the same thing. Scarcity is an **objective** concept that describes a factual situation in which the limited nature of our resources keeps us from being able to completely fulfill our desires for goods and services. In contrast, poverty is a **subjective** concept that refers to a personal opinion of whether someone meets an arbitrarily defined level of income. This distinction is made even clearer when you realize that different people have vastly different ideas of what it means to be poor. The average family in the United States that meets the federal government's definition of being "in poverty" would be considered wealthy in most any country in Africa. Even in the United States as recently as the 1950s, a family was considered fairly wealthy if it had central heat and air conditioning, or more than one automobile or television set. In the United States today, the majority of families officially classified as in poverty have many, if not most, of the items that would have been viewed as symbols of wealth only fifty years ago.

The distinction between "needs" and "wants" helps us understand why it is impossible to define poverty objectively. Most people would agree that an absence of poverty means that some basic level of needs has been met. But they would disagree on what constitutes needs versus wants. In the 1920s, less than half of all households in the United States had electricity, and even fewer had a telephone or an automobile. Still, people survived and prospered. Would you consider electricity a need or a want? How about gasoline? How about other items that you generally hear people say they need, like cable television, a computer, and a $100 pair of tennis shoes—are they really needs? Although food and water are necessary for human survival, no one item (such as pizza, steak, a Big Mac, or a $1 bottle of spring water) is essential.

People always want more and better goods for themselves and others they care about—medical care, schooling, and national security are examples. Scarcity is the constraint that prevents us from having as much of *all* goods as we would like, but it is not the same as poverty. Even if every individual were rich, scarcity would still be present.

Scarcity Necessitates Rationing

Scarcity makes **rationing** a necessity. When a good or resource is scarce, some criterion must be used to determine who will receive it and who will go without. The choice of which method is used will, however, have an influence on human behavior. When rationing is done through the government sector, a person's political status and ability to manipulate the political process are the key factors. Powerful interest groups and those in good favor with influential politicians will be the ones who obtain goods and resources. When this method of rationing is used, people will devote time and resources to lobbying and favor seeking with those who have political power, rather than to productive activities.

When the criterion is first-come, first-served, goods are allocated to those who are fastest at getting in line or willing to spend the longest time waiting in line. Many colleges use this method to ration tickets to sporting events, and the result is students waiting in long lines. Sometimes, as at Duke University during basketball season, they even camp out for multiple nights to get good tickets! Imagine how the behavior of students would change if tickets were instead given out to the students with the highest grade point average.

In a market economy, price is generally used to ration goods and resources only to those who are willing and able to pay the prevailing market price. Because only those goods that are scarce require rationing, in a market economy, one easy way to determine whether a good or resource is scarce is to ask if it sells for a price. If you have to pay for something, it is scarce.

Scarcity Leads to Competitive Behavior

Competition is a natural outgrowth of scarcity and the desire of human beings to improve their conditions. Competition exists in every economy and every society. It exists both when goods are allocated by price in markets and when they are allocated by other means—political decision making, for example.

Objective
A fact based on observable phenomena that is not influenced by differences in personal opinion.

Subjective
An opinion based on personal preferences and value judgments.

Rationing
Allocating a limited supply of a good or resource among people who would like to have more of it. When price performs the rationing function, the good or resource is allocated to those willing to give up the most "other things" in order to get it.

How goods are rationed influences what competitive techniques people will use to get them. When the rationing criterion is price, individuals will engage in income-generating activities that enhance their ability to pay the price needed to buy the goods and services they want. Thus, one benefit of using price as a rationing mechanism is that it encourages individuals to engage in the production of goods and services to generate income. In contrast, rationing on the basis of first-come, first-served encourages individuals to waste a substantial amount of time waiting in line, while rationing through the political process encourages individuals to waste time and other resources in competing with others to influence the political process.

Within a market setting, the competition that results from scarcity is an important ingredient in economic progress. Competition among business firms for customers results in newer, better, and less expensive goods and services. Competition between employers for workers results in higher wages, benefits, and better working conditions. Further, competition encourages discovery and innovation, two important sources of growth and higher living standards.

The Economic Way of Thinking

It [economics] is a method rather than a doctrine, an apparatus of the mind, a technique of thinking which helps its possessor to draw correct conclusions.

—John Maynard Keynes[4]

Economic theory

A set of definitions, postulates, and principles assembled in a manner that makes clear the "cause-and-effect" relationships.

One does not have to spend much time around economists to recognize that there is an "economic way of thinking." Admittedly, economists, like others, differ widely in their ideological views. A news commentator once remarked that "any half-dozen economists will normally come up with about six different policy prescriptions." Yet, in spite of their philosophical differences, the approaches of economists reflect common ground.

That common ground is **economic theory**, developed from basic principles of human behavior. Economic researchers are constantly involved in testing and seeking to verify their theories. When the evidence from the testing is consistent with a theory, eventually that theory will become widely accepted among economists. Economic theory, like a road map or a guidebook, establishes reference points indicating what to look for and how economic issues are interrelated. To a large degree, the basic economic principles are merely common sense. When applied consistently, however, these commonsense concepts can provide powerful and sometimes surprising insights.

Eight Guideposts to Economic Thinking

The economic way of thinking requires incorporating certain guidelines—some would say the building blocks of basic economic theory—into your own thought process. Once you incorporate these guidelines, economics can be a relatively easy subject to master. Students who have difficulty with economics have almost always failed to assimilate one or more of these principles. The following are eight principles that characterize the economic way of thinking. We will discuss each of these principles in more depth throughout the book so that you will be sure to understand how and when to apply them.

1. THE USE OF SCARCE RESOURCES IS COSTLY, SO DECISION MAKERS MUST MAKE TRADE-OFFS. Economists sometimes refer to this as the "there is no such thing as a free lunch" principle. Because resources are scarce, the use of resources to produce one good diverts those resources from the production of other goods. A parcel of undeveloped land could be used for a new hospital or a parking lot, or it could simply be left undeveloped. No option is free of cost—there is always a trade-off. A decision to pursue any one of these options means that the decision maker must sacrifice the others. The

---

[4]John Maynard Keynes (1883–1946) was an English economist whose writings during the 1920s and 1930s exerted an enormous impact on both economic theory and policy. Keynes established the terminology and the economic framework that are still widely used when economists study problems of unemployment and inflation.

When a scarce resource is used to meet one need, other competing needs must be sacrificed. The forgone shoe store is an example of the opportunity cost of building the new drugstore.

highest valued alternative that is sacrificed is the **opportunity cost** of the option chosen. For example, if you use one hour of your scarce time to study economics, you will have one hour less time to watch television, read magazines, sleep, work at a job, or study other subjects. Whichever one of these options you would have chosen had you *not* spent the hour studying economics is your highest valued option forgone. If you would have slept, then the opportunity cost of this hour spent studying economics is a forgone hour of sleep. In economics, the opportunity cost of an action is the highest valued option given up when a choice is made.

It is important to recognize that the use of scarce resources to produce a good is always costly, regardless of who pays for the good or service produced. In many countries, various kinds of schooling are provided free of charge *to students*. However, provision of the schooling is not free *to the community as a whole*. The scarce resources used to produce the schooling—to construct the building, hire teachers, buy equipment, and so on—could have been used instead to produce more recreation, entertainment, housing, medical care, or other goods. The opportunity cost of the schooling is the highest valued option given up because the resources required for its production were instead used for schooling.

By now, the central point should be obvious. As we make choices, we always face trade-offs. Using resources to do one thing leaves fewer resources to do another.

Consider one final example. Mandatory air bags in automobiles save an estimated 400 lives each year. Economic thinking, however, forces us to ask ourselves if the $50 billion spent on air bags could have been used in a better way—perhaps say, for cancer research that could have saved *more* than 400 lives per year. Most people don't like to think of air bags and cancer research as an "either/or" proposition. It's more convenient to ignore these trade-offs. But if we want to get the most out of our resources, we have to consider all of our alternatives. In this case, the appropriate analysis is not simply the lives saved with air bags versus dollars spent on them, but also the number of lives that could have been saved (or other things that could have been accomplished) if the $50 billion had been used differently. A candid consideration of hard trade-offs like this is essential to using our resources wisely.

2. INDIVIDUALS CHOOSE PURPOSEFULLY—THEY TRY TO GET THE MOST FROM THEIR LIMITED RESOURCES. People try not to squander their valuable resources deliberately. Instead, they try to choose the options that best advance their personal desires and goals at the least possible cost. This is called **economizing behavior**. Economizing behavior is the result of purposeful, or rational, decision making. When choosing among things of equal benefit, an economizer will select the cheapest option. For example, if a pizza, a lobster dinner, and a sirloin steak are expected to yield identical benefits for Mary (including the enjoyment of eating them), economizing behavior implies that Mary will select the cheapest of the three alternatives, probably the pizza. Similarly, when choosing among alternatives of equal cost, economizing decision makers will select the option that yields the greatest benefit. If the prices of several dinner specials are equal, for example, economizers will choose the one they like the best. Because of economizing behavior, the desires or preferences of individuals are revealed by the choices they make.

Opportunity cost
The highest valued alternative that must be sacrificed as a result of choosing an option.

Economizing behavior
Choosing the option that offers the greatest benefit at the least possible cost.

Utility

The subjective benefit or satisfaction a person expects from a choice or course of action.

Purposeful choosing implies that decision makers have some basis for their evaluation of alternatives. Economists refer to this evaluation as **utility**—the benefit or satisfaction that an individual expects from the choice of a specific alternative. Utility is highly subjective, often differing widely from person to person. The steak dinner that delights one person may be repulsive to another (a vegetarian, for example).

The idea that people behave rationally to get the greatest benefit at the least possible cost is a powerful tool. It can help us understand their choices. However, we need to realize that a rational choice is not the same thing as a "right" choice. If we want to understand people's choices, we need to understand their own subjective evaluations of their options *as they see them.* As we have said, different people have different preferences. If Joan prefers $50 worth of chocolate to $50 worth of vegetables, buying the chocolate would be the rational choice for her, even though some outside observer might say that Joan is making a "bad" decision. Similarly, some motorcycle riders choose to ride without a helmet because they believe the enjoyment they get from riding without one is greater than the cost (the risk of injury). When people weigh the benefits they receive from an activity against its cost, they are making a rational choice—even though it might not be the choice you or I would make in the same situation.

3. INCENTIVES MATTER—CHOICE IS INFLUENCED IN A PREDICTABLE WAY BY CHANGES IN INCENTIVES. This is probably the most important guidepost in economic thinking. It is sometimes called the basic postulate of all economics. On the one hand, as the personal benefits from an option increase, a person will be more likely to choose it. On the other hand, as the personal costs associated with an option increase, a person will be less likely to choose it. This guidepost also applies to groups of people, and suggests that making an option more beneficial will predictably cause more of them to choose it. Similarly, making an option more costly will cause fewer of them to choose it.

This basic idea is a powerful tool because its usefulness is practically universal. Incentives affect behavior in virtually all aspects of our lives, ranging from market decisions about what to buy to political choices concerning for whom to vote. If beef prices rise, making beef consumption more expensive relative to other goods, consumers will be less likely to buy it. The "incentives matter" postulate also explains why a person would be unlikely to vote for a political candidate who, if elected, would raise taxes to fund a new government program he or she didn't like very much.

Most errors in economic reasoning occur because people overlook this postulate or fail to apply it consistently. With economic applications generally focusing on people trying to satisfy material desires, casual observers often argue that incentives matter only in cases of human selfishness. This view is false. People are motivated by a variety of goals, some humanitarian and some selfish, and incentives matter equally in both. Even an unselfish individual would be more likely to attempt to rescue a drowning child from a three-foot swimming pool than the rapid currents approaching Niagara Falls. Similarly, people are more likely to give a needy person their hand-me-downs rather than their favorite new clothes.

It is clear that incentives, whether monetary or nonmonetary, matter in human decision making. People will be less likely to walk down a dark alleyway than a well-lit one; they will be more likely to take a job if it has good benefits and working conditions than if it doesn't; and they will be more likely to bend down and pick up a quarter lying on the sidewalk than they will a penny. Even a person who normally bends down to pick up pennies on the sidewalk probably would be less likely to if late for an important appointment, or on a first date.

Just how far can we push the idea that incentives matter? If asked what would happen to the number of funerals performed in your town if the price of funerals rose, how would you respond? The "incentives matter" postulate predicts that the higher cost would reduce the number of funerals. While the same number of people will still die each year, the number of funerals performed will still fall as more people choose to be cremated or buried in cemeteries in other towns. Substitutes are everywhere—even for funerals. Individuals also

© Getty Images

respond to incentives when committing crimes—precisely the reason why people put signs in their yard saying "this house protected by XYZ security."

4. INDIVIDUALS MAKE DECISIONS AT THE MARGIN.   When making a choice between two alternatives, individuals generally focus on the *difference* in the costs and benefits between alternatives. Economists describe this process as **marginal** decision making, or "thinking at the margin." The last time you went to eat fast food, you probably faced a decision that highlights this type of thinking. Will you get the $1.50 cheeseburger and the $1.00 medium drink, or instead get the $3.00 value meal that has the cheeseburger and drink and also comes with a medium order of fries? Naturally, individual decision making focuses on the difference between the alternatives. The value meal costs 50 cents more (its marginal cost) but will give you one extra food item—the fries (its marginal benefit). Your marginal decision is whether it is worth the extra 50 cents to have the fries. If you pay attention, you'll notice yourself frequently thinking at the margin. Next time you find yourself asking a salesclerk "How much *more* is this one?" when you are choosing between two items, you are doing a marginal analysis.

Marginal choices always involve the effects of net additions to or subtractions from current conditions. In fact, the word *additional* is often used as a substitute for *marginal*. For example, a business decision maker might ask, "What is the additional (or marginal) cost of producing one more unit?" Marginal decisions may involve large or small changes. The "one more unit" could be a new factory or a new stapler. It is marginal because it involves additional costs and additional benefits. Given the current situation, what marginal benefits (additional sales revenues, for example) can be expected from the new factory, and what will be the marginal cost of constructing it? What is the marginal benefit versus marginal cost of purchasing a new stapler? The answers to these questions will determine whether building the new factory or buying the new stapler is a good decision.

It is important to distinguish between *average* and *marginal*. A manufacturer's average cost of producing automobiles (which would be the total cost of production divided by the total number of cars the manufacturer produces) may be $25,000, but the marginal cost of producing an additional automobile (or an additional 1,000 automobiles) might be much lower, say, $10,000 per car. Costs associated with research, testing, design, molds, heavy equipment, and similar factors of production must be incurred whether the manufacturer is going to produce 1,000 units, 10,000 units, or 100,000 units. Such costs will clearly

Marginal

Term used to describe the effects of a change in the current situation. For example, a producer's marginal cost is the cost of producing an additional unit of a product, given the producer's current facility and production rate.

contribute to the average cost of an automobile, but they will change very little as additional units are produced. Thus, the marginal cost of additional units may be substantially less than the average cost. Should production be expanded or reduced? That choice should be based on marginal costs, which indicate the *change* in total cost due to the decision.

Confusion between marginal and total benefits or costs can also be a source of error. Almost all of the choices we make are marginal, rather than all-or-nothing decisions. For example, we don't make decisions between eating or wearing clothes—dining well in the nude versus starving in style. Instead, we choose between having a little more food at the cost of a little less clothing, or a little less of something else. So the relevant comparison is not between the total value of food and the total value of clothing but between their marginal values.

People commonly ignore the implications of marginal thinking in their comments, but seldom in their actions. Thus, the concept is far better at explaining how people act than what they say. Students are often overheard telling other students that they shouldn't skip class because they have paid to enroll in it. Of course, the tuition is not a factor relevant at the margin—it will be the same whether or not the student attends class on that particular day. The only real marginal considerations are what the student will miss that day (a quiz, information for the exam, etc.) versus what he or she could do with the extra time by skipping class. This explains why even students who tell others they paid too much for the class to skip it will ignore the tuition costs when they themselves decide to skip class.

When we confront a decision, the *marginal benefit* and *marginal cost* associated with the choice will determine our decision. Marginal analysis will be used extensively throughout this course. As we develop this concept further, you should pay special attention to understanding how to use it properly.

5. ALTHOUGH INFORMATION CAN HELP US MAKE BETTER CHOICES, ITS ACQUISITION IS COSTLY.
Information that helps us make better choices is valuable. However, the time needed to gather it is scarce, making information costly to acquire. As a result, people economize on their search for information just like they do anything else. For example, when you purchase a pair of jeans, you might evaluate the quality and prices of jeans at several different stores. At some point, though, you will decide that additional comparison shopping is simply not worth the trouble. You will make a choice based on the limited information you already have.

The process is similar when individuals search for a restaurant, a new car, or a roommate. They will seek to acquire some information, but at some point, they will decide that the expected benefit derived from gathering still more information is simply not worth the cost. When differences among the alternatives are important to decision makers, they will spend more time and effort gathering information. People are much more likely to read a consumer ratings magazine before purchasing a new automobile than they are before purchasing a new can opener. Because information is costly for people to acquire, limited knowledge and uncertainty about the outcome generally characterize the decision-making process.

6. BEWARE OF THE SECONDARY EFFECTS: ECONOMIC ACTIONS OFTEN GENERATE INDIRECT AS WELL AS DIRECT EFFECTS.
In addition to direct effects that are quickly visible, people's decisions often generate indirect, or "secondary," effects that may be observable only with time. Failure to consider secondary effects is one of the most common economic errors because these effects are often quite different from initial, or direct, effects. Frédéric Bastiat, a nineteenth-century French economist, stated that the difference between a good and a bad economist is that the bad economist considers only the immediate, visible effects, whereas the good economist is also aware of the **secondary effects**. The true cause of these secondary effects might not be seen, even later, except by those using the logic of good economics.

Perhaps a few simple examples that involve both immediate (direct) and secondary (indirect) effects will help illustrate the point. The immediate effect of an aspirin is a bitter taste in one's mouth. The secondary effect, which is not immediately observable, is relief from a headache. The short-term direct effect of drinking twelve cans of beer might be a warm, jolly feeling. In contrast, the secondary effect is likely to be a sluggish feeling the next morning, and perhaps a pounding headache.

Secondary effects

The indirect impact of an event or policy that may not be easily and immediately observable. In the area of policy, these effects are often both unintended and overlooked.

THE FAMILY CIRCUS®   **By Bil Keane**

© Bil Keane, Inc. Reprinted with special permission of King Features Syndicate.

3-25

Copyright 1988
Cowles Syndicate, Inc

"Everybody wants to be sick.
I'm using M&M's for pills."

Sometimes actions change the incentives people face and they respond accordingly, creating secondary effects that were not intended.

Sometimes, as in the case of the aspirin, the secondary effect—headache relief—is actually an intended consequence of the action. In other cases, however, the secondary effects are unintended. Changes in government policy often alter incentives, indirectly affecting how much people work, earn, invest, consume, and conserve for the future. When a change alters incentives, *unintended consequences* that are quite different from the intended consequences may occur.

Let's consider a couple of examples that illustrate the potential importance of unintended consequences. In an effort to reduce gasoline consumption, the federal government mandates that automobiles be more fuel efficient. Is this regulation a sound policy? It may be, but when evaluating the policy's overall impact, one should not overlook its secondary effects. To achieve the higher fuel efficiency, auto manufacturers reduced the size and weight of vehicles. As a result, there are more highway deaths—about 2,500 more per year—than would otherwise occur because these lighter cars do not offer as much protection for occupants. Furthermore, because the higher mileage standards for cars and light trucks make driving cheaper, people tend to drive more than they otherwise would. This increases congestion and results in a smaller reduction in gasoline consumption than was intended by the regulation. Once you consider the secondary effects, the fuel efficiency regulations are much less beneficial than they might first appear.

Trade restrictions between nations have important secondary effects as well. The proponents of tariffs and quotas on foreign goods almost always ignore the secondary effects of their policies. Import quotas restricting the sale of foreign-produced sugar in the U.S. market, for example, have resulted in domestic sugar prices that have often been two or three times the price in the rest of the world. The proponents of this policy—primarily sugar producers—argue that the quotas "save jobs" and increase employment. No doubt, the employment of sugar growers in the United States is higher than it otherwise would be. But what about the secondary effects? The higher sugar prices mean it's more expensive for U.S. firms to produce candy and other products that use a lot of sugar. As a result, many candy producers, including the makers of Life Savers, Jaw Breakers, Red Hots, and Fannie May and Fanny Farmer chocolates, have moved to countries like Canada and Mexico, where sugar can be purchased at its true market price. Thus, employment among sugar-using firms in the United States is reduced. Further, because foreigners sell less sugar in the United States, they have less purchasing power with which to buy products we export to them. This, too, reduces U.S. employment.

Once the secondary effects of trade restrictions like the sugar quota program are taken into consideration, we have no reason to expect that U.S. employment will increase as a result. There may be more jobs in favored industries, but there will be less employment in others. Trade restrictions reshuffle employment rather than increase it. But those who unwittingly fail to consider the secondary effects will miss this point. Clearly, consideration of the secondary effects is an important ingredient of the economic way of thinking.

7. THE VALUE OF A GOOD OR SERVICE IS SUBJECTIVE. Preferences differ, sometimes dramatically, between individuals. How much is a ticket to see a performance of the Bolshoi Ballet worth? Some people would be willing to pay a very high price, while others might prefer to stay home, even if tickets were free! Circumstances can change from day to day, even for a given individual. Alice, a ballet fan who usually would value the ticket at more than its price of $100, is invited to a party and suddenly becomes uninterested in attending the ballet. Now what is the ticket worth? If she knows a friend who would give her $40 for the ticket, it is worth at least that much. If she advertises the ticket on eBay and gets $60 for it, a higher value is created. But if someone who doesn't know of the ticket would have been willing to pay even more, then a potential trade creating even more value is missed. If that particular performance is sold out, perhaps someone in town would be willing to pay $120. One thing is certain: The value of the ticket depends on several things, including who uses it and under what circumstances.

Economics recognizes that people can and do value goods differently. Mike may prefer to have a grass field rather than a parking lot next to his workplace and be willing to bear the cost of walking farther from his car each day. Kim, on the other hand, may prefer the parking lot and the shorter walk. As a science, economics does not place any inherent moral judgment or value on one person's preferences over another's—in economics, all individuals' preferences are counted equally. Because the subjective preferences of individuals differ, it is difficult for one person to know how much another will value an item.

Think about how hard it is to know what would make a good gift for even a close friend or family member. Thus, arranging trades, or otherwise moving items to higher valued users and uses, is not a simple task. The entrepreneurial individual, who knows how to locate the right buyers and arranges for goods to flow to their highest valued use, can sometimes create huge increases in value from existing resources. In fact, moving goods toward those who value them most and combining resources into goods that individuals value more highly are primary sources of economic progress.

Scientific thinking

Developing a theory from basic principles and testing it against events in the real world. Good theories are consistent with and help explain real-world events. Theories that are inconsistent with the real world are invalid and must be rejected.

8. THE TEST OF A THEORY IS ITS ABILITY TO PREDICT. Economic thinking is **scientific thinking**. The proof of the pudding is in the eating. How useful an economic theory is depends on how well it predicts the future consequences of economic action. Economists develop economic theories using scientific thinking based on basic principles. The idea is to predict how incentives will affect decision makers and compare the predictions against real-world events. If the events in the real world are consistent with a theory, we say that the theory has *predictive value* and is therefore valid.

If it is impossible to test the theoretical relationships of a discipline, the discipline does not qualify as a science. Because economics deals with human beings who can think and respond in a variety of ways, can economic theories really be tested? The answer to this question is yes, if, on average, human beings respond in predictable and consistent ways to changes in economic conditions. The economist believes that this is the case, even though not all individuals will respond in the specified manner. Economists usually do not try to predict the behavior of a specific individual; instead, they focus on the general behavior of a large number of individuals.

In the 1950s, economists began to do laboratory experiments to test economic theories. Individuals were brought into laboratories to see how they would act in buying and selling situations, under differing rules. For example, cash rewards were given to individuals who, when an auction was conducted, were able to sell at high prices and buy at low prices, thus approximating real-world market incentives. These experiments have verified many of the important propositions of economic theory.

Laboratory experiments, however, cannot duplicate all real economic interactions. How can we test economic theory when controlled experiments are not feasible? This is a problem, but economics is no different from astronomy in this respect. Astronomers can use theories tested in physics laboratories, but they must also deal with the world as it is. They cannot change the course of the stars or planets to see what impact the change would have on the gravitational pull of Earth. Similarly, economists cannot arbitrarily change the prices of cars or unskilled-labor services in real markets just to observe the effects on quantities purchased or levels of employment. However, economic conditions (for example, prices, production costs, technology, and transportation costs), like the location of the planets, do change from time to time. As actual conditions change, an economic theory can be tested by comparing its predictions with real-world outcomes. Just as the universe is the main laboratory of the astronomer, the real-world economy is the primary laboratory of the economist.

Positive and Normative Economics

As a social science, economics is concerned with predicting or determining the impact of changes in economic variables on the actions of human beings. Scientific economics, commonly referred to as **positive economics**, attempts to determine "what is." Positive economic statements involve potentially verifiable or refutable propositions. For example: "If the price of gasoline rises, people will buy less gasoline." We can statistically investigate (and estimate) the relationship between gasoline prices and gallons sold. We can analyze the facts to determine the correctness of a positive economic statement. Remember, a positive economic statement need not be correct; it simply must be testable.

In contrast, **normative economics** is about "what ought to be," given the preferences and philosophical views of the advocate. Value judgments often result in disagreement about normative economic matters. Two people may differ on a policy matter because one is from one political party and the other is from another, or because one wants cheaper food while the other favors organic farming (which is more expensive), and so on. They may even agree about the expected outcome of altering an economic variable (that is, the positive economics of an issue), but disagree as to whether that outcome is desirable.

Unlike positive economic statements, normative economic statements can neither be confirmed nor proven false by scientific testing. "Business firms should not be concerned with profits." "We should have fewer parking lots and more green space on campus." "The price of gasoline is too high." These normative statements cannot be scientifically tested because their validity rests on value judgments.

Normative economic views can sometimes influence our attitude toward positive economic analysis, however. When we agree with the objectives of a policy, it's easy to overlook the warnings of positive economics. Although positive economics does not tell us which policy is best, it can provide evidence about the likely effects of a policy. Sometimes proponents unknowingly support policies that are actually in conflict with their own goals and objectives. Positive economics, based on sound economic logic, can help overcome this potential problem.

Economics can expand our knowledge of how the real world operates, in both the private and the public (government) sectors. If we do not fully understand the implications, including the secondary effects, of alternative actions, we will not be able to choose intelligently. Yet, it is not always easy to use economic thinking to isolate the impact of a change. Let's now consider some pitfalls to avoid in economic thinking.

A positive science may be defined as a body of systematized knowledge concerning what is; a normative or regulative science is a body of systematized knowledge relating to criteria of what ought to be, and concerned therefore with the ideal as distinguished from the actual.

—*John Neville Keynes*[5]

Positive economics

The scientific study of "what is" among economic relationships.

Normative economics

Judgments about "what ought to be" in economic matters. Normative economic views cannot be proven false because they are based on value judgments.

---

[5]John Neville Keynes, *The Scope and Method of Political Economy*, 4th ed. (London: Macmillan, 1917), 34–35.

Pitfalls to Avoid in Economic Thinking

Violation of the *Ceteris Paribus* Condition Can Lead One to Draw the Wrong Conclusion

Ceteris paribus

A Latin term meaning "other things constant" that is used when the effect of one change is being described, recognizing that if other things changed, they also could affect the result. Economists often describe the effects of one change, knowing that in the real world, other things might change and also exert an effect.

Economists often qualify their statements with the words *ceteris paribus*. *Ceteris paribus* is a Latin term meaning "other things constant." An example of a *ceteris paribus* statement would be the following: "*Ceteris paribus,* an increase in the price of housing will cause buyers to reduce their purchases of housing." Unfortunately, we live in a dynamic world, so things seldom remain constant. For example, as the price of housing rises, the income of consumers might also increase for unrelated reasons. Each of these factors—higher housing prices and increasing consumer income—will have an impact on housing purchases. In fact, we would generally expect them to have opposite effects: Higher prices are likely to reduce housing purchases, whereas higher consumer incomes are likely to increase them. We point out this pitfall because sometimes statistical data (or casual observations) do not support economic theories. In most of these cases, other factors have also changed. The effects observed simply reflect the combined effect of these changes.

The task of sorting out the effects of two or more variables that change at the same time is difficult. However, with a strong grip on economic theory, some ingenuity, and enough data, it can usually be done. This is, in fact, precisely the day-to-day work of many professional economists.

Good Intentions Do Not Guarantee Desirable Outcomes

There is a tendency to believe that if the proponents of a policy have good intentions, their proposals must be sound. This is not necessarily the case. Proponents may be unaware of some of the adverse secondary effects of their proposals, particularly when they are indirect and observable only over time. Even if their policies would be largely ineffective, politicians may still find it advantageous to call attention to the severity of a problem and propose a program to deal with it. In other cases, proponents of a policy may actually be seeking a goal other than the one they espouse. They may tie their arguments to objectives that are widely supported by the general populace. Thus, the fact that an advocate says a program will help the economy, expand employment, help the poor, increase wages, improve health care, or achieve some other highly desirable objective does not necessarily make it so.

Let's begin with a couple of straightforward examples. Federal legislation has been introduced that would require all children, including those under age two, to be fastened in a child safety seat when traveling by air. Proponents argue the legislation will increase the survival rate of children in the case of an airline crash and thereby save lives. Certainly, saving lives is a highly desirable objective, but will this really be the case? *Some* lives will probably be saved. But what about the secondary effects? The legislation would mean that a parent traveling with a small child would have to purchase an additional ticket, which will make it more expensive to fly. As a result, many families will choose to travel by auto rather than air. Because the likelihood of a serious accident per mile traveled in an automobile is several times higher than for air travel, more automobile travel will result in more injuries and fatalities. In fact, studies indicate that the increase in injuries and fatalities from additional auto travel will exceed the number of lives saved by airline safety seats.[6] Thus, even though the intentions of the proponents may well be lofty, there is reason to believe that the net impact of their proposal will be more fatalities and injuries than would be the case in the absence of the legislation.

The stated objective of the Endangered Species Act is to protect various species that are on the verge of extinction. Certainly, this is an admirable objective, but there is nonetheless reason to question the effectiveness of the act itself. The Endangered Species Act allows the government to regulate the use of individual private property if an endangered species is

[6]For a detailed analysis of this subject, see Thomas B. Newman, Brian D. Johnston, and David C. Grossman, "Effects and Costs of Requiring Child-Restraint Systems for Young Children Traveling on Commercial Airplanes," *Archives of Pediatrics and Adolescent Medicine* 157 (October 2003): 969–74.

found present on *or* near an individual's land. To avoid losing control of their property, many landowners have taken steps to make their land less attractive as a natural habitat for these endangered species. For example, the endangered red-cockaded woodpecker nests primarily in old trees within southern pine ecosystems. Landowners have responded by cutting down trees the woodpeckers like to nest in to avoid having one nest on their land, which would result in the owner losing control of this part of their property. The end result is that the habitat for these birds has actually been disappearing more rapidly.

As you can see, good intentions are not enough. An unsound proposal will lead to undesirable outcomes even if it is supported by proponents with good intentions. In fact, many economists believe that the recent financial crisis is a secondary effect of well-intended government policies that lowered mortgage lending standards in order to expand homeownership. Sound economic reasoning can help us better anticipate the secondary effects of policy changes and avoid the pitfall of thinking that good intentions are enough.

Association Is Not Causation

In economics, identifying cause-and-effect relationships is very important. But statistical association alone cannot establish this causation. Perhaps an extreme example will illustrate the point. Suppose that each November, a witch doctor performs a voodoo dance designed to summon the gods of winter, and that soon after the dance is performed, the weather in fact begins to turn cold. The witch doctor's dance is associated with the arrival of winter, meaning that the two events appear to have happened in conjunction with one another. But is this really evidence that the witch doctor's dance actually caused the arrival of winter? Most of us would answer no, even though the two events seemed to happen in conjunction with one another.

Those who argue that a causal relationship exists simply because of the presence of statistical association are committing a logical fallacy known as the *post hoc propter ergo hoc* fallacy. Sound economics warns against this potential source of error.

The Fallacy of Composition: What's True for One Might Not Be True for All

What is true for the individual (or subcomponent) may not be true for the group (or the whole). If you stand up for an exciting play during a football game, you will be better able to see. But what happens if everyone stands up at the same time? Will everyone be better able to see? The answer is, of course, no. Thus, what is true for a single individual does not necessarily apply to the group as a whole. When everyone stands up, the view for individual spectators fails to improve; in fact, it may even become worse.

People who mistakenly argue that what is true for the part is also true for the whole are said to be committing the **fallacy of composition**. What is true for the individual can be misleading and is often fallacious when applied to the entire economy. The fallacy of composition highlights the importance of considering both a micro view and a macro view in the study of economics. **Microeconomics** focuses on the decision making of consumers, producers, and resource suppliers operating in a narrowly defined market, such as that for a specific good or resource. Because individual decision makers are the moving force behind all economic action, the foundations of economics are clearly rooted in a micro view.

As we have seen, however, what is true for a small unit may not be true in the aggregate. **Macroeconomics** focuses on how the aggregation of individual micro-units affects our analysis. Like microeconomics, it is concerned with incentives, prices, and output. Macroeconomics, however, aggregates markets, lumping together all 115 million households in this country. Macroeconomics involves topics like total consumption spending, saving, and employment, in the economy as a whole. Similarly, the nation's 25 million business firms are lumped together in "the business sector." What factors determine the level of aggregate output, the rate of inflation, the amount of unemployment, and interest rates? These are macroeconomic questions. In short, macroeconomics examines the forest rather than the individual trees. As we move from the micro-components to a macro view of the whole, it is important that we beware of the fallacy of composition.

Fallacy of composition

Erroneous view that what is true for the individual (or the part) will also be true for the group (or the whole).

Microeconomics

The branch of economics that focuses on how human behavior affects the conduct of affairs within narrowly defined units, such as individual households or business firms.

Macroeconomics

The branch of economics that focuses on how human behavior affects outcomes in highly aggregated markets, such as the markets for labor or consumer products.

Economics as a Career

If you find yourself doing well in this course and discover that economics interests you, you may want to think about majoring in it. Graduating with a major in economics provides a variety of career choices. Many students go on to graduate school in economics, business, public administration, or law. Graduate M.B.A. and law programs find economics majors particularly attractive because of their strong analytical skills—economics majors score the highest on the LSAT among common majors taking the exam.

A graduate degree (a master's or doctorate) in economics is typically required to pursue a career as a professional economist. About one-half of all professional economists are employed by colleges and universities as teachers and researchers. Professional economists also work for the government or private businesses. Most major corporations have a staff of economists to advise them. Governments employ economists to analyze the impact of policy alternatives. The federal government's Council of Economic Advisers provides the president with analyses of how the activities of the government influence the economy.

Students who major in economics but who do not pursue graduate school still have many job opportunities. Because economics is a way of thinking, knowledge of it is a valuable decision-making tool that can be used in almost any job. Undergraduate majors in economics typically work in business, government service, banking, or insurance. Opportunities for people with undergraduate economics degrees to teach the subject at the high school level are also increasing. Arnold Schwarzenegger, Mick Jagger, and Ronald Reagan are among the long list of famous undergraduate economics majors!

The average salary of an economics graduate is comparable to that of finance and accounting graduates and is generally higher than those with management or marketing degrees. Median salaries for economists range from $50,000 for those with a bachelor's degree to $90,000 for those with a Ph.D. in economics. Professional economists with graduate degrees in economics who work in private businesses generally earn more than those who choose to work as teachers and researchers at colleges and universities. Although salaries vary substantially, the point is that a career in economics can be rewarding both personally and financially.

Even if you choose not to major in economics, you will find that your economics courses will broaden your horizons and increase your ability to understand and analyze what is going on around you in the worlds of politics, business, and human relations. Economics is a social science that often overlaps with the fields of political science, sociology, and psychology. Because the economic way of thinking is so useful in making sense of the world around us, economics has sometimes been called the "queen of the social sciences." Reflecting this, economics is the only social science for which a Nobel Prize of the Swedish Academy of Science is awarded.

Looking ahead

The primary purpose of this book is to encourage you to develop the economic way of thinking so that you can separate sound reasoning from economic nonsense. Once you have developed the economic way of thinking, economics will be relatively easy. Using the economic way of thinking can also be fun. Moreover, it will help you become a better citizen. It will give you a different and fascinating perspective on what motivates people, why they act the way they do, and why their actions sometimes go against the best interest of the community or nation. It will also give you valuable insight into how people's actions can be rechanneled for the benefit of the community at large.

KEY POINTS

▼ Scarcity and choice are the two essential ingredients of economic analysis. A good is scarce when the human desire for it exceeds the amount freely available from nature. Scarcity requires us to choose among available alternatives. Every choice entails a trade-off.

▼ Every society will have to devise some method of rationing scarce resources among competing uses. Markets generally use price as the rationing device. Competition is a natural outgrowth of the need to ration scarce goods.

▼ Scarcity and poverty are not the same thing. Absence of poverty implies that some basic level of need has been met. An absence of scarcity implies that our desires for goods are fully satisfied. We may someday eliminate poverty, but scarcity will always be with us.

▼ Economics is a way of thinking that emphasizes eight points:

1. The use of scarce resources to produce a good always has an opportunity cost.

2. Individuals make decisions purposefully, always seeking to choose the option they expect to be most consistent with their personal goals.

3. Incentives matter. The likelihood of people choosing an option increases as personal benefits rise and personal costs decline.

4. Economic reasoning focuses on the impact of marginal changes because it is the marginal benefits and marginal costs that influence choices.

5. Because information is scarce, uncertainty is a fact of life.

6. In addition to their direct impact, economic changes often generate secondary effects.

7. The value of a good or service is subjective and varies with individual preferences and circumstances.

8. The test of an economic theory is its ability to predict and explain events in the real world.

▼ Economic science is positive; it attempts to explain the actual consequences of economic actions or "what is." Normative economics goes further, applying value judgments to make suggestions about what "ought to be."

▼ Microeconomics focuses on narrowly defined units, while macroeconomics is concerned with highly aggregated units. When shifting focus from micro to macro, one must beware of the fallacy of composition: What's good for the individual may not be good for the group as a whole.

▼ The origin of economics as a science dates to the publication of *An Inquiry into the Nature and Causes of the Wealth of Nations* by Adam Smith in 1776. Smith believed a market economy would generally bring individual self-interest and the public interest into harmony.

CRITICAL ANALYSIS QUESTIONS

1. Indicate how each of the following changes would influence the incentive of a decision maker to undertake the action described.
   a. A reduction in the temperature from 80° to 50° on one's decision to go swimming
   b. A change in the meeting time of the introductory economics course from 11:00 A.M. to 7:30 A.M. on one's decision to attend the lectures
   c. A reduction in the number of exam questions that relate directly to the text on the student's decision to read the text
   d. An increase in the price of beef on one's decision to buy steak
   e. An increase in the rental rates of apartments on one's decision to build additional rental housing units

2. "The government should provide such goods as health care, education, and highways because it can provide them for free." Is this statement true or false? Explain your answer.

3. a. What method is used to ration goods in a market economy? How does this rationing method influence the incentive of individuals to supply goods, services, and resources to others?

b. How are grades rationed in your economics class? How does this rationing method influence student behavior? Suppose the highest grades were rationed to those whom the teacher liked best. How would this method of rationing influence student behavior?

*4. In recent years, both the personal exemption and child tax credit have been increased in the United States. According to the basic principles of economics, how will the birthrate be affected by policies that reduce the taxes imposed on those with children?

*5. "The economic way of thinking stresses that good intentions lead to sound policy." Is this statement true or false? Explain your answer.

6. Self-interest is a powerful motivator. Does this necessarily imply that people are selfish and greedy? Do self-interest and selfishness mean the same thing?

*7. Congress and government agencies often make laws to help protect the safety of consumers. New cars, for example, are required to have many safety features before they can be sold in the United States. These rules do indeed provide added safety for buyers, although they also add to the cost of making and price of buying the new vehicles. What secondary effects can you see happening as the result of mandating that automobiles have airbags? What incentives do you see changing for drivers as the result of making cars safer? Do you think the millions of dollars spent by consumers on air bags each year could be better spent elsewhere to save even more lives?

*8. "Individuals who economize are missing the point of life. Money is not so important that it should rule the way we live." Evaluate this statement.

*9. "Positive economics cannot tell us which agricultural policy is better, so it is useless to policy makers." Evaluate this statement.

*10. "I examined the statistics for our basketball team's wins last year and found that, when the third team played more, the winning margin increased. If the coach played the third team more, we would win by a bigger margin." Evaluate this statement.

*11. Which of the following are positive economic statements and which are normative?
   a. The speed limit should be lowered to 55 miles per hour on interstate highways.
   b. Higher gasoline prices cause the quantity of gasoline that consumers buy to increase.
   c. A comparison of costs and benefits should not be used to assess environmental regulations.
   d. Higher taxes on alcohol result in less drinking and driving.

12. "Economics is about trade-offs. If more scarce resources are used to produce one thing, fewer will be available to produce others." Evaluate this statement.

13. Do individuals "economize"? If so, what are they trying to do? Do you economize when you shop at the mall? Why or why not?

*14. Should the United States attempt to reduce air and water pollution to zero? Why or why not?

*Asterisk denotes questions for which answers are given in Appendix B.

A D D E N D U M

Understanding Graphs

Economists often use graphs to illustrate economic relations. Graphs are like pictures. They are visual aids that can communicate valuable information in a small amount of space. A picture may be worth a thousand words, but only to a person who understands the picture (and the graph).

This addendum illustrates the use of simple graphs as a way to communicate. Many students, particularly those with some mathematics background, are already familiar with this material, and can safely ignore it. This addendum is for those who need to be assured that they can understand graphic illustrations of economic concepts.

The Simple Bar Graph

A simple bar graph helps us visualize comparative relationships and understand them better. It is particularly useful for illustrating how an economic indicator varies among countries, across time periods, or under alternative economic conditions.

EXHIBIT A-1 is a bar graph illustrating economic data. The table in part (a) presents data on the income per person in 2007 for several countries. Part (b) uses a bar graph to illustrate the same data. The horizontal scale of the graph indicates the total income per person. A bar is made for indicating the income level (see the dollar scale on the *x*-axis) of each country. The length of each bar is in proportion to the per-person income of the country. Thus, the length of the bars provides a visual illustration of how per capita income varies across the countries. For example, the extremely short bar for Nigeria shows immediately that income per person there is only a small fraction of the comparable income figure for the United States, Japan, Switzerland, and several other countries.

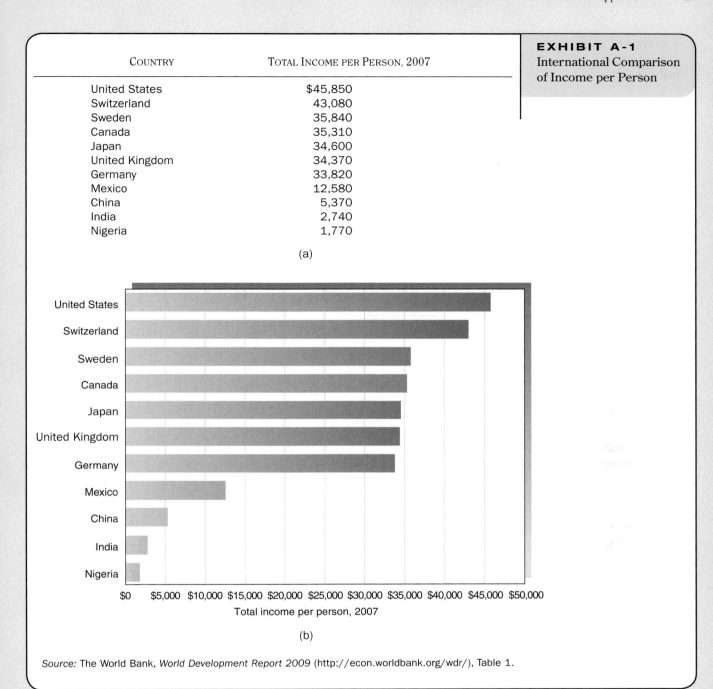

EXHIBIT A-1
International Comparison
of Income per Person

COUNTRY	TOTAL INCOME PER PERSON, 2007
United States	$45,850
Switzerland	43,080
Sweden	35,840
Canada	35,310
Japan	34,600
United Kingdom	34,370
Germany	33,820
Mexico	12,580
China	5,370
India	2,740
Nigeria	1,770

(a)

(b)

Source: The World Bank, *World Development Report 2009* (http://econ.worldbank.org/wdr/), Table 1.

Linear Graphic Presentation

Economists often want to illustrate variations in economic variables with the passage of time. A linear graph with time on the horizontal axis and an economic variable on the vertical axis is a useful tool to indicate variations over time. **EXHIBIT A-2** illustrates a simple linear graph of changes in consumer prices (the inflation rate) in the United States between 1960 and 2008. The table of the exhibit presents data on the percentage change in consumer prices for each year. Beginning with 1960, the horizontal axis indicates the time period (year). The inflation rate is plotted vertically above each year. Of course, the height of the plot (line) indicates the inflation rate during that year. For example, in 1975 the inflation rate was 9.1 percent. This point is plotted at the 9.1 percent vertical distance directly above the year 1975. In 1976, the inflation rate fell to 5.8 percent. Thus, the vertical plot of the 1976 inflation rate is lower than that for 1975. The inflation rate for each year shown in part (a) is plotted at the corresponding height directly above the year in part (b). The linear graph is simply a line connecting the points plotted for each of the years.

EXHIBIT A-2
Changes in the Level of
Prices in United States

*The tabular data (a) of the infla-
tion rate are presented in graphic
form in (b).*

Year	Percentage Change in Consumer Prices	Year	Percentage Change in Consumer Prices
1960	1.7	1984	4.3
1961	1.0	1985	3.6
1962	1.0	1986	1.9
1963	1.3	1987	3.6
1964	1.3	1988	4.1
1965	1.6	1989	4.8
1966	2.9	1990	5.4
1967	3.1	1991	4.2
1968	4.2	1992	3.0
1969	5.5	1993	3.0
1970	5.7	1994	2.6
1971	4.4	1995	2.8
1972	3.2	1996	3.0
1973	6.2	1997	2.3
1974	11.0	1998	1.6
1975	9.1	1999	2.2
1976	5.8	2000	3.4
1977	6.5	2001	2.8
1978	7.6	2002	1.6
1979	11.3	2003	2.3
1980	13.5	2004	2.7
1981	10.3	2005	3.4
1982	6.2	2006	3.2
1983	3.2	2007	2.8
		2008	3.8

(a)

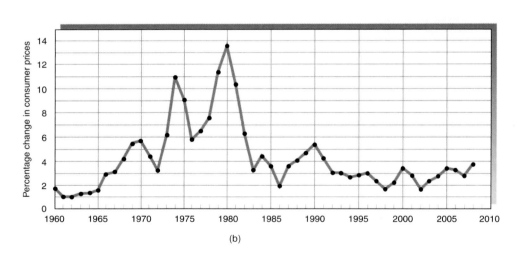

(b)

Source: Bureau of Labor Statistics (http://www.bls.gov/cpi/).

The linear graph is a visual aid to understanding what happens to the inflation rate during the period. As the graph shows, the inflation rate rose sharply between 1967 and 1969, 1972 and 1974, and 1978 and 1980. It was substantially higher during the 1970s than in the early 1960s or the mid-1980s and 1990s. Most importantly, the inflation rate has been lower and more stable since 1983 than in the period before. Although the linear graph does not communicate any information not in the table, it does make it easier to see the pattern of the data. Thus, economists often use simple graphs rather than tables to communicate information.

Direct and Inverse Relationships

Economic logic often suggests that two variables are linked in a specific way. Suppose an investigation reveals that, other things being constant, farmers supply more wheat as the price of wheat increases. **EXHIBIT A-3** presents hypothetical data on the relationship between the price of wheat and the quantity supplied by farmers, first in tabular form in part (a) and then as a simple two-dimensional graph in part (b). Suppose we measure the quantity of wheat supplied by farmers on the *x*-axis (the horizontal axis) and the price of wheat on the *y*-axis (the vertical axis). Points indicating the value of *x* (quantity supplied) at alternative values of *y* (price of wheat) can then be plotted. The line (or curve) linking the points illustrates the relationship between the price of wheat and the amount supplied by farmers.

In the case of price and quantity supplied of wheat, the two variables are directly related. When the *y*-variable increases, so does the *x*-variable. When two variables are directly related, the graph illustrating the linkage between the two will slope upward to the right, as in the case of *SS* in part (b).

Sometimes the *x*-variable and the *y*-variable are inversely related. A decline in the *y*-variable is associated with an increase in the *x*-variable. Therefore, a curve picturing the inverse relationship between *x* and *y* slopes downward to the right. **EXHIBIT A-4** illustrates this case. As the data of the table indicate, consumers purchase more as the price in wheat declines. Measuring the price of wheat on the *y*-axis (by convention, economists always place price on the *y*-axis) and the quantity of wheat purchased on the *x*-axis, the relationship between these two variables can also be illustrated graphically. If the price of

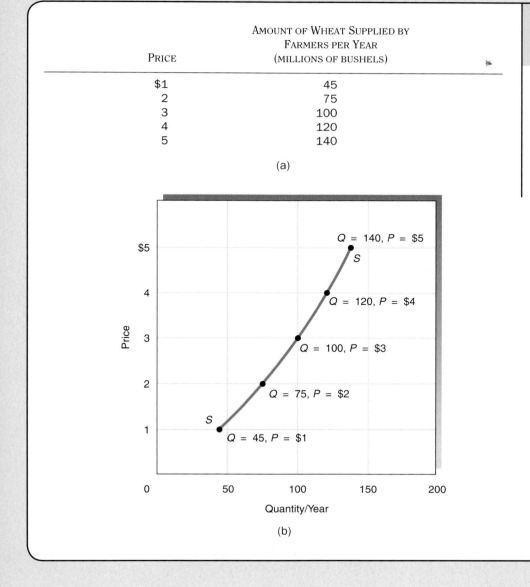

PRICE	AMOUNT OF WHEAT SUPPLIED BY FARMERS PER YEAR (MILLIONS OF BUSHELS)
$1	45
2	75
3	100
4	120
5	140

(a)

(b)

EXHIBIT A-3
Direct Relationship between Variables

As the table (a) indicates, farmers are willing to supply more wheat at a higher price. Thus, there is a direct relationship between the price of wheat and the quantity supplied. When the x- and y-variables are directly related, a curve mapping the relationship between the two will slope upward to the right like SS.

EXHIBIT A-4
Inverse Relationship between Variables

As the table (a) shows, consumers will demand (purchase) more wheat as the price declines. Thus, there is an inverse relationship between the price of wheat and the quantity demanded. When the x- and y-variables are inversely related, a curve showing the relationship between the two will slope downward to the right like DD.

PRICE	AMOUNT OF WHEAT DEMANDED BY CONSUMERS PER YEAR (MILLIONS OF BUSHELS)
$1	170
2	130
3	100
4	75
5	60

(a)

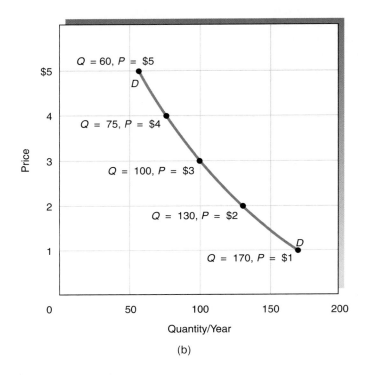

(b)

wheat were $5 per bushel, only 60 million bushels would be purchased by consumers. As the price declines to $4 per bushel, annual consumption increases to 75 million bushels. At still lower prices, the quantity purchased by consumers will expand to larger and larger amounts. As part (b) illustrates, the inverse relationship between price and quantity of wheat purchased generates a curve that slopes downward to the right.

Complex Relationships

Sometimes the initial relationship between the *x*- and *y*-variables will change. **EXHIBIT A-5** illustrates more complex relationships of this type. Part (a) shows the typical relationship between annual earnings and age. As a young person gets work experience and develops skills, earnings usually expand. Thus, initially, age and annual earnings are directly related; annual earnings increase with age. However,

beyond a certain age (approximately age 55), annual earnings generally decline as workers approach retirement. As a result, the initial direct relationship between age and earnings changes to an inverse relationship. When this is the case, annual income expands to a maximum (at age 55) and then begins to decline with years of age.

Part (b) illustrates an initial inverse relationship that later changes to a direct relationship. Consider the impact of travel speed on gasoline consumption per mile. At low speeds, the automobile engine will not be used efficiently. As speed increases from 5 mph to 10 mph and on to a speed of 40 mph, gasoline consumption per mile declines. In this range, there is an inverse relationship between speed of travel (*x*) and gasoline consumption per mile (*y*). However, as speed increases beyond 40 mph, air resistance increases and more gasoline per mile is required to maintain the additional speed. At very high speeds, gasoline consumption

(a) A direct relationship changing
to inverse

(b) An inverse relationship changing
to direct

EXHIBIT A-5
Complex Relationships
between Variables

At first, an increase in age (and work experience) leads to a higher income, but later earnings decline as the worker approaches retirement (a). Thus, age and annual income are initially directly related, but at approximately age 55 an inverse relationship emerges. Part (b) illustrates the relationship between travel speed and gasoline consumption per mile. Initially, gasoline consumption per mile declines as speed increases (an inverse relationship), but as speed increases above 40 mph, gasoline consumption per mile increases with the speed of travel (direct relationship).

per mile increases substantially with speed of travel. Thus, gasoline consumption per mile reaches a minimum, and a direct relationship between the x- and y-variables describes the relationship beyond that point (40 mph).

Slope of a Straight Line

In economics, we are often interested in how much the y-variable changes in response to a change in the x-variable. The slope of the line or curve reveals this information. Mathematically, the slope of a line or curve is equal to the change in the y-variable divided by the change in the x-variable.

EXHIBIT A-6 illustrates the calculation of the slope for a straight line. The exhibit shows how the daily earnings (y-variable) of a worker change with hours worked (the x-variable). The wage rate of the worker is $10 per hour, so when 1 hour is worked, earnings are equal to $10. For 2 hours of work, earnings jump to $20, and so on. A 1-hour change in hours worked leads to a $10 change in earnings. Thus, the slope of the line ($\Delta y/\Delta x$) is equal to 10.

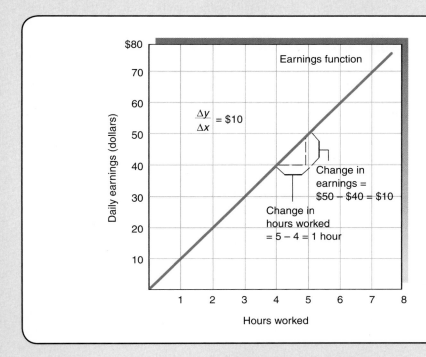

EXHIBIT A-6
Slope of a Straight Line

The slope of a line is equal to the change in y divided by the change in x. The line opposite illustrates the case in which daily earnings increase by $10 per hour worked. Thus, the slope of the earnings function is 10 ($10 ÷ 1 hr). For a straight line, the slope is constant at each point on the line.

EXHIBIT A-7
Slope of a Nonlinear Curve

The slope of a curve at any point is equal to the slope of the straight line tangent to the curve at the point. As the lines tangent to the curve at points A and B illustrate, the slope of a curve will change from point to point along the curve.

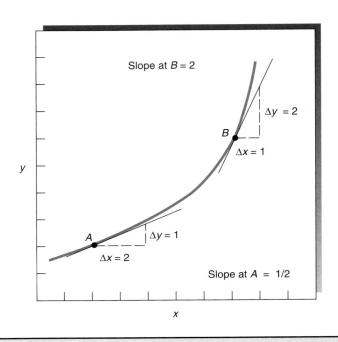

Slope at B = 2

Δy = 2

B

Δx = 1

y

A

Δy = 1

Δx = 2

Slope at A = 1/2

x

(The symbol Δ means "change in.") In the case of a straight line, the change in y, per unit change in x, is equal for all points on the line. Thus, the slope of a straight line is constant for all points along the line. Exhibit A-6 illustrates a case in which a direct relationship exists between the x- and y-variables. For an inverse relationship, the y-variable decreases as the x-variable increases. So, when x and y are inversely related, the slope of the line will be negative.

Slope of a Curve

In contrast with a straight line, the slope of a curve is different at each point along the curve. The slope of a curve at a specific point is equal to the slope of a line tangent to the curve at the point, meaning a line that just touches the curve.

EXHIBIT A-7 illustrates how the slope of a curve at a specific point is determined. First, consider the slope of the curve at point A. A line tangent to the curve at point A indicates that y changes by one unit when x changes by two units at point A. Thus, the slope ($\Delta y/\Delta x$) of the curve at A is equal to 0.5.

Now consider the slope of the curve at point B. The line tangent to the curve at B indicates that y changes by two units for each one-unit change in x at point B. Thus, at B the slope ($\Delta y/\Delta x$) is equal to 2. At point B, a change in the x-variable leads to a much larger change in y than it does at point A. The greater slope of the curve at B reflects this greater change in y per unit change in x at B relative to A.

Graphs Are Not a Substitute for Economic Thinking

By now, you should have a fairly good understanding of how to read a graph. If you still feel uncomfortable with graphs, try drawing (graphing) the relationship between several things with which you are familiar. If you work, try graphing the relationship between your hours worked (x-axis) and your weekly earnings (y-axis). Exhibit A-3 could guide you with this exercise. Can you graph the relationship between the price of gasoline and your expenditures on gasoline? Graphing these simple relationships will give you greater confidence in your ability to grasp more complex economic relationships presented in graphs.

This text uses only simple graphs. Thus, there is no reason for you to be intimidated. Graphs look much more complex than they really are. In fact, they are nothing more than a simple device to communicate information quickly and concisely. Nothing can be communicated with a graph that cannot be communicated verbally.

Most important, graphs are not a substitute for economic thinking. Although a graph may illustrate that two variables are related, it tells us nothing about the cause-and-effect relationship between the variables. To determine probable cause and effect, we must rely on economic theory. Thus, the economic way of thinking, not graphs, is the power station of economic analysis.

Some Tools of the Economist

- **What is opportunity cost? Why do economists place so much emphasis on it?**

- **Why do people engage in exchange?**

- **How does private ownership affect the use of resources? Will private owners pay any attention to the desires of others?**

- **What does a production possibilities curve demonstrate?**

- **What are the sources of gains from trade? How does trade influence our modern living standards?**

- **What are the two major methods of economic organization? How do they differ?**

The key insight of Adam Smith's Wealth of Nations is misleadingly simple: if an exchange between two parties is voluntary, it will not take place unless both believe they will benefit from it. Most economic fallacies derive from the neglect of this simple insight, from the tendency to assume that there is a fixed pie, that one party can gain only at the expense of another.

—Milton and Rose Friedman[1]

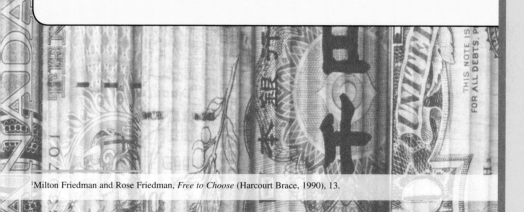

[1]Milton Friedman and Rose Friedman, *Free to Choose* (Harcourt Brace, 1990), 13.

n the preceding chapter, you were introduced to the economic way of thinking. We will now begin to apply that approach. This chapter focuses on five topics: opportunity cost, trade, property rights, the potential output level of an economy, and the creation of wealth. These seemingly diverse topics are in fact highly interrelated. For example, the opportunity cost of goods determines which ones an individual or a nation should produce and which should be acquired through trade. In turn, the ways in which trade and property rights are structured influence the amount of output and wealth an economy can create. These tools of economics are important for answering the basic economic questions: what to produce, how to produce it, and for whom it will be produced. We will begin by first explaining in more detail what opportunity cost is. ∎

What Shall We Give Up?

Because of scarcity, we can't have everything we want. As a result, we constantly face choices that involve trade-offs between our competing desires. Most of us would like to have more time for leisure, recreation, vacations, hobbies, education, and skill development. We would also like to have more wealth, a larger savings account, and more consumable goods. However, all these things are scarce, in the sense that they are limited. Our efforts to get more of one will conflict with our efforts to get more of others.

Opportunity Cost

An unpleasant fact of economics is that the choice to do one thing is, at the same time, a choice *not* to do something else. Your choice to spend time reading this book is a choice not to spend the time playing video games, listening to a math lecture, or going to a party. These things must be given up because you decided to read this book instead. As we indicated in Chapter 1, the highest valued alternative sacrificed in order to choose an option is called the *opportunity cost* of that choice. In economics when we refer to the "cost" of an action, we are referring to its opportunity cost.

Opportunity costs are subjective because they depend on how the decision maker values his or her options. They are also based on the expectations of the decision maker—what he or she expects the value of the forgone alternatives will be. Because of this, opportunity cost can never be directly measured by someone other than the decision maker. Only the person choosing can know the value of what is given up.[2] This makes it difficult for someone other than the decision maker—including experts and elected officials—to make choices on that person's behalf. Moreover, not only do people differ in the trade-offs they prefer to make, but their preferences also change with time and circumstances. Thus, the decision maker is the only person who can properly evaluate the options and decide which is the best, given his or her preferences and current circumstances.

Monetary costs can be measured objectively in terms of dollars and cents (or Japanese yen, English pounds, and so forth). They also represent an opportunity cost. If you spend $20 on a new CD, you must now forgo the other items you could have purchased with the $20—a new shirt, for example. However, it is important to recognize that monetary costs do not represent the total opportunity cost of an option. The total cost of attending a football

[2]See James M. Buchanan, *Cost and Choice* (Chicago: Markham, 1969), for a classic work on the relationship between cost and choice.

game, for example, is the highest valued opportunity lost as a result of both the time you spend at the game and the amount of money you pay for your ticket. In cases like the online purchase of a music album, for which there is minimal outlay of time, effort, and other resources to make the purchase, the monetary cost will approximate the total cost. Contrast this with a decision to sit on your sofa and listen to your new music, which involves little or no monetary cost, but has a clear opportunity cost of your time. In this second case, the monetary cost is a poor measure of the total cost.

Opportunity Cost and the Real World

Is real-world decision making influenced by opportunity costs? Consider your own decision to attend college. Your opportunity cost of going to college is the value of the next best alternative, which could be measured as the salary you would earn if you had chosen to go directly into full-time work instead. Every year you stay in college, you give up what you could have earned by working that year. Typically, students incur opportunity costs of $80,000 or more in forgone income during their stay in college.

But what if the opportunity cost of attending college changes? How will it affect your decision? Suppose, for example, that you received a job offer today for $250,000 per year as an athlete or an entertainer, but the job would require so much travel that school would be impossible. Would this change in the opportunity cost of going to college affect your choice as to whether to continue in school? It likely would. Going to college would mean you would have to say good-bye to the huge salary you've been offered. (See the accompanying illustration on LeBron James for a good example.) You can clearly tell from this example that the monetary cost of college (tuition, books, and so forth) isn't the only factor influencing your decision. Your opportunity cost plays a part, too.

Even when their parents pay all the monetary expenses of their college education, some students are surprised to learn that they are actually incurring more of the total cost of going to college than their parents. For example, the average monetary cost (tuition, room and board, books, and so forth) for a student attending college is about $10,000 per year ($40,000 over four years). Even if the student's next best alternative were working at a job that paid only $15,000 per year, over four years, that would amount to $60,000 in forgone earnings, So, the total cost of the student's education would be $100,000 ($40,000 in monetary costs paid by the parents and $60,000 in opportunity costs incurred by the student).[3]

Now consider another decision made by college students—whether to attend a particular class meeting. The monetary cost of attending class (bus fare, parking, gasoline costs, and so on) remains fairly constant from day to day. Why then do students choose to attend class on some days and not on others? Even though the monetary cost of attending class is fairly constant, a student's opportunity cost can change dramatically from day to day. Some days, the next best alternative to attending class may be sleeping in or watching TV. Other days, the opportunity cost may be substantially larger, perhaps the value of attending a big football game, getting an early start on spring break, or having additional study time for a crucial exam in another class. As options like these increase the cost of attending class, more students will decide not to attend.

Elsa/Getty Images

LeBron James understands opportunity cost. As a high school player, James was already one of the best basketball players in the nation. He had received numerous scholarship offers and was considering attending college at Ohio State, the University of North Carolina, Michigan State, or the University of California. However, after high school graduation, LeBron decided to go directly into the NBA because the opportunity cost of college was simply too high. He was selected as the first pick in the 2003 NBA draft, signing a three-year contract worth almost $13 million, with an option for a fourth year at $5.8 million. Had he decided to go to college instead, James would have incurred an opportunity cost of at least $19 million in forgone income to earn a four-year college degree! Would you have skipped college if your opportunity cost had been that high?

---

[3]From the standpoint of the family's total economic cost of sending a child to college, some of the monetary costs, such as room and board, are not costs of choosing to go to college. The cost of living does have to be covered, but it would be incurred whether or not the student went to college.

Failure to consider opportunity cost often leads to unwise decision making. Suppose that your community builds a beautiful new civic center. The mayor, speaking at the dedication ceremony, tells the world that the center will improve the quality of life in your community. People who understand the concept of opportunity cost may question this view. If the center had not been built, the resources might have funded construction of a new hospital, improvements to the educational system, or housing for low-income families. Will the civic center contribute more to the well-being of the people in your community than these other facilities? If so, it was a wise investment. If not, your community will be worse off than it would have been if decision makers had chosen a higher valued project.

Trade Creates Value

Why do individuals trade with each other, and what is the significance of this exchange? We have learned that value is subjective. It is wrong to assume that a particular good or service has a fixed objective value just because it exists.[4] The value of goods and services generally depends on who uses them, and on circumstances, such as when and where they are used, as well as on the physical characteristics. Some people love onions, whereas others dislike them very much. Thus, when we speak of the "value of an onion," this makes sense only within the context of its value to a specific person. Similarly, to most people an umbrella is more valuable on a rainy day than on a sunny one.

OUTSTANDING ECONOMIST

Thomas Sowell (1930–)

Thomas Sowell, a senior fellow at the Hoover Institution, recognizes the critical importance of the institutions—the "rules of the game"—that shape human interactions. His book *Knowledge and Decisions* stresses the role of knowledge in the economy and how different institutional arrangements compare at using scarce information. Sowell is the author of many books and journal articles and writes a nationally syndicated column that appears in more than 150 newspapers. His writings address subjects ranging from race preferences and cultural differences to the origins and ideology of political conflict.

Consider the case of Janet, who loves tomatoes but hates onions, and Brad, who loves onions but hates tomatoes. They go out to dinner together and the waiter brings their salads. Brad turns to Janet and says, "I'll trade you the tomatoes on my salad for the onions on yours." Janet gladly agrees to the exchange. This simple example will help us illustrate two important aspects of voluntary exchange.

1. WHEN INDIVIDUALS ENGAGE IN A VOLUNTARY EXCHANGE, BOTH PARTIES ARE MADE BETTER OFF. In the previous example, Janet has the option of accepting or declining Brad's offer of a trade. If she accepts his offer, she does so *voluntarily*. Janet would agree to this exchange only if she expects to be better off as a result. Because she likes tomatoes better than onions, Janet's enjoyment of her salad will be greater with this trade than without it. On the other side, Brad has voluntarily made this offer of an exchange to Janet because Brad believes he will also be better off as a result of the exchange.

People tend to think of making, building, and creating things as productive activities. Agriculture and manufacturing are like this. On the one hand, they create something genuinely new, something that was not there before. On the other hand, trade—the mere exchange of one

---

[4]An illuminating discussion of this subject, termed the "physical fallacy," is found in Thomas Sowell, *Knowledge and Decisions* (New York: Basic Books, 1980), 67–72.

thing for another—does not create new material items. You might be tempted to think that if goods are merely being traded, one party will be better off and the other worse off. A closer look at the motivation for trade helps us see through this popular fallacy. Exchange takes place because both parties expect it will make them better off. If they didn't, they wouldn't agree to do it. For example, if Janet liked onions better than tomatoes, she wouldn't have traded with Brad. The fact that she agreed to the trade means she thinks she has something to gain by doing so. Brad thinks the same thing when it comes to his tomatoes. In other words, because their exchange is voluntary, *both* Janet and Brad are made better off. As the chapter-opening quotation illustrates, most errors in economic reasoning happen when we forget that voluntary trades, like the one between Janet and Brad, make both parties better off.

2. BY CHANNELING GOODS AND RESOURCES TO THOSE WHO VALUE THEM MOST, TRADE CREATES VALUE AND INCREASES THE WEALTH CREATED BY A SOCIETY'S RESOURCES. Because preferences differ among individuals, the value of an item can vary greatly from one person to another. Therefore, trade can create value by moving goods from those who value them less to those who value them more. The simple exchange between Janet and Brad also illustrates this point. Imagine for a moment that Brad and Janet had never met and instead were both eating their salads alone. Without the ability to engage in this exchange, both would have eaten their salads but not had as much enjoyment from them. When goods are moved to individuals who value them more, the total value created by a society's limited resources is increased. The same two salads create more value when the trade occurs than when it doesn't.

It is easy to think of material things as wealth, but material things are not wealth until they are in the hands of someone who values them. A highly technical book on electronics that is of no value to an art collector may be worth several hundred dollars to an engineer. Similarly, a painting that is unappreciated by an engineer may be of great value to an art collector. Therefore, a voluntary exchange that moves the electronics book to the engineer and the painting to the art collector will increase the value of both goods. By channeling goods and resources toward those who value them most, trade creates wealth for both the trading partners and for the nation.

Transaction Costs—A Barrier to Trade

How many times have you been sitting home late at night, hungry, wishing you had a meal from your favorite fast-food restaurant? You would gladly pay the $4 price for the value meal you have in mind, but you feel it is just not worth the time and effort to get dressed and make that drive. The costs of the time, effort, and other resources necessary to search out, negotiate, and conclude an exchange are called **transaction costs**. High transaction costs can be a barrier to potentially productive exchange.

Transaction costs

The time, effort, and other resources needed to search out, negotiate, and complete an exchange.

Twentieth Century Fox/The Kobal Collection

ECONOMICS *At The Movies*

Wall Street (1987)

Michael Douglas won an Oscar for his performance in *Wall Street*, but he gets a failing grade for his understanding of economics. In response to a question Charlie Sheen poses to him about how much money is "enough," Michael Douglas replies: "It's not a question of enough, pal. It's a zero-sum game. Somebody wins; somebody loses. Money itself isn't lost or gained, it's simply transferred from one person to another." Wrong! In the real world, even on Wall Street, voluntary exchanges occur only when both parties expect to gain. Voluntary trade is a positive-sum game, meaning that wealth is created. It is not a zero-sum game, in which the gains to one person result in losses to another.

Because of transaction costs, we should not expect all potentially valuable trades to take place, any more than we expect all useful knowledge to be learned, all safety measures to be taken, or all potential "A" grades to be earned. Frequent fliers know that if they never miss a flight, they are probably spending too much time waiting in airports. Similarly, the seller of a car, a house, or a ballet ticket knows that finding the one person in the world willing to pay the most money for the good is not worth the enormous effort it would take to find him or her. Information is costly. That is one reason that perfection in exchange, as in most things we do, is seldom worth achieving.

The Internet has significantly lowered transaction costs. The auction Web site eBay helps sellers to reach millions of potential buyers with little effort and few costs. Buyers can easily search eBay for items they want to buy, even if the items are located halfway around the world. Other Web sites, such as BizRate and PriceGrabber, scour online shopping sites for the lowest prices so buyers don't have to. Consumers can also readily find detailed information about products on any number of sites. Amazon.com posts prices, product information provided by manufacturers, and reviews from other buyers. By reducing transaction costs, the Internet creates value and wealth. It expands the number of trades that are made, and makes it faster and easier to make them.

The Middleman as a Cost Reducer

Middleman

A person who buys and sells goods or services or arranges trades. A middleman reduces transaction costs.

Because it is costly for buyers and sellers to find each other and to negotiate the exchange, an entrepreneurial opportunity exists for people to become **middlemen**. Middlemen provide buyers and sellers information at a lower cost and arrange trades between them. Many people think middlemen just add to the buyer's expense without performing a useful function. However, because of transaction costs, without middlemen, many trades would never happen (nor would the gains from them be realized). An auto dealer, for example, is a middleman. An auto dealer helps both the manufacturer and the buyer. The dealer helps buyers by maintaining an inventory of vehicles for them to choose from. Knowledgeable salespeople hired by the dealer help car shoppers quickly learn about the vehicles they're interested in and the pros and cons of each. Car buyers also like to know that a local dealer will honor the manufacturer's warranty and provide parts and service for the car. The dealer helps manufacturers by handling tasks like these so they can concentrate on designing and making better cars.

Grocers are also middlemen. Each of us could deal with farmers directly to buy our food—probably at a lower monetary cost. But that would have a high opportunity cost. Finding and dealing with different farmers for every product we wanted to buy would take a lot of time. Alternatively, we could form consumer cooperatives, banding together to eliminate the middleman, using our own warehouses and our own volunteer labor to order, receive, display, distribute, and collect payment for the food. In fact, some cooperatives like this do exist. But most people prefer instead to pay a grocer to provide all of the goods they want rather than trying to trade with different farmers.

Stockbrokers, realtors, publishers, and merchants of all sorts are other kinds of middlemen. For a fee, they reduce transaction costs for both buyers and sellers. By making exchanges cheaper and more convenient, middlemen cause more efficient trades to happen. In so doing, they themselves create value.

The Importance of Property Rights

Property rights

The rights to use, control, and obtain the benefits from a good or resource.

The buyer of an apple, a CD, a television set, or an automobile generally takes the item home. The buyer of a steamship or an office building, though, may never touch it. When exchange occurs, it's really the **property rights** of the item that change hands.

PRIVATE OWNERSHIP

Private ownership provides people with a strong incentive to take care of things and develop resources in ways that are highly valued by others.

Private-property rights involve three things:

1. the right to exclusive use of the property (that is, the owner has sole possession, control, and use of the property, including the right to exclude others);

2. legal protection against invasion from other individuals who would seek to use or abuse the property without the owner's permission; and

3. the right to transfer, sell, exchange, or mortgage the property.

Private owners can do anything they want with their property as long as they do not use it in a manner that invades or infringes on the rights of another. For example, I cannot throw the hammer that I own through the television set that you own. If I did, I would be violating your property right to your television. The same is true if I operate a factory spewing out pollution harming you or your land.[5] Because an owner has the right to control the use of property, the owner also must accept responsibility for the outcomes of that control.

In contrast to private ownership, common-property ownership occurs when multiple people simultaneously have or claim ownership rights to a good or resource. If the resource is open to all, none of the common owners can prevent the others from using or damaging the property. Most beaches, rivers, and roads are examples of commonly owned property. The distinction between private- and common-property ownership is important because common ownership does not create the same powerful incentives for conservation and efficient use as private ownership. Economists are fond of saying that when everybody owns something, nobody owns it.

Clearly defined and enforced private-property rights are a key to economic progress because of the powerful incentive effects that private ownership generates. The following four incentives are particularly important:

1. PRIVATE OWNERS CAN GAIN BY EMPLOYING THEIR RESOURCES IN WAYS THAT ARE BENEFICIAL TO OTHERS, AND THEY BEAR THE OPPORTUNITY COST OF IGNORING THE WISHES OF OTHERS. Realtors often advise homeowners to use neutral colors for countertops and walls in their house because they will improve the resale value of the home. As a private owner, you could install bright green fixtures and paint your walls deep purple, but you will bear the cost (in terms of a lower selling price) of ignoring the wishes of others who might want to buy your house later. Conversely, by fixing up a house and doing things to it that others find beneficial, you can reap the benefit of a higher selling price. Similarly, you could spray paint orange designs all over the outside of your brand-new car, but private ownership gives you an incentive not to do so because the resale value of the car depends on the value that *others* place on it.

Consider a parcel of undeveloped, privately owned land near a university. The private owner of the land can do many things with it. For example, she could leave it undeveloped, turn it into a metered parking lot, erect a restaurant, or build rental housing. Will the wishes and desires of the nearby students be reflected in her choice, even though they are not the owners of the property? Yes. Whichever use is more highly valued by potential customers will earn her the highest investment return. If housing is relatively hard to find but there are plenty of other restaurants, the profitability of using her land for housing will be higher than the profitability of using it for a restaurant. Private ownership gives her a strong incentive to use her property in a way that will also fulfill the wishes of others. If she decides to leave the property undeveloped instead of erecting housing that would benefit the students, she will bear the opportunity cost of forgone rental income from the property.

As a second example, consider the owner of an apartment complex near your campus. The owner may not care much for swimming pools, workout facilities, study desks, washers

"Their house looks so nice. They must be getting ready to sell it."

A private owner has a strong incentive to do things with his or her property that increase its value to others.

---

[5]For a detailed explanation of how property rights protect the environment, with several real-world examples, see Roger E. Meiners and Bruce Yandle, *The Common Law: How It Protects the Environment* (Bozeman, MT: PERC, 1998), available online at http://www.perc.org.

and dryers, or green areas. Nonetheless, private ownership provides the owner with a strong incentive to provide these items if students and other potential customers value them more than it costs to provide them. Why? Because tenants will be willing to pay higher rents to live in a complex with amenities that they value. The owners of rental property can profit by providing an additional amenity that tenants value as long as the tenants are willing to pay enough additional rent to cover the cost of providing it. Because renters differ in their preferences and willingness to pay for amenities, some will prefer to live in less expensive apartments with fewer amenities, whereas others will prefer to live in more expensive apartments with a greater range of amenities. By choosing among potential apartment complexes, renters are able to buy as few or as many of these amenities as they wish.

2. PRIVATE OWNERS HAVE A STRONG INCENTIVE TO CARE FOR AND PROPERLY MANAGE WHAT THEY OWN. Will Ed regularly change the oil in his car? Will he see to it that the seats don't get torn? Probably so, because being careless about these things would reduce the car's value, both to him and to any future owner. The car and its value—the sale price if he sells it—belong just to Ed, so he would bear the burden of a decline in the car's value if the oil ran low and ruined the engine, or if the seats were torn. Similarly, he would capture the value of an expenditure that improved the car, like a new paint job. As the owner, Ed has both the authority and the incentive to protect the car against harm or neglect and even to enhance its value. Private-property rights give owners a strong incentive for good stewardship.

Do you take equally good care not to damage an apartment you rent as you would your own house? If you share an apartment with several roommates, are the common areas of the apartment (such as the kitchen and living room) as neatly kept as the bedrooms? Based on economic theory, we guess that the answer to both of these questions is probably "No."

A few years ago, the student government association at Berry College in Georgia purchased twenty bicycles to be placed around campus for everyone's use.[6] These $200 Schwinn Cruiser bicycles were painted red and were marked with a plate reading "Berry Bike." The bikes were available on a first-come, first-served basis, and students were encouraged to take them whenever they needed them and leave them anywhere on campus for others to use when they were finished. What do you think happened to these bikes? Within two months, most of these high-quality bikes were severely damaged or lost. The campus newspaper reported on the "mangled corpses of twisted red metal that lie about campus." Over the summer break, the student government replaced or fixed the bikes, but despite its pleas to "treat the bikes as if they were your own property," the same thing happened the following fall precisely because the bikes weren't the students' own property. It wasn't that the students at Berry College were inherently destructive; after all, there were no problems on campus with privately owned bikes being lost or abused during this time. It was a matter of the different incentives they faced. The student government association eventually abandoned the program and began leasing the remaining bikes to individual students instead. As you can see, there is no denying the strong incentive that private ownership creates for owners to care for their property (or the lack of incentive when private ownership is not clearly defined and enforced).

When apartments and other investment properties are owned privately, the owner has a strong incentive to provide amenities that others value highly relative to their cost.

Kzenon, 2009/Used under license from Shutterstock.com

© Compassionate Eye Foundation/ Getty Images

[6]Daniel L. Alban and E. Frank Stephenson, "The 'Berry Bikes': A Lesson in Private Property," *Ideas on Liberty* 49, no. 10 (October 1999): 8–9.

The incentive for owners to care for and properly manage their property is strong. The owner of a hotel doesn't want to neglect fixing electrical or plumbing problems if it means fewer repair costs due to electrical fires or water leaks in the future. The owner knows travelers aren't going to want to stay in a charred or water-damaged hotel. Poor management will reduce the hotel's value and the owner's personal wealth. This gives the owner an incentive to manage the asset properly.

3. PRIVATE OWNERS HAVE AN INCENTIVE TO CONSERVE FOR THE FUTURE— PARTICULARLY IF THE PROPERTY IS EXPECTED TO INCREASE IN VALUE. People have a much stronger incentive to conserve privately owned property than they do commonly owned property. For example, when Steven was in college, the general rule among his roommates was that any food or drink in the house was common property—open game for the hungry or thirsty mouth of anyone who stumbled across it. There was never a reason for Steven to conserve food or drinks in the house because it would be quickly consumed by a roommate coming in later that night. When Steven first started living alone, he noticed a dramatic change in his behavior. When he ordered a pizza, he would save some for the next day's lunch rather than eating it all that night. Steven began counting his drinks before he had one to make sure there were enough left for the next day. When Steven was the sole owner, he began delaying his current consumption to conserve for the future because he was the one, not his roommates, who reaped the benefit from his conservation.

Similarly, when more than one individual has the right to drill oil from an underground pool of oil, each has an incentive to extract as much as possible, as quickly as possible. Any oil conserved for the future will probably be taken by someone else. In contrast, when only one owner has the right to drill, the oil will be extracted more slowly. The same applies to the common-property problems involved in overfishing of the sea compared with fisheries that use privately owned ponds.

Someone who owns land, a house, or a factory has a strong incentive to bear costs now, if necessary, to preserve the asset's value for the future. The owner's wealth is tied up in the value of the property, which reflects nothing more than the net benefits that will be available to a future owner. Thus, the wealth of private owners is dependent upon their willingness and ability to look ahead, maintain, and conserve those things that will be more highly valued in the future. This is why private ownership is particularly important for the optimal conservation of natural resources.

4. PRIVATE OWNERS HAVE AN INCENTIVE TO LOWER THE CHANCE THAT THEIR PROPERTY WILL CAUSE DAMAGE TO THE PROPERTY OF OTHERS. Private ownership links responsibility with the right of control. Private owners can be held accountable for damage done to

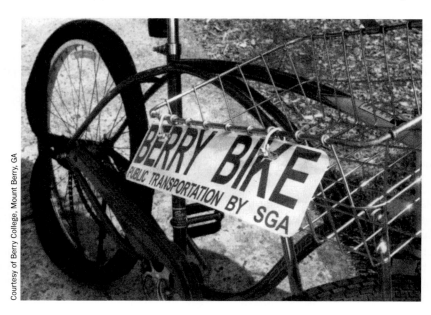

Courtesy of Berry College, Mount Berry, GA

Without clearly defined private-property rights, there is less of an incentive to take proper care of things—as the student government administration at Berry College found out when it provided common-property bikes to be used around campus.

others through the misuse of their property. A car owner has a right to drive his car, but will be held accountable if the brakes aren't maintained and the car damages someone else's property. Similarly, a chemical company has control over its products, but, exactly for that reason, it is legally liable for damages if it mishandles the chemicals. Courts of law recognize and enforce the authority granted by ownership, but they also enforce the responsibility that goes with that authority. Because private-property owners can be held accountable for damages they cause, they have an incentive to use their property responsibly and take steps to reduce the likelihood of harm to others. A property owner, for example, has an incentive to cut down a dying tree before it falls into a neighbor's house and to leash or restrain his or her dog if it's likely to bite others.

Private Ownership and Markets

Private ownership and competitive markets provide the foundation for cooperative behavior among individuals. When private-property rights are protected and enforced, the permission of the owner must be sought before anyone else can use the property. Put another way, if you want to use a good or resource, you must either buy or lease it from the owner. This means that each of us must face the cost of using scarce resources. Furthermore, market prices give private owners a strong incentive to consider the desires of others and use their resources in ways others value.

Friedrich Hayek, the winner of the 1974 Nobel Prize in economics, used the expression "the extended order" to refer to the tendency for markets to lead perfect strangers from different backgrounds around the world to cooperate with one another. Let's go back to the example of the property owner who has the choice of leaving her land idle or building housing to benefit students. The landowner might not know any students in her town nor particularly care about providing them housing. However, because she is motivated by market prices, she might build an apartment complex and eventually do business with a lot of students she never intended to get to know. In the process, she will purchase materials, goods, and services produced by other strangers.

Things are different in countries that don't recognize private-ownership rights or enforce them. In these countries, whoever has the political power or authority can simply seize property from whomever might have it without compensating them. In his book *The Mystery of Capital*, economist Hernando de Soto argues that the lack of well-defined and enforced property rights explains why some underdeveloped countries (despite being market based) have made little economic progress. He points out that in many of these nations, generations of people have squatted on the land without any legal deed giving them formal ownership. The problem is these squatters cannot borrow against the land or the homes they built on it to generate capital because they don't have a deed to it, nor can they prevent someone else from arbitrarily taking the land away from them.

Private ownership and markets can also play an important role in environmental protection and natural-resource conservation. Ocean fishing rights, tradable rights to pollute, and private ownership of endangered species are just some examples. The accompanying Applications in Economics feature, "Protecting Endangered Species with Private-Property Rights," explores some of these issues.

Production Possibilities Curve

People try to get the most from their limited resources by making purposeful choices and engaging in economizing behavior. This can be illustrated using a conceptual tool called the **production possibilities curve**. The production possibilities curve shows the maximum amount of any two products that can be produced from a fixed set of resources, and the possible trade-offs in production between them. The real economy obviously produces more than just two products, but this highly simplified production possibilities curve can help us understand a number of important economic ideas.

Production possibilities curve

A curve that outlines all possible combinations of total output that could be produced, assuming (1) a fixed amount of productive resources, (2) a given amount of technical knowledge, and (3) full and efficient use of those resources. The slope of the curve indicates the amount of one product that must be given up to produce more of the other.

APPLICATIONS IN ECONOMICS

Protecting Endangered Species with Private-Property Rights

Tom Brakefield/Getty Images

Have you ever wondered why the wild tiger is endangered in much of the world but most cats are thriving? Or why spotted owls are threatened in the Pacific Northwest but chickens are not? Why have elephant and rhinoceros populations declined in number but not cattle or hogs? The incentives accompanying private ownership provide the answer.

To understand why many wild animals are scarce, consider what happens with animals that provide food, most of which are privately owned. Suppose that people decided to eat less beef. Beef prices would fall, and the incentive for individuals to dedicate land and other resources to raise cattle would decline. The result would be fewer cows. The market demand for beef *creates* the incentive for suppliers to maintain herds of cattle and to protect them under a system of private ownership.

In some ways, the rhinoceros is similar to a cow. A rhino, like a large bull in a cattle herd, may charge if disturbed. At 3,000 pounds, a charging rhino can be very dangerous to humans. Also like cattle, rhinos can be valuable to people—a single horn from a black rhino, used for artistic carvings and medicines, can sell for up to $30,000. But when hunting rhinos and selling their horns is illegal, rhinos become a favorite target of poachers—people who hunt illegally. Poachers are sometimes even assisted by local people eager to see fewer rhinos present because rhinos make life risky for humans and they also compete for food and water.

Rhinos are very different from cattle in one important respect: In most of Africa where they naturally range, private ownership of the rhino is prohibited. Since 1977, many nations have outlawed rhino hunting and forbidden the sale of rhino parts. But this approach has only made things worse for the rhino: between 1970 and 1994, the number of black rhinos declined by 95%.[1] According to South African economist Michael 't Sas-Rolfes, the trade ban "has not had a discernible effect on rhino numbers and does not seem to have stopped the trade in rhino horn. If anything, the . . . listings led to a sharp increase in the black market price of rhino horn, which simply fuelled further poaching and encouraged speculative stockpiling of horn."

But what if the powerful incentives created by private ownership were instead brought to bear on the rhino? That actually happened for a while in Zimbabwe. Landowners were allowed to fence and manage game animals on their property. Because they could profit from protecting the big animals, some ranchers shifted their operations from producing cattle to wildlife protection, ecotourism, and hunting, often in cooperation with neighboring landowners. Under these rules, the black rhino population climbed dramatically. And because ranchers were allowed to cooperate and combine operations, they could reduce fencing between ranches and manage the larger preserves as a unit, better helping not only rhinos but other valued wildlife as well.

Indeed, several parts of southern Africa have a tradition, extending back to the 1960s, of allowing ownership of wildlife. Namibia, for example, gave those rights to private landholders in the 1960s and extended them to communal lands in the mid-1990s. "These institutional reforms led to wildlife becoming an economically valued land use at the local level," says wildlife specialist Fred Nelson. "For example, in 2003, Namibia's local communal landholders earned over US $1 million from wildlife-based enterprises such as tourism and hunting."[2] Landholders had invested in conservation measures to speed up the recovery that made these revenues possible.

Nelson reports that wildlife on private lands in Namibia increased by an estimated 80% from 1972 to 1992 as a result of the new policies. Where similar policy changes have occurred, wildlife has increased, says Nelson. "In South Africa, Namibia, Botswana, and Zimbabwe (prior to its sociopolitical collapse, 2000–present), the proportion of large herbivore species that are increasing or stable substantially exceeds the number that are declining." Clearly, property rights to ownership or use are one key to conservation.

---

[1]See Michael De Alessi, *Private Conservation and Black Rhinos in Zimbabwe: The Savé Valley and Bubiana Conservancies*, available online at http://www.cei.org/gencon/025,01687.cfm.
[2]Fred Nelson, "Are Large Mammal Declines in Africa Inevitable?" *African Journal of Ecology*, 46 (2007): 3–4.

EXHIBIT 1 illustrates the production possibilities curve for Susan, an intelligent economics major. This curve indicates the combinations of English and economics grades that she thinks she can earn if she spends a total of ten hours per week studying for the two subjects. Currently, she is choosing to study the material in each course that she expects will help her grade the most for the time spent, and she is allocating five hours of study time

EXHIBIT 1
Production Possibilities
Curve for Susan's
Grades in English and
Economics

*The production possibilities for
Susan, in terms of grades, are illustrated for ten hours of total study
time. If Susan studied ten hours
per week in these two classes, she
could attain a D in English and an
A in economics (point S), a
B in English and a B in economics
(point T), or a D in economics
and an A in English (point U).*

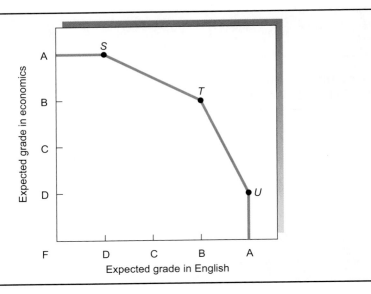

to each course. She expects that this amount of time, carefully spent on each course, will allow her to earn a B grade in both, indicated at point *T*. But if she were to take some time away from studying one of the two subjects and spend it studying the other, she could raise her grade in the course receiving more study time. However, it would come at the cost of a lower grade in the course she spends less time studying for. If she were to move to point *S* by spending more hours on economics and fewer on English, for example, her expected economics grade would rise, while her expected English grade would fall. This illustrates the first important concept shown in the production possibilities framework—the idea of trade-offs in the use of scarce resources. Whenever more of one thing is produced, there is an opportunity cost in terms of something else that now must be forgone.

You might notice that Susan's production possibilities curve indicates that the additional study time required to raise her economics grade by one letter, from a B to an A (moving from point *T* to point *S*), would require giving up two letter grades in her English class, not just one, reducing her English grade from a B to a D. If, alternatively, Susan were to move from point *T* to point *U*, the opposite would be true—she would improve her English grade by one letter at the expense of two letter grades in economics. You can understand this by thinking about your own studying behavior. When you have only a limited amount of time to study a subject, you begin by studying the most important (grade-increasing) material first. As you spend additional time on that subject, you begin studying topics that are of decreasing importance for your grade. Thus, adding an hour of study time to the subject Susan studies least will have a larger impact on her grade than will taking away an hour from the subject on which she currently spends more time.

This idea of increasing opportunity cost is reflected in the slope of the production possibilities curve. The curve is flatter to the left of point *T*, and steeper to the right, showing that, as Susan takes more and more of her resources (time, in this case) from one course and puts it into the other, she must give up greater and greater amounts of productivity in the course getting fewer resources.

Of course, Susan could study more economics *without* giving up her English study time, if she gave up some leisure, or study time for other courses, or her part-time job in the campus bookstore. If she gave up leisure or her job and added those hours to the ten hours of study time for economics and English, the entire curve in Exhibit 1 would shift outward. She could get better grades in both classes by having more time to study.

Can the production possibilities concept be applied to the entire economy? Yes. We can grow more soybeans if we grow less corn, because both can be grown on the same land. Beefing up the nation's military would mean we would have to produce fewer nonmilitary goods than we could otherwise. When scarce resources are being used efficiently, getting more of one requires that we sacrifice others.

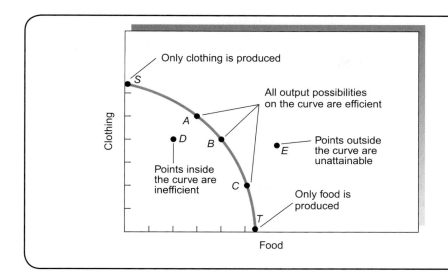

EXHIBIT 2
Concept of Production
Possibilities Curve for
an Economy

*When an economy is using its
limited resources efficiently, production of more clothing requires
that the economy give up some
other goods—such as food in
this example. In time, improved
technology, more resources, or
improvement in its economic
organization could make it possible to produce more of both
goods by shifting the production
possibilities curve outward.*

EXHIBIT 2 shows a hypothetical production possibilities curve for an economy with a limited amount of resources that produces only two goods: food and clothing. The points along the curve represent all possible combinations of food and clothing that could be produced with the current level of resources and technology of the economy (assuming the resources are being used efficiently). A point outside the production possibilities curve (such as point *E*) would be considered unattainable at the present time. A point inside the production possibilities curve (such as point *D*) is attainable, but producing that amount would mean that the economy is not making maximum use of its resources (some resources are being underutilized). Thus, point *D* is considered inefficient.

More specifically, the production possibilities curve shows all of the maximum combinations of two goods that an economy will be able to produce: (1) given a fixed quantity of resources, (2) holding the level of technology constant, and (3) assuming that all resources are used efficiently.

When these three conditions are met, the economy will be at the edge of its production possibilities frontier (where points *A*, *B*, and *C* lie), and producing more of one good will necessitate producing less of others. If condition 3 above is not met, and resources are being used inefficiently, an economy would be operating inside its production possibilities curve. If the level of resources and technology change (conditions 1 and 2), it will result in an outward shift in the production possibilities curve. We will return to these factors that can shift the production possibilities curve in a moment.

Notice that the production possibilities curve is concave (or bowed out) to the origin, just as Susan's was in Exhibit 1 because of the concept of increasing opportunity cost. Here, the curved shape reflects the fact that an economy's resources are not equally well suited to produce food and clothing. If an economy were using all its resources to produce clothing (point *S*), transferring those resources least suited for producing clothing toward food production would reduce clothing output a little but increase food output a lot. Because the resources transferred would be those better suited for producing food and less suited for producing clothing, the opportunity cost of producing additional food (in terms of clothing forgone) is low—near point *S*. However, as more and more resources are devoted to food production and successively larger amounts of food are produced (moving the economy from *S* to *A* to *B* and so on), the opportunity cost of food will rise. This is because, as more and more food is produced, additional food output can be achieved only by using resources that are less and less suitable for the production of food relative to clothing. Thus, as food output is expanded, successively larger amounts of clothing must be forgone per unit of additional food. This is similar to what happened to Susan when she diverted study hours from one course to another. Only this time, we are talking about an entire economy.

Shifting the Production Possibilities Curve Outward

What restricts an economy—once its resources are fully utilized—from producing more of everything? Why can't we get more of something produced without having to give up the production of something else? The same constraint that kept Susan from simultaneously making a higher grade in both English and economics: a lack of resources. As long as all current resources are being used efficiently, the only way to get more of one good is to sacrifice some of the other. Over time, however, it is possible for a country's production possibilities curve to shift outward, making it possible for more of all goods to be produced. There are four factors that could potentially shift the production possibilities curve outward.

1. AN INCREASE IN THE ECONOMY'S RESOURCE BASE WOULD EXPAND OUR ABILITY TO PRODUCE GOODS AND SERVICES. If we had more or better resources, we could produce a greater amount of all goods. Resources such as machinery, buildings, tools, and education are human-made, and thus we can expand our resource base by devoting some of our efforts to producing them. This **investment** would provide us with better tools and skills and increase our ability to produce goods and services in the future. However, like with the production of other goods, devoting effort and resources toward producing these long-lasting physical assets means fewer resources are available to produce other things, in this case goods for current consumption. Thus, the choice between using resources to produce goods for current consumption and using them to produce investment goods for the future can also be illustrated within the production possibilities framework. The two economies illustrated in **EXHIBIT 3** begin with identical production possibilities curves (*RS*). Notice that Economy A dedicates more of its output to investment (shown by I_A) than Economy B (shown by I_B). Economy B, on the other hand, consumes more than Economy A. Because Economy A allocates more of its resources to investment and less to consumption, A's production possibilities curve shifts outward over time by a greater amount than B's. In other words, the growth rate of Economy A—the expansion of its ability to produce goods—is enhanced by this investment. But more investment in machines and human skills requires a reduction in current consumption.

2. ADVANCEMENTS IN TECHNOLOGY CAN EXPAND THE ECONOMY'S PRODUCTION POSSIBILITIES. **Technology** determines the maximum amount of output an economy can produce given the resources it has. New and better technology makes it possible for us to get more output from our resources. An important form of technological change is **invention**—the use of science and engineering to create new products or processes. In recent years, for example, inventions have allowed us to develop photographs faster and more cheaply,

Investment

The purchase, construction, or development of resources, including physical assets, such as plants and machinery, and human assets, such as better education. Investment expands an economy's resources. The process of investment is sometimes called capital formation.

Technology

The technological knowledge available in an economy at any given time. The level of technology determines the amount of output we can generate with our limited resources.

Invention

The creation of a new product or process, often facilitated by the knowledge of engineering and science.

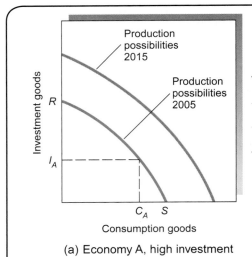

(a) Economy A, high investment

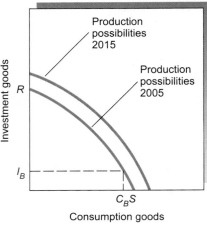

(b) Economy B, low investment

EXHIBIT 3

Investment and Production Possibilities in the Future

Here we illustrate two economies (A and B) that initially confront identical production possibilities curves (RS). Economy A allocates a larger share of its output to investment (I_A, compared to I_B for Economy B). As a result, the production possibilities curve of the high-investment economy (Economy A) will tend to shift outward by a larger amount over time than the low-investment economy's will.

process data more rapidly, get more oil from existing fields, and send information instantly and cheaply by satellite. Such technological advances increase our production possibilities, shifting our economy's entire production possibilities curve outward.

An economy can also benefit from technological change through **innovation**—the practical and effective adoption of new techniques. Such innovation is commonly carried out by an **entrepreneur**—a person who introduces new products or improved techniques to satisfy consumers at a lower cost. To make a profit, an entrepreneur must convert or rearrange resources in a way that increases their value. This also pushes the production possibilities curve outward.

Take, for example, Henry Ford, an entrepreneur who changed how cars were made by pioneering the assembly line. With the same amount of labor and materials, Ford made more cars more cheaply. Another entrepreneur, the late Ray Kroc, purchased a hamburger restaurant from Richard and Maurice McDonald and built it into the world's largest fast-food chain. Kroc revolutionized fast food by offering attractive food at economical prices. He also developed a franchising system that resulted in uniform quality across the many different McDonald's restaurants worldwide. More recently, entrepreneurs like Steven Jobs (Apple Computer) and Bill Gates (Microsoft) helped develop the personal computer and software programs that dramatically increased their usefulness to businesses and households.

Through entrepreneurial discovery and innovation, new products and methods of production are continuously replacing old ones. The great Harvard economist, Joseph Schumpeter, called this process **creative destruction**. The compact disc, for example, rendered vinyl records obsolete, while the automobile caused the demise of the horse and buggy industry. Although this process destroys some businesses or industries, it creates new and arguably better ones in their place. Creative destruction is a powerful force leading to economic growth and prosperity.

3. AN IMPROVEMENT IN THE RULES UNDER WHICH THE ECONOMY FUNCTIONS CAN ALSO INCREASE OUTPUT. The legal system of a country influences the ability of people to cooperate with one another and produce goods. Changes in legal institutions that promote social cooperation and motivate people to produce what others want will also push the production possibilities curve outward. However, poor institutions can reduce both the level of resources used (shifting the curve inward) and how efficiently they are used (causing the economy to operate inside its production possibilities curve).

Historically, legal innovations have been an important source of economic progress. During the eighteenth century, a system of patents was established in Europe and North America, giving inventors private-property rights to their ideas. At about the same time, laws were passed allowing businesses to establish themselves legally as corporations, reducing the cost of forming large firms that were often required for the mass production of manufactured goods. Both of these legal changes allowed improved forms of economic organization and accelerated the growth of output by shifting the production possibilities curve outward more rapidly.

Sometimes governments, perhaps because of ignorance or prejudice, adopt legal institutions that reduce production possibilities. Laws that restrict or prohibit trade are one example. For almost a hundred years following the American Civil War, the laws of several southern states prohibited hiring African Americans for certain jobs and restricted other economic exchanges between blacks and whites. The legislation not only was harmful to African Americans; it also retarded economic progress and reduced the production possibilities of these states.

4. BY WORKING HARDER AND GIVING UP CURRENT LEISURE, WE COULD INCREASE OUR PRODUCTION OF GOODS AND SERVICES. Hypothetically, the production possibilities curve would shift outward if everyone worked more hours and took less leisure time. Strictly speaking, however, leisure is also a good, so we would simply be giving up leisure to have more of other things. If we were to construct a production possibilities curve for leisure versus other goods, this would be shown as simply a movement along the curve. However, if we restrict our model to only material goods and services, a change in the amount we work would be shown as a shift in the curve.

Innovation

The successful introduction and adoption of a new product or process; the economic application of inventions and marketing techniques.

Entrepreneur

A person who introduces new products or improved technologies and decides which projects to undertake. A successful entrepreneur's actions will increase the value of resources and expand the size of the economic pie.

Creative destruction

The replacement of old products and production methods by innovative new ones that consumers judge to be superior. The process generates economic growth and higher living standards.

How much people work depends not only on their personal preferences but also on public policy. For example, high tax rates on personal income may cause people to work less. This is because high tax rates reduce the payoff from working. When this happens, people spend more time doing other, untaxed activities—like leisure activities. This will move the production possibilities curve for material goods inward because the economy can't produce as much when people work less.

Production Possibilities and Economic Growth

Within the production possibilities framework, economic growth is simply an outward shift in the curve through time. The more rapidly the curve shifts outward, the more rapid is economic growth. There are other economic models that are used to analyze economic growth; however, they all share the production possibilities curve as a foundation. Economic growth is one of the most important topics in modern economics for good reason. On the one hand, an economic growth rate of 3 percent per year will result in living standards doubling approximately every twenty-three years. On the other hand, in a country experiencing an economic growth rate of only 1 percent, it will take approximately seventy years for living standards to double.

Trade, Output, and Living Standards

GAINS FROM TRADE

Trade makes it possible for people to generate more output through specialization and division of labor, large-scale production processes, and the dissemination of improved products and production methods.

As we previously discussed, trade creates value by moving goods from people who value them less to people who value them more. However, this is only part of the story. Trade also makes it possible for people to expand their output through specialization and **division of labor**, large-scale production, and the dissemination of better products and production methods.

Gains from Specialization and Division of Labor

Division of labor

A method that breaks down the production of a product into a series of specific tasks, each performed by a different worker.

Businesses can achieve higher output levels and greater productivity from their workers through specialization and division of labor. More than 200 years ago, Adam Smith noted the importance of this factor. Observing the operation of a pin manufacturer, Smith noted that when each worker specialized in a separate function needed to make pins, 10 workers together were able to produce 48,000 pins per day, or 4,800 pins per worker. Smith doubted an individual worker could produce even 20 pins per day working alone from start to finish on each pin.[7]

The division of labor separates production tasks into a series of related operations. Each worker performs one or a few of perhaps hundreds of tasks necessary to produce something. This process makes it possible to assign different tasks to those individuals who are able to accomplish them most efficiently (that is, at the lowest cost). Furthermore, a worker who specializes in just one narrow area becomes more experienced and more skilled in that task over time.

Law of comparative advantage

A principle that states that individuals, firms, regions, or nations can gain by specializing in the production of goods that they produce cheaply (at a low opportunity cost) and exchanging them for goods they cannot produce cheaply (at a high opportunity cost).

Trading partners can also benefit from specialization and the division of labor. The **law of comparative advantage**, developed in the early 1800s by the great English economist David Ricardo, explains why this is true. *The law of comparative advantage states that the total output of a group of individuals, an entire economy, or a group of nations will be*

---

[7]See Adam Smith, *An Inquiry into the Nature and Causes of the Wealth of Nations* (1776; Cannan's ed., Chicago: University of Chicago Press, 1976), 7–16, for additional detail on the importance of the division of labor.

greatest when the output of each good is produced by the person (or firm) with the lowest opportunity cost for that good.

Comparative advantage applies to trade among individuals, business firms, regions, and even nations. When trading partners are able to use more of their time and resources to produce the things each is best at, they will be able to produce more together than would otherwise have been possible. In turn, the mutual gains they get from trading will result in higher levels of income for each. It's a win-win situation for both.

If a good or service can be obtained more economically through trade, it makes sense to get it that way rather than producing it for yourself. For example, even though most doctors might be good at record keeping and arranging appointments, it's generally better for them to hire someone to perform these services for them. That's because the time doctors spend keeping records is time they could have spent seeing patients. The revenue forgone, reflecting the services lost to patients as a result of seeing fewer patients, would be greater than the cost of hiring the worker. The issue is not whether doctors are better record keepers than the assistants they could hire, but rather how they should use their time most efficiently.

If you think about it, the law of comparative advantage is common sense. If someone else is willing to supply you with a good at a lower cost than you can produce it yourself, doesn't it make sense to trade for it and use your time and resources to produce more of the things you can produce most efficiently? Consider the situation of Andrea, an attorney who earns $100 per hour providing legal services. She has several documents that need to be typed, and she is thinking about hiring a typist earning $15 per hour to do it. Andrea is an excellent typist, much faster than the prospective employee. She could do the job in 20 hours, whereas the typist would take 40 hours.

Because of her greater typing speed, some might think Andrea should handle the job herself. This is not the case. If she types the documents, the job will cost her $2,000—the opportunity cost of 20 hours of practicing law at $100 per hour. Alternatively, the cost of having the documents typed by the typist is only $600 (40 hours at $15 per hour). Andrea's comparative advantage lies in practicing law. By hiring the typist, she will increase her own productivity for clients and will make more money.

The implications of the law of comparative advantage are universal. Any group will be able to produce more output from its available resources when each good or service is produced by the person with the lowest opportunity cost. This insight is particularly important in understanding the way a market economy works. Purposeful decision making indicates that buyers will try to get the most for their money. They will not knowingly choose a high-cost option when a lower-cost alternative of the same value is available. This places low-cost suppliers at a competitive advantage. Thus, they will generally survive and prosper in a market economy. As a result, the production of goods and resources will naturally tend to be allocated according to comparative advantage.

Most people recognize that Americans benefit from trade among the nation's fifty states. For example, the residents of Nebraska and Florida are able to produce a larger joint output and achieve higher income levels when Nebraskans specialize in producing corn and other grain products and Floridians specialize in producing oranges and other citrus products. The same is true for trade among nations. Like Nebraskans and Floridians, people in different nations will be better off if they specialize in the goods and services they can produce at a low cost and trade them for goods they produce at a high cost. See the addendum to this chapter for additional evidence on this point.

Gains from Mass Production Methods

Trade also promotes economic progress by making it possible for firms to lower their per-unit costs with mass production. Say a nation isolated itself and refused to trade with other countries. In an economy like this, self-sufficiency and small-scale production would be the norm. If trade were allowed, however, the nation's firms could sell their products to customers around the world. This would make it feasible for the firms to adopt more efficient, large-scale production processes. Mass production often leads to labor and machinery efficiencies that increase enormously the output per worker. But without trade, these gains could not be achieved.

Trade channels goods to those who value them most. Trade also helps disseminate ideas for improved products and makes production methods such as specialization, the division of labor, and mass production more feasible. Over the years, trade has enabled us to produce more with our limited resources, dramatically improving our living standards.

Sandra Baker/Photographer's Choice/Getty Images

Gains from Innovation

Trade also makes it possible to realize gains from the discovery and dissemination of innovative products and production processes. Economic growth involves brain power, innovation, and the application of technology. Without trade, however, the gains derived from the discovery of better ways of doing things would be stifled. Furthermore, observing and interacting with other people using different and better technologies often encourage others to copy successful approaches. People also modify the technology they observe, adapting it for their own purposes. This sometimes results in new, and even better, technologies. Again, gains from these sources would be far more limited in a world without trade.

Can you imagine the difficulty involved in producing your own housing, clothing, and food, to say nothing of radios, television sets, dishwashers, automobiles, and telephone services? Yet, most families in North America, Western Europe, Japan, and Australia enjoy all these conveniences. They are able to do so largely because their economies are organized in such a way that individuals can cooperate, specialize, and trade, thereby reaping the benefits of the enormous increases in output—in both quantity and diversity—that can be generated. In contrast, countries that impose obstacles that retard exchange—either domestic or international—hinder their citizens from achieving these gains and more prosperous lives.

Human Ingenuity and the Creation of Wealth

HUMAN INGENUITY

Economic goods are the result of human ingenuity and action; thus, the size of the "economic pie" is variable, not fixed.

The size of a country's "economic pie" is most easily thought of as the total dollar value of all goods and services produced during some period of time. This economic pie is the total amount of wealth (or value) created in the economy. It is not some fixed total waiting to be divided up among people. It is simply a statistic—a grand total, calculated by adding up the wealth created by each of the individuals in the economy.

Errors in economic reasoning often stem from the incorrect notion that the size of the economic pie is fixed. On the contrary, the size of the economic pie reflects the physical effort and ingenuity of human beings. It is not an endowment from nature. Economic output expands as we discover better ways of doing things. So over time, it is human knowledge and ingenuity—perhaps more than anything else—that limit our economic progress. If Jim, a local farmer who normally produces $30,000 worth of corn each year, finds a better growing method enabling him to produce $40,000 of corn per year, he has created additional wealth. But Jim has actually created more than the $10,000 in extra wealth. The $10,000 is only his share of the gains from the additional trades made possible by the extra corn he grew. Exchange makes both buyer and seller better off, so the total wealth created by Jim includes not only his $10,000 but also the gains of all of the buyers who purchased corn from him as well.

This highlights an important point: in a market economy, a larger income for one person does not mean a smaller income for a trading partner. In fact, it is just the opposite. When a person earns income, he or she expands the economic pie by more than the amount of the slice that he or she gets, making it possible for the rest of us to have a bigger slice, too. When a wealthy entrepreneur, such as Bill Gates or Henry Ford, has an income of, say, $1 billion per year earned through voluntary exchanges in the marketplace, he has enlarged the economic pie for others by an even larger amount. Here's how: suppose that Linda, a freelance graphic artist, pays $175 for a new software program developed by Bill Gates. As a result, she can do twice as much work in the same amount of time. Because she's more productive, Linda can earn more than enough additional income with the software to justify her purchase. In addition, the businesses she serves are also likely to be better off because the software makes it possible for her to give them more and better service and a lower price. More is produced in total. Thus, while Bill Gates gained, so, too, did Linda and her customers.

Similarly, although Henry Ford certainly became rich, he also greatly increased our ability to transport goods, services, and people. In the process, he made it possible for many others to achieve higher living standards than would have been possible in his absence. Had Stephen King never written a novel, not only would he not be as rich, but we would all be poorer for never having had the opportunity to read his novels. When income is acquired through voluntary exchange, people who earn income also help others earn more income and live better, too.

Economic Organization

Every economy faces three basic questions: (1) What will be produced? (2) How will it be produced? and (3) For whom will it be produced? These questions are highly interrelated. Throughout the book, we will consider how different types of economies solve them. There are two broad ways that an economy can be organized: markets and government (political) planning. Let us briefly consider each.

Market Organization

Private ownership of productive assets, voluntary contracts (often verbal), and market prices are the distinguishing features of **market organization**. Market organization is also known as **capitalism**.[8] Under market organization, private parties are permitted to buy and sell ownership rights of their assets at mutually acceptable prices. The government plays the limited role of rule maker and referee. It develops the rules, or the legal structure, that recognize, define, and protect private ownership rights. It helps individuals enforce contracts and protects people from violence and fraud. But in this role, the government is not an active player in the economy. Ideally, it avoids modifying market outcomes in an attempt to favor some people at the expense of others. For example, it doesn't prevent sellers from slashing prices or improving the quality of their products to attract customers from other competitors. Nor does it prevent

Market organization

A method of organization in which private parties make their own plans and decisions with the guidance of unregulated market prices. The basic economic questions of consumption, production, and distribution are answered through these decentralized decisions.

Capitalism

An economic system in which productive resources are owned privately and goods and resources are allocated through market prices.

[8]*Capitalism* is a term coined by Karl Marx.

buyers from outbidding others for products and productive resources. No legal restraints limit potential buyers or sellers from producing, selling, or buying in the marketplace.

Under market organization, no single individual or group of individuals guides the economy. There is no central planning authority, only individual planning. The three basic questions are solved independently in the marketplace by individual buyers and sellers making their own decentralized decisions. Buyers and sellers decide on their own what to produce, how to produce it, and whom to trade it to, based on the prices they themselves decide to charge.

In markets, individual buyers and sellers communicate their desires and preferences both directly and indirectly. They directly voice their desires when they buy or sell by advertising, whether in print or broadcast, or informally by word of mouth, on bulletin boards, and by letters of request and complaint and other means. They communicate indirectly by exiting or entering exchange relationships, as when they stop purchasing Coca-Cola and switch to Pepsi. The indirect, or "exit," option gives special power to their voiced, or direct, statements. Indeed, sellers, when markets are competitive, often hire experts to seek out the statements and desires of potential buyers. Buyers, too, are eager to know what sellers want—special terms of payment or delivery, for example—hoping that sellers might be willing to reward cooperation with a better deal.

Political Planning

Collective decision making

The method of organization that relies on public-sector decision making (voting, political bargaining, lobbying, and so on) to resolve basic economic questions.

Socialism

A system of economic organization in which (1) the ownership and control of the basic means of production rest with the state, and (2) resource allocation is determined by centralized planning rather than market forces.

The major alternative to market organization is **collective decision making**, whereby the government, through the political process, makes decisions for buyers and sellers in an attempt to solve the basic economic questions facing the economy. The government may maintain private ownership but uses taxes, subsidies, and regulations to resolve the basic economic questions. Alternatively, an economic system in which the government also owns the income-producing assets (machines, buildings, and land) and directly determines what goods will be produced is called **socialism**. Either way, individual planning and decisions are replaced by central planning and decisions made through the political process. These decisions can be made by a single dictator or a group of experts, or through democratic voting. Political rather than market forces direct the economy, and government officials and planning boards hand down decisions to expand or contract the output of education, medical services, automobiles, electricity, steel, consumer durables, and thousands of other commodities.

This is not to say that the preferences of individuals carry no weight. If the government officials and central planners are influenced by the democratic process, they must consider how their actions will influence their reelection prospects. That means they will listen to the voices of the voters to win over a majority of them. Otherwise, like the firm in a market economy that produces a product that consumers do not want, their tenure of service is likely to be short. However, under central planning, the indirect exit method of communicating is much more difficult. Although people can use the direct or voice method to communicate their preferences by lobbying government officials or casting votes in an election, they generally cannot use the indirect exit option because they cannot refuse to pay taxes or to quit purchasing a good or service that is provided by government. For example, families who send their children to private school must continue to pay the same amount in taxes to support the public school system as they would if they kept their child in public school. Often, people "vote with their feet" and leave one political jurisdiction to move to another. This is frequently seen when people move to better school districts. It is much easier, however, to move between school districts than between states or nations.

In summary, both market organization and central planning face the same basic economic questions. A basic difference between them is that the market system, with its exit option, allows for a wider variety of products and creates constant competition among suppliers, whereas the central planning system, in a democracy, responds primarily to the votes of the majority. In varying degrees, all economies use a combination of both of these methods of economic organization. Even predominantly market economies will still use taxes, subsidies, and some government ownership to direct and control resources. Similarly, predominantly socialist economies will, to some degree, use markets to allocate certain goods and services.

Looking ahead

The next two chapters present an overview of the market sector and explain how supply and demand for goods and services work. Chapters 5 and 6 focus on potential shortcomings of the market and how the collective decision-making process works in a democracy. As we proceed, the tools of economics will be used to analyze both the market and political sectors. We think this approach is important and that you will find it both interesting and enlightening.

! KEY POINTS

▼ The highest valued activity sacrificed when a choice is made is the opportunity cost of the choice; differences (or changes) in opportunity costs help explain human behavior.

▼ Mutual gain is the foundation of trade. When two parties engage in voluntary exchange, they are both made better off. Trade creates value because it channels goods and resources to those who value them the most.

▼ Transaction costs—the time, effort, and other resources necessary to search out, negotiate, and conclude an exchange—hinder the gains from trade in an economy. Middlemen perform a productive function by reducing transaction costs.

▼ Private-property rights motivate owners to use their resources in ways that benefit others and avoid doing harm to them. These rights also motivate owners to take proper care of their resources and conserve them.

▼ The production possibilities curve shows the maximum combination of any two products that can be produced with a fixed quantity of resources.

▼ Over time, the production possibilities curve of an economy can be shifted outward by (1) investment,

(2) technological advances, (3) improved institutions, and (4) greater work effort (forgoing leisure). The size of the economic pie is variable, not fixed. It can grow (or shrink) over time.

▼ The law of comparative advantage indicates that the joint output of individuals, regions, and nations will be maximized when each productive activity is undertaken by the low-opportunity-cost supplier. When a good can be acquired through trade more economically than it can be produced directly, it makes sense to trade for it.

▼ In addition to the gains that occur when goods are moved toward those who value them most, trade also makes it possible to expand output through specialization, division of labor, mass production processes, and innovation. These improved production techniques have contributed greatly to our modern living standards.

▼ Economies can either be organized by decentralized markets (capitalism) or they can be centrally planned by government through political decision making. Under central planning, buyers and sellers are more limited in their ability to communicate their desires.

? CRITICAL ANALYSIS QUESTIONS

1. "If Jones trades a used car to Smith for $5,000, nothing new is created. Thus, there is no way the transaction can improve the welfare of people." Is this statement true? Why or why not?

*2. Economists often argue that wage rates reflect productivity. Yet, the wages of house painters have increased nearly as rapidly as the national average, even though these workers use approximately the same production methods as they did fifty years

ago. Can you explain why the wages of painters have risen substantially even though their productivity has changed so little?

3. It takes one hour to travel from New York City to Washington, D.C., by air, but it takes five hours by bus. If the airfare is $110 and the bus fare is $70, which would be cheaper for someone whose opportunity cost of travel time is $6 per hour? For someone whose opportunity cost is $10 per hour? $14 per hour?

*4. "People in business get ahead by exploiting the needs of their consumers. The gains of business are at the expense of suffering imposed on their customers." Evaluate this statement.

5. What is the objective of the entrepreneur when it comes to the use of his or her resources? What is the major function of the middleman? Is the middleman an entrepreneur?

6. If you have a private-ownership right to something, what does this mean? Does private ownership give you the right to do anything you want with the things that you own? Explain. How does private ownership influence the incentive of individuals to (a) take care of things, (b) conserve resources for the future, and (c) develop and modify things in ways that are beneficial to others? Explain.

7. What is the law of comparative advantage? According to the law of comparative advantage, what should be the distinguishing characteristics of the goods a nation produces? What should be the distinguishing characteristics of the goods a nation imports? How will international trade influence people's production levels and living standards? Explain.

*8. Does a 60-year-old tree farmer have an incentive to plant and care for Douglas fir trees that will not reach optimal cutting size for another fifty years?

*9. What forms of competition does a private-property, market-directed economy authorize? What forms does it prohibit?

10. What are the major sources of gains from trade? Why is exchange important to a nation's prosperity? How does trade influence the quantity of output that trading partners are able to produce? In a market economy, will there be a tendency for both resources and products to be supplied by low-cost producers? Why or why not? Does this matter? Explain.

*11. Chick-fil-A's "Eat Mor Chikin" advertising campaign features three cows holding signs that say things like: "Save the cows, eat more chicken." If consumers began eating more chicken and less beef, would the cattle population increase or decrease? Explain.

*12. In many states, ticket scalping, or reselling tickets to entertainment events at prices above the original purchase price, is prohibited. Who is helped and who is hurt by such prohibitions? How can owners who want to sell their tickets get around the prohibition? Do you think it would be a good idea to prohibit the resale of other things—automobiles, books, works of art, or stock shares—at prices higher than the original purchase price? Why or why not?

13. Consider the choices of two groups of women ages thirty to fifty. All the women in one group have a college education. All the women in the other group have less than a high school education. Which of the two groups will participate more in the workforce? Which of the two groups will bear a larger number of children on average? Explain your answers based on the concept of opportunity cost.

14. Consider the following questions:
    a. Do you think that your work effort is influenced by whether there is a close link between personal output and personal compensation (reward)? Explain.
    b. Suppose the grades in your class were going to be determined by a random drawing at the end of the course. How would this influence your study habits?
    c. How would your study habits be influenced if everyone in the class was going to be given an A grade? How about if grades were based entirely on examinations composed of the multiple-choice questions in the coursebook for this textbook?
    d. Do you think the total output of a nation will be influenced by whether or not there is a close link between the productive contribution of individuals and their personal reward? Why or why not?

15. In this chapter, it was stated that a private-property right also involves having the right to transfer or exchange what you own with others. However, selling your organs is a violation of federal law, a felony punishable by up to five years in prison or a $50,000 fine. In 1999, eBay intervened when a person put one of his kidneys up for sale on the auction site (the bidding reached $5.7 million before the auction was halted). Does this lack of legal ability to exchange mean that individuals do not own their own organs? Explain.

16. During the last three decades, entrepreneurs like Michael Dell, Sam Walton, and Ted Turner have earned billions of dollars. Do you think the average American is better or worse off as the result of the economic activities of these individuals? Explain your response.

*17. As the skill level (and therefore earnings rate) of, say, an architect, computer specialist, or chemist increases, what happens to his or her opportunity cost of doing other things? How is the time spent on leisure likely to change?

18. Two centuries ago, there were more buffalo than cattle in the United States. Even though millions of cattle are killed for beef consumption each year, the

cattle population continues to grow while the buffalo are virtually extinct. Why?

19. *This question pertains to the addendum to Chapter 2.* The following tables show the production possibilities for two hypothetical countries, Italia and Nire. Which country has the comparative advantage in producing butter? Which country has the comparative advantage in producing guns? What would be a mutually agreeable rate of exchange between the countries?

Italia		Nire	
Guns	**Butter**	**Guns**	**Butter**
12	0	16	0
8	2	12	1
4	4	8	2
0	6	4	3
		0	4

*Asterisk denotes questions for which answers are given in Appendix B.

A D D E N D U M

Comparative Advantage, Specialization, and Gains from Trade

This addendum is for instructors who want to assign a more detailed numerical example demonstrating comparative advantage, specialization, and mutual gains from trade. Students who are uncertain about their understanding of these topics may also find this material enlightening. The international-trade chapter later in the text provides still more information on trade and how it affects our lives.

We begin with hypothetical production possibilities curves for two countries, Slavia and Lebos, shown in **EXHIBIT A-1**. The numerical tables represent selected points from each country's production possibilities curve. To make calculations easier, we have assumed away increasing opportunity costs in production so that the production possibilities curves are linear.

Without trade, each country would be able to consume only what it can produce for itself. Let's arbitrarily assume that for survival, Slavia requires three units of food and Lebos requires six units of food. As can be seen by point *A* in the exhibit, if Slavia were to produce the three units of food it requires, it would have enough resources remaining to produce two units of clothing. Similarly, if Lebos were to produce the six units of food it requires, it would have enough resources left to produce six units of clothing, again shown by point *A* in the exhibit. As we proceed, we will use this outcome as our benchmark outcome that occurs in the absence of specialization and trade between the countries.

Economic analysis suggests that both countries could gain if each were to specialize in the production of the good for which it has the comparative advantage and then trade for the other. First, let's figure out which country has a comparative advantage in the production of clothing. Doing so requires calculating the opportunity cost of producing clothing for each country. Because, in this example, the opportunity costs are constant at all points along the production possibilities curve, rather than increasing, this can be found by first selecting any two points on the production possibilities curve (or equivalently by comparing any two rows of numbers in the numerical tables given in the exhibit). For Slavia, moving from the point of producing six food units and one clothing unit to the alternative point of producing three food units and two clothing units, we see that Slavia gains one clothing unit but must give up three units of food. For simplicity, the opportunity cost for Slavia can be written as 1C = 3F, where C stands for clothing and F for food. You might note that this same numerical trade-off is true for Slavia anywhere along its production possibilities curve (for example, beginning from nine food units and zero clothing units, it would also have to give up three food units to gain one unit of clothing).

Using a similar approach (taking any two points or two rows in the table) for Lebos shows that for every three units of clothing the country wishes to produce, it must give up three units of food (3C = 3F). This can be treated as any other mathematical equation, and can be simplified by dividing both sides by three, resulting in an opportunity cost of one clothing unit equals one food unit (1C = 1F). Now, compare this to the opportunity cost for Slavia (1C = 3F). Slavia must give up the production of three units of food for every one unit of clothing it produces, whereas Lebos must give up only one unit of food for every one unit of clothing it produces. Thus, Lebos gives up the production of *less* food for every unit of clothing. Lebos is the low-opportunity-cost producer of clothing, and thus it has a comparative advantage in the production of clothing.

Because comparative advantage is a relative comparison, if one country has the comparative advantage in the production of one of the products, the other country must have the comparative advantage for the other good. Thus, because Lebos has the comparative advantage in clothing, it will be true that Slavia has the comparative advantage in food. However, it is worthwhile to show this here as well. To produce one unit of food, Lebos must give up one unit of clothing (recall the 1C = 1F opportunity cost). To produce one unit of food, Slavia must give up the production of only one-third of a unit of clothing (recall the 1C = 3F opportunity cost and rewrite the equation as 1/3 C = 1F by dividing both sides of the equation by 3). Thus, Slavia gives up the production of *less* clothing for every unit of food produced. Slavia is the low-opportunity-cost producer of food, and thus has a comparative advantage in the production of food.

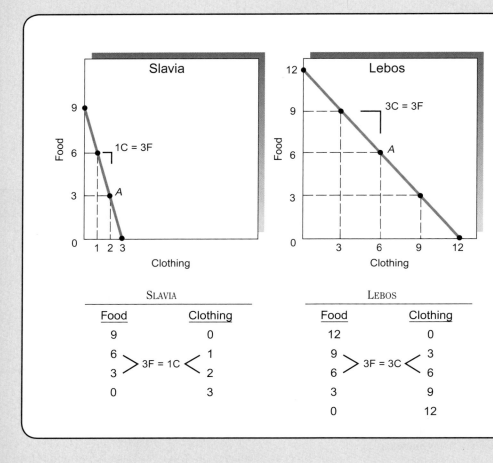

EXHIBIT A-1
Production Possibilities
for Slavia and Lebos

For Slavia, the opportunity cost of producing one unit of clothing is equal to three units of food (1C = 3F). For Lebos, the opportunity cost of producing three units of clothing is equal to three units of food (3C = 3F or 1C = 1F). The difference in the opportunity costs of production will make possible mutually beneficial trade between the countries, with each specializing in its area of comparative advantage.

SLAVIA				LEBOS		
Food		Clothing		Food		Clothing
9		0		12		0
6	3F = 1C	1		9	3F = 3C	3
3		2		6		6
0		3		3		9
				0		12

Suppose that, according to their comparative advantages, Lebos specializes in producing clothing and Slavia in food. From the last row of the table for Lebos, you can see that it can produce twelve units of clothing (and zero food) if it specializes in producing only clothing. From the top row of the table for Slavia, you can see that it can produce nine units of food (and zero clothing) if it specializes in producing only food. Note that this joint output (nine food and twelve clothing) is greater than the benchmark joint output (nine food and eight clothing) produced and consumed without trade.

If they are to trade, the countries now must find a mutually agreeable rate of exchange. Any rate of exchange *between* the two opportunity costs of 1C = 3F and 3C = 3F would be mutually agreeable. Here we will use 2C = 3F.

Recall that Slavia requires three units of food for survival. Now, however, they are specializing and producing nine units of food. Using this rate of exchange, Slavia would send its extra six units of food to Lebos in exchange for four units of clothing. After trade, Slavia would then have three units of food and four units of clothing. Compare this to the situation that existed before specialization and trade, in which Slavia had only three units of food and two units of clothing to consume. Specialization and trade have created two additional units of clothing for Slavia that it would not have had without trade.

With specialization, Lebos is producing twelve units of clothing. In the trade with Slavia, Lebos gave up four units of clothing to obtain six units of food. After trade, Lebos has eight units of clothing remaining and six units of food imported from Slavia. Compare this to the situation that existed before specialization and trade, in which Lebos had only six units of food and six units of clothing to consume. For Lebos, specialization and trade have also created two additional units of clothing that it would not have had without trade.

As this simple example shows, total output is greater and *both* countries are better off when they specialize in the area in which they have a comparative advantage. By doing so, each is able to consume a bundle of goods and services that exceeds what it could have achieved in the absence of trade. This concept applies equally to individuals, states, or nations. The typical worker could not begin to produce alone all of the things he or she can afford to buy with the money earned in a year by specializing and working in a single occupation. As our world has become more integrated over the past several hundred years, the gains that have occurred from specialization and trade are at the root of the significant improvements in well-being that we have experienced.

Markets and Government

Economics has a great deal to say about how both markets and governments allocate scarce resources. It gives us insight about the conditions under which each will likely work well (and each will likely work poorly). The next four chapters will focus on this topic.

There are two primary methods of allocating scarce resources: markets and governments

Market Allocation of Resources

Business firms purchase resources like materials, labor services, tools, and machines from households in exchange for income, bidding the resources away from their alternate uses. The firms then transform the resources into products like shoes, automobiles, food products, and medical services and sell them to households. In a market economy, businesses will continue to supply a good or service only if the revenues from the sale of the product are sufficient to cover the cost of the resources required for its production.

Government Allocation of Resources

Resource allocation by the government involves a more complex, three-sided exchange. In a democratic political setting, a legislative body levies taxes on voter–citizens, and these revenues are subdivided into budgets, which are allocated to government bureaus and agencies. In turn, the bureaus and agencies use the funds from their budgets to supply goods, services, and income transfers to voter–citizens. The legislative body is like a board of directors elected by the citizens. The competitive pressure to get elected gives legislators a strong incentive to cater to the wishes of voters. In turn, voters will be more likely to support a legislator if the value of the goods, services, and transfers received by them is high relative to the taxes they have to pay. In other words, goods, services, and income transfers will be supplied by the government if, and only if, a majority of legislators believe it will improve their election prospects.

This section will first analyze the operation of markets and then turn to the political process.

Supply, Demand, and the Market Process

I am convinced that if [the market system] were the result of deliberate human design, and if the people guided by the price changes understood that their decisions have significance far beyond their immediate aim, this mechanism would have been acclaimed as one of the greatest triumphs of the human mind.

—Friedrich Hayek,
Nobel Laureate[1]

From the point of view of physics, it is a miracle that [7 million New Yorkers are fed each day] without any control mechanism other than sheer capitalism.

—John H. Holland, scientist,
Santa Fe Institute[2]

CHAPTER FOCUS

- **What are the laws of demand and supply?**

- **How do consumers decide whether to purchase a good? How do producers decide whether to supply it?**

- **How do buyers and sellers respond to changes in the price of a good?**

- **What role do profits and losses play in an economy? What must a firm do to make a profit?**

- **How is the market price of a good determined?**

- **How do markets adjust to changes in demand? How do they adjust to changes in supply?**

- **What is the "invisible hand" principle?**

[1]Friedrich Hayek, "The Use of Knowledge in Society," *American Economic Review* 35 (September 1945): 519–30.
[2]As quoted by Russell Ruthen in "Adapting to Complexity," *Scientific American* 268 (January 1993): 132.

To those who study art, the *Mona Lisa* is much more than a famous painting of a woman. Looking beyond the overall picture, they see and appreciate the brush strokes, colors, and techniques embodied in the painting. Similarly, studying economics can help you to gain an appreciation for the details behind many things in your everyday life. During your last visit to the grocery store, you probably noticed the fruit and vegetable section. Next time, take a moment to ponder how potatoes from Idaho, oranges from Florida, apples from Washington, bananas from Honduras, kiwi fruit from New Zealand, and other items from around the world got there. Literally thousands of different individuals, *working independently*, were involved in the process. Their actions were so well coordinated, in fact, that the amount of each good was just about right to fill exactly the desires of your local community. Furthermore, even the goods shipped from halfway around the world were fresh and reasonably priced.

How does all this happen? The short answer is that it is the result of market prices and the incentives and coordination that flow from them. To the economist, the operation of markets—including your local grocery market—is like the brush strokes underlying a beautiful painting. Reflecting on this point, Friedrich Hayek speculates that if the market system had been deliberately designed, it would be "acclaimed as one of the greatest triumphs of the human mind." Similarly, computer scientist John H. Holland argues that, from the viewpoint of physics, the feeding of millions of New Yorkers day after day with very few shortages or surpluses is a miraculous feat (see the quotations at the chapter opening).

Amazingly, markets coordinate the actions of millions of individuals *without* central planning. There is no individual, political authority, or central planning committee in charge. Considering that there are nearly 300 million Americans with widely varying skills and desires, and roughly 25 million businesses producing a vast array of products ranging from diamond rings to toilet paper, the coordination derived from markets is indeed an awesome achievement.

This chapter focuses on supply, demand, and the determination of market prices. For now, we will analyze the operation of competitive markets—that is, markets in which buyers and sellers are free to enter and exit. We will also assume that the property rights are well defined. Later, we will consider what happens when these conditions are absent.

The produce section of your local grocery store is a great place to see economics in action. Literally millions of individuals from around the world have been involved in the process of getting these goods to the shelves in just the right quantities. Market prices underlie this feat.

Kayte M. Deioma/PhotoEdit

On eBay, sellers enter their reserve prices—the minimum prices they will accept for goods; buyers enter their maximum bids—the maximum prices they are willing to pay for goods. The process works the same way when a person runs a newspaper ad to sell a car. The seller has in mind a minimum price he or she will accept for the car. A potential buyer, on the other hand, has in mind a maximum price he or she will pay for the car. If the buyer's maximum price is greater than the seller's minimum price, the exchange will occur at a price somewhere in between. As these examples show, the buyers' and sellers' desires and incentives determine prices and make markets work. We will begin with the demand (buyer's) side, and then turn to the supply (seller's) side of the market. ■

Consumer Choice and the Law of Demand

Clearly, prices influence our decisions. As the price of a good increases, we have to give up more of *other* goods if we want to buy it. Thus, as the price of a good rises, its opportunity cost increases (in terms of other goods that must be forgone to purchase it).

Law of demand

A principle that states there is an inverse relationship between the price of a good and the quantity of it buyers are willing to purchase. As the price of a good increases, consumers will wish to purchase less of it. As the price decreases, consumers will wish to purchase more of it.

A basic principle of economics is that if something becomes more costly, people will be less likely to buy it. This principle is called the **law of demand**. *The law of demand states that there is an inverse (or negative) relationship between the price of a good or service and the quantity of it that consumers are willing to purchase.* This inverse relationship means that price and the quantity consumers wish to purchase move in opposite directions. As the price increases, buyers purchase less—and as the price decreases, buyers purchase more.

The availability of **substitutes**—goods that perform similar functions—helps explain this inverse relationship. No single good is absolutely essential; everything can be replaced with something else. A chicken sandwich can be substituted for a cheeseburger. Wood, aluminum, bricks, and glass can take the place of steel. Going to the movies, playing tennis, watching television, and going to a football game are substitute forms of entertainment. When the price of a good increases, people cut back on their purchases of it and turn to substitute products.

Substitutes

Products that serve similar purposes. An increase in the price of one will cause an increase in demand for the other (examples are hamburgers and tacos, butter and margarine, Microsoft Xbox and Sony PlayStation, Chevrolets and Fords).

The Market Demand Schedule

The lower portion of **EXHIBIT 1** shows a hypothetical *demand schedule* for cellular telephone service.[3] A demand schedule is simply a table listing the various quantities of something consumers are willing to purchase at different prices. In Exhibit 1, notice that the price is the average monthly cost of purchasing cellular phone service. The quantity demanded is the number of people willing to subscribe to cellular service at each price. When the price of cell phone service is $143 per month, just over 2 million people subscribe. As the price falls to $85, the quantity of subscribers rises to 11 million; when the price falls to $41 per month, the quantity of subscribers increases to just over 69 million.

The upper portion of Exhibit 1 shows what the demand schedule would look like if the various prices and corresponding quantity of subscribers were plotted on a graph and connected by a line. This is called the *demand curve*. When representing the demand schedule graphically, economists measure price on the vertical or *y*-axis, and the amount demanded on the horizontal or *x*-axis. Because of the inverse relationship between price and amount purchased, the demand curve will have a negative slope—that is, it will slope downward to the right. More of a good will be purchased as its price decreases. This is the law of demand.

---

[3]These data are actual prices (adjusted to 2000 dollars) and quantities annually for 1988 to 1998 taken from *Statistical Abstract of the United States* (Washington, DC: U.S. Bureau of the Census, various years). *If we could assume that other demand determinants (income, prices of related goods, and so on) had remained constant*, then this hypothetical demand schedule would be accurate for that time period. Because it is possible that some of these other factors changed, we treat the numbers as hypothetical, depicting alternative prices and quantities *at a given time*.

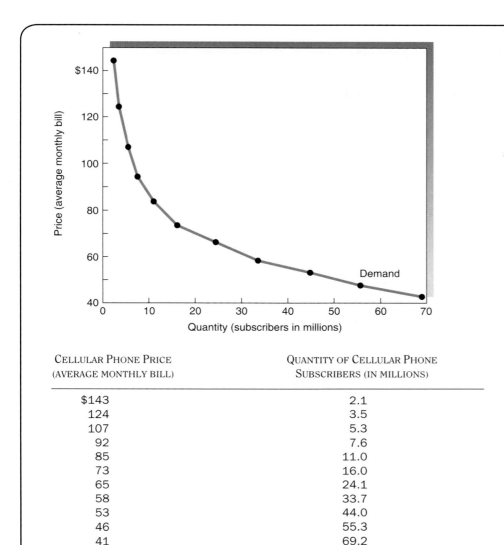

EXHIBIT 1
Law of Demand

As the demand schedule shown in the table indicates, the number of people subscribing to cellular phone service (just like the consumption of other products) is inversely related to price. The data from the table are plotted as a demand curve in the graph. The inverse relationship between price and amount demanded reflects the fact that consumers will substitute away from a good as it becomes more expensive.

CELLULAR PHONE PRICE (AVERAGE MONTHLY BILL)	QUANTITY OF CELLULAR PHONE SUBSCRIBERS (IN MILLIONS)
$143	2.1
124	3.5
107	5.3
92	7.6
85	11.0
73	16.0
65	24.1
58	33.7
53	44.0
46	55.3
41	69.2

Read horizontally, the demand curve shows how much of a particular good consumers are willing to buy at a given price. Read vertically, the demand curve shows how much consumers value the good. The height of the demand curve at any quantity shows the maximum price consumers are willing to pay for an additional unit. If consumers value highly an additional unit of a product, they will be willing to pay a large amount for it. Conversely, if they place a low value on the additional unit, they will be willing to pay only a small amount for it.

Because the amount a consumer is willing to pay for a good is directly related to the good's value to them, the demand curve indicates the marginal benefit (or value) consumers receive from additional units. (Recall that we briefly discussed marginal benefit in Chapter 1.) When viewed in this manner, the demand curve reveals that as consumers have more and more of a good or service, they value additional units less and less.

Consumer Surplus

Previously, we indicated that voluntary exchanges make both buyers and sellers better off. The demand curve can be used to illustrate the gains to consumers. Suppose you value a particular good at $50, but you are able to purchase it for only $30. Your net gain from buying the good is the $20 difference. Economists call this net gain of buyers **consumer surplus**. Consumer surplus is simply the difference between the maximum amount consumers would be willing to pay and the amount they actually pay for a good.

Consumer surplus

The difference between the maximum price consumers are willing to pay and the price they actually pay. It is the net gain derived by the buyers of the good.

EXHIBIT 2
Consumer Surplus

Consumer surplus is the area below the demand curve but above the actual price paid. This area represents the net gains to buyers from market exchange.

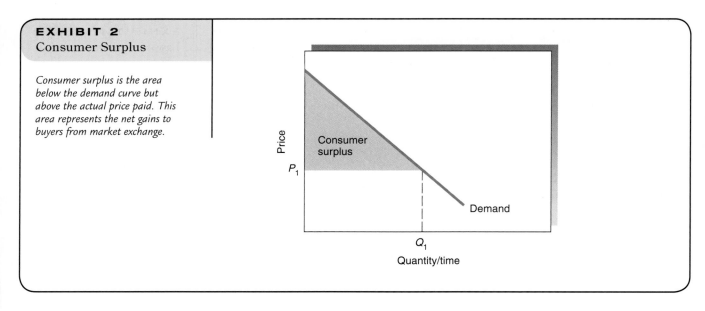

EXHIBIT 2 shows the consumer surplus for an entire market. The height of the demand curve measures how much buyers in the market value each unit of the good. The price indicates the amount they actually pay. The difference between these two—the triangular area below the demand curve but above the price paid—is a measure of the total consumer surplus generated by all exchanges of the good. The size of the consumer surplus, or triangular area, is affected by the market price. If the market price for the good falls, more of it will be purchased, resulting in a larger surplus for consumers. Conversely, if the market price rises, less of it will be purchased, resulting in a smaller surplus (net gain) for consumers.

Because the value a consumer places on a particular unit of a good is shown by the corresponding height of the demand curve, we can use the demand curve to clarify the difference between the *marginal value* and *total value* of a good—a distinction we introduced briefly in Chapter 1. Returning to Exhibit 2, if consumers are currently purchasing Q_1 units, the marginal value of the good is indicated by the height of the demand curve at Q_1—the last unit consumed (or purchased). So at each quantity, the height of the demand curve shows the marginal value of that unit, which as you can see declines along a demand curve. The *total* value of the good, however, is equal to the combined value of all units purchased. This is the sum of the value of each unit (the heights along the demand curve) on the *x*-axis, out to and including unit Q_1. This total value is indicated graphically as the entire area under the demand curve out to Q_1 (the triangular area representing consumer surplus *plus* the unshaded rectangular area directly below it).

You can see that the total value to consumers of a good can be far greater than the marginal value of the last unit consumed. When additional units are available at a low price, the marginal value of a good may be quite low, even though its total value to consumers is exceedingly high. This is usually the case with water, for example, because it is essential for life. The value of the first few units of water consumed per day will be exceedingly high. The consumer surplus derived from these units will also be large when water is plentiful at a low price. As more and more units are consumed, however, the *marginal value* of even something as important as water will fall to a low level. When water is cheap, then, people will use it not only for drinking, cleaning, and cooking but also for washing cars, watering lawns, flushing toilets, and maintaining fish aquariums. Thus, although the total value of water is rather large, its marginal value is quite low.

Consumers will tend to expand their consumption of a good until its price and *marginal value* are equal (which occurs at Q_1 in Exhibit 2 at a price of P_1). Thus, the price of a good (which equals marginal value) reveals little about the *total value* derived from the consumption of it. This is the reason that the market price of diamonds (which reflects their high marginal value) is greater than the market price of water (which has a low marginal value), even though the total value of diamonds is far less than the total value of water. Think of it this way: beginning from your current levels of consumption, if you were offered a choice between one diamond or one gallon of water right now, which would you take? You would probably take the diamond, because at the margin it has more value to you than additional water. However, if given a choice between giving up *all* of the water you use or *all* of the diamonds you have, you would probably keep the water over diamonds, because water has more total value to you.

Responsiveness of Quantity Demanded to Price Changes: Elastic and Inelastic Demand Curves

As we previously noted, the availability of substitutes is the main reason why the demand curve for a good slopes downward. Some goods, however, are much easier than others to substitute away from. As the price of tacos rises, most consumers find hamburgers a reasonable substitute. Because of the ease of substitutability, the quantity of tacos demanded is quite sensitive to a change in their price. Economists would say that the demand for tacos is relatively *elastic* because a small price change will cause a rather large change in the amount purchased. Alternatively, goods like gasoline and electricity have fewer close substitutes. When their prices rise, it is harder for consumers to find substitutes for these products. When close substitutes are unavailable, even a large price change may not cause much of a change in the quantity demanded. In this case, an economist would say that the demand for such goods is relatively *inelastic*.

Graphically, this different degree of responsiveness is reflected in the steepness of the demand curve, as shown in **EXHIBIT 3**. The flatter demand curve (D_1, left frame) is for a product like tacos, for which the quantity purchased is highly responsive to a change in price. As the price increases from \$1.50 to \$2.50, the quantity demanded falls sharply from ten to four units. The steeper demand curve (D_2, right frame) is for a product like gasoline, for which the quantity purchased is much less responsive to a change in price. For gasoline, an increase in price from \$1.50 to \$2.50 results in only a small reduction in the quantity purchased (from ten to eight units). An economist would say that the flatter

EXHIBIT 3
Elastic and Inelastic Demand Curves

The responsiveness of consumer purchases to a change in price is reflected in the steepness of the demand curve. The flatter demand curve (D_1) for tacos shows a higher degree of responsiveness and is called relatively elastic, while the steeper demand curve (D_2) for gasoline shows a lower degree of responsiveness and is called relatively inelastic.

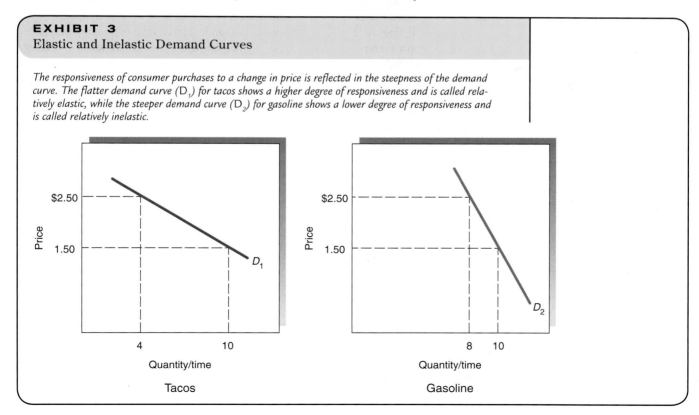

demand curve D_1 is "relatively elastic," whereas the steeper demand curve D_2 is "relatively inelastic." The availability of substitutes is the main determinant of a product's elasticity or inelasticity and thus how flat or steep its demand curve is.

What would a demand curve that was perfectly vertical represent? Economists refer to this as a "perfectly" inelastic demand curve. It would mean that the quantity demanded of the product never changes—regardless of its price. Although it is tempting to think that the demand curves are vertical for goods essential to human life (or goods that are addictive), this is inaccurate for two reasons. First, in varying degrees, there are substitutes for everything. As the price of a good rises, the incentive increases for suppliers to invent even more substitutes. Thus, even for goods that currently have few substitutes, if the price were to rise high enough, alternatives would be invented and marketed, reducing the quantity demanded of the original good. Second, our limited incomes restrict our ability to afford goods when they become very expensive. As the price of a good rises to higher and higher levels, if we do not cut back on the quantity purchased, we will have less and less income to spend on other things. Eventually, this will cause us to cut back on our purchases of it. Because of these two reasons, the demand curve for every good will slope downward to the right.

Changes in Demand versus Changes in Quantity Demanded

The purpose of the demand curve is to show what effect a price change will have on the quantity demanded (or purchased) of a good. Economists refer to a change in the quantity of a good purchased in response solely to a price change as a "change in *quantity demanded*." A change in quantity demanded is simply a movement along a demand curve from one point to another.

Changes in factors other than a good's price—such as consumers' income and the prices of closely related goods—will also influence the decisions of consumers to purchase a good. If one of these other factors changes, the entire demand curve will *shift* inward or outward. Economists refer to a shift in the demand curve as a "change in *demand*."

Failure to distinguish between a change in demand and a change in quantity demanded is one of the most common mistakes made by beginning economics students.[4] ***A change in demand is a shift in the entire demand curve. A change in quantity demanded is a movement along the same demand curve.*** The easiest way to distinguish between these two concepts is the following: If the change in consumer purchases is caused by a change in the price of the good, it is a change in quantity demanded—a movement along the demand curve. If the change in consumer purchases is due to a change in anything other than the price of the good (a change in consumer income, for example), it is a change in demand—a shift in the demand curve.

Let us now take a closer look at some of the factors that cause a "change in demand"—an inward or outward shift in the entire demand curve.

1. CHANGES IN CONSUMER INCOME. An increase in consumer income makes it possible for consumers to purchase more goods. If you were to win the lottery, or if your boss were to give you a raise, you would respond by increasing your spending on many products. Alternatively, when the economy goes into a recession, falling incomes and rising unemployment cause consumers to reduce their purchases of many items. A change in consumer income will result in consumers buying more or less of a product at all possible prices. When consumer income increases, in the case of most goods, individuals will purchase more of the good even if the price is unchanged. This is shown by a shift to the right—an outward shift—in the demand curve. Such a shift is called an increase in demand. A reduction in consumer income generally causes a shift to the left—an inward shift—in the demand curve, which

---

[4]Questions designed to test the ability of students to make this distinction are favorites of many economics instructors. A word to the wise should be sufficient.

EXHIBIT 4
Change in Demand versus Change in Quantity Demanded

Panel (a) shows a change in quantity demanded, a movement along the demand curve D₁, in response to a change in the price of DVDs. Panel (b) shows a change in demand, a shift of the entire curve, in this case due to an increase in consumer income.

is called a decrease in demand. Note that the appropriate terminology here is an increase or decrease in demand, not an increase or decrease in quantity demanded.

EXHIBIT 4 highlights the difference between a change in demand and a change in quantity demanded. The demand curve D_1 indicates the initial demand curve for DVDs. At a price of $30, consumers will purchase Q_1 units. If the price were to decline to $10, the *quantity demanded* would increase from Q_1 to Q_3. The arrow in panel (a) indicates the change in *quantity demanded*—a movement along the original demand curve D_1 in response to the change in price. Now, alternatively suppose there were an increase in income that caused the *demand* for DVDs to shift from D_1 to D_2. As indicated by the arrows in panel (b), the entire demand curve would shift outward. At the higher income level, consumers would be willing to purchase more DVDs than before. This is true at a price of $30, $20, $10, and every other price. The increase in income leads to an increase in *demand*—a shift in the entire curve.

2. CHANGES IN THE NUMBER OF CONSUMERS IN THE MARKET. Businesses that sell products in college towns are greatly saddened when summer arrives. As you might expect in these towns, the demand for many items—from pizza delivery to beer—falls during the summer. **EXHIBIT 5** shows how the falling number of consumers in the market caused by students going home for the summer affects the demand for pizza delivery. With fewer customers, the demand curve shifts inward from D_1 to D_2. There is a decrease in demand; pizza stores sell fewer pizzas than before regardless of what price they originally charged. Had their original price been $20, then demand would fall from 200 pizzas per week to only 100. Alternatively, had their original price been $10, then demand would fall from 300 pizzas to 200. When autumn arrives and the students come back to town, there will be an increase in demand that will restore the curve to about its original position. As cities grow and shrink, and as international markets open up to domestic firms, changes in the number of consumers affect the demand for many products.

3. CHANGES IN THE PRICE OF A RELATED GOOD. Changes in prices of closely related products also influence the choices of consumers. Related goods may be either

EXHIBIT 5
A Decrease in Demand

In college towns, the demand for pizza delivery decreases substantially when students go home for the summer. A decrease in demand is a leftward shift in the entire demand curve. Fewer pizzas are demanded at every price.

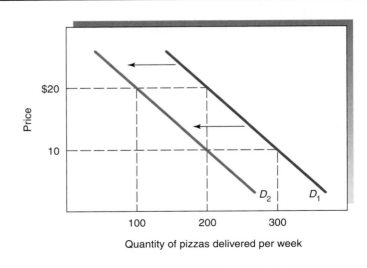

substitutes or complements. When two products perform similar functions or fulfill similar needs, they are substitutes. Economists define goods as substitutes when there is a direct relationship between the price of one and the demand for the other—meaning an increase in the price of one leads to an increase in demand for the other (they move in the same direction). For example, margarine is a substitute for butter. If the price of butter rises, it will increase the demand for margarine as consumers substitute margarine for the more expensive butter. Conversely, lower butter prices will reduce the demand for margarine, shifting the entire demand curve for margarine to the left.

Gasoline and hybrid cars provide another example of a substitute relationship. As gasoline prices have risen in recent years, the demand for gas–electric hybrid cars has increased. Beef and chicken, pencils and pens, apples and oranges, and coffee and tea provide other examples of substitutes.

Note that although a change in the price of butter shifts the demand curve for margarine (a change in demand), it will only result in a movement along the demand curve for butter (a change in the quantity demanded). The reason is that the demand curve for butter already shows the relationship between the price of butter and the quantity of butter desired. An increase in the price of butter makes consumers willing to purchase more margarine, holding constant the price of margarine.

Other products are consumed jointly, so the demands for them are linked together as well. Examples of goods that "go together" include peanut butter and jelly, DVDs and DVD players, hot dogs and hot dog buns, and tents and other camping equipment. These goods are called **complements**. For complements, a decrease in the price of one will not only increase its quantity demanded, it will also increase the demand for the other good. For example, lower prices for DVD players over the past decade have substantially increased the demand for movies on DVD. The reverse is also true. As a complement becomes more expensive, the quantity demanded of it will fall, and so will the demand for its complements. For example, if the price of steak rises, grocery stores can expect to sell fewer bottles of steak sauce, even if the price of steak sauce remains unchanged.

Complements

Products that are usually consumed jointly (for example, bread and butter, hot dogs and hot dog buns). A decrease in the price of one will cause an increase in demand for the other.

4. CHANGES IN EXPECTATIONS. Consumers' expectations about the future also can affect the current demand for a product. If consumers begin to expect that a major hurricane will strike their area, the current demand for batteries and canned food will rise. Expectations about the future direction of the economy can also affect current demand. If consumers are pessimistic about the economy, they start spending less, causing the current demand for goods to fall. Perhaps most important is how a change in the expected

THUMBNAIL SKETCH

Factors That Cause Changes in Demand and Quantity Demanded

This factor changes the quantity demanded of a good:

1. The price of the good: A higher price decreases the quantity demanded; a lower price increases the quantity demanded.

These factors change the demand for a good:

1. Consumer income: Lower consumer income decreases demand; higher consumer income increases demand.
2. Number of consumers in the market: Fewer consumers decreases demand; more consumers increases demand.
3a. Price of a substitute good: A decrease in the price of a substitute decreases the demand for the original good; an increase in the price of a substitute increases the demand for the original good.

3b. Price of a complementary good: An increase in the price of a complement decreases the demand for the original good; a decrease in the price of a complement increases the demand for the original good.
4. Expected future price of the good: If the price of a good is expected to fall in the future, the current demand for it will decrease; if the price of a good is expected to rise in the future, the current demand for it will increase.
5. Demographic changes: Population trends in age, gender, race, and other factors can increase or decrease demand for specific goods.
6. Consumer preferences: Changes in consumer tastes and preferences can increase or decrease demand for specific goods.

future price of a good affects current demand. When consumers expect the price of a product to rise in the future, their current demand for it will increase. Gasoline is a good example. If you expect the price to increase soon, you'll want to fill up your tank now before the price goes up. In contrast, consumers will delay a purchase if they expect the item to decrease in price. No doubt you have heard someone say, "I'll wait until it goes on sale." When consumers expect the price of a product to fall, current demand for it will decline.

5. DEMOGRAPHIC CHANGES. The demand for many products is strongly influenced by the demographic composition of the market. An increase in the elderly population in the United States in recent years has increased the demand for medical care, retirement housing, and vacation travel. The demand curves for these goods have shifted to the right. During the 1980s, the number of people aged 15–24 fell by more than 5 million. Because young people are a major part of the U.S. market for jeans, the demand for jeans fell by more than 100 million pairs over the course of the decade.[5] More recently, the increased use of cell phones and iPods among teenagers has led to a reduction in the demand for wristwatches.

6. CHANGES IN CONSUMER TASTES AND PREFERENCES. Why do preferences change? Preferences change because people change and because people acquire new information. Consider how consumers are responding to the popularity of the Atkins diet. The demand for high-carbohydrate foods like white bread has fallen substantially, whereas the demand for low-carbohydrate foods like beef has risen. This is a major change from the 1990s, when the demand for beef fell because of the "heart-healthy" eating habits consumers preferred then. Trends in the markets for clothing, toys, collectibles, and entertainment are constantly causing changes in the demand for these products as well. Firms may even try to change consumer preferences for their own products through advertising and information brochures.

The accompanying **Thumbnail Sketch** summarizes the major factors that cause a change in *demand*—a shift of the entire demand curve—and points out that quantity *demanded* (but not demand) will change in response to a change in the price of a good.

---

[5]These figures are from Suzanne Tregarthen, "Market for Jeans Shrinks," *The Margin* 6, no. 3 (January–February 1991): 28.

Producer Choice and the Law of Supply

Now let's shift our focus to producers and the supply side of the market. How does the market process determine the amount of each good that will be produced? To figure this out, we first have to understand what influences the choices of producers. Producers convert resources into goods and services by doing the following:

1. organizing productive inputs and resources, like land, labor, capital, natural resources, and intermediate goods;

2. transforming and combining these inputs into goods and services; and

3. selling the final products to consumers.

Producers have to purchase the resources at prices determined by market forces. Predictably, the owners of these resources will supply the resources only at prices at least equal to what they could earn elsewhere. Put another way, each resource the producers buy to make their product has to be bid away from all other potential uses. Its owner has to be paid its opportunity cost. The sum of the producer's cost of each resource used to produce a good will equal the **opportunity cost of production**.

Opportunity cost of production

The total economic cost of producing a good or service. The cost component includes the opportunity cost of all resources, including those owned by the firm. The opportunity cost is equal to the value of the production of other goods sacrificed as the result of producing the good.

There is an important difference between the opportunity cost of production and standard accounting measures of cost. Accountants generally do not count the cost of the firm's assets, such as its buildings, equipment, and financial resources, when they calculate a product's cost. But economists do. Economists consider the fact that these assets could be used some other way—in other words, that they have an opportunity cost. Unless these opportunity costs are covered, the resources will eventually be used in other ways.

The opportunity cost of these assets to the firm is the amount of money the firm could earn from the assets if they were used another way. Consider a manufacturer that invests $10 million in buildings and equipment to produce shirts. Instead of buying buildings and equipment, the manufacturer could simply put the $10 million in the bank and let it draw interest. If the $10 million were earning, say, 10 percent interest, the firm would make $1 million on that money in a year's time. This $1 million in forgone interest is part of the firm's opportunity cost of producing shirts. Unlike an accountant, an economist will take that $1 million opportunity cost into account. If the firm plans to invest the money in shirt-making equipment, it had better earn more from making the shirts than the $1 million it could earn by simply putting the money in the bank. If the firm can't generate enough to cover all of its costs, including the opportunity cost of assets owned by the firm, it will not continue in business.

The Role of Profits and Losses

PROFITS AND LOSSES

Profits direct producers toward activities that increase the value of resources; losses impose a penalty on those who reduce the value of resources.

Profit

An excess of sales revenue relative to the opportunity cost of production. The cost component includes the opportunity cost of all resources, including those owned by the firm. Therefore, profit accrues only when the value of the good produced is greater than the value of the resources used for its production.

Firms earn a **profit** when the revenues from the goods and services that they supply exceed the opportunity cost of the resources used to make them. Consumers will not buy goods and services unless they value them at least as much as their purchase price. For example, Susan would not be willing to pay $40 for a pair of jeans unless she valued them by at least that amount. At the same time, the seller's opportunity cost of supplying a good will reflect the value consumers place on *other* goods that could have been produced with those same resources. This is true precisely because the seller has to bid those resources away from other producers wanting to use them.

Think about what it means when, for example, a firm is able to produce jeans at a cost of $30 per pair and sell them for $40, thereby reaping a profit of $10 per pair. The $30 opportunity cost of the jeans indicates that the resources used to produce the jeans could have been used to produce other items worth $30 to consumers (perhaps a denim backpack). In turn, the profit indicates that consumers value the jeans more than other goods that might have been produced with the resources used to supply the jeans.

The willingness of consumers to pay a price greater than a good's opportunity cost indicates that they value the good more than other things that could have been produced with the same resources. Viewed from this perspective, profit is a reward earned by entrepreneurs who use resources to produce goods consumers value more highly than the other goods those resources could have produced. In essence, this profit is a signal that an entrepreneur has increased the value of the resources under his or her control.

Business decision makers will seek to undertake production of goods and services that will generate profit. However, things do not always turn out as expected. Sometimes business firms are unable to cover their costs. **Losses** occur when the revenue derived from sales is insufficient to cover the opportunity cost of the resources used to produce a good or service. Losses indicate that the firm has reduced the value of the resources it has used. In other words, consumers would have been better off if those resources had been used to produce something else. In a market economy, losses will eventually cause firms to go out of business, and the resources they previously utilized will be directed toward other things valued more highly, or to other firms who can produce those same goods at a lower cost.

Profits and losses play a very important role in a market economy. They determine which products (and firms) will expand and survive, and which will contract and be driven from the market. Clearly, there is a positive side to business failures. As our preceding discussion highlights, losses and business failures free up resources being used unwisely so they can be put to use by other firms providing consumers with more value.

Loss

A deficit of sales revenue relative to the opportunity cost of production. Losses are a penalty imposed on those who produce goods even though they are valued less than the resources required for their production.

Supply and the Entrepreneur

Entrepreneurs organize the production of new products. In doing so, they take on significant risk in deciding what to produce and how to produce it. Their success or failure depends on how much consumers eventually value the products they develop relative to other products that could have been produced with the resources. Entrepreneurs figure out which projects are likely to be profitable and then try to persuade a corporation, a banker, or individual investors to invest the resources needed to give their new idea a chance. Studies indicate, however, that only about 55 to 65 percent of the new products introduced are still on the market five years later. Being an entrepreneur means you have to risk failing.

To prosper, entrepreneurs must convert and rearrange resources in a manner that will increase their value. A person who purchases 100 acres of raw land, puts in streets and a sewage-disposal system, divides the plot into 1-acre lots, and sells them for 50 percent more than the opportunity cost of all resources used is clearly an entrepreneur. This entrepreneur profits because the value of the resources has increased. Sometimes entrepreneurial activity is less complex, though. For example, a 15-year-old who purchases a power mower and sells lawn services to his neighbors is also an entrepreneur seeking to profit by increasing the value of his resources—time and equipment.

Market Supply Schedule

How will producer–entrepreneurs respond to a change in product price? Other things constant, a higher price will increase the producer's incentive to supply the good. Established producers will expand the scale of their operations, and over time new entrepreneurs, seeking personal gain, will enter the market and begin supplying the product, too.

Alex Maclean/Photonic/Getty Images

An entrepreneur who buys raw land, puts in streets and sewer lines, and divides up the land into lots for sale will earn a profit because they have increased the value of the resources under their control.

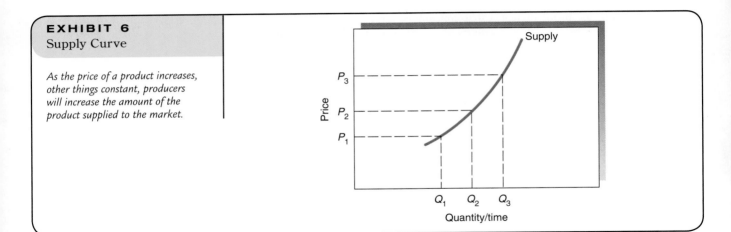

EXHIBIT 6
Supply Curve

As the price of a product increases, other things constant, producers will increase the amount of the product supplied to the market.

Law of supply

A principle that states there is a direct relationship between the price of a good and the quantity of it producers are willing to supply. As the price of a good increases, producers will wish to supply more of it. As the price decreases, producers will wish to supply less.

The law of supply states that there is a direct (or positive) relationship between the price of a good or service and the amount of it that suppliers are willing to produce. This direct relationship means that price and the quantity producers wish to supply move in the same direction. As the price increases, producers will supply more—and as the price decreases, they will supply less.

Like the law of demand, the law of supply reflects the basic economic principle that incentives matter. Higher prices increase the reward entrepreneurs get from selling their products. The more profitable it is to produce a product, the more of it entrepreneurs will be willing to supply. Conversely, as the price of a product falls, so do its profitability and the incentive to supply it. Just think about how many hours of tutoring services you would be willing to supply for different prices. Would you be willing to spend more time tutoring students if instead of $8 per hour, tutoring paid $50 per hour? The law of supply suggests you would, and producers of other goods and services are no different.

EXHIBIT 6 illustrates the law of supply. The curve shown in the exhibit is called a *supply curve*. Because there is a direct relationship between a good's price and the amount offered for sale by suppliers, the supply curve has a positive slope. It slopes upward to the right. Read horizontally, the supply curve shows how much of a particular good producers are willing to produce and sell at a given price. Read vertically, the supply curve reveals important information about the cost of production. The height of the supply curve indicates both (1) the minimum price necessary to induce producers to supply that additional unit and (2) the opportunity cost of producing that additional unit. These are both measured by the height of the supply curve because the minimum price required to induce a supplier to sell a unit is precisely the marginal cost of producing it.

Producer Surplus

We previously used the demand curve to illustrate consumer surplus, the net gains of buyers from market exchanges. The supply curve can be used in a similar manner to illustrate the net gains of producers and resource suppliers. Suppose that you are an aspiring musician and are willing to perform a two-hour concert for $500. If a promoter offers to pay you $750 to perform the concert, you will accept, and receive $250 more than your minimum price. This $250 net gain represents your **producer surplus**. In effect, producer surplus is the difference between the amount a supplier actually receives (based on the market price) and the minimum price required to induce the supplier to produce the given units (their marginal cost). The measurement of producer surplus for an entire market is illustrated by the shaded area of **EXHIBIT 7**.

Producer surplus

The difference between the price suppliers actually receive and the minimum price they would be willing to accept. It measures the net gains to producers and resource suppliers from market exchange. It is not the same as profit.

It's important to note that producer surplus represents the gains received by all parties contributing resources to the production of a good. In this respect, producer surplus is fundamentally different from profit. Profit accrues to the owners of the business firm producing the good, whereas producer surplus encompasses the net gains derived by all people who help produce the good, including those employed by or selling resources to the firm.

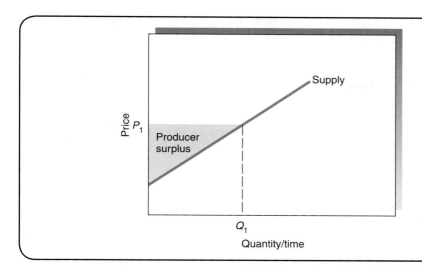

EXHIBIT 7
Producer Surplus

Producer surplus is the area above the supply curve but below the actual sales price. This area represents the net gains to producers and resource suppliers from production and exchange.

Responsiveness of Quantity Supplied to Price Changes: Elastic and Inelastic Supply Curves

Like the quantity demanded, the responsiveness of the quantity supplied to a change in price is different for different goods. The supply curve is said to be elastic when a modest change in price leads to a large change in quantity supplied. This is generally true when the additional resources needed to expand output can be obtained with only a small increase in their price. Consider the supply of soft drinks. The contents of soft drinks—primarily carbonated water, sugar, and flavoring—are abundantly available. A sharp increase in the use of these ingredients by soft drink producers is unlikely to push up their price much. Therefore, as **EXHIBIT 8** illustrates, if the price of soft drinks were to rise from $1 to $1.50, producers would be willing to expand output sharply from 100 million to 200 million cans per month. A 50 percent increase in price leads to a 100 percent expansion in quantity supplied. The larger the increase in quantity in response to a higher price, the more elastic the supply curve. The flatness of the supply curve for soft drinks reflects the fact that it is highly elastic.

In contrast, when the quantity supplied is not very responsive to a change in price, supply is said to be inelastic. Physicians' services are an example. If the earnings of doctors increase from $100 to $150 per hour, there will be some increase in the quantity of the services they provide. Some physicians will work longer hours; others may delay

(a)

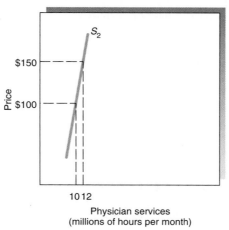

(b)

EXHIBIT 8
Elastic and Inelastic Supply Curves

Frame (a) illustrates a supply curve that is relatively elastic and therefore the quantity supplied is highly responsive to a change in price. Soft drinks provide an example. Frame (b) illustrates a relatively inelastic supply curve, one in which the quantity supplied increases by only a small amount in response to a change in price. This is the case for physician services.

retirement. Yet, these adjustments are likely to result in only a small increase in the quantity supplied because it takes a long time to train a physician and the number of qualified doctors who are working in other occupations or who are outside of the labor force is small. Therefore, as Exhibit 8 (right frame) shows, a 50 percent increase in the price of physician services leads to only a 20 percent expansion in the quantity supplied. Unlike soft drinks, higher prices for physician services do not generate much increase in quantity supplied. Economists would say that the supply of physician services is relatively inelastic.

Changes in Supply versus Changes in Quantity Supplied

Like demand, it is important to distinguish between a change in the *quantity supplied* and a change in *supply*. When producers change the number of units they are willing to supply in response to a change in price, this movement along the supply curve is called a "change in *quantity supplied*." A change in any factor *other than the price* shifts the supply curve and is called a "change in *supply*."

As we previously discussed, profit-seeking entrepreneurs will produce a good only if its sales price is expected to exceed its opportunity cost of production. Therefore, changes that affect the opportunity cost of supplying a good will also influence the amount of it producers are willing to supply. These other factors, such as the prices of resources used to make the good and the level of technology available, are held constant when we draw the supply curve. The supply curve itself reflects quantity changes only in response to price changes. Changes in these other factors shift the supply curve. Factors that increase the opportunity cost of providing a good will discourage production and decrease supply, shifting the entire curve inward to the left. Conversely, changes that lower the opportunity cost of producers will encourage production and increase supply, shifting the entire curve outward to the right.

Let us now take a closer look at the primary factors that will cause a change in supply and shift the entire curve right or left.

1. CHANGES IN RESOURCE PRICES. How will an increase in the price of a resource, such as wages of workers or the materials used to produce a product, affect the supply of a good? Higher resource prices will increase the cost of production, reducing the profitability of firms supplying the good. The higher cost will induce firms to reduce their output. With time, some may even be driven out of business. As **EXHIBIT 9** illustrates, higher resource prices will reduce the supply of the good, causing a shift to the left in the supply curve from S_1 to S_2. Alternatively, a reduction in the price of a resource used to produce a good will cause an increase in supply—a rightward shift in the supply curve—as firms expand output in response to the lower costs and increased profitability of supplying the good.

2. CHANGES IN TECHNOLOGY. Like lower resource prices, technological improvements—the discovery of new, lower-cost production techniques—reduce production costs, and thereby increase supply. Technological advances have affected the cost of almost everything. Before the invention of the printing press, books had to be handwritten. Just imagine the massive reduction in cost and increase in the supply of books caused by this single invention. Similarly, improved farm machinery has vastly expanded the supply of agricultural products through the years. Robotics have reduced the cost of producing airplanes, automobiles, and other types of machinery. Better computer chips have drastically reduced the cost of producing electronics. Less than forty years ago, a simple calculator cost more than $100, a microwave oven almost $500, and a VCR approximately $1,000. When introduced in the mid-1980s, a cellular telephone cost more than $4,000. You have probably noticed that the prices of flat-screen computer monitors and plasma-screen televisions have fallen substantially in recent years. Again, technological advances explain the changes.

3. ELEMENTS OF NATURE AND POLITICAL DISRUPTIONS. Natural disasters and changing political conditions can also alter supply, sometimes dramatically. In some years, good weather leads to "bumper crops," increasing the supply of agricultural products. At other times, freezes or droughts lead to poor harvests, reducing supply. War and political unrest in the Middle East region have had a major impact on the supply of oil several times during the past few decades. Factors such as these will alter supply.

4. CHANGES IN TAXES. If the government increases the taxes on the sellers of a product, the result will be the same as any other increase in the cost of doing business. The added tax that sellers have to pay will reduce their willingness to sell the product at any given

THUMBNAIL SKETCH

Factors That Cause Changes in Supply and Quantity Supplied

This factor changes the quantity supplied of a good:

1. The price of the good: A lower price decreases the quantity supplied; a higher price increases the quantity supplied.

These factors change the supply of a good:

1. Resource prices (the prices of things used to make the good): Lower resource prices increase supply; higher resource prices decrease supply.

2. Technological change: A technological improvement increases supply; a technological setback decreases supply.

3. Weather or political conditions: Favorable weather or good political conditions increase supply; adverse weather conditions or poor political conditions decrease supply.

4. Taxes imposed on the producers of a good: Lower taxes increase supply; higher taxes decrease supply.

price. Each unit must now be sold for a price that covers not only the opportunity cost of production, but also the tax. For example, the Superfund law placed a special tax on petroleum producers based on their output. That raised the cost of producing petroleum products, decreasing the amount producers were willing to supply.

The accompanying **Thumbnail Sketch** summarizes the major factors that change *supply*—a shift of the entire supply curve; and quantity supplied—a movement along the supply curve.

How Market Prices Are Determined: Supply and Demand Interact

Consumer–buyers and producer–sellers make decisions independent of each other, but market prices coordinate their choices and influence their actions. To the economist, a **market** is not a physical location but an abstract concept that encompasses the forces generated by the decisions of buyers and sellers. A market may be quite narrow (for example, the market for grade A jumbo eggs), or it may be quite broad like when we lump diverse goods into a single market, such as the market for all "consumer goods." There is also a wide range of sophistication among markets. The New York Stock Exchange is a highly formal, computerized market. Each weekday, buyers and sellers, who seldom meet, electronically exchange corporate shares they own worth billions of dollars. In contrast, a neighborhood market for babysitting services or tutoring in economics may be highly informal, bringing together buyers and sellers primarily by word of mouth.

Equilibrium *is a state in which the conflicting forces of supply and demand are in balance. When a market is in equilibrium, the decisions of consumers and producers are brought into harmony with one another, and the quantity supplied will equal the quantity demanded*. In equilibrium, it is possible for both buyers and sellers to realize their choices simultaneously. What could bring these diverse interests into harmony? We will see that the answer is market prices.

Market Equilibrium

As we have learned, a higher price will reduce the quantity of a good demanded by consumers. Conversely, a higher price will increase the quantity of a good supplied by producers. The market price of a good will tend to change in a direction that will bring the quantity of a good consumers want to buy into balance with the quantity producers want to sell. If the price is too high, the quantity supplied by producers will exceed the quantity demanded. They will be unable to sell as much as they would like unless they reduce their price. Alternatively, if the price is too low, the quantity demanded by consumers will exceed the quantity supplied. Some consumers will be unable to get as much as they would like, unless they are willing to pay a higher price to bid some of the good away from other potential customers. Thus, there will be a tendency for the price in a market to move toward the price that brings the two into balance.

People have a tendency to think of consumers wanting lower prices and producers wanting higher prices. Although this is true, price changes frequently trend toward the middle of the two extremes. When a local store has an excess supply of a particular item, how does it get rid of it? By having a sale or somehow otherwise lowering its price (a "blue-light special"). Firms often lower their prices in order to get rid of excess supply.

In contrast, excess demand is solved by consumers bidding up prices. Children's toys around Christmas provide a perfect example. When first introduced, items such as the Nintendo Wii, Webkinz, and the Tickle-Me-Elmo doll were immediate successes. The firms producing these products had not anticipated the overwhelming demand; every child wanted one for Christmas. Some stores raised their prices, but the demand was so strong that lines of parents were forming outside stores before they even opened. Often, only the first few in line were able to get the toys (a sure sign that the store had set the price below equilibrium). Out in the parking

Market

An abstract concept encompassing the forces of supply and demand, and the interaction of buyers and sellers with the potential for exchange to occur.

Equilibrium

A state in which the conflicting forces of supply and demand are in balance. When a market is in equilibrium, the decisions of consumers and producers are brought into harmony with one another, and the quantity supplied will equal the quantity demanded.

lots, in the classified ads, and on eBay, parents were offering to pay even higher prices for these items. If stores were not going to set the prices right, parents in these informal markets would! These examples show that rising prices are often the result of consumers bidding up prices when excess demand is present. A similar phenomenon can be seen in the market for tickets to a World Series game or a popular music group's upcoming concert, as the immediate value of a ticket on the resale market can be much higher than the original retail price if, at that price, the original quantity supplied is not adequate to meet the quantity demanded.

As these examples illustrate, whenever quantity supplied and quantity demanded are not in balance, there is a tendency for price to change in a manner that will correct the imbalance. It is possible to show this process graphically with the supply and demand curves we have developed in this chapter. **EXHIBIT 10** shows the supply and demand curves in the market for a basic calculator. At a high price—$12, for example—producers will plan to supply 600 calculators per day, whereas consumers will choose to purchase only 450. An excess supply of 150 calculators (shown by distance *ab* in the graph) will result. Unsold calculators will push the inventories of producers upward. To get rid of some of their calculators in inventory, some producers will cut their price to increase their sales. Other firms will have to lower their price, too, as a result, or sell even fewer calculators. This lower price will make supplying calculators less attractive to producers. Some of them will go out of business. Others will reduce their output or perhaps produce other products. How low will the price of calculators go? As the figure shows, when the price has declined to $10, the quantity supplied by producers and the quantity demanded by consumers will be in balance at 550 calculators per day. At this price ($10), the quantity demanded by consumers just equals the quantity supplied by producers, and the choices of the two groups are brought into harmony.

What will happen if the price per calculator is lower—$8, for example? In this case, the amount demanded by consumers (650 units) will exceed the amount supplied by producers (500 units). An excess demand of 150 units (shown by the distance *cd* in the graph) will be the result. Some consumers who are unable to purchase the calculators at $8 per

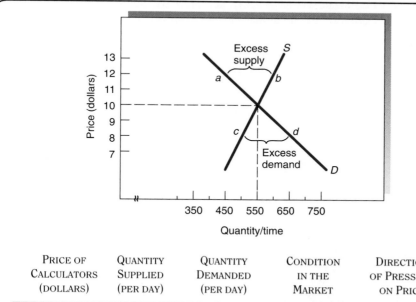

EXHIBIT 10
Supply and Demand

The table indicates the supply and demand conditions for calculators. These conditions are also illustrated by the graph. When the price exceeds $10, an excess supply is present, which places downward pressure on price. In contrast, when the price is less than $10, an excess demand results, which causes the price to rise. Thus, the market price will tend toward $10, at which point the quantity demanded will be equal to the quantity supplied.

PRICE OF CALCULATORS (DOLLARS)	QUANTITY SUPPLIED (PER DAY)	QUANTITY DEMANDED (PER DAY)	CONDITION IN THE MARKET	DIRECTION OF PRESSURE ON PRICE
$13	625	400	Excess supply	Downward
12	600	450	Excess supply	Downward
11	575	500	Excess supply	Downward
10	550	550	Balance	Equilibrium
9	525	600	Excess demand	Upward
8	500	650	Excess demand	Upward
7	475	700	Excess demand	Upward

unit because of the inadequate supply would be willing to pay a higher price. Recognizing this fact, producers will raise their price. As the price increases to $10, producers will expand their output and consumers will cut down on their consumption. At the $10 price, equilibrium will be restored.

Efficiency and Market Equilibrium

Economic efficiency

A situation in which all of the potential gains from trade have been realized. An action is efficient only if it creates more benefit than cost. With well-defined property rights and competition, market equilibrium is efficient.

When a market reaches equilibrium, all the gains from trade have been fully realized and **economic efficiency** is present. Economists often use economic efficiency as a standard to measure outcomes under alternative circumstances. The central idea of efficiency is a cost-versus-benefit comparison. On the one hand, undertaking an economic action will be efficient only if it generates more benefit than cost. On the other hand, undertaking an action that generates more cost than benefit is inefficient. For a market to be efficient, all trades that generate more benefit than cost need to be undertaken. In addition, economic efficiency requires that no trades creating more cost than benefit be undertaken.

A closer look at the way in which markets work can help us understand the concept of efficiency. The supply curve reflects producers' opportunity cost. Each point along the supply curve indicates the minimum price for which the units of a good could be produced without a loss to the seller. Assuming no other third parties are affected by the production of this good, then the height of the supply curve represents the opportunity cost to society of producing and selling the good. On the other side of the market, each point along the demand curve indicates how consumers value an extra unit of the good—that is, the maximum amount the consumer is willing to pay for the extra unit. Again assuming that no other third parties are affected, the height of the demand curve represents the benefit to society of producing and selling the good. Any time the consumer's valuation of a unit (the benefit) exceeds the producer's minimum supply price (the cost), producing and selling the unit is consistent with economic efficiency. The trade will result in mutual gain to both parties. When property rights are well defined and only the buyers and sellers are affected by production and exchange, competitive market forces will automatically guide a market toward an equilibrium level of output that satisfies economic efficiency.

EXHIBIT 11 illustrates why this is true. Suppliers of bicycles will produce additional bicycles as long as the market price exceeds their opportunity cost of production (shown by the height of the supply curve). Similarly, consumers will continue to purchase additional bikes as long as their benefit (shown by the height of the demand curve) exceeds the market price. Eventually, market forces will result in an equilibrium output level of Q and a price of P. At this point, all the bicycles providing benefits to consumers that exceed the costs to suppliers will be produced. Economic efficiency is met because all of the potential

---

EXHIBIT 11
Economic Efficiency

When markets are competitive and property rights are well defined, the equilibrium reached by a market satisfies economic efficiency. All units that create more benefit (the buyer's valuation shown by the height of the demand curve) than cost (opportunity cost of production shown by the height of the supply curve) are produced. This maximizes the total gains from trade, the combined area represented by consumer and producer surplus.

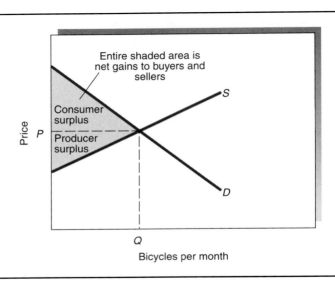

ECONOMICS *at The Movies*

Pretty Woman (1990)

In *Pretty Woman*, Julia Roberts agrees to spend the week as Richard Gere's companion for $3,000. After Roberts and Gere agree on the price, she tells him that she would have been willing to do it for $2,000. His reply is that he would have been willing to pay $4,000. With this additional information, we know that the exchange netted Roberts' character $1,000 in producer surplus and Gere's character $1,000 in consumer surplus. This scene illustrates mutual gains from trade.

consumer and producer gains from exchange (shown by the shaded area) have occurred. As you can see, the point of market equilibrium is also the point where the combined area showing consumer and producer surplus is the greatest.

When fewer than Q bicycles are produced, some bicycles valued more by consumers than the opportunity cost of producing them are not being produced. This is not consistent with economic efficiency. On the other hand, if output is expanded beyond Q, inefficiency will also result because some of the bicycles cost more to produce than consumers are willing to pay for them. Prices in competitive markets eventually guide producers and consumers to the level of output consistent with economic efficiency.

How Markets Respond to Changes in Demand and Supply

How will a market adjust to a change in demand? **EXHIBIT 12** shows the market adjustment to an increase in the demand for eggs around Easter. Demand D_1 and supply S are typical throughout much of the year. During the two weeks before Easter, however, consumer demand for eggs rises because people purchase them to decorate, too. This shifts egg demand from D_1 to D_2 during that time of year. As you can see, the increase in demand pushes the price upward from P_1 to P_2 (typically by about 20 cents per dozen), and results in a larger equilibrium quantity traded (Q_2 rather than Q_1—an increase of typically around 600 million eggs). There is a new equilibrium at point b around Easter (versus point a during the rest of the year).

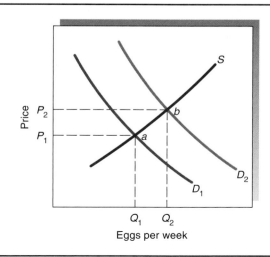

EXHIBIT 12
Market Adjustment to Increase in Demand

Here, we illustrate how the market for eggs adjusts to an increase in demand such as generally occurs around Easter. Initially (before the Easter season), the market for eggs reflects demand D₁ and supply S. The increase in demand (shift from D₁ to D₂) pushes price up and leads to a new equilibrium at a higher price (P₂ rather than P₁) and larger quantity traded (Q₂).

APPLICATIONS IN ECONOMICS

Supply, Demand, and the Price of a Bride

The Chinese family planning policy initiated in 1979 has increased the supply of males and reduced the supply of females. Among the Chinese population under age 20, there were 32 million more males than females in 2005. By way of comparison, 32 million is roughly the population of Canada. Customarily, in China the groom's family pays the bride's family a set amount—known as cai li—while the bride furnishes a dowry of mostly simple household items. In the 1980s, when there was more balance between men and women in the youthful population, the cai li payments were small, something like a couple of sets of clothes.

In the 1990s, cai li prices rose to several thousand yuan (about $200 to $400). There is now a huge supply of men relative to women among the Chinese population approaching the typical age of marriage. This has generated a strong demand for brides, causing cai li prices to spike upward to the 6,000 to 10,000 yuan range. The soaring prices for brides is even affecting the saving rate in areas with the largest excess supply of youthful men, as families save more in order to be in a position to pay the high cai li prices. Supply, demand, and prices affect behavior even for something as sacred as marriage.

Source: Mei Fong, "It's Cold Cash, Not Cold Feet, Motivating Runaway Brides in China," *Wall Street Journal*, June 5, 2009.

The tradition of coloring and hunting for eggs causes an increase in demand for eggs around Easter. As Exhibit 12 illustrates, this leads to higher egg prices and costly actions by producers to supply a larger quantity during this period.

Hub.-Wilh, 2009/Used under license from Shutterstock.com

Although consumers may not be happy about paying a higher price for eggs around Easter, the higher price serves two essential purposes. First, it encourages consumers to conserve on their usage of eggs. Some consumers may purchase only two dozen eggs to color, rather than three; other consumers may skip having an omelet for breakfast and have yogurt instead. These steps on the consumer side of the market help make the eggs that are available around Easter go farther. Second, the higher price is precisely what results in the additional 600 million eggs being supplied to the market to satisfy this increased consumer demand. Without the price increase, excess demand would be present, and many consumers would simply be unable to find eggs to purchase around Easter. If the price remained at P_1 (the equilibrium price throughout most of the year), consumers at Easter time would want to purchase more eggs than producers would be willing to supply. At the higher P_2 price, however, the quantity suppliers are willing to sell is again in balance with the quantity consumers wish to purchase.

Why were suppliers unwilling to supply the additional 600 million eggs at the original price of P_1? Because at the original equilibrium price of P_1, suppliers were already producing and selling all the eggs that cost less to produce than that price. The additional eggs desired by consumers around Easter all cost more to produce than the old market price of P_1. The higher price of P_2 is what allows suppliers to cover their higher production costs associated with these extra eggs. Around Easter, farmers take costly steps to avoid having the hens molt because hens lay fewer eggs when they are molting. They do this by changing the quantity and types of feed and by increasing the lighting in the birds' sheds—both of which mean higher production costs. Farmers also try to build up larger than normal inventories of eggs before Easter. Eggs are typically about two days old when consumers buy them at the store, but can be up to seven days old around Easter time. Building up and maintaining this additional inventory are costly, too.

In a market economy, when the demand for a good increases, its price will rise, which will (1) motivate consumers to search for substitutes and cut back on additional purchases of the good and (2) motivate producers to supply more of the good. These two forces will eventually bring the quantity demanded and quantity supplied back into balance.

It's important to note that this response on the supply side of the egg market is not a shift in the supply curve. The supply curve remains unchanged. Rather, there is a movement along the original supply curve—a change in *quantity* supplied. The only reason suppliers are willing to alter their behavior (produce more eggs) is because the increased demand has pushed up the price of eggs. Notice that it is the change in demand (a shift of the demand curve) that leads to the change in quantity supplied (a movement along the supply curve). Producers are simply responding to the price movement caused by the change in demand. A movement along one curve (a change in quantity supplied *or* a change in quantity demanded) happens in response to a shift in the other curve (a change in demand or a change in supply).

When the demand for a product declines, the adjustment process sends buyers and sellers just the opposite signals. Take a piece of paper and see if you can diagram a decrease in demand and how it will affect price and quantity in a market. If you've done it correctly, a decline in demand (a shift to the left in the demand curve) will lead to a lower price and a lower quantity traded. What's going on in the diagram is that the lower price (caused by lower consumer demand) is reducing the incentive of producers to supply the good. When consumers no longer want as much of a good, falling market prices signal producers to cut back production. The reduced output allows these resources to be freed up to go into the production of other goods consumers want more.

How will markets respond to changes in supply? **EXHIBIT 13** shows the market's adjustment to a decrease in the supply of lemons, such as happened during January 2007 when freezing temperatures in California destroyed a large portion of the lemon crop. A reduction in supply (shift from S_1 to S_2) will cause the price of lemons to increase sharply (P_1 to P_2). Because of the higher price, consumers will cut back on their consumption of lemons (the movement along the demand curve from *a* to *b*). Some will switch to substitutes—in this case, probably other varieties of citrus. The higher price also encourages the remaining

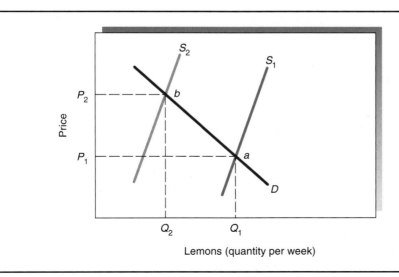

EXHIBIT 13
Market Adjustment to a Decrease in Supply

Here, using lemons as an example, we illustrate how a market adjusts to a decrease in supply. Assume adverse weather conditions substantially reduce the supply (shift from S_1 to S_2) of lemons. The reduction in supply leads to an increase in the equilibrium price (from P_1 to P_2) and a reduction in the equilibrium quantity traded (from Q_1 to Q_2).

THUMBNAIL SKETCH

How Changes in Demand and Supply Affect Market Price and Quantity

Changes in Demand

1. An increase in demand—shown by a rightward shift of the demand curve—will cause an increase in both the equilibrium price and quantity.
2. A decrease in demand—shown by a leftward shift of the demand curve—will cause a decrease in both the equilibrium price and quantity.

Changes in Supply

1. An increase in supply—shown by a rightward shift of the supply curve—will cause a decrease in the equilibrium price and an increase in the equilibrium quantity.
2. A decrease in supply—shown by a leftward shift of the supply curve—will cause an increase in the equilibrium price and a decrease in the equilibrium quantity.

lemon suppliers to take additional steps—like more careful harvesting techniques or using more fertilizer—that allow them to produce more lemons than otherwise would be the case. The higher prices will rebalance the quantity demanded and quantity supplied.

As the lemon example illustrates, a decrease in supply will lead to higher prices and a lower equilibrium quantity. How do you think the market price and quantity would adjust to an increase in supply, as might be caused by a breakthrough in the technology used to harvest the lemons? Again, try to draw the appropriate supply and demand curves to illustrate this case. If you do it correctly, the graph you draw will show an increase in supply (a shift to the right in the supply curve) leading to a lower market price and a larger equilibrium quantity.

The accompanying **Thumbnail Sketch** summarizes the effect of changes—both increases and decreases—in demand and supply on the equilibrium price and quantity. The cases listed in the thumbnail sketch, however, are for when only a single curve shifts. But sometimes market conditions simultaneously shift both demand and supply. For example, consumer income might increase at the same time that a technological advance in production occurs. These two changes will cause both demand and supply to increase at the same time—both curves will shift to the right. The new equilibrium will definitely be at a larger quantity, but the direction of the change in price is indeterminate. The price may either increase or decrease, depending on whether the increase in demand or increase in supply is larger—which curve shifted the most, in other words.

What will happen if supply increases but demand falls at the same time? Price will definitely fall, but the new equilibrium quantity may either increase or decrease. Draw the supply and demand curves for this case and make sure that you understand why.

Invisible Hand Principle

INVISIBLE HAND PRINCIPLE

Market prices coordinate the actions of self-interested individuals and direct them toward activities that promote the general welfare.

More than 230 years ago, Adam Smith, the father of economics, stressed that personal self-interest *when directed by market prices* is a powerful force promoting economic progress. In a famous passage in his book *An Inquiry into the Nature and Causes of the Wealth of Nations*, Smith put it this way:

> Every individual is continually exerting himself to find out the most advantageous employment for whatever [income] he can command. It is his own advantage, indeed, and not that of the society which he has in view. But the

study of his own advantage naturally, or rather necessarily, leads him to prefer that employment which is most advantageous to society. . . . He intends only his own gain, and he is in this, as in many other cases, led by an invisible hand to promote an end which was not part of his intention. By pursuing his own interest he frequently promotes that of the society more effectually than when he really intends to promote it.[7]

Smith's fundamental insight was that market forces would tend to align the actions of self-interested individuals with the best interests of society. The tendency of market forces to channel the actions of self-interested individuals into activities that promote the general betterment of society is now known as the **invisible hand principle**. Let's take a closer look at this important principle.

Prices and Market Order

The invisible hand principle can be difficult to grasp because there is a natural tendency to associate order with central direction and control. Surely some central authority must be in charge. But this is not the case. The pricing system, reflecting the choices of literally millions of consumers, producers, and resource owners, provides the direction. The market process works so automatically that most of us give little thought to it. We simply take it for granted.

Perhaps one example from your everyday life will help you better understand the invisible hand principle. Visualize a busy retail store with ten checkout lanes. No individual assigns shoppers to checkout lanes. Shoppers are left to choose for themselves. Nonetheless, they do not all try to get in the same lane. Why? Individuals are always alert for adjustment opportunities that offer personal gain. When one lane gets long or is held up by a price check, some shoppers will shift to other lanes and thereby smooth out the flow among the lanes. Even though central planning is absent, this process of mutual adjustment by self-interested individuals results in order and social cooperation. In fact, the degree of social cooperation is generally well beyond what could be achieved if central coordination were attempted—if, for example, stores hired someone to assign shoppers to checkout lanes in the interest of getting everyone out as quickly as possible. Shoppers *acting in their own interests* promote the most orderly and quickest flow for everyone. A similar phenomenon occurs on busy interstate highways as drivers switch between lanes for personal gain, with the end result being the quickest flow of traffic for everyone and for the group as a whole.

Market participation is a lot like checking out at a retail store or driving on the freeway. Like the number of people in a lane, profits and losses provide market participants with information about the advantages and disadvantages of different economic activities. Losses indicate that an economic activity is congested, and, as a result, producers are unable to cover their costs. In such a case, successful market participants will shift their resources away from such activities toward other, more valuable uses. Conversely, profits are indicative of an open lane, the opportunity to experience gain if one shifts into an activity in which the price is high relative to the per-unit cost. As producers and resource suppliers shift away from activities characterized by congestion and into those characterized by the opportunity for profit, they smooth out economic activity and enhance its flow. Remarkably, even though individuals are motivated by self-interest, market prices direct their actions toward activities that promote both order and economic progress. This is precisely the message of Smith's "invisible hand."

Is the concept of the invisible hand really valid? Next time you sit down to have a nice dinner, think about all the people who help make it possible. It is unlikely that any of them, from the farmer to the truck driver to the grocer, was motivated by a concern that you have

What's the single most important thing to learn from an economics course today? What I tried to leave my students with is the view that the invisible hand is more powerful than the hidden hand. Things will happen in well-organized efforts without direction, controls, or plans. That's the consensus among economists.

—Lawrence Summers,[6] Economist and former Secretary of the Treasury

Invisible hand principle

The tendency of market prices to direct individuals pursuing their own interests to engage in activities promoting the economic well-being of society.

---

[6]Quoted in Daniel Yergen and Joseph Stanislaw, *The Commanding Heights: The Battle between Government and the Marketplace That Is Remaking the Modern World* (New York: Simon and Schuster, 1998), 150.

[7]Adam Smith, *An Inquiry into the Nature and Causes of the Wealth of Nations* (New York: Modern Library, 1937), 423.

an enjoyable meal. Market prices, however, bring their interest into harmony with yours. Farmers who raise the best beef or turkeys receive higher prices; truck drivers and grocers earn more money if their products are delivered fresh and in good condition; and so on. An amazing degree of cooperation and order is created by market exchanges—all without the central direction of any government official.

How do markets bring the interests of individuals into harmony with economic progress? Consider the following three vitally important functions performed by market prices.

1. PRICES COMMUNICATE INFORMATION TO DECISION MAKERS. Suppose a drought in Brazil severely reduces the supply of coffee. Coffee prices will rise. Even if consumers do not know about the drought, the higher prices will provide them with all the information they need to know—it's time to cut back on coffee consumption. *Market prices register information derived from the choices of millions of consumers, producers, and resource suppliers, and provide them with everything they need to know to make wise decisions.*

Market prices provide producers with up-to-date information about which goods consumers most intensely desire, and with important information about the abundance of the resources used in the production process. The cost of production, driven by the opportunity cost of resources, tells the business decision maker the relative importance others place on the alternative uses of those resources. A boom in the housing market might cause lumber prices to rise. In turn, furniture makers seeing these higher lumber prices will utilize substitute raw materials such as metal and plastic in their production processes. Because of market prices, furniture makers will conserve on their use of lumber, just as if they had known that lumber was now more urgently needed for constructing new housing.

2. PRICES COORDINATE THE ACTIONS OF MARKET PARTICIPANTS. Market prices also coordinate the choices of buyers and sellers, bringing their decisions into line with each other. Excess supply will lead to falling prices, which discourage production and encourage consumption until the excess supply is eliminated. Alternatively, excess demand will lead to price increases, which encourage consumers to economize on their uses of the good and suppliers to produce more of it, eliminating the excess demand. Changing market prices induce responses on both sides of the market in the proper direction to help correct these situations.

The combination of product and resource prices will determine profit (and loss) rates for alternative projects and thereby direct entrepreneurs to undertake the production projects that consumers value most intensely (relative to their cost). If consumers really want more of a good—for example, luxury apartments—the intensity of their demand will lead to a market price that exceeds the opportunity cost of constructing the apartments. The profitable opportunity thus created will soon be discovered by entrepreneurs who will undertake the construction, expanding the availability of the apartments. In contrast, if consumers want less of a good, such as large cars, the sales revenue from their production will be less than the opportunity cost of supplying them, penalizing those who undertake such unprofitable production.

3. PRICES MOTIVATE ECONOMIC PLAYERS. Market prices establish a reward–penalty (profit–loss) structure that encourages people to work, cooperate with others, use efficient production methods, supply goods that are intensely desired by others, and invest for the future. Self–interested entrepreneurs will seek to produce only the goods consumers value enough to pay a price sufficient to cover production cost. Self-interest will also encourage producers to use efficient production methods and adopt cost-saving technologies because lower costs will mean greater profits. Firms that fail to do so will be unable to compete successfully in the marketplace.

At the beginning of this chapter, we asked you to reflect on why the grocery stores in your local community generally have on hand about the right amount of milk, bread, vegetables, and other goods. Likewise, how is it that refrigerators, automobiles, and CD players, produced at different places around the world, make their way to stores near you in approximately the same numbers that they are demanded by consumers? The invisible hand principle provides the answer, and it works without political direction. No government agency needs to tell decision makers to keep costs low or produce those goods most intensely desired by consumers. Similarly, no one has to tell individuals that they should develop skills that are highly valued by others. Once again the profit motive—in this case, higher earnings—will do the job. Many of the things we take for granted in our ordinary lives reflect the invisible hand at work.

Qualifications: Competition and Property Rights

As we noted earlier in this chapter, our focus so far has been on markets in which rival firms can freely enter and exit, and private-property rights are clearly defined and enforced. *The efficiency of market organization is, in fact, dependent upon these two things: (1) competitive markets and (2) well-defined and enforced private-property rights.*

Competition, the great regulator, can protect both buyer and seller. It protects consumers from sellers who would charge a price substantially above the cost of production or withhold a vital resource for an exorbitant amount of money. Similarly, it protects employees (sellers of their labor) from the power of any single employer (the buyers of labor). Competition equalizes the bargaining power between buyers and sellers.

When property rights are well defined, secure, and tradable, suppliers of goods and services have to pay resource owners for their use. They will not be permitted to seize and use scarce resources without compensating the owners. Neither will they be permitted to use violence (for example, to attack or invade the property of another) to get what they want. The efficiency of markets hinges on the presence of property rights—after all, people can't easily exchange or compete for things they don't have or can't get property rights to. Without well-defined property rights, markets simply cannot function effectively.

Looking ahead

Although we incorporated numerous examples designed to enhance your understanding of the supply-and-demand model throughout this chapter, we have only touched the surface. In various modified forms, this model is the central tool of economics. The following chapter will explore several specific applications and extensions of this important model.

KEY POINTS

▼ The law of demand states that there is an inverse (or negative) relationship between the price of a good or service and the quantity of it that consumers are willing to purchase. The height of the demand curve at any quantity shows the maximum price that consumers are willing to pay for that unit.

▼ The degree of responsiveness of consumer purchases to a change in price is shown by the steepness of the demand curve. The more responsive buyers are to a change in price, the flatter, or more elastic, the demand curve will be. Conversely, the less responsive buyers are to a change in price, the steeper, or more inelastic, the demand curve will be.

▼ A movement along a demand curve is called a change in quantity demanded. A shift of the entire curve is called a change in demand. A change in *quantity demanded* is caused by a change in the price of the good (generally in response to a shift of the supply curve). A change in *demand* can be caused by several things, including a change in consumer income or a change in the price of a closely related good.

▼ The opportunity cost of producing a good is equal to the cost of bidding away the resources needed for its production from alternative uses. Profit indicates that the producer has increased the value of the resources used, whereas a loss indicates that the producer has reduced the value of the resources used.

▼ The law of supply states that there is a direct (or positive) relationship between the price of a good or service and the quantity of it that producers are willing to supply. The height of the supply curve at any quantity shows the minimum price necessary to induce suppliers to produce that unit—that is, the opportunity cost of producing it.

▼ A movement along a supply curve is called a change in quantity supplied. A change in *quantity supplied* is caused by a change in the price of the good (generally in response to a shift of the demand curve). A shift of the entire supply curve is called a change in supply. A change in *supply* can be caused by several factors, such as a change in resource prices or an improvement in technology.

▼ The responsiveness of supply to a change in price is shown by the steepness of the supply curve. The more willing producers are to alter the quantity supplied in response to a change in price, the flatter, or more elastic, the supply curve. Conversely, the less willing producers are to alter the quantity supplied in response to a change in price, the steeper, or less elastic, the supply curve.

▼ Prices bring the conflicting forces of supply and demand into balance. There is an automatic tendency for market prices to move toward the equilibrium price, at which the quantity demanded equals the quantity supplied.

▼ Consumer surplus represents the net gain to buyers from market trades. Producer surplus represents the net gain to producers and resource suppliers from market trades. In equilibrium, competitive markets maximize these gains, a condition known as economic efficiency.

▼ Changes in the prices of goods are caused by changes in supply and demand. An increase in demand will cause the price and quantity supplied to rise. Conversely, a decrease in demand will cause the price and quantity supplied to fall. An increase in supply, however, will cause the price to fall and quantity demanded to rise. Conversely, a decrease in supply will cause the price to rise and quantity demanded to fall.

▼ Market prices communicate information, coordinate the actions of buyers and sellers, and motivate decision makers to act. As the invisible hand principle indicates, market prices are generally able to bring the self-interest of individuals into harmony with the general welfare of society. The efficiency of the system is dependent upon two things, however: (1) competitive market conditions and (2) well-defined and secure property rights.

 CRITICAL ANALYSIS QUESTIONS

*1. Which of the following do you think would lead to an increase in the current demand for beef?
   a. higher pork prices
   b. higher consumer income
   c. higher prices of feed grains used to feed cattle
   d. widespread outbreak of mad cow or hoof-and-mouth disease
   e. an increase in the price of beef

2. What is being held constant when a demand curve for a specific product (shoes or apples, for example) is constructed? Explain why the demand curve for a product slopes downward to the right.

3. What is the law of supply? How many of the following "goods" do you think conform to the general law of supply? Explain your answer in each case.
   a. gasoline
   b. cheating on exams
   c. political favors from legislators
   d. the services of heart specialists
   e. children
   f. legal divorces

*4. Are prices an accurate measure of a good's total value? Are prices an accurate measure of a good's marginal value? What's the difference? Can you think of a good that has high total value but low marginal value? Use this concept to explain why professional wrestlers earn more than nurses, despite the fact that nurses probably create more total value to society.

5. What is being held constant when the supply curve is constructed for a specific good like pizza or automobiles? Explain why the supply curve for a good slopes upward to the right.

6. Define consumer and producer surplus. What is meant by economic efficiency, and how does it relate to consumer and producer surplus?

7. Recent tax reforms make college tuition partially tax deductible for certain families. This should motivate more people to attend college. How will this higher demand for a college education affect tuition prices? How will it affect the cost of college for families who don't qualify for the tax deduction?

*8. "The future of our industrial strength cannot be left to chance. Somebody has to develop notions about which industries are winners and which are losers." Is this statement by a newspaper columnist true? Who is the "somebody"?

9. What factors determine the cost of producing a good or service? Will producers continue to supply a good or service if consumers are unwilling to pay a price sufficient to cover the cost?

*10. "Production should be for people and not for profit." Answer the following questions concerning this statement:
   a. If production is profitable, are people helped or harmed? Explain.
   b. Are people helped more if production results in a loss than if it leads to profit? Is there a conflict between production for people and production for profit?

11. What must an entrepreneur do to earn a profit? How do the actions of firms earning profits influence the value of resources? What happens to the value of resources when losses are present? If a firm making losses goes out of business, is this bad? Why or why not?

*12. What's wrong with this way of thinking? "Economists claim that when the price of something goes up, producers increase the quantity supplied to the market. But last year, the price of oranges was really high and the supply of them was really low. Economists are wrong!"

13. What is the invisible hand principle? Does it indicate that self-interested behavior within markets will result in actions that are beneficial to others? What conditions are necessary for the invisible hand to work well? Why are these conditions important?

*14. What's wrong with this way of thinking? "Economists argue that lower prices will result in fewer units being supplied. However, there are exceptions to this rule. For example, in 1972, a very simple ten-digit electronic calculator sold for $120. By 2000, the price of the same type of calculator had declined to less than $5. Yet business firms produced and sold many more calculators in 2000 than they did in 1972. Lower prices did not result in less production or in a decline in the number of calculators supplied."

15. What is the difference between substitutes and complements? Indicate two goods that are substitutes for each other. Indicate two goods that are complements.

16. How is the market price of a good determined? When the market for a product is in equilibrium, how will consumers value an additional unit compared to the opportunity cost of producing that unit? Why is this important?

*17. Do business firms operating in competitive markets have a strong incentive to serve the interest of consumers? Are they motivated by a strong desire to help consumers? Are "good intentions" necessary if individuals are going to engage in actions that are helpful to others? Discuss.

18. How do higher gasoline prices affect each of the following? Explain your answers.
   a. the incentive to invest in developing alternative fuels (such as coal liquefaction or solar energy)
   b. use of mass transit and carpooling
   c. the development of hybrid cars

19. If General Motors (GM) is earning losses, should the government step in to keep them in business with a taxpayer subsidy? What does the presence of losses say about how consumers value the company's output relative to its cost of production? Be sure to address the effects of the policy on GM's competitors, both domestic and foreign.

*Asterisk denotes questions for which answers are given in Appendix B.

Supply and Demand: Applications and Extensions

The division of labour, from which so many advantages are derived, is not originally the effect of any human wisdom, which foresees and intends that general opulence to which it gives occasion. It is the necessary, though very slow and gradual consequence of a certain propensity in human nature...; the propensity to truck, barter, and exchange one thing for another.

—Adam Smith[1]

Nations stumble upon establishments, which are indeed the result of human action, but not the execution of any human design.

—Adam Ferguson[2]

CHAPTER FOCUS

- How broadly can the supply and demand framework be used?

- What happens when prices are set by law above or below the market equilibrium level?

- How do rent controls affect the maintenance and quality of rental housing? How do minimum-wage rates influence the job opportunities of low-skilled workers?

- What are "black markets"? How does the lack of a well-structured legal environment affect their operation?

- How does a tax or subsidy affect a market? What determines the distribution of the tax burden (or subsidy benefit) between buyers and sellers?

- What is the Laffer curve? What does it indicate about the relationship between tax rates and tax revenues?

[1]Adam Smith, *An Inquiry into the Nature and Causes of the Wealth of Nations* (New York: Modern Library, 1937), 13.
[2]Adam Ferguson, *An Essay on the History of Civil Society* (Edinburgh: A. Millar and T. Caddel, London, 1767), 187.

arkets are everywhere. They exist in many different forms and degrees of sophistication. In elementary schools, children trade Pokémon cards; in households, individuals trade chores ("I'll clean the bathroom, if you'll clean the kitchen"); and in the stock market, individuals who have never met exchange shares of corporate stock and other financial assets worth billions of dollars each business day. Even making an activity illegal does not eliminate the market for it. Instead, the market is merely pushed underground. The exchange of illegal drugs or tickets to a big game at illegal prices illustrates this point.

Trading with other individuals is a natural part of human behavior that exists regardless of legal and societal conditions. As Adam Smith put it more than 230 years ago, human beings have a natural propensity "to truck, barter, and exchange one thing for another" (see the quotation at the chapter opening). We all want to improve our standard of living, and trade with others helps us achieve this goal—by allowing us to get the goods and services we really want and giving us the opportunity to earn the income necessary to buy them. Further, as Adam Ferguson points out, markets are a result of human action, not human design.[3] They arise because people can improve their lives by trading with others.

Market prices coordinate the actions of buyers and sellers, but sometimes the "price" of a good or service in a particular market is called something different. For example, in the labor market, the price is often called the "wage rate." In the loanable funds market, the price is generally referred to as the "interest rate." However, as Juliet observes in Shakespeare's *Romeo and Juliet,* "What's in a name? That which we call a rose by any other name would smell as sweet." The same is true for prices. When the price of something is referred to by another term, such as the wage or interest rate, it will still play the same role. Therefore, when these special terms are used, we put them along the vertical axes of supply and demand diagrams, just as we do "price"—because that's what they are.

In the previous chapter, we saw how the forces of supply and demand determine market prices and coordinate the actions of buyers and sellers in the absence of government intervention. In this chapter, we turn our attention to using the supply and demand model to understand more fully what happens when governments intervene in markets by implementing price controls, taxes, and subsidies. ■

The Link between Resource and Product Markets

Understanding the interrelationship among markets is vitally important. A change in one market will also lead to changes in other markets. This section addresses the link between the labor and product markets.

The production process generally involves (1) the purchase of resources—like raw materials, labor services, tools, and machines; (2) transformation of the resources into products (goods and services); and (3) sale of the goods and services in a product market. Production is generally undertaken by business firms. Typically, business firms will demand resources, and households will supply them. Firms demand resources *because* they contribute to the production of goods and services. In turn, households supply them in order to earn income.

---

[3]This theme was a focus of much of the work of Nobel Prize–winning economist Friedrich Hayek.

Resource market

The market for inputs used to produce goods and services.

Just as in product markets, the demand curve in a **resource market** is typically downward-sloping and the supply curve upward-sloping. The inverse relationship between the amount of a resource demanded and its price exists because businesses will substitute away from a resource as its price rises. In contrast, there will be a direct relationship between the amount of a resource supplied and its price because a higher price means greater rewards to those who provide more. As in product markets, prices will coordinate the choices of buyers and sellers in resource markets, bringing the quantity demanded toward balance with the quantity supplied.

The labor market is a large component of the broader resource market. Actually, there is not just one market for labor, but rather there are many labor markets, one for each different skill–experience–occupational category. Let's look at the labor market for waitstaff (waiters and waitresses). **EXHIBIT 1** shows how resource and product markets are linked. The supply of young workers in many occupations, including waitstaff, has declined in recent years in many areas of the United States. This lower supply has caused the wages (tip-inclusive wages) of waitstaff to increase (for example, from $8 to $10 in Exhibit 1a). The higher price of this resource increases the cost of producing restaurant meals. This higher cost, in turn, reduces the supply (shifting S_1 to S_2) of restaurant meals, pushing the price upward (Exhibit 1b). When the price of a resource increases, it will lead to higher production costs, lower supply, and higher prices for the goods and services produced with the resource.

Of course, lower resource prices have the opposite effect. Lower resource prices reduce costs and expand the supply of consumer goods made with the lower-priced resources (shifting the supply curve to the right). The increase in supply will lead to a lower price in the product market. ***Thus, when the price of a resource—such as labor—changes, the prices of goods and services produced with that resource will change in the same direction.***

Changes in product markets will also influence resource markets. There is a close relationship between the demand for products and the demand for the resources required for their production. An increase in demand for a consumer good—automobiles, for example—will lead to higher auto prices, which will increase the profitability of producing automobiles and give automakers an incentive to expand output. But the expansion in automobile output will require additional resources, causing an increase in the demand for, and prices of, the resources required for their production (steel, rubber, plastics, and the labor services of autoworkers, for example). The higher prices of these resources will cause other industries to conserve on their use, freeing them up for more automobile production.

Of course, the process will work in reverse if demand for a product falls. A decrease in demand will not only reduce the price of the product but will also reduce the demand

---

EXHIBIT 1
Resource Prices, Opportunity Cost, and Product Markets

When the supply of young workers falls, it pushes the wage rates of waiters and waitresses upward (a). In the product market (b), the higher wage rates will increase the opportunity costs of restaurants, reducing supply (shift from S_1 to S_2), thus leading to higher meal prices.

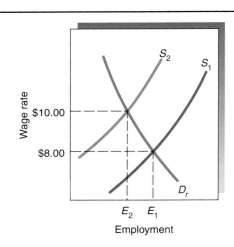

(a) Resource market
(waiters and waitresses)

(b) Product market
(restaurant meals)

for and prices of the resources used to produce it. ***Thus, when the demand for a product changes, the demand for (and prices of) the resources used to produce it will change in the same direction.***

The Economics of Price Controls

Buyers often complain that prices are too high, while sellers complain that they are too low. Unhappy with the prices established by market forces, various groups might try to persuade the government to intervene and impose **price controls**. Price controls force buyers or sellers to alter the prices of certain products. Price controls may be either price ceilings, which set a maximum legal price for a product, or price floors, which impose a minimum legal price. Imposing price controls might seem like a simple, easy way for the government to help buyers at the expense of sellers (or vice versa). The problem is that doing so typically creates secondary effects that, over time, make *both* sides worse off.

Despite good intentions, price controls can, in fact, harm the very people they were intended to help because they undermine the exchange process and reduce the gains from trade. The regulation of automated teller machine (ATM) surcharge fees is one example. Many states, after being lobbied by consumer groups, enacted regulations forbidding or severely restricting the ability of ATM owners to charge fees for using their machines. The unintended consequence of these regulations is that there are now fewer ATMs available to consumers in these states because there's less incentive to own and operate them. Consumers in these states benefit by paying lower ATM fees, but they also bear the cost of reduced ATM access.

The Impact of Price Ceilings

EXHIBIT 2 shows the impact of imposing a **price ceiling** (P_1) for a product below its equilibrium level (P_0). At the lower price, the quantity supplied by producers is lower on the supply curve, at Q_S, while the quantity demanded by consumers is greater, at Q_D, on the demand curve. A **shortage** ($Q_D - Q_S$) of the good will result because the quantity demanded by consumers exceeds the quantity supplied by producers at the new controlled price. After the price ceiling is imposed, the quantity of the good exchanged declines from the equilibrium quantity to Q_S, and the gains from trade (consumer and producer surplus) fall as well.

Normally, a higher price would ration the good to the buyers most willing to pay for it. Because the price ceiling keeps this from happening, though, other means must be used to allocate the smaller quantity Q_S among consumers wanting to purchase Q_D. Predictably, nonprice factors will become more important in the rationing process. Sellers will ration their goods and services to eager buyers on the basis of factors other than their willingness to pay. For example, sellers will be more inclined to sell their products to their friends, to buyers who do them favors, and even buyers willing to make illegal "under-the-table" payments. (The accompanying Applications in Economics box, "The Imposition of Price Ceilings After Hurricanes," highlights this point.) Time might also be used as the rationing device, with those willing to wait in line the longest being the ones able to purchase the good. In addition, the below-equilibrium price reduces the incentive of sellers to expand the future supply of the good. At the lower price, suppliers will direct resources away from production of the good and into other, more profitable areas. As a result, the product shortage will worsen over time.

What other secondary effects can be expected? ***In the real world, there are two ways that sellers can raise prices. First, they can raise their money price, holding quality constant. Or, second, they can hold the money price constant while reducing the quality of the good.*** (The latter might also include reducing the size of the product, say, for example, a candy bar or a loaf of bread.) Faced with a price ceiling, sellers will use quality reductions as a way to raise their prices. Because of the government-created shortage, many consumers will buy the lower quality good rather than do without it.

Price controls

Government-mandated prices that are generally imposed in the form of maximum or minimum legal prices.

Price ceiling

A legally established maximum price sellers can charge for a good or resource.

Shortage

A condition in which the amount of a good offered for sale by producers is less than the amount demanded by buyers at the existing price. An increase in price would eliminate the shortage.

EXHIBIT 2
The Impact of a Price Ceiling

When a price ceiling like P₁ pushes the price of a product (rental housing, for example) below the market equilibrium, a shortage will develop. Because prices are not allowed to direct the market to equilibrium, non-price elements will become more important in rationing the good.

APPLICATIONS IN ECONOMICS

The Imposition of Price Ceilings after Hurricanes

Major hurricanes, such as Katrina (which hit the Gulf Coast in 2005), Andrew (south Florida in 1992), and Hugo (Charleston, South Carolina, in 1989), not only cause massive property damage and widespread power outages but also dramatically increase the local demand for items such as lumber, gasoline, ice, batteries, chain saws, and electric generators. As a result, the prices of these items rise significantly in the wake of a hurricane. After Hurricane Hugo, for example, a bag of ice that sold for $1 before the hurricane went up in price to as much as $10, the price of plywood rose to about $200 per sheet, chain saws soared to the $600 range, and gasoline sold for as much as $10.95 per gallon.

These higher prices play two important roles. First, they encourage suppliers to bring more of these items to the disaster area. John Shepperson from Kentucky, for example, found it worthwhile to take time away from his normal job to buy nineteen generators, rent a truck, and drive it 600 miles to the Katrina-damaged area of Mississippi, expecting to sell the generators for twice the price he paid for them. Second, higher prices also encourage consumers to curtail consumption of these items, both in the disaster area and in other areas of the country where prices also rise when goods are diverted to the disaster area. The higher prices begin to subside once additional supplies flow into the disaster area, but it is precisely these higher prices that encourage this response in the first place.

In response to consumer complaints of "price gouging," state and local officials sometimes impose price controls in the wake of a disaster. After Hurricane Hugo, the mayor of Charleston signed emergency legislation making it a crime,

punishable by up to thirty days in jail and a $200 fine, to sell goods at prices higher than their prehurricane levels in the city.[1] Similarly, Mississippi's attorney general announced a crackdown on price gouging after Hurricane Katrina. No matter what it is called, legislation of this type is a price control and it prohibits mutually advantageous exchange. Remember those nineteen generators John Shepperson brought to storm-ravaged Mississippi? They were confiscated by police and Shepperson was arrested for price gouging. He was held by police for four days, and his generators were kept in police custody and never made it to consumers with urgent needs who desperately wanted to buy them.

While price ceilings may be motivated by a desire to help consumers by keeping prices low, they still exert secondary effects that often retard the recovery processs. At the lower mandated prices, consumer demand quickly outstrips the available supplies creating artificial shortages. The controls reduce the flow of goods into the area. Shipments that do arrive are greeted by long lines of consumers, many of whom end up without anything after waiting in lines for hours. Many of the people at the front of these lines who are able to buy the goods before supplies run out then drive those goods back out of the disaster area to sell them at the higher, uncontrolled prices in areas outside of the jurisdiction in order to obtain money to pay for much-needed repairs to their home. Shortages often become so bad that military guards are needed to protect shipments of goods and maintain order when shipments arrive.

The price controls result in serious misallocations of resources. Electric generators provide one of the best examples. The lack of electric power after a hurricane means that gasoline pumps, refrigerators, cash registers, ATMs, and many other types of electrical equipment do not work. Grocery stores can't open and inside thousands of dollars worth of food spoils. Although gas stations have gasoline in their underground storage tanks, it can't be pumped out without electricity. ATMs and banks can't operate without electricity, so people can't get to their own money, which is critical because almost all transactions in post-hurricane environments are made with cash.

Hardware stores that sell gasoline-powered electric generators typically have only a few in stock, but after a hurricane suddenly hundreds of businesses and residents want to buy them. In the absence of price controls, the price of these generators would rise and thereby allocate the limited supply to those expecting to derive the most value from them. At the higher prices, individual homeowners would generally be outbid by businesses, which can put the generators to use operating stores, gas stations, and ATMs. It is these uses that would yield enough revenue to cover the high price of the generators because they facilitate the provision of other goods and services that people desperately want. Given the large

sums grocery stores, gasoline stations, and others with urgent needs would be willing to pay, some with generators at home would even find it attractive to sell them to businesses.

However, price ceilings will prevent the generators from being allocated to those most willing to pay for them. Instead, people keep their generators at home, and it is commonplace for hardware store owners with a few generators on hand to take one home for their family and then sell the others to their close friends, neighbors, and relatives. In the absence of price rationing, nonprice factors play a larger role in the allocation process. The electric generators so critical for grocery stores, gasoline stations, and banks to open are instead used by households for tasks such as running television sets, lighting, electric razors, hair dryers, and so on. As a result, hundreds of thousands of consumers can't get goods they urgently want. Moreover, the flow of generators into the disaster area effectively stops, and many generators are actually taken out of the city to be sold in the less-damaged, outlying areas where price controls are not in effect.

If price controls were not imposed, the price of generators would quickly be bid up to the point where they were (1) purchased by those with the most urgent and valuable uses for them, and (2) imported into the area fairly rapidly because of the high prices they command. The dramatic change in conditions that often accompanies a hurricane highlights the role prices play. It also illustrates how the secondary effects accompanying price controls can magnify the damage generated by hurricanes.

---

[1]For supporting evidence in the case of Hurricane Hugo, see David N. Laband, "In Hugo's Path, a Man-Made Disaster," *Wall Street Journal*, September 27, 1989, A22; and Tim Smith, "Economists Spurn Price Restrictions," *Greenville News*, September 28, 1989, C1.

It is important to note that a shortage is not the same as scarcity. ***Scarcity is inescapable.*** Scarcity exists whenever people want more of a good than nature has provided. This means, of course, that almost everything of value is scarce. ***Shortages, on the other hand, are a result of prices being set below their equilibrium values—a situation that is avoidable if prices are permitted to rise.*** Removing the price ceiling will allow the price to rise back to its equilibrium level (P_0 rather than P_1 in Exhibit 2). This will stimulate additional production, discourage consumption, and increase the incentive of entrepreneurs to search for and develop substitute goods. This combination of forces will eliminate the shortage.

Rent Control: A Closer Look at a Price Ceiling

Rent controls are a price ceiling intended to protect residents from high housing prices. Rent controls are currently in place in many U.S. cities, including New York City; Washington, D.C.; Newark, New Jersey; and San Jose, California. Most of these measures were enacted during either World War II or the 1970s, when inflation was high. Rent

Rent controls lead to shortages, poor maintenance, and deterioration in the quality of rental housing.

controls peaked in the mid-1980s. At that time, more than 200 cities, encompassing about 20 percent of the nation's population, imposed rent controls.

Because rent controls push the price of rental housing below the equilibrium level, the amount of rental housing demanded by consumers will exceed the amount landlords will make available. Initially, if the mandated price is only slightly below equilibrium, the impact of rent controls may be barely noticeable. Over time, however, the effects will worsen. Inevitably, rent controls that continue will lead to the following results.

1. SHORTAGES AND BLACK MARKETS WILL DEVELOP. Because the quantity of housing demanded will exceed the quantity supplied, some people who value rental housing highly will be unable to find it. Frustrated by the shortage, they will try to induce landlords to rent to them. Some will agree to prepay their rent, including a substantial damage deposit. Others might agree to rent or buy the landlord's furniture at exorbitant prices in order to get an apartment. Still others will make under-the-table (black market) payments to secure housing.

2. THE FUTURE SUPPLY OF RENTAL HOUSES WILL DECLINE. The below-equilibrium price will discourage entrepreneurs from constructing new rental housing units, and private investment will flow elsewhere. In the city of Berkeley, rental units available to students at the University of California dropped by 31 percent in the first five years after the city adopted rent controls in 1978.[4] In contrast, removal of rent controls will often lead to a sharp increase in rental housing construction, as builders seek to expand the supply that lagged behind as the result of the controls. This happened in both Boston and Santa Monica following their repeal of controls in the late 1990s.

3. THE QUALITY OF RENTAL HOUSING WILL DETERIORATE. When apartment owners are not allowed to raise their prices, they will use quality reductions to achieve this objective. Normal maintenance and repair service will deteriorate. Tenant parking lots will be eliminated (or rented out). Eventually, the quality of the rental housing will reflect the controlled price. Cheaper housing will be of cheaper quality.

[4]William Tucker, *The Excluded Americans* (Washington, DC: Regnery Gateway, 1990), 162. For additional information on rent controls, see William Tucker, "Rent Control Drives Out Affordable Housing," in *USA Today Magazine* (July 1998) and Walter Block, "Rent Controls," in *Fortune Encyclopedia of Economics,* ed. David Henderson (New York: Warner Books, 1993). The latter publication can also be found online at http://www.econlib.org.

4. NONPRICE METHODS OF RATIONING WILL BECOME MORE IMPORTANT. Because price no longer rations rental housing, other forms of competition will develop. Landlords will rely more heavily on nonmonetary discriminating devices. They will favor friends, people of influence, and those whose lifestyles resemble their own. In contrast, applicants with many children or unconventional lifestyles, and perhaps racial minorities, will find fewer landlords who will rent to them. Because the cost to landlords of discriminating against those they do not like is lower, discrimination will become more prevalent in the rationing process. In New York City, where rent controls are in force, a magazine article suggested that "joining a church or synagogue" could help people make the connections they need to get an apartment. Can you imagine having to devote this amount of effort to finding an apartment? If your city enacts rent controls, you just might have to.

5. INEFFICIENT USE OF HOUSING SPACE WILL RESULT. The tenant in a rent-controlled apartment will think twice before moving. Why? Even though the tenant might want a larger or smaller space or an apartment closer to work, he or she will be less likely to move because it will be much more difficult to find a unit that's vacant. Turnover will be lower, and many people will find themselves in locations and in apartments not well suited to their needs. In a college town, students who live in the local area will have an advantage over newcomers. Local students and their parents will be more likely to have connections with apartment owners in the area. Many students from farther away, including those who value the apartments more highly, will find it extremely difficult to locate a place to rent.

Imposing rent control laws may sound like a simple way to deal with high housing prices. However, the secondary effects are so damaging that many cities have begun repealing them. In the words of Swedish economist Assar Lindbeck: "In many cases, rent control appears to be the most efficient technique presently known to destroy a city—except for bombing."[5] Though this may overstate the case, both economics and experience show that the controls adversely impact the quantity and quality of rental housing.

The Impact of Price Floors

A **price floor** establishes a minimum price that can legally be charged. The government imposes price floors on some agricultural products, for example, in an effort to artificially increase the prices that farmers receive. When a price floor is imposed above the current market equilibrium price, it will alter the market's operation. **EXHIBIT 3** illustrates the impact of imposing a price floor (P_1) for a product above its equilibrium level (P_0). At the higher price, the quantity supplied by producers increases along the supply curve to Q_S, while the quantity demanded by consumers decreases along the demand curve to Q_D. A **surplus** ($Q_S - Q_D$) of the good will result, as the quantity supplied by producers exceeds the quantity demanded by consumers at the new controlled price. Just like a price ceiling, a price floor reduces the quantity of the good exchanged, and reduces the gains from trade.

As in the case of the price ceiling, nonprice factors will play a larger role in the rationing process. But because there is a surplus rather than a shortage, this time buyers will be in a position to be more selective. Buyers will purchase from sellers willing to offer them nonprice favors—better service, discounts on other products, or easier credit terms, for example. When it's difficult to alter the product's quality—in this case, improve it to make it more attractive for the price that must be charged—some producers will be unable to sell it.

It is important to note that a surplus doesn't mean the good is no longer scarce. People still want more of the good than is freely available from nature, even though they want less of it *at the controlled price* than sellers want to bring to the market. A decline in price would eliminate the surplus, but the item will be scarce in either case.

Price floor

A legally established minimum price buyers must pay for a good or resource.

Surplus

A condition in which the amount of a good offered for sale by producers is greater than the amount that buyers will purchase at the existing price. A decline in price would eliminate the surplus.

[5]Assar Lindbeck, *The Political Economy of the New Left* (New York: Harper & Row, 1972), 39.

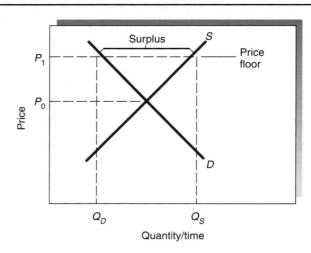

EXHIBIT 3
The Impact of a Price Floor

When a price floor such as P₁ keeps the price of a good or service above the market equilibrium, a surplus will result.

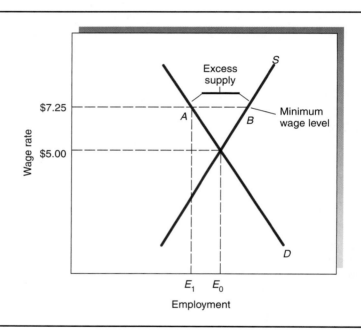

EXHIBIT 4
Employment and the Minimum Wage

If the market wage of a group of employees is $5.00 per hour, a $7.25-per-hour minimum wage will increase the earnings of workers able to retain their jobs, but reduce the employment opportunities of others as the number of jobs available shrinks from E₀ to E₁.

Minimum Wage: A Closer Look at a Price Floor

Minimum wage

Legislation requiring that workers be paid at least the stated minimum hourly rate of pay.

In 1938, Congress passed the Fair Labor Standards Act, which mandated a national **minimum wage** of 25 cents per hour. During the past seventy years, the minimum wage has been increased many times. Most recently, in July 2009, the minimum wage was increased to $7.25 per hour. Numerous states, including California, Washington, Oregon, and Connecticut, have their own higher minimum-wage rates ranging up to over $8 per hour.

A minimum wage is a price floor. Because most employees in the United States earn wages in excess of the minimum, their employment opportunities are largely unaffected by the minimum wage law. However, low-skilled and inexperienced workers whose equilibrium wage rates are lower than the minimum wage will be affected. **EXHIBIT 4** shows the direct effect of a $7.25-per-hour minimum wage on the employment opportunities of a group of low-skilled workers.

Without a minimum wage, the supply of and demand for these low-skilled workers would be in balance at some lower wage rate; here we use $5.00. Because the minimum wage makes low-skilled labor more expensive, employers will substitute machines and more highly skilled workers for the now more expensive low-skilled employees. Fewer low-skilled workers will be hired when the minimum wage pushes their wages up. Graphically, this is reflected in the movement up along the demand curve in Exhibit 4 from the equilibrium point to the point associated with the higher, $7.25 wage rate (point *A*). The result will be a reduction in employment of low-skilled workers from E_0 to E_1.

On the supply side of the market, as the wages of low-skilled workers are pushed above equilibrium, there will be more unskilled workers looking for jobs. Graphically, this is reflected in the movement up along the supply curve in Exhibit 4 from the equilibrium point to the point associated with the higher, $7.25 wage rate (point *B*). At the $7.25 wage rate, the quantity of workers searching for jobs will exceed the quantity of jobs available, causing excess supply.

In a labor market, an excess supply will take the form of a abnormally high rate of unemployment. Thus, *economic analysis indicates that minimum-wage legislation will lead to high unemployment rates among low-skilled workers.* The exceedingly high unemployment rate of teenagers in the United States (a group with limited skills because they lack work experience) is consistent with this analysis. In the United States, the unemployment rate for teenagers is more than three times the average for all workers, and the unemployment rate for black youth has generally exceeded 30 percent in recent years.

It is important to remember that the market price—the wage rate—is only one dimension of the transaction. When a price floor pushes the wage rate above equilibrium, employers will have less incentive to offer nonwage benefits to employees because they will have no trouble hiring low-skilled workers. Predictably, a higher minimum wage will lead to a deterioration of the nonwage qualities of minimum-wage jobs, and so workers in these jobs will experience less convenient working hours, fewer training opportunities, and less continuous employment.

The adverse impact of the minimum wage on the opportunity of youthful workers to acquire work experience and on-the-job training is a particularly important unintended consequence of minimum-wage laws. Low-paying, entry-level jobs can provide workers with experience that will help them move up the job ladder to higher-paying positions. Employment experience obtained at an early age, even on menial tasks, can help people acquire self-confidence, good work habits, and skills that make them more valuable to future employers. The minimum wage makes this more difficult. Not only does the minimum wage make it harder for low-skilled workers to find jobs, it also reduces their on-the-job training opportunities. In order to pay the higher wage rate required by the law, employers will have to find other ways to cut employment costs, like reducing the amount of job training. Not surprisingly, most minimum-wage jobs are dead-end positions with little opportunity for future advancement.[6]

Workers who are able to maintain their employment at the higher minimum-wage rate—most likely the better qualified among those with low skill levels—gain from a minimum wage. But other low-skilled workers are harmed by the minimum wage, particularly those with the lowest skill levels who will find it more difficult to get jobs.

How many fewer low-skilled workers are hired because of the minimum wage? Studies indicate that a 10 percent increase in the minimum wage reduces the employment of low-skilled workers by 1 to 3 percent. Minimum-wage supporters argue that the higher wages for low-skilled workers are worth this reduction in employment and job-training opportunities. Critics argue, however, that the reduced job opportunities for the lowest-skilled workers are reason enough to eliminate the minimum wage.

Does the minimum wage help the poor? According to the U.S. Department of Labor, most minimum wage earners are young, part-time workers and relatively few live below the poverty line. About one-half of minimum wage workers are between the ages of 16 to 24 years and approximately three-fifths hold a part-time job. Fewer than

---

[6]For evidence that the minimum wage limits training opportunities, see David Neumark and William Wascher, "Minimum Wages and Training Revisited," *Journal of Labor Economics* 19 (July 2001): 563–95.

20 percent of minimum wage workers are from families below the poverty line, and only about one out of every four minimum wage workers is married. Therefore, even if the adverse effects of a higher minimum wage on employment and training opportunities are small, a higher minimum wage does little to help the poor, making it a much less attractive antipoverty program than other alternatives.[7]

Black Markets and the Importance of the Legal Structure

When price controls are imposed, exchanges at prices outside of the range set by the government are illegal. Governments may also make it entirely illegal to buy and sell certain products. This is the case with drugs like marijuana and cocaine in the United States. Similarly, prostitution is illegal in all states except Nevada. However, controlling prices and making a good or service illegal doesn't eliminate market forces. When demand is strong and gains from trade can be had, markets will develop and exchanges will occur in spite of the restrictions. People will also engage in illegal exchanges in order to evade taxes. For example, the $3.00 per-pack cigarette tax in New York City has made cigarette smuggling in that city a thriving business.

Black market

A market that operates outside the legal system in which either illegal goods are sold or legal goods are sold at illegal prices or terms.

Markets that operate outside the legal system are called **black markets**. How do black markets work? Can markets function without the protection of the law? As in other markets, supply and demand will determine prices in black markets, too. However, because black markets operate outside the official legal structure, enforcement of contracts and the dependability of quality will be less certain. Furthermore, participation in black markets involves greater risk, particularly for suppliers. Prices in these markets will have to be higher than they otherwise would be to compensate suppliers for the risks they are taking—the threat of arrest, possibility of a fine or prison sentence, and so on. Perhaps most important, in black markets there are no legal channels for the peaceful settlement of disputes. When a buyer or seller fails to deliver, it is the other party who must try to enforce the agreement, usually through the use or threat of physical force.

Compared with normal markets, black markets are characterized by a higher incidence of defective products, higher profit rates (for those who do not get caught), and more violence. The incidence of phony tickets purchased from street dealers selling them at illegal prices and deaths caused by toxic, illicit drugs are reflections of the high presence of defective goods in these markets. Certainly, the expensive clothes and automobiles of many drug dealers suggest that monetary profits are high in black markets. Evidence of violence as a means of settling disputes arising from black-market transactions is widespread. Crime statistics in urban areas show that a high percentage of the violent crimes, including murder, are associated with illegal trades gone bad and competition among dealers in the illegal drug market.

The prohibition of alcohol in the United States from 1920 to 1933 vividly illustrates how violence, deception, and fraud plague markets that operate outside the law. When the production and sale of alcohol were illegal during the Prohibition era, gangsters dominated the alcohol trade, and the murder rate soared to record highs. There were also problems with product quality (tainted or highly toxic mixtures, for example) similar to the ones present in modern-day illegal-drug markets. When Prohibition was repealed and the market for alcoholic beverages began operating once again within the legal framework, these harmful secondary effects disappeared.

The operation of black markets highlights a point often taken for granted: *A legal system that provides for secure private-property rights, contract enforcement, and*

---

[7]See David Neumark and William Wascher, "Do Minimum Wages Fight Poverty?" *Economic Inquiry* 40 (July 2002): 315–33; David Neumark and William Wascher, "The Effects of Minimum Wages Throughout the Wage Distribution," *Journal of Human Resources* 39 (April 2004): 425–50; and Richard V. Burkhauser and Joseph J. Sabia, "The Effectiveness of Minimum-Wage Increases in Reducing Poverty: Past, Present, and Future," *Contemporary Economic Policy* 25 (April 2007): 262-81, for evidence of this point.

access to an unbiased court system for settling disputes is vitally important for the smooth operation of markets. Markets will exist in any environment, but they can be counted on to function efficiently only when property rights are secure and contracts are impartially enforced.

The analysis of black markets also provides insights into the economies of Russia, Ukraine, and other parts of the former Soviet Union. Following the collapse of communism, the legal systems in these areas reflected the prior socialist nature of these economies. Both the protection of private property and the enforcement of contracts between private parties were highly uncertain. People with political connections were often able to escape their contractual responsibilities and obtain favorable rulings from legal and regulatory authorities. As a result, markets in these countries operated much like

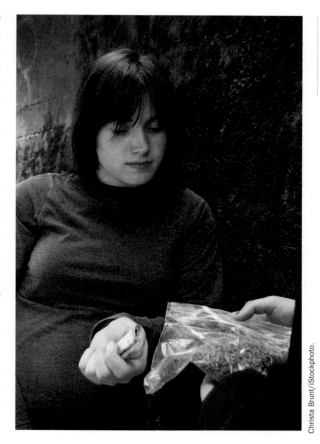

Christa Brunt/iStockphoto.

Black markets like those for illegal drugs are characterized by less dependable product quality and the greater use of violence to settle disputes between buyers and sellers.

black markets. Fraud and deception were commonplace, and the incidence of violence related to business dealings was widespread. The uncertainty accompanying this legal environment was a major contributor to the poor performance of these economies in the aftermath of communism.

The Impact of a Tax

How do taxes affect market exchange? When governments tax goods, who bears the burden? Economists use the term **tax incidence** to indicate how the burden of a tax is *actually* shared between buyers (who pay more for what they purchase) and sellers (who receive less for what they sell). When a tax is imposed, the government can make either the buyer or the seller legally responsible for payment of the tax. The legal assignment is called the *statutory incidence* of the tax. However, the person who writes the check to the government—that is, the person statutorily responsible for the tax—is not always the one who bears the tax burden. The *actual incidence* of a tax may lie elsewhere. If, for example, a tax is placed statutorily on a seller, the seller might simply increase the price of the product. In this case, the buyers end up bearing some, or all, of the tax burden through the higher price.

To illustrate, **EXHIBIT 5** shows how a $1,000 tax placed on the sale of used cars would affect the market. (To simplify this example, let's assume all used cars are identical.) Here, the tax has statutorily been placed on the seller. When a tax is imposed on the seller, it shifts the supply curve upward by exactly the amount of the tax—$1,000, in this example. To understand why, remember that the height of the supply curve at a particular quantity shows the minimum price required to cause enough sellers to offer that quantity of cars for sale. Suppose you were a potential seller, willing to sell your car for any price

Tax incidence

The way the burden of a tax is distributed among economic units (consumers, producers, employees, employers, and so on). The actual tax burden does not always fall on those who are statutorily assigned to pay the tax.

over $6,000, but you would keep it unless you could pocket at least $6,000 from the sale. Because you now have to pay a tax of $1,000 when you sell your car, the minimum price you will accept *from the buyer* will rise to $7,000, so that after paying the tax, you will retain $6,000. Other potential sellers will be in a similar position. The tax will push the minimum price each seller is willing to accept upward by $1,000. Thus, the after-tax supply curve will shift vertically by this amount.

Sellers would prefer to pass the entire tax on to buyers by raising prices by the full amount of the tax, rather than paying any part of it themselves. However, as sellers begin to raise prices, customers respond by purchasing fewer units. At some point, to avoid losing additional sales, some sellers will find it more profitable to accept part of the tax burden themselves (in the form of a lower price net of tax), rather than to raise the price by the full amount of the tax. This process is shown in Exhibit 5.

Before the tax was imposed, used cars sold for a price of $7,000 (at the intersection of the original supply and demand curves shown by point *A*). After the $1,000 tax is imposed, the equilibrium price of used cars will rise to $7,400 (to point *B,* the intersection of the new supply curve including the tax, and the demand curve). Thus, despite the tax being statutorily imposed on sellers, the higher price shifts some of the tax burden to buyers. Buyers will now pay $400 more for used cars. Sellers now receive $7,400 from the sale of their used cars. However, after sending $1,000 in taxes to the government, they retain only $6,400. This is exactly $600 less than the seller would have received had the tax not been imposed. Because the distance between the supply curves is exactly $1,000, this net price can be found in Exhibit 5 by following the vertical line down from the new equilibrium (point *B*) to the original supply curve (point *C*) and over to the price axis. In this case, each $1,000 of tax revenue transferred to the government imposes a burden of $400 on buyers (in the form of higher used-car prices) and a $600 burden on sellers (in the form of lower net receipts from a car sale), even though sellers are responsible for actually sending the $1,000 tax payment to the government.

The tax revenue derived from a tax is equal to the **tax base** (in this case, the number of used cars exchanged) multiplied by the **tax rate**. After the tax is imposed, the quantity

Tax base

The level or quantity of an economic activity that is taxed. Higher tax rates reduce the level of the tax base because they make the activity less attractive.

Tax rate

The per-unit amount of the tax or the percentage rate at which the economic activity is taxed.

EXHIBIT 5
The Impact of a Tax Imposed on Sellers

When a $1,000 tax is imposed statutorily on the sellers of used cars, the supply curve shifts vertically upward by the amount of the tax. The price of used cars to buyers rises from $7,000 to $7,400, resulting in buyers bearing $400 of the burden of this tax. The price received by a seller falls from $7,000 to $6,400 ($7,400 minus the $1,000 tax), resulting in sellers bearing $600 of the burden.

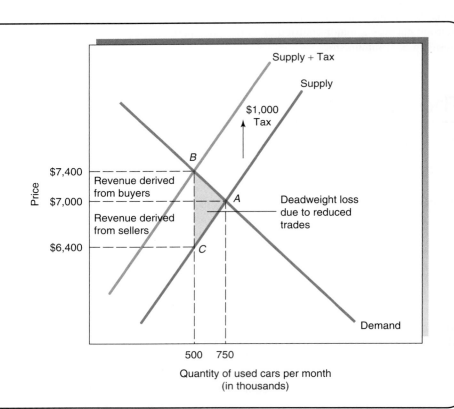

exchanged will fall to 500,000 cars per month because some buyers will choose not to purchase at the $7,400 price, and some sellers will decide not to sell when they are able to net only $6,400. Given the after-tax quantity sold, the monthly revenue derived from the tax will be $500 million (500,000 cars multiplied by $1,000 tax per car).

The Deadweight Loss Caused by Taxes

As Exhibit 5 shows, a $1,000 tax on used cars causes the number of units exchanged to fall from 750,000 to 500,000. It reduces the quantity of units exchanged by 250,000 units. Remember, trade results in mutual gains for both buyers and sellers. The loss of the mutual benefits that would have been derived from these additional 250,000 units also imposes a cost on buyers and sellers. But this cost—the loss of the gains from trade eliminated by the tax—does not generate any revenue for the government. Economists call this the **deadweight loss** of taxation. In Exhibit 5, the size of the triangle *ABC* measures the deadweight loss. The deadweight loss is a burden imposed on buyers and sellers over and above the cost of the revenue transferred to the government. Sometimes it is referred to as the **excess burden of taxation**. It is composed of losses to both buyers (the lost consumer surplus consisting of the upper part of the triangle *ABC*) and sellers (the lost producer surplus consisting of the lower part of the triangle *ABC*).

The deadweight loss to sellers includes an indirect cost imposed on the people who supply resources to that industry (such as its suppliers and employees). The 1990 luxury-boat tax provides a good example. Supporters of the luxury-boat tax assumed the tax burden would fall primarily on wealthy yacht buyers. The actual effects were quite different, though. Because of the tax, luxury-boat sales fell sharply and thousands of workers lost their jobs in the yacht-manufacturing industry. The deadweight loss triangle might seem like an abstract concept, but it wasn't so abstract to the employees in the yacht industry who lost their jobs! Their losses are part of what is reflected in the triangular area. Moreover, because luxury-boat sales declined so sharply, the tax generated only a meager amount of revenue. The large deadweight loss (or excess burden) combined with meager revenue for the government eventually led to the repeal of the tax.

Actual versus Statutory Incidence

Economic analysis indicates that the actual burden of a tax—or more precisely, the split of the burden between buyers and sellers—does not depend on whether the tax is statutorily placed on the buyer or the seller. To see this, we must first look at how the market responds to a tax statutorily placed on the buyer. Continuing with the auto tax example, let's suppose that the government places the $1,000 tax on the buyer of the car, rather than the seller. After making a used-car purchase, the buyer must send a check to the government for $1,000. Imposing a tax on buyers will shift the demand curve downward by the amount of the tax, as shown in **EXHIBIT 6**. This is because the height of the demand curve represents the maximum price a buyer is willing to pay for the car. If a particular buyer is willing and able to pay only $5,000 for a car, the $1,000 tax would mean that the most the buyer would be willing to pay *to the seller* would be $4,000. This is because the total cost to the buyer is now the purchase price plus the tax.

As Exhibit 6 shows, the price of used cars falls from $7,000 (point *A*) to $6,400 (point *B*) when the tax is statutorily placed on the buyer. Even though the tax is placed on buyers, the reduction in demand that results causes the price received by sellers to fall by $600. Thus, $600 of the tax is again borne by sellers, just as it was when the tax was placed statutorily on them. From the buyer's standpoint, a car now costs $7,400 ($6,400 paid to the seller plus $1,000 in tax to the government). Just as when the tax was imposed on the seller, the buyer now pays $400 more for a used car.

A comparison of Exhibits 5 and 6 makes it clear that the actual burden of the $1,000 tax is independent of its statutory incidence. In both cases, buyers pay a total price of $7,400 for the car (a $400 increase from the pretax level), and sellers receive $6,400 from the sale (a $600 decrease from the pretax level). Correspondingly, the revenue

Deadweight loss

The loss of gains from trade to buyers and sellers that occurs when a tax is imposed. The deadweight loss imposes a burden on both buyers and sellers over and above the actual payment of the tax.

Excess burden of taxation

Another term for deadweight loss. It reflects losses that occur when beneficial activities are forgone because they are taxed.

EXHIBIT 6
The Impact of a Tax
Imposed on Buyers

When a $1,000 tax is imposed statutorily on the buyers of used cars, the demand curve shifts vertically downward by the amount of the tax. The price of used cars falls from $7,000 to $6,400, resulting in sellers bearing $600 of the burden. The buyer's total cost of purchasing the car rises from $7,000 to $7,400 ($6,400 plus the $1,000 tax), resulting in buyers bearing $400 of the burden of this tax. The incidence of this tax on used cars is the same regardless of whether it is statutorily imposed on buyers or sellers.

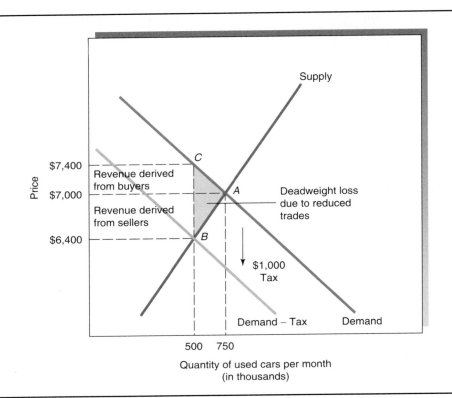

derived by the government, the number of sales eliminated by the tax, and the size of the deadweight loss are identical whether the law requires payment of the tax by the sellers or by the buyers. A similar phenomenon occurs with any tax. The 15.3 percent Social Security payroll tax, for example, is statutorily levied as 7.65 percent on the employee and 7.65 percent on the employer. The impact is to drive down the net pay received by employees and raise the employers' cost of hiring workers. Economic analysis tells us that the actual burden of this tax will probably differ from its legal assignment, and that it will be the same regardless of how the tax is statutorily assigned. Because market prices (here, workers' gross wage) will adjust, the incidence of the tax will be identical regardless of whether the 15.3 percent is levied on employees or on employers or is divided between the two parties.

Elasticity and the Incidence of a Tax

If the actual incidence of a tax is independent of its statutory assignment, what does determine the incidence? The answer: The incidence of a tax depends on the responsiveness of buyers and of sellers to a change in price. When buyers respond to even a small increase in price by leaving the market and buying other things, they will not be willing to accept a price that is much higher than it was prior to the tax. Similarly, if sellers respond to a small reduction in what they receive by shifting their goods and resources to other markets, or by going out of business, they will not be willing to accept a much smaller payment, net of tax. The burden of a tax—its incidence—tends to fall more heavily on whichever side of the market has the least attractive options elsewhere—the side of the market that is less sensitive to price changes, in other words.

In the preceding chapter, we saw that the steepness of the supply and demand curves reflects how responsive producers and consumers are to a price change. Relatively inelastic demand or supply curves are steeper (more vertical), indicating less responsiveness to a change in price. Relatively elastic demand or supply curves are flatter (more horizontal), indicating a higher degree of responsiveness to a change in price.

"THIS NEW TAX PLAN SOUNDS PRETTY GOOD... WE GET A 9% CUT AND BUSINESS PICKS UP THE BURDEN...."

The actual burden of a tax is independent of whether it is imposed on buyers or sellers.

Using gasoline as an example, part (a) of **EXHIBIT 7** illustrates the impact of a tax when demand is relatively inelastic and supply is relatively elastic. It will not be easy for gasoline consumers to shift—particularly in the short run—to other fuels in response to an increase in the price of gasoline. The inelastic demand curve shows this. When a 50-cent per gallon tax is imposed on gasoline (roughly the current average of combined federal and state taxes), buyers end up paying 40 cents more per gallon ($3.00 instead of $2.60), while the net price received by sellers is only 10 cents less ($2.50 instead of $2.60). *When demand is relatively inelastic, or supply is relatively elastic, buyers will bear the larger share of the tax burden.*

Conversely, when demand is relatively elastic and supply is inelastic, more of the tax burden will fall on sellers and resource suppliers. The luxury-boat tax illustrates this point. As we mentioned earlier, Congress imposed a tax on the sale of luxury boats in 1990. Later, the tax was repealed because of its adverse impact on sales and employment in the industry. There are many things wealthy potential yacht owners can spend their money on other than luxury boats *sold in the United States.* For one thing, they can buy a yacht someplace else, perhaps in Mexico, England, or the Bahamas. Or they can spend more time on the golf course, travel to exotic places, or purchase a nicer car or a vacation home. Because there are attractive substitutes, the demand for domestically produced luxury boats is relatively elastic compared with supply. Therefore, as Exhibit 7b illustrates, when a $25,000 tax is imposed on luxury boats, prices rise by only $5,000 (from $100,000 to $105,000), but output falls substantially (from 10,000 to 5,000 boats). The net price received by sellers falls by $20,000 (from $100,000 to $80,000 per boat). *When demand is relatively elastic, or supply is relatively inelastic, sellers (including resource suppliers) will bear the larger share of the tax burden.*

Elasticity and the Deadweight Loss

We have seen that the elasticities of supply and demand determine how the burden of a tax is distributed between buyer and seller. They also influence the size of the deadweight loss caused by the tax because they determine the total reduction in the quantity exchanged. When either demand or supply is relatively inelastic, fewer trades will be eliminated by the tax, so the deadweight loss will be smaller. From a policy perspective, the excess burden of a tax system will therefore be lower if taxes are levied on goods and services for which either demand or supply is highly inelastic.

EXHIBIT 7
How the Burden of a Tax Depends on the Elasticities of Demand and Supply

In part (a), when demand is relatively more inelastic than supply, buyers bear a larger share of the burden of the tax.
In part (b), when supply is relatively more inelastic than demand, sellers bear a larger share of the tax burden.

(a) Tax on gasoline

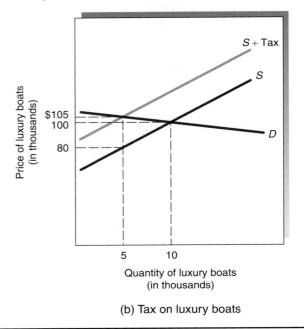

(b) Tax on luxury boats

Tax Rates, Tax Revenues, and the Laffer Curve

It is important to distinguish between the average and marginal rates of taxation. They can be very different, and both provide important information. The average tax rate is generally used to examine how different income groups are burdened by a tax, whereas the marginal tax rate is the key to understanding the negative economic effects created by a tax. Both can be computed with simple equations. The **average tax rate (ATR)** can be expressed as follows:

$$\text{ATR} = \frac{\textbf{Tax liability}}{\textbf{Taxable income}}$$

For example, if a person's tax liability was $3,000 on an income of $20,000, her average tax rate would be 15 percent ($3,000 divided by $20,000). The average tax rate is simply the percentage of income that is paid in taxes.

In the United States, the personal income tax provides the largest single source of government revenue. This tax is particularly important at the federal level. You may have heard that the federal income tax is "progressive." A **progressive tax** is defined as a tax in which the average tax rate rises with income. In other words, people with higher income pay a larger *percentage of their income* in taxes. Alternatively, taxes can be proportional or regressive. A **proportional tax** is defined as a tax in which the average tax rate remains the same across income levels. Under a proportional tax, everyone pays the same percentage of their income in taxes. Finally, a **regressive tax** is defined as a tax in which the average tax rate falls with income. If someone making $100,000 per year paid $30,000 in taxes (an ATR of 30 percent) while someone making $30,000 per year paid $15,000 in taxes (an ATR of 50 percent), the tax code would be regressive. Note that a regressive tax merely means that the *percentage* paid in taxes declines with income; the actual dollar amount of the tax bill might still be higher for those with larger incomes.

Average tax rate (ATR)

Tax liability divided by taxable income. It is the percentage of income paid in taxes.

Progressive tax

A tax in which the average tax rate rises with income. People with higher incomes will pay a higher percentage of their income in taxes.

Proportional tax

A tax in which the average tax rate is the same at all income levels. Everyone pays the same percentage of income in taxes.

Regressive tax

A tax in which the average tax rate falls with income. People with higher incomes will pay a lower percentage of their income in taxes.

Although the average tax rate is useful in determining whether an income tax is progressive, proportional, or regressive, it is the marginal tax rate that concerns individuals when they are making decisions. It is the marginal tax rate that determines how much of an additional dollar of income must be paid in taxes (and thus, also, how much one gets to keep). An individual's marginal tax rate can be very different from his or her average tax rate. The **marginal tax rate (MTR)** can be expressed as follows:

$$\text{MTR} = \frac{\text{Change in tax liability}}{\text{Change in taxable income}}$$

The MTR reveals both how much of one's *additional* income must be turned over to the tax collector and how much is retained by the individual taxpayer. For example, when the MTR is 25 percent, $25 of every $100 of additional earnings must be paid in taxes. The individual is permitted to keep only $75 of his or her additional income, in other words. The marginal tax rate is vitally important because it affects the incentive to earn additional income. The higher the marginal tax rate, the less incentive individuals have to earn more income. At high marginal rates, for example, many spouses will choose to stay home rather than take a job, and others will choose not to take on second jobs or extra work. **EXHIBIT 8** shows the calculation of both the average and marginal tax rates within the framework of the 2008 income tax tables provided to taxpayers.

Generally, a person's income is subject to several different taxes, and it is the combined marginal tax rate of all of them that matters when it comes to decision making. For example, a recent college graduate with $33,000 in taxable income living in Baltimore, Maryland, would face a 25 percent marginal federal income tax rate, a 7.65 percent marginal Social Security payroll tax rate, a 4.75 percent marginal state income tax rate, and a 3.05 percent marginal local income tax rate. If we ignore the relatively small deductions that one tax can generate in calculating certain others, the result is a combined marginal tax rate of 40.45 percent, meaning that an additional $100 of gross income would result in only a $59.55 increase in net take-home income.

Governments generally levy taxes to raise revenue. The revenue derived from a tax is equal to the tax base multiplied by the tax rate. As we previously noted, taxes will lower the level of the activity taxed. When an activity is taxed more heavily, people will choose to do less of it. The higher the tax rate, the greater the shift away from the activity. If taxpayers can easily escape the tax by altering their behavior (perhaps by shifting to substitutes), the tax base will shrink significantly as rates are increased. This erosion in the tax base in response to higher rates means that an increase in tax rates will generally lead to a less-than-proportional increase in tax revenue.

Economist Arthur Laffer popularized the idea that, beyond some point, higher tax rates will shrink the tax base so much that tax revenue will actually begin to decline when tax rates are increased. The curve illustrating the relationship between tax rates and tax revenues is called the **Laffer curve**. **EXHIBIT 9** illustrates the concept of the Laffer curve as it applies to income taxes. Obviously, tax revenue would be zero if the income tax rate were zero. What isn't so obvious is that tax revenue would also be zero (or at least very close to zero) if the tax rate were 100 percent. Confronting a 100 percent tax rate, most individuals would go fishing or find something else to do rather than engage in taxable productive activity, since the 100 percent tax rate would eliminate all personal reward derived from earning taxable income. Why work when you have to give every penny of your earnings to the government?

As tax rates are reduced from 100 percent, the incentive to work and earn taxable income increases, income expands, and tax revenue rises. Similarly, as tax rates increase from zero, tax revenue expands. Clearly, at some rate greater than zero but less than 100 percent, tax revenue will be maximized (point *B* in Exhibit 9). This is not to imply that the tax rate that maximizes revenue is the ideal, or optimal, tax rate from the standpoint of the economy as a whole. Although it might be the tax rate that generates the most revenue for government, we must also consider the welfare reductions imposed on individuals by the deadweight loss created by the tax. As rates are increased and the maximum revenue point (*B*) is approached, relatively large tax rate increases will be necessary to expand tax

Marginal tax rate (MTR)

The additional tax liability a person faces divided by his or her additional taxable income. It is the percentage of an extra dollar of income earned that must be paid in taxes. It is the marginal tax rate that is relevant in personal decision making.

Laffer curve

A curve illustrating the relationship between the tax rate and tax revenues. Tax revenues will be low at both very high and very low tax rates. When tax rates are quite high, lowering them can increase tax revenue.

EXHIBIT 8
Average and Marginal Tax Rates in the Income Tax Tables

This excerpt from the 2008 federal income tax table shows that in the 25 percent federal marginal income tax bracket, each $100 of additional taxable income a single taxpayer earns ($33,000 versus $33,100, for example) causes his or her tax liability to increase by $25 (from $4,600 to $4,625). Note that the average tax rate for a single taxpayer at $33,000 is about 14 percent ($4,600 divided by $33,000), even though the taxpayer's marginal rate is 25 percent.

2008 Tax Table–Continued

If line 43 (taxable income) is—		Single	Married filing jointly	Married filing sepa-rately	Head of a house-hold
At least	But less than				
		Your tax is—			
33,000					
33,000	**33,050**	4,600	4,151	4,600	4,381
33,050	**33,100**	4,613	4,159	4,613	4,389
33,100	**33,150**	4,625	4,166	4,625	4,396
33,150	**33,200**	4,638	4,174	4,638	4,404
33,200	**33,250**	4,650	4,181	4,650	4,411
33,250	**33,300**	4,663	4,189	4,663	4,419
33,300	**33,350**	4,675	4,196	4,675	4,426
33,350	**33,400**	4,688	4,204	4,688	4,434
33,400	**33,450**	4,700	4,211	4,700	4,441
33,450	**33,500**	4,713	4,219	4,713	4,449
33,500	**33,550**	4,725	4,226	4,725	4,456
33,550	**33,600**	4,738	4,234	4,738	4,464
33,600	**33,650**	4,750	4,241	4,750	4,471
33,650	**33,700**	4,763	4,249	4,763	4,479
33,700	**33,750**	4,775	4,256	4,775	4,486
33,750	**33,800**	4,788	4,264	4,788	4,494
33,800	**33,850**	4,800	4,271	4,800	4,501
33,850	**33,900**	4,813	4,279	4,813	4,509
33,900	**33,950**	4,825	4,286	4,825	4,516
33,950	**34,000**	4,838	4,294	4,838	4,524

$100 of additional income . . .

. . . results in $25 of additional tax liability.

revenue by even a small amount. In this range, the deadweight loss of taxation in the form of reductions in gains from trade will be exceedingly large relative to the additional tax revenue. Thus, the ideal tax rate will be well below the rate that maximizes revenue.

The Laffer curve shows that it is important to distinguish between changes in tax rates and changes in tax revenues. Higher rates will not always lead to more revenue for the government. Similarly, lower rates will not always lead to less revenue. ***When tax rates are already high, a rate reduction may increase tax revenues. Correspondingly, increasing high tax rates may lead to less tax revenue.***

Evidence from the sharp reduction in marginal tax rates imposed on those with high incomes during the 1980s supports the Laffer curve. The top marginal rate was reduced from 70 percent at the beginning of the decade to 33 percent by the end of the decade. Even though the top rates were cut sharply, tax revenues and the share of the personal income tax paid by high-income earners actually rose as a result. During the decade, revenue collected from the top 1 percent of earners rose a whopping 51.4 percent (after adjusting for infla-tion). In 1980, 19 percent of the personal income tax was collected from the top 1 percent of earners. By 1990, at the lower tax rates, the top 1 percent of earners accounted for more than

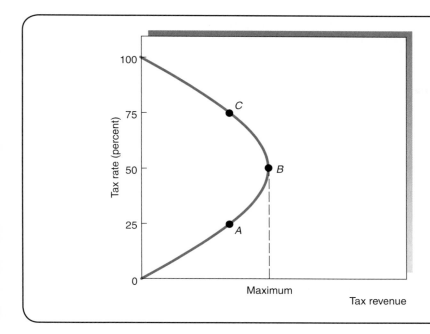

EXHIBIT 9
Laffer Curve

Because taxing an activity affects the amount of it people will do, a change in tax rates will not lead to a proportional change in tax revenues. As the Laffer curve indicates, beyond some point (B), an increase in tax rates will cause tax revenues to fall. At high tax rates, revenue can be increased by lowering tax rates. The tax rate that maximizes tax revenue is higher than the ideal tax rate for the economy as a whole because of the large dead-weight loss of taxation as tax rates increase toward point B.

APPLICATIONS IN ECONOMICS

The Laffer Curve and Mountain-Climbing Deaths

The Laffer curve can be used to illustrate many other relationships besides just tax rates and tax revenues. Economists J. R. Clark and Dwight Lee have used it to analyze the relationship between the safety of mountain climbing and mountain-climbing deaths on Mt. McKinley, North America's highest peak. As the risk of dying from climbing Mt. McKinley fell due to greater search-and-rescue efforts by national park personnel, the number of people seeking to "conquer the mountain" rose significantly. The increase in the number of climbers attempting to conquer the mountain offset the lower risk, leading to a Laffer curve-type relationship. In other words, greater search–an—rescue efforts led to a *higher* number of total deaths on the mountain.

Let's look at the problem numerically. Assume that if the probability of death from an attempted climb were 90 percent, only 100 people would attempt to climb the mountain each year, leading to an annual death rate of 90. Now suppose that greater search-and-rescue efforts lower the probability of death to 50 percent. Because incentives matter, the increased safety will result in an increase in the number of people attempting to climb the mountain.

Suppose that the number of climbers increases from 100 to 200. With 200 climbers and a 50 percent probability of death, the annual number of fatalities would increase to 100, 10 more than before rescue efforts were improved. The total number of mountain-climbing deaths is actually lowest when there is both a very high and a very low probability of death—just as the Laffer curve predicts. The number of deaths is largest in the middle probability ranges. Making a very risky mountain safer can therefore result in more rather than fewer fatalities.

Clark and Lee have also explored a similar relationship between average lengths of prison sentences and total prison space occupied. Other economists have explored the Laffer curve relationship between the minimum wage and the earnings of minimum-wage workers, as well as the regulatory costs of protecting endangered species and the habitat acres available to them.[1]

[1]See J. R. Clark and Dwight R. Lee, "Too Safe to Be Safe: Some Implications of Short- and Long-Run Rescue Laffer Curves," *Eastern Economic Journal*, 23 no. 2 (Spring 1997): 127–37; Russell S. Sobel, "Theory and Evidence on the Political Economy of the Minimum Wage," *Journal of Political Economy*, 107 no. 4 (August 1999): 761–85; and Richard L. Stroup, "The Endangered Species Act: The Laffer Curve Strikes Again," *The Journal of Private Enterprise*, vol. XIV (Special Issue 1998): 48–62.

25 percent of income tax revenues. The top 10 percent of earners paid just over 49 percent of total income taxes in 1980, but by 1990 the share paid by these earners had risen to 55 percent. Thus, the reduction in the exceedingly high rates increased the revenue collected from high-income taxpayers. Additional evidence on the impact of these tax changes in the 1980s is provided in Special Topic 1. However, recently proposals have been made to significantly increase marginal tax rates back to the levels from the early 1990s or even higher, and it will be interesting to see what happens to tax revenue from the rich as a result.

The Impact of a Subsidy

Subsidy

A payment the government makes to either the buyer or seller, usually on a per-unit basis, when a good or service is purchased or sold.

The supply and demand framework can also be used to analyze the impact of a government **subsidy**. A subsidy is a payment to either the buyer or seller of a good or service, usually on a per-unit basis. Subsidies are often granted in an effort to help buyers afford a good or service, or to increase the profitability of producers in an industry. As we have seen in other cases, however, the effect of a government program often differs substantially from its original intent. Because prices change when subsidies are imposed (just as when taxes are imposed), the benefit of a subsidy can be partially, or totally, shifted from buyer to seller, or vice versa.

Suppose that the government, in an effort to make textbooks more affordable, gives college students (buyers) a $20 subsidy for each book they buy. **EXHIBIT 10** shows the effect of the program. Before the subsidy was instituted, 100 million textbooks were sold each year at an average price of $80 per book. The $20-per-book subsidy paid to the buyers will increase demand by the amount of the subsidy (shift from D_1 to D_2). As the result of the subsidy, the equilibrium price will increase from $80 to $90, and the total quantity purchased will expand to 110 million textbooks per year.

The subsidy program reduces the students' out-of-pocket cost of a textbook (from $80 to $70), but the net gain to them is less than the amount of the subsidy. Why? Even though the textbook subsidy is granted to buyers, substantial benefits also accrue to sellers. Because the subsidy program increases the demand for textbooks, pushing their price

---

EXHIBIT 10
The Impact of a Subsidy Granted to Buyers

When a $20-per-textbook subsidy is given to students, the demand curve for textbooks shifts vertically upward by the amount of the subsidy. The market price of textbooks rises from $80 to $90 (new gross price). With the $20 subsidy, buyers now pay a net price of $70 per textbook (the new $90 price minus the $20 subsidy), which is $10 less than before. Textbook buyers get only $10 of the benefit of the subsidy; the remaining $10 benefit accrues to the supply side of the market (sellers and resource suppliers) in the form of higher textbook prices. The distribution of the benefit from the subsidy between buyers and sellers would be the same, whether it was granted to buyers or sellers.

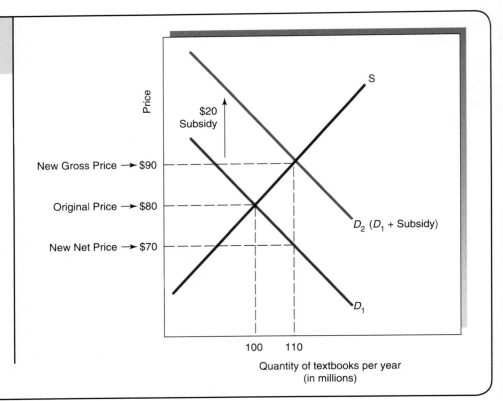

upward by $10, half of the benefits are captured by sellers (including resource suppliers like copy editors, authors, and paper suppliers).

Alternatively, if textbook suppliers had been granted a $20 payment from the government for each textbook sold, the supply curve would have shifted downward by the amount of the subsidy. This would cause the market price of textbooks to decline to $70. In this case, buyers pay $10 less than before the subsidy program, while the sellers receive $10 more (the sellers now get $90 for each book sold—the $70 market price plus the $20 government subsidy). Just like a tax, a subsidy results in the same outcome, regardless of whether the subsidy is granted to buyers or sellers.

Elasticity and the Benefit of Government Subsidy Programs

In this example, the benefit of the $20-per-textbook subsidy was split evenly between buyers and sellers. However, the actual distribution of this benefit will depend on the elasticities of supply and demand—just as it does with a tax. The greater share of the benefit of a subsidy will always be shifted toward the more inelastic side of the market. Thus, the more inelastic the supply, the larger the share of the benefit that will accrue to sellers. Conversely, the more inelastic the demand, the larger the share of the benefit that will accrue to buyers. Using our earlier examples from the section on taxation, consumers would be the main beneficiary of a subsidy on gasoline (a good for which the demand is relatively inelastic, and supply elastic), while suppliers would be the main beneficiary of a subsidy on luxury boats (a good for which demand is relatively elastic, and supply inelastic). Economic analysis indicates that the true benefit of a subsidy will (1) be the same regardless of whether the subsidy is granted to the buyers or sellers in a market, and (2) will depend on the elasticities of supply and demand.

The Cost of Government Subsidy Programs

Policy makers and citizens alike often complain that the cost of government subsidy programs almost invariably exceeds initial projections. One reason for this is the increase in the quantity of the good purchased resulting from the subsidy. Prior to the enactment of the textbook subsidy, 100 million textbooks were sold annually. With a subsidy of $20 per textbook, one might be inclined to think that the annual cost of the program will be $2 billion ($20 × 100 million). This figure, however, will underestimate the true cost. Once the subsidy is in place, textbook sales will increase to 110 million, driving the overall cost of the program up to $2.2 billion ($20 × 110 million).

Furthermore, the expenditures on the subsidies will understate their total costs. To finance the subsidies, the government will have to raise the funds through taxation. A new subsidy granted in one market will require greater taxation in other markets. As we have previously discussed, the taxes will generate a deadweight loss over and above the revenues transferred to the government. This excess burden is also a cost of the subsidy payments.

Real-World Subsidy Programs

The United States has a vast array of subsidy programs. Spending on these programs and the taxes that finance them are major items in the government budget. Some subsidy programs, such as Medicare and food stamps, provide payments to buyers. Others, such as the subsidies to the arts, public broadcasting, sports stadiums, and ethanol are directed toward suppliers. As we discussed, however, the party granted the subsidy may not be the one who captures the larger share of the actual benefit from the subsidy.

Still other subsidy programs are combined with price controls. Many agriculture subsidies fall into this category. The government fixes the prices of products like wheat, corn, cotton, and tobacco above the market equilibrium. To maintain the above-equilibrium price, the government purchases any amount produced that cannot be sold at the artificially high price. The government also restricts the acreage farmers are permitted to plant for these crops. If it were not for the planting restrictions, huge surpluses of these products would develop.

Sometimes government subsidies are granted only to a select group, or subset, of buyers (or sellers). Consider the structure of healthcare subsidies in the United States. The Medicare program subsidizes the healthcare purchases of senior citizens, and the Medicaid program provides subsidies to low-income households. These subsidies increase the demand for health care and drive up the prices of medical service for all consumers, including those ineligible for either program. When only some of the buyers in a market are subsidized, groups that are ineligible for the subsidies will generally be harmed because they will have to pay higher prices for the good or service than they would otherwise have to, even though they do not receive a subsidy.

Ethanol, a biofuel alternative to gasoline made from corn, provides another example of a product that is heavily subsidized in the United States. Ethanol subsidies, which amount to approximately $1.25 per gallon, have a direct cost to taxpayers of almost $6 billion per year. Ethanol is significantly more costly to produce than gasoline. In effect, the ethanol subsidies channel resources into production of a good that is valued less than its production cost. Ethanol's environmental benefits over gasoline are highly questionable. Why does the government subsidize ethanol? The ethanol subsidies increase the demand for corn, driving up its price. Corn farmers derive major benefits from the program, while the cost is spread thinly across taxpayers (who fund the subsidies) and consumers (who pay higher prices for the many products made from corn—from tortillas to soft drinks). As we will discuss later, politicians can derive political gain by supporting programs of this type even when the programs are inefficient. Further, the largest corn-producing state is Iowa, which also happens to hold early caucuses and elect the first delegates to the presidential nominating conventions. Like many other subsidies, the ethanol program is driven by political forces rather than sound economics.

Subsidy programs are often highly complex, and it is sometimes difficult to determine whom they really benefit. As we proceed, we will analyze several of these programs in more detail. The supply and demand model presented here will facilitate our analysis.

Looking ahead

This chapter focused on how government-mandated price controls, taxes, subsidies, and prohibitions affect market outcomes. The next two chapters will apply the basic tools of economics to the political process more generally. In the chapters that follow, we will consider when intervention by the government is likely to enhance the well-being of citizens, and when it is likely to make them worse off. We will also analyze how the political process works and explain why it is sometimes a source of economic inefficiency.

KEY POINTS

▼ Resource markets and product markets are closely linked. A change in one will generally result in changes in the other.

▼ Legally imposed price ceilings result in shortages, and legally imposed price floors will cause surpluses. Both also cause other harmful secondary effects. Rent controls, for example, will lead to shortages,

less investment, poor maintenance, and deterioration in the quality of rental housing.

▼ The minimum wage is a price floor for low-skilled labor. It increases the earnings of some low-skilled workers but also reduces employment and leads to fewer training opportunities and nonwage job benefits for other low-skilled workers.

▼ Because black markets operate outside the legal system, they are often characterized by deception, fraud, and the use of violence as a means of enforcing contracts. A legal system that provides secure private-property rights and unbiased enforcement of contracts enhances the operation of markets.

▼ The division of the actual tax burden between buyers and sellers is determined by the relative elasticities of demand and supply rather than on whom the tax is legally imposed.

▼ In addition to the cost of the tax revenue transferred to the government, taxes will reduce the level of the activity taxed, eliminate some gains from trade, and thereby impose an excess burden, or deadweight loss.

▼ As tax rates increase, the size of the tax base will shrink. Initially, rates and revenues will be directly related—revenues will expand as rates increase. However, as higher and higher rates are imposed, eventually an inverse relationship will develop—revenues will decline as rates are increased further. The Laffer curve illustrates this pattern.

▼ The division of the benefit from a subsidy is determined by the relative elasticities of demand and supply rather than to whom the subsidy is actually paid.

CRITICAL ANALYSIS QUESTIONS

*1. How will a substantial increase in demand for housing affect the wages and employment of carpenters, plumbers, and electricians?

2. Suppose that college students in your town persuaded the town council to enact a law setting the maximum price for rental housing at $400 per month. Will this help or hurt college students who rent housing? In your answer, address how this price ceiling will affect (a) the quality of rental housing; (b) the amount of rental housing available; (c) the incentive of landlords to maintain their properties; (d) the amount of racial, gender, and other types of discrimination in the local rental housing market; (e) the ease with which students will be able to find housing, and, finally; (f) whether a black market for housing would develop.

3. What is the difference between a price ceiling and a price floor? What will happen if a price ceiling is imposed below the market equilibrium? If a price ceiling for a good is set below the market equilibrium, what will happen to the quality and future availability of the good? Explain.

*4. To be meaningful, a price ceiling must be below the market price. Conversely, a meaningful price floor must be above the market price. What impact will a meaningful price ceiling have on the quantity exchanged? What impact will a meaningful price floor have on the quantity exchanged? Explain.

5. Congress recently passed a new program that will subsidize the purchase of prescription drugs by the elderly. What impact will this program have on the demand for and price of prescription drugs? How will people who are not elderly be affected by this program? Explain.

*6. Analyze the impact of an increase in the minimum wage from the current level to $10 per hour. How would the following be affected?
    a. employment of people previously earning less than $10 per hour
    b. the unemployment rate of teenagers
    c. the availability of on-the-job training for low-skilled workers
    d. the demand for high-skilled workers who are good substitutes for low-skilled workers

7. What is a black market? What are some of the main differences in how black markets operate relative to legal markets?

8. How do you think the markets for organ donation and child adoption would be affected if they were made fully legal with a well-functioning price mechanism? What would be the advantages and disadvantages relative to the current system?

9. What is meant by the incidence of a tax? Explain why the statutory and actual incidence of a tax can be different.

10. What conditions must be met for buyers to bear the full burden of a tax? What conditions would cause sellers to bear the full burden? Explain.

*11. What is the nature of the deadweight loss accompanying taxes? Why is it often referred to as an "excess burden"?

12. The demand and supply schedules for a hypothetical labor market are given in the accompanying table.
    a. Find the equilibrium wage and number of workers hired.

b. Suppose that a new law is passed requiring employers to pay an unemployment insurance tax of $1.50 per hour for every employee. What happens to the equilibrium wage rate and number of workers hired? How is this tax burden distributed between employers and workers?

c. Now suppose that rather than being paid by employers, the tax must be paid by workers. How does this affect the equilibrium wage rate and number of workers hired? How is this tax burden distributed between employers and workers?

d. Does it make a difference who is statutorily liable for the tax?

Demand		Supply	
Wage	**Quantity Demanded**	**Wage**	**Quantity Supplied**
$10.00	1,000	$10.00	1,900
9.50	1,200	9.50	1,800
9.00	1,400	9.00	1,700
8.50	1,600	8.50	1,600
8.00	1,800	8.00	1,500
7.50	2,000	7.50	1,400

13. Currently, the Social Security payroll tax is legally imposed equally on workers and employers: 7.65 percent for employees and 7.65 percent for employers. Show this graphically, being careful to distinguish between the total cost to the employer of hiring a worker, the employee's gross wage, and the employee's net wage. Show how the outcome would differ if all 15.3 percent were imposed on the employee or if all 15.3 percent were imposed on the employer.

*14. Suppose Congress were to pass legislation requiring that businesses employing workers with three or more children pay these employees at least $15 per hour. How would this legislation affect the employment level of low-skilled workers with three or more children? Do you think some workers with large families might attempt to conceal the fact? Why?

15. "We should impose a 20 percent luxury tax on expensive automobiles (those with a sales price of $50,000 or more) in order to collect more tax revenue from the wealthy." Will the burden of the proposed tax fall primarily on the wealthy? Why or why not?

*16. Should policy makers seek to set the tax on an economic activity at a rate that will maximize the revenue derived from the tax? Why or why not? Explain.

*17. During the summer of 2001, the combination of city and state taxes on cigarettes sold in New York City rose from $1.19 to more than $3.00 per pack. How will this tax increase affect (a) the quantity of cigarettes sold in New York City, (b) the revenue derived by the city and state from the tax, (c) the Internet purchases of cigarettes by New Yorkers, and (d) the incidence of smoking by New Yorkers?

*Asterisk denotes questions for which answers are given in Appendix B.

Difficult Cases for the Market, and the Role of Government

CHAPTER FOCUS

- What is economic efficiency and how can it be used to evaluate markets?

- Why is it generally undesirable to pursue any goal to perfection?

- What is the role of government in a market economy?

- What are externalities? What are public goods?

- Why might markets fail to allocate goods and services efficiently?

- If the market has shortcomings, does this mean the government should intervene?

The principal justification for public policy intervention lies in the frequent and numerous shortcomings of market outcomes.

—Charles Wolf, Jr.[1]

[1]Charles Wolf, Jr., *Markets or Government* (Cambridge, MA: MIT Press, 1988), 17.

As we previously discussed, markets and government planning are the two main alternatives for the organization of economic activity. Chapters 3 and 4 introduced you to how markets work and demonstrated how the invisible hand of the market process directs the self-interest of individuals toward activities in the best interest of society. Throughout, we noted that some qualifications were in order, in terms of both the "rules of the game" that must be in place for markets to work well and the existence of special cases, in which the invisible hand might not function effectively. In this chapter, we turn our attention to discussing these potential problem areas for the market and consider their implications with regard to the role of government. In the following chapter, we will analyze how the political process works more directly. ■

A Closer Look at Economic Efficiency

Economic efficiency

A situation that occurs when (1) all activities generating more benefit than cost are undertaken, and (2) no activities are undertaken for which the cost exceeds the benefit.

Economists use the standard of **economic efficiency** to assess the desirability of economic outcomes. We briefly introduced the concept in Chapter 3. We now want to explore it in more detail. The central idea of economic efficiency is straightforward. For any given level of cost, we want to obtain the largest possible benefit. Alternatively, we want to obtain any particular benefit for the least possible cost. Economic efficiency means getting the most value from the available resources—making the largest pie from the available set of ingredients, so to speak.

Economists acknowledge that individuals generally do not regard the efficiency of the entire economy as a primary goal for themselves. Rather, each person is interested in enlarging the size of his or her own slice. But if resources are used more efficiently, the overall size of the pie will be larger, and therefore, at least potentially, *everyone* could have a larger slice. For an outcome to be consistent with ideal economic efficiency, two conditions are necessary:

Rule 1. *Undertaking an economic action is efficient if it produces more benefits than costs.* To satisfy economic efficiency, all actions generating more benefits than costs must be undertaken. Failure to undertake all such actions implies that a potential gain has been forgone.

Rule 2. *Undertaking an economic action is inefficient if it produces more costs than benefits.* To satisfy economic efficiency, no action that generates more costs than benefits should be undertaken. When such counterproductive actions are taken, society is worse off because even better alternatives were forgone.

Economic efficiency results only when both of these conditions have been met. *Either failure to undertake an efficient action (Rule 1) or the undertaking of an inefficient action (Rule 2) will result in economic inefficiency.* To illustrate, consider **EXHIBIT 1**, which shows the benefits and costs associated with expanding the amount of any particular activity. We have avoided using a specific example here to ensure you understand the general idea of efficiency without linking it to a specific application. As we will show, the concept has wide-ranging applications, from the evaluation of government policy to how long you choose to brush your teeth in the morning.[2]

---

[2]Note to students who may pursue advanced study in economics: Using the concept of efficiency to compare alternative policies typically requires that the analyst estimate costs and benefits that are difficult or impossible to measure. Costs and benefits are the values of opportunities forgone or accepted by individuals, *as evaluated by those individuals.* Then, these costs and benefits must be added up across all individuals and compared. But does a dollar's gain for one individual really compensate for a dollar's sacrifice by another? Some economists simply reject the validity of making such comparisons. They say that neither the estimates by the economic analyst of subjectively determined costs and benefits nor the adding up of these costs and benefits across individuals is meaningful. Their case may be valid, but most economists today nevertheless use the concept of efficiency as we present it. No other way to use economic analysis to compare policy alternatives has been found.

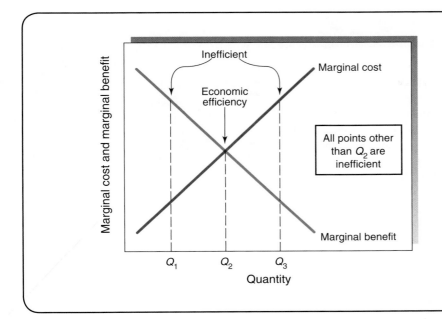

EXHIBIT 1
Economic Efficiency

As we use more time and resources to expand the level of an activity, the marginal benefits will generally decline and the marginal costs rise. From the viewpoint of efficiency, the activity should be expanded as long as the marginal benefits exceed the marginal costs. Therefore, quantity Q_2 is the economically efficient level of this activity. Q_1 is inefficient because some production that could generate more benefits than costs is not undertaken. Q_3 is also inefficient because some units are produced even though their costs exceed the benefits they create. Thus, either too much or too little of an activity will result in inefficiency.

In Exhibit 1, the marginal benefit curve shows the additional benefit associated with expanding the activity. The marginal cost curve shows the cost—including any opportunity costs—of spending additional time, effort, and resources on the activity. At Q_1, the height of the marginal benefit curve exceeds the height of the marginal cost curve. Thus, at that point, the additional benefits of expanding the activity past Q_1 exceed the additional costs. According to Rule 1 of economic efficiency, we should continue to expand the activity until we reach Q_2. Beyond Q_2 (at Q_3, for example), the height of the marginal benefit curve is less than the height of the marginal cost curve. The additional benefits from expanding activity to that point are smaller than the additional costs. According to Rule 2, at Q_3, we have gone too far and should cut back on the activity. Q_2 is the only point consistent with both rules of economic efficiency.

If It's Worth Doing, It's Worth Doing Imperfectly

Eliminating pollution. Earning straight As. Being completely organized. Cleaning your apartment until it sparkles. Making automobiles completely safe. Making airplanes fully secure against terrorist attacks. All of these are worthwhile goals, right? Well, they are until you consider the costs of actually achieving them. The heading for this section is, of course, a play on the old saying, "If it's worth doing, it's worth doing to the best of your ability." Economics suggests, however, that this is not a sensible guideline. At some point, the gains from doing something even better will not be worth the cost. It will make more sense to stop short of perfection.

Exhibit 1 can also be used to illustrate this point. As more resources are dedicated to an activity, the marginal improvements (benefits) will become smaller and smaller, while the marginal costs will rise. The optimal time and effort put into the activity will be achieved at Q_2, and this will nearly always be well below one's best effort. Note that inefficiency results when either too little (for example, Q_1) or too much (for example, Q_3) time and effort are put into the activity.

Do you make decisions this way? Last time you cleaned your car or apartment, why did you decide to leave some things undone? Once the most important areas were clean,

ECONOMICS *at The Movies*

Along Came Polly (2004)

Ben Stiller and Jennifer Aniston struggle to find the efficient (optimal) amount of organization in their lives. In one scene, they use a knife to destroy pillows after Aniston convinces Stiller that the eight minutes a day he spends arranging decorative pillows on his bed (that nobody else sees) isn't worth the effort. In the next scene, Aniston's inefficiently low level of organization is illustrated when she spends a lot of time searching for her car keys. At the margin, Stiller's time spent arranging his pillows isn't generating enough benefit to justify the cost. Meanwhile, if Aniston were to spend just a little more time getting organized, the benefits to her would exceed the costs. The two of them would both be more efficient, and they'd probably get along better, too!

you likely began to skip over other areas (like on top of the refrigerator or under the bed), figuring that the benefits of cleaning these areas were simply not worth the cost. Very few people live in a perfectly organized and clean house, wash their hands enough to prevent all colds, brush their teeth long enough to prevent all cavities, or make their home as safe as Fort Knox. They recognize that the benefit of perfection in these, and many other areas, is simply not worth the cost.

Economics is about trade-offs; it is possible to pursue even worthy activities beyond the level that is consistent with economic efficiency. People seem to be more aware of this in their personal decision making than when evaluating public policy. It is not uncommon to hear people say things like, "We ought to eliminate all pollution" or "No price is too high to save a life."

If we want to get the most out of our resources, we need to think about both marginal benefits and marginal costs and recognize that there are alternative ways of pursuing objectives. Consequently, economists do not ask whether eliminating pollution or saving lives is worth the cost *in terms of dollars* per se, but whether it is worth the cost in terms of giving up other things that could have been done with those dollars—the opportunity cost. Spending an extra $10 billion on worker safety requirements to save 100 lives isn't efficient if the funds could have been spent differently and saved 500 lives. It is no more efficient for the government to pursue perfection than for individuals to do so. Regardless of sector, achievement of perfection is virtually never worth the cost.

Thinking about The Economic Role of Government

For centuries, philosophers, economists, and other scholars have debated the proper role of government. While the debate continues, there is substantial agreement that at least two functions of government are legitimate: (1) protecting individuals and their property against invasions by others and (2) providing goods that cannot easily be provided through private markets. These two functions correspond to what Nobel laureate James M. Buchanan conceptualizes as the protective and productive functions of government.

Protective Function of Government

The most fundamental function of government is the protection of individuals and their property against acts of aggression. As John Locke wrote more than three centuries ago, individuals are constantly threatened by "the invasions of others." Therefore, each individual "is willing to join in society with others, who are already united, or have a mind to unite, for the mutual preservation of their lives, liberties, and estates."[3] *The protective function of government involves the maintenance of a framework of security and order—an infrastructure of rules within which people can interact peacefully with one another.* Protection of person and property is crucial. It entails providing police protection and prosecuting aggressors who take things that do not belong to them. It also involves providing for a national defense designed to protect against foreign invasions. The legal enforcement of contracts and rules against fraud are also central elements of the protective function. People and businesses that write bad checks, violate contracts, or knowingly supply others with false information, for example, are therefore subject to legal prosecution.

© Bettmann/Corbis

The English philosopher John Locke argued that people own themselves and, as a result of this self-ownership, they also own the fruits of their labor. Locke stressed that individuals are not subservient to governments. On the contrary, the role of governments is to protect the "natural rights" of individuals to their person and property. This view, also reflected in the "unalienable rights" section of the U.S. Declaration of Independence, is the basis for the protective function of government.

It is easy to see the economic importance of the protective function. When it is performed well, the property of citizens is secure, freedom of exchange is present, and contracts are legally enforceable. When people are assured that they will be able to enjoy the benefits of their efforts, they will be more productive. In contrast, when property rights are insecure and contracts unenforceable, productive behavior is undermined. Plunder, fraud, and economic chaos result. Governments set and enforce the "rules of the game" that enable markets to operate smoothly.

Productive Function of Government

The nature of some goods makes them difficult to provide through markets. Sometimes it is difficult to establish a one-to-one link between the payment and receipt of a good. If this link cannot be established, the incentive of market producers to supply these goods is weak. In addition, high transaction costs—particularly, the cost of monitoring use and collecting fees—can sometimes make it difficult to supply a good through the market. When either of these conditions is present, it may be more efficient for the government to supply the good and impose taxes on its citizens to cover the cost.

One of the most important productive functions of government is providing a stable monetary and financial environment. If markets are going to work well, individuals have to know the value of what they are buying or selling. For market prices to convey this information, a stable monetary system is needed. This is especially true for the many market exchanges that involve a time dimension. Houses, cars, consumer durables, land, buildings, equipment, and many other items are often paid for over a period of months or even years. When the purchasing power of money fluctuates wildly, previously determined prices do not represent their intended values. Under these circumstances, exchanges involving long-term commitments are hampered, and the smooth operation of markets is undermined.

The government's tax, spending, and monetary policies exert a powerful influence on the stability of the overall economy. If properly conducted, these policies contribute to economic stability, full and efficient utilization of resources, and stable prices.

---

[3]John Locke, *Treatise of Civil Government,* 1690, ed. Charles Sherman (New York: Appleton-Century-Crofts, 1937), 82.

However, improper stabilization policies can cause massive unemployment, rapidly rising prices, or both. For those pursuing a course in macroeconomics, these issues will be central to that analysis.

Potential Shortcomings of the Market

As we previously discussed, the invisible hand of market forces generally gives resource owners and business firms a strong incentive to use their resources efficiently and undertake projects that create value. Will this always be true? The answer to this question is "No." There are four major factors that can undermine the invisible hand and reduce the efficiency of markets: (1) lack of competition, (2) externalities, (3) public goods, and (4) poorly informed buyers or sellers. We will now consider each of these factors and explain why they may justify government intervention.

Lack of Competition

Competition is vital to the proper operation of the pricing mechanism. The existence of competing buyers and sellers reduces the power of both to rig or alter the market in their own favor. Although competition is beneficial from a social point of view, individually each of us would prefer to be loosened from its grip. Students do not like stiff competitors in their romantic lives, at exam time, or when they're trying to get into graduate school. Buyers on eBay hope for few competing bidders so they can purchase the items they're bidding on at lower prices. Similarly, sellers prefer fewer competing sellers so they can sell at higher prices.

EXHIBIT 2 illustrates how sellers can gain from restricting competition. In the absence of any restrictions on competition in the market, the price P_1 and output Q_1 associated with the competitive supply curve (S_1) will prevail. Here, Q_1 is the level of output consistent with economic efficiency. If a group of sellers is able to restrict competition, perhaps by forcing some firms out of the market and preventing new firms from entering, the group would be able to gain by raising the price of the product. This is illustrated by the price P_2 and output Q_2 associated with the restricted supply (S_2). Even though the output is smaller, the total revenue (price P_2 times quantity Q_2) derived by the sellers at the restricted output level is greater than at the competitive price P_1. Clearly, the sellers gain because, at the higher price, they are being paid more to produce less.

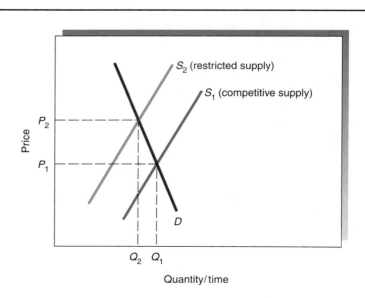

EXHIBIT 2
Lack of Competition and Problems for the Market

If a group of sellers can restrict competition, the group may be able to gain by reducing supply (to S₂, for example) and raising the price (to P₂, for example) rather than charging the competitive market price of P₁. Under these circumstances, output will be less than the economically efficient level.

The restricted output level, however, is clearly less efficient. At the competitive output level Q_1, all units that were valued more than their cost are produced and sold. But this is not the case at Q_2. The additional units between Q_2 and Q_1 are valued more than their cost. Nonetheless, they will not be produced if suppliers are able to limit competition and restrict output. When competition is absent, there is a potential conflict between the interests of sellers and the efficient use of resources.

What can the government do to ensure that markets are competitive? The first guideline might be borrowed from the medical profession: Do no harm. A productive government will refrain from using its powers to impose licenses, discriminatory taxes, price controls, tariffs, quotas, and other entry and trade restraints that lessen the intensity of competition. In the vast majority of markets, sellers will find it difficult or impossible to limit the entry of rival firms (including rival producers from other countries). Thus, most suppliers will not be able to limit competition unless they get the government to impose various types of entry restrictions or mandates that provide them with an advantage relative to rivals. Predictably, private firms and interest groups will lobby for government action of this type. When governments succumb to these pressures and engage in actions that limit competition, however, economic inefficiency will result.

When entering a market is very costly and there are only a few existing sellers, it may be possible for these sellers by themselves to restrict competition. In an effort to deal with cases like this, the United States has enacted a series of "antitrust laws," most notably the Sherman Antitrust Act (1890) and the Clayton Act (1914), making it illegal for firms to collude or attempt to monopolize a market.

Virtually all economists favor competitive markets, but there is considerable debate about the impact of government action in this area. Many economists believe that, by and large, government policy in this area has been ineffective. Others stress that government policies have often been misused to actually limit competition, rather than promote it. Laws are often adopted that restrict entry into markets, protect existing producers from competitors, and limit price competition. For those taking a microeconomics course, noncompetitive markets and related policy alternatives will be analyzed in greater detail later.

Externalities—A Failure to Account for All Costs and Benefits

When property rights are unclear or poorly enforced, the actions of an individual or group may "spill over" onto others and thereby affect their well-being without their consent. These spillover effects are called **externalities**. You are probably familiar with externalities. For example, when your neighbor's loud stereo makes it hard for you to study, you are experiencing an externality firsthand. Although your neighbors do not have a right to come in to your apartment and turn on your stereo, they do have a right to listen to their own stereo, and their listening may interfere with the quietness in your apartment. Their actions impose a cost on you, and they also raise an issue of property rights. Do your neighbors have a property right to play their stereo as loudly as they please? Or do you have a property right to quietness in your own apartment? When questions like these arise, how should the boundaries of property rights be determined, and what steps should be taken to ensure adequate enforcement? Although the volume of your neighbor's stereo may not be a major economic issue, it nonetheless illustrates the nature of the problems that arise when property rights are unclear and externalities are present.

The spillover effects may either impose a cost or create a benefit for third parties—people not directly involved in the transaction, activity, or exchange. Economists use the term **external cost** to describe a situation in which the spillover effects harm third parties. If the spillover effects enhance the welfare of the third parties, an **external benefit** is present. We will analyze both external costs and external benefits and consider why both of them can lead to problems.

Externalities

Spillover effects of an activity that influence the well-being of nonconsenting third parties.

External costs

Spillover effects that reduce the well-being of nonconsenting third parties.

External benefits

Spillover effects that generate benefits for nonconsenting third parties.

External Costs

Economists worry about external costs because they may result in economic inefficiency. For example, resources may be used to produce goods that are valued less than their production costs, including the costs imposed on the nonconsenting third parties. Consider the production of paper. The firms in the market operate mills and purchase labor, trees, and other resources to produce the paper. But they also emit pollutants into the atmosphere that impose costs on residents living around the mills. The pollutants cause paint on buildings to deteriorate more rapidly. They make it difficult for some people to breathe normally, and perhaps cause other health hazards. If the residents living near a pulp mill can prove they have been harmed, they could take the mill to court and force the paper producer to cover the cost of their damages. But it might be difficult to prove that they were harmed and that the pulp mill is responsible for the damage. As you can see, the residents' property rights to clean air may be difficult to enforce, particularly if there are many parties emitting pollutants into the air.

If the residents are unable to enforce their property rights, the production of paper will generate an external cost that will be ignored by markets. **EXHIBIT 3** illustrates the implications of these external costs within the supply and demand framework. As the result of the external cost, the market supply curve S_1 will understate the true cost of producing paper. It reflects only the cost actually paid by the firms, and ignores the uncompensated costs imposed on the nearby residents. Under these circumstances, the firm will expand output to Q_1 (the intersection of the demand curve D and supply curve S_1) and the market price P_1 will emerge. Is this price and output consistent with economic efficiency? The answer is clearly "No." If all of the costs of producing the paper, including those imposed on third parties, were taken into account, the supply curve S_2 would result. From an efficiency standpoint, only the smaller quantity Q_2 should be produced. The units beyond Q_2 on out to Q_1 cost more than their value to consumers. People would be better off if the resources used to produce those units (beyond Q_2) were used to produce other things. Nonetheless, profit-maximizing firms will expand output into this range. Thus, when external costs are present, the market supply curve will understate production costs, and output will be expanded beyond the quantity consistent with economic efficiency. Moreover, resources for which property rights are poorly enforced will be overutilized and sometimes polluted. This is often the case with air and water when the property rights to these resources are poorly enforced.

What should be done about external costs? These costs arise because property rights are poorly defined or imperfectly enforced. Initially, therefore, it makes sense to think seriously about how property rights might be better defined and enforced. However, the

---

EXHIBIT 3
External Costs and
Output That Is Greater
Than the Efficient Level

When an activity such as paper production imposes external costs on nonconsenting third parties, these costs will not be registered by the market supply curve (S_1). As a result, output will be beyond the economically efficient level. The units between Q_2 and Q_1 will be produced, even though their cost exceeds the value they provide to consumers.

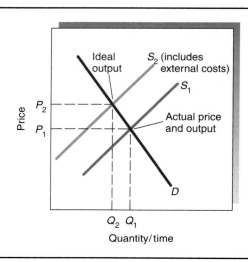

nature of some goods will make the defining and enforcement of property rights extremely difficult. This will certainly be the case for resources like clean air and many fish species in the ocean. In cases that involve a relatively small number of people, the parties involved may be able to agree to rules and establish procedures that will minimize the external effects. For example, property owners around a small lake will generally be able to control access to the lake and prevent each other, as well as outsiders, from polluting or overfishing the lake.

However, in cases that involve large numbers of people, the transaction costs of arriving at an agreement will be prohibitively high, so it is unrealistic to expect that private contracts among the parties will handle the situation satisfactorily. For example, this will be the case when a large number of automobiles and firms emit pollutants into the atmosphere. In these "large-number" cases, government regulations may be the best approach. At this point, we want you to see the nature of the problem when external costs are present. As we proceed, we will analyze a number of problems in this area in detail and consider alternative approaches that might improve economic efficiency.

External Benefits

As we mentioned, sometimes the actions of individuals and firms generate external benefits for others. The homeowner who keeps a house in good condition and maintains a neat lawn improves the beauty of the entire community. A flood-control dam built by upstream residents for their benefit might also generate gains for those who live downstream. Scientific theories benefit their authors, but the knowledge can also help others who did not contribute to the development of them.

From the standpoint of efficiency, why might external benefits be a problem? Here, inefficiency may arise because potential producers may fail to undertake productive activities because they are unable to fully capture the benefits their actions create for others. Suppose a pharmaceutical company develops a vaccine protecting users against a contagious virus or some other communal disease. Of course, the vaccine can easily be marketed to users who will benefit directly from it. However, because of the communal nature of the virus, as more and more people take the vaccine, nonusers will also be less likely to get the flu. But it will be very difficult for the pharmaceutical companies to capture any of the benefits derived by the nonusers. As a result, too little of the vaccine may be supplied.

External costs resulting from poorly defined and enforced property rights underlie the problems of excessive air and water pollution.

Sfyn/Dreamstime LLC

EXHIBIT 4
External Benefits and Output That Is Less Than the Efficient Level

A vaccine that protects users against the flu will also help nonusers by making it less likely that they will catch it. But this benefit will not be registered by the market demand curve (D$_1$). In cases where external benefits like this are present, output will be less than the economically efficient level. Even though the units between Q$_1$ and Q$_2$ generate more benefits than costs, they will not be supplied because sellers are unable to capture the value of these external benefits.

EXHIBIT 4 illustrates the impact of external benefits like those generated by the vaccine within the framework of supply and demand. The market demand curve reflects the benefits derived by the users of the vaccine, while the supply curve reflects the opportunity cost of providing it. Market forces result in an equilibrium price of P_1 and output of Q_1. Is this outcome consistent with economic efficiency? Again, the answer is "No." The market demand curve D_1 will register only the benefits derived by the users. Those benefits that accrue to nonusers, who are now less likely to contract the flu, will not be taken into account by decision makers. The producer of the vaccine makes it more likely that these people will not get sick, but it doesn't derive any benefit (sales revenue) from having done so. Thus, market demand D_1 understates the total benefits derived from the production and use of the vaccine. Demand D_2 provides a measure of these total benefits, including those that accrue to the nonusers. The units between Q_1 and Q_2 are valued more highly than what it costs to produce them. Nonetheless, they will not be supplied because the suppliers of the vaccine will be unable to capture the benefits that accrue to the nonusers. Thus, when external benefits are present, market forces may supply less than the amount consistent with economic efficiency.

While external benefits are a potential source of inefficiency, entrepreneurs have a strong incentive to figure out ways to capture more fully the gains their actions generate for others. In some cases, they are able to capture what would otherwise be external benefits by extending the scope of the firm. The accompanying Application in Economics, "Capturing External Benefits: The Case of Walt Disney World," provides an interesting and informative illustration of this point.

Public Goods and Why They Pose a Problem for the Market

Public goods

Goods for which rivalry among consumers is absent and exclusion of nonpaying customers is difficult.

What are public goods? **Public goods** have two distinguishing characteristics; they are: (1) nonrival in consumption and (2) nonexcludable. Let's take a closer look at both of these characteristics.

Nonrivalry in consumption means that making the good available to one consumer does not reduce its availability to others. In fact, providing it to one person simultaneously makes it available to other consumers. A radio broadcast signal provides an example. The same signal can be shared by everyone within the listening range. Having additional listeners tune in does not detract from the availability of the signal. Clearly, most goods do not have this shared consumption characteristic, but are instead rival-in-consumption. For example, two individuals cannot simultaneously consume the same pair of jeans. Further, if one person purchases a pair of jeans, there is one less pair available for someone else.

APPLICATIONS IN ECONOMICS

Capturing External Benefits: The Case of Walt Disney World

Charles W Luzier/Reuters/Landov

Sometimes projects that generate more benefits than cost are still unattractive because a substantial share of the benefits is external and therefore difficult to capture. If an entrepreneur could figure out a way to capture more of these benefits, an otherwise unprofitable project might be transformed into a profitable one. Sometimes this can be done by extending the scope of a project.

The development of golf courses is an example. Because of the beauty and openness of the courses, many people find it attractive to live nearby. Thus, constructing a golf course typically generates an external benefit—an increase in the value of the nearby property. In recent years, golf course developers have figured out how to capture this benefit. Now, they typically purchase a large tract of land around the planned course *before it is built*. This lets them resell the land at a higher price after the golf course has been completed and the surrounding land has increased in value. By extending the scope of their activities to include

real estate as well as golf course development, they are able to capture what would otherwise be external benefits.

Florida's Walt Disney World is an interesting case study in entrepreneurial ingenuity designed to capture external benefits more fully. When Walt Disney developed Disneyland in California, the market value of the land in the immediate area soared as a result of the increase in demand for services (food, lodging, gasoline, and so on). Because the land in the area was owned by others, the developers of Disneyland were unable to capture these external benefits. In addition, Disney felt as if some of the adult nightclubs that had opened around his existing Disneyland park were imposing external costs on him by detracting from the family image his park was trying to attain.

Because of his experience with these externalities, when Walt Disney World was developed outside of Orlando, Florida, in the mid-1960s, Walt Disney purchased far more land than was needed for the amusement park. This enabled him to capture the increased land value surrounding his development (when he resold the land for a higher price), and reduce the negative externalities imposed on him via his control of the surrounding property.

The purchases were made as secretly as possible to prevent speculators from driving up the land prices if Disney's actions were detected. Disney even created a handful of smaller companies, with names like the Latin-American Development and Managers Corporation and the Reedy Creek Ranch Corporation, to purchase the land. After his first major land purchase of 12,400 acres, Walt Disney was at a meeting at which he was offered an opportunity to purchase an additional 8,500 acres. Walt Disney's assistant was rumored to have said, "But Walt, we already own 12,000 acres, enough to build the park." Disney replied, "How would you like to own 8,000 acres around our existing Disneyland facility right now?" His assistant immediately responded, "Buy it!"

After another major acquisition of 1,250 acres, Disney began concentrating on buying smaller land parcels around his main property. By June 1965, Disney had purchased 27,400 acres, or about 43 square miles—an area 150 times larger than his existing Disneyland park, and about twice as big as Manhattan. In October 1965, when an Orlando newspaper finally broke the story that Disney was behind the land purchases, the remaining land prices around his property jumped from $183 an acre to $1,000 an acre overnight. But by then, except for several small parcels he was unable to acquire, Walt Disney had purchased all of the land he wanted.

Florida eventually gave Walt Disney permission to create an autonomous Reedy Creek Improvement District, outside the authority of any local government in Florida.

In a very real sense, Walt Disney World is a jurisdiction of its own, separate from any other local government authority. Because of this, Walt Disney World can write its own zoning restrictions and building codes. It can also plan its own roadways, lakes, security, sidewalks, airports, and recreational areas. Walt Disney World is able to provide goods and services like these—that might normally be considered public goods—by charging general admission fees to its park. This helped Disney overcome the potential free-rider problems sometimes associated with producing these goods.

Just as Disney expected, the value of the land surrounding Walt Disney World soared as the demand for hotels, restaurants, and other businesses increased along with the development of the amusement park. Through the years, the resale of land near the park has been a major source of revenue for the company. To a large degree, the success of the Disney Corporation reflects Walt Disney's entrepreneurial ability to deal with externality and public-good problems.

The second characteristic of a public good—nonexcludability—means that it is impossible (or at least very costly) to exclude nonpaying customers from receiving the good. Suppose an antimissile system were being built around the city in which you live. How could some people in the city be protected by the system and others excluded? Most people will realize there is no way the system can protect their neighbors from incoming missiles without providing similar protection to other residents. Thus, the services of the antimissile system have the nonexcludability characteristic.

It is important to note that it is the characteristic of the good, not the sector in which it is produced, that determines whether it qualifies as a public good. There is a tendency to think that if a good is provided by the government, then it is a public good. This is not the case. Many of the goods provided by governments clearly do not have the characteristics of public goods. Medical services, education, mail delivery, trash collection, and electricity come to mind. Although these goods are often supplied by governments, they do not have either nonrivalry or nonexcludability characteristics. Thus, they are not public goods.

Why are public goods difficult for markets to allocate efficiently? The nonexcludability characteristic provides the answer. Because those who do not pay cannot be excluded, sellers are generally unable to establish a one-to-one link between the payment and receipt of these goods. Realizing they cannot be excluded, potential consumers have little incentive to pay for these goods. Instead, they have an incentive to become **free riders**, people who receive the benefits of the good without helping to pay for its cost. But, when a large number of people become free riders and revenues thus are low, not very much of the good is supplied. This is precisely the problem: markets will tend to undersupply public goods, even when the population in aggregate values them highly relative to their cost.

Suppose national defense were provided entirely through the market. Would you voluntarily help to pay for it? Your contribution would have little impact on the total supply of defense available to each of us, even if you made a large personal contribution. Many citizens, even though they might value defense highly, would become free riders, and few funds would be available to finance national defense.

For most goods, it is easy to establish a link between payment and receipt. If you do not pay for a gallon of ice cream, an automobile, a television set, a DVD player, and literally thousands of other items, suppliers will not provide them to you. Thus, there are very few public goods. National defense is the classic example of a public good. Radio and TV signals, software programs, flood-control projects, mosquito abatement programs, and perhaps some scientific theories also have public good characteristics. But beyond this short list, it is difficult to think of additional goods that qualify.

Just because a good is a public good does not necessarily mean that markets will fail to supply it. When the benefit of producing these goods is high, entrepreneurs will attempt to find innovative ways to gain by overcoming the free-rider problem. For example, radio

Free rider

A person who receives the benefit of a good without paying for it. Because it is often virtually impossible to restrict the consumption of public goods to those who pay, these goods are subject to free-rider problems.

and television broadcasts, which have both of the public good characteristics, are still produced well by the private sector. The free-rider problem is overcome through the use of advertising (which generates indirect revenue from listeners), rather than directly charging listeners. Private entrepreneurs have developed things like scrambling devices (so nonpaying customers can't tune into broadcasts free of charge), copy protection on DVDs, and tie-in purchases (for example, tying the purchase of a software instruction manual to the purchase of the software itself) to overcome the free-rider problem. The marketing of computer software provides an interesting illustration. Because the same software program can be copied without reducing the amount available, and it is costly to prevent consumption by nonpayers, software clearly has public good characteristics. Nonetheless, Bill Gates became the richest man in the world by producing and marketing it!

In spite of the innovative efforts of entrepreneurs, however, the quantity of public goods supplied strictly through market allocation might still be smaller than the quantity consistent with economic efficiency. This creates a potential opportunity for government action to improve the efficiency of resource allocation.

Potential Information Problems

Like other goods, information is scarce. Thus, when making purchasing decisions, people are sometimes poorly informed about the price, quality, durability, and side effects of alternative products. Imperfect knowledge is not the fault of the market. In fact, the market provides consumers with a strong incentive to acquire information. If they mistakenly purchase a "lemon," they will suffer the consequences. Furthermore, sellers have a strong incentive to inform consumers about the benefits of their products, especially in comparison with competing products. However, circumstances will influence the incentive structure confronted by both buyers and sellers.

The consumer's information problem is minimal if the item is purchased regularly. Consider the purchase of soap. There is little cost associated with trying different brands. Because soap is a regularly purchased product, trial and error is an economical means of determining which brand is most suitable to one's needs. Regularly purchased items such as toothpaste, most food products, lawn service, and gasoline provide additional examples of **repeat-purchase items**. When purchasing items like these, the consumer can use past experience to acquire accurate information and make wise decisions.

Repeat-purchase item
An item purchased often by the same buyer.

Furthermore, the sellers of repeat-purchase items also have a strong incentive to supply consumers with accurate information about them because failing to do so will adversely affect future sales. Because future demand is directly related to the satisfaction level of current customers, sellers of repeat-purchase items will want to help their customers make satisfying long-run choices. This helps harmonize the interests of buyers and sellers.

But harmony will not always occur. Conflicting interests, inadequate information, and unhappy customers can arise when goods are either (1) difficult to evaluate on inspection and seldom repeatedly purchased from the same producer, or (2) potentially capable of serious and lasting harmful side effects that cannot be predicted by a typical consumer. Under these conditions, consumers might make decisions they will later regret.

When customers are unable to distinguish between high-quality and low-quality goods, business entrepreneurs have an incentive to cut costs by reducing quality. Businesses that follow this course may survive and even prosper. Consider the information problem when an automobile is purchased. Are consumers capable of properly evaluating the safety equipment? Most are not. Of course, some consumers will seek the opinion of experts, but this information will be costly and difficult to evaluate. In this case, it might be more efficient to have the government regulate automobile safety and require certain safety equipment.

Similar issues arise with regard to product effectiveness. Suppose a new wonder drug promises to reduce the probability a person will be stricken by cancer or heart disease. Even if the product is totally ineffective, many consumers will waste their money trying it. Verifying the effectiveness of the drug will be a complicated and lengthy process. Consequently, it may be better to have experts certify its effectiveness. The federal Food and Drug Administration was established to perform this function. However, letting the experts decide is also a less than ideal solution. The certification process is likely to be costly and lengthy. As a result, the introduction of products that are effective may be delayed for years, and they are likely to be more costly than they would be otherwise.

Information as a Profit Opportunity

Consumers are willing to pay for information that will help them make better decisions. This presents a profit opportunity. Entrepreneurial publishers and other providers of information help consumers find what they seek by offering product evaluations by experts. For example, dozens of publications provide independent expert opinions about automobiles and computers at a low cost to potential purchasers. Laboratory test results and detailed product evaluations on a wide variety of goods are provided by *Consumer Reports* and other publications.

Franchises are another way entrepreneurs have responded to the need of consumers for more and better information. A **franchise** is a right or license granted to an individual to market a company's goods or services (or use their brand name). Fast-food restaurants like McDonald's and Wendy's are typically organized as franchises. The individual restaurants are independently owned, but the owner pays for the right to use the company name and must offer specific products and services in a manner specified by the franchiser. Franchises help give consumers reliable information. The tourist traveling through an area for the first time with very little time to search out alternatives may find that eating at a franchised restaurant and sleeping at a franchised motel are the cheapest ways to avoid annoying and costly mistakes that might come from patronizing an unknown local establishment. The franchiser sets the standards for all firms in the chain and establishes procedures, including continuous inspections designed to maintain the standards. Franchisers have a strong incentive to maintain their reputation for quality, because if it declines, their ability to sell new franchises and to collect ongoing franchise fees is adversely affected. Even though the tourist may visit a particular establishment only once, the franchise turns that visit into a "repeat purchase," because the reputation of the entire national franchise operation is at stake.

Similarly, advertising a brand name nationally puts the brand's reputation at stake each time a purchase is made. How much would the Coca-Cola Company pay to avoid the sale of a dangerous bottle of Coke? Surely, it would be a large sum. Interbrand, a branding consulting agency that evaluates and ranks the top brand names in the world, estimated that Coca-Cola's brand name was worth $67 billion in 2008. The value of that brand name is a hostage to quality control. The firm would suffer enormous damage if it failed to maintain the quality of its product. For example, in 2000 and 2001, Firestone's brand name suffered an immense reduction in value after only a few Firestone tires were suspected of being defective. Firestone is still attempting to recover fully from its loss in brand name value.

Enterprising entrepreneurs have found ways to assure buyers that products meet high standards of quality, even when the producer is small and not so well known. Consider the case of Best Western Motels.[4] Best Western owns no motels; however, building on the franchise idea, it publishes rules and standards with which motel owners must comply if they are to use the Best Western brand name and the reservation service that the company also operates. To protect its brand name, Best Western sends out inspectors to see that each Best Western Motel meets these standards. Every disappointed customer harms the reputation and reduces the value of the Best Western name, which reduces the willingness of motel owners to pay for use of the name. The standards are designed to keep customers satisfied. Even though each motel owner has only a relatively small operation, renting the Best Western name provides the small operator with the kind of international reputation formerly available only to large firms. In effect, Best Western acts as a regulator of all motels bearing its name. It profits by requiring efficient standards—those that produce maximum visitor satisfaction for every dollar spent by the motels utilizing the franchise name. As it does so, it helps eliminate problems in the market that result from imperfect information.

Underwriters Laboratories, Inc. (UL) is another example of private-sector regulation aimed at overcoming potential information problems. UL is a private-sector corporation

Franchise

A right or license granted to an individual to market a company's goods or services or use its brand name. The individual firms are independently owned but must meet certain conditions to continue to use the name.

---

[4]This section draws from Randall G. Holcombe and Lora P. Holcombe, "The Market for Regulation," *Journal of Institutional and Theoretical Economics* 142, no. 4 (1986): 684–96.

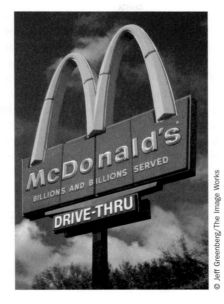

Brand names (like Coca-Cola), franchises (like McDonald's or Best Western), consumer-ratings magazines (like Consumer Reports*), and private-sector certification firms (like Underwriters Laboratories, Inc.) are ways the private sector helps buyers overcome potential information problems.*

that has been testing and certifying products for more than 100 years based on its own set of quality standards. You have probably seen the UL mark on many of your household appliances. Sellers pay a fee to have UL evaluate their products for possible certification. The value of the UL brand depends on its careful evaluation of every product it certifies. If UL allows defective products to carry its mark, its brand value will diminish.

Information published by reliable sources, franchising, and brand names can help consumers make better-informed decisions. Although these options are effective, they will not always provide an ideal solution. Government regulation may sometimes be able to improve the situation, but this, too, has some predictable shortcomings. As with other things, there is no general solution to imperfect information problems.

Pulling Things Together

Throughout this textbook, we have stressed that a sound legal system—one that protects individuals and their property and provides access to evenhanded courts for the enforcement of contracts and settlement of disputes—is vitally important for the smooth operation of markets. So, too, is a monetary regime that provides people with access to a sound currency—money that maintains its value across time periods. Beyond these functions, however, there is little justification for government action when there is reason to expect that markets will allocate resources efficiently. But a lack of competition, externalities, public goods, and information problems often pose challenges and sometimes undermine the efficient operation of markets. Market shortcomings due to these factors raise the possibility that government intervention beyond the protective function might improve things. But before jumping to that conclusion, we need better knowledge about how the political process works. We are now ready to move on to that topic.

Looking ahead

Political decision making is complex, but the tools of economics can enhance our understanding of how it works. This is the subject matter of the next chapter.

KEY POINTS

▼ Economists use the standard of economic efficiency to assess the desirability of economic outcomes. Efficiency requires: (1) that all actions generating more benefit than cost be undertaken, and (2) that no actions generating more cost than benefit be undertaken.

▼ Although perfection is a noble goal, it is rarely worth achieving because additional time and resources devoted to an activity generally yield smaller and smaller benefits and cost more and more. Inefficiency can result when either too little or too much effort is put into an activity.

▼ Governments can enhance economic well-being by performing both protective and productive functions.

The protective function involves (1) the protection of individuals and their property against aggression and (2) the provision of a legal system for the enforcement of contracts and settlement of disputes. The productive function of government can help people obtain goods that would be difficult to supply through markets.

▼ When markets fail to meet the conditions for ideal economic efficiency, the problem can generally be traced to one of four sources: absence of competition, externalities, public goods, or poor information.

▼ Externalities reflect a lack of fully defined and enforced property rights. When external costs are present, output can be too large—units are produced even though their costs exceed the benefits they generate. In contrast, external benefits can lead to an output that is too small—some units are not produced even though the benefits of doing so would exceed the cost.

▼ Public goods are goods for which (1) rivalry in consumption is absent and (2) it is difficult to exclude those who do not pay. Because of the difficulties involved in establishing a one-to-one link between

payment and receipt of such goods, the market supply of public goods will often be less than the economically efficient quantity.

▼ Entrepreneurs in markets have an incentive to find solutions to each market problem, and new solutions are constantly being discovered. But problems remain that can potentially be improved through government action.

CRITICAL ANALYSIS QUESTIONS

*1. Why is it important for producers to be able to prevent nonpaying customers from receiving a good?

2. In response to the terrorist attacks of September 11, 2001, airline security screening has increased dramatically. As a result, travelers must now spend considerably more time being screened before flights. Would it make economic sense to devote enough resources to completely prevent any such future attacks? Why or why not?

3. What are the distinguishing characteristics of "public goods"? Give two examples of a public good. Why are public goods difficult for markets to allocate efficiently?

*4. Which of the following are public goods? Explain, using the definition of a public good.
   a. an antimissile system surrounding Washington, D.C.
   b. a fire department
   c. tennis courts
   d. Yellowstone National Park
   e. elementary schools

5. Explain in your own words what is meant by external costs and external benefits. Why may market outcomes be less than ideal when externalities are present?

6. English philosopher John Locke argued that the protection of each individual's person and property (acquired without the use of violence, theft, or fraud) was the primary function of government. Why is this protection important to the efficient operation of an economy?

7. "If it's worth doing, it's worth doing to the best of your ability." What is the economic explanation for why this statement is frequently said but rarely followed in practice? Explain.

8. "Unless quality and price are regulated by government, travelers would have no chance for a fair deal. Local people would be treated well, but the traveler would have no way to know, for example, who offers a good night's lodging at a fair price." Is this true or false? Explain.

*9. If sellers of toasters were able to organize themselves, reduce their output, and raise their prices, how would economic efficiency be affected? Explain.

10. What are external costs? When are they most likely to be present? When external costs are present, what is likely to be the relationship between the market output of a good and the output consistent with ideal economic efficiency?

*11. "Elementary education is obviously a public good. After all, it is provided by the government." Evaluate this statement.

12. What are the necessary conditions for economic efficiency? In what four situations might a market fail to achieve ideal economic efficiency?

13. Suppose that Abel builds a factory next to Baker's farm, and air pollution from the factory harms Baker's crops. Is Baker's property right to the land being violated? Is an externality present? What if the pollution invades Baker's home and harms her health? Are her property rights violated? Is an externality present? Explain.

*14. Apply the economic efficiency criterion to the role of government. When would a government intervention be considered economically efficient? When would a government intervention be considered economically inefficient?

*Asterisk denotes questions for which answers are given in Appendix B.

The Economics of Collective Decision Making

[Public choice] analyzes the motives and activities of politicians, civil servants and government officials as people with personal interests that may or may not coincide with the interest of the general public they are supposed to serve. It is an analysis of how people behave in the world as it is.

—Arthur Seldon[1]

It does not follow that whenever laissez faire falls short government interference is expedient; since the inevitable drawbacks of the latter may, in any particular case, be worse than the shortcomings of private enterprise.

—Harry Sidgwick, 1887[2]

CHAPTER FOCUS

- How large is the government sector, and what are the main activities undertaken by government?

- What are the differences and similarities between market and government actions?

- What insights can economics provide about the behavior of voters, politicians, and bureaucrats? How will their actions affect political outcomes?

- When is democratic representative government most likely to lead to economic efficiency?

- Why will there sometimes be a conflict between winning politics and economic efficiency?

- How does economic organization influence the efficiency of resource use?

[1]Preface to Gordon Tullock, *The Vote Motive* (London: Institute of Economic Affairs, 1976), x.
[2]Quoted in Charles Wolf, Jr., *Markets or Government* (Cambridge, MA: MIT Press, 1988), 17.

As we have previously discussed, the protection of property rights, evenhanded enforcement of contracts, and provision of a stable monetary environment are vital for the smooth and efficient operation of markets. Governments that perform these functions well will help their citizens prosper and achieve higher levels of income. Governments may also help allocate goods difficult for markets to handle. However, it is crucially important to recognize that government is simply an alternative form of economic organization. In most industrialized nations, the activities of governments are directed by the democratic political process. In this chapter, we will use the tools of economics to analyze how this process works. ■

The Size and Growth of the U.S. Government

What exactly does government do? Has its role in the economy shrunk or grown over time? Data on government spending shed light on these questions. As **EXHIBIT 1** illustrates, total government expenditures (federal, state, and local combined) were only 9.4 percent of the U.S. economy in 1930. (*Note:* GDP is generally how economists measure the size of the economy. The term will be explained more fully in a macroeconomics course.) In that year, federal government spending by itself was only 3 percent of the economy. At the time, this made the federal government about half the size of all state and local governments combined.

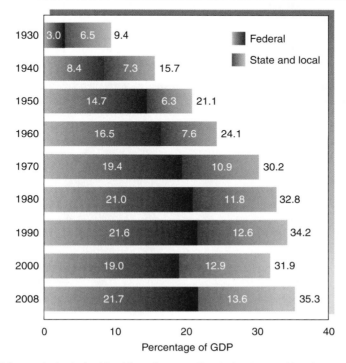

EXHIBIT 1

The Growth of Government Spending between 1930 and 2008

U.S. government expenditures as a share of the economy's gross domestic product have risen dramatically over the past seventy-five years. They are now about one-third of the U.S. economy.

Source: Bureau of Economic Analysis, http://www.bea.gov. Grants to state and local governments are included in federal expenditures. Individual data may not add to total due to rounding.

However, between 1930 and 1980, the size of government grew very rapidly. By 1980, government expenditures had risen to 32.8 percent of the economy, *more than three times* the level of 1930. Moreover, the federal government grew to about twice the size of all state and local governments combined, despite the fact that they were growing rapidly, too. Since 1980, total government spending as a share of the economy has been relatively constant at approximately one-third of GDP.

EXHIBIT 2 shows the major categories of government spending for both the federal government and state and local governments. The major categories of federal spending are health care, Social Security, national defense, and other income transfers. Education, administration, and public welfare and health constitute the largest areas of spending for state and local governments.

Transfer payments are transfers of income from some individuals (who pay taxes) to others (who receive government payments). Social Security, unemployment benefits, and welfare are examples of transfer payments. Direct income transfers now account for almost 45 percent of the total spending of the government. As **EXHIBIT 3** illustrates, government spending on income transfers has grown rapidly. In 1930, income transfers summed to only 1.1 percent of total income. By 1970, the figure had jumped to 7.7 percent; by 2008, it had risen to 15.9 percent of national income. Obviously, the government has become much more involved in tax-transfer activities during the past seventy years.

Given the size and growth of government, understanding how the political process works and how it is likely to affect the economy is vitally important. The remainder of this chapter will address this issue.

Transfer payments

Payments to individuals or institutions that are not linked to the current supply of a good or service by the recipient.

EXHIBIT 2
Government Spending by Category

The major categories of federal government spending are health care, Social Security, national defense, and income security (welfare programs). The major categories of state and local government spending are education, health and welfare programs, and administration.

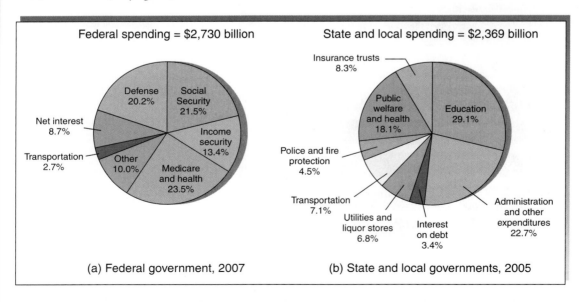

Federal spending = $2,730 billion

Defense 20.2%
Social Security 21.5%
Net interest 8.7%
Income security 13.4%
Transportation 2.7%
Other 10.0%
Medicare and health 23.5%

(a) Federal government, 2007

State and local spending = $2,369 billion

Insurance trusts 8.3%
Public welfare and health 18.1%
Education 29.1%
Police and fire protection 4.5%
Transportation 7.1%
Utilities and liquor stores 6.8%
Interest on debt 3.4%
Administration and other expenditures 22.7%

(b) State and local governments, 2005

Source: Economic Report of the President, 2009, and Statistical Abstract of the United States, 2009.

EXHIBIT 3
The Growth of Government Transfer Payments

The government taxes approximately 16 percent of national income away from some people and transfers it to others. Means-tested income transfers—those directed toward the poor—account for only about one-sixth of all income transfers. Government income-transfer activities have grown substantially over the past seventy years.

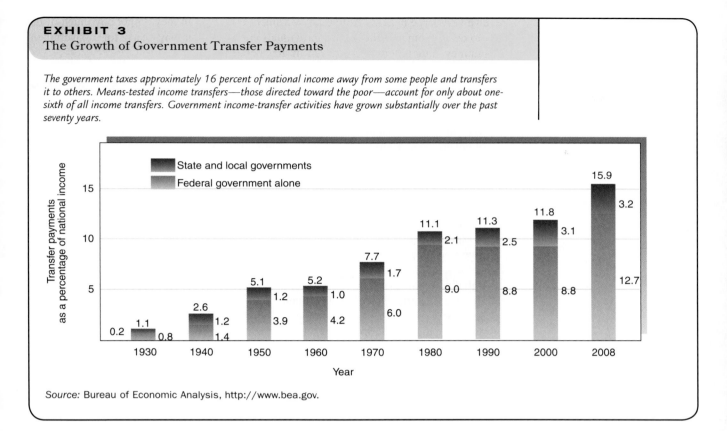

Source: Bureau of Economic Analysis, http://www.bea.gov.

The Differences and Similarities between Governments and Markets

When political decisions are made democratically, or in a representative democracy, as we assume in this chapter, the choices of individuals will influence outcomes in the government sector, just as they do in the market sector. Therefore, when we analyze the political process, we focus on individuals and how incentives influence their choices, just as we do when we analyze markets. There are both differences and similarities between political and market decision making. Let's take a look at six of them.

1. COMPETITIVE BEHAVIOR IS PRESENT IN BOTH THE MARKET AND PUBLIC SECTORS. The nature of the competition and the criteria for success differ between the two sectors, but people compete in both. Politicians compete for elective office. Bureau chiefs and agency heads compete for taxpayer dollars and the authority to regulate others to meet their bureau or agency goals. Public-sector employees compete for promotions, higher incomes, and additional decision-making authority, just as they do in the private sector. Lobbyists compete for program funding, for favorable bureaucratic rulings, and for legislation favorable to the interest groups they represent, including both private and government clients. The nature of the competition may differ between the two sectors, but it is present in both. (See Applications in Economics: Perspectives on the Cost of Political Competition.)

2. PUBLIC-SECTOR ORGANIZATION CAN BREAK THE INDIVIDUAL CONSUMPTION–PAYMENT LINK. In the market sector, goods are allocated to those who are willing to pay the price: there is a one-to-one relationship between a person's payment and receipt of a good. This is often not the case when decisions are made politically. Sometimes people receive very large benefits from the government even though they do not pay much of the cost to cover them. In other cases, individuals are required to pay dearly for a government program even though they derive few, if any, benefits.

3. SCARCITY IMPOSES THE AGGREGATE CONSUMPTION–PAYMENT LINK IN BOTH SECTORS. Although the government can break the link between a person's payment for a good and the right to consume it, the reality of the *aggregate consumption–aggregate payment link* remains. Resources the government uses for one purpose have alternative uses, in and out of government. Therefore, it is costly to provide goods and services through the government. This is true even if the good is provided "free of charge" to certain consumers.

4. PRIVATE-SECTOR ACTION IS BASED ON MUTUAL AGREEMENT; PUBLIC-SECTOR ACTION IS BASED ON MAJORITY RULE. In the market sector, when two parties engage in trade, their actions are voluntary and motivated by the expectation of mutual gain. Corporations like Exxon and Microsoft, no matter how large or powerful, cannot take income from you or force you to buy their products. Mutual gain is the foundation for market exchange. Conversely, in a democratic setting, collective action is based on majority rule, either through direct voting or through legislative procedures involving elected representatives. If a legislative majority decides on a particular policy, the minority must accept the policy and help pay for it, even if they strongly object. Even democratic political action creates "losers" as well as "winners." Further, as we will explain, there is no assurance that the gains the winners derive from a project will exceed the losses imposed on the losers.

5. WHEN COLLECTIVE DECISIONS ARE MADE LEGISLATIVELY, VOTERS MUST CHOOSE AMONG CANDIDATES WHO REPRESENT A BUNDLE OF POSITIONS ON ISSUES. On election day, the voter cannot choose the views of one politician on poverty and business welfare and simultaneously choose the views of a different politician on national defense and tariffs. This greatly limits the voter's power to make his or her preferences count on specific issues. Because the average elected representative is asked to vote on roughly 2,000 different issues during a two-year term, the size of the problem is obvious. The situation in markets, however, is quite different. A buyer can purchase some groceries or clothing from one store, while choosing related items from different suppliers. There is seldom a bundle-purchase problem in markets.

APPLICATIONS IN ECONOMICS

Perspectives on the Cost of Political Competition: What Does It Cost to Get Elected?

Competition for elective office is fierce and campaigns are expensive. For example, in recent years, candidates for U.S. House of Representatives and Senate positions raised and spent more than $1 billion. This amounts to approximately $2 million per congressional seat! Races for highly contested seats are often far more expensive.

During and after an election, lobbying groups compete for the attention of elected officials. In fact, the greatest portion of campaign funds raised by incumbents is not raised at election time; rather, it accrues over their entire term in office. A large campaign contribution may not be able to "buy" a vote, but it certainly enhances the lobbyist's

chance to sit down with the elected official to explain "the power and the beauty" of the contributor's position. In the competitive world of politics, the politician who does not at least listen to helpful "friends of the campaign" is less likely to survive.

The U.S. Congress controls approximately $3.5 trillion in spending annually and imposes regulations that cost another $1 trillion. That's a huge amount of money and influence, allocated politically. As long as Congress wields the power to spend these sums, huge expenditures designed to influence the policies representatives make will continue.[1]

---

[1]More details on campaign finance can be found in Michael Barone and Grant Ujifusa, *The Almanac of American Politics* (Washington, DC: National Journal, annual), or at the Federal Election Commission's Web site.

6. INCOME AND INFLUENCE ARE DISTRIBUTED DIFFERENTLY IN THE TWO SEC-TORS. People who supply more highly valued resources in the marketplace have larger incomes. The number of these dollar "votes" earned by a person in the marketplace will reflect his or her abilities, ambitions, skills, past savings, inheritance, good fortune, and willingness to produce for others, among other things. Bill Gates is a good example. Many people have "voted" for his products, making Gates quite wealthy as a result. This process results in an unequal distribution of income and power in the market sector.

However, in a democratic government, one citizen, one vote is the rule. But there are ways other than voting to influence political outcomes. People can donate their money and time to help a campaign. They can also try to influence friends and neighbors, write letters to legislators, and speak in public on behalf of a candidate or cause. The greatest rewards of the political process go to those best able and most willing to use their time, persuasive skills, organizational abilities, and financial contributions to help politicians get votes. People who have more money and skills of this sort—and are willing to spend them in the political arena—can expect to benefit themselves and their favorite causes more handsomely. Thus, while the sources of success and influence differ between sectors, both generate an unequal distribution of influence and power.

Political Decision Making: An Overview

Public-choice analysis is a branch of economics that applies the principles and methodology of economics to the operation of the political process. Public-choice analysis links the theory of *individual* behavior to political action, analyzes the implications of the theory, and tests them against events in the real world. Over the past fifty years, research in this area has greatly enhanced our understanding of political decision making.[3] Just as economists have used the idea of self-interest to analyze markets, public-choice economists use it to analyze political choices and the operation of government. After all, the same people make decisions in both sectors. If self-interest and the structure of incentives influence market choices, there is good reason to expect that they will also influence choices in a political setting.

The collective decision-making process can be thought of as a complex interaction among voters, legislators, and bureaucrats. Voters elect a legislature, which levies taxes and allocates budgets and regulatory authority to various government agencies and bureaus. The bureaucrats in charge of these agencies utilize the funds to supply government services and income transfers, and to exercise regulatory authority as well. In a representative democracy, voter support determines who is elected to the legislature. A majority vote of the legislature is generally required for the passage of taxes, budget allocations, and regulatory legislation. Let's take a closer look at the incentive structure confronting the three primary political players—voters, legislators, and bureaucrats—and consider how they affect the operation of the political process.

Incentives Confronted by the Voter

How do voters decide whom to support? Self-interest dictates that voters, like market consumers, will ask, "What can you do for me and my goals, and how much will it cost me?" The greater the voter's perceived net personal gain from a particular candidate's election, the more likely it is that the voter will favor that candidate. In contrast, the greater the perceived net economic cost imposed on the voter by the positions of a candidate, the less inclined the voter will be to support the candidate. Other things being equal, voters will tend to support those candidates who they believe will provide

Public-choice analysis
The study of decision making as it affects the formation and operation of collective organizations, like governments. In general, the principles and methodology of economics are applied to political science topics.

[3]The contributions of Kenneth Arrow, James Buchanan, Duncan Black, Anthony Downs, Mancur Olson, Robert Tollison, and Gordon Tullock have been particularly important. Public choice is something of a cross between economics and political science. Thus, advanced courses are generally offered in both departments.

the most government services and transfer benefits to them and their favorite causes, net personal costs.

How well will voters be informed about political issues and candidates? When decisions are made collectively, the choices of a single person will not be decisive. The probability that an individual vote will decide a city, state, or national election is virtually zero. Realizing that their votes will not affect the outcome, individual voters have little incentive to spend much effort seeking the information needed to cast an informed ballot. Economists refer to this lack of incentive as the **rational ignorance effect**.

As the result of the rational ignorance effect, most voters simply rely on information supplied to them freely by candidates (via political advertising) and the mass media, as well as conversations with friends and coworkers. Surveys, in fact, indicate that huge numbers of voters are unable even to identify their own congressional representatives, much

Rational ignorance effect

Because it is highly unlikely that an individual vote will decide the outcome of an election, a rational individual has little or no incentive to search for and acquire the information needed to cast an informed vote.

Voters, politicians, and bureaucrats are the primary decision makers in the political arena.

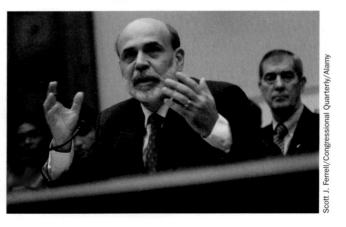

less know where they stand on issues like Social Security reform, tariffs, and agricultural price supports. Given that voters gain little from casting a more informed vote, their meager knowledge of political candidates and issues is not surprising.

In contrast, when people can put information to good use in serving their own goals, they will put forth more effort to acquire it. Consider the incentive of an automobile purchaser to make a well-informed choice. The model, the dealer, and the financial terms are a matter of personal preference and consumer choice. The individual consumer who makes a bad choice will personally bear the consequences. As a result, auto consumers have a strong incentive to make informed decisions. Thus, they often take different models for test drives, review consumer publications, and consult with various car experts about them in order to learn more. Yet the voter gains little or nothing in terms of a changed result from a more informed political choice. For the person whose vote is unlikely to decide the outcome of an election, a mistake in casting an uninformed ballot won't make much difference. Thus, it is actually *reasonable* to expect people to be far better informed when choosing a car than a senatorial, congressional, or other political candidate.

The fact that citizens realize their individual votes will not sway the outcome of an election also explains why so many of them don't vote. Even in a presidential election, only about half of all voting-age Americans take the time to register and vote. The turnout for state and local elections is generally still lower. Given the low probability that one's vote will be decisive, low voter turnout is an expected result.

Incentives Confronted by the Politician

What motivates political candidates and officeholders? Economics indicates that the pursuit of votes will primarily shape politicians' actions and political positions. No doubt, many of them genuinely care about the "public interest" and the quality of government, but they need to be elected to achieve their objectives, whatever they might be. To be successful, a candidate's positive attributes must be brought to the attention of rationally ignorant voters focused on their families, jobs, various civic activities, and local sports teams (which are probably more entertaining). The successful candidate needs an expert staff, sophisticated polling techniques to uncover popular issues and positions, and high-quality advertising to shape his or her image favorably. This, of course, will be costly. It is not unusual for an incumbent candidate to the U.S. Senate to spend $15 million or more to get reelected. In other words, votes are the necessary objective of politicians, but money helps them get those votes. Predictably, the pursuit of campaign contributions then shapes the actions of politicians, too.

Are we implying that politicians are selfish, caring only for their pocketbooks and reelection chances? The answer is "No." Factors other than personal political gain, narrowly defined, may well influence their actions. Sometimes an elected official may feel so strongly about an issue that he or she will knowingly take a position that is politically unpopular and damaging to his or her future electoral prospects. None of this is inconsistent with the economic view of the political process. Over time, however, the politicians most likely to remain in office are the ones who focus on how their actions will influence their reelection prospects. Just as profits are the lifeblood of the market entrepreneur, votes are the lifeblood of the politician.

Politicians face competition for elected office from other candidates. Just like market suppliers, political suppliers have an incentive to find ways to gain an advantage over their competitors. Catering to the strongly held views of voters and contributors is one way of doing that. Enacting rules that put potential challengers at a disadvantage is another. When geographic political districts are redrawn, for example, politicians frequently manipulate the process to increase their chances of reelection—a process known as "gerrymandering." Incumbents can also attempt to use government resources for their reelection campaigns, an advantage challengers do not have. Campaign finance "reforms" that make it more difficult for a challenger to raise funds may also provide incumbents with an additional advantage.

Just as the general does not want his Camp Swampy budget cut, most heads of agencies want expanded budgets to help them do more and do it more comfortably.

Incentives Confronted by the Government Bureaucrat

Like other people, bureaucrats who staff government agencies, especially those who rise to decision-making levels, have narrowly focused interests.[4] They usually want to see their own agency's goals furthered. Doing so, however, requires larger budgets or greater authority to regulate or both. In turn, larger budgets and more authority lead to more satisfaction, prestige, and career opportunities for the bureaucrats. Economic analysis suggests there is a strong tendency for government bureaucrats and employees to want to expand their budgets and their authority well beyond what would be economically efficient. Indeed, analysts recognize that bigger programs often have strong, organized political backing. In contrast "efficiency has no political constituency."

Legislative bodies are in charge of overseeing these bureaus, but the individual legislators themselves generally know little about the true costs of agency decisions, especially the costs to those regulated. This makes it even more likely that bureaucrats will be able to get funding and authority beyond what's economically efficient.

In summary, the political process, which begins with voter-driven elections and proceeds to legislative decisions and bureaucratic actions, brings about results that please some voters and displease others. The goals of the three major categories of participants—voters, politicians, and bureaucrats—frequently conflict with one another. Each group wants more of the government's limited supply of resources. Coalitions form and the members of each coalition hope to enhance their ability to get the government to do what they want. Sometimes this results in productive activities on the part of the government, and sometimes it does not.

When the Political Process Works Well

Under what conditions are voting and representative government most likely to result in productive actions? People have a tendency to believe that support by a majority makes a political action productive. However, if a government project is truly productive, it will always be possible to find a way to allocate the cost so that *all* voters gain. This would mean that, even if voting rules required unanimity or near unanimity, all truly productive government projects would pass if the costs were allocated in the right manner. **EXHIBIT 4** helps illustrate this point. Column 1 presents hypothetical data on the distribution of benefits from a government road construction project. These benefits sum to $40, which exceeds the $25 cost of the road, so the project is productive. But if the project's $25 cost were allocated equally among the voters (plan A), Adams and Chan gain substantially, but Green, Lee, and Diaz lose. If the fate of the project is decided by majority vote, the project will be defeated by the "no" votes of Green, Lee, and Diaz. This productive government project fails to obtain a majority vote in this case because of the way that the costs have been allocated.

Because the project is indeed productive, there is an alternative way to allocate its costs so that Adams, Chan, Green, Lee, and Diaz all benefit. This can be accomplished

---

[4]The economic analysis of bureaucracy was pioneered by William Niskanen. Reprints of some of his classic articles along with recent updated material can be found in William A. Niskanen, Jr., *Bureaucracy and Public Economics* (Aldershot, U.K.: Edward Elgar Publishing, 1994).

EXHIBIT 4
The Benefits Derived by Voters from a Hypothetical Road Construction Project

When taxes are levied in proportion to benefits received (tax plan B), any efficient project can pass unanimously (and any inefficient project will fail unanimously). When taxes are not levied in accordance with benefits received (tax plan A), efficient projects can fail to win a majority vote (or inefficient projects can pass in a majority vote).

| | | TAX PAYMENT | |
| | BENEFITS RECEIVED | PLAN A | PLAN B |
VOTER	(1)	(2)	(3)
Adams	$20	$5	$12.50
Chan	12	5	7.50
Green	4	5	2.50
Lee	2	5	1.25
Diaz	2	5	1.25
Total	**$40**	**$25**	**$25.00**

by allocating the cost of the project among voters in proportion to the benefits that they receive (plan B). Under this arrangement, Adams would pay half ($12.50) of the $25 cost, because he receives half ($20) of the total benefits ($40). The other voters would all pay in proportion to the benefits they receive. Under this plan, all voters would gain from the proposal. Even though the proposal could not secure a majority when the costs were allocated equally among voters, it will be favored by all five voters when they are taxed in proportion to the benefits they receive (plan B).

This simple illustration highlights an extremely important point about voting and the efficiency of government action. ***When voters pay in proportion to benefits received, all voters will gain if the government action is productive, and all will lose if it is unproductive.***[5] ***When the benefits and costs derived by individual voters are closely related, the voting process will enact efficient projects while rejecting inefficient ones. When voters pay in proportion to the benefits they receive, there will tend to be harmony between good politics and sound economics.***

How might the cost of a government service be linked to the benefits received? **User charges**, which require people who use a service more to pay a larger share of the cost, provide one way. User charges are most likely to be levied at the local level. Local services such as electricity, water, and garbage collection are generally financed with user charges. Sometimes the intensity of the use of a service and the amount paid for it can be linked by specifying that the revenue from a specific tax be used for a designated purpose. For example, most states finance road construction and maintenance with the revenue collected from taxes on gasoline and other motor fuels. The more an individual drives—getting more benefits from the roads—the more that individual pays.

EXHIBIT 5 provides a useful way to look at the possible linkage between the benefits and costs of government programs. The benefits from a government action may be either widespread among the general public or concentrated among a small subgroup (for example, farmers, students, business interests, senior citizens, or members of a labor union). Similarly, the costs may be either widespread or highly concentrated among voters. Thus, as the exhibit shows, there are four possible patterns of voter benefits and costs: (1) widespread benefits and widespread costs, (2) concentrated benefits and widespread costs, (3) concentrated benefits and concentrated costs, and (4) widespread benefits and concentrated costs.

User charges

Payments users (consumers) are required to make if they want to receive certain services provided by the government.

---

[5]The principle that productive projects generate the potential for political unanimity was initially articulated by Swedish economist Knut Wicksell in 1896. See Wicksell, "A New Principle of Just Taxation," in *Public Choice and Constitutional Economics*, James Gwartney and Richard Wagner (Greenwich, CT: JAI Press, Inc., 1988). Nobel laureate James Buchanan has stated that Wicksell's work provided him with the insights that led to his large role in the development of modern public-choice theory.

EXHIBIT 5
Distribution of Benefits and Costs among Voters

It is useful to visualize four possible combinations for the distribution of benefits and costs among voters to consider how the alternative distributions affect the operation of representative governments. When the distribution of benefits and costs is both widespread among voters (type 1) or both concentrated among voters (type 3), representative government will tend to undertake projects that are productive and reject those that are unproductive. In contrast, when the benefits are concentrated and the costs are widespread (type 2), representative government is biased toward the adoption of inefficient projects. Finally, when benefits are widespread but the costs concentrated (type 4), the political process may reject projects that are productive.

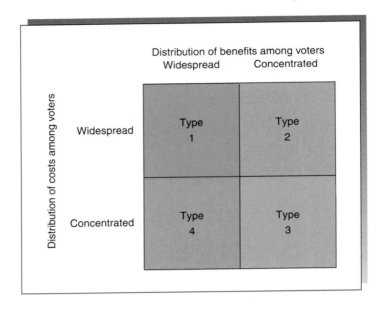

When both the benefits and costs are widespread among voters (type 1 issue), essentially everyone benefits and everyone pays. Although the costs of type 1 measures may not be precisely proportional to the benefits individuals receive, there will be a rough relationship. When type 1 measures are productive, almost everyone gains more than they pay. There will be little opposition, and political representatives have a strong incentive to support such proposals. In contrast, when type 1 proposals generate costs in excess of benefits, almost everyone loses, and representatives will face pressure to oppose such issues. Thus, for type 1 projects, the political process works pretty well. Productive projects will tend to be accepted and unproductive ones rejected.

Similarly, there is reason to believe that the political process will work fairly well for type 3 measures—those for which both benefits and costs are concentrated on one or more small subgroups. In some cases, the concentrated beneficiaries may be the same group of people paying for the government to provide them a service. In other cases, the subgroup of beneficiaries may differ from the subgroup footing the bill. Even in this case, however, when the benefits exceed the costs, the concentrated group of beneficiaries will have an incentive to expend more resources lobbying for the measure than those harmed by it will expend opposing it. Thus, when the benefits and costs are both concentrated, there will be a tendency for productive projects to be adopted and unproductive ones to be rejected.

When the Political Process Works Poorly

Although the political process yields reasonable results when there is a close relationship between the receipt of benefits and the payment of costs, the harmony between good politics and sound economics breaks down when the beneficiaries differ from those bearing the costs (type 2 and type 4 projects). Inefficiency may also arise from other sources when governments undertake economic activities. In this section, we consider four major reasons why the political allocation of resources will often result in inefficiency.

Special-Interest Effect

Trade restrictions that limit the import of steel and lumber from abroad; subsidies for sports stadiums, the arts, and various agricultural products; federal spending on an indoor rain forest in Coralville, Iowa; a tattoo-removal program in San Luis Obispo County, California; a "bridge to nowhere" in Alaska; a golf awareness program in St. Augustine, Florida; and therapeutic horseback riding in Apple Valley, California: These seemingly diverse programs funded by tax dollars from the federal government have one thing in common—they reflect the attractiveness of special interests to vote-seeking politicians. A **special-interest issue** is one that generates substantial personal benefits for a small number of constituents while spreading the costs widely across the bulk of citizens (type 2 projects). Individually, a few people gain a great deal, but many others lose a small amount. In aggregate, the losses may exceed the benefits.

How will a vote-seeking politician respond to special-interest issues? Because their personal stake is large, members of the interest group (and lobbyists representing their interests) will feel strongly about such issues. Many of the special-interest voters will vote for or against candidates strictly on the basis of whether they are supportive of their positions. In addition, interest groups are generally an attractive source of campaign resources, including financial contributions. In contrast, most other rationally ignorant voters will either not know or will care little about special-interest issues. Even if voters know about some of these programs, it will be difficult for them to punish their legislators because each politician represents a bundle of positions on many different issues. Politicians have little to gain by supporting the rationally ignorant and unorganized majority, but organized interest groups are eager to provide cooperative politicians with vocal supporters, campaign workers, and, most important, financial contributions.

As a result, politicians have a strong incentive to support legislation that provides concentrated benefits to special-interest groups at the expense of disorganized groups (like the bulk of taxpayers and consumers). Even if supporting such legislation is counterproductive economically, politicians can often gain by supporting programs favored by special interests. For a real-world illustration of how the special-interest effect works, see Applications in Economics, "Sweet Subsidies to Sugar Growers: A Case Study of the Special-Interest Effect."

The power of special interests is further strengthened by logrolling and pork-barrel legislation. **Logrolling** involves the practice of trading votes by a politician to get the necessary support to pass desired legislation. **Pork-barrel legislation** is the term used to describe the bundling of unrelated projects benefiting many interests into a single bill. Both logrolling and pork-barrel legislation will often make it possible for special-interest projects to gain legislative approval, even though these projects themselves are counterproductive and individually would be unable to muster the needed votes.

EXHIBIT 6 provides a numeric illustration of the forces underlying logrolling and pork-barrel legislation. Here we analyze the operation of a five-member legislature considering three projects: construction of a post office in district A, dredging of a harbor in district B, and spending on a military base in district C. For each district, the net benefit or cost is shown—that is, the benefit to the district minus the tax cost imposed on it. The total cost of each of the three projects exceeds the benefits (as shown by the negative number in the total row at the bottom of the table); therefore, each, is counterproductive. If the projects were voted on separately, each would lose by a 4-to-1 vote because only one district would gain, and the other four would lose. However, when the projects are bundled together through either logrolling (representatives A, B, and C could agree to trade votes) or pork-barrel legislation (all three programs put on the same bill), they can all pass, despite the fact that all are inefficient.[6] This can be seen by noting that the total combined net benefit is positive for representatives A, B, and C. Given the weak incentive for voters to acquire information, those harmed by pork-barrel and other special-interest policies are unlikely to even be aware of them. Furthermore, spending projects that favor specific groups will help legislators raise campaign funds. **Earmarking** is a technique that is widely used for this purpose. See boxed feature, "Earmarking, Congressional Favors, and Political Contributions." Thus, the incentive to support special interest projects, including those that are counterproductive, is even stronger than is implied by the simple numeric example of Exhibit 6.

Special-interest issue

An issue that generates substantial individual benefits to a small minority while imposing a small individual cost on many other citizens. In total, the net cost to the majority might either exceed or fall short of the net benefits to the special-interest group.

Logrolling

The exchange between politicians of political support on one issue for political support on another.

Pork-barrel legislation

A package of spending projects benefiting local areas financed through the federal government. The costs of the projects typically exceed the benefits in total, but the projects are intensely desired by the residents of a particular district who get the benefits without having to pay much of the costs.

Earmarking

The direction of budgeted funds to specific projects, programs, and locations. The technique is costly but provides major benefits to business firms and other concentrated constituent groups, and to the districts where the spending takes place. The benefits are often targeted to those willing to make substantial campaign contributions.

---

[6]Logrolling and pork-barrel policies can sometimes lead to the adoption of productive measures. However, if a project is productive, there would always be a pattern of finance that would lead to its adoption even if logrolling and pork-barrel policies were absent. Thus, the tendency for logrolling and pork-barrel policies to result in the adoption of inefficient projects is the more significant point.

APPLICATIONS IN ECONOMICS

Sweet Subsidies to Sugar Growers: A Case Study of the Special-Interest Effect

For many years, the price of sugar in the United States has been two or three times as high as the world price. Why? Because the U.S. government severely restricts the quantity of sugar imported. This keeps the domestic price of sugar high. As a result, the roughly 60,000 sugar growers in the United States gain about $1.9 billion. That's more than $30,000 per grower! Most of these benefits are reaped by large growers with incomes far above the national average. In contrast, these subsidies cost the average American household about $20 in the form of higher prices for products containing sugar. Even more important, the resources of Americans are wasted producing a good we are ill-suited to produce and one that could be obtained at a substantially lower cost through trade. As a result, Americans are worse off.

Why does Congress support this program year after year? Given the sizable impact the restrictions have on the personal wealth of sugar growers, it is perfectly sensible for the growers, particularly the large ones, to use their wealth and political clout to help politicians who support their interests. This is precisely what they have done. During the 2000 and 2004 election cycles, the sugar lobby contributed more than $16 million to candidates and political action committees. Yet it makes no sense for the average voter to investigate this issue or give it any significant weight when deciding for whom to vote. In fact, most voters are unaware that this program is costing them money. Here, as in several other areas, politicians have a strong incentive to support policies favored by special interests, solicit those parties for political contributions, and use the funds to attract the support of other voters, most of whom know nothing about the sugar program. Even though the sugar program is counterproductive, it is still a political winner.

The sugar growers are not the only ones benefiting from government programs that are economically inefficient. Taxpayers and consumers spend approximately $20 billion annually to support grain, cotton, peanut, wool, and dairy programs, all of which have structural characteristics similar to those of the sugar program. The political power of special interests also explains the presence of tariffs and quotas on steel, textiles, lumber, and many other products. Federally funded irrigation projects, subsidized agricultural grazing rights, subsidized business loans, numerous pork-barrel spending projects (the list goes on and on) are all policies rooted in the special-interest effect rather than economic efficiency and net benefits to Americans. Although each such program individually imposes only a small drag on the economy, together they exert a sizeable negative impact on our income levels and living standards.

Glow Images/Getty Images

EXHIBIT 6

Trading Votes and Passing Counterproductive Legislation

All three projects are inefficient and would not pass majority vote individually. However, representatives from districts A, B, and C could trade votes (logrolling) or put together pork-barrel legislation that would result in all three projects passing.

		NET BENEFITS (+) OR COSTS (−) TO VOTERS IN DISTRICT		
VOTERS OF DISTRICT[a]	CONSTRUCTION OF POST OFFICE IN A	DREDGING HARBOR IN B	CONSTRUCTION OF MILITARY BASE IN C	TOTAL
A	+$10	−$ 3	−$ 3	+$ 4
B	−$ 3	+$10	−$ 3	+$ 4
C	−$ 3	−$ 3	+$10	+$ 4
D	−$ 3	−$ 3	−$ 3	−$ 9
E	−$ 3	−$ 3	−$ 3	−$ 9
Total	−$ 2	−$ 2	−$ 2	−$ 6

[a]We assume the districts are of equal size.

APPLICATIONS IN ECONOMICS

Earmarking, Congressional Favors, and Political Contributions

Pork-barrel spending and the power of special interests is often accomplished through earmarking, detailed directives written into spending bills that require budgeted funds to be spent in specific locations, or on specific projects or programs. In effect, earmarks let members of Congress direct federal spending to specific firms, districts, and states. These directives are often inserted into bills late in the legislative process by powerful committee members or through logrolling as a means of obtaining needed votes for legislative passage. Not surprisingly, firms and groups benefiting substantially from the earmarks are often those making large contributions to the political campaigns of the senators and representatives inserting the earmarks. In recent years, the national defense, transportation, energy, and homeland security bills have been "stuffed" with spending of this type.

Implicitly, earmarking involves the use of taxpayer funds to provide government favors in exchange for campaign contributions. The process borders on corruption and has been widely condemned by political leaders in both major parties, particularly when they are in the minority and less able to use the tool. But it provides incumbents with a major source of campaign contributions. Aggressive use of earmarking by a member of Congress also lets lobbyists and other favor seekers know that the member is cooperative, while unwillingness to use the tool lets them know that their campaign contributions can be used more effectively elsewhere. Thus, willingness to use the technique provides members of Congress with a competitive advantage. Given this incentive structure, it is not surprising that while the tool is criticized, Congress fails to curtail it.

Why don't representatives oppose measures that force their constituents to pay for projects that benefit others? There is some incentive to do so, but the constituents of any one elected representative would capture only a tiny portion of the benefits of tax savings from improved efficiency. The savings, after all, would be spread nationwide among all taxpayers. We would not expect the president of a corporation to devote any significant amount of the firm's resources toward projects that chiefly benefit other firms. Neither should we expect an elected representative to devote political resources to projects like defeating pork-barrel programs when the bulk of benefits from spending reductions and tax savings will be derived by constituents in other districts. Instead, the representative of each district has a strong incentive to work for programs that concentrate benefits in that district, especially to organized interest groups that can help the representative be reelected. Indeed, for programs with spending primarily in the representative's district, to constituents who gain jobs or profits as a result, the cost of the program IS the benefit. There is a strong incentive for each representative to focus on getting more such spending for district constituents while ignoring the costs, which are spread nationally. Heeding such incentives is a key to gaining votes to survive the next election.

When the benefits of a governmental action are spread far and wide among the unorganized, and the costs are highly concentrated (type 4 of Exhibit 5), special-interest groups—those who stand to bear the cost—are likely to oppose and lobby strongly against even an efficient project. Most other voters will be largely uninformed and uninterested. Once again, politicians will have an incentive to respond to the views of the concentrated interests. A proposal to reduce or eliminate a tariff (tax) on an imported good would be an example of this type of legislation. Although many thousands of consumers would benefit from the lower prices that result, the domestic firms that compete with the imported good would devote substantial resources toward lobbying to keep the tariff in place. Projects of this type will tend to be rejected even when they are productive, that is, when they would generate larger benefits than costs.

The bottom line is clear: ***Public-choice analysis indicates that majority voting and representative democracy work poorly when concentrated interests can benefit at the expense of the general public. In the case of special-interest issues, there is a conflict between good politics—getting elected—and the efficient use of resources***. The special-interest effect helps explain the presence of numerous government programs that increase the size of government but reduce the overall size of the economic pie. As we discuss diverse topics throughout this text, counterproductive political action that has its foundation in the special-interest effect will arise again and again.

Shortsightedness Effect

Because voters have a weak incentive to acquire information, current economic conditions will have a major impact on their choices at election time. Complex issues, like reforming Social Security or restructuring health care programs that involve future benefits and costs, will be difficult for voters to assess. Thus, incumbent politicians will want to make sure economic conditions look good on election day. To accomplish this, they will favor policies that provide current benefits voters can easily identify at the expense of future costs that are complicated and difficult to identify. Similarly, they will tend to oppose legislation that involves immediate and easily identifiable costs (and higher taxes) but yields future benefits that are complex and difficult to identify. Economists refer to this bias inherent in the political process as the **shortsightedness effect**.

As a result of the shortsightedness effect, politicians will tend to favor programs that generate highly visible current benefits, even when the true cost of these programs outweighs the benefits. In contrast, their incentive is weak to support efficient programs that generate future benefits but involve current costs.

The shortsightedness effect sheds light on why legislators find debt financing so attractive. Debt financing makes it possible for officeholders to provide visible benefits to their constituents without having to levy an equivalent amount of taxes. Since 1960, the federal budget has been in deficit forty-four times; there have been only five surpluses (1969 and 1998–2001). The bias toward budget deficits is a predictable result; it reflects the shortsighted nature of the political process. Similarly, the shortsightedness effect indicates that vote-seeking politicians will find it attractive to promise future benefits without levying a sufficient amount of taxes to finance them. This has been the case with both the Social Security and Medicare programs. The unfunded liabilities of these two programs are now more than *four times* the size of the official outstanding federal debt. By the time the higher taxes (or benefit cuts) for these programs are confronted, the politicians who gained votes from the promised benefits will be long gone.

It is worth taking a moment to consider the differences between the public and private sectors in terms of how future benefits and costs are considered in current decisions. As we explained in Chapter 2, private-property rights provide a means by which the value of future benefits can be immediately captured (and costs must be borne) by a property owner. Owners who do not invest now to properly maintain their homes or cars, for example, will bear the consequences of the reduced value of those assets. Correspondingly, the value of a firm's stock will immediately rise (or fall), depending on the shareholders' perception of the expected future benefits and costs of an action taken by the company's executives today. In contrast, there is no such market indicator or incentive in the public sector, so decision makers there naturally tend to place more weight on current benefits and costs and less weight on the future. In areas for which the primary benefits are in the future and property rights can be well defined and enforced, there is good reason to believe that the private sector will do a better job than the government sector.

Rent Seeking

There are two ways individuals can acquire wealth: production and plunder. When individuals produce goods or services and exchange them for income, they not only enrich themselves but they also enhance the wealth of the society. Sometimes the rules—or lack of rule enforcement—also allow people to get ahead by taking, or plundering, what others have produced. This method not only fails to generate additional income—the gain of one is a loss to another—but it also consumes resources and thereby reduces the wealth of the society.

Rent seeking is the term economists use to describe actions taken by individuals and groups seeking to use the political process to take the wealth of others.[8] Perhaps

---

Shortsightedness effect

The misallocation of resources that results because public-sector action is biased (1) in favor of proposals yielding clearly defined current benefits in exchange for difficult-to-identify future costs and (2) against proposals with clearly identifiable current costs that yield less concrete and less obvious future benefits.

When buying and selling are controlled by legislation, the first things bought and sold are legislators.

—P. J. O'Rourke[7]

Rent seeking

Actions by individuals and groups designed to restructure public policy in a manner that will either directly or indirectly redistribute more income to themselves or the projects they promote.

---

[7]Quoted in P. J. O'Rourke, *Insight Magazine*, Jan. 15–25: 35.
[8]See the classic work of Charles K. Rowley, Robert D. Tollison, and Gordon Tullock, *The Political Economy of Rent-Seeking* (Boston: Kluwer Academic Publishers, 1988) for additional details on rent seeking.

To get elected (or reelected), politicians have a strong incentive to provide transfers to important interest groups to secure their support.

"favor seeking" would be a more descriptive term for this type of activity, which generally involves "investing" resources in lobbying and other activities designed to gain favors from the government. The incentive for individuals to spend time and effort in rent seeking will be determined by how rewarding it is. Rent seeking will be unattractive when constitutional constraints prevent politicians from taking the property of some and transferring it to others (or forcing some to pay for things desired by others).

When a government fails to allocate the costs of public-sector projects to the primary beneficiaries (through user fees, for example), or when it becomes heavily involved in transfer activities, people will spend more time organizing and lobbying politicians and less time producing goods and services. Resources that would otherwise be used to create wealth and generate income are wasted as people fight over slices of the economic pie, a pie that is smaller than it could be if they were engaged in productive activities instead. When the government grants favors to some people at the expense of others (instead of simply acting as a neutral force protecting property rights and enforcing contracts), counterproductive activities will expand while productive activities will shrink. As a result, the overall income level will fall short of its potential.

There is ample evidence that rent seeking consumes a substantial amount of resources. Washington, D.C., is full of organizations seeking subsidies and other favors from the federal government. More than 3,000 trade associations have offices in Washington, and they employ nearly 100,000 people seeking to alter the actions of Congress. Of course, business and labor organizations are well represented, but so, too, are agricultural interests, health care providers, trial lawyers, senior citizens, export industries, and many others.

The recent response to the current crisis and bailout of banks, insurance companies, and automobile manufacturers illustrates this point. With billions of dollars in additional government spending up for grabs, business executives and their lobbyists descended on Washington, D.C., seeking to obtain money for their organizations. Companies such as General Motors and AIG have spent tens of millions of dollars on lobbying activities and other efforts to influence political decisions over the allocation of this spending. Just as economic theory would have predicted, when government increased its role in allocating resources and redistributing money from taxpayers to politically favored groups, the return to these unproductive rent seeking activities increased, and companies shifted their efforts away from production and toward favor seeking.

It is important to remember that the unproductive activities encouraged by political allocation of resources extend well beyond the lobbying, campaign contributions, and other favor seeking directed toward politicians. Many government programs have specific qualifications or requirements that must be met, and thereby create incentives for organizations to waste resources in order to qualify for government money. For example, a small airport in West Virginia flew in a Boeing 757 from Newark, New Jersey, and offered free 30-minute sightseeing flights in order to meet the 10,000 minimum annual passenger requirement needed to secure a $1 million federal airport improvement grant. Rather than competing by offering consumers more for their money, rent seekers compete by using resources to obtain more funds from taxpayers. As a result, more resources are squandered on unproductive activities and fewer are available for productive use.

As we noted earlier, income transfers have grown substantially during the last several decades. The government now uses taxation to take approximately one out of every seven dollars citizens earn, and transfer it to someone else. Rent seeking is the political "fuel" for most of these transfer activities. Interestingly, *means-tested transfers*, those directed toward the poor, constitute only about one-sixth of all transfers. No income test is applied to the other five-sixths of income transfers. These transfers are generally directed toward groups that are either well organized (like businesses and labor union interests) or easily identifiable (like the elderly and farmers). The people receiving these transfers often have incomes well above the average person.

Within the framework of public-choice analysis, the relatively small portion of income transfers directed toward the poor is not surprising. There is little reason to believe that transfers to the poor will be particularly attractive to vote-seeking politicians. After all, in the United States, the poor are less likely to vote than middle- and upper-income recipients. They are also less likely to be well informed on political issues and candidates. They are not a source of large political contributions. Politicians often argue that their proposed policies will help the poor, but there is little reason to believe that such help will be a high priority for most of them.

There are three major reasons why government transfer activity will reduce the size of the economic pie. First, *income redistribution weakens the link between productive activity and reward.* When taxes take a larger share of a person's income, the reward from hard work and productive activity is reduced. Second, *as public policy redistributes a larger share of income, more resources will flow into wasteful rent-seeking activities.* Resources used for lobbying and other rent-seeking activities will not be available to increase the size of the economic pie. Third, *higher taxes to finance income redistribution and an expansion in rent seeking will induce taxpayers to focus less on income-producing activities and more on actions to protect their income*. More accountants, lawyers, and tax-shelter experts will be retained as people seek to limit the amount of their income taken for redistribution to others. Like the resources allocated to rent seeking, resources allocated to protecting one's wealth from the reach of government will also be unavailable for productive activity. Predictably, the incentives created by government redistribution policies will exert a negative impact on the level of economic activity.

Inefficiency of Government Operations

Will government goods and services be produced efficiently? The pride of a job well done is likely to motivate both public- and private-sector suppliers. However, the incentive to reduce costs and operate efficiently differs substantially between the two. In the private sector, there is a strong incentive to produce efficiently because lower costs mean higher profits, and high costs mean losses and going out of business. Similarly, the value of better products is reflected in buyers' increased willingness to pay. Both forces reward increasing the value of output, relative to the value (cost) of inputs. This index of performance (profit) is unavailable in the public sector. Missing also are signals from the capital market. When a corporation announces a strategy or a plan that vigilant, personally committed investors believe to be faulty, they can personally gain by selling their stock and buying other assets, and the price of the corporation's stock will drop. There is no mechanism similar to the asset market (including the stock market) in the public sector allowing vigilant voters to gain personally from their vigilance. Furthermore, direct competition in the form of other firms trying to woo the customers—as a revenue source or constituents—as political supporters of a government agency or enterprise is absent in most of the public sector. As a result, bureaucrats can pursue their narrow goals and interests without a strong regard for the control of costs relative to the benefits delivered to the public.

Bankruptcy weeds out inefficiency (where costs of resource inputs exceed benefits as measured by customer payments) in the private sector, but there is no parallel mechanism to eliminate inefficiency in the public sector. In fact, failure to achieve a targeted objective (for example, a lower crime rate or improvement in student achievement scores) is often used as an argument for *increased* public-sector funding of an agency or its programs. Furthermore, public-sector managers are seldom in a position to gain personally from measures that reduce costs. The opposite is often true, in fact. If an agency fails to spend its entire budget for a given year, not only does it have to return the extra money, but its budget for the next year is likely to be cut. Because of this, government agencies typically

THE FAMILY CIRCUS   **By Bil Keane**

Family Circus © Reprinted by permission of King Features Syndicate

1-26
©1998 Bil Keane, Inc.
Dist. by Cowles Synd., Inc.

"Daddy, could you buy a new metal detector? I dropped my quarter in the snow."

Just as the boy considers the quarter (his quarter) more important than the far greater cost (to the father) of the metal detector, so, too, does the leader of a bureau often consider the bureau's goals more important than the costs, even if the latter are far greater.

go on a spending spree near the end of a budget period if they discover they have failed to spend all the current year's allocated funds.

It is important to note that the argument of internal inefficiency is not based on the assumption that employees of a bureaucratic government are lazy or less capable. Many agency managers are highly capable, diligent, and focused strongly on their mission within the agency. Rather, the inefficiency stems from the incentives and opportunities that such managers and workers confront. Government firms do not have owners that are risking their wealth on the future success of the firm. No decision maker in the firm can reap substantial economic gain if the firm produces more efficiently or incorporates a new product or service highly valued relative to its costs. Is the product or service delivered at the best time and place, and of the appropriate quality? Because the profitability criteria are absent, the value of performance on behalf of those who pay is difficult to evaluate. There are no tests to define economic inefficiency or measure it accurately much less to eliminate it. These perverse incentives are bound to affect efficiency.

The empirical evidence is consistent with this view. Economies dominated by government control, like those of the former Soviet bloc, Indonesia, Syria, and Nigeria (and many other African countries), have performed poorly. The level of output per unit of resource input in countries with numerous government enterprises is low. Similarly, when private firms are compared with government agencies providing the same goods or services (like garbage collection, hospitals, electric and water utilities, weather forecasting, and public transportation), studies indicate that private firms generally provide the services more economically.

It is clear that both the sector in which the good or service is produced and whether or not consumers directly pay for it influence efficiency. The addendum to this chapter explores this concept in more detail.

The Economic Way of Thinking about Government

Both the market and the political process have shortcomings. In Chapter 5, we focused on the shortcomings of the market and explained why markets sometimes fail to achieve the efficient use of resources. This chapter provides a parallel analysis for the political process. The accompanying **Thumbnail Sketch** lists the major deficiencies of both sectors.

When analyzing the operation of markets and government, it is vitally important to keep two points in mind. First, the government's protective role provides the foundation for the smooth operation of markets. A government that protects private property, enforces contracts evenhandedly, maintains monetary stability, and refrains from regulations that restrict entry into markets is central to the efficient operation of markets. Second, when governments move beyond the protective function and become actively involved in real-locating resources toward politically favored businesses or special interest groups, political outcomes will often conflict with the efficient and productive use of resources. This will be the case even when political decisions are made democratically.

It is informative to compare and contrast markets and government with regard to the incentive of decision makers to undertake productive projects and refrain from counterproductive ones. In a market economy, businesses that use resources to produce goods and services that are valued more highly than the resources required for their production will earn profits, which in turn provide them with the incentive to continue and expand. In contrast, when businesses produce goods that consumers do not value enough to cover the cost of the resources used in their production, losses will occur and eventually bring such unproductive activities to a halt through business failure. Thus, the profit and loss mechanism of a market economy tends to direct resources toward productive projects and away from those that are unproductive.

The political process does not have a parallel mechanism that can be counted on to provide decision makers with the incentive to engage in productive, and refrain from counterproductive, projects. Instead, when government moves beyond the establishment of a legal and monetary environment conducive for the smooth operation of markets, political allocation is largely about various coalitions trading contributions and other forms of support with politicians in exchange for subsidies, spending programs, and regulations that provide them with favors at the expense of others. As this happens, more resources will be channeled toward lobbying and other rent-seeking activities and fewer toward the production and development of more and better products within the private sector. The businesses (and other organizations) who are most effective at lobbying will expand, rather than those who are employing resources most productively. Predictably, this will lead to a decline in the productive use of resources and an expansion in counterproductive activities, reducing overall income and prosperity as a result.

The framers of the U.S. Constitution were aware that even a democratic government might undertake counterproductive actions. Thus, they incorporated restraints on the economic role of government. They enumerated the permissible tax and spending powers of the central government (Article I, Section 8) and allocated all other powers to the states and the people (Tenth Amendment). They also prohibited states from adopting legislation "impairing the obligation of contracts" (Article I, Section 10). Furthermore, the Fifth Amendment specifies that private property shall not be "taken for public use without just compensation." Over time, however, these restraints have been significantly eroded, due in part to Supreme Court decisions that have effectively reinterpreted the Constitution.

There is a tendency to idealize democratic governance—to focus on the stated objectives of political officials rather than the actual effects of their policies. Public choice analysis

THUMBNAIL SKETCH

What Weakens the Case for Market-Sector Allocation Versus Public-Sector Intervention, and Vice Versa?

These factors weaken the case for market-sector allocation:
1. lack of competition
2. externalities
3. public goods
4. poor information

These factors weaken the case for public-sector intervention:
1. the special-interest effect
2. the shortsightedness effect
3. rent seeking
4. weak incentives for operational efficiency

uses the tools of economics to enhance our understanding of how the political process really works. It also highlights the importance of institutions, constitutional rules, and procedures that encourage productive political actions and restrain those that are counterproductive. Higher income levels and living standards can be achieved if political structures more consistent with economic progress are instituted. Clearly, this is one of our most important future challenges.

Looking ahead

Cases involving potential government intervention will be discussed repeatedly throughout this book. The tools presented in this chapter and the previous one will help us better understand both the potential and the limitations of public policy as a source for economic progress.

KEY POINTS

▼ In recent years, government spending has been about one-third the size of the U.S. economy.

▼ There are both similarities and differences between markets and governments. Competition is present in both sectors. The government can use its taxing power to break the link between payment and receipt of a good for an individual, but not for the economy as a whole. In the public sector, voters face a "bundle" purchase problem; they are unable to vote for some policies favored by one candidate and other policies favored by the candidate's opponent. Power and income are distributed differently in the public sector than in the private sector.

▼ In a representative democracy, government is controlled by voters who elect politicians to set policy and hire bureaucrats to run government agencies. The incentives faced by all three classes of participants influence political outcomes.

▼ Voters have a strong incentive to support the candidate who offers them the greatest gain relative to their personal costs. Because collective decisions break the link between the choice of the individual

and the outcome of the issue, voters are likely to be poorly informed on most political matters.

▼ Politicians have a strong incentive to follow a strategy that will enhance their chances of getting elected (and reelected). Political competition more or less forces them to focus on how their actions influence their support among voters and potential contributors.

▼ The distribution of the benefits and costs among voters influences how the political process works. When voters pay in proportion to the benefits they receive from a public-sector project, productive projects tend to be approved and counterproductive ones rejected. When the costs of a policy are distributed among voters differently than are the benefits, democratic decision making will tend to be less efficient.

▼ Government actions will often lead to economic inefficiency as the result of (1) the special-interest effect, (2) the shortsightedness effect, (3) rent seeking, and (4) weak incentives to keep costs low within government enterprises and agencies. Thus, just as the market sometimes fails to allocate goods efficiently, so, too, will the government.

CRITICAL ANALYSIS QUESTIONS

1. Are voters likely to be well informed on issues and the positions of candidates? Why or why not?

*2. "The government can afford to take a long view when it needs to, while a private firm has a short-

term outlook. Corporate officers, for example, typically care about the next 3 to 6 months, not the next 50 to 100 years. Government, not private firms, should own things like forests, which take decades to develop." Evaluate this view.

3. "If there are problems with markets, government will generally be able to intervene and correct the situation." Is this statement true or false? Explain your response.

*4. "The political process sometimes leads to economic inefficiency because we elect the wrong people to political office. If the right people were elected, a democracy governed by majority rule would allocate resources efficiently." Evaluate this statement.

5. What is rent seeking? When is it likely to be widespread? How does it influence economic efficiency? Explain.

*6. "The average person is more likely to make an informed choice when he or she purchases a personal computer than when he or she votes for a congressional candidate." Evaluate this statement.

7. "Government action is based on majority rule, whereas market action is based on mutual consent. The market allows for proportional representation of minorities, but minorities must yield to the views of the majority when activities are undertaken through government." In your own words, explain the meaning of this statement. Is the statement true? Why or why not?

*8. "Voters should simply ignore political candidates who play ball with special-interest groups and vote instead for candidates who will represent all the people when they are elected. Government will work far better when this happens." Evaluate this view.

9. If a project is efficient (if its total benefits exceed its total costs), would it be possible to allocate the cost of the project in a manner that would provide net benefits to each voter? Why or why not? Explain. Will efficient projects necessarily be favored by a majority of voters? Explain.

*10. "When an economic function is turned over to the government, social cooperation replaces personal self-interest." Is this statement true? Why or why not?

11. What is the shortsightedness effect? How does the shortsightedness effect influence the efficiency of public-sector action?

*12. What's wrong with this way of thinking? "Public policy is necessary to protect the average citizen from the power of vested interest groups. In the absence of government intervention, regulated industries such as airlines, railroads, and trucking will charge excessive prices; products will be unsafe; and the rich will oppress the poor. Government curbs the power of special-interest groups."

13. "Since government-operated firms do not have to make a profit, they can usually produce at a lower cost and charge a lower price than privately owned enterprises." Evaluate this view.

14. What percentage of government income transfer payments go to the poor? Do you think that the political process in general works to the advantage of the poor? Why or why not?

15. Why does representative democracy often tax some people in order to provide benefits to others? When governments become heavily involved in tax-transfer activities, how will this involvement affect economic efficiency?

*16. The United States imposes highly restrictive sugar import quotas that result in a domestic price that is generally two or three times the world price. The quotas benefit sugar growers at the expense of consumers. Given that there are far more sugar consumers than growers, why aren't the quotas abolished? Has government action in this area improved the living standards of Americans? Why or why not?

17. "The United States is rich because it is a political democracy where the people decide what policies will be followed." Is this statement true or false? Discuss.

18. If the power of special interests were reduced, for example, through the adoption of a supra-majority voting rule, would economic efficiency improve? How would contributions to political campaigns be affected? Do you think politicians are very interested in curtailing the power of special interests? Why or why not?

19. Suppose that in the election campaign of 2010, incumbent Representative Earmark is shown to have proposed and helped to pass twenty programs in her previous term, all of which were funded by the federal government, but delivered benefits only in her district—benefits that were estimated to be only 50 percent as large as the federal costs. How would this charge by her opponent, who provided good evidence of the validity of the charge, be likely to affect Representative Earmark's likelihood of reelection? Explain.

20. If a senator trades his or her vote on an issue for a $10,000 payment, would you consider this corruption? If a senator votes a certain way in "exchange" for a $10,000 contribution to his political campaign, would you consider this corruption? Is there a major difference between the two? Discuss.

*Asterisk denotes questions for which answers are given in Appendix B.

A D D E N D U M

Incentives and Economic Organization: Who Produces, Who Pays, and Why It Matters

The first six chapters of this book have introduced you to the basic economic insight that the incentives faced by individuals, in both the private and public sectors, help to shape economic outcomes. Here, we bring the ideas of these chapters together in a more unified framework regarding how the structures of production and consumption influence economic outcomes.

Goods and services can be either produced by private enterprises or supplied by the government. They can be paid for either by the consumer directly or by the taxpayer or some other third party. As **EXHIBIT A-1** shows, there are four possible combinations of production and consumption. Let's take a closer look at each and consider the impact on the allocation of resources and the incentive to economize. As we do so, think about how the incentive confronted by consumers and producers influences their behavior. *If personal incentives and economic efficiency are not aligned, waste and output below its potential will result.*

In quadrant 1, goods are produced by private firms and purchased by consumers with their own money. Because they are spending their own funds, consumers have a strong incentive to economize. They will compare value with cost and will make purchases only when they value items more than their purchase price. Correspondingly, profits and losses provide the owners of private enterprises with a strong incentive to both cater to the views of

consumers and supply goods efficiently. Net revenues can be increased if the output can be produced at a lower cost. Producers will continue to supply goods if, and only if, consumers are willing to pay an amount sufficient to cover their production costs. Essentially, the supply and demand analysis of Chapter 3 focused on quadrant 1 cases. As we discussed in that chapter, under these conditions, market forces will bring the self-interest of both consumers and producers into alignment with economic efficiency.

Quadrant 2 represents the case in which goods are produced privately but are paid for by the taxpayer or some other third party. Providing health care to citizens financed primarily by government (Medicare and Medicaid) or insurance is an example. Because someone else is paying the bill, consumers have little incentive to care much about the price of their health care services. Instead of economizing, many consumers will simply purchase from suppliers they believe offer the highest quality or greatest convenience, even when the price is higher. The behavior of producers will also be affected. When consumers are largely insensitive to prices, producers have less reason to control costs and offer services at low prices. In this case, the personal self-interest of consumers and producers is in conflict with the efficient use of resources. Waste and inefficiency will result.

Quadrant 3 represents the situation in which consumers pay for a good or service, but production is handled by the government. First-class mail delivery via the U.S. Postal Service, water and electricity sold by municipal governments on a monopoly basis, and the operation of

	Good is paid for by:	
Good is produced by:	Consumer-Purchaser	Taxpayer or Other Third Party
Private Enterprises	(1) Examples: apples, oranges, television sets, food, housing, most other goods	(2) Examples: health care, food purchased with food stamps
Government Enterprises or Contracting	(3) Examples: Post Office, water and electricity in many cities, toll roads, many hospitals	(4) Examples: public schools, streets and roads, national defense, law enforcement

EXHIBIT A-1
The Private- and Government-Sector Matrix of Production and Payment

The incentive to economize is influenced by who produces a good and who pays for it. Economizing behavior will be strongest when consumers use their own money to purchase goods produced by private firms (quadrant 1). The incentive to economize is reduced when payment is made by a third party and when production is handled by the government.

toll roads without close substitutes are examples that fall into this category. When consumers pay for a good or service directly, they will economize and seek the most value per dollar they spend. This will be true whether their purchases are from private or government enterprises. As we discussed earlier in this chapter, however, the managers of government-operated firms will often be influenced by political considerations when tax dollars, not just revenues from buyers, are in their budgets. Further, compared with private firms, the incentive to keep costs low and provide consumers with quality service is weaker for government-operated firms. Given this incentive structure, some inefficiency is likely, particularly if the government firm is subsidized and has no private-sector rivals.

Quadrant 4 represents the case in which the government both provides the service and covers its costs through taxation. In this case, the political process determines what will be produced, how it will be produced, and how it will be allocated to the general public. Under these circumstances, individual consumers are in a very weak position to either discipline the suppliers or alter their production. The incentive to produce efficiently is weak, and there is likely to be a disconnect between the goods produced and the preferences of consumers. The expected result is high costs of production and widespread dissatisfaction among the consumers of the good. The U.S. experience with government provision of K-12 education reflects this incentive structure.

As we discussed in the previous chapter, the nature of public goods—items such as national defense—may make it difficult to supply them through markets. This makes the quadrant 4 option, government provision financed by taxes, more attractive. However, even here, the structure of incentives indicates that problems will arise. There is nothing similar to profit and loss that can be counted on to direct the government to produce the proper amount, provide it in the best location, and produce it with the appropriate technology and least-cost resource combination. Difficulties involved in closing redundant military bases, continuation of ineffective weapon systems produced in the districts or states of powerful legislators, and purchase of materials at exorbitant prices (for example, the infamous $600 toilet seat purchased by the Defense Department) are consistent with this view. Thus, while markets may handle public goods poorly, there are also problems with government provision.

Most goods and services in the United States are allocated under conditions approximating those of quadrant 1. Thus, most of economic analysis focuses on this case. However, a sizable portion of economic activity takes place under conditions present in the other three quadrants, where the incentive structure often creates problems.

What might be done to reduce the inefficiency accompanying the economic organization of quadrants 2, 3, and 4? The special topic features on health care, school choice, and Social Security will address this question in more detail. A few general points, however, can be made now. For quadrant 2 cases, inefficiency can be reduced by providing consumers with a specific subsidy rather than paying for whatever amount of the good they would like to purchase. When this is done, consumers will face the cost and compare it with the value received for purchases beyond the specified subsidy. Thus, their choices in this range will be consistent with economic efficiency. This is essentially what the food stamp program does. Depending on income level, people are provided with a finite dollar amount of food stamps; they must pay for purchases beyond that amount with their own money. Another option would be to have consumers pay for a significant fraction, 50 percent for example, of the price of the subsidized good. This would provide incentive to shop for value relative to price, which would also increase the incentive of producers to keep their prices low.

For quadrant 3 cases, competition from private-sector producers, both actual and potential, can improve the cost efficiency of government-operated firms. If consumers have private sector options, government firms will have to operate efficiently in order to compete. For example, the presence of UPS and FedEx helps to keep the package delivery service of the U.S. Postal Service on its toes. Similarly, competition from private power-generating firms will improve the efficiency of government firms in this sector. Further, the option of contracting provision of a government-provided service out to a private supplier can also improve the competitiveness and efficiency in the quadrant 3 area.

In quadrant 4, consumers can sometimes be subsidized without forcing them to buy the good from the government. Doing so would enhance the consumers' ability to obtain what they want, through increased competition. This will increase the incentive of both private and government firms in the area to operate more efficiently. In recent years, there has been some movement in this direction in the area of K-12 education (e.g., school vouchers).

Inefficiency generally results because decision makers do not have to bear the full cost of their choices or because they are unable to capture fully the benefits their actions could generate for others. This is an important point to keep in mind when thinking about economic organization and the potential of government intervention to improve the quality of our lives.

Core Macroeconomics

Macroeconomics is about growth of the economy and fluctuations in output, employment, and the general level of prices. Growth of output is extremely important because it makes higher levels of consumption and living standards possible. Fluctuations in output and prices can retard growth and generate economic hardship. What causes economic fluctuations? What can economic policy do to promote more stability? Why do some countries grow and achieve high levels of income while others remain poor? Part 3 will focus on these questions and related issues.

Growth of output is the key to a higher living standard

Taking the Nation's Economic Pulse

CHAPTER FOCUS

- What is GDP? How is GDP calculated?

- When making comparisons over time, why is it important to adjust nominal GDP for the effects of inflation?

- What do price indexes measure? How can they be used to adjust for changes in the general level of prices?

- Is GDP a good measure of output? What are its strengths and weaknesses?

[1]As quoted by Milton Friedman in *Economic Freedom: Toward a Theory of Measurement*, edited by Walter Block (Va British Columbia: The Fraser Institute, 1991), 11.

O ur society likes to keep score. The sports pages supply us with the win–loss records that reveal how well the various teams are doing. We also keep score on the performance of our economy. The scoreboard for economic performance is the *national-income accounting system*. Just as a firm's accounting statement provides information on its performance, national-income accounts supply performance information for the entire economy.

Simon Kuznets, the winner of the 1971 Nobel Prize in economics, developed the basic concepts of national-income accounting during the 1920s and 1930s (see the Outstanding Economist feature). Through the years, these procedures have been modified and improved. In this chapter, we will explain how the flow of an economy's output (and income) is measured. We will also explain how changes in the quantity of goods and services produced are separated from changes that reflect merely inflation (higher prices). Finally, we will analyze the strengths and weaknesses of the measurement tools used to assess the performance of our national economy. ■

GDP—A Measure of Output

The **gross domestic product (GDP)** is the market value of final goods and services produced within a country during a specific time period, usually a year. GDP is the most widely used measure of economic performance. The GDP figures are closely watched both by policy makers and by those in the business and financial communities. In the United States, the numbers are prepared quarterly and released a few weeks following the end of each quarter.

GDP is a "flow" concept. By analogy, a water gauge measures the amount of water that flows through a pipe each hour. Similarly, GDP measures the market value of production that "flows" through the economy's factories and shops each year (or quarter).

Gross domestic product (GDP)

The market value of all final goods and services produced within a country during a specific period.

What Counts toward GDP?

First and foremost, GDP is a measure of output. Thus, it cannot be arrived at merely by summing the totals on the nation's cash registers during a period. The key phrases in the definition of GDP—"market value" of "final goods and services" "produced" "within a country" "during a specific time period"—reveal a great deal about what should be included in and excluded from the calculation of GDP. Let's take a closer look at this issue.

ONLY FINAL GOODS AND SERVICES COUNT. If output is to be measured accurately, all goods and services produced during the year must be counted once and only once. Most goods go through several stages of production before they end up in the hands of their ultimate users. To avoid double-counting, one must take care to differentiate between **intermediate goods**—goods in intermediate stages of production—and **final market goods and services**—those purchased for final use rather than for resale or further processing.

Sales at intermediate stages of production are not counted by GDP because the value of the intermediate goods is embodied within the final-user good. Adding the sales price of both the intermediate good and the final-user good would exaggerate GDP. For example, when a wholesale distributor sells steak to a restaurant, the final purchase price paid by

Intermediate goods

Goods purchased for resale or for use in producing another good or service.

Final market goods and services

Goods and services purchased by their ultimate user.

the patron of the restaurant for the steak dinner will reflect the cost of the meat. Double-counting would result if we included both the sale price of the intermediate good (the steak sold by the wholesaler to the restaurant) and the final purchase price of the steak dinner.

EXHIBIT 1 will help clarify the accounting method for GDP. Before the final good, bread, is in the hands of the consumer, it will go through several intermediate stages of production. The farmer produces a pound of wheat and sells it to the miller for 30 cents. The miller grinds the wheat into flour and sells it to the baker for 65 cents. The miller's actions have *added* 35 cents to the value of the wheat. The baker combines the flour with other ingredients, makes a loaf of bread, and sells it to the grocer for 90 cents. The baker has *added* 25 cents to the value of the bread. The grocer stocks the bread on the grocery shelves and provides a convenient location for consumers to shop. The grocer sells the loaf of bread for $1, *adding* 10 cents to the value of the final product. Only the final market value of the product—the $1 for the loaf of bread—is included in GDP. This price reflects the value added at each stage of production. The 30 cents *added* by the farmer, the 35 cents by the miller, the 25 cents by the baker, and the 10 cents by the grocer sum to the $1 purchase price.

EXHIBIT 1
GDP and the Stages of Production

Most goods go through several stages of production. This chart illustrates both the market value of a loaf of bread as it passes through the various stages of production (column 1) and the additional value added by each intermediate producer (column 2). GDP counts only the market value of the final product. Of course, the amount added by each intermediate producer (column 2) sums to the market value of the final product.

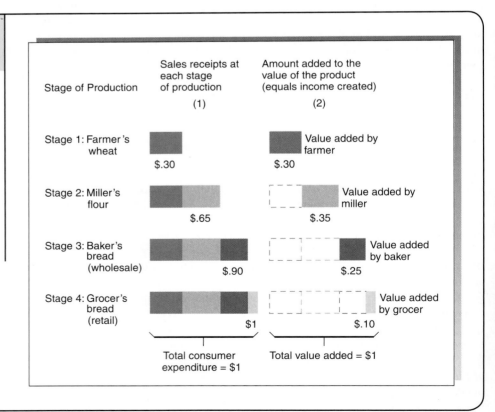

ONLY TRANSACTIONS INVOLVING PRODUCTION COUNT. Remember, GDP is a measure of goods and services "produced." Financial transactions and income transfers are excluded because they merely move ownership from one party to another. They do not involve current production and are therefore not included in GDP. (*Note*: If a financial transaction involves a sales commission, the commission is included in GDP because it involves a service rendered during the current period.)

Thus, the purchases and sales of stocks, bonds, and U.S. securities are not included in GDP. Neither are private- and public-sector income transfers. If your aunt sends you $100 to help pay for your college expenses, your aunt has less wealth and you have more, but the transaction adds nothing to current production. Government income transfer payments, such as Social Security, welfare, and veterans payments, are also omitted. The recipients of these transfers are not producing goods in return for the transfers. Therefore, it would be inappropriate to add them to GDP.

ONLY PRODUCTION WITHIN THE COUNTRY IS COUNTED. GDP is a measure of "domestic product." Therefore, it counts only goods and services produced within the geographic borders of the country. When foreigners earn income within U.S. borders, it adds to the GDP of the United States. For example, the incomes of Canadian engineers and Mexican baseball players earned in the United States are included in the U.S. GDP. However, the earnings of Americans abroad—for example, an American college professor teaching in England—do not count toward the U.S. GDP because this income is not generated within the borders of the United States.

ONLY GOODS PRODUCED DURING THE CURRENT PERIOD ARE COUNTED. As the definition indicates, GDP is a measure of output "during the current period." Transactions involving the exchange of goods or assets produced during earlier periods are omitted because they do not reflect current production. For example, the purchases of "second-hand" goods, such as a used car or a home built five years ago, are not included in this year's GDP. Production of these goods was counted at the time they were produced and initially purchased. Resale of such items produced during earlier years merely changes the ownership of the goods or assets. It does not add to current production. Thus, these transactions should not be included in current GDP. (*Note:* As in the case of financial transactions, sales commissions earned by those helping to arrange the sale of used cars, homes, or other assets are included in GDP because they reflect services provided during the current period.)

Dollars Are the Common Denominator for GDP

In elementary school, each of us was taught the difficulties of adding apples and oranges. Yet, this is precisely the nature of aggregate output. Literally millions of different commodities and services are produced each year. How can the production of apples, oranges, shoes, movies, roast beef sandwiches, automobiles, dresses, legal services, education, heart transplants, haircuts, and many other items be added together? Answer: The "market value" of each is added to GDP.

The vastly different goods and services produced in our modern world have only one thing in common: Someone pays a price for them. Therefore, when measuring output, units of each good are weighted according to their market value—the purchase price of the good or service. If a consumer pays $25,000 for a new automobile and $25 for a nice meal, production of the automobile adds 1,000 times as much to output as production of the meal. Similarly, production of a television set that is purchased for $1,000 will add 1/25 as much to output as the new automobile and 40 times the amount of the meal.

Each good produced increases output by the amount the purchaser pays for the good. The total spending on all goods and services produced during the year is then summed, in dollar terms, to obtain the annual GDP.

GDP as a Measure of Both Output and Income

There are two ways of looking at and measuring GDP. First, ***the GDP of an economy can be reached by totaling the expenditures on goods and services produced during the year.*** National-income accountants refer to this method as the *expenditure approach.* Alternatively, ***GDP can be calculated by summing the income payments to the resource suppliers of the things used to produce those goods and services.*** Production of goods and services is costly because the resources required for their production must be bid away from their alternative uses. These costs generate incomes for resource suppliers. Thus, this method of calculating GDP is referred to as the *resource cost–income approach.*

The prices used to weight the goods and services included in GDP reflect both the market value of the output and the income generated by the resources. From an accounting viewpoint, when a good is produced and sold, the total payments to the factors of production (including the producer's profit or loss) must be equal to the sales price generated by the good.[2] For example, consider a beauty salon operator who leases a building and equipment, purchases various cosmetic products, and combines these items with labor to provide hairdressing services for which customers pay $500 per day. The market value of the output, $500 per day, is added to GDP. The $500 figure is also equal to the income resource owners receive from the provision of the service.

The link between the market value of a good and the income (including the profit or loss) earned by resource suppliers occurs for each good or service produced. This same link is also present in the aggregate economy. In accounting terms, the idea can be illustrated as follows:

The dollar flow of expenditures on final goods = The dollar flow of income (and indirect cost) from final goods

GDP is a measure of the value of the goods and services that were purchased by households, investors, governments, and foreigners. These purchasers valued the goods and services more than the purchase price; otherwise they would not have purchased them. GDP is also a measure of aggregate income. Production of the goods involves human toil, wear and tear on machines, use of natural resources, risk, managerial responsibilities, and other of life's unpleasantries. Resource owners have to be compensated with income payments in order to induce them to supply these resources.

Thus, GDP is a measure of both (1) the market value of the output produced and (2) the income generated by those who produced the output. This highlights a very important point: Increases in output and growth of income are linked. An expansion in output—that is, the additional production of goods and services that people value—is the source of higher income levels.

EXHIBIT 2 summarizes the components of GDP for both the expenditure and resource cost–income approaches. Except for a few complicating elements that we will discuss in a moment, the revenues business firms derive from the sale of goods and services are paid directly to resource suppliers in the form of wages, self-employment income, rents, profits, and interest. We now turn to an examination of these components and the two alternative ways of deriving GDP.

Deriving GDP by the Expenditure Approach

When derived by the expenditure approach, GDP has four components: (1) personal consumption expenditures, (2) gross private domestic investment, (3) government consumption

---

[2]In the national-income accounts, the terms profit and corporate profit are used in the accounting sense. Thus, they reflect both the competitive rate of return on assets (opportunity cost of capital) and the firm's economic profit and loss, which were discussed in Chapter 3.

EXHIBIT 2
Two Ways of Measuring GDP

There are two methods of calculating GDP. It can be calculated either by summing the expenditures on the "final-user" goods and services purchased by consumers, investors, governments, and foreigners (net exports) or by summing the income payments and direct cost items that accompany the production of goods and services.

EXPENDITURE APPROACH

PERSONAL CONSUMPTION
EXPENDITURES
+
GROSS PRIVATE DOMESTIC
INVESTMENT
+
GOVERNMENT CONSUMPTION AND
GROSS INVESTMENT
+
NET EXPORTS OF GOODS AND
SERVICES
=
GDP

RESOURCE COST–INCOME APPROACH

AGGREGATE INCOME
Compensation of employees
(wages and salaries)
Income of self-employed
proprietors
Rents
Profits
Interest
+
NONINCOME COST ITEMS
Indirect business taxes
Depreciation
+
NET INCOME OF FOREIGNERS
=
GDP

and gross investment, and (4) net exports to foreigners. The left side of **EXHIBIT 3** presents the values of these four components in 2008. Later, we will discuss the right side, which deals with the resource cost–income approach.

CONSUMPTION PURCHASES. **Personal consumption** purchases are the largest component of GDP; in 2008, they amounted to $10,058 billion. Most consumption expenditures are for nondurable goods or services. Food, clothing, recreation, medical and legal services, and fuel are included in this category. These items are used up or consumed in a relatively short time. Durable goods, such as appliances and automobiles, constitute

Personal consumption

Household spending on consumer goods and services during the current period. Consumption is a flow concept.

EXHIBIT 3
Two Ways of Measuring GDP—2008 Data (billions of dollars)

The left side shows the flow of expenditures and the right side the flow of income payments and indirect costs. Both procedures yield GDP.

EXPENDITURE APPROACH			RESOURCE COST–INCOME APPROACH	
Personal Consumption		$10,058	Employee Compensation	$8,055
Durable goods	$1,023		Proprietors' Income	$1,072
Nondurable goods	$2,965		Rents	$64
Services	$6,070		Corporate Profits	$1,477
Gross Private Investment		$1,994	Interest Income	$683
Fixed Investment	$2,041		Indirect Business Taxes	$1,080
Inventories	−$47		Depreciation (Capital Consumption)[a]	$1,967
Gov. Cons. and Gross Inv.		$2,882	Net Income of Foreigners	−$133
Federal	$1,072			$14,265
State and local	$1,810			
Net Exports		−$669		
Gross Domestic Product		$14,265	Gross Domestic Product	$14,265

[a]Includes $1,523 billion for the depreciation of privately owned capital, $308 billion for the depreciation of government-owned assets, and plus $136 billion for statistical discrepancy.
Source: U.S. Department of Commerce. These data are also online at http://www.bea.gov.

approximately one-ninth of all consumer purchases. These products are consumed over a longer period of time, even though they are fully counted when they are purchased.

Private investment

The flow of private-sector expenditures on durable assets (fixed investment) plus the addition to inventories (inventory investment) during a period. These expenditures enhance our ability to provide consumer benefits in the future.

GROSS PRIVATE INVESTMENT. The next item in the expenditure approach, **private investment**, is the production or construction of capital goods that provide a "flow" of future service. Unlike food or medical services, they are not immediately "used." Business plants and equipment are investment goods because they will help produce goods and services in the future. Similarly, a house is an investment good because it will also provide a stream of services long into the future. Increases in business inventories are also classified as investment because they will provide future consumer benefits.

Gross investment includes expenditures for both (1) the replacement of machinery, equipment, and buildings worn out during the year and (2) net additions to the stock of capital assets. Net investment is simply gross investment minus an allowance for **depreciation** and obsolescence of machinery and other physical assets during the year.

Depreciation

The estimated amount of physical capital (for example, machines and buildings) that is worn out or used up producing goods during a period.

Net investment is an important indicator of the economy's future productive capability. A substantial amount of net investment indicates that the capital stock of the economy is growing, thereby enhancing the economy's future productive potential (shifting the economy's production possibilities frontier outward). In contrast, a low rate of net investment, or even worse, a negative net investment, implies a stagnating or even contracting economy. Of course, the impact of investment on future income will also be affected by the productivity of investment—whether the funds invested are channeled into wealth-creating projects. Other things being the same, however, countries with a large net investment rate will tend to grow more rapidly than those with a low (or negative) rate of net investment. In 2008, gross private investment expenditures in the United States were $1,994 billion, 14.0 percent of GDP. Of course, a large portion ($1,967 billion) of this figure was for the replacement of private assets worn out during the year. Thus, net private investment was $161 billion, only 1.1 percent of GDP.

Inventory investment

Changes in the stock of unsold goods and raw materials held during a period.

Because GDP is designed to measure current production, allowance must be made for goods produced but not sold during the year—that is, for **inventory investment**, or changes during the year in the market value of unsold goods on shelves and in warehouses. If business firms have more goods on hand at the end of the year than they had at the beginning of the year, inventory investment will be positive. This inventory investment must be added to GDP. Conversely, a decline in inventories would indicate that the purchases of goods and services exceeded current production. In this case, inventory *disinvestment* would be a subtraction from GDP. In 2008, the United States disinvested $47 billion in additional inventories.

GOVERNMENT CONSUMPTION AND GROSS INVESTMENT. In 2008, federal, state, and local government consumption and investment in the United States summed to $2,882 billion, approximately 20 percent of total GDP. The purchases of state and local governments exceeded those of the federal government by a wide margin. The government component includes both (1) expenditures on items like office supplies, law enforcement, and the operation of veterans hospitals, which are "consumed" during the current period, and (2) the purchase of long-lasting capital goods, like missiles, highways, and dams for flood control. (Remember, transfer payments are excluded from GDP because they do not involve current production.) As a result, the government's total expenditures are substantially higher than its total consumption and investment expenditures. Unlike the other components of GDP, government purchases are counted at their *cost* to taxpayers rather than their *value* to those receiving them. In cases in which the value of the item to citizens is low relative to the tax cost of providing it, the government expenditures will overstate the value derived from the item.

Net exports

Exports minus imports.

Exports

Goods and services produced domestically but sold to foreigners.

Imports

Goods and services produced by foreigners but purchased by domestic consumers, businesses, and governments.

NET EXPORTS. The final item in the expenditure approach is **net exports**, or total exports minus imports. **Exports** are domestically produced goods and services sold to foreigners. **Imports** are foreign-produced goods and services purchased domestically.

Remember, GDP is a measure of domestic production—output produced within the borders of a nation. Therefore, when measuring GDP by the expenditure approach, we must (1) add exports (goods produced domestically that were sold to foreigners) and (2) subtract imports (goods produced abroad that were purchased by Americans). For national-income accounting purposes, we can combine these two factors into a single entry:

$$\text{Net exports} = \text{Total exports} - \text{Total imports}$$

Net exports may be either positive or negative. When we sell more to foreigners than we buy from them, net exports are positive. In recent years, however, net exports have been negative, indicating we were buying more goods and services from foreigners than we were selling to them. In 2008, net exports were *minus* $669 billion.

Deriving GDP by the Resource Cost–Income Approach

The right side of Exhibit 3 illustrates how, rather than summing the flow of expenditures on final goods and services, we could reach GDP by summing the flow of costs incurred and income generated. Labor services play a very important role in the production process. It is therefore not surprising that employee compensation, $8,055 billion in 2008, provides the largest source of income generated by the production of goods and services.

Self-employed proprietors undertake the risks of owning their own business and simultaneously provide their own labor services to their firm. Their earnings in 2008 contributed $1,072 billion to GDP, 7.5 percent of the total. Together, employees and self-employed proprietors accounted for approximately two-thirds of GDP.

Machines, buildings, land, and other physical assets also contribute to the production process. Rents, corporate profits, and interest are payments to people who provide either the physical resources or the financial resources required for the purchase of physical assets. Rents are returns to resource owners who permit others to use their assets during a time period. Corporate profits are earned by stockholders, who bear the risk of the business undertaking and provide the financial capital the firm needs to purchase resources. Interest is a payment to parties who extend loans to producers.

Not all cost components of GDP result in an income payment to a resource supplier. In order to get to GDP, we also need to account for three other factors: indirect business taxes, the cost of depreciation, and the net income of foreigners.

INDIRECT BUSINESS TAXES. Taxes imposed on the sale of a good that increase the cost of the good to consumers are called **indirect business taxes**. The sales tax is a clear example. When you make a $1.00 purchase in a state with a 5 percent sales tax, the purchase actually costs you $1.05. The $1.00 goes to the seller to pay wages, rent, interest, and managerial costs. The 5 cents goes to the government. Indirect business taxes boost the market price of goods when GDP is calculated by the expenditure approach. Similarly, when looked at from the factor-cost viewpoint, taxes are an indirect cost of supplying the goods to the final consumers.

DEPRECIATION. As machines are used to produce goods, they wear out and become less valuable. Even though this decline in the value of capital assets is a cost of producing goods during the current period, it does not involve a direct payment to a resource owner. Thus, it must be estimated. Depreciation is an estimate, based on the expected life of the asset, of the decline in the asset's value during the year. In 2008, depreciation (sometimes called *capital consumption allowance*) of private- and public-sector capital amounted to $1,968 billion, approximately 13.8 percent of GDP.

NET INCOME OF FOREIGNERS. The sum of employee compensation, proprietors' income, rents, corporate profits, and interest yields **national income**, the income of Americans, whether earned domestically or abroad. If depreciation and indirect business

Indirect business taxes

Taxes that increase a business firm's costs of production and, therefore, the prices charged to consumers. Examples are sales, excise, and property taxes.

National income

The total income earned by a country's nationals (citizens) during a period. It is the sum of employee compensation, self-employment income, rents, interest, and corporate profits.

Gross national product (GNP)

The total market value of all final goods and services produced by the citizens of a country. It is equal to GDP minus the net income of foreigners.

Net income of foreigners

The income that foreigners earn by contributing labor and capital resources to the production of goods within the borders of a country minus the income the nationals of the country earn abroad.

taxes—the two indirect cost components—are added to national income, the result will be **gross national product (GNP)**, the output of Americans, whether generated in the United States or abroad. Put another way, GNP counts the income that Americans earn abroad, but it omits the income foreigners earn in the United States.

Because GDP is a measure of domestic output, the net income earned by foreigners must be added when GDP is derived using the resource cost-income approach. The **net income of foreigners** is equal to the income foreigners earn in the United States minus the income that Americans earn abroad. If Americans earn more abroad than foreigners earn in the United States, the net income of foreigners will be negative. In recent years, this has been the case. The net income of foreigners is generally small. In 2008, it was *minus* $133 billion, about 1 percent of GDP. As Exhibit 3 indicates, when this figure is added to the other components, the sum is equal to GDP.

The Relative Size of GDP Components

EXHIBIT 4 shows the relative size of each of the GDP components during 2005–2008. When the expenditure approach is used, personal consumption is by far the largest component of GDP. Consumption accounted for 70 percent of GDP during 2005–2008, compared with only 16 and 19 percent for private investment and government purchases, respectively. When GDP is measured using the resource cost–income approach, compensation to employees is the dominant component (57 percent of GDP). During 2005–2008, corporate profits and interest combined accounted for 17 percent of GDP.

EXHIBIT 4
The Major Components of GDP in the United States, 2005–2008

The relative sizes of the major components of GDP usually fluctuate within a fairly narrow range. The average proportion of each component during 2005–2008 is demonstrated here for both (a) the expenditure and (b) the resource cost–income approaches.

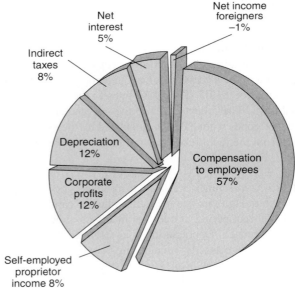

(a) Expenditure approach

(b) Resource cost–income approach[a]

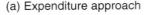

[a]Rental income was negligible.
Source: http://www.economagic.com.

Adjusting for Price Changes and Deriving Real GDP

GDP was developed to help us better assess what is happening to output (and income) over time. This is important because expansion in the production of goods and services people value is the source of higher incomes and living standards. When comparing GDP across time periods, however, we confront a problem; the nominal value of GDP may increase as the result of either (1) an expansion in the quantity of goods produced or (2) higher prices. Because only the former will improve our living standards, it is very important to distinguish between the two.

When tracking the path of GDP and other income measures across time periods, economists use price indexes to adjust **nominal values** (or *money values*, as they are often called) for the effects of inflation—an increase in the general level of prices over time. When the term **real** accompanies GDP and income data (for example, *real GDP* or *real wages*), this means that the data have been adjusted for changes in the general level of prices through time. When comparing data at different points in time, it is nearly always the real changes that are of most interest.

What precisely is a price index, and how can it be used to adjust GDP and other figures for the effects of inflation? A price index measures the cost of purchasing a market basket (or "bundle") of goods at a point in time relative to the cost of purchasing the identical market basket during an earlier reference period. A base year (or period) is chosen and assigned a value of 100. As prices increase and the cost of purchasing the reference bundle of goods rises relative to the base year, the price index increases proportionally. Thus, a price index of 110 indicates that the general level of prices is 10 percent higher than during the base period. An index of 120 implies 20 percent higher prices than the base period, and so on. *Note*: See the Addendum at the end of this chapter for additional details on how price indexes are constructed.

Two Key Price Indexes: The Consumer Price Index and the GDP Deflator

Price indexes indicate what is happening to the general level of prices. The two most widely used are the consumer price index (CPI) and the GDP deflator. Because the construction of the CPI is simpler, we will begin with it.

*The **consumer price index (CPI)** is designed to measure the impact of price changes on the cost of the typical bundle of goods purchased by households.* A bundle of 211 items that constitute the "typical bundle" purchased by urban consumers during the 1982–1984 base period provides the foundation for the CPI. The quantity of each good reflects the quantity actually purchased by the typical household during the base period. Every month, the Bureau of Labor Statistics surveys approximately 26,400 stores representative of the urban United States to derive the average price for each of the food items, consumer goods and services, housing, and property taxes included in the index. The cost of purchasing this 211-item market basket at current prices is then compared with the cost of purchasing the same market basket at base-year prices. The result is a measure of current prices compared with 1982–1984 base-period prices. In 2008, the value of the CPI was 215.3, compared with 100 during the 1982–1984 base period. This indicates that the price level in 2008 was 115.3 percent higher than the price level of 1982–1984.

*The **GDP deflator** is a broader price index than the CPI. It is designed to measure the change in the average price of the market basket of goods included in GDP.* In addition to consumer goods, the GDP deflator includes prices for capital goods and other goods and services purchased by businesses and governments. Therefore, in addition to consumer goods, the bundle used to construct the GDP deflator will include such items as large computers, airplanes, welding equipment, and office space. The overall bundle is intended to be representative of those items included in GDP.

Nominal values

Values expressed in current dollars.

Real values

Values that have been adjusted for the effects of inflation.

Consumer price index (CPI)

An indicator of the general level of prices. It attempts to compare the cost of purchasing the market basket bought by a typical consumer during a specific period with the cost of purchasing the same market basket during an earlier period.

GDP deflator

A price index that reveals the cost during the current period of purchasing the items included in GDP relative to the cost during a base year (currently 2000). Unlike the consumer price index (CPI), the GDP deflator also measures the prices of capital goods and other goods and services purchased by businesses and governments. Because of this, it is thought to be a more accurate measure of changes in the general level of prices than the CPI.

The cost of purchasing the typical bundle of goods included in this year's GDP is always compared with the cost of purchasing that same bundle at last year's prices. Each year's percentage change in prices, based on the updated bundle, is then used to chain together the index. Because of this constant updating of the typical bundle, the impact of price increases is reduced when purchasers substitute away from goods that have risen in price. As a result, the GDP deflator is thought to yield a slightly more accurate measure of changes in the general level of prices than the CPI. As in the case of the CPI, a base year (currently it is the year 2000) is chosen for the GDP deflator and assigned a value of 100. Values of the GDP deflator above 100 indicate that the general level of prices is higher than during the base period.

The annual inflation rate is simply the percentage change from one year to the next in the general level of prices. Both the CPI and the GDP deflator can be used to estimate the rate of **inflation**. When using either price index (PI):

Inflation

An increase in the general level of prices of goods and services. The purchasing power of the monetary unit, such as the dollar, declines when inflation is present.

$$\text{Inflation rate} = \frac{\text{This year's PI} - \text{Last year's PI}}{\text{Last year's PI}} \times 100$$

If the price index this year was 220, compared with 200 last year, for example, the inflation rate would equal 10 percent:

$$\frac{220 - 200}{200} \times 100 = 10$$

EXHIBIT 5 presents data during 1983–2008 for both the CPI and GDP deflator and uses each to estimate the annual rate of inflation. Even though the two price indexes are based on different market baskets and procedures, their estimates for the annual rate of inflation

EXHIBIT 5 The Consumer Price Index and GDP Deflator: 1983–2008	YEAR	CPI (1982–84 = 100)	INFLATION RATE (%)	GDP DEFLATOR (2000 = 100)	INFLATION RATE (%)
	1983	99.6	3.2	65.2	4.0
	1984	103.9	4.3	67.7	3.8
	1985	107.6	3.6	69.7	3.0
	1986	109.6	1.9	71.3	2.2
	1987	113.6	3.6	73.2	2.7
	1988	118.3	4.1	75.7	3.4
	1989	124.0	4.8	78.6	3.8
	1990	130.7	5.4	81.6	3.9
	1991	136.2	4.2	84.4	3.5
	1992	140.3	3.0	86.4	2.3
	1993	144.5	3.0	88.4	2.3
	1994	148.2	2.6	90.3	2.1
	1995	152.4	2.8	92.1	2.0
	1996	156.9	3.0	93.9	1.9
	1997	160.5	2.3	95.4	1.7
	1998	163.0	1.5	96.5	1.1
	1999	166.6	2.2	97.9	1.4
	2000	172.2	3.4	100.0	2.2
	2001	177.1	2.8	102.4	2.4
	2002	179.9	1.6	104.2	1.7
	2003	184.0	2.3	106.4	2.1
	2004	188.9	2.7	109.5	2.9
	2005	195.3	3.4	113.0	3.3
	2006	201.6	3.2	116.7	3.2
	2007	207.3	2.8	119.8	2.7
	2008	215.3	3.8	122.4	2.2

Source: http://www.economagic.com.

are similar. The difference between the two alternative measures is usually only a few tenths of a percentage point.

The CPI and GDP deflator were designed for different purposes. Choosing between the two depends on what we are trying to measure. If we want to determine how rising prices affect the money income of consumers, the CPI would be most appropriate because it includes only consumer goods. However, if we want an economy-wide measure of inflation with which to adjust GDP data, the GDP deflator is clearly the appropriate index because it includes a broader set of goods and services.

Using the GDP Deflator to Derive Real GDP

We can use the GDP deflator together with **nominal GDP** to measure **real GDP**, which is GDP in dollars of constant purchasing power. If prices are rising, we simply deflate the nominal GDP during the latter period to account for the effects of inflation.

EXHIBIT 6 illustrates how real GDP is measured and why it is important to adjust for price changes. Between 2000 and 2008, the nominal GDP of the United States increased from $9,817 billion to $14,265 billion, an increase of 45.3 percent. However, a large portion of this increase in nominal GDP reflected inflation rather than an increase in real output. When making GDP comparisons across time periods, we generally do so in terms of the purchasing power of the dollar during the base year of the GDP deflator, currently 2000. The GDP deflator, the price index that measures changes in the cost of all goods included in GDP, increased from 100.0 in 2000 to 122.4 in 2008. This indicates that prices rose by 22.4 percent between 2000 and 2008. To determine the real GDP for 2008 in terms of 2000 dollars, we deflate the 2008 nominal GDP for the rise in prices:

Nominal GDP

GDP expressed at current prices. It is often called money GDP.

Real GDP

GDP adjusted for changes in the price level.

$$\text{Real GDP}_{2008} = \text{Nominal GDP}_{2008} \times \frac{\text{GDP deflator}_{2000}}{\text{GDP deflator}_{2008}}$$

EXHIBIT 6
Changes in Prices and Real GDP in the United States, 2000–2008

Between 2000 and 2008, nominal GDP increased by 45.3 percent. But when the 2008 GDP is deflated to account for price increases, we see that real GDP increased by only 18.7 percent.

	NOMINAL GDP (BILLIONS OF DOLLARS)	PRICE INDEX (GDP DEFLATOR, 2000 = 100)	REAL GDP (BILLIONS OF 2000 DOLLARS)
2000	$9,817	100.0	$9,817
2008	14,265	122.4	11,654
Percentage Increase	45.3	22.4	18.7

Source: http://www.economagic.com.

APPLICATIONS IN ECONOMICS

Converting Prior Data to Current Dollars: The Case of Gasoline

We have explained how the GDP deflator can be used to convert nominal GDP data to real GDP (measured in terms of the dollar's purchasing power during the base year of the GDP deflator). Sometimes, however, it makes more sense to convert income or other data during prior years to the purchasing power of the dollar during the current year. A price index can also be used to accomplish this task. To convert an earlier observation to current dollars, just multiply the observation by the price index during the current period and then divide it by the price index during the earlier period. If prices have risen in recent years, this will "inflate" the data for the earlier year and thereby bring it into line with the current purchasing power of the dollar.

Let's illustrate this point and at the same time analyze the changes in gasoline prices during the last several decades. As gas prices rose sharply during 2007, the media reported that they had risen to an all-time high in the United States. In nominal terms, this was indeed the case, but what about the real price of gasoline?

The accompanying table presents data for the nominal price (column 1) of a gallon of unleaded regular gasoline for various years since 1973. The parallel data for the consumer price index (CPI) are presented in column 2. The nominal price of gasoline in 1973 was 39 cents. To convert this figure to the purchasing power of the dollar in April 2009, multiply the 39 cents by the ratio of the CPI in April 2009 divided by the CPI in 1973. This

real price (shown in column 3), measured in terms of the 2009 price level, is equal to $1.87 (0.39 times the ratio of 212.7/44.4).

Both crude oil prices and gasoline prices rose sharply throughout the 1970s. By 1980, the nominal price of gasoline had risen to $1.25. This would make the real price of gasoline measured in 2009 dollars equal to $3.23 ($1.25 times the ratio of 212.7/82.4), even higher than the price in 2009. What was the real price of gasoline in 1976, 1985, 1990, 1995, and 2005? As an exercise, derive these figures to make sure that you understand how to convert data from an earlier time period into the purchasing power of the dollar during the current year.

Price of a Gallon of Regular Unleaded Gasoline

Year	Nominal Price (1)	CPI (1982–84 = 100) (2)	Real Price (3)
1973	$0.39	44.4	$1.87
1976	0.61	56.9	?
1980	1.25	82.4	3.23
1985	1.20	107.6	?
1990	1.16	130.7	?
1995	1.15	152.4	?
2000	1.51	172.2	1.87
2005	2.30	195.3	?
2009 (April)	2.31	212.7	2.31

Source: U.S. Energy Information Administration, *Monthly Energy Review.* The data for regular unleaded gasoline were unavailable prior to 1976. Thus, the 1973 observation is for regular leaded gasoline, which was slightly cheaper during that period.

Because prices were rising, the latter ratio is less than 1. Measured in terms of 2000 dollars, the real GDP in 2008 was $11,654 billion, only 18.7 percent more than in 2000. So although money GDP (nominal GDP) expanded by 45.3 percent, real GDP increased by only 18.7 percent.

Data on both money GDP and price changes are essential for meaningful output comparisons between two time periods. By itself, a change in money GDP tells us nothing about what is happening to the rate of real production. For example, not even a doubling of money GDP would lead to an increase in real output if prices more than doubled during the time period. On the other hand, money income could remain constant while real GDP increased if there were a reduction in prices. Knowledge of both nominal GDP and the general level of prices is required for real income comparisons over time.

Problems with GDP as a Measuring Rod

Even real GDP is an imperfect measure of current output and income. Some productive activities are omitted because their value is difficult to determine. The introduction of new products complicates the use of GDP as a measuring rod. Also, when production involves harmful side effects that are not fully registered in the market prices, GDP will fail to measure the level of output accurately. Let's take a closer look at some of the limitations of GDP.

Nonmarket Production

GDP does not count household production because it does not involve a market transaction. As a result, the household services of millions of people are excluded. If you mow the yard, repair your car, paint your house, pick up relatives from school, or perform similar productive household activities, your efforts add nothing to GDP because no market transaction is involved. Such nonmarket productive activities are sizable—10 percent to 15 percent of total GDP.

Excluding household production results in some oddities in national-income accounting. Suppose, for example, that a woman marries her gardener, and, after the marriage, the spouse-gardener works for love rather than for money. GDP will decline because the services of the spouse-gardener no longer involve a market transaction and therefore no longer contribute to GDP. In contrast, if a family member decides to enter the labor force and hires someone to perform services previously provided by household members, there will be a double-barreled impact on GDP. It will rise as a result of (1) the market earnings of the new labor-force entrant plus (2) the amount paid to the person hired to perform the services that were previously supplied within the household.

Most important, omitting household production makes income comparisons across lengthy time periods less meaningful. Compared with the situation today, fifty years ago Americans were far more likely to produce sizable amounts of their own food and clothing. Only a small proportion of married women worked, and child care services were almost exclusively provided within the household. Today, people are also more likely to eat out at a restaurant than prepare their own food; hire a lawn service than mow their own lawn; and purchase an automatic dishwasher than do the dishes by hand. These and many other similar changes involve the substitution of a market transaction, which adds to GDP. Because the share of total production provided within the household has declined relative to production that involves market transactions, current GDP, even in real dollars, is overstated relative to the earlier period. Correspondingly, this factor causes an upward bias to the growth rate of real GDP.

Underground Economy

Some people attempt to conceal various economic activities in order to evade taxes or because the activities themselves are illegal. Economists call these activities, which are unreported and therefore difficult to measure, the **underground economy**.

Because cash transactions are hard for government authorities to trace, they are the lifeblood of the underground economy. This is why drug trafficking, smuggling, prostitution, and other illegal activities are generally conducted in cash. Not all underground economic activity is illegal. A large portion of the underground economy involves legal goods and services that go unreported so that people can try to evade taxes. The participants in this legal-if-reported portion of the underground economy are quite diverse. Taxicab drivers and wait staff may pocket fees and tips. Small-business owners may fail to ring up and report various cash sales. Craft and professional workers may fail to report cash income. Employees ranging from laborers to bartenders may work "off the books" and accept payment in cash in order to qualify for income-transfer benefits or evade taxes (or allow their employers to evade taxes).

Even though they are often productive, these unreported underground activities are not included in GDP. Estimates of the size of the underground economy in the United States range from 10 percent to 15 percent of total output. The available evidence indicates that the size of the underground economy is even larger in Western Europe (where tax rates are higher) and South America (where regulations often make it more costly to operate a business legally).

Underground economy

Unreported barter and cash transactions that take place outside recorded market channels. Some are otherwise legal activities undertaken to evade taxes. Others involve illegal activities, such as trafficking drugs and prostitution.

Leisure and Human Costs

GDP excludes leisure and the human cost associated with the production of goods and services. Only output matters; no allowance is made for how long or how hard people work to generate it. Simon Kuznets, the "inventor" of GDP, believed that these omissions substantially reduced the accuracy of GDP as a measure of economic well-being.

The average number of hours worked per week in the United States has declined through the years. The average nonagricultural production worker spent only 33.3 hours per week on the job in 2008, compared with more than 40 hours in 1947—a 15 percent reduction in weekly hours worked. Clearly, this reduction in the length of the workweek raised the American standard of living, even though it did not enhance GDP.

GDP also fails to take into account human costs. On average, jobs today are less physically strenuous and are generally performed in a safer, more comfortable environment than they were a generation ago.[3] To the extent that working conditions have improved through the years, GDP figures understate the growth of real income.

Quality Variation and the Introduction of New Goods

If GDP is going to measure accurately changes in real output, changes in the price level must be measured accurately. This is a difficult task in a dynamic world where new and improved products are constantly replacing old ones. Think about how much more functional today's computers are compared with yesterday's typewriters, for example. Even after adjusting for inflation, today's personal computer probably costs more than the typewriter of 1980. But there is also a huge difference between the quality of the two products. Thus, a portion of the higher price of improved products like computers is due to quality improvements rather than pure inflation. Although statisticians attempt to make some allowance for quality improvements and new products, they are generally thought to be inadequate. Most economists believe that price indexes, including the GDP deflator, overestimate the rate of inflation by approximately 1 percent *annually* because quality improvements aren't accounted for accurately. If so, annual changes in output are underestimated by a similar amount. Although 1 percent per year might seem small, errors of this size make a huge difference over long time periods.

Harmful Side Effects and Economic "Bads"

GDP makes no adjustment for harmful side effects that sometimes arise from production, consumption, and the destructive acts of man and nature. If they do not involve market transactions, economic "bads" are ignored in the calculation of GDP. Yet, in a modern industrial economy, production and consumption sometimes generate side effects that either detract from current consumption or reduce our future production possibilities. When property rights are defined imperfectly, air and water pollution are sometimes side effects of economic activity. For example, an industrial plant may pollute the air or water while producing goods. Automobiles may put harmful chemicals into the atmosphere while providing us with transportation. GDP makes no allowance for these negative side effects. In fact, expenditures on the cleanup of air and water pollution, should they be undertaken, will add to GDP.

Similarly, GDP makes no allowance for various acts of destruction. Consider the impact of the September 11, 2001, terrorist attacks. In addition to roughly 3,000 fatalities, property losses were estimated at approximately $20 billion, including the destruction of the World Trade Center, portions of the Pentagon, and the four commercial planes hijacked. But GDP makes no allowance for these losses. Therefore, none of this destruction influenced GDP. In fact, the cleanup cost, which continued for months, actually added

---

[3]For evidence on this point, see "Have a Nice Day," *2001 Annual Report, Federal Reserve Bank of Dallas* (available online at http://www.dallasfed.org).

to GDP. Of course, GDP was indirectly adversely affected by the attacks: some people and businesses weren't able to function for some time afterward, if ever. Air travel and tourism spending fell. Other responses to the attacks, like the increase in expenditures on security, national defense, and the reconstruction of the Pentagon, enhanced GDP. But the GDP numbers did not reflect the loss of property or life. The same is true for destruction accompanying hurricanes, earthquakes, and other acts of nature. Even if billions of dollars of assets are destroyed, there will be no adjustment made to the GDP numbers.

Differences in GDP over Time

Per capita GDP is simply GDP divided by population. It is a measure of income per person or the average level of income. As real per capita GDP increases, so too does the average level of real income. **EXHIBIT 7** presents the data for per capita real GDP (measured in 2000 dollars) for the United States for various years since 1930. In 2008, per capita GDP was more than twice the figure of 1970 and six times the figure for 1930. What do these figures reveal? As we previously discussed, some of the measurement deficiencies of GDP will result in an overstatement of current real GDP relative to earlier periods. For example, current per capita GDP is biased upward because, compared with earlier periods, more output now takes place in the market sector and less in the household sector. Other biases, however, are in the opposite direction. Reductions in both time and strenuousness of work as well as the introduction of improved products and new technologies provide examples of the latter. On balance, the direction of the overall bias is uncertain.

However, one thing is clear: GDP comparisons are less meaningful when there is a dramatic difference in the bundle of goods available. This is generally the case when comparisons are made across distant time periods. Consider the 1930s, compared with today. In the 1930s, there were no jet planes, television programs, automatic dishwashers,

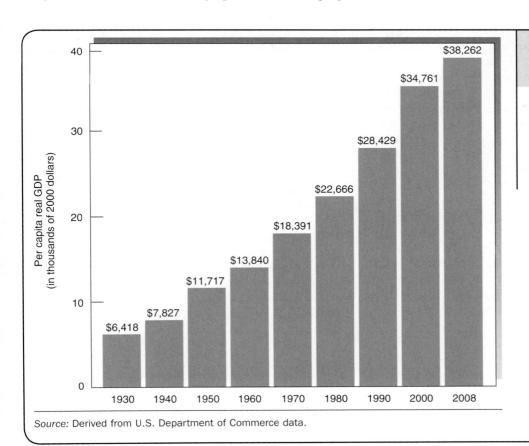

EXHIBIT 7
Per Capita GDP: 1930–2008

In 2008, per capita real GDP was 2.8 times the 1960 level, 4.9 times the 1940 level, and 6.0 times the 1930 level. What do these numbers reveal about income today relative to the earlier years?

Source: Derived from U.S. Department of Commerce data.

personal computers, or MP3 players. In 1930, even a millionaire could not have purchased the typical bundle consumed by the average American in 2006.[4] When the potential goods available differ substantially between time periods (or countries), comparative GDP statistics lose some of their precision.

Shortcomings aside, however, there is evidence that GDP per person is a broad indicator of general living standards. As per capita GDP in the United States has increased over time, the quality of most goods has increased while the amount of work time required for their purchase has declined. In many cases, the changes have been dramatic. (See the boxed feature, "The Time Cost of Goods: Today and Yesterday.") Like per capita GDP, these data indicate that our income levels and living standards have improved. Various quality-of-life variables paint a similar picture. For example, as per capita GDP has risen in the United States and other countries, life expectancy and leisure time have gone up, while illiteracy and infant mortality rates have gone down. This suggests that increases in per capita GDP and improvements in living standards are closely related.

APPLICATIONS IN ECONOMICS

The Time Cost of Goods: Today and Yesterday

Many of you have heard stories from your parents or grandparents about how low prices were when they were young. A bottle of soda cost only a nickel, and a brand-new car was less than $2,000. In this chapter, you have learned that there is a difference between nominal and real values. Economists generally use the CPI or GDP deflator to adjust the nominal prices of earlier periods and figure out if a good is now cheaper or more expensive. There is, however, an alternative way of looking at this issue: you could estimate how long a person working at the average wage rate would have to work in order to earn enough to purchase various items at different points in time. For example, just after telling you that a soda used to cost a nickel, your grandfather might have noted that he used to earn only 25 cents per hour. Thus, for an hour's worth of work, he could earn enough money to purchase five bottles of soda. Today, the price of a soda is approximately $1. To earn the same real wage as your grandfather, you would need to earn only $5 per hour (exactly enough to purchase five sodas with your hour's wage).

Over time, the productivity of the average worker in America has increased substantially. This increased worker productivity is the key to higher real incomes and improved living standards. When people are able to produce more per hour of work, they will be able to achieve a higher living standard.

Using average wage rates, W. Michael Cox and Richard Alm of the Federal Reserve Bank of Dallas have computed the time of work required for the typical worker to purchase many common items. Their analysis shows that Americans today are able to acquire most goods with much less work time than was previously the case. Some examples are shown in the accompanying table.

In 1908, a new automobile cost $850, which took the average worker 4,696 hours to earn. In 1955, a new automobile costing $3,030 took 1,638 hours of work, and by 1997, a $17,995 new automobile cost a typical worker only 1,365 hours of work. The time cost of a new car today is less than 30 percent of the time cost in 1908. Furthermore, even today's most economical model is light–years away from the 1908 version with regard to power, performance, and dependability.

The prices of technology products, such as computers, calculators, and cellular phones, in particular, have fallen dramatically in recent years. Cellular phones and computers now cost only a small fraction of the time required for their purchase just a few years ago. In 1984, it took the average worker more than 10 weeks of work to purchase a cellular phone; by 1997, the work time cost had fallen to 9 hours, and the figure is still lower today. In 1901, spending on food, clothing, and shelter consumed 76 percent of the typical worker's paycheck. Because of greater productivity and higher real earnings, today the average worker spends only 38 percent of earnings on these items.

---

[4]The following quotation from the late Mancur Olson, longtime professor of economics at the University of Maryland, illustrates this point:

> The price level has risen about eight times since 1932, so a $25,000 income then would be the "equivalent" of an income of $200,000 today—one could readily afford a Rolls-Royce, the best seats in the theater, and the care of the best physicians in the country. But the 1932 Rolls-Royce, for all its many virtues, does not embody some desirable technologies available today in the humblest Ford. Nor would the imposing dollar of 1932 buy a TV set or a home videocassette recorder. And if one got an infection, the best physicians in 1932 would not be able to prescribe an antibiotic.

APPLICATIONS IN ECONOMICS

As worker productivity grows, real incomes increase, and the time cost required to purchase products falls. This process generates higher living standards and brings goods that used to be luxuries, costing weeks' or months' worth of a worker's salary, within the reach of most Americans. The next time you call home, remind your parents that in 1915, a 3-minute, coast-to-coast, long distance telephone call cost more than 2 weeks' worth of wages. Today, it costs only 1.8 minutes of work. Your parents will be happy to hear that, particularly if you are calling collect.

The Cost of Products to an Average-Wage Worker in Minutes or Hours of Work

Item	Old Cost	Cost in 1997
Eggs (1 dozen)	80 minutes in 1919	5 minutes
Sugar (5 lbs.)	72 minutes in 1919	10 minutes
Coffee (1 lb.)	55 minutes in 1919	17 minutes
Bread (1 lb.)	13 minutes in 1919	4 minutes
Mattress and box spring (twin)	161 hours in 1929	24 hours
Refrigerator	3,162 hours in 1916	68 hours
Clothes washer and dryer	256 hours in 1956	52 hours
Automobile	4,696 hours in 1908	1,365 hours
Coast-to-coast air flight	366 hours in 1930	16 hours
Big Mac	27 minutes in 1940	9 minutes
Long-distance call (3 min.)	90 hours in 1915	1.8 minutes
Calculator	31 hours in 1972	46 minutes
Microwave oven	97 hours in 1975	15 hours
Cellular phone	456 hours in 1984	9 hours
Personal computer	435 hours in 1984	76 hours

Source: W. Michael Cox and Richard Alm, "Time Well Spent: The Declining Real Cost of Living in America," *1997 Annual Report, Federal Reserve Bank of Dallas:* 2–24. Also see Michael Cox, *Myths of Rich and Poor* (New York: Basic Books, 1999).

Is an automobile really more expensive now than it was in 1955? You might be surprised to learn that in 1955 it took a typical worker 1,638 hours of work time to purchase a car. Today, a vastly improved model can be purchased after only 1,365 hours of work.

The Great Contribution of GDP

Although GDP is a broad indicator of income levels and living standards, this is not its major purpose. ***GDP was designed to measure the value of the goods and services produced during a time period. In spite of its limitations, real GDP is a reasonably precise measure of the rate of output and the year-to-year changes in that output.***

Adjusted for changes in prices, annual and quarterly GDP data provide the information required to track the economy's performance level. These data allow us to compare the current rate of output with that of the recent past. Without this information, policy makers would be less likely to adopt productive policies, and business decision makers would be less able to determine the future direction of the demand for their products.

Looking ahead

GDP provides us with a measure of economic performance. In the next chapter, we will take a closer look at the path of real GDP in the United States and introduce other indicators of economic performance. Later, we will investigate the factors that underlie both the level of and fluctuations in real GDP.

KEY POINTS

▼ Gross domestic product (GDP) is a measure of the market value of final goods and services produced within the borders of a country during a specific time period, usually a year.

▼ Income transfers, purely financial transactions, and exchanges of goods and assets produced during earlier periods are not included in GDP because they do not involve current production.

▼ When derived by the expenditure approach, GDP has four major components: (1) personal consumption, (2) gross private investment, (3) government consumption and gross investment, and (4) net exports.

▼ When derived by the resource cost–income approach, GDP equals (1) the direct income components (wages and salaries, self-employment income, rents, interest, and corporate profits), plus (2) indirect business taxes, depreciation, and the net income of foreigners.

▼ Price indexes measure changes in the general level of prices over time. They can be used to adjust nominal values for the effects of inflation. The two most widely used price indexes are the GDP deflator and the consumer price index (CPI).

▼ The following formula can be used to convert the nominal GDP data of the current period (2) to real GDP measured in terms of the general level of prices of an earlier period (1):

$$\text{Real GDP}_2 = \text{Nominal GDP}_2 \times \frac{\text{GDP deflator}_1}{\text{GDP deflator}_2}$$

▼ Even real GDP is an imperfect measure of current production. It excludes household production and the underground economy, fails to take leisure and human costs into account, and adjusts imperfectly for quality changes.

▼ Real GDP is vitally important because it is a reasonably accurate measure of how well the economy is doing. Per capita GDP is a broad indicator of income levels and living standards across time periods.

CRITICAL ANALYSIS QUESTIONS

*1. Indicate how each of the following activities will affect this year's GDP:
   a. the sale of a used economics textbook to the college bookstore
   b. Smith's $500 doctor bill for setting her son's broken arm
   c. family lawn services provided by Smith's 16-year-old child
   d. lawn services purchased by Smith from the neighbor's 16-year-old child who has a lawn-mowing business
   e. a $5,250 purchase of 100 shares of stock at $50 per share plus the sales commission of $250
   f. a multibillion-dollar discovery of natural gas in Oklahoma
   g. a hurricane that causes $10 billion of damage in Florida
   h. $60,000 of income earned by an American college professor teaching in England

2. If nominal GDP increased by 6 percent during a year, while the GDP deflator increased by 4 percent, by how much did real GDP change during the year?

*3. A large furniture retailer sells $100,000 of household furnishings from inventories built up last year. How does this sale influence GDP? How are the components of GDP affected?

4. Suppose a group of British investors finances the construction of a plant to manufacture skateboards in St. Louis, Missouri. How will the construction of the plant affect GDP? Suppose the plant generates $100,000 in corporate profits this year. Will these profits contribute to GDP? Why or why not?

*5. Why might even real GDP be a misleading index of changes in output between 1950 and 2008 in the United States?

6. What are price indexes designed to measure? Outline how they are constructed. When GDP and other income figures are compared across time periods, explain why it is important to adjust for changes in the general level of prices.

*7. In 1982, the average hourly earnings of private nonagricultural production workers were $7.87 per hour. By 2008, the average hourly earnings had risen to $18.08. In 2008, the CPI was 215.3, compared with 96.5 in 1982. What were the real earnings of private nonagricultural production workers in 2008 measured in 1982 dollars?

8. The receipts and year of release of the four movies with the largest nominal box office revenues, along with the CPI data of each year are presented below. Assuming that the receipts for each of the movies were derived during their year of release, convert the receipts for each to real dollars for the year 2008 (2008 CPI 215.3). Which movie had the largest real box office receipts?

Movies	Box Office Receipts (millions)	Year Released	CPI in Year Released
Titanic	$600.8	1997	160.5
Star Wars	461.0	1977	60.6
Shrek 2	437.2	2004	188.9
E. T.: The Extra-Terrestrial	399.9	1982	96.5

*9. How much do each of the following contribute to GDP?
   a. Jones pays a repair shop $1,000 to rebuild the engine of her automobile.
   b. Jones spends $200 on parts and pays a mechanic $400 to rebuild the engine of her automobile.
   c. Jones spends $200 on parts and rebuilds the engine of her automobile herself.
   d. Jones sells her four-year-old automobile for $5,000 and buys Smith's two-year-old model for $10,000.
   e. Jones sells her four-year-old automobile for $5,000 and buys a new car for $20,000.

10. What is the difference between the consumer price index (CPI) and the GDP deflator? Which would be better to use if you want to measure whether your hourly earnings this year were higher than they were last year? Why?

*11. Indicate whether the following statements are true or false:
   a. "For the economy as a whole, inventory investment can never be negative."
   b. "The net investment of an economy must always be positive."
   c. "An increase in GDP indicates that the standard of living of people has risen."

*12. How do the receipts and expenditures of a state-operated lottery affect GDP?

13. GDP does not count productive services, such as child care, food preparation, cleaning, and laundry, provided within the household. Why are these things excluded? Is GDP a sexist measure? Does it understate the productive contributions of women relative to men? Discuss.

*14. Indicate how each of the following will affect this year's GDP:
   a. You suffer $10,000 of damage when you wreck your automobile.
   b. You win $10,000 in a state lottery.
   c. You spend $5,100 in January for 100 shares of stock ($5,000 for the stock and $100 for the sales commission) and sell the stock in August for $8,200 ($8,000 for the stock and $200 for the sales commission).
   d. You pay $500 for this month's rental of your apartment.
   e. You are paid $300 for computer services provided to a client.
   f. You receive $300 from your parents.
   g. You get a raise from $8 to $10 per hour and simultaneously decide to reduce your hours worked from 20 to 16 per week.
   h. You earn $4,000 working in Spain as an English instructor.

15. The accompanying chart presents 2008 data from the national-income accounts of the United States.

Component	Billions of Dollars
Personal consumption	$10,057.9
Employee compensation	8,055.1
Rents	64.4
Gov't consumption & investment	2,882.4
Imports	2,528.6
Depreciation	1,968.1
Corporate profits	1,476.5
Interest income	682.7
Exports	1,859.4
Gross private investment	1,993.5
Indirect business taxes	1,078.6
Self-employment income	1,072.4
Net income of foreigners	−133.2

   a. Indicate the various components of GDP when it is derived by the expenditure approach. Calculate GDP using the expenditure approach.
   b. Indicate the various components of GDP when it is derived by the resource cost–income approach. Calculate GDP using the resource cost–income approach.

*16. Fill in the blanks in the following table:

Year	Nominal GDP (in billions)	GDP Deflator (2000 = 100)	Real GDP (Billions of 2000 dollars)
1960	$526.4	21.0	a. _____
1970	$1,038.5	27.5	b. _____
1980	$2,789.5	c. _____	$5,165.7
1990	d. _____	81.6	$7,112.5
1995	$7,397.7	e. _____	$8,032.2
2000	$9,817.0	100.0	f. _____
2008	$14,265	122.4	g. _____

*Asterisk denotes questions for which answers are given in Appendix B.

A D D E N D U M

The Construction of a Price Index

Price indexes are designed to measure the magnitude of changes in the general level of prices through time. The price index during the current year (PI_2) is

$$PI_2 = \frac{\text{Cost of purchasing the typical bundle this year}}{\text{Cost of purchasing the same bundle during the base year}} \times 100$$

The typical (representative) bundle might be the bundle actually chosen during the earlier base year. Alternatively, it could be the bundle chosen this year. *In either case, the quantities of the various goods do not change from year to year; only the prices change.*

Let's suppose that the bundle used to calculate the index was the quantity of each good actually chosen during the base year. This is how the consumer price index is calculated. In this case, the cost of purchasing the base-year bundle this year would be the sum of the price of each good this year (P_2) multiplied by the quantity consumed during the base year (Q_1). The cost of purchasing the *same bundle* during the base year would be the sum of the price of each good during the base year (P_1) multiplied by the quantity of each good chosen during the base year (Q_1). Therefore, the mathematical formula for the price index during the current year (PI_2) could be written:

$$PI_2 \times \frac{\sum P_2 Q_1}{\sum P_1 Q_1} \times 100$$

If prices on average are higher during the current period than they were during the base year, then this expression will be greater than 100. This indicates that it is now more costly to purchase the representative bundle than it was during the base year. Correspondingly, if the general level of prices is currently lower today than during the base period, then PI_2 would be less than 100. Thus, the current price index indicates how the current level of prices compares with the level during the base period.

Let's consider a simple example that illustrates more fully how price indexes are constructed. Suppose that your typical daily consumption bundle is two hamburgers, one order of french fries, and three Coca-Colas. Initially, the price of a hamburger was $3, french fries $1, and Coca-Cola $1. The price index during this base period is assigned a value of 100. Your expenditures on the bundle during the base period (the denominator in the previous formula) were $10 ($6 for the two hamburgers, $1 for the french fries, and $3 for the three Coca-Colas).

Now consider the implications if prices in the current period are $3.50 for a hamburger, $1.75 for french fries, and 75 cents for a Coca-Cola. Now the cost of purchasing this bundle (numerator in the previous formula) is $11 ($7 for the two hamburgers, $1.75 for the french fries, and $2.25 for the three Coca-Colas). This would yield a price index of 110 ($11 divided by $10 multiplied by 100). The price index of 110 indicates that the general level of prices for the three-good bundle is now 10 percent higher than it was during the base period.

Of course, the number of goods and the quantities included in the consumer price index (CPI) and GDP deflator are far greater than the bundle we considered in this simple illustration. Nonetheless, the general idea is the same. The cost of purchasing the typical bundle in the current period is compared with the cost of purchasing the same bundle during a base year, which is assigned a value of 100. If the cost of purchasing the bundle is now higher than it was during the base period, then the value of this year's price index will be greater than 100. As the price index changes from year to year, it indicates the magnitude of the change in the general level of prices.

Economic Fluctuations, Unemployment, and Inflation

CHAPTER FOCUS

- What is a business cycle? How much economic instability has the United States experienced?

- Why do economies experience unemployment? Are some types of unemployment worse than others?

- What do economists mean by full employment? How is full employment related to the natural rate of unemployment?

- How are anticipated and unanticipated inflation different? What are some of the dangers that accompany inflation?

Prosperity is when the prices of things that you sell are rising; inflation is when the prices of things that you buy are rising. Recession is when other people are unemployed; depression is when you are unemployed.

—Anonymous

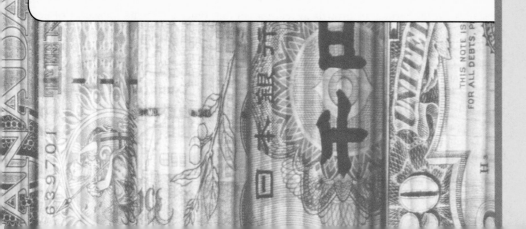

As we have already discussed, macroeconomics is about growth of income and fluctuations in that growth. The primary objectives of macroeconomic policy are to help promote rapid and stable growth, a high level of employment, and stability in the general level of prices. These goals are generally considered desirable. However, there is sometimes controversy about how they can best be achieved. As we proceed, we will analyze both economic growth and stability in detail and consider how both of these objectives can be attained.

The performance of the economy influences our job opportunities, income levels, and quality of life. Thus, key indicators of economic performance, such as growth of real GDP, the rate of unemployment, and the inflation rate, are closely watched by investors, politicians, and the media. This chapter will focus on how several key economic indicators are derived and explain how changes in these measures influence our lives. ■

Swings in the Economic Pendulum

During the last hundred years, the annual growth rate of real GDP in the United States has averaged approximately 3 percent. But there have also been considerable fluctuations in year-to-year growth. During the Great Depression of the 1930s, economic growth plunged. Real GDP declined by 7.5 percent or more each year from 1930 to 1932. In 1933, it was almost 30 percent less than it was in 1929. The 1929 level of real GDP was not reached again until 1939. World War II was characterized by a rapid expansion of GDP, which was followed by a decline after the war. Real GDP did not reach its 1944 level again until 1953, although the output of consumer goods did increase significantly in the years immediately following the war.

EXHIBIT 1 presents the growth rate figures (four-quarter moving average) for real GDP for 1960–2009. Real GDP grew rapidly throughout most of the 1960s; the periods 1972–1973, 1976–1977, and 1983–1988; and most of the 1990s. Since 1960, however, there have also been seven periods (1960, 1970, 1974–1975, 1980, 1982, 1991, 2001 and 2008–2009) of falling real GDP. Although the economic ups and downs have continued, the fluctuations have been less severe in recent decades than during the first fifty years of the twentieth century. Figures on GDP and related data can be obtained from the Bureau of Economic Analysis on the Internet at http://www.bea.gov/.

A Hypothetical Business Cycle

The United States and other industrial economies have been characterized by instability when it comes to the growth of real GDP. Inevitably, real GDP growth has been followed by economic slowdowns. Economists refer to these swings in the rate of output as the **business cycle**. Periods of growth in real output and other aggregate measures of economic activity followed by periods of decline are the characteristics of business cycles.

EXHIBIT 2 shows a hypothetical business cycle. When most businesses are operating at capacity level and real GDP is growing rapidly, a *business peak,* or boom, is present. As business conditions slow, the economy begins the *contraction,* or recessionary, phase of a business cycle. During the contraction, the sales of most businesses decline, real GDP grows at a slower rate or perhaps falls, and unemployment in the labor market increases.

The bottom of the contraction phase is referred to as the *recessionary trough.* After the downturn reaches bottom and economic conditions begin to improve, the economy enters the *expansion* phase of the cycle. Here business sales rise, GDP grows rapidly,

Business cycle

Fluctuations in the general level of economic activity as measured by variables such as the rate of unemployment and changes in real GDP.

EXHIBIT 1

Instability in the Growth of Real GDP, 1960-2009

Although real GDP in the United States fluctuates substantially, periods of positive growth outweigh the periods of declining real GDP. Since 1960, the U.S. growth rate of real GDP has averaged approximately 3 percent annually. Economists refer to periods of declining real GDP as recessions. The recessionary periods are shaded.

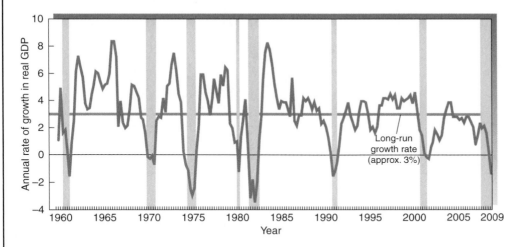

Source: Economic Report of the President (Washington, DC: Government Printing Office, various issues).

During economic expansions, construction and investment are increasing. In contrast, recessions are characterized by plant closings and high unemployment.

and the rate of unemployment declines. Eventually, the expansion blossoms into another business peak. The peak, however, inevitably ends and turns into a contraction, beginning the cycle anew.

The term **recession** is widely used to describe conditions during the contraction and recessionary trough phases of the business cycle. This is a period during which real GDP declines. Often, a recession is defined as a decline in real GDP for two or more consecutive quarters.[1] When a recession is prolonged and has a sharp decline in economic activity, it is called a **depression**.

Recession

A downturn in economic activity characterized by declining real GDP and rising unemployment. In an effort to be more precise, many economists define a recession as two consecutive quarters in which there is a decline in real GDP.

Depression

A prolonged and very severe recession.

---

[1]See Geoffrey H. Moore, "Recessions," in *The Fortune Encyclopedia of Economics*, ed. David R. Henderson (New York: Time Warner, Inc., 1993), for additional information on recessions in the United States. This publication is also available online at http:/www.econlib.org/.

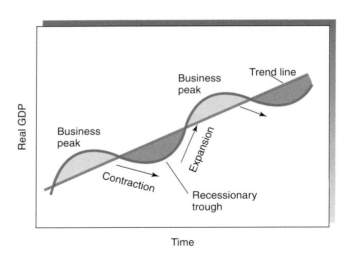

EXHIBIT 2
The Business Cycle

In the past, ups and downs have often characterized aggregate business activity. Despite these fluctuations, there has been an upward trend in real GDP in the United States and other industrial nations.
During economic expansions, construction and investment are increasing. In contrast, recessions are characterized by plant closings and high unemployment.

Civilian labor force

The number of people sixteen years of age and over who are either employed or unemployed. To be classified as unemployed, a person must be looking for a job.

Unemployed

The term used to describe a person not currently employed who is either (1) actively seeking employment or (2) waiting to begin or return to a job.

Labor force participation rate

The number of people in the civilian labor force sixteen years of age or over who are either employed or actively seeking employment as a percentage of the total civilian population sixteen years of age and over.

In one important respect, the term *business cycle* is misleading. The word *cycle* is often used to describe events of similar time length that occur regularly, like the seasons of the year, for example. As Exhibit 1 illustrates, this is not the case with the business cycle. The expansions and contractions last varying lengths of time, and the swings differ in terms of their magnitude. For example, the recessions of 1961, 1982, and 1990 were followed by eight years or more of uninterrupted growth of output. In contrast, the recession of 1980 was followed by an expansion that lasted only twelve months. The expansionary phase following the recessions of 1970 and 1974–1975 fell between these two extremes. Clearly, the duration of real-world expansions and contractions is varied and unpredictable.

How can we know where an economy is in the business cycle? Of course, changes in real GDP will tell us. However, these numbers are available only quarterly, and it usually takes four to six weeks after the quarter is over before reliable figures are released. Various measures that are available monthly or more often can provide clues. For example, auto sales, new housing starts, new factory orders, and even the stock market will generally increase during an expansion and decline when the economy dips into a recession. As a result, these indicators are monitored carefully.

Economic Fluctuations and the Labor Market

Fluctuations in real GDP influence the demand for labor and employment. In our modern world, people are busy with jobs, household work, school, and other activities. **EXHIBIT 3** illustrates how economists classify these activities in relation to the **civilian labor force**, defined as the number of people aged sixteen years and over who are either employed or seeking employment. The noninstitutional civilian adult population is divided into two broad categories: (1) people not in the labor force and (2) people in the labor force. There are various reasons why people aren't in the labor force. Some are retired. Others are working in their own households or attending school. Still others are not working because they are ill or disabled. Although many of these people are quite busy, their activities lie outside the market labor force.

As Exhibit 3 shows, **unemployed** workers who are seeking work are included in the labor force along with employed workers. The **labor force participation rate** is the number of people in the civilian labor force (including both those who are employed and those who are unemployed) as a percentage of the civilian population sixteen years of age

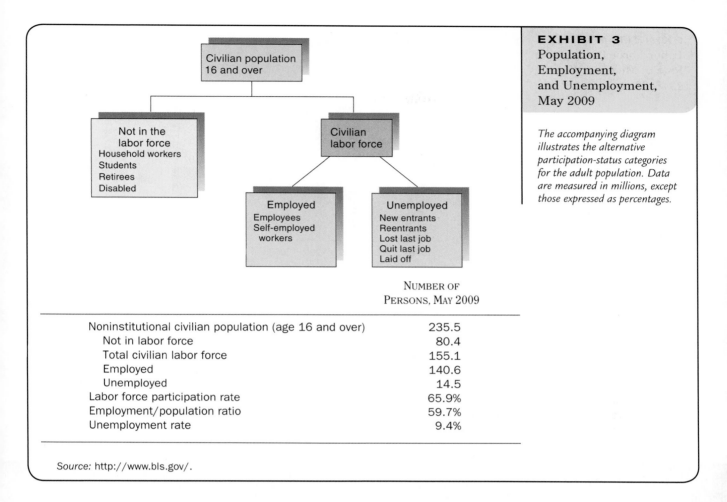

EXHIBIT 3
Population, Employment, and Unemployment, May 2009

The accompanying diagram illustrates the alternative participation-status categories for the adult population. Data are measured in millions, except those expressed as percentages.

	NUMBER OF PERSONS, MAY 2009
Noninstitutional civilian population (age 16 and over)	235.5
Not in labor force	80.4
Total civilian labor force	155.1
Employed	140.6
Unemployed	14.5
Labor force participation rate	65.9%
Employment/population ratio	59.7%
Unemployment rate	9.4%

Source: http://www.bls.gov/.

and over. In May 2009, the population (sixteen years of age and over) of the United States was 235.5 million, 155.1 million of whom were in the labor force. Thus, the U.S. labor force participation rate was 65.9 percent (155.1 million divided by 235.5 million).

The labor force participation rate varies substantially across countries. For example, in 2008, the labor force participation rate of fifteen- to sixty-four-year-olds was 75.3 percent in the United States, 78.8 percent in Canada, and 80.2 percent in Sweden. In contrast, the labor force participation rate was only 62.2 percent in Mexico and 63.0 percent in Italy. The percentage of married women in the labor force is generally smaller in countries like Italy and Mexico that have low labor force participation rates.

In the United States, one of the most interesting labor force developments in recent decades is the dramatic increase in the labor force participation rate of women. **EXHIBIT 4** illustrates this point. In 2008, 59.5 percent of adult women worked outside the home, up from 32.7 percent in 1948. Married women accounted for most of this increase. More than half of all married women now are in the labor force, compared to only 20 percent immediately following World War II. While the labor force participation of women rose, the rate for men fell. In 2008, the labor force participation rate of men was 73.0 percent, down from 83.3 percent in 1960 and 86.6 percent in 1948. Clearly, the composition of workforce participation within the family has changed substantially during the past six decades.

The **unemployment rate** is a key barometer of conditions in the aggregate labor market. This not withstanding, the term is often misunderstood. It is important to note that unemployment is different from not working. As we previously discussed, there are several reasons—including household work, school attendance, retirement, and illness or disability—why a person may be neither employed nor looking for a job. These people, though not employed, are not counted as unemployed.

Unemployment rate

The percentage of people in the labor force who are unemployed. Mathematically, it is equal to the number of people unemployed divided by the number of people in the labor force.

EXHIBIT 4
Labor Force Participation Rate of Men and Women, 1948–2008

As the chart illustrates, the labor force participation rate for women has been steadily increasing for several decades, while the rate for men has been declining.

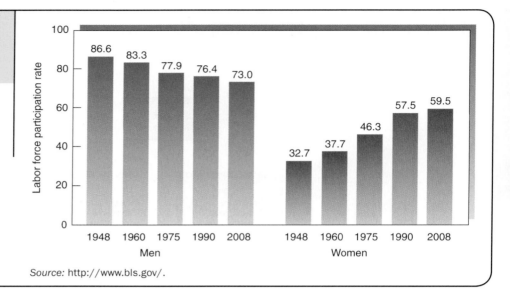

Source: http://www.bls.gov/.

Moreover, only people employed or unemployed are counted as part of the labor force. Part-time as well as full-time workers are counted as employed members of the labor force. The rate of unemployment is the number of people unemployed expressed as a percentage of the labor force. In May 2009, the rate of unemployment in the United States was 9.4 percent (14.5 million out of a labor force of 155.1 million). (See the accompanying Measures of Economic Activity feature for information on how the Bureau of Labor Statistics derives the unemployment rate.)

MEASURES OF ECONOMIC ACTIVITY

Deriving the Unemployment Rate

Each month, the Bureau of Labor Statistics (BLS) contacts a sample of 50,000 households that reflects the population characteristics of the United States. Specially trained interviewers pose identical questions designed to determine whether each of the approximately 90,000 adults in these households is employed, unemployed, or not in the labor force. People aged sixteen years and over are considered employed if they (1) worked at all (even as little as 1 hour) for pay or profit during the survey week, (2) worked 15 hours or more without pay in a family-operated enterprise during the survey week, or (3) have a job at which they did not work during the survey week because of illness, vacation, industrial disputes, bad weather, time off, or personal reasons. People are considered unemployed if they (1) do not have a job, (2) are available for work, and (3) have actively looked for work during the past four weeks. Looking for work may involve any of the following activities: (1) registering at a public or private employment office, (2) meeting with prospective employers, (3) checking with friends or relatives, (4) placing or answering advertisements, (5) writing letters of application, or (6) being in a union or on a professional register. In addition, those not working

are classified as unemployed if they are either waiting to start a new job within thirty days or waiting to be recalled from a layoff. The BLS uses its survey data to calculate the unemployment rate and other employment-related statistics each month. States use the BLS survey and employment figures from industries covered by unemployment insurance to construct state and area employment statistics. These labor market figures are published by the U.S. Department of Labor in the *Monthly Labor Review* and on the Internet at http://www.bls.gov/.

THUMBNAIL SKETCH

Formulas for Key Labor Market Indicators

1. **Labor force** = Employed + Unemployed
2. **Labor force participation rate** = Number in labor force/ Population (aged 16 and over)
3. **Unemployment rate** = Number unemployed/Number in labor force
4. **Employment/population ratio** = Number employed/ Population (aged 16 and over)

In addition to the rate of unemployment, many economists also use the **employment/ population ratio**—the number of people employed expressed as a percentage of the population sixteen years old and over—to monitor labor market conditions. This ratio will tend to rise during an expansion and fall during a recession. Both the number of people employed and the population aged sixteen and over are well defined and readily measurable. Their measurement does not require a subjective judgment as to whether a person is actually "available for work" or "actively seeking employment." Thus, some believe that the employment/population ratio is a more objective measure of job market conditions than the rate of unemployment. The employment/population ratio was 59.7 percent in May 2009. The accompanying **Thumbnail Sketch** shows the formulas that are used to calculate the major indicators of labor market conditions.

Employment/population ratio

The number of people sixteen years of age and over employed as civilians divided by the total civilian population sixteen years of age and over. The ratio is expressed as a percentage.

Dynamic Change and Reasons for Unemployment

In a dynamic world, where information is scarce and people are free to choose among jobs, some unemployment is inevitable. As new products are introduced and new technologies developed, some firms are expanding while others are contracting. Similarly, some firms will be starting operations, while others will be going out of business. This process results in the creation of new jobs and the disappearance of old ones. At the same time, some potential workers will be switching from school or other nonwork activities to the labor force, while others are retiring or taking a leave from the labor force. Furthermore, workers are mobile. At any point in time, some will voluntarily quit and search for better opportunities. Although some unemployment will always be present, there is a positive side to the unemployment–job search process: it makes it possible for individuals to better match their skills and preferences with the job requirements of employers. Better-matched employees and employers increase both productivity and earnings.

Unemployment may occur for reasons other than the loss of a job, however. For example, people often experience periods of unemployment as they enter and reenter the labor force. The Department of Labor lists five reasons why workers may experience unemployment. **EXHIBIT 5** shows the share of unemployed workers in each of these five categories in May 2009. Interestingly, 6.6 percent of the unemployed workers were first-time entrants into the labor force; 21.8 percent were reentering the labor force after exiting it to obtain additional schooling, do household work, or for other reasons. Therefore, 28.4 percent of the unemployed workers—over one-quarter—were unemployed because they were entering or reentering the labor force. About one out of every sixteen unemployed workers (6.2 percent) quit their job. People laid off and waiting to return to their previous positions contributed 12.6 percent to the total. Workers dismissed from their job accounted for about one-half (52.8 percent) of the total number of unemployed workers.

Young workers often switch jobs and move between schooling and the labor force as they search for a career path that best fits their abilities and preferences. As the result of this job switching, the unemployment rate of younger workers is substantially higher than that of more established workers. As **EXHIBIT 6** shows, the unemployment rate of workers twenty to twenty-four years of age in May 2009 was nearly twice the rate for their counterparts aged twenty-five years and over. Further, the unemployment rate for

EXHIBIT 5
Composition of the Unemployed by Reason

This chart indicates the various reasons that people were unemployed in May 2009. About one-half (52.8 percent) of the people unemployed were dismissed from their last job. More than one-quarter (28.4 percent) of the unemployed workers were either new entrants or reentrants into the labor force.

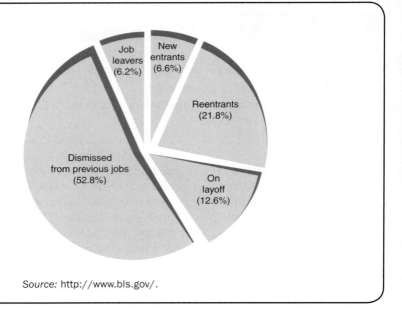

Source: http://www.bls.gov/.

EXHIBIT 6
The Unemployment Rate by Age and Gender, May 2009

GROUP	CIVILIAN RATE OF UNEMPLOYMENT MAY 2009 (PERCENTAGE)
Total, all workers	9.4
Men, Total	10.5
Ages 16–19	26.7
Ages 20–24	17.5
Ages 25 and over	9.0
Women, Total	8.0
Ages 16–19	18.6
Ages 20–24	12.2
Ages 25 and over	7.0

Source: http://www.bls.gov/.

teenagers was approximately three times the rate for those twenty-five years and older. The unemployment rates for men were higher than women for all age groups.

Three Types of Unemployment

Although some unemployment is consistent with economic efficiency, this is not always the case. Abnormally high rates of unemployment generally reflect weak demand conditions for labor, counterproductive policies, and/or the inability or lack of incentive on the part of potential workers and potential employers to arrive at mutually advantageous agreements. To clarify matters, economists divide unemployment into three categories: frictional, structural, and cyclical. Let us take a closer look at each of these three classifications.

Frictional Unemployment

Frictional unemployment

Unemployment due to constant changes in the economy that prevent qualified unemployed workers from being immediately matched up with existing job openings. It results from imperfect information and search activities related to suitably matching employees with employers.

Unemployment that is caused by constant changes in the labor market is called **frictional unemployment**. It occurs because (1) employers are not fully aware of all available workers and their job qualifications and (2) available workers are not fully aware of the jobs being offered by employers. In other words, the main cause of frictional unemployment is imperfect information.

For example, an employer looking for a new worker seldom hires the first applicant who walks into the employment office. The employer wants to find the "best available" worker to fill the opening. It is costly to hire workers who perform poorly. It is sometimes even costly to terminate their employment. So, employers search—they expend time and resources screening applicants in an effort to find the best-qualified workers who are willing to accept their wage and employment conditions.

Similarly, job seekers search for their best option among the potential alternatives. They make telephone calls, search newspaper ads and Internet sites, submit to job interviews, use employment services, and so on. The pursuit of personal gain—landing jobs that are more attractive than the current options they face—motivates job seekers to engage in job search activities.

However, as a job seeker finds out about more and more potential job opportunities, it becomes less likely that additional searching will uncover a more attractive option. Therefore, the *marginal benefit* derived from a job search declines with the time spent searching for a job because it becomes less likely that it will lead to a better position. The *marginal cost* of a job search rises as a more lengthy search leads to the discovery of more attractive job opprtunities.

As the marginal benefit of the job search declines and the marginal costs rise, eventually a rational job seeker will conclude that additional search is no longer worth the cost. He or she will then accept the best alternative available at that point. However, this process will take time, and during this time the job seeker is contributing to the frictional unemployment of the economy.

It is important to note that, even though frictional unemployment is a side effect, the job search process typically leads to improved economic efficiency and a higher real income for employees (see the accompanying Myths of Economics feature).

Changes that affect the costs and benefits of a job search influence the level of unemployment. The Internet has had an interesting effect on the job search process. Increasingly, both employers and employees are using Internet sites as a means of communicating with each other. Employers provide information about job openings in various skill and occupational categories, and employees supply information about their education, skills, and experience. This electronic job search process reduces information costs and makes it possible for both employers and employees to consider quickly a wide range of alternatives. As this method of employment search becomes more widespread, it will tend to shorten the job search process and improve the matches between employers and employees. As a result, frictional unemployment might be lower in the future.

On the other hand, a change that makes it cheaper to reject available opportunities and continue searching for jobs will increase the level of unemployment. For example, an increase in unemployment benefits would make it less costly to continue looking for a preferred job. As a result, job seekers will expand the length of their search time, and the unemployment rate will rise.

Structural Unemployment

In the case of **structural unemployment**, changes in the basic characteristics of the economy prevent the "matching up" of available jobs with available workers. It is not always easy to distinguish between frictional and structural unemployment. In each case, job openings and potential workers searching for jobs are both present. The crucial difference between the two is that with frictional unemployment, workers possess the necessary skills to fill the job openings; with structural unemployment, they do not. Essentially, the primary skills of a structurally unemployed worker have been rendered obsolete by changing market conditions and technology. Realistically, the structurally unemployed worker faces the prospect of either a career change or prolonged unemployment. For older workers in particular, these are bleak alternatives.

Structural unemployment

Unemployment due to the structural characteristics of the economy that make it difficult for job seekers to find employment and for employers to hire workers. Although job openings are available, they generally require skills many unemployed workers do not have.

There are many causes of structural unemployment. The introduction of new products and production technologies can substantially alter the relative demand for workers with various skills. Changes of this type can affect the job opportunities of even highly skilled workers, particularly if their skills are not easily transferable to other industries and occupations. The "computer revolution" has dramatically changed the job opportunities of many workers. The alternatives available to workers with the skills required to operate and maintain high-tech equipment have improved substantially, while the prospects of those without such skills have, in some cases, deteriorated drastically.

Shifts in public-sector priorities can also cause structural unemployment. For example, environmental regulations designed to improve air quality led to a reduction in the demand for coal during the 1990s. As a result, many coal miners in West Virginia, Kentucky, and other coal-mining states lost their jobs. Unfortunately, the skills of many of the job losers were ill-suited for employment in expanding industries. Structural unemployment was the result.

Institutional factors can also make it difficult for some workers to find jobs. For example, minimum-wage legislation may push the wages of low-skilled workers above their productivity levels and thereby severely retard the job opportunities available to them. High unemployment benefits reduce the opportunity cost of unemployment and may also lead to higher levels of structural unemployment. See Applications in Economics for a suggested policy alternative that would reduce the adverse unintended consequences of the current unemployment benefit system.

MYTHS OF ECONOMICS

"Unemployment would not exist if the economy were operating efficiently."

Nobody likes unemployment. Certainly, an extended period of unemployment can be a very painful experience. Looking for a job, however, performs an important labor market function: It leads to improved matches between workers' skills and employers' job requirements.

Job searchers are "shopping"—they are searching for information about the job opportunity that best fits their skills, earning capabilities, and preferences. Similarly, employers shop when they are seeking labor services. They, too, acquire information about available workers that will help them select employees whose skills and preferences match the demands of the job.

This shopping results in some unemployment, but it also provides both employees and employers with information that will help them make better choices. If the resources of an economy are going to be used effectively, the skills of workers must be matched well with the jobs of employers. Waste will result if, for example, a person with high-level computer skills ends up working as a janitor while someone else with minimal computer skills is employed as a computer programmer. Moreover, as workers try to find jobs for which their skills are well suited, they achieve higher wage rates, and the economy is able to generate a larger output.

Perhaps thinking about the housing market will help you better understand why search time can be both beneficial and productive. Like the employment market, the housing market is characterized by imperfect information and dynamic change. New housing structures are built; older structures depreciate and are torn down. Families move from one community to another. In this dynamic world, it makes sense for renters to shop around from time to time to find the housing quality, price, and location that best fit their preferences and budgets. Similarly, landlords search among renters, seeking to rent their accommodations to those who value them most highly. As a result of this shopping, housing vacancies inevitably occur. But does this mean the housing market is inefficient? No. It is the result of imperfect information and the search for a more efficient match on the part of both landlords and renters.

Of course, some types of unemployment, particularly cyclical unemployment, are indicative of inefficiency. However, this is not the case with frictional unemployment. The job searching (as well as the frictional unemployment that accompanies it) helps both job seekers and employers make better choices, and it leads to a more efficient match of applicants with job openings than would otherwise be possible. It is perfectly consistent with economic efficiency.

APPLICATIONS IN ECONOMICS

Would Personal Savings Accounts Reduce the Rate of Unemployment?

Under the current unemployment insurance system, workers and their employers are required to pay taxes on wages and salaries, which are used to finance benefits for unemployed workers covered by the program. Typically, the benefits replace about 50 percent of a worker's prior pretax earnings for up to twenty-six weeks. During recent recessions, Congress has extended benefits for an additional thirteen weeks. In Europe, however, unemployment benefits are even higher, and people are permitted to draw the benefits for longer time periods—often two or three years.

Unfortunately, unemployment programs have an unintended secondary effect: They increase the unemployment rate. The benefits make it less costly for an unemployed worker to turn down available jobs and continue searching while receiving the payments. They also reduce the incentive of the unemployed to switch occupations or move to another location in order to find employment. As a result, workers stay unemployed longer and the overall unemployment rate is higher than it would be otherwise. In fact, empirical evidence indicates that there is a spike in the number of unemployed workers obtaining employment just prior to and immediately after their unemployment benefits are exhausted. The persistently higher unemployment rates in Europe (see Exhibit 8), where the benefits are more generous, also indicate that the program pushes the unemployment rate upward, perhaps by as much as 2 or 3 percentage points.

To deal with this problem, Lawrence Brunner and Stephen Colarelli have proposed that a system of personal savings accounts be substituted for the current system.[1] Instead of paying a payroll tax, employees and their employers would make equivalent payments into an unemployment personal savings account owned by the employee. Workers could then access the funds in their accounts during periods of unemployment. Upon retirement, any funds remaining in the account would be available to the worker, and, in case of death, unused funds would be passed along to the worker's heirs. Because this system would mean that workers would be using their own funds rather than the government's during periods of unemployment, the approach would eliminate the perverse incentive structure caused by the current system.

Question for Thought

1. Would the proposed reform increase the incentive to search for and accept employment rather than undergo lengthy periods of unemployment? Why or why not? Can you think of problems this system would create compared with the current system?

[1]Lawrence Brunner and Stephen M. Colarelli, "Individual Unemployment Accounts," *Independent Review* 8 (Spring 2004): 569–85.

Cyclical Unemployment

When there is a general downturn in business activity, **cyclical unemployment** arises. Because fewer goods are being produced, fewer workers are required to produce them. Employers lay off workers and cut back employment.

An unexpected fall in the general level of demand for goods and services will cause cyclical unemployment to rise. In a world of imperfect information, adjustments to unexpected declines in demand are often painful for people. When the demand for labor declines, workers will at first not know whether they are being laid off because their employer is experiencing lower demand or if the reduction in demand is widespread throughout the economy. Similarly, they will not immediately know whether their poor current employment opportunities are temporary or long-term. If a reduction in demand is limited to only a few employers, the dismissed workers will generally be able to find jobs with other employers in a short period of time. The situation is different, however, when there is a general decline in demand. Many employers will lay off workers and few other employers will be hiring. Under these circumstances, workers' search efforts will be less fruitful, and the duration of their unemployment abnormally long. Unemployment of this type is referred to as cyclical unemployment. As we proceed, we will consider the causes of cyclical unemployment and analyze how it might be reduced.

Cyclical unemployment

Unemployment due to recessionary business conditions and inadequate labor demand.

Employment Fluctuations—
The Historical Record

Employment and output are closely linked over the business cycle. If we are going to produce more goods and services, we must either increase the number of workers or increase the output per worker. Although productivity, or output per worker, is the primary source of long-term economic growth, it changes slowly from year to year. Consequently, rapid increases in output, such as those that occur during a strong business expansion, generally require an increase in employment. As a result, output and employment tend to be positively related. Conversely, there is an inverse relationship between growth of output and the rate of unemployment.

The empirical evidence is consistent with this view. As **EXHIBIT 7** shows, the unemployment rate generally increases during a recession (indicated by shading), and declines during periods of expansion in output. During the recession of 1960–1961, the rate of unemployment rose to approximately 7 percent. In contrast, it declined throughout the economic boom of the 1960s, only to rise again during the recession of 1970. During the recession of 1974–1975, the unemployment rate jumped to more than 9 percent. Similarly, it soared to nearly 11 percent during the severe recession of 1982 and to over 9 percent during the 2008–2009 recession. Conversely, it declined substantially during the expansions of 1983–1989, 1992–2000, and 2002–2006.

Full Employment and the Natural Rate of Unemployment

Full employment, a term widely used by economists and public officials alike, does not mean zero unemployment. As we have noted, in a world of imperfect information, both employees and employers will "shop" before they agree to accept a job or hire a new

Full employment

The level of employment that results from the efficient use of the labor force taking into account the normal (natural) rate of unemployment due to information costs, dynamic changes, and the structural conditions of the economy. For the United States, full employment is thought to exist when approximately 95 percent of the labor force is employed.

EXHIBIT 7
The Unemployment Rate, 1960–2009

Here, we illustrate the rate of unemployment during the 1960–2009 period. As expected, the unemployment rate rose rapidly during each of the seven recessions. (The shaded years indicate recessions.) In contrast, soon after each recession ended, the unemployment rate began to decline as the economy moved to an expansionary phase of the business cycle. Also note that the actual rate of unemployment was substantially greater than the natural rate during and immediately following each recession.

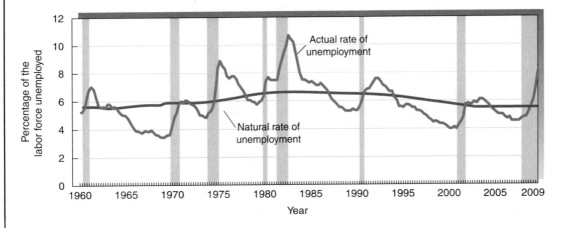

Source: http://www.bls.gov/; and Robert J. Gordon, *Macroeconomics* (Boston: Addison-Wesley, 2009).

worker. Much of this shopping is efficient, because it leads to better matches between the skills of employees and the skills employers need. Some unemployment is therefore necessary for a dynamic labor market to operate efficiently. *Consequently, economists define full employment as the level of employment that results when the rate of unemployment is "normal," considering both frictional and structural factors.* In the United States, full employment is currently believed to be approximately 95 percent of the labor force, or perhaps just slightly above this figure.

Closely related to the concept of full employment is the **natural rate of unemployment**, the amount of unemployment reflected by job shopping and imperfect information. *The natural rate of unemployment is not a temporary high or low; it is a rate that is sustainable. Economists sometimes refer to it as the unemployment rate accompanying the economy's "maximum sustainable" rate of output.* When unemployment is at its natural rate, full employment is present, and the economy is achieving the highest rate of output that it can sustain.

The natural rate of unemployment, however, is not fixed. It is affected by the structure of the labor force and by changes in public policy. Over time, changes in the demographic composition of the labor force will influence the natural rate. The natural rate of unemployment increases when youthful workers expand as a proportion of the workforce. Because youthful workers change jobs and move in and out of the labor force often, they experience high rates of unemployment (see Exhibit 6). Therefore, the overall rate of unemployment is pushed upward as they become a larger share of the labor force. This is what happened during the 1960s and 1970s. In 1960, youthful workers (ages sixteen to twenty-four) constituted only 16 percent of the labor force. But as the postwar baby boom generation entered the labor market, youthful workers as a share of the labor force rose dramatically. By 1980, one out of every four workers was in the youthful-worker grouping. In contrast, prime-age workers (over age twenty-five) declined from 84 percent of the U.S. workforce in 1960 to only 75 percent in 1980. As a result of these demographic changes, studies indicate that the natural rate of unemployment rose from approximately 5 percent in the late 1950s to more than 6 percent in the mid-1980s.

Since the late 1980s, the situation has reversed. The natural rate of unemployment has declined as the baby boomers moved into their prime working years and youthful workers shrank as a share of the labor force. Today, most researchers estimate that the natural rate is once again about 5 percent, or perhaps even a little lower.

Public policy also affects the natural rate of unemployment. When public policy makes it more costly to employ workers and/or less costly for people to remain unemployed, it increases the natural rate of unemployment. The economies of France, Germany, Italy, and Spain illustrate this point. Labor markets in these four countries are characterized by generous unemployment benefits and regulations that both increase the cost of dismissing workers and mandate uniform wages nationwide. Regulations of this type reduce the flexibility of labor markets and make it more costly to hire and employ workers. Persistently high rates of unemployment will result, as can be seen in **EXHIBIT 8**. The unemployment rates of the countries with highly regulated labor markets were substantially higher during the last decade than the comparable figures for the United States, Japan, and the United Kingdom, where labor markets are less regulated. High unemployment rates over lengthy time periods are indicative of structural rather than cyclical factors.

The relationship between the *actual* unemployment rate and the *natural* unemployment rate for the United States over the last four decades can be observed in Exhibit 7. Note that the actual unemployment rate fluctuates around the natural rate in response to cyclical economic conditions. The actual rate generally rises above the natural rate during a recession and falls below the natural rate when the economy is in the midst of an economic boom. For example, the actual rate of unemployment was substantially above the natural rate during the recessions of 1974–1975, 1982, and 2008–2009. The reverse was true during the latter stages of the lengthy expansions of the 1960s, 1980s, 1990s, and 2000s. As we proceed, we will often compare the actual and natural rates of unemployment. In a very real sense, macroeconomics studies why the actual and natural rates differ and attempts to discern the factors that cause the natural rate to change over time.

Natural rate of unemployment

The "normal" unemployment rate due to frictional and structural conditions in labor markets. It is the unemployment rate that occurs when the economy is operating at a sustainable rate of output. The current natural rate of unemployment in the United States is thought to be approximately 5 percent.

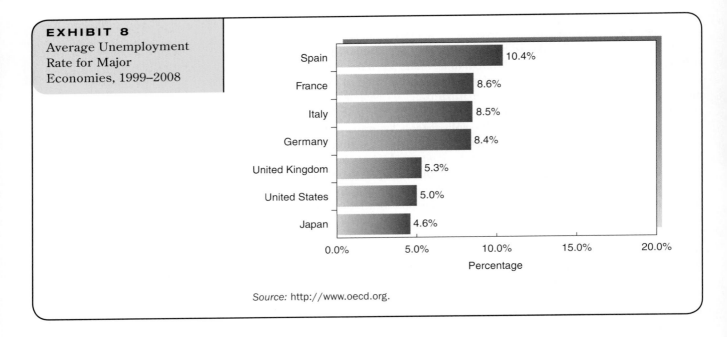

EXHIBIT 8
Average Unemployment Rate for Major Economies, 1999–2008

Source: http://www.oecd.org.

Actual and Potential GDP

If an economy is going to realize its potential, full employment is essential. When the actual rate of unemployment exceeds the natural rate, the actual output of the economy will fall below its potential. Potential output does not represent the absolute maximum level of production that could, for example, be generated in wartime or other situations during which the level of aggregate demand is abnormally high. Rather, it is the rate that would be expected under more normal circumstances.

Potential output can therefore be thought of as the maximum *sustainable* output level consistent with the full employment of resources currently available in the economy. To estimate the economy's potential output level, we need to look at three factors: the size of the labor force, the quality (productivity) of labor, and the natural rate of unemployment. Because these factors cannot be estimated with certainty, some variation exists in the estimated values of the potential rate of output.

EXHIBIT 9 shows the relationship between the actual and potential output of the United States since 1960. The relationship between actual and potential GDP reflects the business cycle. Note the similarity of the actual real GDP data of Exhibit 9 and the hypothetical data of an idealized business cycle of Exhibit 2. Although the actual data of Exhibit 9 are irregular compared to the hypothetical data, periods of expansion and economic boom followed by contraction and recession are clearly observable. During the boom phase, actual output expands rapidly and may temporarily exceed the economy's long-run potential. In contrast, recessions are characterized by an actual real GDP that is less than its potential. As we proceed, we will focus on how we can achieve maximum potential output while minimizing economic instability.

Potential output

The level of output that can be achieved and sustained in the future, given the size of the labor force, its expected productivity, and the natural rate of unemployment consistent with the efficient operation of the labor market. Actual output can differ from the economy's potential output.

The Effects of Inflation

Inflation is a sustained increase in the general level of prices. When inflation is on the rise, it costs more to purchase a typical bundle of goods and services. Of course, even when the general level of prices is stable, some prices will be rising and others will be falling. During a period of inflation, however, the impact of the rising prices will outweigh the impact of falling prices. Because of the higher prices (on average), a dollar will purchase

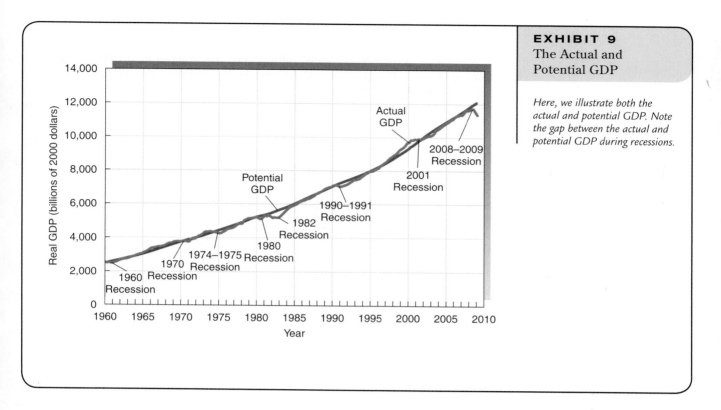

less than it did previously. Inflation, therefore, can also be defined as a decline in the value (the purchasing power) of money.

How do we determine whether prices are generally rising or falling? Essentially, we answered that question in the preceding chapter when we indicated how a price index is constructed. When the general level of prices is rising, the price index will also rise. In turn, the annual rate of inflation is merely the year-to-year change in an index of the general level of prices. The consumer price index (CPI) and the GDP deflator are the price indexes most widely used to measure the inflation rate in the United States. As discussed earlier, these two measures of the rate of inflation tend to follow a similar path.

It's important to note that inflation affects the prices of things we sell as well as the prices of goods we buy. Both resource and product prices are influenced by inflation. Before we become too upset about inflation "robbing us of the purchasing power of our paychecks," we need to realize that inflation influences the size of those paychecks. For example, the weekly earnings of employees would not have risen at a sharp annual rate of 7 percent during the 1970s if the rate of inflation hadn't increased rapidly during the period, too. Wages are also a price. Inflation raises both prices and wages.

How rapidly has the general level of prices risen in the United States? Using the annual rate of change in the CPI, **EXHIBIT 10** shows the U.S. inflation rate since the mid-1950s. During the 1950s and into the mid-1960s, the annual inflation rate was generally low. The average inflation rate during the 1956–1965 period, for example, was just 1.6 percent. Beginning in the latter half of the 1960s, however, inflation began to accelerate upward, jumping to 12 percent or more during 1974, 1979, and 1980. During the 1973–1981 period, the inflation rate averaged 9.2 percent. Price increases moderated again in the mid-1980s, and the inflation rate averaged 3.1 percent during the period 1983–2009. Additional details on inflation and related measures can be obtained on the Internet at http://www.bls.gov/.

The rate of inflation varies widely among countries. **EXHIBIT 11** provides data on the annual inflation rates during 2002–2008 for Canada, Germany, Singapore, the United Kingdom, and the United States—five countries with low rates of inflation. The annual inflation rates of these countries were generally less than 4 percent during this period;

moreover, the year-to-year variations in inflation were relatively small—typically no more than 1 or 2 percent.

Exhibit 11 also presents parallel inflation rate data for five high-inflation countries: Romania, Russia, Turkey, Uruguay, and Venezuela. In contrast with the low-inflation countries, the inflation rate of the high-inflation countries was not only higher but it also varied substantially more from one year to another. For example, consider the data for

---

EXHIBIT 10

The Inflation Rate, 1956–2009

Here, we present the annual rate of inflation since 1956. Between 1956 and 1965, prices increased at an annual rate of only 1.6 percent. In contrast, the inflation rate averaged 9.2 percent during the 1973–1981 era, reaching double-digit rates in several years. Since 1982, the rate of inflation has been lower (the average annual rate was 3.1 percent during the period 1983–2009) and more stable.

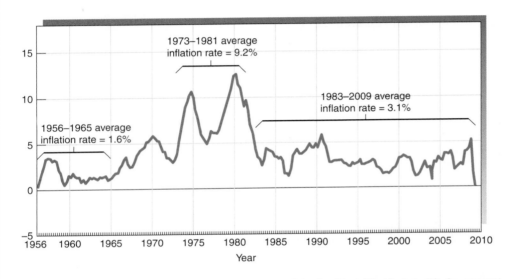

Source: http://www.bls.gov/. Also see *Economic Report of the President* (Washington, DC: Government Printing Office, published annually).

EXHIBIT 11

Variations in the Annual Inflation Rates of Selected Countries, 2002–2008

COUNTRY	2002	2003	2004	2005	2006	2007	2008
LOW INFLATION							
Canada	2.3	2.7	1.8	2.2	2.0	2.1	2.4
Germany	1.4	1.0	1.8	1.9	1.8	2.3	2.8
Singapore	−0.4	0.5	1.7	0.5	1.0	2.1	6.5
United Kingdom	1.3	1.4	1.3	2.0	2.3	2.3	3.6
United States	1.6	2.3	2.7	3.4	3.2	2.9	3.8
HIGH INFLATION							
Romania	22.5	15.3	11.9	9.0	6.6	4.8	7.8
Russia	15.8	13.7	10.9	12.7	9.7	9.0	14.1
Turkey	45.1	25.3	8.6	8.2	9.6	8.8	10.4
Uruguay	14.0	19.4	9.2	4.7	6.4	8.1	7.9
Venezuela	22.4	31.1	21.7	16.0	13.7	18.7	30.4

Source: International Monetary Fund, http://www.imf.org.

Venezuela. The inflation rate in Venezuela jumped from 22.4 in 2002 to 31.1 in 2003. It then receded to 13.7 by 2006 and rose again to reach 30.4 in 2008. The other countries in the high-inflation group also experienced wide fluctuations in their annual rates of inflation. The data of Exhibit 11 reflect a general pattern. ***High rates of inflation are almost always associated with substantial year-to-year swings in the inflation rate.***

Unanticipated and Anticipated Inflation

Before we examine the effects of inflation, it is important that we distinguish between unanticipated and anticipated inflation. **Unanticipated inflation** is an increase in the price level that comes as a surprise, at least to most individuals. For example, suppose that, based on the recent past, most people anticipate an inflation rate of 3 percent. If the actual inflation rate turns out to be 10 percent, it will catch people off guard. When the inflation rate is high and variable, it will be virtually impossible for people to anticipate it accurately.

Anticipated inflation, on the other hand, is a change in the price level that is widely expected. Decision makers are generally able to anticipate slow, steady rates of inflation—like those in Canada, Germany, Singapore, the United Kingdom, and the United States during the period 2002–2008—with a high degree of accuracy. When the general level of prices is more stable, this will exert a positive impact on real output and the level of prosperity. The experience of the United States illustrates this point. During the 1983–2008 period, U.S. inflation was low and relatively stable. This period was characterized by strong growth and only seventeen months of recession. In contrast, when the inflation rate was high and variable during the 1970s, the United States experienced two recessions (1974–1975 and 1979–1980) and sluggish growth of real GDP.

Why Does Inflation Adversely Affect the Economy?

People will not be able to predict high and variable rates of inflation. There are three major reasons why such rates will adversely affect GDP and the overall health of the economy.

1. HIGH AND VARIABLE INFLATION REDUCES INVESTMENT. Unanticipated inflation alters the outcomes of long-term projects, such as the purchase of a machine or an investment in a business; it will increase the risks and retard the level of such productive activities. For example, when the price level rises 15 percent one year and 40 percent the next year and then increases again by 20 percent the following year, no one knows what to expect. Unanticipated changes of even 5 percent or 10 percent in the rate of inflation can often turn an otherwise profitable project into a personal economic disaster. Given the uncertainty that it creates, many decision makers will simply forgo capital investments and other transactions involving long-term commitments when the rate of inflation is highly variable and therefore unpredictable. As a result, mutually advantageous gains from trade will be lost and the efficiency of markets reduced.

2. INFLATION DISTORTS THE INFORMATION DELIVERED BY PRICES. Prices communicate important information concerning the relative scarcity of goods and resources. Some prices can be easily and regularly changed. But this will not be true for others, particularly those set by long-term contracts. For example, time delays will occur before the prices accompanying rental lease agreements, items sold in catalogs, mortgage interest rates, and collective bargaining contracts can be changed. Because some prices will respond quickly to inflation whereas others will change more slowly, an unanticipated change in the rate of inflation will change *relative prices* as well as the *general price level*. The distorted relative prices will be a less reliable indicator of relative scarcity. As a result of these unreliable price signals, producers and resource suppliers will often make choices that they will later regret, and the allocation of resources will be less efficient than it would have been if the general level of prices had been more stable.

Unanticipated inflation

An increase in the general level of prices that was not expected by most decision makers.

Anticipated inflation

An increase in the general level of prices that was expected by most decision makers.

3. HIGH AND VARIABLE INFLATION RESULTS IN LESS PRODUCTIVE USE OF RESOURCES. Failing to anticipate accurately the inflation rate can have a substantial effect on one's wealth. Because of this, when the inflation rate is high, people will spend more of their time and money trying to predict and cope with the future rate of inflation. These are resources that could have been used to produce goods and services demanded by the marketplace. For example, managers will spend more time coping with frequent price changes and less time improving production methods and products. Speculative market practices will occur as people try to outguess one another about the future direction of prices. As a result, funds will flow into speculative-type investments instead of more productive ones that increase output.

What Causes Inflation?

We need to acquire some additional tools of analysis before we can answer in detail the question of what causes inflation. However, at this point we can list two particular causes. First, economists emphasize the link between aggregate demand and supply. If aggregate demand rises more rapidly than supply, prices will rise. Second, nearly all economists believe that a rapid expansion in a nation's stock of money causes inflation. The old saying is that prices will rise because "there is too much money chasing too few goods." The hyperinflation experienced by South American countries and, more recently, by Russia and several other countries of the former Soviet Union has mainly been the result of monetary expansion. Once we develop additional knowledge about the operation of our economy, we will consider this issue in more detail.

Looking ahead

In this chapter, we looked at business cycles and how they affect employment, and how inflation, both anticipated and unanticipated, affects output. In the next chapter, we will begin to develop a macroeconomic model that will help us better understand the factors that influence these indicators of economic performance.

KEY POINTS

▼ During the past century, real GDP in the United States has grown at an average annual rate of approximately 3 percent. Cyclical movements in real GDP have accompanied this growth of output.

▼ The four phases of the business cycle are *expansion, peak (or boom), contraction*, and *recession*. A recession is defined as two back-to-back quarters of declining real GDP. If a recession is quite severe, it is called a depression.

▼ There are three types of unemployment: (1) frictional unemployment, (2) structural unemployment, and (3) cyclical unemployment.

In a world of imperfect information and dynamic change, some unemployment is inevitable.

▼ Full employment is the employment level consistent with the economy's natural rate of unemployment. Both full employment and the natural rate of unemployment are associated with the economy's maximum sustainable rate of output.

▼ Potential output is the maximum *sustainable* output level consistent with the economy's resource base and current institutional arrangements.

▼ Inflation is an increase in the general level of prices. It is important to distinguish between anticipated and unanticipated inflation. Unanticipated changes in the rate of inflation often alter the intended terms of long-term agreements and cause people to regret choices they have previously made.

▼ Inflation, particularly unanticipated inflation, has harmful effects. These include (1) adverse impact on investment and other time-dimension contracts, (2) distortion of relative prices, and (3) the shift of productive resources into activities designed to prevent inflation from eroding one's wealth.

CRITICAL ANALYSIS QUESTIONS

1. List the major phases of the business cycle and indicate how real GDP, employment, and unemployment change during these phases. Are the time periods of business cycles and the duration of the various phases relatively similar and therefore highly predictable?

*2. Explain why even an efficiently functioning economic system will have some unemployed resources.

*3. Classify each of the following as employed, unemployed, or not in the labor force:
   a. Brown is not working; she applied for a job at Wal-Mart last week and is awaiting the result of her application.
   b. Martinez is vacationing in Florida during a layoff at a General Motors plant due to a model changeover, but he expects to be recalled in a couple of weeks.
   c. Green was laid off as a carpenter when a construction project was completed. He is looking for work but has been unable to find anything except an $8-per-hour job, which he turned down.
   d. West works seventy hours per week as a homemaker for her family of nine.
   e. Carson, a seventeen-year-old, works six hours per week as a delivery person for the local newspaper.
   f. Chang works three hours in the mornings at a clinic and for the last two weeks has spent the afternoons looking for a full-time job.

4. What is full employment? When full employment is present, will the rate of unemployment be zero? Explain.

5. Is the natural rate of unemployment fixed? Why or why not? How are full employment and the natural rate of unemployment related? Is the actual rate of unemployment currently greater or less than the natural rate of unemployment? Why?

*6. How are the following related to one another?
   a. the actual rate of unemployment
   b. the natural rate of unemployment
   c. cyclical unemployment
   d. potential GDP

*7. Use the following data to calculate (a) the labor force participation rate, (b) unemployment rate, and (c) the employment/population ratio:

Population (aged 16 and over)	10,000
Labor force	6,000
Not currently working	4,500
Employed full-time	4,000
Employed part-time	1,500
Unemployed	500

*8. People are classified as unemployed if they are not currently working at a job and if they made an effort to find a job during the past four weeks. Does this mean that there were no jobs available? Does it mean that there were no jobs available for which the unemployed workers were qualified? What does it mean?

9. What impact will high and variable rates of inflation have on the economy? How will they influence the risk accompanying long-term contracts and related business decisions?

*10. The nominal salary paid to the president of the United States along with data for the consumer price index (CPI) are given for various years below.

Year	Presidential Salary	CPI (2000 = 100)
1920	$75,000	11.6
1940	75,000	8.1
1960	100,000	17.2
1980	200,000	47.9
2000	400,000	100.0

   a. Calculate the president's real salary measured in the purchasing power of the dollar in 2000.
   b. In which year was the real presidential salary the highest?
   c. The president's nominal salary was constant between 1920 and 1940. What happened to the real salary? Can you explain why?

11. "When employees are dismissed from employment for reasons other than poor performance,

unemployment benefits should replace 100 percent of their prior earnings while they are searching for a new job." Evaluate this statement. Do you think the idea expressed is a good one? Would it influence how quickly laid-off workers would find new jobs? What impact would it have on the unemployment rate?

12. Suppose that the consumer price index at year-end 2009 was 150 and by year-end 2010 had risen to 160. What will be the inflation rate during 2010?

*13. "My money wage rose by 6 percent last year, but inflation completely erased these gains. How can I get ahead when inflation continues to wipe out my increases in earnings?" What's wrong with this way of thinking?

14. Data for nominal GDP and the GDP deflator (2000 = 100) in 2007 and 2008 for six major industrial countries are presented in the accompanying Table A.
   a. Use the data provided to calculate the 2007 and 2008 real GDP of each country measured in 2000 prices. Place the figures in the blanks provided.

b. Use the data for the GDP deflator to calculate the inflation rate of each country. Put your answers in the blanks provided.
c. Which country had the highest growth rate of real GDP? Which had the lowest?
d. Which countries had the highest and the lowest inflation rates?
e. Which one of the countries had the most inflation during this period?

15. The following Table B presents the 2008 population, employment, and unemployment data among persons aged fifteen to sixty-four for several countries.
   a. Calculate the number of people in the labor force for each country, and put the figures in the blanks provided.
   b. Calculate the labor force participation rate for each country, and put the figures in the blanks provided. Which country had the highest labor force participation rate? Which country had the lowest?
   c. Calculate the unemployment rate for each country, and put the figures in the blanks provided. Which country had the highest unemployment rate? Which had the lowest?

*Asterisk denotes questions for which answers are given in Appendix B.

TABLE A

COUNTRY	NOMINAL GDP (BILLIONS OF LOCAL CURRENCY UNITS)		GDP DEFLATOR (2000 = 100)		REAL GDP (IN 2000 CURRENCY UNITS)		INFLATION RATE
	2007	2008	2009	2006	2008	2008	2008
United States	13,807.6	14,264.6	119.8	122.4	——	——	——
Canada	1,535.6	1,602.5	116.4	120.9	——	——	——
Japan	515,805.0	507,614.8	92.0	91.1	——	——	——
Germany	2,422.9	2,492.0	108.1	109.7	——	——	——
France	1,892.4	1,947.0	115.8	118.3	——	——	——
United Kingdom	1,400.5	1,442.9	110.6	113.1	——	——	——

Source: International Monetary Fund, http://www.imf.org.

TABLE B

COUNTRY	POPULATION (IN MILLIONS)	NUMBER EMPLOYED (IN MILLIONS)	NUMBER UNEMPLOYED	RATE OF LABOR FORCE PARTICIPATION (PERCENTAGE)	RATE OF UNEMPLOYMENT (PERCENTAGE)
United States	196.6	139.4	8.7	——	——
Canada	22.7	16.7	1.1	——	——
Japan	82.4	58.3	2.5	——	——
Germany	54.2	38	3.1	——	——
France	40	25.8	2.1	——	——
Australia	14.4	10.5	0.5	——	——
Italy	39.2	23	17	——	——

Source: http://www.oecd.org. Data are based on persons aged 15 to 64.

An Introduction to Basic Macroeconomic Markets

CHAPTER FOCUS

- What is the circular flow of income? What are the major markets that coordinate macroeconomic activities?

- Why is the aggregate demand for goods and services inversely related to the price level?

- Why is an increase in the price level likely to expand output in the short run, but not in the long run?

- What determines the equilibrium level of GDP of an economy? When equilibrium is present, how will the actual rate of unemployment compare with the natural rate?

- What is the difference between the real interest rate and the money interest rate? Does inflation help borrowers relative to lenders?

- What determines the exchange rate? How is a nation's trade balance related to the attractiveness of the economy to investors?

Macroeconomics is interesting... because it is challenging to reduce the complicated details of the economy to manageable essentials. Those essentials lie in the interactions among the goods, labor, and assets [loanable funds] markets of the economy.

—Rudiger Dornbusch and Stanley Fischer[1]

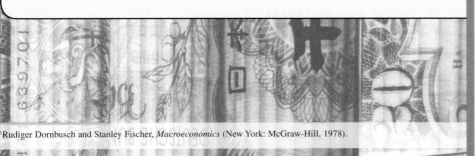

[1]Rudiger Dornbusch and Stanley Fischer, *Macroeconomics* (New York: McGraw-Hill, 1978).

M acroeconomics is primarily about economic growth and fluctuations in output, employment, and the general level of prices. As previously noted, the U.S. economy has historically grown at an annual rate of about 3 percent. This growth has improved the living standards of Americans. The growth, however, has been uneven. In some years, the economy has grown by more than the 3 percent. In others, it has grown by much less. In still other years—during recessions, for example—it has actually declined. As noted in Chapter 8, the U.S. economy has also experienced fluctuations in employment and inflation rates. Other countries' experiences are similar. All countries experience short-term fluctuations in output and employment, and varying degrees of inflation.

It is one thing to describe these fluctuations and another to understand their causes. In this chapter, we will develop a simple macroeconomic model that explains the factors underlying output, employment, and the general level of prices. In subsequent chapters, we will use this model to analyze economic fluctuations and what might be done about them. ■

Understanding Macroeconomics: Our Game Plan

A model is like a road map: it illustrates relationships. The simple model developed in this chapter will help us better understand macroeconomic relationships. It will also help us analyze the impact of policy changes on important economic variables, such as output, employment, and the general level of prices.

Macroeconomic policy is usually divided into two components: fiscal policy and monetary policy. **Fiscal policy** relates to the government's taxation and spending policies to achieve macroeconomic goals. In the United States, fiscal policy is conducted by Congress and the president. It is thus a reflection of the political process. **Monetary policy** encompasses actions that alter the **money supply**—the amount of cash in our billfolds and deposits in our checking accounts. The direction of monetary policy is determined by a nation's central bank, the Federal Reserve System in the United States. Ideally, both monetary and fiscal policy are used to promote business stability, high employment, the growth of output, and a stable price level.

Initially, as we develop our basic macroeconomic model, we will assume that monetary and fiscal policies are unchanged—that Congress and the president aren't making fiscal policy changes and that the Federal Reserve is keeping the money supply constant. Of course, changes in government expenditures, taxes, and the money supply are potentially important. We will investigate their impact in detail in subsequent chapters.

Four Key Markets: Resources, Goods and Services, Loanable Funds, and Foreign Exchange

Businesses generally purchase resources from households and use them to produce goods and services. In turn, households generally use a substantial portion of the income they earn from the sale of their productive services to purchase goods and services supplied by

Fiscal policy
The use of government taxation and expenditure policies for the purpose of achieving macroeconomic goals.

Monetary policy
The deliberate control of the money supply, and, in some cases, credit conditions, for the purpose of achieving macroeconomic goals.

Money supply
The supply of currency, checking account funds, and traveler's checks. These items are counted as money because they are used as the means of payment for purchases.

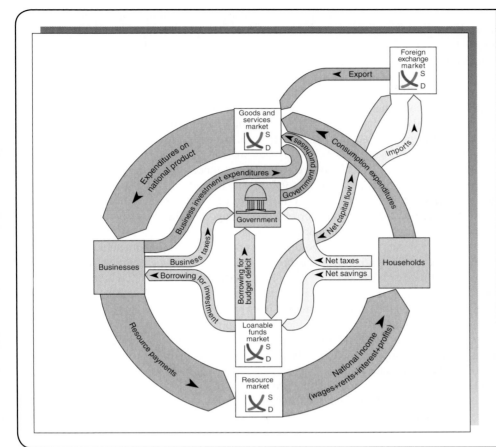

EXHIBIT 1
Four Key Markets and the
Circular Flow of Income

The circular-flow diagram is a visual model of the economy. The circular flow of income is coordinated by four key markets. First, the resource market (bottom loop) coordinates businesses demanding resources and households supplying them in exchange for income. Second, the loanable funds market (lower center) brings the net saving of households plus the net inflow of foreign capital into balance with the borrowing by businesses and governments. Third, the foreign exchange market (top right) brings the purchases (imports) from foreigners into balance with sales (exports plus net inflow of capital) to them. Finally, the goods and services market (top loop) coordinates the demand (consumption, investment, government purchases, and net exports) with the supply of domestically produced goods and services (real GDP).

businesses. ***Thus, there is a circular flow of output and income between these two key sectors, businesses and households. This circular flow of income is coordinated by four key macroeconomic markets: (1) goods and services, (2) resources, (3) loanable funds, and (4) foreign exchange.***

EXHIBIT 1 illustrates both the circular flow of income between the household and business sectors and the interrelationships among the key macroeconomic markets. This is a very important exhibit and really much less complicated than it might first appear. It essentially depicts the macroeconomic model explained in this chapter and used to analyze the economy. It will help you see more clearly the various spending flows and interrelationships among the key markets—where the money comes from and where it goes.

The bottom loop of this circular-flow diagram depicts the **resource market**, a highly aggregated market that includes the markets for labor services, natural resources, and physical capital. In the resource market, business firms demand resources because they need them to produce goods and services. Households supply labor and other resources in exchange for income. The forces of demand and supply determine prices in the resource market. The payments made to households and the suppliers of other resources sum to national income. Some of that income is taxed and used to finance the expenditures of governments. A portion is generally saved, but most of us use the bulk of our income to buy goods and services.

The **goods and services market** constitutes the top loop of the circular-flow diagram. In this market, sometimes called the *product market,* businesses supply goods and services in exchange for sales revenue. This market counts all items in the economy's GDP. As the arrows flowing into the goods and services market (top loop) show, there are four major

Resource market

A highly aggregated market encompassing all resources (labor, physical capital, land, and entrepreneurship) contributing to the production of current output. The labor market is the largest component of this market.

Goods and services market

A highly aggregated market encompassing the flow of all final-user goods and services. The market counts all items that enter into GDP. Thus, real output in this market is equal to real GDP.

sources of expenditures in this market: (1) household expenditures on consumption (and new housing), (2) business investment, (3) government purchases, and (4) net exports. The expenditures of households, business investors, governments, and foreigners (net exports) compose the aggregate (total) demand for domestic output. As you can see, the goods and services market is a highly diverse market. It includes items such as cheeseburgers, pizza, hairstyling, movie tickets, clothing, television sets, and DVD players—goods purchased primarily by consumers. It also includes investment goods such as tools, manufacturing equipment, and office buildings, generally purchased by business firms. Finally, things like highways, fire protection, and national defense, which are usually purchased by governments, are also part of the goods and services market.

Loanable funds market

A general term used to describe the market that coordinates the borrowing and lending decisions of business firms and households. Commercial banks, savings and loan associations, the stock and bond markets, and insurance companies are important financial institutions in this market.

Two other key markets help direct the flow of income between households and businesses. One is the **loanable funds market**. The loanable funds market is the market in which money is borrowed and loaned. It matches people who want to borrow money with those who want to lend it. If you borrow money to go to college or buy a car, you are participating in the loanable funds market.

The net **saving** of the household sector supplies funds to the loanable funds market. The demand for funds arises from businesses to finance investment projects and from government to finance budget deficits. In an open economy like the United States, people also borrow from and lend money to foreigners. Notice the net inflow of capital from foreign economies into the loanable funds market in Exhibit 1. If the funds borrowed from foreigners exceed the loans made to them, there will be a net inflow of funds. This will increase the supply of funds that can be loaned to borrowers. However, if foreigners borrow more money than they supply, there will be a net outflow of funds. The price in the loanable funds market is the interest rate. Like prices in other markets, the interest rate will tend to bring the quantity demanded (funds borrowed by businesses and governments) into balance with the quantity supplied (the net saving of households plus the net inflow of capital from foreigners). When the borrowed funds are spent on investment goods and government purchases, they return to the circular flow.

Saving

The portion of after-tax income that is not spent on consumption. Saving is a "flow" concept.

Foreign exchange market

The market in which the currencies of different countries are bought and sold.

The other key market is the **foreign exchange market**. The foreign exchange market determines the rate—or price—at which two countries' currencies are exchanged. Firms generally want to be paid in their local currency. International transactions, therefore, generally require one of the trading partners to convert its domestic currency to that of the other partner. Exchanges like this take place in the foreign exchange market. For example, if an American firm purchases glassware from a Mexican supplier, the firm would typically exchange dollars for pesos and then use the pesos to pay for the glassware. This generates demand for pesos. Conversely, when foreigners buy U.S. products, it generates demand for U.S dollars. The **exchange rate**—the price of one currency relative to another—brings the purchases from foreigners into balance with the sales to them because rates of exchange are also subject to the laws of supply and demand.

Exchange rate

The price of one unit of foreign currency in terms of the domestic currency. For example, if it takes $1.50 to purchase an English pound, the dollar–pound exchange rate is 1.50.

Look closely at the right side of Exhibit 1 to determine what happens to the flow of income received by households. A major portion of household income is used to purchase consumer goods from domestic producers. These expenditures flow directly into the goods and services market. However, there are three types of "leakages" that can occur: households will use some of their income to purchase imports; some of the income will be taxed away by the government; and some of it will be saved. Imports, net taxes, and net saving are leakages from the circular flow of income.

However, these income leakages don't just evaporate into thin air. They tend to be channeled into the loanable funds and foreign exchange markets and back into the circular flow. The loanable funds market will tend to direct the net saving of households toward business investment and government purchases. The foreign exchange market will tend to direct import expenditures toward either spending by foreigners on exports or supplying funds to the loanable funds market. As we proceed, we will investigate in more detail how the loanable funds and foreign exchange markets influence the leakages from and injections to the circular flow of income.

As we noted in Chapter 7, there are two ways of measuring gross domestic product (GDP), the aggregate domestic output of an economy. First, GDP can be measured by adding up the spending of consumers, investors, governments, and foreigners (net exports) on goods and services produced during the year. This method is equivalent to measuring the flow of output as it moves through the top loop—the goods and services market—of the circular-flow diagram. Alternatively, GDP can be measured by summing the income payments, both direct and indirect, received by the resource suppliers who produced the goods and services. This method uses the bottom loop—the resource market—to measure the flow of output.

Aggregate Demand for Goods and Services

What goes on in the aggregate goods and services market is central to the health of an economy. Indeed, if we could keep our eye on just one market in an economy, we would choose the goods and services market. It is important to note that the "quantity" and "price" in this highly aggregated, or combined, market differ from their counterparts in markets for specific goods. In the aggregate market for goods and services, the "quantity" (graphed on the *x*-axis) refers to the output of the entire economy—its GDP, in other words. The "price" (graphed on the *y*-axis) refers to the price level in the entire economy, which is measured by a general price index (such as the GDP deflator or consumer price index).

Demand and supply can help us understand highly aggregated markets just as they do markets for specific goods (say, for MP3 players or Starbucks coffee). Because demand in the goods and services market aggregates, or combines together, the purchases of all consumers, investors, governments, and foreigners, it is called "aggregate demand." The **aggregate demand curve** shows the various quantities of *domestically produced* goods and services purchasers are willing to buy at different price levels. As **EXHIBIT 2** illustrates, the aggregate demand curve (*AD*) slopes downward to the right, indicating an inverse relationship between the amount of goods and services demanded and the price level.

Aggregate demand curve

A downward-sloping curve showing the relationship between the price level and the quantity of domestically produced goods and services all households, business firms, governments, and foreigners (net exports) are willing to purchase.

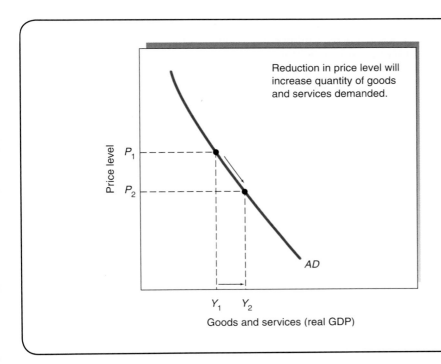

Reduction in price level will increase quantity of goods and services demanded.

Price level

P_1

P_2

AD

Y_1 Y_2

Goods and services (real GDP)

EXHIBIT 2
The Aggregate Demand Curve

The quantity of goods and services purchased will increase (to Y_2) as the price level declines (to P_2). Other things being constant, the lower price level will increase the wealth of people holding money, lead to lower interest rates, and make domestically produced goods cheaper relative to foreign goods. All these factors will tend to increase the quantity of goods and services purchased at the lower price level.

Why Does the Aggregate Demand Curve Slope Downward?

The reason the aggregate demand curve slopes downward is different from the reason the demand curve for a single product does. The inverse relationship between price and the amount demanded of a specific commodity—television sets, for example—reflects the fact that consumers will buy the good in lieu of substitute goods when its price goes down. This is because the good becomes less expensive relative to others. In contrast, a price reduction in the aggregate goods and services market indicates that the level of prices in the entire economy has declined. When this happens, the prices of *all* goods are lower. When the prices of all goods produced domestically fall by the same proportion, there will be no incentive for *domestic* buyers to substitute one good for another.

Nonetheless, there will still be an inverse relationship between price and quantity in the goods and services market. There are three major reasons a lower price level will lead to an increase in the aggregate quantity of goods and services demanded by purchasers.

1. A LOWER PRICE LEVEL WILL INCREASE THE PURCHASING POWER OF MONEY. As the level of prices declines, the purchasing power of money increases. For example, suppose that you have $2,000 in your bank account. Consider how a 20 percent reduction in the level of prices will influence your wealth and spending. At the lower price level, your $2,000 will buy more goods and services. In fact, your $2,000 will buy as much as $2,500 would have purchased at the previous higher price level. Other people will be in the same position you are. They will be wealthier and able to buy more. (*Note:* Remember we are assuming that the supply of money is fixed—that the Federal Reserve is keeping the money supply constant.) Because of this increase in wealth, people will purchase more goods and services.

2. THE INTEREST-RATE EFFECT: A LOWER PRICE LEVEL WILL REDUCE THE DEMAND FOR MONEY AND LOWER THE REAL INTEREST RATE, WHICH WILL STIMULATE ADDITIONAL PURCHASES. When the average price of everything is lower, consumers and businesses will need less money to conduct their normal activities. Households will be able to get by just fine with a smaller money balance because, at the lower price level, they will be spending a smaller amount on food, clothing, and other items they regularly purchase. Similarly, businesses will need less money to pay employee wages, taxes, and other business expenses. At the lower price level, both consumers and businesses will attempt to reduce their money balances and shift more funds to interest-earning assets like bonds and savings deposits. This will channel more funds into the loanable funds market, placing downward pressure on interest rates.

What impact will a lower interest rate have on the demand for goods and services? A reduction in the interest rate will make it cheaper to purchase goods and services on credit. Both households and businesses will demand more goods and services as a result. Households can be expected to increase their purchases of interest-sensitive consumption goods, like automobiles and consumer durables. Similarly, firms will invest more in business expansion and new construction. This effect through the interest rate also contributes to the downward slope of the aggregate demand curve.

3. OTHER THINGS BEING CONSTANT, A LOWER PRICE LEVEL WILL MAKE DOMESTICALLY PRODUCED GOODS LESS EXPENSIVE RELATIVE TO FOREIGN GOODS. As a result, if prices fall in the United States, for example, imports will decline as Americans find that many domestically produced goods are now cheaper than products produced abroad. At the lower price level, Americans will tend to purchase fewer Japanese automobiles, Korean textiles, Italian shoes, and other imports because these items are now more expensive relative to domestically produced goods. At the same time, foreigners will increase their purchases of American-made goods that are now relatively cheaper. Therefore, net exports (exports minus imports) will tend to rise.[2] The increase in net exports at the lower U.S.

[2]An increase in exports and a decline in imports will place some upward pressure on the foreign exchange value of the currency. However, the lower interest rates (point 2 above) will result in an outflow of capital, which will place downward pressure on the foreign exchange value of the currency. Most economists believe that this latter effect will dominate. If it does, a depreciation in the nation's currency will stimulate net exports, which will also increase the quantity demanded of goods and services.

price level will directly increase the quantity demanded of domestically produced goods. This international-substitution effect is a third reason the aggregate demand curve slopes downward.

The Downward-Sloping Aggregate Demand Curve: A Summary

The accompanying **Thumbnail Sketch** summarizes the reasons why a lower price level increases the quantity demanded of domestically produced goods and services. A lower price level will (1) increase the purchasing power of money, (2) lower interest rates, and (3) reduce the price of domestically produced goods relative to goods produced abroad. Each of these factors will tend to increase the quantity demanded in the goods and services market.

If the price level were to rise, the effects would be just the opposite. At a higher price level, (1) the wealth of people holding money would be less; (2) the demand for money would be greater, which would lead to higher interest rates; and (3) domestic goods would be more expensive relative to those produced abroad. Each of these factors would tend to reduce the quantity demanded of domestically produced goods.

Aggregate Supply of Goods and Services

In light of our discussion of aggregate demand, it shouldn't surprise you that the general shape of the **aggregate supply curve** differs from the shape of the supply curve for a single good. As we already noted, when the price level rises, the prices of all goods rise, rather than the price of one good relative to other goods. Thus, the general shape of the aggregate supply (*AS*) curve is not a reflection of changes in the relative prices of goods.

When we examine aggregate supply, it is particularly important to distinguish between the short run and the long run. In the short run, some prices, particularly those in labor markets, are set by prior contracts and agreements. Households and businesses are unable to adjust these prices when unexpected changes occur, including unexpected changes in the price level. In contrast, the long run is a time period long enough that people are able to modify their behavior in response to price changes. We now consider both the short-run and long-run aggregate supply curves.

Aggregate supply curve

The curve showing the relationship between a nation's price level and the quantity of goods supplied by its producers. In the short run, it is an upward-sloping curve, but in the long run the aggregate supply curve is vertical.

Aggregate Supply in the Short Run

The short-run aggregate supply (**SRAS**) *curve shows the various quantities of goods and services domestic firms will supply in response to changing demand conditions that alter the level of prices in the goods and services market*. As **EXHIBIT 3** part (a) shows, the *SRAS*

THUMBNAIL SKETCH

Why Is The Aggregate Quantity Demanded Inversely Related to the Price Level?

A decrease in the price level will raise the aggregate quantity demanded because:

1. The real wealth of people holding money will increase when prices fall; this will encourage additional consumption.

2. A fall in the demand for money at the lower price level will reduce interest rates, which will encourage current investment and consumption.

3. Net exports will expand (because the prices of domestic goods will have fallen relative to foreign goods).

curve in the goods and services market slopes upward to the right. The upward slope reflects the fact that, in the short run, an unanticipated increase in the price level will, on average, improve the profitability of firms. They will respond with an expansion in output.

The *SRAS* curve is based on a specific expected price level, P_{100} in the case of Exhibit 3, and rate of inflation that generates that price level. When the expected price level is actually achieved, the profitability rate of firms, on average, will be normal, and they will supply output Y_0.

Consider how firms would respond if strong demand led to an unexpected increase in the price level (to P_{105}, for example). Important components of producers' costs are determined by long-term contracts. These components include interest rates on their loans, collective bargaining agreements with their employees, lease agreements on buildings and machines, and other contracts with resource suppliers. The prices incorporated into these long-term contracts at the time of the agreement are based on the expectation of price level (P_{100}) for the current period and tend to be temporarily fixed. So, in the short run, the higher prices enhance producers' profitability because the prices for which they can sell their products rise but some of their costs (like labor) don't. When this happens, firms will happily respond by expanding their output (to Y_1). Their profits will be higher if they do.[3]

EXHIBIT 3
The Aggregate Supply Curve

The short-run aggregate supply (SRAS) curve shows the relationship between the price level and the quantity supplied of goods and services by domestic producers (part a). In the short run, firms will generally expand output as the price level increases; the higher prices will improve their profit margins because many of their cost components will be temporarily fixed as the result of prior long-term commitments. However, once people have had time to adjust their prior long-term commitments, resource markets (and costs) will adjust to the higher level of prices, and firms will no longer have an incentive to supply a larger output at the higher price level. The vertical long-run aggregate supply (LRAS) curve in part (b) illustrates this point. The economy's full-employment rate of output—Y_F, the maximum output rate that is sustainable—is determined by the supply of resources, level of technology, and structure of institutions, factors that are insensitive to changes in the price level.

(a) Short-run aggregate supply

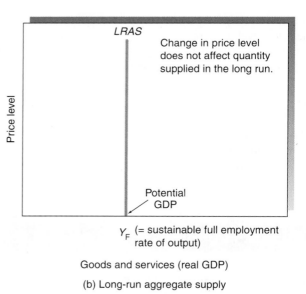

(b) Long-run aggregate supply

---

[3]Other factors may also contribute to the positive relationship between the price level and output in the short run. In response to a general increase in demand, some firms may expand output without much of an increase in price because they believe that their current strong sales are only temporary and that a price increase would drive some of their regular customers to rival suppliers. Other firms may expand output because they mistakenly believe that the demand for their product has increased relative to other products. In the long run, higher costs relative to product prices will make it impossible to sustain such expansions in output.

Conversely, an unexpected reduction in the price level to P_{95} will have the opposite effect. It will decrease product prices relative to costs and thereby reduce profitability. In response, firms will reduce output to Y_2. Thus, as Exhibit 3(a) illustrates, there is a direct relationship between the amount producers will supply and the price level in the goods and services market in the short run.

Aggregate Supply in the Long Run

Things are different, though, when it comes to aggregate supply in the long run. In the long run, a higher price level won't change the relationship between product and resource prices. Once people have time to adjust their prior commitments fully, competitive forces will restore the usual relationship between product prices and costs. Profit rates will return to normal, and firms will not have any additional incentive to pump out extra goods and services. ***The long-run aggregate supply (LRAS) curve shows the relationship between the price level and quantity of output after decision makers have had time to adjust their prior commitments, or take steps to counterbalance them, when the price level changes***. Therefore, as Exhibit 3 part (b) illustrates, the *LRAS* curve is vertical.

In the long run, once people have time to adjust their choices, the forces that provide for an upward-sloping *SRAS* curve are no longer present. Costs that are temporarily fixed as the result of contractual agreements will eventually rise. With time, the long-term contracts will expire and be renegotiated. Once the contracts are renegotiated, resource prices will increase in the same proportion as product prices. A proportional increase in costs and product prices will leave the incentive to produce unchanged. Consider how a firm with a selling price of $50 and per-unit costs of $50 will be affected when both the price it can sell its product for and the resources used to make it double. After the price increase, the firm's sales price per unit will be $100, but so, too, will its per-unit costs. Thus, neither the firm's profit rate nor its incentive to produce more of the good has changed. Therefore, in the long run, an increase in the price level will fail to exert a lasting impact on aggregate output.

As we discussed in Chapter 2, at a point in time, the production possibilities of a nation are constrained by the supply of resources, level of technology, and institutional arrangements that influence the efficiency of resource use. The long-run aggregate supply curve is an alternative way to visualize the economy's production possibilities. Rather than showing the output of physical units like the production possibilities curve does, the long-run aggregate supply curve shows the real dollar value of the units produced. The vertical long-run supply curve indicates that a change in the price level doesn't loosen the constraints limiting our production possibilities. For example, a doubling of prices will

THUMBNAIL SKETCH

Why Is the Short-Run Aggregate Quantity Supplied Directly Related to the Price Level?

As the general level of sales prices for products increases, profit margins will improve because some costs of production are temporarily fixed by long-term contracts.

Why is the long-run aggregate supply curve vertical?

1. Once people have had time to adjust fully to a new price level, the normal relationship between product prices and resource costs will be restored.

2. The sustainable potential output of an economy is determined by its quantity of resources, level of technology, and the efficiency of its institutional structures—not by the price level.

not improve technology. Neither will it expand the availability of productive resources, nor improve the efficiency of our economic institutions.

Thus, there is no reason a higher price level would increase our ability to produce goods and services in the long run. Firms are going to continue to produce the same amount of goods and services they're able to, given their resources, no matter what the price level is. This is precisely what the vertical *LRAS* curve implies. The temporary hike in aggregate supply—shown by the upward slope of the *SRAS* curve—is purely a short-run phenomenon. It can't last. The accompanying **Thumbnail Sketch** summarizes the factors that underlie both the short-run and long-run aggregate supply curves.

Equilibrium in the Goods and Services Market

Equilibrium

A balance of forces permitting the simultaneous fulfillment of plans by buyers and sellers.

We are now ready to combine our analysis of aggregate demand and aggregate supply to see how they determine the price level and rate of output in the economy. When a market is in **equilibrium**, the forces exerted by buyers and sellers balance one another. Buyers are willing to purchase all the units that sellers are willing to supply *at the current price level*. Because the equilibrium price clears the market—all units produced are sold—some refer to it as the "market-clearing price."

Equilibrium in the Short Run

As **EXHIBIT 4** illustrates, short-run equilibrium is present in the goods and services market at the price level *P*, at which the aggregate quantity demanded is equal to the aggregate quantity supplied. This occurs at the output rate *Y*, where the *AD* and *SRAS* curves intersect. At the price level *P*, the amount that buyers want to purchase is just equal to the quantity that sellers are willing to supply.

If a price level lower than *P* were present, the aggregate quantity demanded would exceed the aggregate quantity supplied. Purchasers would want to buy more goods and services than producers would be willing to produce. This excess demand would place upward pressure on prices, causing the price level to rise toward *P*. In contrast, at a price level greater than *P*, the aggregate quantity supplied would exceed the aggregate quantity demanded. Producers would be unable to sell all the goods they produce. This would result

EXHIBIT 4
Short-Run Equilibrium in the Goods and Services Market

Short-run equilibrium in the goods and services market occurs at the price level P, where the AD and SRAS curves intersect. If the price level were lower than P, excess demand in goods and services markets would push prices upward. Conversely, if the price level were higher than P, excess supply would result in falling prices.

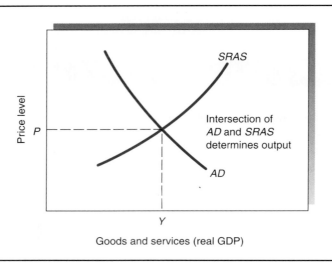

in downward pressure (toward P) on prices. Only at the price level P will there be a balance of forces between the amount of goods demanded by consumers, investors, governments, and foreigners, and the amount supplied by domestic firms.

Equilibrium in the Long Run

In the short run, the goods and services market will gravitate toward a price level that brings quantity demanded and quantity supplied in the economy into balance. ***However, a second condition is required for long-run equilibrium: decision makers who agreed to long-term contracts influencing current prices and costs must have correctly anticipated the current price level at the time they arrived at the agreements.*** If this is not the case, buyers and sellers will want to modify the agreements when their long-term contracts expire. In turn, their modifications will affect costs, profit margins, and output.

EXHIBIT 5 illustrates a long-run equilibrium in the goods and services market. As in Exhibit 3, the subscripts attached to the *SRAS* and *AD* curves indicate the price level (the price index) that decision makers anticipated at the time they made their decisions about their long-term contracts. In this case, when buyers and sellers made their purchasing and production choices, they anticipated that the price level during the period would be P_{100}. As the intersection of the *AD* and *SRAS* curves reveals, P_{100} was actually attained. In long-run equilibrium, aggregate demand (*AD*) intersects with *SRAS* along the economy's vertical *LRAS*.

When the price level expectations about the long-term contracts turn out to be correct, then the current resource prices and real interest rates will tend to persist into the future. Profit rates will be normal. The choices of buyers and sellers will

---

EXHIBIT 5
Long-Run Equilibrium in the Goods and Services Market

When the goods and services market is in long-run equilibrium, two conditions must be present. First, the quantity demanded must equal the quantity supplied at the current price level. Second, the price level anticipated by decision makers must equal the actual price level. The subscripts on the SRAS and AD curves indicate that buyers and sellers alike anticipated the price level P_{100}, where the 100 represents an index of prices during an earlier base year. When the anticipated price level is actually attained, current output (Y_F) will equal the economy's potential GDP, and full employment will be present.

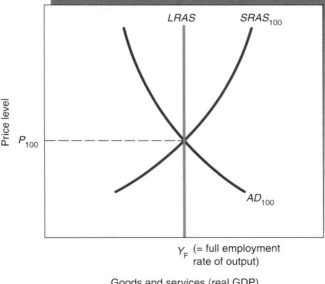

harmonize, and neither will have reason to modify their previous contractual agreements when they come up for renegotiation. Thus, the current rate of output (Y_F) is sustainable in the future. This also corresponds to full employment in the economy. Long-run equilibrium is present, and it will persist into the future until changes in other factors alter *AD* or *SRAS*.

Long-Run Equilibrium, Potential Output, and Full Employment

As we discussed in Chapter 8, potential GDP is equal to the economy's *maximum sustainable output* consistent with its resource base, current technology, and institutional structure. Potential GDP is neither a temporary high nor an abnormal low. When long-run equilibrium is present, the actual output achieved is equal to the economy's potential GDP.

The long-run equilibrium output rate (Y_F in Exhibit 5) also corresponds with the full employment of resources. When full-employment output is present, the job search time of unemployed workers will be normal, given the characteristics of the labor force and the institutional structure of the economy. Only frictional and structural unemployment will be present; cyclical unemployment will be absent.

When an economy is in long-run equilibrium, the *actual* rate of unemployment will be equal to the natural rate. Remember, the *natural* rate of unemployment reflects the normal job search process of employees and employers, given the structure of the economy and the laws and regulations that affect the operation of markets. It is a rate that is neither abnormally high nor abnormally low; it can be sustained into the future. If long-run equilibrium is present, unemployment will be at its natural rate.

Let's summarize what we've learned: In long-run equilibrium, (1) output will be equal to its potential, (2) full employment will be achieved, and (3) the actual rate of unemployment will be equivalent to the natural rate of unemployment. It is this long-run maximum sustainable output that economists are referring to when they speak of "full-employment output" or "potential GDP."

What Happens When the Economy's Output Differs from Its Long-Run Potential?

SCENARIO 1: OUTPUT IS GREATER THAN LONG-RUN POTENTIAL. What happens when changes in the price level catch buyers and sellers by surprise? When the actual price level differs from the level forecast by buyers and sellers, some decision makers will enter into agreements that they will later regret—agreements that they will want to change as soon as they have an opportunity to do so.

Consider the situation when the price level *increases* more than was anticipated. Failing to foresee the strong demand and higher product prices, many resource suppliers will have agreed to long-term contracts that are not as attractive as they initially thought they would be. For example, many union officials and employees will have made commitments to money wages that are now unattractive, given the strong demand and higher general level of prices. Other resource suppliers will find themselves in a similar position. In the short run, the atypically low resource costs relative to product prices make profit margins abnormally high. In this case, firms will pump out more output to boost their profits. Employment expands and unemployment falls below its natural rate.

An economic boom is present, but the abnormally large output and high level of employment are not sustainable. The "mistakes," based on a failure to predict the strength of current demand, will be recognized and corrected when contracts expire. Real wages (and other resource prices) will increase and eventually reflect the higher price level and rate of inflation. Profit margins will return to normal. When these adjustments are completed, the temporarily large output rate and high employment level will decline and return to normal.

How can output, even temporarily, be pushed beyond the economy's potential GDP? Remember, potential GDP is a sustainable rate of output; it can be maintained. Motivated by strong demand and high profitability, firms can expand output through intensive supervision, more overtime work, a reduction in downtime for maintenance, and similar measures. However, this intense pace cannot be maintained over lengthy periods. The situation is much like that of students who stay up later, watch less television, and spend less time on social and leisure activities in order to increase their study time prior to a major exam. They are able to increase their "productivity" temporarily, but the intense schedule cannot be maintained. Similarly, business firms can temporarily push output beyond long-run potential. But, given the constraints of the current resource base, the higher output rate cannot be sustained. Markets will adjust and output will recede to its long-run potential.

SCENARIO 2: OUTPUT IS LESS THAN LONG-RUN POTENTIAL. What will happen if product prices either decline or increase less rapidly than anticipated? Given the lower than expected price level, many employers will find themselves committed to wages and other resource prices that are extremely high relative to the prices they can get for their products. Profit margins will be squeezed, causing producers to reduce output and lay off employees. Unemployment will rise above its *natural rate,* and current output will fall short of the economy's potential GDP. Recessionary conditions will be present.

But the weak demand for resources and abnormally high unemployment will place downward pressure on resource prices and, as long-term contracts are eventually renegotiated, resource prices will fall. In turn, this will reduce costs, and eventually the lower cost will make it possible for firms to once again earn normal returns. As this happens, the economy will be directed back to its long-run equilibrium output and employment rates. Clearly, this adjustment process will take time, several quarters or perhaps even a year or two.

Again, let's summarize what we've learned: An unexpected change in the price level (rate of inflation) will alter the rate of output in the short run. An unexpected *increase* in the price level will stimulate output and employment during the next year or two, whereas an unexpected *decrease* in the price level will cause output and employment to fall.

As we have said, in addition to the aggregate goods and services market, the resource market, loanable funds market, and foreign exchange market help coordinate the circular flow of income between households and businesses. All four of these markets are interrelated—changes in one will have repercussions in the others. We will now turn to an analysis of the resource, loanable funds, and foreign exchange markets and how they work in tandem with the goods and services market.

The expected rate of inflation influences the prices incorporated into long-term contracts, like collective bargaining agreements. If the actual price level differs from what was expected, output will differ from long-run equilibrium.

Resource Market

The resource market is the place where labor services, raw materials, machines, and other factors of production are bought and sold. Within the framework of our circular-flow analysis, households supply resources (like their labor) in exchange for income. Business firms demand resources to produce goods and services, as Exhibit 1 showed. By far, labor is the largest component of the resource market. In the United States, labor costs make up approximately 70 percent of production costs. Because of the labor market's size and importance, we will focus considerable attention on it.

An increase in the price of labor and other resources will increase the cost of production and make it less profitable for firms to employ resources. As a result, businesses will demand less labor and other resources as the prices of those resources increase. Thus, the demand curve in the resource market will have the usual downward slope to the right. Although working and supplying resources generate income, they also require a person to give up other things—like leisure. Higher resource prices—like higher wages—will make it more attractive for people to give up some leisure and supply labor and other resources instead. Therefore, the quantity supplied of labor and other resources expands as resource prices increase.

As **EXHIBIT 6** illustrates, there will be a tendency to move toward a price level that will bring the amount of resources demanded by business firms into balance with the amount supplied by resource owners, just as goods and services are brought into balance between consumers and producers. At this price (P_r), the choices of both buyers and sellers in the aggregate resource market harmonize—they are consistent with each other. If either excess demand or excess supply were present, the market would move back toward equilibrium.

The markets for resources and products are closely related. The demand for resources is directly linked to the demand for goods and services. An increase in demand in the goods and services market will generate additional demand for resources. Similarly, a reduction in aggregate demand in the goods and services market will reduce the demand for resources.

Changes in resource markets will also exert an effect on the goods and services market. The cost of producing goods and services is influenced directly by the price of resources. Other things constant, an increase in resource prices will increase costs and squeeze profit margins, causing the supply curve (*SRAS*) in the product market to shift to the left. If inputs are costing firms more, higher product prices will be required to provide firms with the same incentive to supply any given level of output. Conversely, a reduction

EXHIBIT 6
Equilibrium in the
Resource Market

In general, as resource prices increase, the amount demanded by producers declines and the amount supplied by resource owners expands. In equilibrium, resource price brings the amount demanded into balance with the amount supplied in the aggregate-resource market. The labor market is a major component of the resource market.

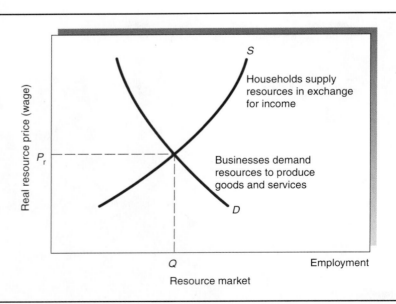

in resource prices will lower costs and improve profit margins in the goods and services market. An increase in aggregate supply (a shift to the right in *SRAS*) will result. As we analyze the macroeconomy, the interrelations between these two markets will arise again and again.

Loanable Funds Market

As we have said, the loanable funds market is the market in which borrowers demand funds and lenders supply them. The price in this market is the interest rate. To keep things simple, we will assume that there is a single interest rate. In reality, of course, borrowers and lenders make deals at many different interest rates. Those interest rates depend on what a person or firm is buying, the length of time they want to borrow the money for, and the level of risk involved. Banks, insurance companies, and brokerage firms often act as intermediaries between lenders and borrowers in the loanable funds market.

Essentially, borrowers are exchanging future income to get purchasing power now. Most of us are impatient; we want things now rather than in the future. *From the viewpoint of borrowers, interest is the price they have to pay to get money now. From the viewpoint of lenders, interest is the reward they get for waiting, for not being able to spend their money now because they've loaned it to someone else.*

As part (a) of **EXHIBIT 7** illustrates, more funds will be borrowed at lower interest rates. A lower interest rate will make it cheaper for households to purchase consumption goods and for businesses to undertake investment projects. They will borrow more at lower rates. As a result, the demand curve for loanable funds slopes downward to the right. Conversely, higher interest rates make it more attractive to save (and lend funds). Thus, the supply curve for loanable funds slopes upward to the right, indicating that there is a direct relationship between the interest rate and the quantity of funds supplied by lenders. The interest rate will coordinate the actions of borrowers and lenders. It will tend to move toward an equilibrium rate (in the case of Exhibit 7(a), 6 percent). This is the rate at which the quantity of funds supplied by lenders just equals the quantity demanded by borrowers.

Banks, savings and loan associations, and brokerage firms help coordinate saving and borrowing in the loanable funds market.

EXHIBIT 7
Interest Rates and the Loanable Funds Market

The interest rate in the loanable funds market will bring the quantity of funds demanded by borrowers into balance with the quantity supplied by lenders (part a). As part (b) illustrates, inflation will influence the nominal interest rate. Suppose that when people expect the general level of prices to be stable (zero inflation) in the future, a 6 percent interest rate brings quantity demanded into balance with quantity supplied. Under these conditions, the money interest rate and real interest rate will be equal. When people expect prices to rise at a 5 percent rate, however, the money rate of interest (i) will rise to 11 percent even though the real interest rate (r) remains constant at 6 percent.

(a) Interest rate determination

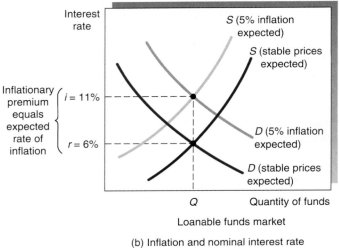

(b) Inflation and nominal interest rate

Money interest rate

The percentage of the amount borrowed that must be paid to the lender in addition to the repayment of the principal. The money interest rate overstates the real cost of borrowing during an inflationary period. When inflation is anticipated, an inflationary premium will be incorporated into this rate. The money interest rate is often called the nominal interest rate.

Real interest rate

The interest rate adjusted for expected inflation: it indicates the real cost to the borrower (and yield to the lender) in terms of goods and services.

It is important to think of the interest rate in two ways. First, there is the **money interest rate**, the percentage of the amount borrowed that must be paid to the lender in addition to the repayment of the principal. Money interest rates are those typically quoted in newspapers and business publications. Second, there is the **real interest rate**, which reflects the actual burden to borrowers and the payoff to lenders after inflation has had an impact.

The rate of inflation expected by borrowers and lenders will influence the attractiveness of various interest rates. Perhaps an example will illustrate this point and highlight the distinction between the money interest rate and the real interest rate. Suppose that a borrower and lender—both anticipating that the general level of prices will be stable—agree to a 6 percent interest rate for a one-year loan of $1,000. After a year, the borrower must pay the lender $1,060—the $1,000 principal plus the 6 percent interest. Now, suppose during the year prices rise 5 percent as the result of inflation. Because of this, the $1,060 repayment after a year commands only about 1 percent more purchasing power than the original $1,000 did when it was loaned. The lender receives only a 1 percent return for making the purchasing power available to the borrower. In this case, the real interest return to the lender (and real cost to the borrower) is just 1 percent. Lenders are unlikely to continue making funds available at such bargain rates. They are going to begin charging higher rates.

When inflation is persistent, people will come to anticipate it. Once borrowers and lenders expect a rate of inflation—5 percent, for example—they will build that rate into their loanable funds agreements. Lenders will demand (and borrowers will agree to pay) a higher money interest rate to compensate for the impact of inflation. This premium for the expected decline in purchasing power of the dollar is called the **inflationary premium**. It is equal to the expected rate of inflation. The relationship between the real interest rate and money interest rate is

Real interest rate = Money interest rate − Inflationary premium

Part (b) of Exhibit 7 illustrates how people's expectations about inflation influence money interest rates. Here, we consider a situation in which a 6 percent market rate of interest would emerge when borrowers and lenders anticipate stable prices. Because the expected rate of inflation is zero, there will be no inflationary premium and, under these conditions, the money interest rate will be equal to the real interest rate. Now consider how a persistent inflation rate of 5 percent will influence the choices of both borrowers and lenders. Compared with the situation in which the inflation rate was zero and the interest rate 6 percent, an 11 percent interest rate will now be required to provide lenders with the same incentive to loan funds. Similarly, an 11 percent interest rate will provide borrowers with the same incentive to demand funds. When people expect a 5 percent rate of inflation, both the supply and demand curves will shift vertically by this amount to compensate for the expected rate of inflation. As a result, the money rate of interest will increase to 11 percent: 5 percent of that is the inflationary premium; 6 percent is the real return that lenders earn.

Of course, the expected rate of inflation and inflationary premium cannot be directly observed. Therefore, neither can the real interest rate. Nonetheless, it is easy to see why the money interest rate can be misleading. It doesn't reflect the real cost of borrowing money. (Remember: *real* always means adjusted for inflation.) What people expect inflation to be and what it actually ends up being can be different. Even though this is problematic, the money interest rate will nonetheless vary directly with what people expect inflation to be. If they expect inflation will be higher, the inflationary premium will be higher, too, as will the money rate of interest. Only the *real* interest rate reflects the true cost of borrowing and the true return of lending money. For a discussion of how inflation affects interest rates and welfare of borrowers and lenders, see the Applications in Economics box: Does Inflation Help Borrowers?

Inflationary premium

A component of the money interest rate that reflects compensation to the lender for the expected decrease, due to inflation, in the purchasing power of the principal and interest during the course of the loan. It is determined by the expected rate of future inflation.

APPLICATIONS IN ECONOMICS

Does Inflation Help Borrowers?

In a world of uncertainty, decision makers will not always be able to forecast accurately the future rate of inflation. If the actual rate of inflation is higher than was expected, borrowers will tend to gain relative to lenders. For example, suppose borrowers and lenders expect a 3 percent future rate of inflation and therefore agree to an 8 percent interest rate on a loan—5 percent representing the real interest rate and 3 percent the inflationary premium. If the actual rate of inflation turns out to be higher than 3 percent—6 percent, for example—the real amount paid by the borrower and received by the lender will decline. ***When the actual rate of inflation is greater than was anticipated, borrowers gain at the expense of lenders.***

But the converse is true when the actual rate of inflation is less than expected. Suppose that after the borrower and lender agree to the 8 percent loan, the price level remains stable. In this case, the borrower ends up paying an 8 percent real interest rate, rather than the 5 percent which was expected. ***When the actual rate of inflation is less than anticipated, lenders gain at the expense of borrowers.***

Some people argue that inflation helps borrowers relative to lenders. But this neglects the fact that loans have an inflationary premium built into them. Borrowers will only gain relative to lenders if both borrowers and lenders underestimate the rate of inflation and don't allow enough of an inflationary premium. This is highly unlikely to happen on a regular basis. Of course, forecasting errors will be made. Sometimes the inflation rate will be higher than decision makers anticipated, whereas in other instances it will be lower. There is no reason, however, to expect that everyone will underestimate inflation and what the inflationary premium should be. Thus, there is no reason why inflation will help either borrowers or lenders in a systematic manner.

Interest Rates and Macroeconomic Markets

The circular-flow diagram (Exhibit 1) illustrates both the inflow and outflow to the loanable funds market. The net saving of households and net capital inflow from foreigners provide the inflow—the supply of funds—into the loanable funds market. Borrowing by businesses and governments generates the demand for loanable funds.

Businesses and governments often borrow money by issuing bonds on which they pay interest. Issuing bonds is simply a method of demanding loanable funds. In turn, the purchasers of bonds are supplying loanable funds. There is an inverse relationship between bond prices and interest rates. When interest rates rise, the market value of bonds previously issued will fall. Conversely, lower interest rates will push the market value of bonds previously issued upward. (For a detailed explanation of this point, see the Applications in Economics box on bonds and interest rates).

In an open economy like that of the United States, domestic residents are also able to borrow from and lend to foreigners. When foreigners supply more loanable funds to the domestic market than Americans supply to foreigners, there will be a net inflow of foreign capital that will supplement domestic saving. Conversely, if Americans are net lenders, there will be a net outflow of capital from the domestic market. The real interest rate in the loanable funds market will move toward the rate that will bring the quantity of funds demanded into equality with the quantity supplied, *including the net inflow or outflow of capital.*

In today's global financial markets, the flow of capital to the domestic loanable funds market will be directly related to the real interest rate. As **EXHIBIT 8** shows, when domestic demand is weak (D_1, for example) and the real interest rate low (r_1), capital will flow outward toward other markets where the rate of return is expected to be higher. In contrast, strong domestic demand (D_2, for example) for loanable funds and high real interest rates will lead to an inflow of capital.

Like the resource market, the loanable funds market is interrelated with the goods and services market. We saw that the interest rate generally falls when the price level falls, which helps explain why the *AD* curve slopes downward to the right. In addition, the real interest rate may change for other reasons. When it does, it will affect the aggregate demand schedule. The real interest rate influences how households allocate their income between saving and current consumption. An increase in the interest rate will discourage current consumption by making it more attractive to save and more expensive to borrow.

EXHIBIT 8

Interest Rates and the Inflow and Outflow of Capital

Demand and supply in the loanable funds market determine interest rates. When the demand for loanable funds is strong (such as D_2), the real interest rate will be high (such as r_2), and there will be a net inflow of capital. In contrast, weak demand (such as D_1) and low interest rates (such as r_1) will lead to net capital outflow.

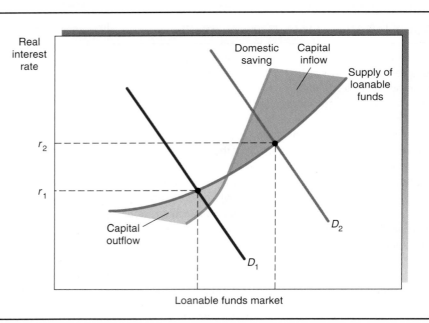

APPLICATIONS IN ECONOMICS

Bonds, Interest Rates, and Bond Prices

Bonds are simply IOUs issued by firms and governments. Issuing bonds is a method of borrowing in the loanable funds market. The entity issuing the bond promises to pay interest at a fixed rate on the amount borrowed (called principal) while the loan is outstanding and to repay the principal on a specified date in the future (for example, five or ten years after the bond is issued). The date when the principal comes due is called the bond's *maturity* date. Each year until that time, the issuing entity usually makes regular interest payments (for example, quarterly or semiannually) to bondholders.

Even though interest rates may change over time, *the bondholder will receive the fixed interest rate specified on the face of the bond*. Although bonds are issued for lengthy periods of time—the U.S. Treasury issues bonds for up to thirty years—they can be sold to another party at any time prior to their maturity. Each day, most of the bonds sold in the bond market are ones that have been issued previously.

When overall interest rates rise, the prices of these previously issued bonds will fall. Suppose you bought a newly issued $1,000 bond that pays 8 percent per year in perpetuity (forever). (*Note*: Bonds that pay interest in

perpetuity are called "consols" and are available in the United Kingdom.) As long as you own the bond, you are entitled to a fixed return of $80 per year. Let's also assume that after you have held the bond for one year and collected your $80 interest for that year, the market rate of interest for newly issued bonds like yours increases to 10 percent. How will this increase in the interest rate affect the market price of your bond? Because bond purchasers can now earn 10 percent interest if they buy newly issued bonds, they will be unwilling to pay more than $800 for your bond, which pays only $80 interest per year. After all, why would anyone pay $1,000 for a bond that yields only $80 interest per year when the same $1,000 will now purchase a bond that yields $100 (10 percent) per year? The increase in the interest rate to 10 percent will therefore cause the *market price* of your $1,000 bond (which earns only 8 percent annually) to fall to $800. At that price, the new owner of your bond would earn the 10 percent market rate of interest. This is why rising market interest rates cause bond prices to fall.

Conversely, falling interest rates will cause bond prices to rise. If the market interest rate had fallen to 6 percent, what would have happened to the market value of your bond? (*Hint*: $80 is 6 percent of $1,333.) As you can see, bond prices and interest rates are inversely linked to each other.

This will reduce aggregate demand. Lower interest rates will have the opposite effect. As we proceed, we will analyze in more detail the interrelationship between the loanable funds market and the goods and services market.

Foreign Exchange Market

Look back at Exhibit 1 and note the various transactions with foreigners. Households import some goods and services from foreigners, reducing the flow of spending into the domestic product market. But foreigners buy some of the goods produced by the domestic firms, and these exports add to the flow of spending into the domestic product market. In addition, there is an inflow of money from foreigners into the loanable funds market and an outflow of money to foreigners. As we just discussed, the size and direction of this net flow of money depend on the real interest rate.

EXHIBIT 9 illustrates how the foreign exchange market tends to bring purchases from foreigners into balance with the sales to them. The dollar price of foreign currency is measured along the vertical axis. A fall in the dollar price of foreign currency—shown by a movement down the vertical axis—means a dollar will buy more units of various foreign currencies. This will make it cheaper for Americans to purchase things from foreigners. Thus, we say that the dollar has **appreciated**, meaning that it will now buy more foreign goods than it previously could. As the dollar price for foreign exchange falls (movement down the vertical axis), Americans buy more from foreigners and therefore demand a

Appreciation

An increase in the value of a currency relative to foreign currencies. An appreciation increases the purchasing power of the currency over foreign goods.

EXHIBIT 9
Foreign Exchange Market

Americans demand foreign currencies to pay for goods and services they import and investments they make abroad. Foreigners supply foreign currency in exchange for U.S. dollars in order to purchase American exports and make investments in the United States. The exchange rate will bring the quantity demanded into balance with the quantity supplied. This will also bring imports plus capital outflow into equality with exports plus capital inflow.

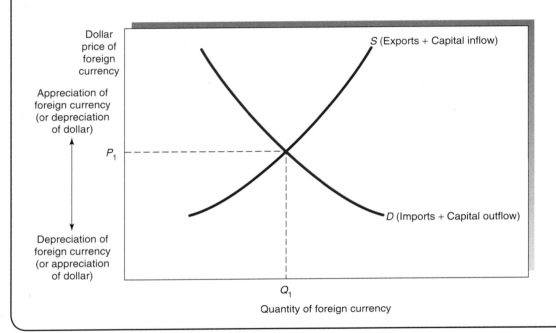

larger quantity of foreign currency in order to make the purchases. The demand curve for foreign currency therefore slopes downward to the right.

In contrast, an increase in the dollar price of foreign currency—shown by movement up the vertical axis—means that more dollars are needed to purchase a unit of foreign currency. This makes foreign purchases more expensive for Americans. Thus, we say the dollar has **depreciated**. As the dollar depreciates, a unit of foreign currency will purchase a larger quantity of dollars. This depreciation in the dollar makes American goods less expensive for foreigners. As the dollar depreciates (movement up the vertical axis), foreigners buy more from Americans and supply more foreign currency in exchange for dollars. The supply curve for foreign currency therefore slopes upward to the right.

The forces of supply and demand in the foreign exchange market will move the exchange rate toward the equilibrium price (P_1 in Exhibit 9). In equilibrium, the quantity demanded of foreign currency will just equal the quantity supplied. Imports plus the outflow of capital for investment abroad to foreign countries will equal exports plus the inflow of capital from the investments of foreigners in the United States.[4] Mathematically, when the exchange market is in equilibrium, the following relationship exists:

Depreciation

A reduction in the value of a currency relative to foreign currencies. A depreciation reduces the purchasing power of the currency over foreign goods.

(9-1)   **Imports + Capital outflow = Exports + Capital inflow**

This relationship can be rewritten as:

(9-2)   **Imports − Exports = Capital inflow − Capital outflow**

---

[4]There are two other small items, gifts to and from foreigners and net income from investments abroad, that also influence the demand for and supply of foreign exchange. Because these factors are so small, however, their omission will not alter the general analysis presented here.

The right side of Equation 9-2 is also called *net capital inflow*. Because it is a net figure, it can be either positive (indicating an inflow of capital) or negative (indicating an outflow of capital).

The left side of the equation (imports minus exports) indicates the nation's balance of trade. On the one hand, when imports exceed exports, this is referred to as a **trade deficit**. On the other hand, when exports exceed imports, this is referred to as a **trade surplus**. There is an interesting relationship between the flow of trade and the flow of capital: When a trade deficit is present, there must be an inflow of capital. The reverse is also true: An inflow of capital implies a trade deficit. Conversely, when a trade surplus (exports are greater than imports) is present, there must also be an outflow of capital.

When the exchange rate is determined by market forces, trade deficits will be closely linked with an inflow of capital. In contrast, trade surpluses will be closely linked with an outflow of capital.

EXHIBIT 10 shows the relationship between the inflow of capital and trade deficits in the United States in recent decades, measured as a share of GDP. Notice how large capital inflows (shown in part a) are closely associated with correspondingly large trade deficits (shown in part b). In the late 1970s and early 1980s, the net inflow of capital was relatively small; so too was the trade deficit. Between 1983 and 1987, the net inflow of capital soared, reaching more than 3 percent of GDP during the latter part of the period. Again, the trade deficit increased by a similar amount. Between 1988 and 1992, the inflow of capital slowed to a trickle and the trade deficit shrank to about to 0.5 percent of GDP. During the last decade, however, the inflow of capital soared once again, reaching 6 percent of GDP; the trade deficit increased hugely, too. Clearly, these two factors are closely related; this is to be expected when a country's exchange rate is determined by market forces.

Are trade deficits bad? The "term" deficit certainly has negative connotations. It is important to recognize that trade deficits may arise for various reasons. If the government is running a large budget deficit, this may push interest rates upward, leading to both an inflow of foreign capital and a trade deficit. However, attractive private investment opportunities may also lead to a trade deficit. When an economy provides a more attractive investment environment than is available in other countries, an inflow of capital and a trade deficit are likely to occur. Clearly, trade deficits arising from this source are not bad. Thus, when analyzing the significance of a trade deficit, it is important to consider the underlying sources of the deficit.

Trade deficit

The situation when a country's imports of goods and services are greater than its exports.

Trade surplus

The situation when a country's exports of goods and services are greater than its imports.

Long-Run Equilibrium

We have now discussed all four basic macroeconomic markets: goods and services, resources, loanable funds, and foreign exchange. Like the legs of a chair, these four macroeconomic markets are dependent upon each other. When an economy is in long-run equilibrium, the interrelationships among these four markets will be in harmony. The relationship among resource prices, interest rates, exchange rates, and product prices will be such that, on average, firms will be just able to cover their costs of production, including a competitive return on their investment. In other words, the typical producer's return to capital must equal the interest rate, that is, the opportunity cost of capital. Higher returns would induce producers to expand output, whereas lower returns would cause them to cut back on production. These market adjustments will move an economy toward long-run equilibrium.

EXHIBIT 10
Net Capital Inflow and
the Trade Deficit

When a country's exchange rate is determined by market forces, the size of the net inflow of capital and trade deficit will be closely linked, as the figures here show. Notice that when the United States has experienced an increase in net capital inflow, its trade deficit has increased by a similar magnitude.

(a)

(b)

Looking ahead

In this chapter, we focused on macroequilibrium. We introduced the four basic macroeconomic markets and analyzed the implications of their equilibriums. However, we live in a world of dynamic change and unexpected events that are constantly disrupting equilibrium. The following chapter will consider what happens when various factors disrupt equilibrium and analyze how these changing conditions influence economic performance.

KEY POINTS

▼ The circular flow of income and expenditures shows how money flows through the four basic markets that make up the macroeconomy. Those four markets are the (a) goods and services market, (b) resources market, (c) loanable funds market, and (d) foreign exchange market.

▼ The aggregate demand curve shows the various quantities of domestically produced goods and services that purchasers are willing to buy at different price levels. It slopes downward to the right because the quantity purchased by consumers, investors, governments, and foreigners (net exports) will be larger at lower price levels.

▼ The aggregate supply (*AS*) curve shows the various quantities of goods and services that domestic suppliers will produce at different price levels. The short-run aggregate supply (*SRAS*) curve will slope upward to the right because higher product prices will improve profit margins when important cost components like labor are temporarily fixed in the short run.

▼ In the long run, output is constrained by the economy's resource base, current technology, and efficiency of its existing institutions. A higher price level does not loosen these constraints. Thus, the long-run aggregate supply (*LRAS*) curve is vertical.

▼ Two conditions are necessary for long-run equilibrium in the goods and services market: (a) the quantity demanded must equal the quantity supplied, and (b) the *actual* price level must equal the price level decision makers *anticipated* when they entered into their long-term agreements. When long-run equilibrium is present, output will be at its maximum sustainable level.

▼ The aggregate demand—aggregate supply model reveals the determinants of the price level and real output. In the short run, price and output will move toward the intersection of the aggregate demand (*AD*) and short-run aggregate supply (*SRAS*) curves. In the long run, price and output will gravitate to the levels represented by the intersection of the *AD, SRAS,* and *LRAS* curves.

▼ When the economy is in long-run equilibrium, potential output will be achieved and full employment will be present (the actual rate of unemployment will equal the natural rate).

▼ It is important to distinguish between real interest rates and money interest rates. The real interest rate reflects the real burden to borrowers and the payoff to lenders after inflation. It is equal to the money rate of interest minus the inflationary premium. The inflationary premium depends on the expected rate of inflation.

▼ When the exchange rate is determined by market forces, trade deficits will be closely linked with an inflow of capital. Conversely, trade surpluses will be closely linked with an outflow of capital.

▼ Macroeconomic equilibrium requires that equilibrium be achieved in all four key macroeconomic markets and that they be in harmony with one another.

CRITICAL ANALYSIS QUESTIONS

1. In your own words, explain why aggregate demand is inversely related to the price level. Why does the explanation for the inverse relationship between price and quantity demanded for the aggregate demand curve differ from that of a demand curve for a specific good?

2. What major factors influence our ability to produce goods and services in the long run? Why is the long-run aggregate supply curve vertical?

3. Why does the short-run aggregate supply curve slope upward to the right? If the prices of both (a) resources and (b) goods and services increased proportionally (by the same percentage), would business firms be willing to expand output? Why or why not?

*4. Suppose prices had been rising at 3 percent annually in recent years. A major union signs a three-year contract calling for increases in money wage rates of 6 percent annually. What will happen to the real wages of the union members if the price level is constant (unchanged) during the next three years? If other unions sign similar contracts, what will probably happen to the unemployment rate?

Why? Answer the same questions under conditions in which the price level increases at an annual rate of 8 percent during the next three years.

5. What is the current money interest rate on ten-year government bonds? Is this also the real interest rate? Why or why not?

*6. If the real interest rate in the loanable funds market increases, what will happen to the net inflow of foreign capital? Explain.

7. Explain why it's possible to temporarily achieve output levels beyond the economy's long-run potential. Why can't the high rates of output be sustained?

*8. If the price level in the current period is higher than buyers and sellers anticipated, what will tend to happen to real wages and the level of employment? How will the profit margins of businesses be affected? How will the actual rate of unemployment compare with the natural rate of unemployment? Will the current rate of output be sustainable in the future? Why or why not?

9. Suppose you purchase a $5,000 bond that pays 7 percent interest annually and matures in five years. If the inflation rate in recent years has been steady at 3 percent annually, what is the estimated real rate of interest? If the inflation rate during the next five years remains steady at 3 percent, what real rate of return will you earn? If the inflation rate during the next five years is 6 percent, what will happen to your real rate of return?

*10. How are the following related to each other?
   a. the long-run equilibrium rate of output
   b. the potential real GDP of the economy
   c. the output rate at which the actual and natural rates of unemployment are equal

11. How will an increase in the inflation rate affect (a) the money rate of interest and (b) the real rate of interest? Explain. Does inflation transfer wealth from lenders to borrowers? Why or why not?

*12. If a bond pays $1,000 per year in perpetuity (each year in the future), what will the market price of the bond be when the long-term interest rate is 10 percent? What would it be if the interest rate were 5 percent?

*13. How are bond prices related to interest rates? Why are they related?

14. When the price of a specific product increases, individual firms can generally expand their output by a larger amount in the long run than in the short run. For the economy as a whole, however,

an unexpected increase in the price level leads to a larger expansion in output in the short run than in the long run. Can you explain this apparent paradox?

15. How is a nation's trade balance related to its net inflow of foreign capital? If an economy provides more attractive investment opportunities than are available in other countries, how will this tend to influence its trade balance?

*16. The following chart indicates the aggregate demand (*AD*) and short-run aggregate supply (*SRAS*) schedules of decision makers for the current period. Both buyers and sellers previously anticipated that the price level during the current period would be P_{105}.
   a. Indicate the quantity of GDP that will be produced during this period.
   b. Will it be a long-run equilibrium level of GDP? Why or why not?
   c. What will the relationship between the actual and natural rates of unemployment be during the period? Explain your answer.

AD_{105}	Price Level	$SRAS_{105}$
6,900	90	4,500
6,600	95	4,800
6,300	100	5,100
6,000	105	5,400
5,700	110	5,700
5,400	115	6,000

17. Consider an economy with the following aggregate demand (*AD*) and short-run aggregate supply (*SRAS*) schedules. Decision makers have previously made decisions anticipating that the price level during the current period will be P_{105}.
   a. Indicate the quantity of GDP that will be produced during the period.
   b. Is it a long-run equilibrium level of GDP? Why or why not?
   c. How will the unemployment rate during the current period compare with the natural rate of unemployment?
   d. Will the current rate of GDP be sustainable into the future? Why or why not?

AD_{105}	Price Level	$SRAS_{105}$
6,300	90	4,500
6,000	95	4,800
5,700	100	5,100
5,400	105	5,400
5,100	110	5,700
4,800	115	6,000

*Asterisk denotes questions for which answers are given in Appendix B.

A D D E N D U M

Leakages and Injections from the Circular Flow of Income

As we explained earlier, there are three leakages of income in the circular-flow diagram: saving, taxes, and imports. However, there are also "injections." Refer again to Exhibit 1 and notice that, in addition to consumption expenditures, there are three other arrows showing flows, or injections, into the goods and services market. They are investment, government purchases, and exports.

For macroequilibrium to be present, the flow of expenditures on goods and services (top loop of Exhibit 1) must equal the flow of income to resource owners (bottom loop). *This will be true if the injections (investment, government purchases, and exports) into the circular flow equal the leakages (saving, taxes, and imports).* Interestingly, this will be the case when the loanable funds and foreign exchange markets are also in equilibrium. Let's analyze why this is so.

As Exhibit 1 shows, the net saving of households plus net capital inflow from foreigners provide the supply in the loanable funds market. Business investment and government borrowing to finance budget deficits generate the demand. When the interest rate brings these two forces into balance, the following relationship is present:

(9-A1)   **Net saving + Net capital inflow = Investment + Budget deficit**

The foreign exchange market brings imports plus capital outflow into equality with exports plus capital inflow (Equation 9-1 in the text). As a result, the net inflow of capital (capital inflow minus capital outflow) is equal to imports minus exports (see Equation 9-2 in the text). Substituting imports minus exports for the net capital inflow in Equation 9-A1 yields

(9-A2)   **Net saving + Imports − Exports = Investment + Budget deficit**

Because the budget deficit is merely government purchases minus net taxes, Equation 9-A2 can be rewritten as

(9-A3)   **Net saving + Imports − Exports = Investment + Government purchases − Taxes**

Finally, moving exports and taxes to opposite sides of the equation yields

(9-A4)   **Net saving + Imports + Taxes = Investment + Government purchases + Exports**

Of course, the derivation of Equation 9-A4 is based on the presence of equilibrium in both the loanable funds and foreign exchange markets. When interest rates and exchange rates bring these markets into equilibrium, they will also bring into balance the leakages from (left side of Equation 9-A4) and injections into (right side of Equation 9-A4) the circular flow of income.

Dynamic Change, Economic Fluctuations, and the *AD–AS* Model

CHAPTER FOCUS

- What factors change aggregate demand? What factors change aggregate supply?

- How will an economy adjust to unanticipated changes in aggregate demand? How will it adjust to unanticipated changes in aggregate supply?

- What causes recessions and booms?

- When an economy is in a recession, will market forces help direct it back to full employment? If so, how rapidly will this adjustment process work?

- What does the *AD–AS* model reveal about the economic crisis of 2008?

Not only will the [aggregate demand and aggregate supply] analysis help us interpret recent episodes in the business cycle, but it will also enable us to understand the debates on how economic policy should be conducted.

—Frederic Mishkin[1]

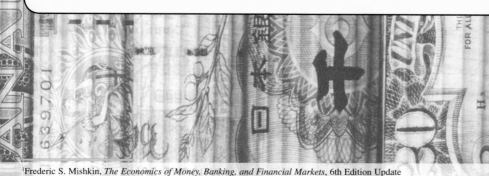

[1]Frederic S. Mishkin, *The Economics of Money, Banking, and Financial Markets*, 6th Edition Update (Boston: Addison Wesley, 2003), 612.

n Chapter 9, we focused on the equilibrium conditions in the four basic macroeconomic markets. Equilibrium is important, but we live in a dynamic world that continually wars against it. Unexpected changes are constantly occurring. New products and technologies are developed; consumers and investors become more optimistic (or pessimistic) about the future; weather affects crop yields; international tensions disrupt or threaten to disrupt the supply of a key resource, and so on. Consequently, equilibrium is continually disrupted. Thus, if we want to understand how the real world works, we need to know how macroeconomic markets adjust to change.

In this chapter, we focus on what happens when the macroequilibrium of an economy is disrupted. The linkage between these disruptions and the ups and downs of the business cycle is also investigated. If economic change throws an economy into a recession, will market forces direct it back to full employment? If so, how quickly will this occur? This chapter will examine these questions and related issues.

We will continue to assume that the government's tax, spending, and monetary policies don't change. The impact of changes in these policy variables will be examined in subsequent chapters. For now, our focus is on the basic macroeconomic markets and how they respond to various disruptions. ■

Anticipated and Unanticipated Changes

Anticipated change

A change that is foreseen by decision makers in time for them to make adjustments.

Unanticipated change

A change that decision makers could not reasonably foresee. The choices they made prior to the change did not take it into account.

In Chapter 8, we stated that it is important to distinguish between price-level changes that are anticipated and those that are not. This distinction is important in several areas of economics. **Anticipated changes** are foreseen by economic participants. Decision makers have time to adjust to them before they occur. For example, suppose that, under normal weather conditions, a new drought-resistant hybrid seed is expected to expand grain production in the Midwest by 10 percent next year. As a result, buyers and sellers will plan for a larger supply of grain and lower grain prices in the future. They will adjust their decision-making behavior accordingly.

In contrast, **unanticipated changes** catch people by surprise. New products are introduced, technological discoveries alter production costs, droughts reduce crop yields, and demand expands for some goods and contracts for others. It is impossible for decision makers to foresee many of these changes. As we will explain in a moment, there is good reason to expect that the path of the adjustment process will be influenced by whether or not a change is anticipated.

Factors That Shift Aggregate Demand

The aggregate demand curve isolates the effect of the price level on the quantity demanded of goods and services. As we discussed in the previous chapter, a reduction in the price level will (1) increase the wealth of people holding a fixed quantity of money, (2) reduce the real rate of interest, and (3) make domestically produced goods cheaper than those produced abroad. All three of these factors will lead to an increase in the quantity of goods and services demanded at the lower price level.

The price level, however, is not the only factor that influences the demand for goods and services. When we constructed the aggregate demand curve, we assumed that several other factors affecting the choices of buyers in the goods and services market were constant. Changes in these "other factors" will shift the entire aggregate demand schedule, altering the amount purchased at each price level. Let us take a closer look at the major factors that alter aggregate demand and shift the aggregate demand (*AD*) curve.

1. CHANGES IN REAL WEALTH. OWNERSHIP OF STOCKS AND HOUSING CONSTITUTES A LARGE SHARE OF THE WEALTH OF AMERICANS. Between 2002 and 2006, stock prices in the United States increased by more than 60 percent. During the same period, housing prices increased by nearly 90 percent. This huge increase in both stock and housing prices increased the wealth of Americans. In contrast, stock prices plummeted by more than 50 percent during the sixteen months following October 2007, and housing prices fell by more than 30 percent between the fourth quarter of 2006 and the fourth quarter of 2008. These price declines reduced the wealth of Americans.

How will changes in the wealth of households affect the demand for goods and services? If the real wealth of households increases, perhaps as the result of higher prices in stock, housing, and/or real estate markets, people will demand more goods and services. As **EXHIBIT 1** illustrates, this increase in wealth will shift the entire *AD* curve to the right (from AD_0 to AD_1). More goods and services are purchased at each price level. Conversely, a reduction in wealth will reduce the demand for goods and services, shifting the *AD* curve to the left (to AD_2).

2. CHANGES IN THE REAL INTEREST RATE. As we discussed in Chapter 9, the major macroeconomic markets are closely related. A change in the real interest rate in the loanable funds market will influence the choices of consumers and investors in the goods and services market. A lower real interest rate makes it cheaper for consumers to buy major appliances, automobiles, and houses now rather than in the future. Simultaneously, a lower interest rate will also stimulate business spending on capital goods (investment). If a firm must borrow, the real interest rate will contribute directly to the cost of a project. Even if the firm uses its own funds, it sacrifices interest that could have been earned by loaning the funds to someone else. Therefore, a lower interest rate reduces the opportunity cost of a project, regardless of whether it is financed with internal funds or by borrowing.

Because a fall in the real interest rate makes both consumer and investment goods cheaper, both households and investors will increase their current expenditures in response.

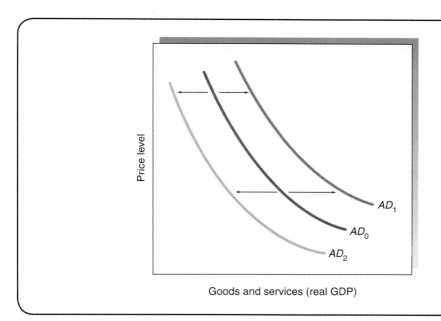

EXHIBIT 1
Shifts in Aggregate Demand

An increase in real wealth that would result from a stock market boom, for example, will increase aggregate demand, shifting the entire curve to the right (from AD_0 to AD_1). In contrast, a reduction in real wealth decreases the demand for goods and services, causing AD to shift to the left (from AD_0 to AD_2).

In turn, their additional expenditures will increase aggregate demand, shifting the entire *AD* curve to the right. In contrast, a higher real interest rate makes current consumption and investment goods more expensive, which leads to a reduction in aggregate demand, shifting the *AD* curve to the left.

3. CHANGES IN THE EXPECTATIONS OF BUSINESSES AND HOUSEHOLDS ABOUT THE FUTURE DIRECTION OF THE ECONOMY.

What people think will happen in the future influences current purchasing decisions. Optimism about the future direction of the economy will stimulate current investment. Business decision makers know that an expanding economy will mean strong sales and improved profit margins. Investment today may be necessary if business firms are going to benefit fully from these opportunities. Similarly, consumers are more likely to buy big-ticket items, such as automobiles and houses, when they expect an expanding economy to provide them with both job security and rising income in the future. Increased optimism encourages additional current expenditures by both investors and consumers, increasing aggregate demand.

Of course, pessimism about the future of the economy exerts just the opposite effect. When investors and consumers expect an economic downturn (a recession), they will cut back on their current spending to avoid overextending themselves. This pessimism leads to a decline in aggregate demand, shifting the *AD* curve to the left.

The University of Michigan conducts a monthly survey of consumers and uses the information to develop a **consumer sentiment index**. **EXHIBIT 2** presents this index for the 1978–2009 period. An increase in the consumer sentiment index indicates that consumers are more optimistic about the future. A decline indicates increased consumer pessimism. Notice how the index fell sharply prior to and during the early stages of the recessions that occurred in this period. The reduction was particularly sharp prior to and during the most recent recession. The index fell to an all-time low of 57.7 in the fourth quarter of 2008.

4. CHANGE IN THE EXPECTED RATE OF INFLATION.

When consumers and investors believe that the rate of inflation will go up in the future, they have an incentive to spend more during the current period. This expectation of higher inflation will stimulate current aggregate demand, shifting the *AD* curve to the right.

In contrast, if people expect inflation to decline in the future, this will discourage current spending. When prices are expected to decline (or at least increase less rapidly), people will have an incentive to wait before they buy things. This expectation of lower inflation will cause current aggregate demand to fall, shifting the *AD* curve to the left.

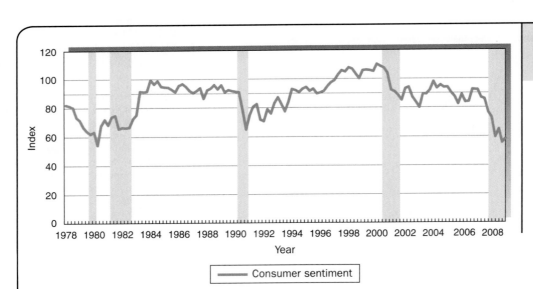

EXHIBIT 2
Consumer Sentiment
Index, 1978–2009

The consumer sentiment index developed by the University of Michigan is shown here. It is designed to measure whether consumers are becoming more optimistic or more pessimistic about the economy. Note how the index has turned down (shaded areas) sharply prior to and during the early stages of recent recessions.

5. CHANGES IN INCOME ABROAD. Changes in the income of a nation's trading partners will influence the demand for its exports. If the income of a nation's trading partners increases rapidly, the demand for its exports will expand. This will stimulate its aggregate demand. For example, rapid growth of income in Europe, Canada, and Mexico increases the demand of consumers in these areas for U.S.-produced goods. This will cause U.S. exports to expand, increasing aggregate demand (shifting the *AD* curve to the right).

Conversely, when a nation's trading partners are experiencing recessionary conditions, citizens in these countries reduce their purchases, including their purchases of foreign-produced goods. Thus, a decline in the income of a nation's trading partners will reduce its exports and the aggregate demand for its products.

Currently, approximately 11 percent of the goods and services produced in the United States are sold to purchasers abroad. Canada, Mexico, and most Western European countries export an even larger share of what they produce. The larger the size of the trade sector, the greater the potential importance of fluctuations in income abroad as a source of instability in aggregate demand. If the demand of foreign buyers does not rise and fall at the same time as domestic demand, the diversity of markets will reduce the fluctuations in demand for a nation's exports and thereby exert a stabilizing effect on aggregate demand. However, when incomes abroad are falling at the same time as domestic demand, this factor will reduce exports, causing domestic demand to fall by an even larger amount. This is precisely what happened during 2008–2009. Most of the world's major economies dipped into a recession at approximately the same time, placing downward pressure on aggregate demand throughout the world.

6. CHANGES IN EXCHANGE RATES. As we previously discussed, changes in exchange rates influence the relative price of both imports and exports. If the dollar appreciates, imported goods will be cheaper for Americans to buy, and goods exported from the United States will be more expensive for foreigners to purchase. As a result, U.S. imports will rise and exports will fall. This decline in net exports (exports minus imports) will reduce aggregate demand (shifting the *AD* curve to the left).

If the dollar depreciates, the effect will be just the opposite. When the value of the dollar falls, foreign-produced goods become more expensive for U.S. consumers, whereas U.S.-produced goods become cheaper for foreigners. This is precisely what happened during the 2003–2007 period, when the dollar depreciated by about 15 percent relative to the euro and several other major currencies. When the dollar depreciates, imports will tend to fall and exports rise. In turn, this increase in net exports will stimulate aggregate demand in the United States (shifting the *AD* curve to the right).[2]

THUMBNAIL SKETCH

What Factors Affect Aggregate Demand?[1]

These factors *increase* aggregate demand (*AD*).
1. An increase in real wealth
2. A decrease in the real rate of interest
3. Optimism about future economic conditions
4. A rise in the expected rate of inflation
5. Higher real incomes abroad
6. A fall in the value of a nation's currency

These factors *decrease* aggregate demand (*AD*).
1. Lower real wealth
2. An increase in the real rate of interest
3. Pessimism about future economic conditions
4. A fall in the expected rate of inflation
5. Lower real incomes abroad
6. A rise in the value of a nation's currency

[1]The impact of macroeconomic policy is considered later.

[2]Later, when discussing international finance, we will analyze the determinants of the exchange rate and consider in more detail how changes in exchange rates affect both trade and macroeconomic markets.

The accompanying **Thumbnail Sketch** summarizes the major factors that change aggregate demand and shift the *AD* curve. Other factors include the government's spending, taxing, and monetary policies. In subsequent chapters, we will analyze the impact of fiscal and monetary policy on aggregate demand and economic performance. We now turn to the analysis of the factors that alter aggregate supply. Then we will be in a position to consider how macroeconomic markets adjust and whether these adjustments will help keep output and employment high.

Shifts in Aggregate Supply

What factors will cause the aggregate supply curve to shift? The answer to this question will differ depending on whether the change in supply is long run and sustainable or short run and only temporary. A long-run change in aggregate supply indicates that it will be possible to achieve and sustain a larger rate of output. For example, the discovery of a lower-cost source of energy would cause a long-run change in aggregate supply. If this happened, both long-run aggregate supply (*LRAS*) and short-run aggregate supply (*SRAS*) would change.

In contrast, changes that temporarily alter the production capacity of an economy will shift the *SRAS* curve, but not the *LRAS* curve. A drought in California would be an example of such a short-run change. The drought will hurt in the short run, but it will eventually end, and output will return to the long-run normal rate. Changes that are temporary in nature shift only the *SRAS* curve. Let's consider the factors that change long-run and short-run aggregate supply in more detail.

Changes in Long-Run Aggregate Supply

Productivity

The average output produced per worker during a specific time period. It is usually measured in terms of output per hour worked.

Remember, the long-run aggregate supply curve shows the maximum rate of sustainable output of an economy, given its current (1) resource base, (2) level of technology, and (3) institutional arrangements that affect its **productivity** and the efficient use of its resources. Changes in any of these three determinants of output will cause the *LRAS* curve to shift.

As part (a) of **EXHIBIT 3** illustrates, changes that increase the economy's production capacity will shift the *LRAS* curve to the right. Over time, net investment will expand the supply of physical capital, natural resources, and labor (human resources). Physical capital investment expands the supply of buildings, machines, and other physical assets. Education and training improve the quality of the labor force and thereby expand the availability of human capital. Because investment in physical and human capital enhances output both now and in the future, it increases both long-run and short-run aggregate supply, causing both curves to shift to the right. However, things can work the other way around, too. Reductions in physical and human capital over time could cause the current and long-term production capacity of an economy to fall, shifting the *SRAS* and *LRAS* curves to the left.

Improvements in technology—the discovery of economical new products or less costly ways of producing goods and services—also permit us to squeeze a larger output from a given resource supply. The enormous improvement in our living standards during the last 250 years is largely the result of the discovery and adoption of technologically superior ways of transforming resources into goods and services. The development of the internal combustion engine, electricity, and nuclear power has vastly altered our energy sources (and consumption). The railroad, automobile, and airplane dramatically changed both the speed and cost of transportation. More recently, high-tech products like personal computers, fax machines, e-mail, and the Internet have cut the cost of doing business and expanded our production capacity. Technological improvements of this type enhance productivity and thereby shift both *LRAS* and *SRAS* curves to the right.

Finally, institutional changes can affect productivity and efficiency and change both short- and long-run aggregate supply. Depending on how well a government's institutional, or policy, changes are designed, they can increase aggregate supply by enhancing economic efficiency and productivity or decrease it by encouraging waste and making production more costly.

EXHIBIT 3
Shifts in Aggregate Supply

Factors like an increase in the stock of capital or an improvement in technology will expand the economy's potential output and shift the LRAS curve to the right as shown in part (a). Factors like favorable weather or falling resource prices (say, a temporary drop in the price of a major import like oil) will shift the SRAS curve to the right, as shown in part (b).

(a) Increase in *LRAS*

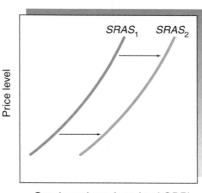

(b) Increase in *SRAS*

The long-run growth of real GDP in the United States has been about 3 percent per year. In other words, we have been able to expand our productivity steadily over the years. Hence, the *LRAS* and *SRAS* curves have gradually drifted to the right at about a 3 percent annual rate, sometimes a little faster and sometimes a little slower.

Changes in Short-Run Aggregate Supply

Changes can sometimes influence current output without altering the economy's long-run capacity. When this is the case, the *SRAS* curve will shift even though the *LRAS* curve remains unchanged. What types of changes would do this?

1. CHANGES IN RESOURCE PRICES. When we derived the *SRAS* schedule in Chapter 9, we held resource prices constant. But a change in resource prices will alter *SRAS*, although not necessarily *LRAS*. A reduction in resource prices will lower production costs and therefore shift the *SRAS* curve to the right, as illustrated in part (b) of Exhibit 3. However, unless the lower cost of resources reflects a long-term increase in their supply, *LRAS* won't change. Conversely, an increase in the price of resources used in production will increase firms' costs, shifting the *SRAS* curve to the left. But unless the higher prices are the result of a long-term reduction in the size of the economy's resource base, they will not reduce *LRAS*.[3]

2. CHANGES IN THE EXPECTED RATE OF INFLATION. As we learned, a change in the expected rate of inflation will affect aggregate demand (*AD*) in the goods and services market. It will also alter short-run aggregate supply (*SRAS*). If sellers in the goods and services market expect the future rate of inflation to increase, they will be less motivated to sell their products at lower prices in the current period. After all, goods that they do not sell today will be available for sale in the future at what they anticipate will be even higher prices because of inflation. But they will have produced them earlier at lower costs. Therefore, an increase in the expected rate of inflation will reduce the *current* supply of

[3]In subsequent chapters, we will explain how stable prices can be achieved as real output increases.

goods, thereby shifting the *SRAS* curve to the left. Of course, a reduction in the expected rate of inflation will have just the opposite effect. When sellers scale back their expectations of future price increases, their incentive to sell in the current period rises. Why should they wait to sell what they've produced now, if prices aren't going to go up very much in the future? Thus, a reduction in the expected rate of inflation will increase short-run aggregate supply, shifting the *SRAS* curve to the right.

Supply shock

An unexpected event that temporarily increases or decreases aggregate supply.

3. SUPPLY SHOCKS. Supply shocks can also alter current output without directly affecting the productive capacity of the economy. Supply shocks are surprise occurrences that temporarily increase or decrease current output. For example, adverse weather conditions, a natural disaster, or a temporary rise in the price of imported resources (for example, oil in the case of the United States) will reduce current supply, even though they do not alter the economy's long-term production capacity. They lower short-run aggregate supply (shift the *SRAS* curve to the left) without directly affecting *LRAS*, in other words. In contrast, favorable weather conditions or a temporary fall in the world price of major resources imported by a country will expand current output, even though the economy's long-run capacity remains unchanged.

The accompanying **Thumbnail Sketch** summarizes the major factors that influence both long-run and short-run aggregate supply. Of course, macroeconomic policy can also influence aggregate supply. Like aggregate demand, we will study the impact macroeconomic policies have on aggregate supply in subsequent chapters.

Steady Economic Growth and Anticipated Changes in Long-Run Aggregate Supply

As we've said, changes that people anticipate affect the economy differently from changes they don't. When a change takes place slowly and predictably, decision makers will make choices based on their anticipation of the event. These changes do not generally disrupt equilibrium in markets. With time, net investment and improvements in technology and institutional efficiency will lead to increases in the sustainable rate of output and shift the economy's *LRAS* curve to the right.

EXHIBIT 4 illustrates the impact of economic growth on the goods and services market. Initially, the economy is in long-run equilibrium at price level P_1 and output Y_{F_1}.

THUMBNAIL SKETCH

What Factors Affect Long-Run and Short-Run Aggregate Supply?[1]

These factors *increase* long-run aggregate supply (*LRAS*).
1. An increase in the supply of resources
2. Technology and productivity improvements
3. Institutional changes that improve the efficiency of resource use

These factors *decrease* long-run aggregate supply (*LRAS*).
1. A decrease in the supply of resources
2. Technology and productivity deteriorations
3. Institutional changes that reduce the efficiency of resource use

These factors *increase* short-run aggregate supply (*SRAS*).
1. A fall in resource prices (production costs)
2. A fall in the expected rate of inflation
3. Favorable supply shocks, such as good weather or lower prices of important imported resources

These factors *decrease* short-run aggregate supply (*SRAS*).
1. A rise in resource prices (production costs)
2. A rise in the expected rate of inflation
3. Unfavorable supply shocks, such as bad weather or higher prices of important imported resources

[1]The impact of macroeconomic policy will be considered later.

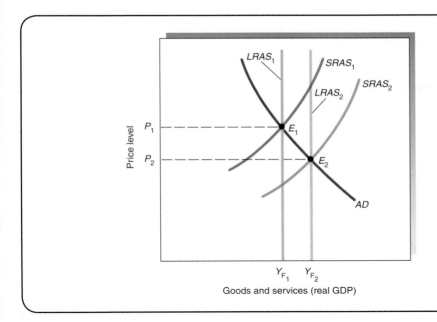

EXHIBIT 4
Growth of Aggregate
Supply

Here, we illustrate the impact of economic growth due to capital formation or a technological advancement, for example. The full-employment output of the economy expands from Y_{F_1} to Y_{F_2}. Thus, both LRAS and SRAS increase (to LRAS$_2$ and SRAS$_2$). A sustainable, higher level of real output and real income is the result. If the money supply is held constant, a new long-run equilibrium will emerge at a larger output rate (Y_{F_2}) and lower price level (P_2).

Goods and services (real GDP)

The growth expands the economy's potential output, shifting both the *LRAS* and *SRAS* curves to the right (to *LRAS$_2$* and *SRAS$_2$*). Because these changes are gradual, decision makers have time to anticipate the changing market conditions and adjust their behavior accordingly.

When economic growth expands the economy's production possibilities, a higher rate of real output can be achieved and sustained. The larger output can be attained even while unemployment remains at its natural rate. If the money supply is held constant, the increase in aggregate supply will lead to a lower price level (P_2).

During the past fifty years, real output has expanded significantly in the United States and other countries. However, contrary to the presentation of Exhibit 4, the price level has generally not declined. This is because monetary policy makers have expanded the supply of money. As we will see later, an increase in the money supply stimulates aggregate demand, shifting *AD* to the right and pushing the price level upward.

Unanticipated Changes and Market Adjustments

In contrast to anticipated changes, unanticipated changes in aggregate demand and aggregate supply will disrupt long-run equilibrium in the goods and services market. If a change isn't anticipated, initially, it may be unclear to decision makers whether the change—an increase in sales, for example—reflects a random occurrence or a real change in demand conditions. Businesses will also take some time to differentiate between temporary fluctuations and more permanent changes. Even after decision makers are convinced that market conditions have changed, it will take some time for them to make new decisions and carry them out. In some cases, long-term contracts will delay the adjustment process.

Equilibrium may be disrupted by unexpected changes in either aggregate demand or aggregate supply. We will begin with the analysis of changes in aggregate demand.

Unanticipated Increases in Aggregate Demand

Part (a) of **EXHIBIT 5** shows how an economy that is initially in long-run equilibrium will adjust to an unanticipated increase in aggregate demand. Initially, at output Y_F and price level P_{100} (point E_1), the economy is in long-run equilibrium. Aggregate demand and

EXHIBIT 5

An Unanticipated Increase in Aggregate Demand

In response to an unanticipated increase in aggregate demand for goods and services that shifts AD₁ to AD₂ (shown in part a), prices will rise to P₁₀₅ in the short run and output will increase temporarily to Y₂, exceeding full-employment capacity. However, over time, prices in resource markets, including the labor market, will rise as the result of the strong demand. The higher resource prices will mean higher production costs, which will reduce aggregate supply to SRAS₂ (as shown in part b). In the long run, a new equilibrium will emerge at a higher price level (P₁₁₀) and an output consistent with the economy's sustainable capacity. Thus, the increase in aggregate demand will expand output only temporarily.

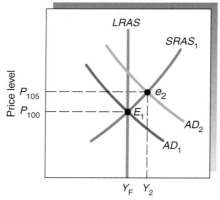

(a) Short-run effects of increase in *AD*

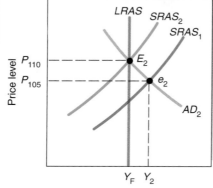

(b) Long-run effects of increase in *AD*

aggregate supply are in balance. Decision makers have correctly anticipated the current price level, and the economy is operating at its full-employment level of output.

What would happen if this equilibrium were disrupted by an unanticipated increase in aggregate demand (a shift from AD_1 to AD_2), which might result for example from a stock market boom or the rapid growth of income abroad? An excess demand for goods and services would result at the initial price level (P_{100}). Responding to the strong sales and excess demand, businesses would increase their prices. Their profit margins would improve (because product prices have increased relative to the cost of the resources used to make them), and they would expand output along the *SRAS* curve. As part (a) of Exhibit 5 shows, the economy would move to a short-run equilibrium (e_2), at a larger output (Y_2) and higher price level (P_{105}). (*Note*: A short-run equilibrium is indicated with a lowercase *e*, whereas a capital *E* is used to designate a long-run equilibrium. This convention will be followed throughout the text.)

In the short run, the economy's output will deviate from full-employment capacity when prices in the goods and services market deviate from the price level people anticipated. This will happen when unusually strong demand pushes prices up more than was expected. For a time, resource prices like wage rates, interest payments, and rents will remain at the initial price level (P_{100}), lagging behind the prices producers can get for their products. The higher price level will temporarily improve firms' profit margins, which will motivate them to expand both output and employment in the short run. As a result, the unemployment rate will drop below its natural rate, and the economy's output will temporarily exceed its long-run potential.[4]

---

[4]The definition of long-run aggregate supply helps clarify why a change in resource prices will affect short-run aggregate supply but not long-run aggregate supply. When an economy is operating on its *LRAS* curve, the relationship between resource prices (costs) and product prices will reflect normal competitive market conditions. Because both profit and unemployment rates are at their normal levels, there is no tendency for resource prices to change relative to product prices when current output is equal to the economy's long-run potential. Therefore, when an economy is operating on its *LRAS* schedule, any change in resource prices will be matched by a proportional change in product prices, leaving the incentive to supply resources (and output) unchanged.

This isn't the end of the story, though. ***The increase in GDP above the economy's long-run potential will last only until temporarily fixed resource prices (and interest rates) can be adjusted upward by people in light of the new stronger demand conditions.*** The strong demand accompanying the high level of output (rates beyond Y_F) will put upward pressure on prices in the resource and loanable funds markets. As part (b) of Exhibit 5 shows, eventually the rising resource prices and costs will shift the short-run aggregate supply curve to the left (to $SRAS_2$). Given sufficient time, wages, other resource prices, and interest rates will completely adjust. When this happens, a new long-run equilibrium (E_2) will be established at a higher price level (P_{110}). Correspondingly, profit margins will return to their normal levels, output will recede to the economy's long-run potential, and unemployment will return to its natural rate.

Notice that because an increase in aggregate demand doesn't change the economy's production capacity, it cannot permanently expand output (beyond Y_F). The increase in demand temporarily expands output, but in the long term, it only increases the price level.

Unanticipated Reductions in Aggregate Demand

How would the goods and services market adjust to an unanticipated reduction in aggregate demand? For example, suppose decision makers become more pessimistic about the future or an unexpected decline in income abroad reduces demand for their products.

EXHIBIT 6 will help us analyze what happens during an unanticipated reduction in aggregate demand. In part (a) of Exhibit 6, the economy is in long-run equilibrium (E_1) at output Y_F and the price level P_{100}. The reduction in demand will shift aggregate demand from AD_1 to AD_2, disrupting the initial equilibrium. As a result of the fall in demand, businesses will be unable to sell Y_F units of output at the initial price level of P_{100}. In the short run, business firms will reduce their output (to Y_2) and cut their prices (to P_{95}) in response to the weak demand conditions. Because many business costs are temporarily fixed, profit margins will fall. Predictably, firms will cut back on output and lay off workers, causing the unemployment rate to rise. The actual rate of unemployment will rise above the economy's natural rate of unemployment. Weak demand and excess supply will

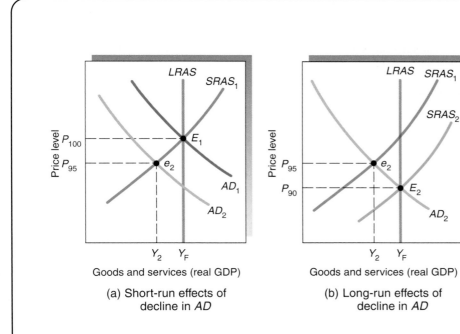

EXHIBIT 6

An Unanticipated Reduction in Aggregate Demand

The short-run impact of an unanticipated fall in aggregate demand, shifting AD_1 to AD_2, will be a decline in output to Y_2 and a lower price level of P_{95} (as shown in part a). Temporarily, profit margins will decline, output will fall, and unemployment will rise above its natural rate. In the long run, weak demand and excess supply in the resource market will lead to lower wages and resource prices. This will lower production costs, leading to an expansion in short-run aggregate supply, shifting it to $SRAS_2$ (as shown in part b). However, this method of restoring equilibrium (E_2) may be both painful and quite lengthy.

(a) Short-run effects of decline in *AD*

(b) Long-run effects of decline in *AD*

be widespread in resource markets. Many firms will have excess production capacity, and the demand for investment funds will be weak. These forces will place downward pressure on both resource prices and interest rates.

If resource prices quickly adjust downward in response to weak demand, then the decline in output to Y_2 will be brief. Lower resource prices will reduce costs and increase aggregate supply, shifting the $SRAS_1$ curve to $SRAS_2$, as part (b) shows. The result will be a new long-run equilibrium (E_2) at the economy's full-employment output rate (Y_F) and a lower price level (P_{90}). Lower interest rates will also help keep the economy on track. Given the excess production capacity of many firms, weak demand for capital goods (investment) will reduce the demand for loanable funds, which will put downward pressure on interest rates. The lower rates will stimulate current spending, which will help offset the lower demand and direct the economy back to full employment.

Resource prices and interest rates, however, may not adjust quickly. Long-term contracts and uncertainty about whether the weak demand is only temporary will slow down the adjustment process. Moreover, workers and unions may be reluctant to accept lower wages. If resource prices are downwardly inflexible, as many economists believe, the adjustment process may be lengthy and painful. Pessimism on the part of both investors and consumers may also complicate the adjustment process. This has been the case in recent recessions. As Exhibit 2 shows, consumer confidence remained at a low level for twelve to eighteen months after the 1990–1991 and 2001 recessions were over. This pessimism acted as a drag on the growth of aggregate demand, and, as a result, the initial recovery from these recessions was sluggish.

Unanticipated Increases in Short-Run Aggregate Supply

Supply shocks catch people by surprise. That is, in part, why they're called "shocks." What would happen if the nation's output expanded because of a favorable shock like good weather conditions or a temporary fall in the world price of oil? **EXHIBIT 7** provides the answer. Because the temporarily favorable supply conditions can't be counted on in the future, they won't change the economy's long-term production capacity. Short-run aggregate supply will increase (to $SRAS_2$), but *LRAS* will remain unchanged. Output (and income) will temporarily expand beyond the economy's full-employment constraints. This increase in current supply will put downward pressure on the price level.

Over time, however, the favorable conditions will come to an end. As this happens, the *SRAS* curve will return to its original position, and long-run equilibrium will be restored. The expansion in output will be only temporary. Knowing this, many households will save

EXHIBIT 7

An Unanticipated, Temporary Increase in Aggregate Supply

Here, we show the impact of an unanticipated, but temporary, increase in aggregate supply that might result from a bumper crop caused by favorable weather, for example. The increase in aggregate supply, shifting it to SRAS₂, will lead to a lower price level of P₉₅ and an increase in current GDP to Y₂. Because the favorable supply conditions cannot be counted on in the future, the economy's long-run aggregate supply will not increase.

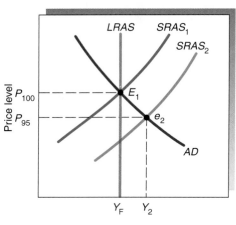

a substantial portion of the extra income they earn during the expansion for a time when things aren't so prosperous.

What would happen if the favorable conditions increasing supply reflected long-term factors? For example, suppose the discovery and development of a huge natural gas field in the United States lowered energy prices and these price reductions were expected to be long-term rather than temporary. In this instance, both the *LRAS* and the *SRAS* would increase (shift to the right). This case would parallel the analysis of Exhibit 4. A new long-run equilibrium at a higher output would result.

Unanticipated Reductions in Short-Run Aggregate Supply

In recent decades, the U.S. economy has been jolted by several unfavorable supply-side factors. During the summer of 1988, the worst drought to hit the country in fifty years made for an extremely poor harvest in the U.S. agricultural belt. In 1973, 1979, 1990, and again in 2000–2001, the United States, which imports more than half of the oil it consumes, was hit with sharply higher oil prices due to instability in the Middle East. The higher oil prices had a significant impact because they raised the transportation costs of virtually everything as well as the production costs of numerous items, such as plastics, fertilizer, and asphalt. Most recently, the world price of crude oil soared to more than $140 per barrel in 2007–2008, and, for the first time in the United States, the average nominal price of a gallon of gasoline rose above $4.

How do unfavorable supply shocks like this affect macroeconomic markets? As **EXHIBIT 8** (part a) illustrates, an unfavorable supply shock, such as might result from adverse weather or a higher world price of oil, will reduce supply (from S_1 to S_2) in the domestic resource market. Resource prices will rise to P'_r. In turn, the higher resource prices will reduce short-

---

EXHIBIT 8
The Effects of an Adverse Supply Shock

Suppose that there's an unanticipated fall in the economy's supply of resources, perhaps because of a crop failure or sharp increase in the price of a major imported resource like oil. Resource prices will rise from P_r to P'_r, as shown in part (a). The higher resource prices will shift the SRAS curve to the left, as shown in part (b). In the short run, the price level will rise to P_{110}, and output will decline to Y_2. What happens in the long run depends on whether the reduction in the supply of resources is temporary or permanent. If it is temporary, resource prices will fall in the future, permitting the economy to return to its initial equilibrium (E_1). Conversely, if it is permanent, the production capacity of the economy will shrink, shifting LRAS to the left, and e_2 will become the new long-run equilibrium.

(a) Resource market

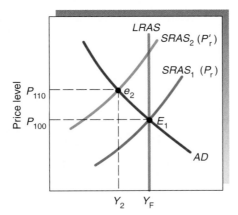

(b) Goods and services (real GDP)

run aggregate supply (the shift from $SRAS_1$ to $SRAS_2$ in part b) in the goods and services market. Because supply shocks of this type are generally unanticipated, initially they will reduce output and put upward pressure on prices in the goods and services market.

If an unfavorable supply shock is expected to be temporary, as will generally be the case, long-run aggregate supply will be unaffected. For example, unfavorable weather conditions for a year or two do not represent a permanent change in the climate. As normal weather returns, supply and prices in the resource market will return to normal, and the economy will return to long-run equilibrium at output Y_F.

When an adverse supply-side factor is more permanent, the long-run supply curve will also shift to the left. For example, an oil price increase that is expected to continue for several years will reduce long-run as well as short-run aggregate supply. Under these circumstances, the economy will have to adjust to a lower level of output. Whether the decline in aggregate supply is temporary or permanent, other things being constant, the price level will rise. Similarly, output will decline, at least temporarily.

The Price Level, Inflation, and the *AD–AS* Model

In the basic *AD–AS* model, the level of prices is measured on the *y*-axis in both the goods and services and resource markets. This approach makes it easier to visualize relative price changes. If prices change in one of the markets, goods and services, for example, this indicates that prices in that market have changed *relative* to those in other markets. It is important to note, however, that this structure implicitly incorporates the assumption that the actual and expected rates of inflation are initially zero.

As we have previously discussed, when persistent inflation is present, it will be anticipated by both buyers and sellers. Moreover, the anticipated inflation will be incorporated into the price agreements of long-term contracts, including those affecting important components of costs. When the actual and anticipated rates of inflation are equal, persistent price increases will be present in both goods and services and resource markets, even though the relative prices between the two markets are unchanged.

However, once decision makers anticipate a given rate of inflation and build it into long-term contracts, an actual rate of inflation that is less than expected is essentially the equivalent of a reduction in the price level when price stability (zero inflation) is anticipated. For example, consider the situation in which 5 percent inflation has been present over a lengthy time period and therefore the 5 percent rate has been built into long-term contracts, including those in resource markets. If weak demand causes the inflation rate to fall to, say, 2 percent, the adjustments will be the same as those for a reduction in product prices when zero inflation is anticipated (see Exhibit 6). In both cases, prices in the goods and services market will fall relative to resource prices. In the short run, profit margins will be squeezed, and firms will cut back on output. Workers will be laid off, and the economy may well fall into a recession.

Similarly, the impact of an inflation rate that is greater than was anticipated will be like that of an increase in the price level when price stability is anticipated. Both will increase product prices relative to resource prices, which will enhance profits and thereby induce firms to expand output and employment.

Unanticipated Changes, Recessions, and Booms

The *AD–AS* model indicates that unanticipated changes will disrupt macroequilibrium and result in economic instability. On the one hand, unanticipated reductions in either aggregate demand or short-run aggregate supply can throw an economy into a recession. On the other hand, unanticipated increases in aggregate demand or short-run aggregate supply can generate an unsustainable economic boom—a temporarily high level of output and employment that cannot be maintained.

However, the model also suggests that changes in resource prices and interest rates will tend to direct an economy back toward full employment following a disruption. Let's take a closer look at these two forces that underlie the self-corrective mechanism of macroeconomic markets.

1. CHANGES IN REAL RESOURCE PRICES WILL HELP DIRECT AN ECONOMY TOWARD EQUILIBRIUM. Price adjustments in the resource market will help keep an economy on an even keel. When an economy is in a recession and its output is less than its full-employment potential, the demand for resources will be weak. Underutilized assets and unemployment of resources will be widespread. However, the weak demand will place downward pressure on resource prices. As real resource prices fall, costs will decline, and this will help restore profit margins and strengthen the incentive of producers to expand output. Thus, the lower resource prices will help direct a recessionary economy back toward full employment.

In contrast, when a booming economy is operating beyond its full-employment capacity—when unemployment is less than the natural unemployment rate—strong demand will push up the real price of labor (wages) and other resources. In turn, the higher resource prices will increase costs and reduce profit margins. As costs increase, firms will cut back their output, directing the economy toward its full-employment potential.

2. CHANGES IN REAL INTEREST RATES HELP STABILIZE AGGREGATE DEMAND AND REDIRECT ECONOMIC FLUCTUATIONS. Real interest rates tend to reflect business conditions. During an economic downturn, businesses borrow less money for new investment projects. The demand for loanable funds is weak, and real interest rates generally fall. In turn, the lower interest rates lead to higher consumption and make investment projects cheaper, motivating businesses to undertake them. This helps offset the decline in aggregate demand and redirect output toward the full-employment level.

Conversely, during an economic boom, businesses borrow more money to invest in projects that will help them meet the stronger demand for their goods and services. The demand for loanable funds will strengthen, putting upward pressure on real interest rates. In turn, the higher interest rates will make it more expensive to purchase consumer durables and undertake investment projects. This helps restrain aggregate demand and redirect output toward the full-employment level.

Interest rate adjustments will also help offset potential economic disturbances arising from shifts in expectations about future business conditions. Suppose consumers and business operators suddenly become more pessimistic and, as a result, reduce their current level of spending. This will lower consumer spending and increase saving. Demand in the loanable funds market will be weak. Thus, the supply of loanable funds will increase relative to the demand. However, this will lead to lower real interest rates, which will help keep the economy on track by offsetting spending reductions caused by the increased pessimism.

Just the opposite will happen if consumers and businesses suddenly became more optimistic. If they suddenly decide to spend more of their current income, this will reduce the supply of loanable funds relative to the demand, causing real interest rates to rise. The higher rates will then make current spending less attractive and will help stabilize aggregate demand.[5]

The implications of the *AD–AS* model with regard to economic instability might be summarized in the following manner.

---

[5]The foreign exchange market may also help stabilize the business cycle. When an economy dips into a recession, investment prospects will deteriorate, leading to a reduction in the inflow of capital from abroad. In turn, the decline in capital inflow will lead to depreciation in the foreign exchange rate, which will stimulate net exports and aggregate demand and thereby help to redirect the economy back toward full employment. Just the opposite will occur during the expansionary phase of the business cycle. However, these adjustments are not likely to be very important in countries like the United States where the international trade sector is a relatively small share of the economy. Thus, we focus on the importance of the interest rate and resource price adjustments as the primary forces that will direct a market economy toward full employment.

Various shocks (unanticipated changes in *AD* or *AS*) can disrupt full-employment equilibrium and lead either to recessionary unemployment or to an inflationary boom. In the short run, long-term contracts and misperceptions about the current price level can lead to output levels that differ from long-run equilibrium. With time, however, changes in real resource prices and interest rates will act as a stabilizing force and direct a market economy back to its full employment potential.

But the *AD–AS* model does not indicate how quickly the market adjustment process will work. This is an area in which the views of economists often differ. Some believe that, if not undermined by harmful policies, market forces will direct the economy back to full employment within a relatively short time frame, and therefore recessions will generally last only a few quarters. Other economists argue that the self-corrective mechanism of markets works slowly, and therefore without appropriate macroeconomic policy changes, recessions will be long and painful. As we proceed, we will present each of these views in detail and examine their policy implications.

Expansions and Recessions: The Historical Record

EXHIBIT 9 shows the time intervals of the expansions and recessions experienced by the U.S. economy since 1950. There have been ten business cycles, periods of expansion followed by a recession, during this period of six decades. The expansions have generally been more lengthy than the recessions. The ten expansions since 1950 have averaged approximately sixty months in length, and three of those expansions have lasted seven years or more. In contrast, the average length of the recessions has been about ten months, and prior to the recession that began in December 2007, none lasted more than sixteen months.

Using the AD–AS Model to Think about the Business Cycle and the Crisis of 2008

The 1930s were a period of extremely high unemployment and depressed economic conditions. The unemployment rate rose to nearly 25 percent of the labor force in 1932 and 1933. Between 1931 and 1940, the rate of unemployment exceeded 14 percent during each year. These extreme conditions explain why this period is referred to as the Great Depression.

The collapse of the U.S. economy and others around the world during 2008 has caused many to wonder if the current conditions will spiral downward and become something like the Great Depression. Clearly, current conditions are not comparable with those of the 1930s, but the downturn may well be the longest and most severe experienced since that painful era. Why did economic conditions deteriorate so rapidly in 2008? The *AD–AS* model provides considerable insight on this issue.

EXHIBIT 9
Expansions and Recessions, 1950–2009

The accompanying table indicates the periods of both economic expansions (rising GDP) and recessions (falling GDP) since 1950. As the table indicates, the length of both varies substantially, but the expansions have clearly been longer.

Period of Expansion	Length (in months)	Period of Recession	Length (in months)
Oct '49 to July '53	44	July '53 to May '54	10
May '54 to August '57	39	August '57 to April '58	9
April '58 to April '60	24	April '60 to February '61	10
February '61 to Dec '69	105	Dec '69 to November '70	10
Nov '70 to Nov '73	36	Nov '73 to March '75	16
March '75 to January '80	58	January '80 to July '80	6
July '80 to July '81	12	July '81 to November '82	16
Nov '82 to July '90	92	July '90 to March '91	9
March '91 to March '01	120	March '01 to November '01	8
November '01 to November '07	73	December '07 to ?[a]	18

[a] To date, this recession has continued through May 2009.
Source: http://www.nber.orga

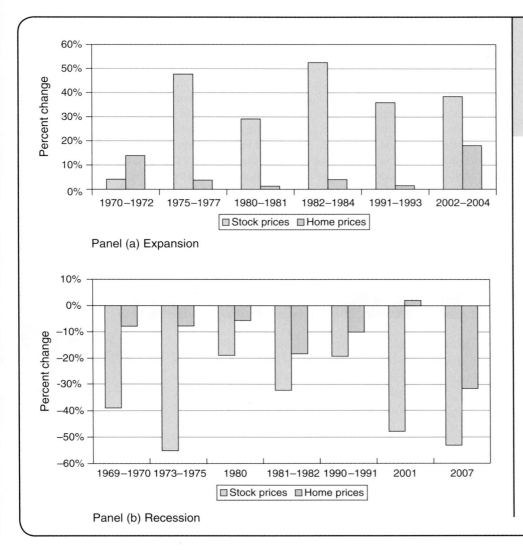

EXHIBIT 10

Changes in the Real Price of Stock Shares and Housing (Single-Family Homes) during Business Cycles since 1969

Both housing and stock prices generally rise during expansions and fall during recessions. Note how the housing price reduction preceding the 2008 recession was substantially greater than during earlier recessions. This is a major reason for the severity of this recession. Stock prices are based on Standard and Poor's monthly opening prices through May 2009. Housing prices prior to 1976 are based on National Association of Realtors median existing home sale prices. Sale prices for 1976 to 1986 are based on Office of Federal Housing Enterprise Oversight quarterly constant quality home price index. The housing prices for 1987 to fourth quarter 2008 are based on the Case-Shiller quarterly housing price index. All prices were adjusted for inflation using the Consumer Price Index. The price changes during the expansion are for the 24 months subsequent to the end of the recession.

Between 2002 and mid-year 2006, there was a sharp increase in housing prices. Nationwide, the average home price increased by 89 percent during this period. At the same time, stock prices were also increasing rapidly. This huge increase in wealth stimulated aggregate demand and generated an economic boom.

But the situation began to change in 2006. Housing prices reversed and began to fall. Mortgage default rates and housing foreclosures started to rise. The construction industry contracted sharply. As housing wealth fell, people became more pessimistic, causing a further reduction in aggregate demand. The depressed conditions in the housing market soon spread to other parts of the economy. In 2008, stocks plummeted, leading to a further erosion in both wealth and the confidence of consumers and businesses. Moreover, the recession quickly spread to other countries, and the falling incomes abroad depressed aggregate demand even more. During 2007 and the first half of 2008, energy prices were soaring. The price of gasoline doubled, and other energy prices also rose sharply. As we previously discussed, unanticipated increases in the prices of key imported resources would reduce short-run aggregate supply. These adverse forces combine to reduce both aggregate demand and supply, and just as the *AD–AS* model indicates, they generated a sharp decline in real output and employment.

EXHIBIT 10 presents data on the change in both real housing and stock prices during the first two years of expansions and contractions since 1969. Note how both housing and stock prices have risen during the expansionary phase of the business cycle. During the first two years of expansions, the average real home price rose by 7 percent, and the average real stock price rose by 35 percent. These higher asset prices increase wealth and stimulate aggregate demand. This will lead to increases in output and employment during this phase of the cycle.

But just the opposite happens during the contraction. During the past seven recessions, the average real home price fell by 11 percent, and the average real stock price fell by 38 percent. When housing and stock prices fall, household wealth will decline, causing a reduction in aggregate demand. In turn, the reductions in wealth and demand will both contribute to the initial downturn and complicate the recovery process.

The housing and stock data provide additional perspective on the 2008 recession. While stock prices fell by similar amounts during the 1973–1975 and 2001 recessions, the decline in housing prices during the 2008 recession was substantially larger than that during the prior downturns. In fact, housing prices fell by more than 30 percent during the most recent recession, which is about three times the average of recessions during the past four decades. Clearly, the housing price boom during 2002–2005, followed by the substantial fall in housing prices that started in mid-year 2006, was a central factor underlying the recession. As we proceed, we will investigate this issue in more detail.

Looking ahead

The AD–AS model enhances our understanding of macroeconomic markets and potential sources of economic fluctuations. It also provides a constructive frame work with which to address key unanswered questions. Can fiscal and monetary policy promote economic stability? Can they help direct an economy out of a recession? If so, how might this be achieved? Has macroeconomic policies sometimes been the source of economic instability? The next four chapters will focus on these questions and related issues.

KEY POINTS

▼ It is important to distinguish between anticipated and unanticipated changes.

▼ An increase in aggregate demand involves a shift of the entire *AD* curve to the right. Major factors causing an increase in aggregate demand (other than government policies) are (1) an increase in real wealth, (2) a lower real interest rate, (3) increased optimism on the part of businesses and consumers, (4) an increase in the expected rate of inflation, (5) higher real income abroad, and (6) a depreciation in the exchange rate. Conversely, if these factors change in the opposite direction, a decrease in aggregate demand will result.

▼ It is important to distinguish between long-run and short-run aggregate supply. The following factors will increase long-run aggregate supply (*LRAS*): (1) increases in the supply of labor and capital resources, (2) improvements in technology and productivity, and (3) institutional changes improving the efficiency of resource use. Changes in resource prices, the expected rate of inflation, and supply

shocks will cause shifts in short-run aggregate supply (*SRAS*).

▼ An increase in output due to economic growth (an increase in the economy's production capacity) will increase both short-run and long-run aggregate supply, permitting the economy to achieve and sustain a larger output level.

▼ Unanticipated changes in either aggregate demand or aggregate supply will disrupt long-run equilibrium and cause current output to differ from the economy's long-run potential.

▼ Unanticipated increases in aggregate demand and favorable supply shocks can cause economic booms that push output beyond the economy's long-run potential and unemployment below its natural rate. However, as decision makers adjust to the strong demand, resource prices and interest rates will rise, and output will recede to long-run capacity.

▼ Unanticipated reductions in aggregate demand and adverse supply shocks can lead to below-capacity output and abnormally high rates of unemployment. Eventually, lower resource prices (and lower real interest rates) will direct the economy back to long-run equilibrium. This adjustment process will take time, and it may be quite lengthy if wages and prices are downwardly inflexible.

▼ Changes in resource prices and interest rates will help keep an economy on track. During a recession, resource prices and interest rates will decline, and this will help direct the economy back toward

full employment. However, there is considerable debate about how rapidly this adjustment process works.

▼ During the past six decades, economic expansions have been far more lengthy than recessions. However, the depth and severity of the recession that started in December 2007 has once again placed the issue of economic instability and recovery from a recession at the forefront of macroeconomics.

CRITICAL ANALYSIS QUESTIONS

*1. Explain how and why each of the following factors would influence current aggregate demand in the United States:
   a. increased fear of recession
   b. increased fear of inflation
   c. rapid growth of real income in Canada and Western Europe
   d. a reduction in the real interest rate
   e. a higher price level (Be careful.)

*2. Indicate how each of the following would influence U.S. aggregate supply in the short run:
   a. an increase in real wage rates
   b. a severe freeze that destroys half the orange trees in Florida
   c. an increase in the expected rate of inflation in the future
   d. an increase in the world price of oil, a major import
   e. abundant rainfall during the growing season in agricultural states

3. What is the difference between the production possibilities constraint and the long-run aggregate supply curve? How would changes in conditions that move the production possibilities curve affect the *LRAS* curve? How have improvements in computer technology affected production possibilities and the long-run aggregate supply curve?

4. When an economy dips into a recession, consumers will often be relatively pessimistic about the future for an extended period of time. How will this pessimism affect the speed and strength of the recovery? Feel free to use the data of Exhibit 2 in your response to this question.

5. What is the difference between an anticipated and an unanticipated increase in aggregate demand? Provide an example of each. Which is more likely to result in a temporary spurt in the growth of real output?

*6. Assume that both union and management representatives agree to wage increases because they expect prices to rise 10 percent during the next year. Explain why the unemployment rate will probably increase if the actual rate of inflation next year is only 3 percent.

7. During 2007, there was a substantial reduction in housing prices, and the world price of crude oil rose sharply. How did these two changes influence aggregate demand and aggregate supply in the United States? Use the *AD–AS* model to indicate the expected impact of these changes on output and the price level.

*8. When actual output exceeds an economy's full-employment output, how will the self-correcting mechanism direct the economy to long-run equilibrium? Why can't the above-normal output be maintained?

9. How will (a) an unexpected 3 percent fall in the price level in the goods and services market differ from (b) 1 percent inflation when 4 percent inflation had been expected? What impact would (a) and (b) have on the real price of resources, profit margins, output, and employment? Explain.

*10. Suppose that an unexpectedly rapid growth in real income abroad leads to a sharp increase in the demand for U.S. exports. What impact will this change have on the price level, output, and employment in the short run in the United States? In the long run?

11. Construct the *AD, SRAS,* and *LRAS* curves for an economy experiencing (a) full employment, (b) an economic boom, and (c) a recession.

12. Consider an economy with the following aggregate demand (*AD*) and aggregate supply (*AS*) schedules. These schedules reflect the fact that, prior to the period we're examining, decision makers entered into contracts and made choices anticipating that the price level would be P_{105}.

AD_{105} (in trillions)	Price Level	$SRAS_{105}$ (in trillions)
$5.1	95	$3.5
4.9	100	3.8
4.7	105	4.2
4.5	110	4.5
4.3	115	4.8

a. Indicate the quantity of GDP that will be produced and the price level that will emerge during this period.
b. Is the economy in long-run equilibrium? Why or why not?
c. How will the unemployment rate during the current period compare with this economy's natural rate of unemployment?
d. What will tend to happen to resource prices in the future? How will this affect the equilibrium rate of output?
e. Will the rate of GDP produced during this period be sustainable into the future? Why or why not?

*13. What effect did the events of September 11, 2001, have on aggregate demand, aggregate supply, and the long-run potential real output of the United States?

*Asterisk denotes questions for which answers are given in Appendix B.

Fiscal Policy: The Keynesian View and Historical Perspective

CHAPTER FOCUS

- How did the Great Depression alter views about the stability of markets?

- Why did it lead to the development of Keynesian Economics?

- What determines the equilibrium level of output in the Keynesian model?

- What is the multiplier? What does it imply about the stability of a market economy?

- How can fiscal policy be used to promote economic stability and full employment?

I believe myself to be writing a book on economic theory which will largely revolutionize not, I suppose, at once but in the course of the next ten years the way the world thinks about economic problems.

—*John Maynard Keynes*[1]

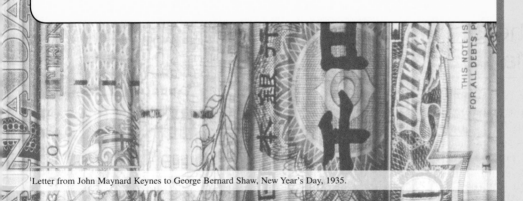

[1]Letter from John Maynard Keynes to George Bernard Shaw, New Year's Day, 1935.

The Great Depression exerted a huge impact on modern macroeconomics. The national income accounts that we use to measure gross domestic product are an outgrowth of this era. Several of the basic concepts of macroeconomics and much of the terminology used today were initially introduced during the 1930s. The Great Depression also led to the development of a theory that provided both an explanation for the prolonged unemployment of the 1930s and a recipe for how to generate a recovery. This theory, developed by the English economist John Maynard Keynes (pronounced "canes"), dominated macroeconomics to such a large extent that the theories he developed were soon known as Keynesian economics.

Keynesian analysis indicated that fiscal policy could be used to maintain a high level of output and employment. The Keynesian view reached a pinnacle in the 1960s. The cover of the December 31, 1965, issue of *TIME* magazine posed the question, "Are we all Keynesians now?" In the midst of strong growth boosted by expansionary fiscal policy, particularly tax reductions, the answer was clearly, "Yes."

But the response proved to be premature. The 1970s were characterized by both high unemployment and inflation. As we will soon illustrate, the Keynesian model provided an explanation for either unemployment or inflation, but it did not account for the simultaneous occurrence of both. The Keynesian theory was designed to explain economic instability and prolonged depressed conditions. Thus, it should not be surprising that its popularity waned even more during the stability of 1982–2007. However, the severity of the plunge in output and employment in 2008 has generated renewed interest and a reexamination of Keynesian economics.

Perhaps surprising to some, active use of fiscal policy is a relatively recent phenomenon. Prior to the 1960s, policy makers focused primarily on how to balance the government's budget, and they generally did so except during times of war or severe recession. Given the limited experience with active use of fiscal policy, the presence of alternative theories and areas of continued debate should not be surprising.

This chapter, and the next, will present both the primary fiscal policy theories and the views of their critics. There are also areas of widespread agreement, and these will be noted as we proceed. In areas in which disagreements remain, we will seek to explain the sources underlying the continuing debate. We will begin with the presentation of the Keynesian view, primarily because it provides historical perspective on the evolution of modern macroeconomics. The following chapter will focus on alternative theories that have arisen over the past four decades. Taken together, these two chapters provide a balanced presentation of current views on the potential and limitations of fiscal policy as a stabilization tool. ■

The Great Depression and the Macroadjustment Process

The 1930s dramatically altered views about the stability of a market economy. Prior to the Great Depression, most economists thought that markets would adjust and direct an economy back to its long-run potential rather quickly. Prolonged recessionary conditions were thought to be impossible. The Great Depression changed all of that.

For those who are familiar only with the relative stability of recent decades, the depth and length of the economic decline during the 1930s are difficult to comprehend: between 1929 and 1933, real GDP in the United States fell by more than 30 percent. In 1933, nearly

Franklin D. Roosevelt Library, courtesy of the National Archives and Records Administration

The Keynesian model was an outgrowth of the great Depression. It provided an explanation for the widespread and prolonged unemployment of the 1930s.

25 percent—one-quarter—of the U.S. labor force was unemployed. The depressed conditions continued throughout the decade. In 1939, a decade after the plunge began, the rate of unemployment was still 17 percent, and per capita income was nearly 10 percent less than that in 1929. Other industrial countries experienced similar conditions during the 1930s.

The Great Depression and Keynesian Economics

Keynesian economics provided a reasonable explanation for the prolonged depressed conditions of the 1930s. Keynes believed that spending motivated firms to supply goods and services. He argued that if total spending fell—as it might, for example, if consumers and investors became pessimistic about the future—then firms would respond by cutting back production. Less spending would thus lead to less output.[2]

Keynes rejected the view that lower wages and interest rates would get the economy back on track and eliminate abnormally high rates of unemployment. He argued that wages and prices are highly inflexible, particularly in a downward direction. Even when demand is weak, Keynes and his followers believed powerful trade unions and large corporations would be able to maintain their wages and prices at a high level. Further, even if wages did decline, this would reduce incomes and exert a negative impact on aggregate demand.

Keynes also rejected the potential effectiveness of interest rate cuts to get the economy back on track. He argued that when excess capacity is widespread and people are extremely pessimistic about the future, lower interest rates will fail to stimulate additional investment. Moreover, when nominal interest rates fall to extremely low levels—rates near zero, for example—significant additional reductions capable of stimulating the economy would be impossible. Keynes believed that all of these conditions were present during the Great Depression. Under these circumstances, he did not believe that market forces would direct the economy back to full employment.

Output, Employment, and Keynesian Economics

Keynes also introduced a different concept of equilibrium and a different mechanism for its achievement. In the Keynesian view, equilibrium takes place when total spending in the economy is equal to current output. When this is the case, business firms will just be able to sell the quantity of goods and services they are currently producing. Their inventories will be neither rising nor falling, and therefore they will have no reason to either expand or contract output.

---

[2]See the classic book by John Maynard Keynes, *The General Theory of Employment, Interest, and Money* (London: Macmillan, 1936), for the presentation of this theory.

Keynesians believe that changes in output rather than changes in prices direct the economy toward equilibrium. An increase in total spending demand would generate expanding sales and reduce the inventories of firms. Businesses would respond with an expansion in output, and the higher level of output would be maintained as long as spending remained at the higher level.

On the other hand, a decline in total spending would lead to a reduction in sales and rising inventories. If total spending fell below the full-employment level of output, business firms would cut back on employment and reduce their output to the level of spending, and, most significantly, the lower level of output and employment would persist as long as the level of spending was unchanged. Therefore, if total spending is deficient—if it is less than full-employment output—high rates of unemployment will be present, output will continue below the economy's potential, and these conditions will persist as long as the spending on goods and services remains weak.

This is exactly what Keynes believed was happening during the 1930s. Consumers were unwilling to spend much because reductions in stock prices and the value of other assets had reduced their wealth and incomes, and they were extremely pessimistic about the future. Businesses responded with reductions in output because there was little demand for their products. Moreover, investment came to a complete standstill because underutilized resources and capacity were abundantly available.

The Multiplier and Economic Instability

Multiplier principle

Concept that an increase in spending on a project will generate income for the resource suppliers, who will then increase their consumption spending. In turn, their additional consumption will generate income for others and lead to still more consumption. As this process goes through successive rounds, total income will expand by a multiple of the initial increase in spending.

Expenditure multiplier

The ratio of the change in equilibrium output to the independent change in investment, consumption, or government spending that brings about the change. Numerically, the multiplier is equal to 1 *divided by* (1 − MPC) when the price level is constant.

Marginal propensity to consume (MPC)

Additional current consumption divided by additional current disposable income

Keynes also argued that market forces could not be counted on to maintain spending levels consistent with full employment because even minor disturbances will often be amplified into major disruptions. The **multiplier principle** can be used to explain his argument. The multiplier principle *builds on the point that one individual's expenditure becomes the income of another.* Predictably, income recipients will spend a portion of their additional earnings on consumption. In turn, their consumption expenditures will generate additional income for others who will also spend a portion of it.

Perhaps an example will illuminate the multiplier concept. Suppose an entrepreneur undertakes a $1 million investment project. The project will increase spending directly by $1 million. This is not the entire story, however. The investment project will require plumbers, carpenters, masons, lumber, cement, and many other resources. The project will generate $1 million of income for the suppliers of these resources. What will they do with this income? After setting aside (saving) a portion of it, the resource suppliers will spend a fraction of the additional income. They will buy food, clothing, recreation, medical care, and thousands of other items. How will this spending influence the incomes of those who supply these products and services? Their incomes will increase, also. These people will save a portion of it and will spend some of it on current consumption. This consumption spending will result in still more additional income generated and received by the suppliers of the additional goods and services.

The term *multiplier* is also used to indicate the number by which the initial investment would be multiplied to obtain the total increase in the economy's income. If the $1 million investment resulted in $4 million of additional income, the **expenditure multiplier** would be 4. The total increase in income would be four times the amount of the initial increase in spending. Similarly, if total income increased by $3 million, the multiplier would be 3.

The size of the multiplier depends on the proportion of the additional income that households choose to spend on consumption.[3] Keynes referred to this fraction as the **marginal propensity to consume (MPC)**. Mathematically,

$$MPC = \frac{\text{Additional consumption}}{\text{Additional income}}$$

[3]For the purposes of simplicity when calculating the size of the multiplier, we will assume that all additions to income are either (1) spent on domestically produced goods or (2) saved. This assumption means that we are ignoring the impact of taxes and spending on imports as income expands via the multiplier process.

For example, if your income increases by $100 and you increase your current consumption expenditures by $75 as a result, your marginal propensity to consume is 75/100, which is 3/4 or 0.75.

EXHIBIT 1 illustrates why the size of the multiplier is dependent upon the MPC. Continuing with the previous example, we consider the impact of the $1 million investment project when the MPC is equal to 3/4. Initially, a $1 million investment will result in $1 million of additional income in round 1 for those undertaking the project. Because the MPC is 3/4, consumption will increase by $750,000 (the other $250,000 will flow into saving) and turn into other people's income in round 2. The recipients of the round 2 income of $750,000 will spend 3/4 of it on current consumption. Hence, their spending will increase income by $562,500 in round 3. Exhibit 1 indicates the additions to income through other rounds. In total, income will increase by $4 million, given an MPC of 3/4. The multiplier is 4.

If the MPC had been greater, income recipients would have spent a larger share of their additional income on current consumption during each round. Thus, the additional income generated in each round would have been greater, increasing the size of the multiplier. There is a precise relationship between the MPC and the multiplier, in other words. The expenditure multiplier, M, is

$$M = \frac{1}{1-MPC}$$

The multiplier concept also works in reverse—reductions in spending will also be magnified and generate even larger reductions in income. Thus, even modest reductions in investment or consumption, perhaps due to increased pessimism about the future, might throw an economy into a recession. Keynesians argue that the multiplier concept indicates that market economies are extremely fragile and that they have a tendency to fluctuate back and forth between excessive and deficient demand.

Adding Realism to the Multiplier

When considering the multiplier, it is important to understand the chain reactions that underlie the concept. Exhibit 1 implicitly assumes that the additional spending will always bring previously idle workers into the labor force. For example, the analysis implies that the electricians, plumbers, masons, and others involved in the initial construction project would not have been working if the project had not been undertaken. When unemployment is exceedingly high, as it was during the Great Depression, this may be largely the case. However, during more normal times when there are fewer unemployed resources, much of

EXPENDITURE STAGE	ADDITIONAL INCOME (DOLLARS)	ADDITIONAL CONSUMPTION (DOLLARS)	MARGINAL PROPENSITY TO CONSUME	**EXHIBIT 1** The Multiplier Principle
Round 1	1,000,000 →	750,000	3/4	
Round 2	750,000	562,500	3/4	
Round 3	562,500	421,875	3/4	
Round 4	421,875	316,406	3/4	
Round 5	316,406	237,305	3/4	
Round 6	237,305	177,979	3/4	
Round 7	177,979	133,484	3/4	
Round 8	133,484	100,113	3/4	
Round 9	100,113	75,085	3/4	
Round 10	75,085	56,314	3/4	
All Others	225,253	168,939	3/4	
Total	4,000,000	3,000,000	3/4	

the additional spending will merely bid resources away from other activities. Under these circumstances, there will be upward pressure on prices, and the additions to income will be smaller, perhaps substantially smaller, than the multiplier analysis implies.

It is also important to consider how the initial addition to spending is derived. If the increase in spending is financed by borrowing, there will be upward pressure on real interest rates, which will reduce spending in other areas. Correspondingly, if the additional spending were the result of a government project financed by taxes, the higher taxes would reduce spending in other areas, at least partially offsetting the impact of the multiplier.[4] These factors indicate that during normal times, the demand stimulus effects of a spending project will be substantially weaker than the multiplier analysis suggests.

Keynes and Economic Instability: A Summary

The central message of Keynes can be summarized as follows: businesses will produce only the quantity of goods and services they believe consumers, investors, governments, and foreigners will plan to buy. If these planned aggregate expenditures are less than the economy's full-employment output, output will fall short of its potential. Moreover, reductions in spending will often be amplified by the multiplier and tend to feed on themselves. Downturns will breed pessimism among both consumers and investors, which will lead to lower prices for assets such as stocks and houses, causing total spending and output to plummet downward by even larger amounts. When total expenditures (aggregate demand) on goods and services are deficient, market economies do not have an automatic mechanism that will return the economy to full employment. Prolonged unemployment will persist. Against the backdrop of the Great Depression, this was a compelling argument.

However, Keynes also indicated that there was a way out of this economic tragedy. Fiscal policy provided the remedy. We now turn to that topic.

OUTSTANDING ECONOMIST

John Maynard Keynes (1883–1946)

Keynes might properly be referred to as the "father of macroeconomics." The son of a prominent nineteenth-century economist (John Neville Keynes), he earned a degree in mathematics from King's College, Cambridge, where he would later return and spend most of his career as an economist. His *General Theory of Employment, Interest, and Money*, published in 1936, revolutionized the way that economists think about macroeconomics. This work, written in the midst of the Great Depression, provided both a plausible explanation for the massive unemployment and a strategy for ending it. Keynes married an idea with a moment in time.

Although Keynes's work was groundbreaking, it was also controversial. Keynes argued that governments should run budget deficits during a recession to stimulate demand and direct the economy back to full employment. But this idea challenged the entrenched views of both policy makers and economists. Nonetheless, his ideas soon triumphed and dominated the thinking of macroeconomists for three decades following his untimely death due to a heart attack in 1946. Most observers would rate Keynes as the most influential economist of the twentieth century.

---

[4]The multiplier analysis is often abused by proponents of government spending projects. For example, proponents of tax-subsidized sports stadiums and industrial development projects often use the multiplier to argue that spending on such projects will generate a huge increase in income and employment for the local economy, while ignoring the offsetting spending reductions as the result of the higher taxes.

The Keynesian View of Fiscal Policy

As we noted in Chapter 9, fiscal policy involves the use of the government's spending, taxing, and borrowing policies. Until now, we have assumed that the government's fiscal policy remained unchanged. We are now ready to relax this assumption and investigate the effect of fiscal policy on output, prices, and employment. We want to isolate the impact of changes in fiscal policy from changes in monetary policy. Thus, we will continue to assume that the monetary authorities are holding the supply of money constant. We will relax this assumption and investigate the impact of monetary policy in subsequent chapters.

The federal budget is the primary tool of fiscal policy. When the supply of money is constant, government expenditures must be financed with either (1) taxes or revenues derived from other sources or (2) borrowing. If the government's revenue from taxes and other sources is equal to its total expenditure, a **balanced budget** is present. The budget need not be in balance, however. A **budget deficit** occurs when total government spending exceeds total government revenue from all sources. When this happens, the government must borrow funds to finance the excess of its spending relative to revenue. It borrows by issuing interest-bearing bonds that become part of what we call the national debt, the total amount of outstanding government bonds. Conversely, a **budget surplus** is present when the government's revenues exceed its total expenditures. The surplus allows the government to reduce its outstanding debt.

While budget conditions are often used to gauge the direction of fiscal policy, it is important to recognize that changes in the size of the deficit or surplus can have two different sources. ***First, changes in the size of the deficit or surplus may merely reflect the state of the economy.*** During a recession, tax revenues generally fall and expenditures on transfer programs increase because of the weak economic conditions. This will shift the budget toward a deficit—even with no changes in fiscal policy. Just the opposite will happen during the expansionary phase of the business cycle. The rapid growth of income during an expansion will increase tax revenues and reduce income transfers, causing the budget to shift toward a surplus (or smaller deficit), even if there has not been any change in fiscal policy. ***Second, changes in the deficit or surplus may reflect discretionary fiscal policy.*** Discretionary fiscal policy requires passage of tax and/or spending legislation by Congress and the president that alter the size of the budget deficit (or surplus). When we speak of "changes in fiscal policy," we are referring to this latter type of action—a deliberate change in tax laws or government spending levels (or both) that affect the budget deficit or surplus.

Fiscal Policy and the Good News of Keynesian Economics

Keynesians argue that the federal budget should be used to promote a level of total spending (aggregate demand) consistent with the full-employment rate of output. How might policy makers use the budget to stimulate aggregate demand? First, an increase in government purchases of goods and services will directly increase aggregate demand. As the government spends more on highways, flood-control projects, education, and national defense, for example, these expenditures will increase demand in the goods and services market. Second, changes in tax policy will also influence aggregate demand. For example, a reduction in personal taxes will increase the current disposable income of households. As their after-tax income rises, people will spend more on consumption. In turn, this increase in consumption will stimulate aggregate demand. Similarly, a reduction in business taxes increases after-tax profitability, which will stimulate both business investment and aggregate demand.

When an economy is operating below its potential capacity, Keynesians believe the government should institute **expansionary fiscal policy**. In other words, the government should increase its purchases of goods and services or cut taxes or both. Of course, this

Balanced budget

A situation in which current government revenue from taxes, fees, and other sources is just equal to current government expenditures.

Budget deficit

A situation in which total government spending exceeds total government revenue during a specific time period, usually one year.

Budget surplus

A situation in which total government spending is less than total government revenue during a time period, usually a year.

Discretionary fiscal policy

A change, in laws or appropriation levels, that alters government revenues and/or expenditures.

Expansionary fiscal policy

An increase in government expenditures and/or a reduction in tax rates, such that the expected size of the budget deficit expands.

policy will increase the government's budget deficit. To finance the enlarged budget deficit, the government will have to borrow from either private domestic sources or foreigners.[5]

EXHIBIT 2 illustrates the case for expansionary fiscal policy when an economy is experiencing abnormally high unemployment caused by deficient aggregate demand. Initially, the economy is operating at e_1. Output is below potential capacity, Y_F, and unemployment exceeds its natural rate. As we discussed in Chapter 10, if there is no change in policy, abnormally high unemployment and excess supply in the resource market will eventually reduce real wages and other resource prices, which will lower costs and direct the economy toward a full-employment equilibrium like E_3. In addition, weak demand for investment goods will place downward pressure on interest rates, which will stimulate aggregate demand and also help to direct the economy back to full employment. However, these adjustments may work slowly.

Rather than depending on the economy's self-corrective mechanism, Keynesians favor a shift to a more expansionary fiscal policy—an increase in government spending or a reduction in taxes, or some combination of the two. In other words, they advocate a deliberate increase in the budget deficit in order to stimulate aggregate demand. Furthermore, they argue that the multiplier process will magnify the initial increase in spending. Suppose that the government holds taxes constant and increases its spending on highways and school construction by $20 billion. The additional spending will generate $20 billion in income for those undertaking the construction projects. As these individuals use a portion of this income to buy consumer goods, the multiplier process indicates that their spending will trigger more income and spending by others. Thus, Keynesians expect that the total increase in aggregate demand will be substantially greater than the initial $20 billion increase in government purchases.

When an economy is operating below its potential capacity, the Keynesian prescription calls for expansionary fiscal policy—a deliberate change in expenditures and/or taxes that will increase the size of the government's budget deficit. An appropriate dose of expansionary fiscal policy, if timed properly, will stimulate aggregate demand (shift the curve to AD_2 in Exhibit 2) and guide the economy to full-employment equilibrium (E_2).

EXHIBIT 2
Expansionary Fiscal Policy to Promote Full Employment

Here, we illustrate an economy operating in the short run at Y_1, below its potential capacity of Y_F. There are two routes to a long-run, full-employment equilibrium. First, policy makers could wait for lower wages and resource prices to reduce costs, increase supply to $SRAS_3$, and restore equilibrium at E_3. Most Keynesians believe this market-adjustment method will be slow and uncertain. Alternatively, expansionary fiscal policy could stimulate aggregate demand (shift it to AD_2) and guide the economy to E_2.

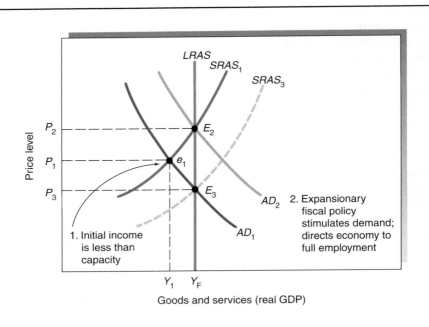

---

[5]Alternatively, the government could borrow from its central bank—the Federal Reserve Bank in the United States. However, as we will see in the following chapter, this method of financing a budget deficit would expand the money supply. Because we want to differentiate between fiscal and monetary effects, we must hold the supply of money constant. So for now, we assume that government deficits must be financed by borrowing from private sources.

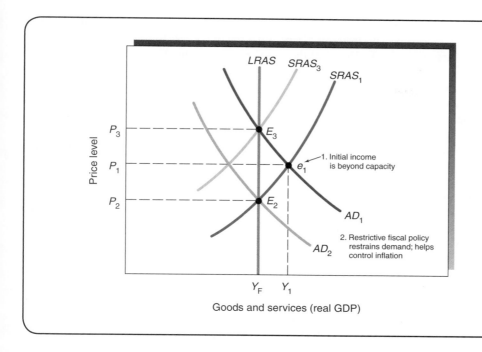

EXHIBIT 3
Restrictive Fiscal Policy
to Combat Inflation

Strong demand such as AD$_1$ will temporarily lead to an output rate beyond the economy's long-run potential (Y$_F$). If the high level of demand persists, it will lead to a long-run equilibrium (E$_3$) at a higher price level. However, restrictive fiscal policy could restrain demand to AD$_2$ (or better still, prevent demand from expanding to AD$_1$ in the first place) and thereby guide the economy to a noninflationary equilibrium (E$_2$).

The Keynesian view also provides a fiscal policy remedy for inflation. Suppose that an economy is experiencing an inflationary economic boom as the result of excessive aggregate demand. As **EXHIBIT 3** illustrates, in the absence of a change in policy, the strong demand (AD_1) will push up wages and other resource prices. In time, the higher resource prices will increase costs, reduce aggregate supply (from $SRAS_1$ to $SRAS_3$), and lead to a higher price level (P_3). Keynesians argue, however, that **restrictive fiscal policy** can be used to reduce aggregate demand (shift it to AD_2) and guide the economy to a noninflationary equilibrium (E_2). A reduced level of government purchases will diminish aggregate demand directly. Alternatively, higher taxes on households and businesses could be used to dampen consumption and private investment. The restrictive fiscal policy—a spending reduction and/or an increase in taxes—will shift the government budget toward a surplus (or smaller deficit). *Keynesians believe that a shift toward a more restrictive fiscal policy is the proper prescription with which to combat inflation generated by excessive aggregate demand.*

The Keynesian theory challenges the view that a responsible government should constrain spending within the bounds of its revenues. *Rather than balancing the budget annually, Keynesians stressed the importance of* **countercyclical policy**, *that is, policy designed to "counter" or offset fluctuations in aggregate demand.* On the one hand, when an economy is threatened by a recession, the government should shift to a more expansionary fiscal policy, increasing spending or reducing taxes in a manner that will increase the size of the budget deficit. On the other hand, fiscal policy should become more restrictive—the budget should be shifted toward a smaller deficit or larger surplus—in response to a threat of inflation. According to the Keynesian view, fluctuations in aggregate demand are the major source of economic disturbances. Moreover, wise use of fiscal policy can help stabilize and maintain demand at or near the full-employment rate of output.

Restrictive fiscal policy

A reduction in government expenditures and/or an increase in tax rates such that the expected size of the budget deficit declines (or the budget surplus increases).

Countercyclical policy

A policy that tends to move the economy in an opposite direction from the forces of the business cycle. Such a policy would stimulate demand during the contraction phase of the business cycle and restrain demand during the expansion phase.

Fiscal Policy Changes and Problems of Timing

In the 1960s, Keynesian economists were highly optimistic that fiscal policy could be instituted in a manner that would smooth the ups and downs of the business cycle. Over time, the earlier optimism has been tempered. If discretionary fiscal policy changes are going to reduce economic instability, they must be timed correctly. Fiscal stimulus must be felt during recessions and restraint during inflationary booms. But proper timing of fiscal policy is not an easy task. There are three major reasons why this is true.

First, a change in fiscal policy will require legislative action. But the political process moves slowly. This is particularly true in a country like the United States that has a number of checks and balances built into its political system. Congressional committees must meet, hear testimony, and draft legislation. Key legislators may choose to delay action in an attempt to amend the legislation so that it benefits their own constituents and supporters. Furthermore, a majority of the lawmakers must be convinced that the legislation will not adversely affect their particular constituents and supporters. Predictably, this will all require a significant amount of time.

Second, a change in policy will not immediately impact the macroeconomy. Even after a policy change is adopted, another six to twelve months will generally pass before it will have much impact on the economy. If government expenditures are going to be increased, time will be required for competitive bids to be submitted and government contracts granted. Contractors might not be able to begin work right away. Although a tax cut might exert some stimulus more quickly, typically several months will pass before the primary effects of the cut are felt throughout the economy.

Third, because of these delays, if fiscal policy is going to exert a stabilizing influence, policy makers need to know what economic conditions are going to be like twelve to eighteen months in the future. However, this is a big problem because our ability to forecast when the economy is about to dip into a recession or experience an economic boom is extremely limited. Therefore, in a world of dynamic change and unpredictable events, macroeconomic policy making is a little bit like lobbing a ball at a target that often moves in unforeseen directions.

Given these time lags and forecasting limitations, policy-making errors will occur. Sometimes fiscal policy changes will end up adding stimulus during periods of strong demand and restraint during periods of recession. Changes of this type would add to rather than reduce economic instability.

Thus, a discretionary change in fiscal policy is like a two-edged sword—it has the potential to do harm as well as good. If timed correctly, it will reduce economic instability. But, when timed incorrectly, a fiscal policy change can also be a source of instability.

Automatic Stabilizers

Fortunately, a few fiscal programs tend automatically to apply demand stimulus during a recession and demand restraint during an economic boom. Programs of this type are called **automatic stabilizers**. They are automatic in that, without any new legislative action, they tend to increase the budget deficit (or reduce the surplus) during a recession and increase the surplus (or reduce the deficit) during an economic boom.

Automatic stabilizers

Built-in features that tend automatically to promote a budget deficit during a recession and a budget surplus during an inflationary boom, even without a change in policy.

The major advantage of automatic stabilizers is that they institute countercyclical fiscal policy without the delays associated with legislative action. They minimize the problem of proper timing, in other words. On the one hand, when unemployment is rising and business conditions are slow, these stabilizers automatically reduce tax revenues collected and increase government spending, giving the economy a shot in the arm. On the other hand, automatic stabilizers help apply the brakes to an economic boom, increasing tax revenues and decreasing government spending. Three of these built-in stabilizers deserve specific mention: unemployment compensation, the corporate profit tax, and the progressive income tax.

UNEMPLOYMENT COMPENSATION. When an economy begins to dip into a recession, the government will pay out more money in unemployment benefits as the number of laid-off and unemployed workers expands. Simultaneously, the receipts from the employment tax that finance the unemployment compensation system will decline because fewer workers are paying into the system. Therefore, this program will automatically run a deficit during a business slowdown. In contrast, during an economic boom, the tax receipts from the program will increase because more people are now working, and the amount paid out in benefits will decline because fewer people are unemployed. Thus, the program will automatically tend to run a surplus during good times. So without any change in policy, the unemployment compensation program has the desired countercyclical effect on aggregate demand.[6]

THE CORPORATE PROFIT TAX. The corporate profit tax is a highly important automatic stabilizer because corporate profits are highly sensitive to cyclical conditions. During a recession, corporate profits decline sharply, and so, too, do corporate tax payments. In turn, the decline in tax revenues will enlarge the size of the budget deficit. In contrast, when the economy is expanding, corporate profits typically increase much more rapidly than wages, income, or consumption. This increase in corporate profits will result in a rapid increase in the "tax take" from the business sector during the expansion phase of the business cycle. Thus, corporate tax payments will go up during an expansion and fall rapidly during a contraction, even though no new legislative action has been instituted.

THE PROGRESSIVE INCOME TAX. When incomes grow rapidly, the average personal income tax liability of individuals and families increases. With rising incomes, more people will find their income above the "no tax due" cutoff. Others will jump up into higher tax brackets. Therefore, during an economic expansion, personal income tax revenues increase more rapidly than income, because income will grow at a more incremental pace. Other things constant, the budget moves toward a surplus (or smaller deficit), even though the economy's tax rate structure is unchanged. Conversely, when incomes decline, many individuals will be taxed at lower rates or not at all. Income tax revenues will fall more rapidly than income, automatically enlarging the size of the budget deficit during a recession.

During the 1960s, it was widely believed that discretionary fiscal policy could be instituted in a manner that would help promote economic stability. Both Keynesian and non-Keynesian economists now recognize that proper timing of fiscal policy is more difficult than was previously thought. Automatic stabilizers minimize the problem of appropriate timing and thereby exert an important stabilizing impact on the economy. However, the timing difficulties mean that the potential of discretionary fiscal policy is substantially more limited. Discretionary changes may have their greatest relevance during severe and lengthy recessions such as the one that began in December of 2007. As we proceed, we will consider the potential of fiscal stimulus to promote the recovery of a highly depressed economy in detail.

The Keynesian Aggregate Expenditure Model[7]

As we have already illustrated, the central elements of Keynesian economics can be presented within the *AD–AS* model we developed in the previous two chapters. An alternative framework—an aggregate expenditure model—can also be used to present these ideas. We will present this alternative model in this section and also illustrate its relationship to the *AD–AS* model more explicitly.

All models make simplifying assumptions. As we develop the *aggregate expenditure (AE) model*, we want to be explicit about several of the key assumptions. First, as with the *AD–AS* model, the *AE* model assumes that there is a specific rate of output associated with full employment. Second, following in the Keynesian tradition, the *AE* model assumes that

---

[6]Although unemployment compensation has the desired countercyclical effect on demand, it also reduces the incentive to accept available employment opportunities. Research in this area indicates that the existing unemployment compensation system increases the length of job search by unemployed workers and thereby increases the long-run natural (normal) unemployment rate.
[7]Some instructors may choose not to cover the aggregate expenditure model. The text has been designed so this section can be omitted and readers may move immediately on to the material of Chapter 12 without any break in continuity.

wages and prices are completely inflexible until full employment is reached. Once full employment is achieved, though, additional demand will lead only to higher prices.

The key to understanding the *AE* model is the concept of *planned* aggregate expenditures. As in the case of aggregate demand, the four components of *planned* aggregate expenditures are consumption, investment, government purchases, and net exports. Let's consider each.

Planned Consumption Expenditures

The largest component of planned aggregate expenditures is *planned* consumption (*C*). Keynes believed that people's current income primarily determines their consumption spending. According to Keynes, disposable income—one's income after taxes—is by far the most important determinant of current consumption. If disposable income increases, consumers will increase their planned expenditures.

Consumption function

The relationship between disposable income and consumption. When disposable income increases, current consumption expenditures rise, but by less than the increase in income.

This positive relationship between disposable income and consumption spending is called the **consumption function**. **EXHIBIT 4** illustrates this relationship for an economy. At low levels of aggregate income (less than $9 trillion), the consumption expenditures of households will exceed their disposable income. When income is low, households *dissave*—they either borrow money or draw from their past savings to purchase consumption goods. As income increases, consumption will also increase, but not as rapidly as income. This indicates that the marginal propensity to consume is less than one; some fraction of additional income is allocated to saving. At $9 trillion, current consumption and income are equal. As income expands beyond $9 trillion, household income will exceed consumption and saving will be positive. Note that the consumption function is flatter than the 45-degree line. This indicates that as income expands, households increase their consumption by less than their increase in income.

Autonomous expenditures

Expenditures that do not vary with the level of income. They are determined by factors such as business expectations and economic policy.

Planned Investment Expenditures

Investment (*I*) encompasses (1) expenditures on fixed assets, such as buildings and machines, and (2) changes in the inventories of raw materials and final products not yet sold. Keynes argued that, in the short run, investment is best viewed as an **autonomous**

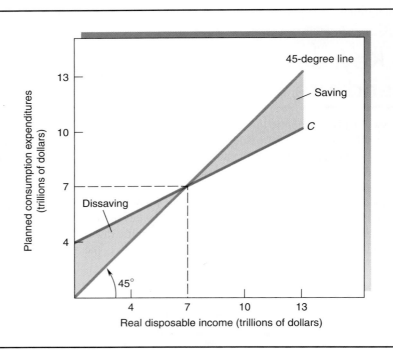

EXHIBIT 4
Aggregate Consumption Function

The Keynesian model assumes that there is a positive relationship between consumption and income. However, as income increases, consumption expands by a smaller amount. Thus, the slope of the consumption function (line C) is less than 1 (less than the slope of the 45-degree line).

expenditure, one that is independent of people's income. In other words, business investment decisions, at least in the short run, don't hinge on people's current income and spending. Instead, investment is primarily a function of current sales relative to plant capacity, expected future sales, and the interest rate. To isolate the forces pushing an economy toward an equilibrium level of output, the Keynesian model assumes that the planned level of investment expenditure is constant with respect to current income.

Planned Government Expenditures

Like investment, planned government (*G*) expenditures in the basic Keynesian model are assumed to be independent of income. These expenditures need not change with the level of income. In the Keynesian model, government expenditures are a policy variable determined by the political process—not consumers' income or spending. Governments can, and often do, spend more than they receive in taxes. As we proceed, we will analyze how changes in government expenditures influence output and employment within the *AE* model.

Planned Net Exports

Exports are dependent upon spending choices and income levels abroad. These decisions are, by and large, unaffected by changes in a nation's domestic output level and spending. Therefore, as **EXHIBIT 5** illustrates, exports remain constant (at $1.2 trillion) when income changes. In contrast, increases in domestic income will induce consumers to purchase more foreign as well as domestic goods. So the level of imports increases as income rises. Because exports remain constant but imports increase as aggregate income expands, a nation's net exports (*NX*) will decline as income rises (see Exhibit 5). Thus, Keynes theorized that there is a negative relationship between a nation's net exports and its aggregate income. When its aggregate income rises, its net exports fall; when its aggregate income falls, its net exports rise.

Planned versus Actual Expenditures

Now let's explain the difference between planned and *actual* expenditures. Planned expenditures reflect the choices of consumers, investors, governments, and foreigners, *given their expectations about the choices of other decision makers*. Planned expenditures, though, need not equal actual expenditures. If buyers spend a different amount on goods and services from what firms anticipate, the firms will experience unplanned changes in inventories.

Consider what would happen if the planned expenditures of consumers, investors, governments, and foreigners on goods and services were less than what business firms thought they would be. If this were the case, business firms would be unable to sell as much of their current output as they had anticipated. Their *actual* inventories would increase as they unintentionally made larger inventory investments than they *planned*. On the other hand, consider what would happen if purchasers bought more goods and services than businesses expected. The unexpected brisk sales would draw down

TOTAL OUTPUT (REAL GDP IN TRILLIONS)	PLANNED EXPORTS (TRILLIONS)	PLANNED IMPORTS (TRILLIONS)	PLANNED NET EXPORTS (TRILLIONS)
$13.4	$1.2	$1.00	$0.20
13.7	1.2	1.05	0.15
14.0	1.2	1.10	0.10
14.3	1.2	1.15	0.05
14.6	1.2	1.20	0.0

EXHIBIT 5
Income and Net Exports

Because exports are determined by income abroad, they are constant at $1.2 trillion. Imports increase as domestic income expands. Thus, planned net exports fall as domestic income increases.

inventories and result in less inventory investment than business firms planned. In this case, *actual* inventory investment would be less than what was *planned* for by business decision makers.

Actual and *planned* expenditures are equal only when purchasers buy the quantity of goods and services that business decision makers anticipated they would purchase. Only then will the plans of buyers and sellers in the goods and services market harmonize.

Keynesian Equilibrium in the *AE* Model

Equilibrium is present in the Keynesian **AE** *model when planned aggregate expenditures equal the value of actual output.* When this is the case, businesses are able to sell the total amount of goods and services that they produce. There are no unexpected changes in inventories. Thus, producers have no incentive to either expand or contract their output during the next period. In equation form, Keynesian macroequilibrium is attained when

$$\underbrace{\text{Total output}}_{\text{Real GDP}} = \underbrace{\text{Planned } C + I + G + NX}_{\text{Planned aggregate expenditures}}$$

For an example of Keynesian macroeconomic equilibrium, let's take a look at the hypothetical economy described by **EXHIBIT 6**. First, look at columns 1 and 2. At what level of total output is this economy in Keynesian macroeconomic equilibrium? Stop now and attempt to figure out the answer.

The answer is $14 trillion, because only the total output is exactly equal to planned aggregate expenditures. When real GDP is equal to $14 trillion, the planned expenditures of consumers, investors, governments, and foreigners (net exports) are precisely equal to the value of the output produced by business firms. To see this, note that only at $14 trillion do columns 3, 4, and 5 combined equal column 1. At $14 trillion in output, the spending plans of purchasers mesh with the production plans of businesses.

What happens at other output levels? At any output other than equilibrium, the plans of producers and purchasers will conflict. If output is $13.7 trillion, for example, planned aggregate expenditures will be $13.85 trillion—$150 billion more than the current level of output. When expenditures (purchases) exceed output, inventories will decline. Firms will then expand their output to get their inventories back up to normal levels. Therefore, when aggregate expenditures exceed current output, there will be a tendency for output to expand toward the equilibrium output ($14 trillion).

Conversely, if aggregate expenditures are less than current output, firms will cut back on production. For example, if output is $14.3 trillion, it will be greater than planned aggregate expenditures, and excess inventories will accumulate. Of course, business firms will not continue to produce goods they cannot sell, so they will reduce production, and output will recede toward the $14 trillion equilibrium.

EXHIBIT 6
Example of Keynesian Macroeconomic Equilibrium

All figures are in trillions of dollars. Column 2 equals the sum of columns 3, 4, and 5.

TOTAL OUTPUT (REAL GDP) (1)	PLANNED AGGREGATE EXPENDITURES (2)	PLANNED CONSUMPTION (3)	PLANNED INVESTMENT + GOVERNMENT EXPENDITURES (4)	PLANNED NET EXPORTS (5)	TENDENCY OF OUTPUT (6)
$13.4	$13.70	$9.1	$4.4	$0.20	Expand
13.7	13.85	9.3	4.4	0.15	Expand
14.0	14.00	9.5	4.4	0.10	Equilibrium
14.3	14.15	9.7	4.4	0.05	Contract
14.6	14.30	9.9	4.4	0.00	Contract

Note: All figures are in trillions of dollars. Column 2 equals the sum of columns 3, 4, and 5.

Equilibrium at Less Than Full Employment

Because Keynesian equilibrium hinges on planned aggregate expenditures and output being equal, it need not take place at full employment. *If an economy is in Keynesian equilibrium, there will be no tendency for output to change—even if output is well below full-employment capacity.*

To see this using our example, assume that full employment is at an output of $14.3 trillion, in Exhibit 6. Given the current planned spending, the economy will fail to achieve full employment. The rate of unemployment will be high. In the Keynesian *AE* model, neither wages nor interest rates will decline in the face of abnormally high unemployment and excess capacity. Therefore, output will remain at less than the full-employment rate as long as insufficient spending prevents the economy from reaching its full potential.

This is precisely what Keynes thought was happening during the Great Depression. He believed that Western economies were in equilibrium at an employment rate substantially below capacity. Unless aggregate expenditures increased, therefore, the prolonged unemployment had to continue—and, in fact, it did, throughout the 1930s.

Keynesian Equilibrium—A Graphic Presentation

The Keynesian analysis is presented graphically in **EXHIBIT 7**. Notice that planned aggregate consumption, investment, government, and net export expenditures are measured on the *y*-axis, and total output is measured on the *x*-axis. The 45-degree line that extends from the origin maps out all the points at which aggregate expenditures (*AE*) are equal to total output (GDP).

Because aggregate expenditures equal total output for all points along the 45-degree line, the line maps out all possible equilibrium income levels. As long as the economy is operating at less than its full-employment capacity, producers will produce any output along the 45-degree line that they believe purchasers will buy. Producers, though, will supply a level of output only if they believe planned expenditures will be large enough to purchase it. Depending on the level of aggregate expenditures, each point along the 45-degree line is a potential equilibrium.

Using the data of Exhibit 6, **EXHIBIT 8** shows the Keynesian equilibrium in our hypothetical economy. The *C + I + G + NX* (*AE*) line indicates the total planned expenditures of consumers, investors, governments, and foreigners (net exports) at each income level.

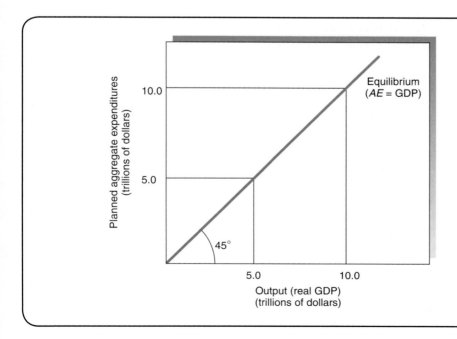

EXHIBIT 7
Aggregate
Expenditures (*AE*)

Aggregate expenditures will be equal to total output for all points along a 45-degree line from the origin. The 45-degree line thus maps out potential equilibrium levels of output for the Keynesian model.

EXHIBIT 8
Aggregate Expenditures and Keynesian Equilibrium

Here the data of Exhibit 6 are presented within the Keynesian graphic framework. The equilibrium level of output is $14.0 trillion because planned expenditures (C + I + G + NX) are just equal to output at that level of income. At a lower level of income, $13.7 trillion, for example, unplanned inventory reduction would cause business firms to expand output (right-pointing arrow). Conversely, at a higher income level, such as $14.3 trillion, accumulation of inventories would lead to lower future output (left-pointing arrow). Given current aggregate expenditures, only the $14.0 trillion output would be sustainable in the future. Note that the $14.0 trillion equilibrium income level is less than the economy's potential of $14.3 trillion.

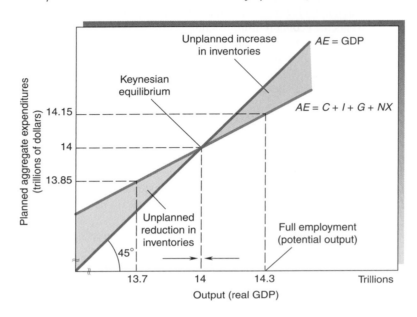

Remember, the aggregate expenditure (*AE*) line is flatter than the 45-degree line because, as income rises, consumption also increases, but by less than the increase in income. Therefore, as income expands, total expenditures increase by less than the expansion in income.

The equilibrium level of output will be $14.0 trillion, the point at which total expenditures (measured vertically) are just equal to total output (measured horizontally). Of course, the aggregate expenditures function $C + I + G + NX$ will cross the 45-degree line at the $14.0 trillion Keynesian equilibrium level of output. As long as the aggregate expenditures function remains unchanged, no other level of output can be sustained. When total output exceeds $14.0 trillion—for example, when it's $14.3 trillion—the aggregate expenditure line ($C + I + G + NX$) lies below the 45-degree line. Remember, when the height of the $C + I + G + NX$ line is less than the height of the 45-degree line, total spending is less than total output. People aren't willing to buy as much as is produced. Excess inventories will accumulate, leading businesses to reduce their future production. Employment will subsequently decline. Output will fall back from $14.3 trillion to the equilibrium level of $14.0 trillion. Note that the change in total spending, followed by changes in output and employment, is what will restore equilibrium in the Keynesian model, not changes in prices.

In contrast, if total output is temporarily below equilibrium, there will be a tendency for aggregate income to rise. Here's how: Suppose output is temporarily at $13.7 trillion. At that output level, the $C + I + G + NX$ function lies above the 45-degree line. At this point, aggregate expenditures exceed aggregate output. Businesses are selling more than they currently produce. Their inventories are falling. Excess demand is present. They will react by hiring more workers and expanding production. This will increase the nation's aggregate income. Only at the equilibrium level—the point at which the $C + I + G + NX$ function crosses the 45-degree line ($14.0 trillion)—though, will the spending plans of consumers, investors, governments, and foreigners equal the output of firms. Only this level of output can be sustained.

Notice (from Exhibit 8) that the economy's equilibrium output of $14.0 trillion is less than the full employment output level ($14.3 trillion). At $14.3 trillion, though, aggregate expenditures are insufficient to purchase the output produced. In the Keynesian model, neither falling wages nor declining interest rates will direct the economy back to full employment. Given the aggregate expenditures function, output will remain below its potential. Unemployment will persist. Within the Keynesian *AE* model, equilibrium need not coincide with full employment.

How Can Full Employment Be Achieved?

If full employment is going to be attained, there must be an increase in aggregate expenditures. As **EXHIBIT 9** illustrates, full employment can be achieved, if the aggregate expenditure schedule shifts upward to AE_2. Expansionary fiscal policy can be used to achieve this objective. An increase in government spending (holding taxes constant) would directly increase *AE*. Correspondingly, a reduction in taxes could be used to increase the net income of households and businesses and thereby stimulate the consumption and investment components of *AE*. Thus, the *AE* model indicates that expansionary fiscal policy can increase total spending and direct an economy to the full-employment rate of output.

What would happen if aggregate expenditures were to exceed the economy's production capacity? For example, suppose aggregate expenditures rose to AE_3. Within the basic Keynesian model, aggregate expenditures in excess of output lead to a higher price level once the economy reaches full employment. Nominal output will increase, but it merely reflects higher prices, rather than additional real output. Total spending in excess of full-employment capacity is inflationary within the Keynesian model.

Aggregate expenditures are the catalyst of the Keynesian model. Changes in expenditures make things happen. If the economy is operating below full employment, supply

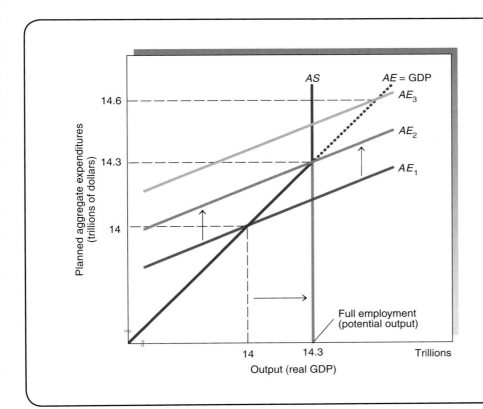

EXHIBIT 9
Shifts in Aggregate Expenditures and Changes in Equilibrium Output

When equilibrium output is less than the economy's capacity, only an increase in expenditures (a shift in AE) will lead to full employment. If consumers, investors, governments, or foreigners would spend more and thereby shift the aggregate expenditures schedule to AE$_2$, output would reach its full-employment potential ($14.3 trillion). Once full employment is reached, further increases in aggregate expenditures, like those shown by the shift to AE$_3$, will lead only to higher prices. Nominal output will expand (the dotted segment of the AE–GDP schedule), but real output will not.

is always accommodative. An increase in aggregate expenditures, caused, for example, by an increase in government expenditures, will thus lead to an increase in real output and employment. Once full employment is reached, though, additional aggregate expenditures lead merely to higher prices.

Keynesians argue that control of aggregate expenditures is the crux of sound macroeconomic policy. If we could ensure that aggregate expenditures were large enough to achieve capacity output, but not so large as to result in inflation, then maximum output, full employment, and price stability could be attained. This central point of Keynesian analysis is easily observable within the framework of the aggregate expenditure model.

The Aggregate Expenditure and *AD—AS* Models

The key implications of the aggregate expenditure model can also be presented within the aggregate demand/aggregate supply (*AD–AS*) framework. The assumptions of the aggregate expenditure model imply that the short-run aggregate supply curve (*SRAS*) will have a distinctive shape. Part (a) of **EXHIBIT 10** illustrates this point. Note that the *SRAS* is completely flat at the existing price level until full-employment capacity is reached. This is because the Keynesian model assumes that, at less than full-employment output levels, prices (and wages) are fixed, because they are inflexible in a downward direction. Economists sometimes refer to this horizontal segment as the *Keynesian range* of the aggregate supply curve. However, just as in the *AE* model, once full employment has been reached, real output cannot be expanded beyond the economy's full-employment capacity. Thus, both *SRAS* and *LRAS* are vertical at the full-employment rate of output (Y_F).

Part (a) of Exhibit 10 clearly illustrates the importance of aggregate demand within the Keynesian analysis. The assumptions of the aggregate expenditure model imply that the *SRAS* will be horizontal until full employment is reached, at which time it becomes vertical. When aggregate demand is less than AD_2 (for example, AD_1), the economy will

---

EXHIBIT 10
Implications of the *AE* Model within the *AD–AS* Framework

As is shown in part (a), the assumptions of the aggregate expenditure model imply that the SRAS will be horizontal until full employment is reached, at which time it becomes vertical. When output is less than capacity (for example, Y_1), an increase in aggregate demand, shown by the shift from AD_1 to AD_2, will expand output without increasing prices. However, increases in demand beyond AD_2 (like the shift to AD_3) lead only to a higher price level (P_2). Part (b) relaxes the assumption of complete price inflexibility and short-run output inflexibility beyond Y_F. Notice that in part (b), the SRAS curve turns from horizontal to vertical more gradually. Part (b) is more realistic of what happens in the real world.

(a) Polar assumption

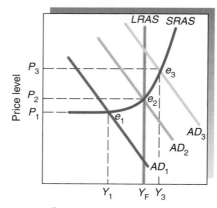

(b) Central implication

languish below potential capacity. Because prices and wages are inflexible downward, below-capacity output rates (Y_1, for example) and abnormally high unemployment will persist unless there is an increase in aggregate demand. When output is below its potential, any increase in aggregate demand (for example, the shift from AD_1 to AD_2) brings previously idle resources into the productive process at an unchanged price level. Of course, once the economy's potential output constraint (Y_F) is reached, increases in demand beyond AD_2 (such as the shift to AD_3) lead only to a higher price level (P_2).

In the real world, prices are unlikely to remain unchanged when output is substantially below capacity as is implied by a horizontal aggregate supply curve. Similarly, in the short run, an unanticipated increase in demand is unlikely to lead to only higher prices as is implied by the vertical portion of the aggregate supply curve.

Part (b) of Exhibit 10 relaxes the polar assumption of complete price inflexibility until full employment is reached and short-run output inflexibility beyond Y_F. Thus, the *SRAS* curve turns from horizontal to vertical more gradually. This reflects a more realistic view of how real-world changes in aggregate demand will influence output and employment under alternative economic conditions. When an economy is operating well below capacity, the primary impact of an increase in aggregate demand will be on output rather than the general level of prices. Therefore, ***under conditions like those of the 1930s—when idle factories and widespread unemployment were present—increases in aggregate demand will exert a strong impact on output. In contrast, however, when an economy is already operating at or near full-employment capacity, additional aggregate demand (for example, the shift to*** AD_3***) will predictably exert its primary impact on prices rather than output.***

Looking ahead

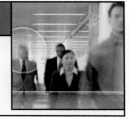

The Keynesian perspective indicates that fiscal policy is highly potent, but there are alternative views on this topic. These views, along with other hotly debated topics concerning the potential and limitations of fiscal policy, will be presented in the following chapter.

KEY POINTS

▼ During the Great Depression, John Maynard Keynes developed a model that implied a market economy could remain below full employment for lengthy periods of time.

▼ In the Keynesian model, firms will produce the amount of goods and services they believe consumers, investors, governments, and foreigners (net exports) plan to buy. This equilibrium need not occur at the full-employment rate of output.

▼ According to the Keynesian view, fluctuations in total spending (aggregate demand) are the major source of economic instability. Keynesians believe that market economies have a tendency to fluctuate between economic booms driven by excessive demand and recessions resulting from insufficient demand. The multiplier concept magnifies these fluctuations.

▼ When an economy is operating below full-employment capacity, increases in aggregate expenditures lead to an expansion in both output and employment. Once capacity is reached, further expansions in expenditures lead only to higher prices. The Keynesian model highlights the importance of maintaining demand at a level consistent with full employment and price stability.

▼ When an economy is in a recession, Keynesians do not believe that reductions in either resource prices or interest rates will promote recovery. As a result, market economies are likely to experience recessions that are both severe and lengthy.

▼ The federal budget is the primary tool of fiscal policy. Rather than balancing the budget annually, Keynesians believe that fiscal policy should reflect business cycle conditions. During a recession, fiscal policy should become more expansionary (a larger deficit should be run). During an inflationary boom, fiscal policy should become more restrictive (shift toward a budget surplus).

▼ Changes in fiscal policy must be timed properly if they are going to exert a stabilizing influence on an economy. The ability of policy makers to time fiscal policy changes in a countercyclical manner is reduced by (1) the inability of the political process to act rapidly, (2) the time lag between when a policy change is instituted and when it affects the economy, and (3) inability to forecast accurately the future direction of the economy.

▼ Automatic stabilizers help promote stability because they are able to add demand stimulus during a recession and restraint during an economic boom without legislative action.

CRITICAL ANALYSIS QUESTIONS

1. What determines the equilibrium rate of output in the Keynesian model? Why did Keynes think the Great Depression lasted so long and the unemployment rate remained so high throughout the 1930s?

2. What do Keynesians think cause fluctuations in output? What must be done to maintain full-employment capacity?

*3. What is the multiplier principle? What determines the size of the multiplier? Does the multiplier make it more or less difficult to stabilize the economy? Explain.

4. What is a budget deficit? How are budget deficits financed? Why do Keynesians believe that budget deficits will increase aggregate demand?

5. From a stabilization standpoint, why is proper timing of a change in fiscal policy important? Is it easy to time fiscal policy changes properly? Why or why not?

*6. According to the Keynesian view, what fiscal policy actions should be taken if the unemployment rate is high and current GDP is well below potential output?

7. Are discretionary changes in fiscal policy likely to be instituted in a manner that will help smooth the ups and downs of the business cycle? Why or why not?

*8. What are automatic stabilizers? Explain their major advantage.

9. "An increase in aggregate demand will tend to increase real output by a larger amount when unemployment is widespread than when the economy is operating at or near full employment." Is this statement true? Explain.

*10. "If we set aside our reluctance to use fiscal policy as a stabilization force, it is quite easy to achieve full employment and price stability. When output is at less than full employment, we run a budget deficit. If inflation is a problem, we run a budget surplus. Quick implementation of proper fiscal policy will stabilize the economy." Evaluate this statement.

11. When output and employment slowed in early 2008, the Bush Administration and the Democratic Congress passed legislation sending households a check for $600 for each adult (and $300 per child). These checks were financed by borrowing. Would a Keynesian favor this action? Why or why not?

*Asterisk denotes questions for which answers are given in Appendix B.

Fiscal Policy: Incentives, and Secondary Effects

CHAPTER FOCUS

- How do the crowding-out and new classical models of fiscal policy modify the Keynesian analysis?

- Is discretionary fiscal policy an effective stabilization tool? Is there broad agreement among Keynesians and non-Keynesians on this issue?

- Will increases in government spending financed by borrowing help promote recovery from a recession?

- Is saving good or bad for the economy?

- Are there supply-side effects of fiscal policy?

The main difference between Keynes and modern economics is the focus on incentives. Keynes studied the relation between macroeconomic aggregates, without any consideration for the underlying incentives that lead to the formation of these aggregates. By contrast, modern economists base all their analysis on incentives.

—Luigi Zingales[1]

[1]Luigi Zingales, Booth School of Business at the University of Chicago, March 10, 2009. Online debate sponsored by *The Economist*.

s we discussed in the previous chapter, Keynesian analysis indicates that fiscal policy provides a potential tool through which aggregate demand can be controlled and maintained at a level consistent with full employment and price stability. During the 1970s, however, the economic instability, along with high rates of both unemployment and inflation, illustrated some of the difficulties involved in the effective use of fiscal policy as a stabilization tool. Moreover, in recent decades, economists have become more aware of secondary effects that reduce the potency of fiscal policy. More attention has also been paid to the incentive effects accompanying fiscal changes, including both changes in the composition of government spending and the supply-side effects of marginal tax rates. The chapter-opening quote by Luigi Zingales highlights these points. This chapter will focus on these topics and investigate how they affect the operation of fiscal policy and its potential to improve the performance of a market economy. The chapter will also address the current debate among economists about the effectiveness of "fiscal stimulus" as a tool with which to promote recovery from a severe recession like that of 2008–2009. ■

Fiscal Policy, Borrowing, and the Crowding-Out Effect

Keynesian analysis indicates that expansionary fiscal policy will exert a powerful impact on aggregate demand, output, and employment. Other economists disagree. When the government runs a budget deficit, the funds will have to come from somewhere. If we rule out money creation (monetary policy), the government will have to finance its deficit by borrowing from either domestic or foreign lenders. But the additional government borrowing will increase the demand for loanable funds, which will push real interest rates upward. In turn, the higher real interest rates will reduce private investment and consumption, thereby dampening the stimulus effects of expansionary fiscal policy. Economists refer to this squeezing out of private spending by a deficit-induced increase in the real interest rate as the **crowding-out effect**.

Crowding-out effect

A reduction in private spending as a result of higher interest rates generated by budget deficits that are financed by borrowing in the private loanable funds market.

Suppose the government increases its spending or reduces taxes and, as a result, runs a budget deficit of $100 billion. As **EXHIBIT 1** shows, the government's additional borrowing will increase demand in the loanable funds market and place upward pressure on real interest rates. How will the higher interest rates influence private spending? Consumers will reduce their purchases of interest-rate–sensitive goods, such as automobiles and consumer durables. A higher interest rate will also increase the opportunity cost of investment projects. Businesses will postpone spending on plant expansions, heavy equipment, and capital improvements. Residential-housing construction and sales will also be hurt. Thus, the higher real interest rates caused by the larger deficit will retard private spending. If it were not for the reduction in private spending, aggregate demand would increase to AD_2 (the dotted curve of part a), but given the reduction in private spending, aggregate demand remains unchanged at AD_1.

The crowding-out effect implies that the demand stimulus effects of budget deficits will be weak because borrowing to finance the deficits will increase interest rates and thereby crowd out private spending on investment and consumption. This reduction in private spending will partially, if not entirely, offset the additional spending financed by

EXHIBIT 1
The Crowding-Out Model—Higher Interest Rates Crowd Out Private Spending

The crowding-out effect indicates that budget deficits will lead to higher interest rates, which will reduce private investment and consumption, offsetting the demand stimulus of expansionary fiscal policy. If the government borrows an additional $100 billion to finance a budget deficit, the demand for loanable funds will increase by this amount (shift from D_1 to D_2 in frame b), leading to higher real interest rates. If it were not for the higher real interest rates, aggregate demand would increase to AD_2 (dotted curve of part a). However, at the higher interest rates, private investment and consumption will decline. As a result, aggregate demand will remain unchanged at AD_1. The crowding-out effect indicates that expansionary fiscal policy will have little or no impact on aggregate demand.

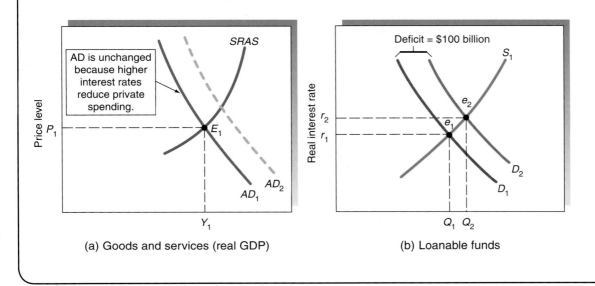

(a) Goods and services (real GDP)

(b) Loanable funds

the deficit. Thus, the net impact of expansionary fiscal policy on aggregate demand, output, and employment will be small.

Furthermore, as private investment is crowded out by the higher interest rates, the output of capital goods will decline. As a result, the future stock of capital (for example, heavy equipment, other machines, and buildings) available to future workers will be smaller than it would have been otherwise. In other words, deficits will have an adverse effect on capital formation and tend to retard the growth of productivity and income.

Keynesians respond that even if crowding out occurs when the economy is at or near full employment, it will be less important during a recession, particularly a serious one. During the severe recession of 2008–2009, short-term interest rates fell to nearly zero even though the federal government was running huge deficits.[2] Under circumstances like these, the immediate crowding-out effect is likely to be small, and therefore the budget deficits will stimulate output and employment just as the Keynesian analysis implies. The proponents of crowding out counter that while this may be true during the recession, the deficits will mean more borrowing and less private spending as the economy begins to recover. As a result, the recovery will be more sluggish than would have been the case if government borrowing had been more restrained.

The implications of the crowding-out analysis are symmetrical. Restrictive fiscal policy will "crowd in" private spending. If the government collects greater tax revenues

[2]Expansionary monetary policy also contributed to the low short-term interest rates of 2008–2009. The impact of monetary policy on interest rates, output, and employment will be discussed in Chapter 14.

and/or reduces spending, the budget will shift toward a surplus (or smaller deficit). As a result, the government's demand for loanable funds will decrease, placing downward pressure on the real interest rate. The lower real interest rate will stimulate additional private investment and consumption. So the fiscal policy restraint will be partially, if not entirely, offset by an expansion in private spending. *As the result of this crowding in, restrictive fiscal policy will be largely ineffective as a weapon against inflation.*

Do Global Financial Markets Minimize the Crowding-Out Effect?

Today, financial capital can rapidly move in and out of countries. Suppose the budget deficit of the United States increases and additional borrowing by the U.S. Treasury pushes real interest rates upward, just as the crowding-out theory implies. Think about how investors will respond to this situation. The higher real interest yields on bonds and other financial assets will attract funds from abroad. In turn, this inflow of financial capital will increase the supply of loanable funds and thereby moderate the rise in real interest rates in the United States.[3]

At first glance, the crowding-out effect would appear to be weakened because the inflow of funds from abroad will moderate the upward pressure on domestic interest rates. Closer inspection, though, reveals that this will not be the case. Foreigners cannot buy more U.S. bonds and financial assets without "buying" more dollars in the foreign exchange market. Thus, additional bond purchases will increase the demand for U.S. dollars (and the supply of foreign currencies) in the foreign exchange market—the market that coordinates exchanges of the various national currencies. As foreigners demand more dollars to buy financial investments in the United States, this will increase the demand for the dollar, causing it to appreciate. The appreciation of the dollar will make imports cheaper for Americans. Simultaneously, it will make U.S. exports more expensive for foreigners. Predictably, the

EXHIBIT 2

A Visual Presentation of the Crowding-Out Effect in an Open Economy

The implications of the crowding-out effect in an open economy are illustrated here. As was shown in the previous exhibit, government borrowing to finance a budget deficit will place upward pressure on real interest rates. This will retard private investment and aggregate demand. In an open economy, the higher interest rates will also increase the inflow of capital from abroad, which will cause the dollar to appreciate and net exports to decline. Thus, in an open economy, the higher interest rates will trigger reductions in both private investment and net exports, which will weaken the expansionary impact of a budget deficit.

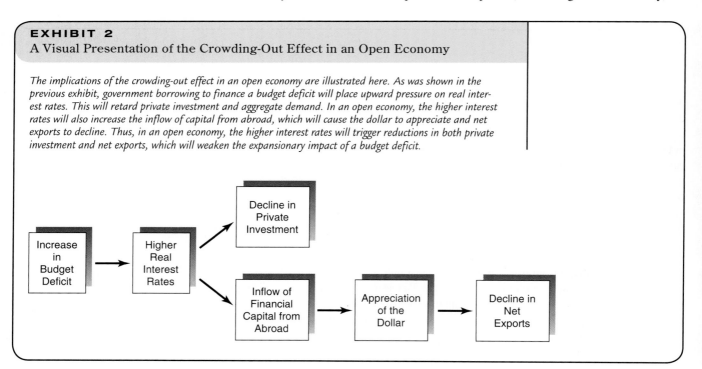

[3]For students who are unsure about the demand for and supply of loanable funds, this would be a good time to review the topic within the framework of our basic macro model outlined by Exhibit 1 in Chapter 9. As this exhibit indicates, household saving and the inflow of financial capital from abroad supply loanable funds. In turn, private investment and borrowing by the government to finance budget deficits generate the demand for these funds.

United States will import more and export less. Thus, net exports will decline (or net imports increase), causing a reduction in aggregate demand. Therefore, while the inflow of capital from abroad will moderate the increase in the interest rate and the crowding out of private domestic investment, it will also reduce net exports and thereby retard aggregate demand.

EXHIBIT 2 summarizes the crowding-out view of budget deficits in an open economy. The additional government borrowing triggered by the budget deficits will cause interest rates to rise, and this will lead to two secondary effects that will dampen the stimulus impact of the deficits. First, the higher interest rates will reduce private investment, which will directly restrain aggregate demand. Second, the higher interest returns will also attract an inflow of foreign capital, which will moderate the increase in interest rates, but it will also cause the dollar to appreciate. In turn, the appreciation of the dollar will reduce both net exports and aggregate demand. ***According to the crowding-out theory, these two factors will largely, if not entirely, offset the stimulus effects of a larger budget deficit.***

Fiscal Policy, Future Taxes, and the New Classical Model

Thus far, we have implicitly assumed that the current consumption and saving decisions of taxpayers are unaffected by budget deficits. This may not be the case. The 1995 Nobel laureate, Robert Lucas (University of Chicago); Thomas Sargent (New York University); and Robert Barro (Harvard University) have been leaders among a group of economists arguing that budget deficits imply higher future taxes and that taxpayers will reduce their current consumption just as they would have if the taxes had been collected during the current period. Because this position has its foundation in classical economics, these economists and their followers are referred to as **new classical economists**.

In the Keynesian model, a tax cut financed by borrowing will increase the current income of households, and they respond by increasing their consumption. New classical economists argue that this analysis is incorrect because it ignores the impact of the higher future tax liability implied by the budget deficit and the interest payments required to service the additional debt. Rather than increasing their consumption in response to a larger budget deficit, new classical economists believe that households will save all or most of their increase in disposable income so that they will be able to pay the higher future taxes implied by the additional government debt. Thus, new classical economists do not believe that budget deficits will stimulate additional consumption and aggregate demand.

The new classical economists stress that debt financing simply substitutes higher future taxes for lower current taxes. Thus, budget deficits affect the timing of the taxes but not their magnitude. A mere change in the timing of taxes will not alter the wealth of households. Therefore, there is no reason to believe that current consumption will change when current taxes are cut and government debt and future taxes are increased by an equivalent amount. This view that taxes and debt financing are essentially equivalent is known as **Ricardian equivalence**, after the nineteenth-century economist, David Ricardo, who initially developed the idea.[4]

Perhaps an illustration will help explain the underlying logic of the new classical view. Suppose you knew that your taxes were going to be cut by $1,000 this year, but that next year they were going to be increased by $1,000 plus the interest on that figure. Would this year's $1,000 tax cut cause you to increase your consumption spending? New classical economists argue that it would not. They believe that most people would recognize that their wealth is unchanged and would therefore save most of this year's tax cut to be better able to pay next year's higher taxes. Correspondingly, new classical economists argue that when debt is substituted for taxes, people will recognize that the additional debt means higher future taxes and that therefore they will save more in order to pay them.

New classical economists

Economists who believe that there are strong forces pushing a market economy toward full-employment equilibrium and that macroeconomic policy is an ineffective tool with which to reduce economic instability.

Ricardian equivalence

The view that a tax reduction financed with government debt will exert no effect on current consumption and aggregate demand because people will fully recognize the higher future taxes implied by the additional debt.

---

[4]See Robert J. Barro, "The Ricardian Approach to Budget Deficits," *Journal of Economic Perspectives* (Spring 1989): 37–44; and John J. Seater, "Ricardian Equivalence," *Journal of Economic Literature* (March 1993): 142–90.

EXHIBIT 3 illustrates the implications of the new classical view on the potency of fiscal policy. Suppose that the fiscal authorities issue $100 billion of additional debt in order to cut taxes by an equal amount. The government borrowing increases the demand for loanable funds (D_1 shifts to D_2 in part b) by $100 billion. If taxpayers didn't think that higher future taxes would result from the debt, they would expand their consumption in response to the lower taxes and the increase in their current disposable income. Under these circumstances, aggregate demand in the goods and services market would expand to AD_2 (part a). In the new classical model, though, this will not be the case. Realizing that the $100 billion in additional debt will mean higher future taxes, taxpayers will maintain their initial level of consumption spending and use the tax cut to increase their savings in order to generate the additional income required to pay the higher future taxes. Because consumption is unchanged, aggregate demand also remains constant (at AD_1). At the same time, the additional saving (to pay the implied increase in future taxes) allows the government to finance its deficit without an increase in the real interest rate.

According to the new classical view, changes in fiscal policy have little effect on the economy. Debt financing and larger budget deficits will not stimulate aggregate demand. Neither will they affect output and employment. Similarly, the real interest rate is unaffected by deficits because people will save more in order to pay the higher future taxes. In the new classical model, fiscal policy is completely impotent.

In Chapter 1, we indicated that failure to consider the secondary effects is one of the most common errors in economics. Once the secondary effects are considered, both the crowding-out and new classical models indicate that spending increases financed by borrowing will provide little if any net stimulus to the economy. Nonetheless, politicians continue to argue that their favorite spending programs will create jobs and improve economic performance. Are they right? The accompanying box feature "Is Job Creation a Good Reason to Support a Government Spending Program?" provides insight on this issue.

EXHIBIT 3

The New Classical View—Higher Expected Future Taxes Crowd Out Private Spending.

New classical economists emphasize that budget deficits merely substitute future taxes for current taxes. If households did not anticipate the higher future taxes, aggregate demand would increase to AD_2. However, demand remains unchanged at AD_1 when house holds fully anticipate the future increase in taxes (part a). Simultaneously, the additional saving to meet the higher future taxes will increase the supply of loanable funds to S_2 and allow the government to borrow the funds to finance its deficit without pushing up the real interest rate (part b). In this model, fiscal policy exerts no effect. The real interest rate, real GDP, and level of employment all remain unchanged.

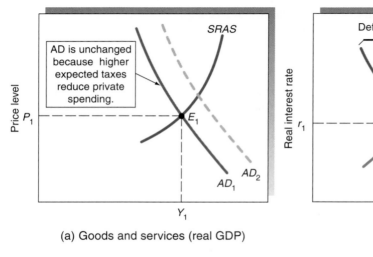

(a) Goods and services (real GDP)

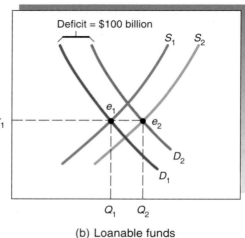

(b) Loanable funds

Is Job Creation a Good Reason to Support a Government Spending Program?

Jobs are typically used to produce goods and services that we value. But we must not forget that it is the value of the goods produced that is important and the jobs are merely a means to that end. If people do not keep their eyes on this basic fact, they may be misled to support projects that destroy wealth rather than create it.

Politicians are fond of talking about the jobs created by their spending programs. Suppose the government spends $50 billion employing one million workers to build a high-speed train linking Los Angeles and Las Vegas. Supporters of projects like this often argue that they should be undertaken because they will create a huge number of jobs. Is this a sound argument? When thinking about the answer to this question, consider the following two points.

First, the government will have to use either taxes or borrowing to finance the project. Taxes of $50 billion will reduce consumer spending and private savings by this amount, and this will diminish employment in other sectors by a magnitude similar to the employment created by the spending on the project. Alternatively, if the project is financed by debt, the additional borrowing will lead to higher interest rates and future taxes to cover interest payments. This will also divert funds away from other projects, both private and public. Thus, the net impact will be primarily a reshuffling of jobs rather than job creation.

Second, what really matters is the value of what is produced, not jobs. If jobs were the key to high incomes, we could easily create as many as we wanted. For example, the government could pay attractive wages hiring the unemployed to dig holes one day and fill them up the next. The program would create jobs, but as a nation we would also be poorer because such jobs would not generate goods and services that people value. Job creation, either real or imagined, is not a sound reason to support a program. Instead, the proper test is opportunity cost: the value of what is produced relative to the value of what is given up. If people value the output generated by the government-spending program more than the production it crowds out, it will increase our incomes and living standards. If the opposite is the case, then the additional spending will make us worse off.

Political Incentives and the Effective Use of Discretionary Fiscal Policy

As we discussed in the last chapter, inability to forecast the future direction of the economy and the time lag between when a fiscal change is needed and when it can be instituted and begin to exert an impact on the economy make it difficult to use discretionary fiscal policy in a stabilizing manner. In addition to these practical problems, the political incentive structure also makes appropriate timing of fiscal changes less likely.

As our analysis of public choice stressed, politicians—at least those who survive for very long—will be attracted to policies that will help them win the next election. Predictably, legislators will be delighted to spend money on programs that benefit their constituents but reluctant to raise taxes because they impose a visible cost on voters. The political incentive structure encourages legislation that increases spending and reduces taxes when the economy is weak. But there is very little incentive to reduce spending and increase taxes when the economy is strong. As a result, deficits will be far more common than surpluses. Thus, discretionary fiscal policy is unlikely to be instituted in a countercyclical manner.

Fiscal Policy: Countercyclical versus Response during a Severe Recession

It is important to distinguish between the use of (1) discretionary fiscal policy as a potential tool with which to combat economic instability and (2) fiscal policy to combat a severe recession. Substantial agreement has emerged between Keynesians and non-Keynesians on the first point, while spirited debate continues on the second. We now turn to the discussion of these topics.

Areas of Agreement about Fiscal Policy as a Stabilization Tool

In recent decades, the effectiveness of fiscal policy as a stabilization tool has been hotly debated and widely analyzed by macroeconomists. A synthesis view has emerged. Most macroeconomists—both Keynesian and non-Keynesian—are now largely in agreement on the following three issues.

1. PROPER TIMING OF DISCRETIONARY FISCAL POLICY IS BOTH DIFFICULT TO ACHIEVE AND CRUCIALLY IMPORTANT. Given our limited ability to forecast ups and downs in the business cycle, the delays that inevitably accompany fiscal changes, and the structure of political incentives, the effectiveness of discretionary fiscal policy as a stabilization tool is limited. Put simply, persistent fiscal changes are unlikely to be instituted in a manner that will smooth the ups and downs of the business cycle. Therefore, most macroeconomists now place less emphasis on the use of discretionary fiscal policy as a stabilization tool.[5]

2. AUTOMATIC STABILIZERS REDUCE FLUCTUATIONS IN AGGREGATE DEMAND AND HELP DIRECT THE ECONOMY TOWARD FULL EMPLOYMENT. Because they are not dependent upon legislative action, automatic stabilizers are able consistently to shift the budget toward a deficit during a recession and toward a surplus during an economic boom. They add needed stimulus during a recession and act as a restraining force during an inflationary boom. Although some economists question their potency, nearly all agree that they exert a stabilizing influence.

3. FISCAL POLICY IS MUCH LESS POTENT THAN THE EARLY KEYNESIAN VIEW IMPLIED. Both the crowding-out and new classical models indicate that there are secondary effects of budget deficits that will substantially, if not entirely, offset their impact on aggregate demand. In the crowding-out model, higher real interest rates and a decline in net exports offset the expansionary effects of budget deficits. In the new classical model, higher future taxes lead to the same result. Both models indicate that fiscal policy will have little, if any, effect on current aggregate demand, employment, and real output during normal economic times.

The Great Debate: Will Fiscal Stimulus Speed Recovery?

Will increases in government spending financed by borrowing speed recovery from a severe recession? Keynesians clearly believe that the answer to this question is "yes." The Keynesian view stresses that private sector spending will decline during a severe recession and that the government needs to expand its spending in order to reignite the private sector. During a severe recession like that of 2008–2009, interest rates may essentially fall to zero, and even these low rates may fail to stimulate much private investment. Under these conditions, crowding out of private spending will be minimal. Moreover, unemployed and underemployed resources will be widespread, and, as a result, the additional government spending will have a substantial multiplier effect. Thus, Keynesians argue that fiscal policy will have its greatest impact under the conditions of a severe recession and it will be a highly effective tool with which to promote recovery.

The non-Keynesian critics argue that the side effects of the increased spending and expanded debt will exert an adverse impact on both the recovery process and long-term growth. They raise three major points in support of their view.

---

[5]As the following statement from Keynes indicates, he did not believe that spending on government projects would be an effective countercyclical tool:

> *Organized public works, at home and abroad, may be the right cure for a chronic tendency to a deficiency of effective demand. But they are not capable of sufficiently rapid organization (and above all cannot be reversed or undone at a later date), to be the most serviceable instrument for the prevention of the trade cycle.*

John Maynard Keynes in *Collected Works, vol. XXVII*, 122.

1. THE EXPANSION IN GOVERNMENT DEBT WILL MEAN HIGHER FUTURE INTEREST PAYMENTS AND TAX RATES, AND THIS WILL RETARD LONG-TERM GROWTH. Even if the government is able to borrow at low interest rates during a recession, as was the case during 2008–2009, some combination of higher interest rates and higher taxes will be required for the financing and refinancing of the larger debt as the economy recovers. The higher interest rates will increase costs and squeeze out private spending, particularly spending on investment. At the same time, the higher taxes will reduce the net income of both households and businesses. All of these factors will weaken the recovery from recession, reduce capital formation, and lead to a slower rate of long-term growth.

2. RECESSIONS REFLECT A COORDINATION PROBLEM RELATED TO THE COMPOSITION OF AGGREGATE DEMAND, NOT JUST ITS LEVEL. *Increases in government spending are likely to increase the severity of this coordination problem rather than reduce it.* Predictably, the increased government spending will be motivated by political considerations and much of it will flow into unproductive projects and areas of full employment. Remember, political decision making does not have anything like profit and loss that will direct resources into productive projects and away from unproductive projects. Political favoritism will become more important, and efficient allocation of resources less.

Moreover, the composition of the politically driven spending is likely to differ substantially from market-directed spending, and, as a result, the unemployed resources will be ill suited to expand production in the politically favored areas. When this is the case, the stimulus spending will increase structural unemployment and lead to a worsening of the coordination problem. For example, as the economy recovers from the 2008–2009 recession, substantial additional spending is being targeted toward health care, education, and wind and solar energy. But the unemployed workers and capital from the auto manufacturing and construction sectors, for example, do not generally have the skills needed for the expansion of output in health care and education. Thus, more spending in these areas will not bring them much relief.

3. MORE POLITICALLY DIRECTED SPENDING WILL LEAD TO MORE RENT SEEKING AND LESS WEALTH-CREATING PRODUCTION. Incentives matter. When the government is spending a lot on subsidies, special projects, and income transfers, businesses and other organized groups will spend more on lobbying, political contributions, and other efforts designed to attract the government funds. As a result, resources will be channeled toward wasteful rent seeking and away from productive activities, those that provide consumers with goods and services that are more highly valued than their cost. Ironically, most of the wasteful rent-seeking activity will add to GDP as it is currently measured. For example, if business executives, lawyers, and even economists are spending more of their time schmoozing government officials, preparing grant proposals, designing politically attractive projects, and so on, such expenditures will enhance GDP. Moreover, the government spending will enter GDP at cost. If it costs $50 billion to construct a railroad from Los Angeles to Las Vegas, the project will add $50 billion to GDP even if the railroad never covers the cost of its operation.

The stimulus critics argue that the Japanese experience during the 1990s is supportive of their view. Like the 2008 recession in the United States, Japan experienced a sharp increase in both stock and real estate prices in the late 1980s, followed by a collapse of those prices and a recession in the early 1990s. Japan responded with a substantial increase in government spending financed by borrowing. Measured as a share of GDP, government spending rose by approximately 6 percentage points. Budget deficits ranged between 6 and 9 percent of GDP throughout most of the 1990s. Despite this huge fiscal stimulus, the Japanese economy continued to stagnate, and, as a result, this is sometimes referred to as Japan's lost decade. (See Special Topic 7, "Lessons from the Japanese Experience of the 1990s" for additional details on this topic.)

Tax Cuts versus Spending Increases

When seeking to promote recovery from a recession, would it be better to reduce taxes than to increase government spending? It is sometimes argued that increases in government spending will expand GDP by more than tax reductions, because 100 percent of an increase in government purchases will be pumped into the economy, whereas part of the tax reduction will be saved or spent abroad. However, the comparison between the two options is more complex than is implied by the mechanics of this simple multiplier exercise.[6]

There are at least four reasons why a tax cut is likely to be more effective than a spending increase as a tool with which to promote recovery and long-term growth. First, a tax cut will generally stimulate aggregate demand more rapidly. As recent experience illustrates, the federal government is able to get checks to people in just two or three months. Even if a substantial portion of the funds is not spent quickly, there will be an immediate positive impact on the financial position of households. In contrast, spending projects are often a lengthy process spread over several years. For example, the Congressional Budget Office estimated that only 15 percent of the spending funded by the stimulus package passed in February 2009 would occur during the initial year, while nearly half (48 percent) would not be spent until 2011 and beyond.

Second, compared to an increase in government spending, a tax cut is less likely to increase structural unemployment and reduce the productivity of resources. New government spending programs will generally change the structure of aggregate demand more than a tax cut, and, other things being constant, this change in the composition of demand will mean more structural unemployment, at least in the short run. Moreover, the additional government spending is likely to be less productive. When households increase their spending as the result of lower taxes, they will not purchase items that are valued less than cost. The assurance that this will be the case for additional government spending is much weaker.

Third, a tax cut will be easier to reverse once the economy has recovered. Once started, the interests undertaking a government project and benefiting from it will lobby for its continuation; therefore, spending projects started during a crisis are likely to continue long after the crisis is history.

Fourth, a reduction in tax rates will increase the incentive to earn, invest, produce, and employ others. These supply-side effects will be examined in detail later in this chapter.

Paradoxes of Thrift and Spending

Is it better to spend than to save? Consumer spending comprises approximately 70 percent of GDP. Because of its size, consumer spending is closely monitored by macroeconomists. When a large number of households try to increase their saving and reduce their consumption, total saving may not increase. Instead, the reduction in consumption may reduce the overall demand for goods and services, causing businesses to reduce output and lay off workers. This is often referred to as the **paradox of thrift**.

Paradox of thrift

The idea that when many households simultaneously try to increase their saving, actual saving may fail to increase because the reduction in consumption and aggregate demand will reduce income and employment.

Within the framework of the *AD–AS* model, the increase in saving by households would increase the supply of loanable funds and reduce interest rates, which would tend to offset the reduction in consumer demand. Keynesians do not believe this will be the case. Perhaps a simple example will help to explain their concerns and the underlying logic of the paradox of thrift. Suppose a family decides to eat out less often and save an additional $200 per month. Keynesians argue that their actions will reduce the incomes of restaurants by $200 per month, and as a result of this reduction in net income, the savings of the restaurant owners will fall by this amount. Thus, the family saves $200 more per month, but the restaurant owners save $200 less, so there is no net change in saving. If numerous families cut back on their consumption spending in an effort to increase their saving, the

---

[6]The empirical evidence on the size of the tax and spending multipliers is mixed. Estimates of the multipliers range from approximately 1 to 3, and some have found the multiplier effects of a tax cut to be stronger than those for an increase in government spending, whereas others have found the reverse. See Valerie A. Ramey, "Identifying Government Spending Shocks: It's All in the Timing," University of California, San Diego, Working Paper, June 2008; Christina D. Romer and David H. Romer, "The Macroeconomic Effects of Tax Changes: Estimates Based on a New Measure of Fiscal Shocks," University of California, Berkeley Working Paper, March 2007; and John F. Cogan, Tobias Cwik, John B. Taylor, and Volker Wieland, "New Keynesian versus Old Keynesian Government Spending Multipliers," NBER Working Paper No. 14782, March 2009.

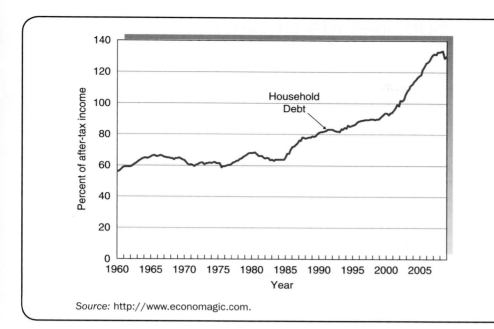

EXHIBIT 4
Household Debt as
a Share of After-Tax
Income: 1960–2008

The household debt to income ratio has increased steadily since the mid-1980s and is now approximately twice the level of that of the 1960s and 1970s. This heavy indebtedness makes it more difficult for households to deal with unexpected expenses and achieve financial security.

Source: http://www.economagic.com.

results would be the same. There would be no increase in saving, but consumption, aggregate demand, and output would decline.[7]

Eventually, the deficient demand, excess capacity, and weak investment would place downward pressure on both interest rates and resource prices, but this might well be a painful process. Keynesians fear that this will be the case, and that is why they have persistently stressed the implications of the paradox of thrift and potential dangers of excessive saving.

However, there is also a paradox of excessive consumption and deficient saving, which is often overlooked. You cannot have a strong, healthy economy if all or most households face financial troubles because they are spending just about everything they earn (or can borrow) on consumption. Even though the incomes of Americans are the highest in history, so too is their financial anxiety. When families and individuals are heavily indebted and have little or no savings, they are in a very poor position to deal with irregular expenses like repairs, health issues, or other financial setbacks that are a part of life.

There is evidence that Americans have saved too little and drifted into excessive debt in recent years. As **EXHIBIT 4** shows, household debt as a share of income has increased steadily during the past quarter of a century. During 1960–1985, household debt fluctuated between 55 and 70 percent of after-tax income. Since the mid-1980s, however, this debt to income ratio has soared, reaching nearly 135 percent in 2007. Clearly, this heavy indebtedness meant that Americans were in a weak position to deal with the financial setbacks accompanying the 2008–2009 recession. The heavy debt load also suggests that consumption is unlikely to rebound sharply as the economy begins to recover from the downturn.

Is saving good or bad for the economy? Straight thinking on this topic is important. While an abrupt increase in saving may exert an adverse impact on the economy in the short run, saving provides the source of investment capital that allows businesses to expand production and the economy to grow. Other things remaining constant, countries that persistently save and invest more will grow more rapidly. Moreover, when households save on a regular basis, live within their means, and avoid excessive debt, they will be better able to deal with unexpected expenses, sustain a steady consumption rate, and achieve greater financial security.

---

[7]For additional details on both the paradox of thrift and the Keynesian perspective, see Interview with Steve Fazzari of Washington University, "On Keynesian Economics," January 12, 2009, EcoTalk.org. at http://www.econtalk.org/archives/2009/01/fazzari_on_keyn.html.

The Supply-Side Effects of Fiscal Policy

Supply-side economists

Economists who believe that changes in marginal tax rates exert important effects on aggregate supply.

So far, we have focused on the potential impact of fiscal policy on aggregate demand. However, when fiscal changes alter tax rates, they influence the incentive of people to work, invest, and use resources efficiently. Thus, tax changes may also influence aggregate supply. Prior to 1980, macroeconomists generally ignored the supply-side effects of changes in tax rates, thinking they were of little importance. **Supply-side economists** challenged this view. The supply-side argument was central to the tax rate reductions of the 1980s, and it also affected tax legislation passed in both 2001 and 2002.

From a supply-side viewpoint, the marginal tax rate is crucially important. As we discussed in Chapter 4, the marginal tax rate determines the breakdown of a person's additional income between tax payments on the one hand and personal income on the other. Lower marginal tax rates mean that individuals get to keep a larger share of their additional earnings. For example, reducing the marginal tax rate from 40 percent to 30 percent allows individuals to keep 70 cents of each additional dollar they earn, instead of only 60 cents. In turn, the lower tax rates and accompanying increase in take-home pay provide them with a greater incentive to earn. Supply-side economists believe that these incentive effects will bring more resources into productive activities. Most significantly, they argue that high marginal rates—for example, rates of 50 percent or more—seriously discourage people from working harder and using their resources productively.

The supply-side effects of a tax change are fundamentally different from the demand-side effects. On the demand side, lower taxes increase the after-tax incomes of consumers and thereby stimulate consumption and aggregate demand. ***On the supply side, lower tax rates increase the incentive of people to work, supply resources, and use them more efficiently and thereby increase aggregate supply.***

EXHIBIT 5 graphically depicts the impact of a supply-side tax cut, one that reduces marginal tax rates. The lower marginal tax rates increase aggregate supply because the new incentive structure encourages taxpayers to earn more and use resources more efficiently. If taxpayers think the cut will be permanent, both long- and short-run aggregate supply (*LRAS* and *SRAS*) will increase. Real output and income will expand. As real income expands, aggregate demand will also increase (shift to AD_2). If the lower marginal rates are

---

EXHIBIT 5
Tax Rate Effects and Supply-Side Economics

Here, we illustrate the supply-side effects of lower marginal tax rates. The lower marginal tax rates increase the incentive to earn and use resources efficiently. Because these are long-run as well as short-run effects, both LRAS and SRAS increase (shift to the right). Real output expands. In turn, the higher income levels accompanying the expansion in real output will stimulate aggregate demand (shift it to AD₂).

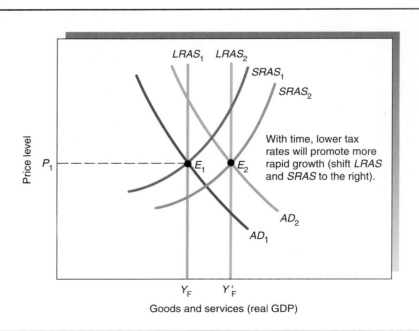

financed by a budget deficit, though, aggregate demand may increase by a larger amount than aggregate supply, putting upward pressure on the price level.

Supply-side economics should not be viewed as a short-run countercyclical tool. It will take time for people to react to the tax cuts and move their resources out of investments designed to lower their taxes and into higher-return, production-oriented activities. The full positive effects of lower marginal tax rates will not be observed until both labor and capital markets have time to adjust fully to the new incentive structure. *Supply-side economics is a long-run, growth-oriented strategy, not a short-run stabilization tool.*

Why Do High Tax Rates Retard Output?

There are three major reasons why high tax rates are likely to retard the growth of output. *First, as we have explained, high marginal tax rates discourage work effort and productivity.* When marginal tax rates soar to 55 or 60 percent, people get to keep less than half of what they earn, so they tend to work less. Some (for example, those with a working spouse) will drop out of the labor force. Others will simply work fewer hours. Still others will decide to take longer vacations, forgo overtime opportunities, retire earlier, or forget about pursuing that promising but risky business venture. In some cases, high tax rates will even drive highly productive citizens to other countries where taxes are lower. In recent years, high-tax countries such as Belgium, France, Sweden, and even Canada have experienced an outflow of highly successful professionals, business entrepreneurs, and athletes.

Second, high tax rates will adversely affect the rate of capital formation and the efficiency of its use. When tax rates are high, foreign investors will look for other places to put their money, and domestic investors will look for investment projects abroad where taxes are lower. In addition, domestic investors will direct more of their time and effort into hobby businesses (like collecting antiques, raising horses, or giving golf lessons) that may not earn much money but are enjoyable and have tax-shelter advantages. This will divert resources away from projects with higher rates of return but fewer tax-avoidance benefits. As a result, scarce capital will be wasted and resources channeled away from their most productive uses.

Third, high marginal tax rates encourage people to substitute less-desired tax-deductible goods for more-desired nondeductible goods. High marginal tax rates make tax-deductible expenditures cheap for people in high tax brackets. Because the personal cost (but not the cost to society) is cheap, these taxpayers will spend more money on pleasurable, tax-deductible items, like plush offices, professional conferences held in favorite vacation spots, and various other fringe benefits (say a company-paid luxury automobile and business entertainment). Because purchasing tax-deductible goods lowers their tax bill, people will often buy them even though they do not value them as much as it costs to produce them.

How Important Are the Supply-Side Effects?

There is considerable debate among economists about the strength of the supply-side incentive effects. Critics of supply-side economics argue that the tax cuts of the 1980s reduced real federal tax revenues and led to large budget deficits, without having much impact on economic growth. This suggests that the supply-side effects are not very strong. Defenders of the supply-side position respond by noting that rate reductions in both the 1960s and the 1980s resulted in impressive growth and lengthy economic expansions. They also stress that the supply-side response in top income brackets—where lower rates have the largest incentive effects—is particularly strong.[8] See the boxed feature "Have Supply-Side Economists Found a Way to Soak the Rich?"

Supply-side critics also point out that most elasticity estimates indicate that a 10 percent change in after-tax wages increases the quantity of labor supplied by only

---

[8]The incentive effects are greater in the upper brackets because a similar percentage rate reduction will have a greater impact on take-home pay in this area. For example, if a 70 percent marginal tax rate is cut to 50 percent, take-home pay per additional dollar of earnings will increase from 30 cents to 50 cents, a 67 percent increase in the incentive to earn. Conversely, if a 14 percent marginal rate is reduced to 10 percent, take-home pay per dollar of additional earnings will increase from 86 cents to 90 cents, only a 5 percent increase in the incentive to earn.

APPLICATIONS IN ECONOMICS

Have Supply-Side Economists Found a Way to Soak the Rich?

Under a progressive rate structure, marginal tax rates rise with income level. The highest marginal tax rates are imposed on those with the largest incomes. The supply-side view stresses that high marginal rates have such a negative effect on the incentive to earn (and the taxable income base) that reducing these high rates can actually increase the revenues collected from high-income taxpayers. The Laffer curve analysis presented in Chapter 4 highlights this point. The Laffer curve indicates that as tax rates are increased from zero,

rate increases will increase the revenue derived from the tax. Eventually, however, higher and higher rates will lead to a maximum revenue point, and rate increases beyond this level will actually reduce the revenue collected. Thus, when tax rates are exceedingly high, more revenue could be collected from these high-income taxpayers if their rates were reduced.

Since 1960, the personal income tax rate imposed on high-income earners has varied considerably. What effect have the rate changes had on the revenue collected from them? **EXHIBIT 6** presents data on the share of the personal income tax collected from the top one-half percent of income recipients. When the top marginal tax rate was sliced from

---

EXHIBIT 6
How Have Changes in Marginal Tax Rates Affected the Share of Taxes Paid by the Rich?

The accompanying graph shows the share of the personal income taxes paid by the top one-half percent of earners from 1960 to 2006. During this period, there were four major reductions in marginal tax rates. First, the Kennedy-Johnson tax cut reduced the top rate from 91 percent in 1963 to 70 percent in 1965. During the Reagan years, the top rate was reduced from 70 percent in 1980 to 50 percent in 1982 and to approximately 30 percent in 1986. In 1997, the capital gains tax rate was sliced from 28 to 20 percent. Interestingly, the share of the tax bill paid by these "super-rich" earners increased after each of these tax cuts. These findings suggest that, at least for this group of high-income recipients, strong supply-side effects accompanied the rate cuts. Perhaps surprising to some, these high-income taxpayers paid a larger portion of the tax bill when the top marginal rate was less than 40 percent (1986–2006) than when it was 70 percent or more.

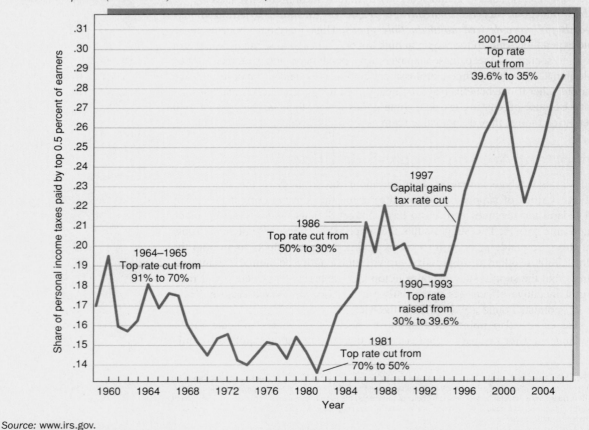

Source: www.irs.gov.

91 percent to 70 percent by the Kennedy–Johnson tax cut of 1964, the share of the personal income tax paid by these high earners rose from 16 percent to 18 percent. In contrast, as inflation pushed more and more taxpayers into higher brackets during the 1970s, the share paid by the top one-half percent declined. When the tax cuts of the 1980s once again reduced the top rates, the share paid by the top one-half percent climbed to more than 20 percent of the total. When the top marginal rate was increased in 1991 and again in 1993, there was little change in the share of taxes paid by the top group. Beginning in 1997, the tax rate on income from capital gains was cut from 28 percent to 20 percent. This rate reduction was accompanied by a substantial increase in revenues derived from the capital gains taxes and personal income taxes collected from high-income taxpayers.[1]

Since 1986, the top marginal personal income tax rate in the United States has been less than 40 percent. In 2004, the top rate was 35 percent, down from 39.6 percent in 2000. In contrast, prior to 1981, the top marginal rate was 70 percent or more. Nonetheless, those with high incomes are now paying more. In fact, the top one-half percent of earners has paid more than 22 percent of the personal income tax every year since 1997. In 2006, the top one-half percent of earners paid 28.7 percent of the federal income tax. Clearly, these recent figures are well above the 14 percent to 19 percent collected from these taxpayers in the 1960s and 1970s, when much higher marginal rates were imposed on the rich.[2]

These data suggest that if you want to collect a lot of revenue from the rich, you better not push the tax rate on their marginal income too high. This sounds counterintuitive. Is it really true? We may have additional evidence on this issue in the near future. The Obama Administration is considering not only allowing the rate reductions passed during the Bush years to expire but also levying the social security payroll tax on earnings greater than $250,000. Once state and local income taxes are added, this change will mean marginal tax rates of more than 50 percent for many high-income taxpayers. The supply-side view suggests that marginal rates of this magnitude will raise little additional revenue from the rich. If the marginal rates are pushed to this level, it will make an interesting economic experiment.

---

[1]High earners also respond to high marginal tax rates imposed by states. A recent study estimated that between 1998 and 2007, more than 1,100 people per day moved from the nine highest income-tax states such as California, New Jersey, New York, and Ohio to the nine states without a personal income tax, including Florida, Nevada, New Hampshire, and Texas. See Arthur Laffer and Stephen Moore, "Soak the Rich, Lose the Rich; Americans Know How To Use The Moving Van To Escape High Taxes," *Wall Street Journal*, May 18, 2009.

[2]For additional evidence on the impact of tax rates on both output and revenue, see Lawrence Lindsey, *The Growth Experiment: How the New Tax Policy Is Transforming the U.S. Economy* (New York: Basic Books, 1990). For additional information on supply-side economics, see James Gwartney, "Supply-side Economics" in *The Encyclopaedia of Economics,* ed. David Henderson (Indianapolis: Liberty Fund, 2007: available online.). For a critical analysis of supply-side economics, see Joel B. Slemrod ed., *Does Atlas Shrug: The Economic Consequences of Taxing the Rich* (New York: Russell Sage Foundation, 2000).

---

1 or 2 percent. This suggests that changes in tax rates exert only a modest impact on the amount of labor supplied. Supply-side advocates, however, argue that these estimates reflect only the adjustments that occur over relatively short time periods. In the long run, they claim that tax cuts increase the labor supply by much more. Recent work by Nobel laureate Edward Prescott at Arizona State University supports this view. Prescott used marginal tax differences between France and the United States to estimate the labor supply response in the long run. Prescott found that the elasticity of labor supply in the long run was substantially greater than in the short run. He also found that France's higher tax rates explained why the labor supply in that country is nearly 30 percent less than it is in the United States.[9]

The supply-side view has exerted considerable impact on tax policy throughout the world. Since 1980, there has been a dramatic shift away from high marginal tax rates. Sixty-two countries imposed a personal income tax with a top marginal rate of 50 percent or more in 1980, but by 2005 only nine countries levied such high rates. Many countries with exceedingly high rates cut them substantially. For example, in 1980 the top marginal rate in the United Kingdom was 83 percent; in 2007 it was 40 percent. In Italy, the top rate was 75 percent in 1980 but only 43 percent in 2007.

---

[9]Prescott concludes, "I find it remarkable that virtually all of the large difference in labor supply between France and the United States is due to differences in tax systems. I expected institutional constraints on the operation of labor markets and the nature of the unemployment benefit system to be more important. I was surprised that the welfare gain from reducing the intratemporal tax wedge is so large." See Edward C. Prescott, "Richard T. Ely Lecture: Prosperity and Depression," *American Economic Review*, Papers and Proceedings 92, no. 2 (May 2002): 9.

The Fiscal Policy of the United States

As we previously mentioned, economists use changes in the size of the deficit or surplus, rather than the absolute amount, to determine whether fiscal policy is shifting toward expansion or restriction. Movement toward a larger deficit (or a smaller surplus) relative to GDP indicates that fiscal policy is becoming more expansionary. Conversely, a reduction in the deficit as a share of GDP (or increase in the surplus) would imply that a more restrictive fiscal policy has been implemented.

EXHIBIT 7 shows federal expenditures, revenues, and deficits in the United States as a share of GDP since 1960. Although the federal government ran deficits throughout most of the 1960s and 1970s, the deficits were small relative to the size of the economy, except during the recessions of 1970 and 1974–1975. Budget deficits have generally increased during recessions (indicated by the shaded bars) and shrunk during expansions. However, the changes in the size of the deficit over the business cycle have been primarily the result of automatic stabilizers rather than discretionary use of fiscal policy.

It is interesting to compare and contrast fiscal policy during the 1980s and 1990s. Propelled by both the Reagan tax cuts and a defense buildup, fiscal policy was highly expansionary during the 1980s. These two factors along with the severe recession of 1982 pushed the federal deficit to peacetime highs in the mid-1980s. As Exhibit 7 shows, the budget deficit was approximately 5 percent of GDP during 1982–1986. In spite of this highly expansionary fiscal policy, the inflation rate fell from the double-digit levels of 1979–1980 to 4 percent in 1983. As the economy rebounded from the 1982 recession, inflation remained in check, and the recovery was both strong and lengthy, lasting nearly eight years.

In contrast with the 1980s, fiscal policy was restrictive in the 1990s. Following the collapse of communism and the end of the Cold War, defense spending was cut sharply and federal spending fell as a share of GDP. Between 1994 and 2000, federal expenditures declined as a share of GDP, and a large budget deficit was transformed into a modest surplus. As during the 1980s, the expansion of the 1990s was both strong and lengthy. Thus, in spite of the differences in fiscal policy between the two decades, the performance of the economy was quite similar. These results do not indicate that fiscal policy—either expansionary or restrictive—exerts a strong impact on either aggregate demand or real output. In that respect, they are more consistent with the crowding-out and new classical theories than the Keynesian view.

The budgetary situation again changed dramatically following the terrorist attacks of September 11, 2001. The combination of the 2001 recession and sluggish recovery, increases in defense spending, and the Bush administration's tax cut quickly moved the budget from surplus to deficit.

It is also informative to compare fiscal policy during the recessions of 1990–1991 and 2001. During the earlier recession, the administrations of both George H. W. Bush and Bill Clinton raised taxes. In both cases, the tax increases were based on the premise that higher taxes would shrink the budget deficit, reduce government borrowing, and lower interest rates. These tax increases were grounded in the crowding-out theory. In contrast, taxes were cut and government expenditures increased during and following the recession of 2001. As Exhibit 7 illustrates, the budget shifted sharply from surplus to deficit during 2001–2003. While the Bush Administration generally used the supply-side argument to buttress support for its tax policy, the budget deficit figures illustrate that it was highly consistent with the Keynesian perspective. Thus, even though the fiscal policy responses to the two recessions were essentially polar opposites, there's little evidence that it made much difference. Both recessions were mild and relatively short (eight to twelve months). Once again, these results are consistent with the view that fiscal policy is not very potent, at least not during relatively normal times.

As the economy slowed and then plunged into the 2008–2009 recession, Congress and the Bush Administration responded with huge increases in federal spending financed through borrowing. A $168 billion stimulus package was passed in early 2008. Most of these funds went for checks of $600 per adult and $300 per child sent to households

EXHIBIT 7

Federal Government Expenditures and Revenues as a Percentage of GDP, 1960–2010

Except during recessions (indicated by shaded bars), budget deficits were small as a share of the economy prior to 1980. After a period of persistently large deficits during the 1980s, the federal deficit shrank, and by the late 1990s a surplus was present. Deficits reemerged in 2002 and skyrocketed starting in the 2008-2009 recession.

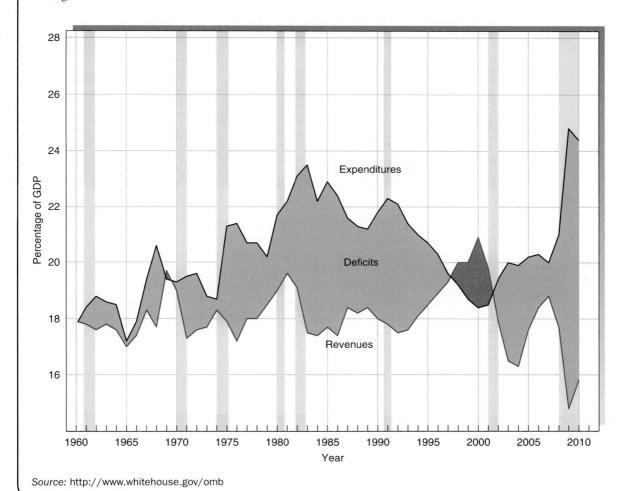

Source: http://www.whitehouse.gov/omb

with incomes of less than $150,000. Later in the year, the Troubled Asset Relief Program (TARP) authorized another $700 billion to bail out troubled financial institutions. When the Obama Administration took over in 2009, still another stimulus package of $787 billion was passed. As Exhibit 7 shows, these programs pushed federal spending to 25 percent of GDP and the budget deficit to 10.0 percent in 2009. During that year, about two-fifths of the federal budget was financed through borrowing. In 2010, the budget of the Obama Administration calls for a federal deficit of 8.9 percent of GDP, and historic high deficits are projected throughout the next decade.

The Great Experiment

We are in the midst of a Great Experiment. The 2009 and 2010 budget deficits are at levels achieved only in the midst of World War II. Moreover, the Obama Administration is projecting both higher levels of government spending and large budget deficits throughout the next decade. The Keynesian view indicates that (1) the budget deficits will stimulate

Fiscal Policy is determined by Congress and the President. They responded to the downturn of 2008-2009 with large spending increases and budget deficits. Will this fiscal policy stimulate recovery and promote future growth?

© Greg mathieson/MAI/Landov

aggregate demand and (2) the adverse secondary effects of the large deficits and growth of government will be small. If the Keynesians are right, the growth of real output and income during the next decade should be strong—at least equal to the 3 percent historic long-term growth of the United States. In contrast, the Keynesian critics argue that the big deficits will mean higher future interest rates and higher taxes just to pay the interest on the government's larger outstanding debt. This will retard future growth. Many non-Keynesians also believe that the growth of government as a share of the economy will lead to less productive allocation of resources, more wasteful rent-seeking activities, and less incentive to earn. Given these adverse secondary and incentive effects, non-Keynesians expect growth below the historic average during the next decade. It will be interesting and informative to observe this experiment unfold.

Looking ahead

Fiscal policy is not the only macroeconomic policy tool. Monetary policy provides another stabilization weapon. We are now ready to integrate the monetary system into our analysis. Chapter 13 will focus on the operation of the banking system and the factors that determine the supply of money. In Chapter 14, we will analyze the impact of monetary policy on real output, interest rates, and the price level.

KEY POINTS

▼ The crowding-out model indicates that expansionary fiscal policy will lead to higher real interest rates and less private spending, particularly for investment. In an open economy, the higher interest rates will also lead to the following secondary effects: an inflow of capital, appreciation of the dollar, and a reduction in net exports. The crowding-out theory implies that these secondary effects will largely offset the demand stimulus of expansionary fiscal policy.

▼ The new classical model stresses that financing government spending with debt rather than taxes changes the timing, but not the level, of taxes. According to this view, people will expect higher future taxes, which will lead to more saving and less private spending. This will tend to offset the expansionary effects of a deficit.

▼ Keynesian and non-Keynesian economists are now largely in agreement on the following three issues: (1) proper timing of discretionary fiscal policy is both difficult to achieve and crucially important; (2) automatic stabilizers reduce the fluctuation of aggregate demand and help promote economic stability; and (3) fiscal policy is much less potent than early Keynesians thought.

▼ Keynesian economists believe that increases in government spending financed by borrowing will increase aggregate demand and help promote recovery from a serious recession like that of 2008–2009.

▼ Non-Keynesian economists argue that increases in government spending financed by borrowing will exert adverse side effects that will retard both the recovery and long-term growth. These side effects include (1) higher future interest rates and taxes, (2) coordination problems that will undermine the effectiveness of the increased spending and lead to an expansion in unproductive activities, and (3) increased rent seeking as groups fight to obtain more funds from the government.

▼ While an abrupt increase in saving may exert an adverse impact on the economy in the short run, saving provides the financing for investment that powers long-term growth. Moreover, a healthy economy is dependent on households saving regularly and avoiding excessive debt.

▼ When fiscal policy changes marginal tax rates, it influences aggregate supply by altering the attractiveness of productive activity relative to leisure and tax avoidance. Other things being constant, lower marginal tax rates will increase aggregate supply. Supply-side economics should be viewed as a long-run strategy, not a countercyclical tool.

▼ We are now in the midst of a Great Experiment. Political decision makers have responded to the 2008–2009 recession with large increases in both government spending and budget deficits. The Keynesian perspective indicates that this will stimulate recovery and generate strong growth. Non-Keynesians believe that this policy will lead to a sluggish recovery and slow future growth. In a few years, we will have additional insights concerning which view is correct.

CRITICAL ANALYSIS QUESTIONS

1. Suppose that you are a member of the Council of Economic Advisers. The president has asked you to prepare a statement on the question, "What is the proper fiscal policy for the next twelve months?" Prepare such a statement, indicating (a) the current state of the economy (that is, the unemployment rate, growth in real income, and rate of inflation) and (b) your fiscal policy suggestions. Should the budget be in balance? Explain the reasoning behind your suggestions.

*2. What is the crowding-out effect? How does it modify the implications of the basic Keynesian model with regard to fiscal policy? How does the new classical theory of fiscal policy differ from the crowding-out model?

3. Suppose that the government provides each taxpayer with a $1,000 tax rebate financed by issuing additional Treasury bonds. Outline alternative views that predict how this fiscal action will influence interest rates, aggregate demand, output, and employment.

4. Will increases in government spending financed by borrowing help promote a strong recovery from a severe recession? Why or why not?

5. Outline the supply-side view of fiscal policy. How does this view differ from the various demand-side theories? Would a supply-side economist be more likely to favor a $500 tax credit or an equivalent reduction in marginal tax rates? Why?

6. Are changes in discretionary fiscal policy likely to be instituted in a manner that will reduce the ups and downs of the business cycle? Why or why not?

7. If uncertainty about the future causes households to increase their saving and reduce their consumption spending during a recession, how will this affect the economy? Explain. If households save little and spend most of their income on current consumption, how will this affect the economy? Explain.

8. If the government becomes more heavily involved in subsidizing some businesses and sectors of the economy while levying taxes on others, how will

this influence the quantity of rent seeking? How will this affect long-term growth? Explain your response.

9. Does fiscal policy have a strong impact on aggregate demand? Did the large budget deficits of the last decade lead to excessive aggregate demand? Did the budget surpluses of the late 1990s restrain aggregate demand? Discuss.

*10. How do persistently large budget deficits affect capital formation and the long-run rate of economic growth? Do the proponents of the Keynesian, crowding-out, and new classical theories agree on the answer to this question? Discuss.

11. During the 1990s, the federal budget moved from a deficit to a surplus. What factors accounted for this change? Were the budget surpluses of the late 1990s good for the economy? Would it have been better to have reduced taxes and balanced the budget during 1999–2000? Why or why not?

12. Marginal tax rates were cut substantially during the 1980s, and although rates were increased in the early 1990s, the marginal rates applicable in the highest income brackets were still well below the top rates of the 1960s and 1970s. How did the lower rates of the 1980s and 1990s affect the share of taxes paid by high-income taxpayers? Were the lower rates of the 1980s and 1990s good or bad for the economy? Discuss.

*13. If the impact on tax revenues is the same, does it make any difference whether the government cuts taxes by (a) reducing marginal tax rates or (b) increasing the personal exemption allowance? Explain.

14. If there is a shift to a more expansionary fiscal policy in order to stimulate recovery from a recession, does it make any difference whether tax rates are cut or government expenditures increased? Explain your answer.

*15. The American Wind Energy Association argues for additional government support because wind-generated electricity creates more employment per kilowatt-hour than the alternatives: 27 percent more jobs than coal and 66 percent more than natural gas. Is this a sound economic argument for increased use of wind power? If the jobs created pay similar wages, what does the statement imply about the cost of generating energy with wind power relative to coal and natural gas?

*Asterisk denotes questions for which answers are given in Appendix B.

Money and the Banking System

CHAPTER FOCUS

- What is money? How is money supply defined?

- What is a fractional reserve banking system? How does it influence the ability of banks to create money?

- What are the major functions of the Federal Reserve System?

- What are the major tools with which the Federal Reserve controls the supply of money?

- How has the Federal Reserve responded to the financial crisis of 2008–2009?

Money is whatever is generally accepted in exchange for goods and services—accepted not as an object to be consumed but as an object that represents a temporary abode of purchasing power to be used for buying still other goods and services.

—Milton Friedman[1]

[1] Milton Friedman, *Money Mischief: Episodes in Monetary History* (New York: Harcourt Brace Jovanovich, 1992), 16.

The simple macroeconomic model we have developed so far has four major markets: (1) the goods and services market, (2) the resources market, (3) the loanable funds market, and (4) the foreign exchange market. When people make exchanges in any of these markets, they generally use money. Money is used to purchase all types of goods, services, physical assets like houses, and financial assets like stocks and bonds. This chapter focuses on the nature of money, how the banking system works, and how the central bank—the Federal Reserve System in the United States—controls the supply of money. ■

What Is Money?

As the chapter opening quote from Milton Friedman indicates, money is the item commonly used to pay for goods, services, assets, and outstanding debts. Most modern money is merely paper or electronic digits indicating funds in a bank account. Paradoxically, money has little or no intrinsic value. Nonetheless, most of us would like to have more of it. Why? Because money is an asset that performs three basic functions: it serves as a medium of exchange, it provides a means of storing value for future use, and it is used as an accounting unit.

Money as a Medium of Exchange

Medium of exchange

An asset that is used to buy and sell goods or services.

Money is one of the most important inventions in human history because of its role as a **medium of exchange**. Money simplifies and reduces the costs of transactions. Think what it would be like to live in a barter economy—one without money, in which goods were traded for goods. If you wanted to buy a pair of jeans, for example, you would first have to find someone willing to trade you the jeans for your labor services or something else you were willing to supply. Such an economy would be highly inefficient.

Money "oils the wheels" of trade and makes it possible for each of us to specialize in the supply of those things that we do best and easily buy the many goods and services we want. It frees us from cumbersome barter procedures.

At various times in the past, societies have used gold, silver, beads, seashells, and other commodities as mediums of exchange. It is costly to use a valuable commodity as money. Here's why. Precious metals, like gold, would be cumbersome to carry around for use as payment. In fact, it might even be dangerous to do so. Moreover, think about how much it costs to create a thousand dollar bill: just a cent or two, perhaps. But if gold bars, for example, were used instead of bills as money, it would take a lot of resources to produce enough of them to facilitate today's current volume of trade. Further, if a precious metal was used as money, people would employ scarce resources producing "money," and as a result, fewer resources would be available to produce desired goods and services.

Fiat money

Money that has neither intrinsic value nor the backing of a commodity with intrinsic value; paper currency is an example.

Thus, most modern nations use **fiat money**—money with no intrinsic value. Why is fiat money valuable? Governments often designate it as "legal tender," meaning it must be accepted as payment for debt. But the value of fiat money is closely linked to trust and its supply. People are willing to accept fiat money because they have confidence it can be used to purchase real goods and services. A limited supply is also important: as we will discuss shortly, if governments expand the supply of money rapidly, its value will diminish.

© Bettmann/Corbis

Money is the item commonly used to buy and sell things. During the Second World War, prisoners of war used cigarettes as money in POW camps.

Money as a Store of Value

Money is also a financial asset—a method of storing value for use in the future. Put another way, it provides readily available purchasing power for dealing with an uncertain future. Thus, most people hold some of their wealth in the form of money. Moreover, it is the most **liquid** of all assets. It can be easily and quickly transformed into other goods at a low transaction cost, usually without an appreciable loss in value.

However, there are some disadvantages of using money as a **store of value**. The value of a unit of money—a dollar, for example—is measured in terms of what it will buy. Its value, therefore, is inversely related to the price level in the economy. When inflation rises, the purchasing power of money declines—as does its usefulness as a store of value. This imposes a cost on people holding money.

Other assets, like land, houses, stocks, or bonds, also serve as a store of value, but they aren't as liquid as money. It will take time to locate an acceptable buyer for a house, a plot of land, or an office building. Stocks and bonds are quite liquid—they can usually be sold quickly for only a small commission—but they are not readily acceptable as a direct means of payment.

Liquid asset

An asset that can be easily and quickly converted to money without loss of value.

Store of value

An asset that will allow people to transfer purchasing power from one period to the next.

Money as a Unit of Account

Money also serves as a **unit of account**. Just as we use yards or meters to measure distance, we use units of money—the dollar in the United States—to measure the exchange value and cost of goods, services, assets, and resources. The value (and cost) of movie tickets, personal computers, labor services, automobiles, houses, and numerous other items is measured in units of money. Money serves as a common denominator for the expression of both costs and benefits. If consumers are going to spend their income wisely, they must be able to compare the costs of a vast array of goods and services. Prices measured in units of money help them make such comparisons. Similarly, sound business decisions require cost and revenue comparisons. Resource prices and accounting procedures measured in money units facilitate this task.

Unit of account

A unit of measurement used by people to post prices and keep track of revenues and costs.

How the Supply of Money Affects Its Value

The main thing that makes money valuable is the same thing that generates value for other commodities: demand relative to supply. People demand money because it reduces the cost of exchange. When the supply of money is limited relative to the demand, money will become more valuable. Conversely, when the supply of money is large relative to demand, it will become less valuable.

If the purchasing power of money is to remain stable over time, its supply must be limited. When the supply of money grows more rapidly than the output of goods and services, prices will rise. In layman's terms, "too much money is chasing too few goods."

When government authorities rapidly expand the supply of money, it becomes less valuable in exchange and is virtually useless as a store of value. The rapid growth in the supply of money in Germany following World War I provides a dramatic illustration of this point. During the period 1922–1923, the supply of German marks increased by 250 percent in some months. The German government was printing money almost as fast as the printing presses would run. Because money became substantially more plentiful in relation to goods and services, it quickly lost its value. As a result, an egg cost 80 billion marks and a loaf of bread 200 billion. Workers picked up their wages in suitcases. Shops closed at the lunch hour to change price tags. The value of money had eroded. More recently, several countries including Poland, Russia, Ukraine, and Zimbabwe have followed this same pattern. These countries expanded the supply of money rapidly to pay for government expenditures and, as a result, experienced very high rates of inflation. Thus, while fiat money is economical to produce, this feature also makes it easier for governments to use money creation to finance expenditures, expand the money supply rapidly, and thereby erode its purchasing power.

How Is the Money Supply Measured?

How is the money supply defined and measured? There is not a single answer to this question. Economists and policy makers have developed several alternative measures. We will briefly describe the two most widely used measures.

The M1 Money Supply

Above all else, money is a medium of exchange. The narrowest definition of the money supply, **M1**, focuses on this function. Based on its role as a medium of exchange, it is clear that **currency**—coins and paper bills—falls into this definition. But currency isn't the only form of money readily used for exchange. If you want to buy something from a store, many will let you pay with either a check or debit card that will transfer funds from your bank account to theirs. Therefore, checkable bank deposits that can easily be used as a means of payment should be included in the M1 money supply measure.

There are two kinds of checkable deposits. First, there are **demand deposits**, non–interest-earning deposits with banking institutions that are available for withdrawal ("on demand") at any time without restrictions. Demand deposits are usually withdrawn either by writing a check or by using a debit card tied to your account. Second, there are **other checkable deposits** that earn interest but carry some restrictions on their transferability. Interest-earning checkable deposits generally either limit the number of checks depositors can write each month or require the depositor to maintain a substantial minimum balance ($1,000, for example).

Like currency and demand deposits, interest-earning checkable deposits are available for use as a medium of exchange. Traveler's checks are also a means of payment. They can be freely converted to cash at parity (equal value). ***Thus, the M1 money supply comprises (1) currency in circulation, (2) checkable deposits (both demand deposits and interest-earning checkable deposits), and (3) traveler's checks.***

M1 (money supply)

The sum of (1) currency in circulation (including coins), (2) checkable deposits maintained in depository institutions, and (3) traveler's checks.

Currency

Medium of exchange made of metal or paper.

Demand deposits

Non–interest-earning checking deposits that can be either withdrawn or made payable on demand to a third party. Like currency, these deposits are widely used as a means of payment.

Other checkable deposits

Interest-earning deposits that are also available for checking.

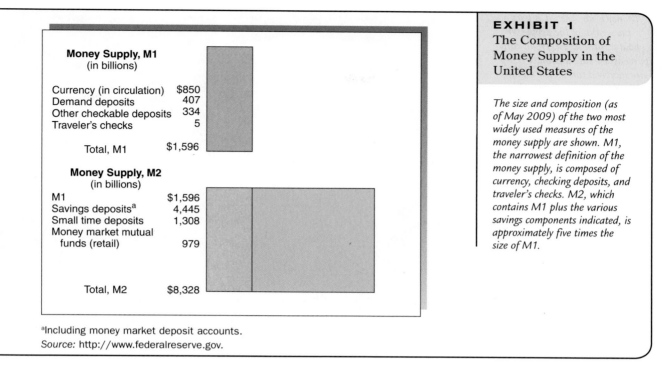

EXHIBIT 1
The Composition of
Money Supply in the
United States

The size and composition (as of May 2009) of the two most widely used measures of the money supply are shown. M1, the narrowest definition of the money supply, is composed of currency, checking deposits, and traveler's checks. M2, which contains M1 plus the various savings components indicated, is approximately five times the size of M1.

As **EXHIBIT 1** shows, the total M1 money supply in the United States was $1,596 billion in May 2009. Demand and other checkable deposits accounted for almost one-half of the M1 money supply. This large share reflects the fact that most of the nation's business is conducted with checks and electronic payment transfers.

The Broader M2 Money Supply

In modern economies, several financial assets can be easily converted into checking deposits or currency; therefore, the line between money and "near monies" is often blurred. Broader definitions of the money supply include various assets that can be easily converted to checking account funds and cash. The most common broad definition of the money supply is **M2**. It includes all the items included in M1 plus (1) savings deposits, (2) time deposits of less than $100,000 at all **depository institutions**, and (3) money market mutual funds.

Although the non-M1 components of the M2 money supply are not generally used as a means of making payment, they can be easily and quickly converted to currency or checking deposits for such use. For example, if you maintain funds in a savings account, you can easily transfer the funds to your checking account. **Money market mutual funds** are interest-earning accounts offered by banks and brokerage firms that pool depositors' funds and invest them in highly liquid short-term securities. Because these securities can be quickly converted to cash, depositors are permitted to write checks against these accounts.

Many economists—particularly those who stress the store-of-value function of money—prefer the broader M2 definition of the money supply to the narrower M1 concept. As Exhibit 1 shows, in May 2009 the M2 money supply was $8,328 billion, about five times the M1 money supply. Other definitions of the money supply have been developed for specialized purposes, but the M1 and M2 definitions are the most important and most widely used.

Credit Cards versus Money

It is important to distinguish between money and credit. Money is a financial asset that provides the holder with future purchasing power. **Credit** is a liability acquired when one borrows funds. This distinction sheds light on a question students frequently ask: "Because

M2 (money supply)

Equal to M1 plus (1) savings deposits, (2) time deposits (accounts of less than $100,000) held in depository institutions, and (3) money market mutual fund shares.

Depository institutions

Businesses that accept checking and savings deposits and use a portion of them to extend loans and make investments. Banks, savings and loan associations, and credit unions are examples.

Money market mutual funds

Interest-earning accounts that pool depositors' funds and invest them in highly liquid short-term securities. Because these securities can be quickly converted to cash, depositors are permitted to write checks (which reduce their share holdings) against their accounts.

Credit

Funds acquired by borrowing.

Money is an asset; it is part of the wealth of the people who hold it. In contrast, credit card purchases create a liability. They are merely a convenient method of arranging a short-term loan.

credit cards are often used to make purchases, why aren't credit card expenditures part of the money supply?" In contrast with money, credit cards do not have purchasing power. They are merely a convenient way of arranging a loan. When you use your Visa or MasterCard to buy a DVD player, for example, you are not really paying for the player. Instead, you are taking out a loan from the institution issuing your card, and that institution is paying for the player. You haven't paid for the DVD player until you've paid your credit card bill down far enough to cover its cost. The same goes for your other credit card purchases. Thus, credit cards are not money because they don't represent purchasing power. Instead, the outstanding balance on your credit card is a liability, money you owe to the company that issued the card.

Although credit cards are not money, their use will influence the amount of money people will want to hold. Credit cards make it possible for people to buy things throughout the month and then pay for them in a single transaction at the end of the month. This makes it possible for people to conduct their regular business affairs with less money than would otherwise be needed. Thus, widespread use of credit cards will tend to reduce the average quantity of money people hold.

The Business of Banking

Federal Reserve System

The central bank of the United States; it carries out banking regulatory policies and is responsible for the conduct of monetary policy.

Central bank

An institution that regulates the banking system and controls the supply of a country's money.

We must understand a few things about the business of banking before we can explain the factors that influence the supply of money. The banking industry in the United States operates under the jurisdiction of the **Federal Reserve System**, the nation's **central bank**. We will discuss the Federal Reserve System in detail later in this chapter.

The banking system is an important component of the capital market. Like other private businesses, banks are profit-seeking operations. Banks provide services (for example, the safekeeping of funds and checking account services) and pay interest to attract both checking and savings depositors. They help bring together people who want to save for the future and those who want to borrow in order to undertake investment projects. The primary source of revenue for banks is the income they derive from their loans and investments.

When deciding whether to extend a loan for a project, bankers have a strong incentive to take into account the project's expected profitability and the borrower's creditworthiness.

If the borrowed funds are channeled into an unprofitable project, the borrower may not be able to repay the loan. This will hurt the bank's profitability. The efficient allocation of investment funds by banks is an important source of economic growth. Profitable business projects increase the value of resources and promote economic growth; unprofitable projects have the opposite effect and tie up resources better used elsewhere. Thus, an efficiently operating capital market is an important ingredient for economic growth, and the banking system plays a central role in the operation of this market.

In the United States, the banking system consists of savings and loan institutions, credit unions, and commercial banks. **Savings and loan associations** accept deposits in exchange for shares that pay dividends. **Credit unions** are cooperative financial organizations composed of individuals with a common affiliation (such as an employer). Credit unions accept deposits, pay interest (or dividends) on them, and generate earnings primarily by extending loans to members. **Commercial banks** offer a wide range of services—including checking and savings accounts and extension of loans—and are owned by stockholders.

Credit unions, savings and loan associations, and commercial banks all accept both checking and savings deposits and extend a wide variety of loans to their customers. All of these institutions are now under the jurisdiction of the Federal Reserve System, which applies similar regulations and offers similar services to each. *Therefore, when we speak of the banking industry, we are referring not only to commercial banks but also to savings and loan associations and credit unions.*

EXHIBIT 2 presents the consolidated balance sheet of commercial banking institutions. These figures illustrate the major banking functions. Note that major liabilities of banks are transaction (checking), savings, and time deposits. *From the viewpoint of a bank,* these are liabilities because they represent an obligation of the bank to its depositors. Outstanding interest-earning loans constitute the major class of banking assets. In addition, most banks own sizable amounts of interest-earning securities—bonds issued by either governments or private corporations. As these figures show, banks use the deposits of their customers to earn income by extending loans. Banks also invest some of the deposits in low-risk assets, such as U.S. government securities.

Banking differs from most businesses in that a large portion of the liabilities are payable on demand. Conceivably, all or most customers might want to withdraw their deposits on the same day, but the probability of this occurring is highly remote. Typically, while

Savings and loan associations

Financial institutions that accept deposits in exchange for shares that pay dividends. Historically, these funds were channeled into residential mortgage loans, but today they offer essentially the same services as a commercial bank.

Credit unions

Financial cooperative organizations of individuals with a common affiliation (such as an employer or a labor union). They accept deposits, including checkable deposits, pay interest (or dividends) on them out of earnings, and lend funds primarily to members.

Commercial banks

Financial institutions that offer a wide range of services (for example, checking accounts, savings accounts, and loans) to their customers. Commercial banks are owned by stockholders and seek to operate at a profit.

EXHIBIT 2
The Functions of Commercial Banking Institutions

The consolidated balance sheet of commercial banks shown here illustrates the primary banking functions. Banks provide services and pay interest to attract deposits (both checking and saving) that are liabilities from the standpoint of the bank. Most of these deposits are invested and loaned out, providing the bank with interest income. Banks hold a portion of their assets as reserves (either cash or deposits with the Fed) to meet their daily obligations toward their depositors.

CONSOLIDATED BALANCE SHEET OF COMMERCIAL BANKING INSTITUTIONS, APRIL 2009 (BILLIONS OF DOLLARS)

ASSETS		LIABILITIES	
Vault cash	$40	Checking deposits	$600
Reserves at the Fed	672	Savings and time deposits	6,851
Loans outstanding	7,051	Borrowings	2,400
U.S. Government securities	1,265	Other liabilities	928
Other securities	1,412	Net worth	1,291
Other assets	1,630		
Total	$12,070	Total	$12,070

Note: Borrowings include loans from other banks, loans from the Federal Reserve, and negotiable certificates of deposit.
Source: http://www.federalreserve.gov.

some individuals are making withdrawals, others are making deposits. These transactions tend to balance out, eliminating sudden changes in deposit levels.

It's important to note that banks maintain only a fraction of their assets in reserve against their checking and saving deposits. As Exhibit 2 illustrates, **bank reserves**—vault cash plus reserve deposits with the Federal Reserve—were $712 billion in April 2009, compared to total checking plus savings deposits of $7.451 trillion. Thus, the reserves of banks are less than 10 percent of the deposits (checking plus savings) of their customers. Savings cannot always be withdrawn immediately, and they are generally more stable than checking deposits. Therefore, banks are required to maintain reserves only against their checking deposits. Prior to the financial crisis of 2008, bank reserves were smaller relative to checking deposits. In 2008, however, the central bank substantially increased the reserves available to banks, and many banks increased their holdings of reserves because of the uncertainty of the times. As a result, the ratio of reserves to checking deposits of the banking system is now substantially higher than in the past. We will now take a closer look at the historical development and operation of a fractional reserve banking system.

Fractional Reserve Banking

Economists often draw an analogy between our current banking system and the goldsmiths of the past. In the past, gold was used as the means of making payments. It was money. People would store their money with a goldsmith for safekeeping, just as many of us open a checking account for safety reasons. Gold owners received a certificate granting them the right to withdraw their gold any time they wished. If they wanted to buy something, they would go to the goldsmith, withdraw gold, and use it as a means of making a payment. Thus, the money supply was equal to the amount of gold in circulation plus the gold deposited with goldsmiths.

It was inconvenient to make a trip to the goldsmith every time one wanted to buy something. Because the certificates were redeemable in gold, they began to circulate as a means of payment. The depositors were pleased with this arrangement because it eliminated the need for a trip to the goldsmith every time something was purchased. As long as they had confidence in the goldsmith, sellers were glad to accept the certificates as payment.

As gold certificates began to circulate, the daily withdrawals and deposits with goldsmiths declined even more. This makes sense because the only way the goldsmiths could earn money was by lending out gold. They made nothing on the gold just sitting in their vaults. Consequently, local goldsmiths would keep only about 20 percent of the total gold deposited with them so they could meet the current requests to redeem the gold certificates in circulation. The remaining 80 percent of their gold deposits would be loaned out to merchants, traders, and other citizens. One hundred percent of the gold certificates were circulating as money, along with that portion of gold that had been loaned out—80 percent of total deposits, in other words. Therefore, the *total* money supply circulating in the economy—gold certificates plus actual gold—was 1.8 times the amount of gold deposited with the goldsmiths. By issuing loans and retaining only a fraction of the total gold in their vaults, goldsmiths were actually able to increase the money supply.

In principle, our modern banking system is very similar to goldsmithing. The United States has a **fractional reserve banking** system. Banks are required to maintain only a fraction of their deposits in the form of vault cash and other reserves. These are called **required reserves**. Just as the early goldsmiths did not have enough gold to pay all their depositors simultaneously, our banks also do not have enough reserves to pay all depositors at once. To make money, the early goldsmiths expanded the money supply by issuing loans. So, too, do present-day bankers.

There are important differences between modern banking and early goldsmithing, though. Today, the actions of individual banks are regulated by a central bank. The central bank is supposed to follow policies designed to promote a healthy economy. It also acts as a lender of last resort. If the customers of a bank all attempted to withdraw their deposits simultaneously, the central bank would intervene and supply the bank with enough funds to meet the demand.

Bank reserves

Vault cash plus deposits of banks with Federal Reserve banks.

Fractional reserve banking

A system that permits banks to hold reserves of less than 100 percent against their deposits.

Required reserves

The minimum amount of reserves that a bank is required by law to keep on hand to back up its deposits. If reserve requirements were 15 percent, banks would be required to keep $150,000 in reserves against each $1 million of deposits.

Bank Runs, Bank Failures, and Deposit Insurance

Compared to other businesses, banks are more vulnerable to failure because their liabilities to depositors are current but most of their assets are illiquid. This means that if a significant share of depositors lose confidence and withdraw their funds from a bank, it will quickly lead to problems. In turn, when a bank fails, it affects not only the bank's owners and employees but its depositors as well. These effects can undermine the operation of an economy if many banks fail.

The U.S. economy has had its share of banking problems. Between 1922 and 1933, more than 10,000 banks (one-third of the total) failed. Most of these failures were the result of "bank runs"—panic withdrawals when people lost confidence in the banking system. Remember, under a fractional reserve system, banks do not have a sufficient amount of reserves to redeem the funds of all (or even most) depositors if they should seek to withdraw their funds at the same time.

The bank failures of the 1920s and 1930s led to the establishment of the **Federal Deposit Insurance Corporation (FDIC)** in 1934. The FDIC guarantees the deposits of banking customers up to some limit—currently $250,000 per account. Even if the bank should fail, depositors will be able to get their money (up to the $250,000 limit). Member banks pay an insurance premium to the FDIC for each dollar deposited with them, and the FDIC uses these premiums to reimburse depositors when a bank fails. The FDIC restored confidence in the banking system and brought bank runs to a halt. Banks still fail today. There were twenty-five bank failures in 2008 and over 100 in 2009. But bank failures are now far less common, and they are almost always the result of bad loans and investments rather than bank runs.

Federal Deposit Insurance Corporation (FDIC)

A federally chartered corporation that insures the deposits held by commercial banks, savings and loans, and credit unions.

How Banks Create Money by Extending Loans

Let us consider a banking system without a central bank, one in which only currency acts as a reserve against deposits. Initially, we will assume that all banks are required by law to maintain 20 percent or more of their deposits as cash in their vaults. This proportion of the percentage of reserves that must be maintained against checkable transaction deposits is called the **required reserve ratio**. The required reserve ratio in our example is 20 percent.

Now suppose that you find $1,000 that your long-deceased uncle had apparently hidden in the basement of his house. You take the bills to the First National Bank and open a checking account. How much will the $1,000 in your newly opened account expand

Required reserve ratio

The ratio of reserves relative to a specified liability category (for example, checkable deposits) that banks are required to maintain.

ECONOMICS *At The Movies*

It's a Wonderful Life (1946)

In this classic movie from 1946 (which often airs on TV during the winter holidays), there is a bank run. When everyone shows up and wants to withdraw their money, James Stewart explains, "Your money is not in the vault. It's in Bert's house and in Ernie's house." Thus, he cannot give everyone their money because the bank uses the deposits to make loans to other people. In essence, Stewart is giving everyone a lesson in fractional reserve banking.

RKO/Thekobal Collection

It's a Wonderful Life

Excess reserves

Actual reserves that exceed the legal requirement.

the economy's money supply? First National is now required to keep $200 of the $1,000 in vault cash—20 percent of your deposit. So after placing $200 in the bank vault, First National has $800 of **excess reserves**—reserves over and above the amount the law requires it to retain. Given its current excess reserves, First National can now extend an $800 loan. Suppose it loans $800 to a local citizen to help pay for a car. At the time the loan is extended, the money supply will increase by $800 as the bank adds the funds to the checking account of the borrower. No one else has less money. You still have your $1,000 checking account, and the borrower has $800 for the car.

When the borrower buys the car, the seller accepts a check and deposits the $800 in a bank, Citizen's State Bank. What happens when the check clears? The temporary excess reserves of the First National Bank will be eliminated when it pays $800 to the Citizen's State Bank. But when Citizen's State Bank receives $800 in currency, it will now have excess reserves. It must keep 20 percent of it, or $160, as required reserves, but the remaining $640 can be loaned out. Because Citizen's State, like other banks, wants to earn income, it will be quite happy to "extend a helping hand" to someone who wants to borrow that money. When the second bank loans out its excess reserves, the deposits of the person borrowing the money will increase by $640. Another $640 has now been added to the money supply. You still have your $1,000, the automobile seller has an additional $800, and the new borrower has just received an additional $640. Because you found the $1,000 and deposited it in the bank, the money supply has increased by $1,440 ($800 + $640).

Of course, the process can continue. **EXHIBIT 3** shows what happens when the money creation process continues through several more stages. When the reserve requirement is 20 percent, the money supply can expand to a maximum of $5,000, the initial $1,000 plus an additional $4,000 in demand deposits that can be created by extending new loans.

Deposit expansion multiplier

The multiple by which an increase in reserves will increase the money supply. It is inversely related to the required reserve ratio.

Potential deposit expansion multiplier

The maximum potential increase in the money supply as a ratio of the new reserves injected into the banking system. It is equal to the inverse of the required reserve ratio.

The multiple by which new reserves increase the stock of money is called the **deposit expansion multiplier**. It is determined by the ratio of required reserves to deposits. In fact, the **potential deposit expansion multiplier** is merely the reciprocal of the required reserve ratio (r). Mathematically, the potential deposit expansion multiplier is equal to $1/r$. In our example, the required reserves are 20 percent or one-fifth of the total deposits. So the potential deposit expansion multiplier is 5. If only 10 percent reserves were required, the potential deposit expansion multiplier would be 10, the reciprocal of one-tenth. *The lower the percentage of reserves required, the larger the potential expansion in the money supply generated by creation of new reserves. However, the fractional reserve requirement puts a ceiling on the expansion in the money supply resulting from the creation of new reserves.*

EXHIBIT 3
Creating Money from New Reserves

When banks are required to maintain 20 percent reserves against demand deposits, the creation of $1,000 of new reserves will potentially increase the supply of money by $5,000.

BANK	NEW CASH DEPOSITS: ACTUAL RESERVES	NEW REQUIRED RESERVES	POTENTIAL DEMAND DEPOSITS CREATED BY EXTENDING NEW LOANS
Initial deposit (Bank A)	$1,000.00	$ 200.00	$ 800.00
Second stage (Bank B)	800.00	160.00	640.00
Third stage (Bank C)	640.00	128.00	512.00
Fourth stage (Bank D)	512.00	102.40	409.60
Fifth stage (Bank E)	409.60	81.92	327.68
Sixth stage (Bank F)	327.68	65.54	262.14
Seventh stage (Bank G)	262.14	52.43	209.71
All others (other banks)	1,048.58	209.71	838.87
Total	$5,000.00	$1,000.00	$4,000.00

The Actual Deposit Multiplier

Will the introduction of new currency reserves fully expand the money supply by the amount of the multiplier? The answer is "No." The actual deposit multiplier will generally be less than its potential for two reasons.

First, the deposit expansion multiplier will be reduced if some people decide to hold the currency rather than deposit it in a bank. For example, suppose the person who borrowed the $800 in the preceding example spends only $700 and stashes the remaining $100 away for a possible emergency. Only $700 can then end up as a deposit in the second stage and contribute to the excess reserves that underlie the expansion of the money supply. The potential of new loans in the second stage and in all subsequent stages will be reduced proportionally. When currency remains in circulation outside of banks, it reduces the size of the deposit expansion multiplier.

Second, the actual deposit multiplier will be less than its maximum potential if banks fail to use all the new excess reserves to extend loans. Banks are in business to make profit, and they will generally be able to increase their net income by extending loans and undertaking investments, rather than holding excess reserves. In the past, this has certainly been the case, and therefore, historically, the excess reserves of banks have been small. However, in the midst of the uncertainty of the financial crisis of 2008, the excess reserves of banks skyrocketed. Moreover, in October 2008 the Federal Reserve acquired the authority to pay interest on bank reserves. This interest rate can be used to affect the excess reserves of banks and the size of the money deposit multiplier. We now turn to an examination of the Federal Reserve and the tools it has to control the money supply of the United States.

The Federal Reserve System

Most countries have a central banking authority that controls the money supply and conducts monetary policy. As we previously noted, the central bank of the United States is the Federal Reserve System. The European Central Bank is the central bank for countries using the euro as their currency. In the United Kingdom, the central bank is the Bank of England; in Canada, it is the Bank of Canada; in Japan, it is the Bank of Japan. Central banks are responsible for the conduct of monetary policy.

Structure of the Fed

The major purpose of the Federal Reserve System (and other central banks) is to regulate the money supply and provide a monetary climate that is in the best interest of the entire economy. Congress has instructed the Federal Reserve, or the Fed, as it is often called, to conduct monetary policy in a manner that promotes both full employment and price stability. Unlike commercial banks, the Federal Reserve is not a profit-making institution. The earnings of the Fed, over and above its expenses, belong to the U.S. Treasury.

EXHIBIT 4 illustrates the structure of the Fed. There are three major centers of decision making within the Federal Reserve: (1) the Board of Governors, (2) the district and regional banks, and (3) the Federal Open Market Committee.

THE BOARD OF GOVERNORS. The Board of Governors is the decision-making hub of the Fed. This powerful board consists of seven members, each appointed to a staggered fourteen-year term by the nation's president with the advice and consent of the U.S. Senate. The president designates one of the seven members as chair for a four-year term.

The Fed chairman directs the Federal Reserve staff, presides over board meetings, and testifies frequently before Congress. Because of the importance of monetary policy and the power of the position, the Fed chair is often said to be the second most influential person—next to the president—in the United States. The current Fed chair

EXHIBIT 4
Structure of Federal Reserve System

The Board of Governors of the Federal Reserve System is at the center of the banking system in the United States. The board sets the rules and regulations for all depository institutions. The seven members of the Board of Governors also serve on the Federal Open Market Committee, which establishes Fed policy with regard to the buying and selling of government securities, the primary mechanism used to control the money supply in the United States.

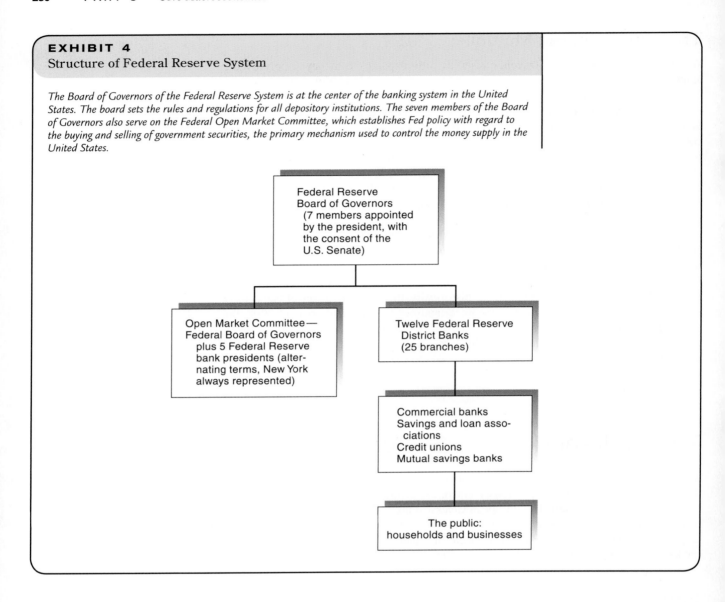

is Ben Bernanke, who was appointed to the position in 2006. Bernanke succeeded Alan Greenspan, who retired after serving as Fed chair for nearly two decades.

The Board of Governors establishes the rules and regulations that apply to all depository institutions. It sets the reserve requirements and regulates the composition of the asset holdings of depository institutions. The board is the rule maker, and often the umpire, of the banking industry.

THE FEDERAL RESERVE DISTRICT BANKS. There are twelve Federal Reserve District banks with twenty-five regional branches spread throughout the nation. **EXHIBIT 5** shows the regions covered by each of the twelve district banks. These district and regional banks operate under the supervision of the Board of Governors. Federal Reserve banks are bankers' banks; they provide banking services for commercial banks. Private citizens and corporations do not bank with the Fed.

The district banks are primarily responsible for the monitoring of the commercial banks in their region. They audit the books of depository institutions regularly to ensure their compliance with reserve requirements and other regulations of the Fed. The district banks also play an important role in the clearing of checks throughout the banking system. Most depository institutions, regardless of their Fed membership status, maintain

EXHIBIT 5
The Twelve Federal Reserve Districts

The map shows the twelve Federal Reserve districts and the city in which the district bank is located. These district banks monitor the commercial banks in their region and assist them with the clearing of checks. If you look at any dollar bill, it will identify the Federal Reserve district bank that initially issued the currency. The Board of Governors of the Fed is located in Washington, D.C.

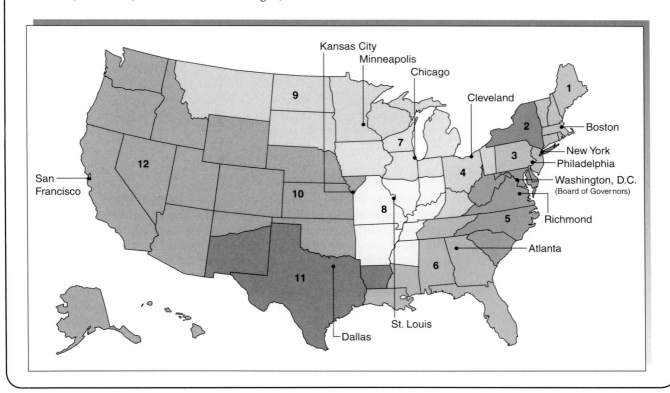

deposits with Federal Reserve Banks. As a result, the clearing of checks through the Federal Reserve System becomes merely an accounting transaction.

THE FEDERAL OPEN MARKET COMMITTEE. The **Federal Open Market Committee (FOMC)** is a powerful committee that determines the Fed's policy with respect to the purchase and sale of government bonds and other financial assets. As we shall soon see, this is the primary tool used by the Fed to control the money supply in the United States. The seven members of the Board of Governors, plus the twelve presidents of the Federal Reserve district banks, participate in the FOMC meetings, but at any point in time, only twelve of the nineteen members will get to vote. The twelve voting members of this important policy-making arm of the Fed are (1) the seven members of the Board of Governors, (2) the president of the New York district bank, and (3) four (of the remaining eleven) additional presidents of the Fed's district banks, who rotate as voting members. The FOMC meets every four to six weeks in the huge conference room of the Federal Reserve Building in Washington, D.C.

THE INDEPENDENCE OF THE FED. Like the Supreme Court, the structure of the Federal Reserve provides it with considerable independence from both Congress and the executive branch of government. Several factors contribute to this independence. The lengthy terms—fourteen years—protect the seven members of the Fed's Board of Governors from political pressures. Because their terms are staggered—a new governor is appointed only every two years—even two-term presidents are well into their second term before they are able to appoint a majority of the Fed's governing board. The Fed's earnings on its

Federal Open Market Committee (FOMC)

A committee of the Federal Reserve system that establishes Fed policy with regard to the buying and selling of government securities—the primary mechanism used to control the money supply. It is composed of the seven members of the Board of Governors and the twelve district bank presidents of the Fed.

financial assets, mostly government bonds, provide it with substantially more funding than is needed to cover its operating costs. Thus, it is not dependent upon Congress for funding allocations. The Fed does not even have to undergo audits from the General Accounting Office, a government agency that audits the books of most government operations. This independence of the Fed is designed to reduce the likelihood that political pressures will adversely affect its ability to follow a stable, noninflationary monetary policy.

Does the independence of a central bank affect policy? There is considerable variation in the independence of central banks. Like the Fed, the European Central bank and the central banks of Japan, England, and Canada also have considerable independence from the other branches of their governments. In other instances, however, central banks are directly beholden to political officials. The central banks of many Latin American countries fall into this category. Studies indicate that central banks that are strongly influenced by political considerations are more likely to follow inflationary policies. Politicians in countries with high budget deficits have often pressured their central banks to expand the money supply in order to finance government spending. When they do so, the result is rapid growth in the money supply and inflation.

How the Fed Controls the Money Supply

The Fed now has four major tools it can use to control the money supply: (1) the establishment of reserve requirements for banks, (2) buying and selling U.S. government securities and other financial assets in the open market, (3) the volume of loans extended to banks and other institutions, and (4) the interest rate it pays banks on funds held as reserves. We will analyze in detail how each of these tools can be used to regulate the amount of money in circulation.

RESERVE REQUIREMENTS. The Federal Reserve System requires banking institutions (including credit unions and savings and loan associations) to maintain reserves against the checking deposits of their customers. The reserves of banking institutions are composed of (1) currency held by the bank (vault cash) and (2) deposits of the bank with the Federal Reserve System. A bank can always obtain additional currency by drawing on its deposits with the Federal Reserve. So, both the bank's cash on hand and its deposits with the Fed can be used to meet the demands of depositors. Both therefore count as reserves.

EXHIBIT 6 indicates the required reserve ratio—the percentage of each deposit category that banks are required to keep in reserve (either as vault cash or deposits with the Fed). As of January 2009, the reserve requirement for checking accounts was set at 3 percent for amounts above $10.3 million up to $44.4 million and 10 percent for amounts in excess of $44.4 million. Currently, banks are not required to keep reserves against their savings and time deposits or against the first $10.3 million of their checking deposits.

EXHIBIT 6
The Required Reserve Ratio of Banking Institutions

Banking institutions are required to maintain 3 percent reserves against checking account deposits of over $10.3 million and up to $44.4 million and 10 percent reserves for transaction deposits over $44.4 million (in effect January 2009).

CHECKING ACCOUNTS[a]		
0–$10.3 MILLION	$10.3–$44.4 MILLION	>$44.4 MILLION
0%	3%	10%

[a]The dividing points are adjusted each year to reflect changes in total checking account deposits in all banking institutions.

Source: http://www.federalreserve.gov.

Why are commercial banks required to maintain assets in the form of reserves? One reason is to prevent imprudent bankers from overextending loans and thereby placing themselves in a poor position to deal with any sudden increase in withdrawals by depositors. The quantity of reserves needed to meet such emergencies is not left totally to the judgment of individual bankers. The Fed imposes the reserve level.

The Fed's control over reserve requirements, however, is important for another reason. By altering reserve requirements, the Fed can alter the funds banks have available to extend loans and undertake other investments. In turn, the volume of these loans and investments will alter the money supply.

If the Fed wanted to increase the supply of money, it would reduce the reserve requirements. The lower reserve requirements would increase the excess reserves of banks, placing them in a position to extend more loans and thereby increase the money supply. During normal times, the profit-seeking banks will use the newly created excess reserves to extend additional credit throughout the economy. As they do so, their actions will expand the money supply.

An increase in the reserve requirements will have the opposite effect. The higher reserve requirements increase the funds that banks must maintain in reserve against the checking deposits of their customers. In order to meet the higher reserve requirements, many banks will reduce their outstanding loans and investments. As the volume of loans (and other forms of credit) extended by banks declines, so, too, will the money supply. ***Thus, an increase in the reserve requirements will reduce the supply of money.***

Banks can maintain reserves in excess of the level required by the Fed. However, they are in business to make money, and it will generally be more profitable for them to hold interest-earning assets like loans and bonds rather than excess reserves. Prior to 2008, most banks shaved their excess reserves to low levels, and, as a result, the excess reserves for the banking system as a whole were minimal. This changed dramatically during the economic crisis of 2008–2009. We will consider this change in more detail as we proceed.

In recent years, the Fed has seldom used its regulatory power over reserve requirements to alter the supply of money. Why? Several factors combine to provide the explanation. First, changes in reserve requirements can be disruptive to banking operations. An increase in the required reserve ratio may force many banks to sell securities quickly or call in loans, even if there has been no change in the level of their deposits. Second, reserve requirement changes are a blunt instrument—small changes in reserve requirements can sometimes lead to large changes in the money supply. Moreover, the magnitude and timing of a change in the money supply resulting from a change in reserve requirements are difficult to predict with precision. For these reasons, the Fed has usually preferred to use other monetary tools.

OPEN MARKET OPERATIONS. The most common tool used by the Fed to alter the money supply is **open market operations**—the buying and selling of U.S. securities and other financial assets on the open market. As we indicated earlier, Fed policy in this area is conducted by the Federal Open Market Committee (FOMC). This committee meets every few weeks to map out the Fed's policy.

Open market operations
The buying and selling of U.S. government securities and other financial assets in the open market by the Federal Reserve.

For six decades following World War II, the Fed purchased and sold only U.S. government securities in its conduct of open market operations. However, since December 2007, the Fed has been buying and selling a broader range of financial assets, including corporate bonds, commercial paper, and mortgage-backed securities. If the Fed wants to expand the money supply, it simply purchases more of these financial assets. It pays for them merely by writing a check on itself. Unlike you and me, the Fed does not have to check to see if it has adequate funds in its account. ***When the Fed buys things, it injects "new money" into the economy in the form of additional currency in circulation and deposits with commercial banks. In essence, the Fed creates money out of nothing.***

Consider the following case. Suppose the Fed purchases $10,000 of U.S. securities from Maria Valdez. The Fed receives the securities, and Valdez receives a check for $10,000. If she merely cashes the check drawn on the Federal Reserve, the amount of currency in circulation would expand by $10,000, increasing the money supply by that amount. If, as is more likely to be the case, she deposits the funds in her checking account at the First National Bank, her checking account will increase by $10,000, and new excess reserves will be created. The First National Bank is required to increase its reserve holdings by only a fraction of Valdez's $10,000 deposit. Assuming that the bank is required to keep 10 percent in reserves, it can now extend new loans of up to $9,000 while maintaining its initial reserve position. As the money deposit multiplier indicates, the extension of the new loans will contribute to a further expansion in the money supply. Part of the new loans will eventually be deposited in other banks, and these banks will also be able to extend additional loans. As the process continues, the money supply expands by a multiple of the securities purchased by the Fed.

Open market operations can also be used to reduce the money supply. *If the Fed wants to reduce the money supply, it sells some of its current holdings of government securities or other assets.* When the Fed sells assets, a buyer like Maria Valdez will pay for them with a check drawn on a commercial bank. As the check clears, both the buyer's checking deposits and the reserves of the bank on which the check was written will decline. Thus, the action will reduce the money supply both directly (by reducing checking deposits) and indirectly (by reducing the quantity of reserves available to the banking system).

EXTENSION OF LOANS BY THE FED. When banking institutions borrow from the Federal Reserve, they must pay interest on the loans. Historically, member banks have borrowed from the Fed primarily to meet temporary shortages of reserves. The interest rate that banks pay on these short-term loans from the Federal Reserve is called the **discount rate**. These loans through the discount window are for brief time periods, a few days or weeks, in order to provide a bank a little time to adjust its loan and investment portfolios and bring its reserves in line with the requirements. Essentially, these discount rate loans are a temporary bridge extended to banks with a short-term liquidity problem, and typically they are repaid in a matter of days or a few months at the most. Other things being constant, an increase in the discount rate will reduce borrowing from the Fed and thereby exert a restrictive impact on the money supply. Conversely, a lower discount rate will make it cheaper for banks to borrow from the Fed and exert an expansionary impact on the supply of money.

The discount rate is closely related to the interest rate in the **federal funds market**. The federal funds market is a private loanable funds market in which banks with excess reserves extend short-term loans (sometimes for as little as a day) to other banks trying to meet their reserve requirements. The interest rate in the federal funds market fluctuates with the demand for loanable funds. In recent years, the Fed has linked the discount rate to the Federal funds rate, typically setting the discount interest rate a fraction of a percent higher than the Fed's target federal funds rate.

Announcements following the regular meetings of the Fed's Board of Governors often focus on the Fed's target for the federal funds rate. If the Fed wants to lower the federal funds interest rate, it will purchase government securities or other financial assets and thereby inject additional reserves into the banking system. This will expand the supply of money and reduce the federal funds rate. Conversely, if the Fed wants to increase the federal funds rate, it will sell some of its asset holdings and thereby drain reserves from the system. In turn, the reduction in the reserves will lower the money supply and place upward pressure on the federal funds rate.

Prior to 2008, the Fed extended only short-term discount rate loans, and they were extended only to member banks. As the Fed responded to the severe downturn of 2008, there was a dramatic change in its loan extension policy. The Fed established several new procedures for the extension of credit. The most important was the **Term Auction Facility (TAF)**. Under the TAF, depository institutions bid for credit provided from the Fed for an eighty-four-day period. The credit is granted to those willing to pay the highest interest rates, as long as the rate exceeds the minimum rate set by the Fed. Furthermore, in 2008 the Fed also began making loans to nonbank financial institutions such as insurance companies and brokerage firms, and these loans have often been for lengthy time periods like five to ten years. Like the discount rate loans, these new types of loans inject additional

Discount rate

The interest rate the Federal Reserve charges banking institutions for short-term loans.

Federal funds market

A loanable funds market in which banks seeking additional reserves borrow short-term funds (generally for seven days or less) from banks with excess reserves. The interest rate in this market is called the federal funds rate.

Term Auction Facility (TAF)

Newly established procedure used by the Fed to auction credit for an eighty-four-day period to depository institutions willing to bid the highest interest rates for the funds.

reserves into the banking system and thereby exert an expansionary impact on the money supply. Some economists worry that these special loans make the Fed vulnerable to political manipulation by large corporations, unions, and other well-organized groups seeking more attractive conditions than could be obtained from private sources.

INTEREST RATE THE FED PAYS BANKS ON RESERVES. Beginning in October 2008, the Fed began paying commercial banks interest on their reserves. As of January 2009, the Fed was paying commercial banks an interest rate equal to the target federal funds rate on both required and excess reserves. However, the Fed can set the interest rate on these reserves at whatever level it chooses. This provides it with another tool with which to conduct monetary policy.

If the Fed wants the banks to expand the money supply by extending more loans, it will set the interest rate paid on excess reserves at a very low level, possibly even zero. This will encourage banks to reduce their excess reserves, extend more loans, and thereby expand the supply of money. On the other hand, if the Fed wants to reduce the money supply, it can increase the interest rate paid on excess reserves and thereby provide commercial banks with a stronger incentive to hold excess reserves rather than extend more loans. This will reduce the money expansion multiplier and thereby reduce the money supply.

CONTROLLING THE MONEY SUPPLY—A SUMMARY. EXHIBIT 7 summarizes the monetary tools of the Federal Reserve. If the Fed wants to increase the money supply, it can decrease reserve requirements, purchase additional financial assets, extend additional loans, and/or lower the interest rate it pays banks on excess reserves. On the other hand, if the Fed wants to reduce the money supply, it can increase the reserve requirements, sell some of its asset holdings, extend fewer loans, and/or pay banks a higher interest rate on

EXHIBIT 7
Summary of Monetary Tools of the Federal Reserve

FEDERAL RESERVE POLICY	EXPANSIONARY MONETARY POLICY	RESTRICTIVE MONETARY POLICY
1. Reserve requirements	*Reduce reserve requirements* because this will create additional excess reserves and induce banks to extend more loans, which will expand the money supply.	*Raise reserve requirements because this* will reduce the excess reserves of banks and induce them to make fewer loans, which will contract the money supply.
2. Open market operations	*Purchase additional U.S. securities and other assets,* which will increase the money supply and also expand the reserves available to banks.	*Sell US. securities and other assets,* which will decrease the money supply and also contract the reserves available to banks.
3. Extension of loans	*Extend more loans* because this will increase bank reserves, encouraging banks to make more loans and expand the money supply.	*Extend fewer loans* because this will decrease bank reserves, discourage bank loans, and reduce the money supply.
4. Interest paid on excess bank reserves	*Reduce the interest paid on excess reserves* because this will induce banks to hold less reserves and extend more loans, which will expand the money supply.	*Increase the interest paid on excess reserves* because this will induce banks to hold more reserves and extend fewer loans, which will contract the money supply.

their excess reserves. Because the Fed typically seeks only small changes in the money stock (or its rate of increase), at any point in time, it typically uses only one of these tools, usually open market operations, to accomplish a desired objective.

Recent Fed Policy, the Monetary Base, and the Money Supply

Federal Reserve policy changed dramatically during the financial crisis of 2008. The Fed moved to both (1) assist troubled institutions the collapse of which might have endangered the stability of financial markets and (2) inject additional reserves into the banking system in order to combat the sharp economic downturn.

EXHIBIT 8 presents data from the Fed's balance sheet indicating its asset holdings at various times during 2006–2009. These figures illustrate several of the dramatic changes in recent Fed policy. First, note the huge increase in the Fed's holdings of securities and outstanding loans during the latter half of 2008. These holdings more than doubled during this six-month period. This sharp increase reflects the Fed's use of open market operations to shift toward a highly expansionary monetary policy. Second, note how the composition of the Fed's security holdings changed. At year-end 2006 and 2007, the overwhelming bulk of the Fed's assets were Treasury securities. During 2008, however, the Fed's holdings of Treasury securities fell from $754 billion to $476 billion, while its holdings of other securities (corporate bonds, mortgage-backed securities, and commercial paper issued by businesses) soared from $40 billion to $433 billion. Finally, note the huge increase in the volume of the Fed's outstanding loans, including those to nonbanking institutions such as brokerage firms and insurance companies. Fed loans to banks and other institutions soared from $25 billion in December 2007 to $197 billion in July 2008 and then skyrocketed to $1,045 billion in December 2008. By June 2009, the Fed's outstanding loans receded to $661 billion, but this figure was still more than 25 times the level of a year and a half earlier.

EXHIBIT 8
Federal Reserve Assets, 2006–2009

Various categories of assets held by the Federal Reserve during 2006–2009 are shown here. Note the vast increase in both the Fed's security holdings and extension of loans during the second half of 2008. Responding to the financial crisis, the Fed sharply increased its purchases of securities (other than U.S. Treasury bonds), such as mortgage-backed securities and commercial paper, and its loans, including those to nonbanking institutions such as brokerage firms and insurance companies.

Asset	December 2006	December 2007	July 2008	December 2008	June 2009
U.S. Treasury bonds	$779	$754	$479	$476	$629
Other securities	$33	$40	$110	$433	$652
Total security holdings	$812	$794	$589	$909	$1,281
Loans to banks	$0	$25	$167	$537	$372
Loans to other institutions	$0	$0	$30	$508	$289
Total outstanding loans	$0	$25	$197	$1,045	$661
Total other assets	$92	$108	$154	$345	$150
Total assets	$904	$926	$940	$2,299	$2,092

Note: Figures are in billions.

The Fed's huge increase in purchase of assets and extension of loans has dramatically increased the monetary base. The **monetary base** is equal to the currency in circulation plus the reserves of commercial banks (vault cash and reserve deposits with the Fed). The monetary base is important because it provides the foundation for the money supply. The currency in circulation contributes directly to the money supply, while the bank reserves provide the underpinnings for checking deposits.

Historically, as the Fed increased its assets, thereby injecting additional reserves into the economy and expanding the monetary base, the money supply increased by a multiple of the additional reserves just as the deposit expansion multiplier implies. Some of the additional reserves would flow into currency and some into bank reserves. Banks would use their additional reserves to extend loans and undertake investments, which, along with the currency expansion, would expand the money supply. Excess reserves would be shaved to near zero because neither vault cash nor deposits with the Fed earned interest. Under these conditions, the (1) monetary base and (2) currency plus required reserves were virtually equal, and they moved up in lockstep together.

EXHIBIT 9 illustrates this pattern during 1990–2009. Note how the monetary base and sum of currency plus required reserves were approximately equal and they gradually increased together year after year prior to the second half of 2008. Throughout this period, as the Fed injected additional reserves into the system and thereby expanded the monetary base, the M1 money supply increased by a similar proportion. As the available reserves expanded, banks used them to extend loans and undertake investments until the excess reserves were negligible.

But all of this changed dramatically during the second half of 2008 as the Fed increased its security holdings and outstanding loans. As Exhibit 9 shows, the monetary base (currency plus the bank reserves) jumped from $828 billion during the second quarter

Monetary base

The sum of currency in circulation plus bank reserves (vault cash and reserves with the Fed). It reflects the purchases of financial assets and extension of loans by the Fed.

EXHIBIT 9

The Monetary Base, the M1 Money Supply, and Excess Reserves, 1990–2009

The monetary base provides the foundation for the money supply. It reflects the Fed's purchase of financial assets and its extension of loans. Prior to mid-year 2008, the monetary base grew gradually year after year and excess reserves were negligible. Thus, the monetary base and the sum of currency plus required reserves were virtually equal. While the M1 money supply was substantially greater than the monetary base, the two expanded together. But, during the second half of 2008, the Fed injected a massive amount of reserves into the banking system and both the monetary base and excess reserves soared. If offsetting action is not taken, how will this dramatic increase in the monetary base affect the money supply in the future?

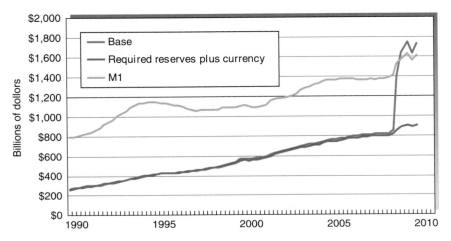

Source: http://www.economagic.com (All figures are in billions.)

of 2008 to $1.63 trillion during the first quarter of 2009. Thus, the monetary base virtually doubled in about six months.

How did this doubling of the monetary base affect the money supply? During the twelve months prior to May 2009, the M1 money supply increased 15 percent, while the M2 money supply grew by 10 percent during the same period. While these money growth rates are high, they are far less than the potential. The growth of the money supply has been substantially less rapid than the monetary base because the banks are holding vast excess reserves rather than using them to extend loans and undertake investments. As Exhibit 9 shows, the excess reserves of banks were $825 billion in the second quarter of 2009, far greater than ever before.

Why aren't the banks using the excess reserves to make loans and investments? Given the weak economy, the demand for loans, particularly low-risk loans, is weak. Further, the Fed has pushed short-term interest rates down to virtually zero. Therefore, the yields available on Treasury bills and other low-risk investments are extremely low.

As the economy begins to recover, however, the huge overhang of excess reserves means that the money supply could soar if banks use these reserves to extend loans and undertake investments. This would lead to inflation, and some fear that this will be the case. If this begins to happen, the Fed hopes to respond in a manner that will control the money supply growth and potential threat of inflation without throwing the economy back into recession. Will they be able to do so? We will analyze this complex question in the next chapter.

The Fed and the Treasury

Many students tend to confuse the Federal Reserve with the U.S. Treasury, probably because both sound like monetary agencies. However, the Treasury is a budgetary agency. If there is a budgetary deficit, the Treasury will issue U.S. securities as a method of financing the deficit. Newly issued U.S. securities are almost always sold to domestic or foreign investors (or government trust funds). Bonds issued by the Treasury to finance a budget deficit are seldom purchased directly by the Federal Reserve. In any case, the Treasury is primarily interested in obtaining funds so that it can pay Uncle Sam's bills. Except for nominal amounts, mostly coins, the Treasury does not issue money. Borrowing—the public sale of new U.S. securities—is the primary method used by the Treasury to cover any excess of expenditures in relation to revenues from taxes and other sources.

Whereas the Treasury is concerned with how the federal government will pay its bills, the Fed is concerned primarily with the availability of money and credit for the entire economy. The Fed does not issue U.S. securities. It merely purchases and sells government securities issued by the Treasury as a means of controlling the economy's money supply. Unlike the Treasury, the Fed can purchase government bonds by writing a check on itself without having deposits, gold, or anything else to back it up. In doing so, the Fed creates money out of thin air. The Treasury does not have this power. The Fed does not have an obligation to meet the financial responsibilities of the U.S. government. That is the domain of the Treasury. Although the two agencies cooperate with each other, they are distinctly different institutions established for different purposes (see the accompanying **Thumbnail Sketch**).

It is important to recognize that the buying and selling of bonds by the Treasury and by the Fed have different effects on the supply of money. The key point here is that the Treasury and the Fed handle revenues collected from the selling of bonds in different ways. When the Treasury issues and sells bonds, it does so in order to generate additional funds to cover its spending. The people who buy the bonds from the Treasury have less money, but when the Treasury spends, the recipients of its spending will have more money. Thus, Treasury borrowing and spending do not change the supply of money.

In contrast, when the Fed sells bonds, in effect, it takes the revenues and holds them, keeping them out of circulation. Because this money is out of circulation and can no longer be used for the purchase of goods and services, the money supply shrinks. However, if the Fed later wishes to increase the money supply, it can buy bonds, which will increase the availability of bank reserves and the money supply.

THUMBNAIL SKETCH

What are the differences between the U.S. Treasury and the Federal Reserve banking system?

The U.S. Treasury

1. Is concerned with the finances of the federal government
2. Issues bonds to the general public to finance the budget deficits of the federal government

3. Does not determine the money supply

The Federal Reserve

1. Is concerned with the monetary climate of the economy
2. Does not issue bonds
3. Controls the money supply and often uses the buying and selling of bonds issued by the U.S. Treasury to do so

Ambiguities in the Meaning and Measurement of the Money Supply

In the past, economists have generally used the *growth rate* of the money supply (either M1 or M2) to gauge the direction of monetary policy. A rapid growth rate of the money supply was indicative of expansionary monetary policy—a policy that was adding stimulus to the economy. Conversely, slow growth, or a decline, in the money stock implied a more restrictive monetary policy. However, financial innovations have altered our methods of payment and the nature of money many times. Sometimes these innovations affect the significance of the growth rate figures for the various measures of the money supply. Consider the changes during the last several decades.

Throughout most of the 1970s, M1 consisted almost entirely of currency and demand deposits. At the time, regulations virtually prohibited banks from offering their customers interest-earning checking accounts. Increased competition from mutual funds led to the repeal of the regulatory restraints in 1980, and, as **EXHIBIT 10** illustrates, this repeal was followed by rapid growth of interest-earning checking deposits. In turn, the growth of these deposits pushed up the growth rate of the M1 money supply. The growth of M1 during the 1980s, however, was deceptive. To a degree, it reflected a change in the nature of the M1 money supply. Interest-earning checking accounts are less costly to hold than currency and demand deposits. In essence, interest-earning checking accounts are partly medium-of-exchange money and partly savings. As a result, the M1 money supply of the 1980s is not precisely comparable with the figures for earlier years.

Another innovation influenced the M1 money supply in the 1990s. Beginning in 1994, a number of banks began to encourage customers to move deposits from interest-earning checking accounts into money market deposit accounts. Each of these accounts provides customers with similar services. However, because interest-earning checking deposits are included in M1 but money market deposits are not, this shift reduced the size of the M1 money supply figures. It was largely responsible for the decline in the M1 money supply during the period 1995–1997 (see Exhibit 10). As with the introduction of interest-earning checking during the 1980s, these shifts distorted the M1 money supply statistics and reduced their comparability across time periods.

Structural changes and financial innovations continue to alter the nature of money and therefore the usefulness of money growth figures (both M1 and M2) as an indicators of monetary policy. Let's consider three additional factors that are continuing to influence the nature and meaning of the money supply figures.

1. WIDESPREAD USE OF THE U.S. DOLLAR OUTSIDE OF THE UNITED STATES. The U.S. dollar is widely used in other countries. To a degree, this has been true for a long time. However, in recent years, many countries have relaxed legal restraints that limited the domestic use of foreign currencies (and the maintenance of foreign currency bank

EXHIBIT 10

Innovations, Changes in the Nature of Money, and Growth of the M1 Money
Supply, 1970–2009

*The M1 money supply is shown here. Innovations have affected the figures. The introduction of interest-earning
checking accounts in the early 1980s caused M1 to grow rapidly. In contrast, a shift of funds from interest-
earning checking accounts to money market mutual funds caused M1 to fall during 1995–1997 because the
former are included in M1 but the latter are not. Because of innovations like these, economists now place less
emphasis on money growth figures as an indicator of monetary policy.*

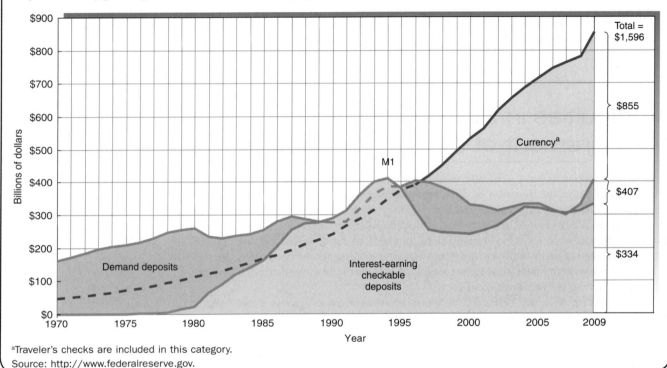

^aTraveler's checks are included in this category.
Source: http://www.federalreserve.gov.

accounts).[2] As noted earlier, the currency component of the M1 money supply was $855
billion in May 2009. According to a recent study by the Federal Reserve, more than one-
half and perhaps as much as two-thirds of this currency is held overseas. The movement
of these funds abroad (and our inability to measure them with any degree of precision)
substantially reduces the reliability of the M1 money supply figures. (*Note:* There is also
some impact on M2. However, because the currency component is a much smaller proportion of M2 than M1, the distortion of M2 is less severe.)

**2. THE INCREASING AVAILABILITY OF LOW-FEE STOCK AND BOND MUTUAL
FUNDS.** Until recently, financial investors were generally required to pay a substantial
start-up, or "load," fee when purchasing stock and bond mutual funds. This reduced their
attractiveness relative to the various savings instruments included in the M2 money supply. No-load stock and bond mutual funds—that is, funds without an initial fee—are now
increasingly available. Because stock and bond mutual fund investments are not counted in
any of the monetary aggregates, movement of funds from various M2 components (money
market mutual funds, for example) will distort the M2 money supply figures.[3]

[2]The number of countries in which it is legal for citizens to maintain a foreign currency bank account rose from thirty-eight in 1985
to seventy-nine in 2007. See James Gwartney and Robert Lawson, *Economic Freedom of the World: 2009 Annual Report* (Vancouver,
British Columbia: Fraser Institute, 2009).
[3]For additional information on this topic, see Sean Collins and Cheryl L. Edwards, "Redefining M2 to Include Bond and Equity
Mutual Funds," Federal Reserve Bank of St. Louis *Review* (November/December 1994): 7–30; and John V. Duca, "Should Bond
Funds Be Included in M2?" *Journal of Banking and Finance* 19 (April 1995): 131–52.

3. SUBSTITUTION OF ELECTRONIC PAYMENTS FOR CHECKS AND CASH.   Increasingly, money is becoming electronic. More and more consumer purchases are being handled with debit cards, credit cards, and electronic transfers rather than by check or cash. Many people have their "pay check" deposited directly into their bank account and make regular payments like those for utilities, mortgage and auto loans, and investment accounts with automatic transfers. With the touch of a few computer keys, you can also shop on the Internet and use your deposits to pay for magazines, financial advice, and numerous consumer goods. Currently, less than half of consumer purchases are paid for with either check or cash, compared to 80 percent just a decade ago. These changes in payment methods make it possible for both individuals and businesses to hold smaller money balances (cash and checking deposits) than would otherwise be the case. They also reduce the comparability across time periods of the money supply data, particularly the M1 figures.

Because of these dynamic changes in the nature of money, economists now place less emphasis on the growth rate of the money supply figures as a monetary policy indicator. Most now rely on a combination of factors to evaluate the direction and appropriateness of monetary policy. We will follow this procedure as we consider the impact of monetary policy in subsequent chapters.

Looking ahead

In this chapter, we focused on the banking industry and the mechanics of monetary policy. The following chapter will analyze how monetary policy affects output, growth, and the general level of prices.

KEY POINTS

▼ Money is a financial asset that is widely accepted as a medium of exchange. It is a means of storing purchasing power for the future and is used as a unit of account. Without money, exchange would be both costly and tedious. Money derives its value from its scarcity (supply) relative to its usefulness (demand).

▼ There are two primary measures of the money supply. The narrowest definition of money supply (M1) includes only (1) currency in the hands of the public, (2) checkable deposits (both demand and interest-earning) held in depository institutions, and (3) traveler's checks. The broader M2 money supply includes M1 plus (1) savings deposits, (2) time deposits (of less than $100,000), and (3) money market mutual fund shares.

▼ Banking is a business. Banks provide their depositors with the safekeeping of money, check-clearing services on demand deposits, and interest payments on time (and some checking) deposits. Banks get most of their income by extending loans and investing in interest-earning securities.

▼ Savings and loan associations and credit unions provide the same services and confront similar regulations as commercial banks. All of these institutions are part of an integrated banking system.

▼ Under a fractional reserve banking system, banks are required to maintain only a fraction of their deposits in the form of reserves (vault cash or deposits with the Fed). Excess reserves may be invested or loaned to customers. When banks extend loans, they create additional deposits and thereby expand the money supply.

▼ The Federal Reserve System is a central banking authority designed to provide a stable monetary framework for the entire economy. The Fed is a banker's bank. The structure of the Fed is designed to insulate it from political pressures so that it will have greater freedom to follow policies more consistent with economic stability.

▼ The Fed has four major tools with which to control the money supply: (1) the establishment of reserve requirements, (2) open market operations, (3) the extension of loans, and (4) setting the interest rate paid to banks on their reserves. If the Fed wanted to increase the money supply, it could decrease the reserves banks are required to hold, buy government bonds and other financial assets in the open market, extend more loans, or reduce the interest rate it pays banks on their excess reserves. Open market operations—the buying or selling of bonds and other assets—have been the primary tool used by the Fed to alter the money supply.

▼ The monetary base provides the foundation for the money supply. The Fed alters the monetary base through its purchases of assets and extension of loans. The monetary base increased sharply—it approximately doubled—during the second half of 2008, as the Fed shifted to a highly expansionary monetary policy to combat the severe downturn.

▼ The Federal Reserve and the U.S. Treasury are distinct agencies. The Fed is concerned primarily with the money supply and the establishment of a stable monetary climate, whereas the Treasury focuses on budgetary matters—tax revenues, government expenditures, and the financing of government debt.

▼ Historically, the rate of change of the money supply has been used to judge the direction and intensity of monetary policy. However, recent financial innovations and other structural changes (for example, the widespread use of U.S. currency in other countries) have blurred the meaning of money and reduced the reliability of the money growth figures as a monetary policy indicator. In the computer age, continued change in this area is likely.

CRITICAL ANALYSIS QUESTIONS

*1. What is meant by the statement, "This asset is illiquid"? List some things you own and rank them from most liquid to most illiquid.

2. What determines whether a financial asset is included in the M1 money supply? Why are interest-earning checkable deposits included in M1, whereas interest-earning savings accounts and Treasury bills are not?

*3. What makes money valuable? Does money perform an economic service? Explain. Could money perform its function better if there were twice as much of it? Why or why not?

4. "People are poor because they don't have very much money. Yet, central bankers keep money scarce. If people had more money, poverty could be eliminated." Evaluate this view. Do you think it reflects sound economics?

5. Why can banks continue to hold reserves that are only a fraction of the demand and saving deposits of their customers? Is your money safe in a bank? Why or why not?

*6. Suppose you withdraw $100 from your checking account. How does this transaction affect (a) the supply of money, (b) the reserves of your bank, and (c) the excess reserves of your bank?

7. The excess reserves of the banking system were quite large during mid-year 2009. If the banks use these excess reserves to extend additional loans, what will happen to the money supply? Explain. Is this a potential problem? Why or why not?

*8. How will the following actions affect the money supply?
   a. a reduction in the discount rate
   b. an increase in the reserve requirements
   c. purchase by the Fed of $100 million in U.S. securities from a commercial bank
   d. sale by the U.S. Treasury of $100 million in newly issued bonds to a commercial bank
   e. an increase in the discount rate
   f. sale by the Fed of $200 million in U.S. securities to a private investor

9. What's wrong with this way of thinking? "When the government runs a budget deficit, it simply pays its bills by printing more money. As the newly printed money works its way through the economy, it waters down the value of paper money already in circulation. Thus, it takes more money to buy things. Budget deficits are the major cause of inflation."

*10. If the Federal Reserve does not take any offsetting action, what would happen to the supply of money if the general public decided to increase its holdings of currency and decrease its checking deposits by an equal amount?

11. What is the federal funds interest rate? If the Fed wants to use open market operations to lower the federal funds rate, what action should it take? Explain.

*12. If the Fed wants to expand the money supply, why is it more likely to do so by purchasing bonds and other financial assets rather than by lowering reserve requirements?

*13. Are the following statements true or false?
   a. "You can never have too much money."
   b. "When you deposit currency in a commercial bank, cash goes out of circulation and the money supply declines."
   c. "If the Fed would create more money, Americans would achieve a higher standard of living."

14. Why is the actual money deposit multiplier generally less than the potential multiplier?

15. How would the following influence the growth rates of the M1 and M2 money supply figures over time?
   a. an increase in the quantity of U.S. currency held overseas
   b. a shift of funds from interest-earning checking deposits to money market mutual funds
   c. a reduction in the holdings of currency by the general public because debit cards have become more popular and widely accepted
   d. the shift of funds from money market mutual funds into stock and bond mutual funds because the fees to invest in the latter have declined

*16. Suppose that the Federal Reserve purchases a bond for $100,000 from Donald Truck, who deposits the proceeds in the Manufacturer's National Bank.
   a. What will be the impact of this transaction on the supply of money?
   b. If the reserve requirement ratio is 20 percent, what is the maximum amount of additional loans that the Manufacturer's Bank will be able to extend as the result of Truck's deposit?
   c. Given the 20 percent reserve requirement, what is the maximum increase in the quantity of

checkable deposits that could result throughout the entire banking system because of the Fed's action?
   d. Would you expect this to happen? Why or why not? Explain.

17. Suppose that the reserve requirement is 10 percent and the balance sheet of the People's National Bank looks like the accompanying example.
   a. What are the required reserves of People's National Bank? Does the bank have any excess reserves?
   b. What is the maximum loan that the bank could extend?
   c. Indicate how the bank's balance sheet would be altered if it extended this loan.
   d. Suppose that the required reserves were 20 percent. If this were the case, would the bank be in a position to extend any additional loans? Explain.

ASSETS		LIABILITIES	
Vault cash	$ 20,000	Checking deposits	$200,000
Deposits at Fed	30,000	Net worth	15,000
Securities	45,000		
Loans	120,000		

*18. Suppose that the reserve requirements are 10 percent and that the Federal Reserve purchases $2 billion in securities on a given day.
   a. How will this transaction affect the M1 money supply?
   b. If the brokerage firm that sold the bonds to the Fed deposits the proceeds of the sale into its account with Nation's Bank, what is the maximum amount of additional loans that Nation's Bank will be able to extend as a result of this deposit?
   c. If additional loans are extended throughout the banking system and the proceeds are always redeposited back into a checking account, by how much will the M1 money supply increase if banks use all their additional reserves to extend new loans?

*Asterisk denotes questions for which answers are given in Appendix B.

Modern Macroeconomics and Monetary Policy

CHAPTER FOCUS

- How does monetary policy affect interest rates, output, and employment?

- Can monetary policy stimulate real GDP in the short run? Can it do so in the long run?

- How does monetary policy affect economic stability? How does it affect inflation?

- Did monetary policy cause the Crisis of 2008? How will current monetary policy affect future economic conditions?

The conventional wisdom once held that money doesn't matter. Now there is wide agreement that monetary policy can significantly affect real economic activity in the short run, though only price level in the long run.

—*Daniel L. Thornton and David C. Wheelock[1]*

[1]Daniel L. Thornton and David C. Wheelock, "Editor's Introduction," *Federal Reserve Bank of St. Louis: Review* (May/June 1995): vii.

n the preceding chapter, we noted that many consider the chair of the Federal Reserve System to be the second most important person—next to the president—in the United States. Why is this so? Along with other members of the Fed's Board of Governors and Federal Open Market Committee, the Fed chairman is in charge of monetary policy. When monetary policy keeps prices stable—that is, when it keeps the inflation rate at a persistently low level—markets operate more smoothly. Conversely, the consequences of monetary instability and high rates of inflation are often disastrous. This makes the conduct of monetary policy extremely important.

Until now, within the framework of the aggregate demand–aggregate supply model, we assumed that the supply of money was constant. We now relax this assumption. The previous chapter outlined the tools the Fed has to alter the supply of money. This chapter focuses on how monetary policy works—how changes in the supply of money affect interest rates, output, and prices. ■

The Impact of Monetary Policy on Output and Inflation

Like the modern view of fiscal policy, the modern view of monetary policy has evolved over the years. In the aftermath of the Great Depression and Keynesian revolution, there was great debate about the importance of monetary policy. During the 1950s and 1960s, many economists argued that monetary policy could be used to control inflation but that it was often ineffective as a means of stimulating aggregate demand. It was popular to draw an analogy between monetary policy and the workings of a string. Like a string, monetary policy could be used to "pull" (hold back) price increases and thereby control inflation. However, just as one cannot "push" with a string, many leading economists did not believe that monetary policy could be used to push (stimulate) aggregate demand.

Beginning in the late 1950s, this view was hotly contested by Nobel laureate Milton Friedman and other economists, who later became known as **monetarists**. The monetarists argued that changes in the money supply had a powerful influence on the economy's output in the short run, but in the long run, monetary policy affected only the general level of prices. Furthermore, monetarists argued that erratic monetary policy was the primary *source* of both economic instability and inflation. Milton Friedman summarized the monetarists' position in his 1967 presidential address to the American Economic Association when he stated:

> "Every major contraction in this country has been either produced by monetary disorder or greatly exacerbated by monetary disorder. Every major inflation episode has been produced by monetary expansion."[2]

A modern view of monetary policy emerged from this debate. While minor disagreements remain, most economists now agree that monetary policy exerts an impact on output, employment, inflation, and economic stability.[3] We now turn to the presentation of this modern consensus view.

Monetarists

A group of economists who believe that (1) monetary instability is the major cause of fluctuations in real GDP and (2) rapid growth of the money supply is the major cause of inflation.

---

[2]Milton Friedman, "The Role of Monetary Policy," *American Economic Review* (March 1968): 12.
[3]The evolution of the views of Paul Samuelson, who might properly be regarded as the father of American Keynesian economics, illustrates the change in the Keynesian view with regard to the relative importance of monetary and fiscal policy. Commenting on the twelfth edition of his classic text in 1985, Samuelson stated: "In the early editions of the book, fiscal policy was top banana. In later editions that emphasis changed to equality. In this edition we've taken a stand that monetary policy is most important."

The Demand and Supply of Money

Why do individuals and businesses want to hold cash and checking-account money rather than bonds, stocks, automobiles, buildings, and consumer durables? As you think about this question, don't confuse (1) the desire to hold money balances with (2) the desire for more wealth (or income). Of course, all of us would like to have more wealth, but we may be perfectly satisfied with our holdings of money in relation to our holdings of other goods, *given our current level of wealth*. When we say people want to hold more (or less) money, we mean that they want to restructure their wealth toward larger (smaller) money balances.

People hold money for several reasons. At the most basic level, we hold money so that we can buy things. Households hold money balances so that they can pay for the weekly groceries, the monthly house payment, gasoline for the car, lunch for the kids, and other items purchased regularly. Businesses demand money so they can pay their workers, buy supplies, and conduct other transactions. People also hold money for unexpected expenses like an accident or a medical emergency. Economists call this the *precautionary motive* for holding money. In addition, money is an asset—a means of storing value. Holding money is a convenient way to set aside purchasing power for future use.

Higher interest rates make it more costly to hold money, however. Consider the cost of holding $1,000 in currency and demand deposits (which do not earn interest) rather than in interest-earning bonds, for example. If the interest rate is 10 percent, it will cost you $100 per year to hold an additional $1,000 of non-interest-earning money. In contrast, if the interest rate is 1 percent, the annual cost of holding the $1,000 money balance will be only $10. Even if you put the $1,000 in an interest-earning checking account, you could probably earn more interest if you purchased a U.S. Treasury Security or some other less liquid form of savings with the funds. Thus, the opportunity cost of holding money is directly related to the nominal interest rate.

A curve that outlines the relationship between the interest rate (measured on the *y*-axis) and the quantity of money (measured on the *x*-axis) is called the **demand for money**. As part (a) of **EXHIBIT 1** shows, there is an inverse relationship between the interest rate

Demand for money

A curve that indicates the relationship between the interest rate and the quantity of money people want to hold. Because higher interest rates increase the opportunity cost of holding money, the quantity of money demanded will be inversely related to the interest rate.

OUTSTANDING ECONOMIST

Milton Friedman (1912–2006)

Milton Friedman, the 1976 recipient of the Nobel Prize, is widely regarded as the most influential spokesman for a free market economy in the twentieth century. More than anyone else, Friedman developed the modern view of monetary policy. At a time when the role of money was largely ignored by the dominant Keynesian perspective, Friedman almost single-handedly convinced the economics profession that monetary policy exerted a strong impact on the economy. His *Monetary History of the United States* (1963) with Anna Schwartz presented powerful evidence that monetary policy not only mattered but it was also the major source of economic instability. The chapter on the Great Contraction illustrated that the Great Depression was primarily, if not exclusively, the result of a perverse monetary policy rather than a defect of market economies. Even his critics eventually concluded that, by and large, his views about the importance of monetary policy were correct.

Friedman's popular books *Capitalism and Freedom* (1962) and *Free to Choose* (1980), coauthored with his wife, Rose, are classic treatises in support of economic freedom. He had an uncanny ability to connect with both the general public and the brightest in his field. After retiring from the University of Chicago, he went on to spend nearly three decades on the faculty of Stanford University. Most people would rate Friedman and John Maynard Keynes as the most influential economists of the twentieth century.

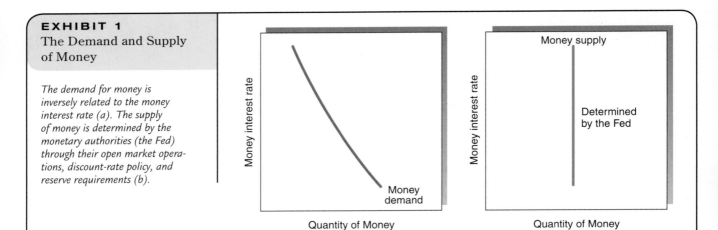

EXHIBIT 1
The Demand and Supply of Money

The demand for money is inversely related to the money interest rate (a). The supply of money is determined by the monetary authorities (the Fed) through their open market operations, discount-rate policy, and reserve requirements (b).

and the quantity of money demanded. This inverse relationship reflects the fact that higher interest rates make it more costly to hold money instead of interest-earning assets like savings deposits and Treasury Securities. Therefore, as interest rates rise, individuals and businesses will try to manage their affairs with smaller money balances.

The demand for money balances will generally increase with the nominal value of transactions. If wages and prices increase, people will need more money in their wallets (or checking accounts) to make their regular daily, weekly, and monthly purchases. Businesses will also require more money to pay their bills. Similarly, if prices remain constant but the quantity of goods bought and sold in the economy increases, larger money balances will be needed to conduct those transactions. In other words, as nominal GDP increases, as the result of *either* higher prices or the growth of real output, the demand for money balances will also increase. When this happens, the entire demand curve for money will shift to the right. Conversely, a decline in nominal GDP will decrease the demand for money, shifting the curve to the left.

Changes in institutional factors can also affect the demand for money. For example, the greater availability and widespread use of credit cards in recent years has made it easier for households to manage their affairs with less money. The increased availability of short-term loans has had a similar effect. Both of these factors have gradually reduced the demand for money (shifting the entire curve to the left).

As we discussed in the previous chapter, monetary policy is conducted by the monetary authorities—the Federal Reserve in the case of the United States. The Fed can use reserve requirements, the extension of loans, and especially open market operations to regulate the supply of money. Changes in the interest rate do not alter the Fed's ability to determine the supply of money. Therefore, as Exhibit 1 (part b) shows, the money supply schedule is vertical. The vertical supply curve reflects that the quantity of money is determined by Fed policy, and the Fed's ability to set the money supply is unaffected by the interest rate.

The Equilibrium between Money Demand and Money Supply

EXHIBIT 2 brings money demand and money supply together and shows how they determine the equilibrium rate of interest. The money interest rate will move toward i_e when the quantity of money demanded by households and businesses is just equal to the quantity supplied by the Fed. At the equilibrium interest rate, people are willing to hold the stock of money the Fed has supplied to the economy.

At an above-equilibrium interest rate, i_2, for example, people will not want to hold as much money as the Fed has supplied. Accordingly, they will try to reduce their money balances. A number of people (and businesses) will do so by using some of their

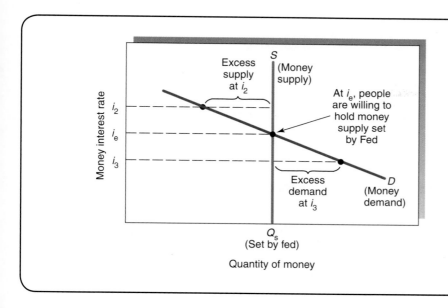

EXHIBIT 2
Money Supply,
Money Demand, and
Equilibrium

The money interest rate will tend to gravitate toward equilibrium, i_e, where the quantity of money demanded by households and businesses will equal the quantity of money supplied by the Fed.

money balances to buy bonds. This increase in the demand for bonds will drive bond prices up and interest rates down. (*Remember:* Higher bond prices imply lower interest rates.) As a result, the money interest rate will move toward the i_e equilibrium. In contrast, at a below-equilibrium money interest rate, i_3, for example, an excess demand for money will be present. People would like to hold a larger quantity of money than the Fed has supplied. In this case, people will sell some of the bonds they own to get more money. In turn, the sale of their bonds will reduce bond prices and put upward pressure on interest rates. This will cause the interest rate to once again move toward i_e.

How Does Monetary Policy Affect the Economy?

How will a change in the money supply affect the economy? As we previously discussed, the Fed typically uses open market operations to control the supply of money. If the Fed wants to shift to a more **expansionary monetary policy**, it will generally buy bonds issued by the U.S. Treasury or a financial institution. The Fed will pay for the bonds by writing a check on itself, thereby creating money out of thin air; and as the check clears, it will also make additional reserves available to the banks.

EXHIBIT 3 shows the impact on the economy. Let's first consider the situation in which the money interest rate (i_1 in the money balances market) is equal to the real interest rate (r_1 in the loanable funds market). This indicates that the expected rate of inflation is zero. When the Fed purchases bonds in order to increase the money supply (shifting S_1 to S_2 in part a), it bids up bond prices and injects additional reserves into the banking system. Profit-seeking banks will generally use the additional reserves to extend more loans and increase their investments. This combination of factors—higher bond prices and excess reserves—will increase the supply of loanable funds (shift from S_1 to S_2 in part b). In the short run, this will cause the real interest rate to fall to r_2.

How will the Fed's bond purchases, the creation of additional bank reserves, and a lower real interest rate influence the demand for goods and services? As part (c) of Exhibit 3 shows, aggregate demand will increase (shift from AD_1 to AD_2). Economists stress the importance of three factors that contribute to this increase in aggregate demand.

1. THE LOWER REAL INTEREST RATE WILL MAKE CURRENT INVESTMENT AND CONSUMPTION CHEAPER. At the lower interest rate, entrepreneurs will undertake some investment projects they otherwise wouldn't have. Spending by firms on structures and equipment will increase. Likewise, consumers will decide to expand their purchases of automobiles and consumer durables, which can now be bought with smaller monthly payments.

Expansionary monetary policy

A shift in monetary policy designed to stimulate aggregate demand. Injection of additional bank reserves, lower short-term interest rates, and an acceleration in the growth rate of the money supply are indicators of a more expansionary monetary policy.

EXHIBIT 3
The Transmission of Monetary Policy

When the Fed shifts to a more expansionary monetary policy, it will generally buy additional bonds. This will supply the banking system with additional reserves. Both the Fed's bond purchases and the banks' use of the additional reserves to extend new loans will increase the supply of loanable funds (shift it from S_1 to S_2, part b) and put downward pressure on the real rate of interest. As the real interest rate falls (to r_2), aggregate demand increases (to AD_2 in part c). Because the effects of the monetary expansion were unanticipated, the expansion in AD leads to both an increase in current output (to Y_2) and higher prices (inflation) in the short run. The increase in output, however, will only be temporary.

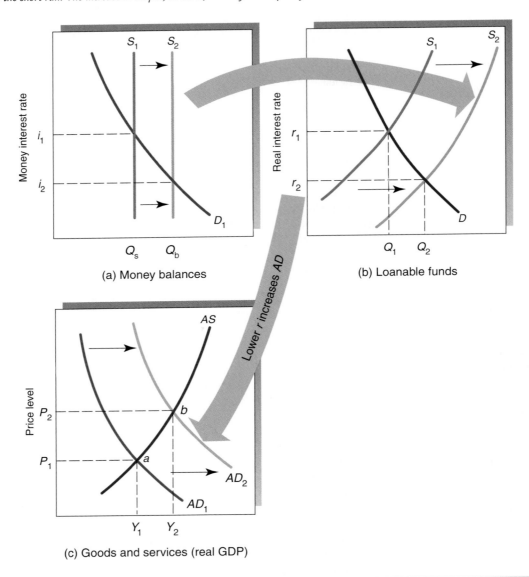

(a) Money balances

(b) Loanable funds

(c) Goods and services (real GDP)

2. THE LOWER INTEREST RATE WILL TEND TO CAUSE FINANCIAL CAPITAL TO MOVE ABROAD, THE FOREIGN EXCHANGE RATE OF THE DOLLAR TO DEPRECIATE, AND NET EXPORTS TO EXPAND. Here's how: As domestic interest rates fall, both domestic and foreign investors will shift some of their financial investments to countries where interest rates are higher and they can get better returns on their investments. As investors shift funds abroad, they will supply dollars and demand foreign currency to purchase the new foreign assets. This will cause the dollar to depreciate in the foreign exchange market. In turn, the depreciation in the exchange-rate value of the dollar will make imports more expensive for Americans and U.S. exports cheaper for foreigners. As a result, U.S. imports will decline and exports will expand. This increase in net exports will also stimulate the nation's aggregate demand as foreigners buy more U.S. goods and services.

3. THE LOWER INTEREST RATE WILL TEND TO INCREASE ASSET PRICES—FOR EXAMPLE, THE PRICES OF STOCKS, HOUSES, AND OTHER STRUCTURES PEOPLE OWN—WHICH WILL ALSO INCREASE AGGREGATE DEMAND. Here's how this works: As the prices of real and financial assets rise because they are now relatively more attractive investments, household wealth will increase. Because people are wealthier, they will, in turn, increase their consumption spending. Further, the higher prices of houses and other physical assets will make their production more profitable and motivate entrepreneurs to expand their investment spending on them. This additional investment by entrepreneurs will also increase aggregate demand.

The **Thumbnail Sketch** on this page outlines the complex sequence of events through which Fed bond purchases expand the money supply and increase aggregate demand. This sequence is sometimes referred to as the interest rate transmission mechanism of monetary policy.[4]

The Effects of an Unanticipated Expansionary Monetary Policy

As we have previously discussed, modern macroeconomic analysis emphasizes whether a change is anticipated or unanticipated. If people do not anticipate the increase in aggregate demand accompanying an expansionary monetary policy, the prices of products will rise more quickly than the costs of producing them in the short run. As a result, the profit margins of businesses will improve, and they will respond by expanding their output (as the increase in real output from Y_1 to Y_2 in part c of Exhibit 3 shows).

THUMBNAIL SKETCH

The Transmission of Monetary Policy—A Summary

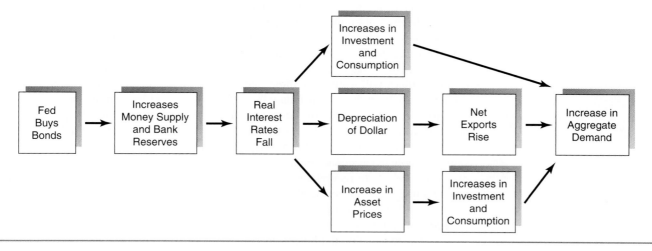

---

[4]There is also a more direct route through which expansionary monetary policy may stimulate aggregate demand. When the Fed expands the supply of money, it will create an "excess supply of money" *at the initial money interest rate.* People may respond by directly increasing their purchases of goods and services in an effort to reduce their money balances to desired levels. Obviously, this will increase aggregate demand. This direct path is most relevant when the government expands the supply of money by paying its bills with newly created currency. Because the money supply of the United States is generally expanded via open market operations and control of short-term interest rates, we have focused on the transmission of monetary policy through the interest rate. The implications of both the direct and indirect paths are identical—both indicate that expansionary monetary policy will stimulate aggregate demand.

EXHIBIT 4
The Effects of Expansionary Monetary Policy

If the impact of an increase in aggregate demand accompanying an expansionary monetary policy is felt when the economy is operating below capacity, the policy will help direct the economy to a long-run full-employment equilibrium (E_2 in Part a). In this case, the increase in output from Y_1 to Y_F will be long term. In contrast, if the stimulus on aggregate demand is imposed on an economy already at full employment (Part b), it will lead to excess demand and higher product prices. Output will temporarily increase (to Y_2). However, in the long run, the strong demand will push up resource prices, shifting short-run aggregate supply to $SRAS_2$. The price level will rise to P_3, and output will recede (to Y_F) from its temporary high.

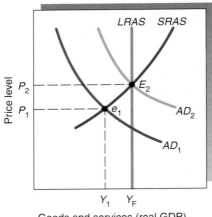

(a) Output is initially at less than full employment

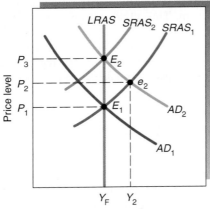

(b) Output is initially at full employment

Thus, an unexpected increase in the supply of money will reduce the real rate of interest, thereby triggering an increase in the demand for goods and services. In turn, the increase in aggregate demand will expand real output and employment in the short run.

EXHIBIT 4 (part a) shows the potential of expansionary monetary policy to direct a recessionary economy to full employment. Consider an economy initially at output Y_1, which is below full-employment capacity (Y_F). Expansionary monetary policy will lower interest rates and increase aggregate demand (to AD_2). Real output will then expand (to Y_F). In essence, the expansionary monetary policy provides an alternative to the economy's self-corrective mechanism. If demand is unchanged, reductions in real interest rates and resource prices will eventually direct the economy back to full employment, but many economists believe that expansionary monetary policy can speed up this process.

How will an expansion of the money supply by the Fed influence the price level and output if the economy is already at full employment? Although this is not a desirable strategy, it is interesting to analyze the outcome. As part (b) of Exhibit 4 shows, an unanticipated shift to a more expansionary monetary policy will increase aggregate demand, causing the prices of products to rise relative to the costs of making them. Keep in mind that important production components, like labor, are sometimes temporarily fixed by long-term contracts. When this is the case, real output will initially increase to Y_2, which is beyond the economy's long-run capacity of Y_F. However, the high rate of output (Y_2) will not be sustainable. Eventually, the long-term contracts based on the previously weaker demand (AD_1) will end, and the new agreements will reflect the new stronger demand. As a result, resource prices (like labor) will rise pushing costs up, which will shift *SRAS* upward and to the left. Eventually, a new long-run equilibrium (E_2) will be established at a higher price level (P_3). Output will fall to Y_F. Thus, when an economy is already at full employment, an unexpected shift to a more expansionary monetary policy will temporarily increase output, but in the long run, it only leads to higher prices.

The Effects of an Unanticipated Restrictive Monetary Policy

Suppose that the Fed moves toward a more **restrictive monetary policy** by selling bonds to the general public. The sale of bonds will reduce both the supply of money and the reserves of banks as people take money out of their accounts to buy the bonds. **EXHIBIT 5** shows the impact of the more restrictive monetary policy on the loanable funds and goods and services markets. The Fed's sale of bonds reduces bond prices because it puts more bonds in the market. It also drains reserves from the banking system as people buy the bonds (reducing the ability of banks to extend loans). As a result, the supply of loanable funds will fall, causing the real interest rate to rise (from r_1 to r_2 in part a of Exhibit 5). The higher real interest rate will reduce spending on both investment goods and consumer durables because they'll be more costly to finance. The higher rate will also cause an inflow of capital from abroad and lead to the appreciation in the exchange rate of the dollar. In turn, this appreciation of the dollar will encourage U.S. citizens to buy imported products (which will become cheaper for them) and discourage foreigners from buying U.S. exports (because they will be more costly for them). This will then lead to lower net U.S. exports (and lower aggregate demand in the United States). The higher interest rates will also reduce housing and other asset prices, discouraging new construction and investment. All of these factors will tend to reduce aggregate demand (shift it from AD_1 to AD_2 in part b of Exhibit 5).

The unexpected decline in the demand for goods and services will put downward pressure on prices, squeeze profit margins, and reduce output. As part (b) of Exhibit 5 shows, the price level will decline (to P_2), and output will fall (to Y_2) as a result of the restrictive monetary policy.

The appropriateness of a restrictive policy depends on the state of the economy. **EXHIBIT 6** illustrates this point. When there is upward pressure on prices because of strong demand, restrictive policy is an effective weapon against inflation. Suppose that, as illustrated by part (a) of Exhibit 6, an economy is temporarily operating at e_1 and Y_1—beyond its full employment real GDP of Y_F. Strong aggregate demand is putting upward pressure on prices. In this case, a restrictive policy will help keep the price level constant and offset the inflationary forces. If a proper "dose" of a restrictive policy is administered at the right time, it will lower aggregate demand (to AD_2) and direct the economy to a noninflationary, long-run equilibrium at P_2 and Y_F (that is, E_2).

As part (b) of Exhibit 6 shows, however, an unanticipated shift to restrictive policy will be damaging to an economy operating at full-employment equilibrium. If the output of an economy is at full employment (or worse still, at less than full employment), a restrictive policy will reduce aggregate demand (shift it to AD_2), and output

(a) Loanable funds market

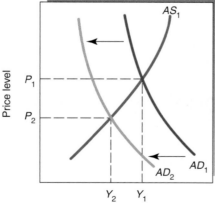

(b) Goods and services (real GDP)

EXHIBIT 5
The Short-Run Effects of a More Restrictive Monetary Policy

When the Fed shifts to a more restrictive policy, it sells bonds, which reduces the reserves available to banks, decreases the supply of loanable funds, and puts upward pressure on interest rates (a). The higher interest rates decrease aggregate demand (shift it to AD_2 in b). When the reduction in aggregate demand is unanticipated, real output will decline (to Y_2) and downward pressure on prices will result.

EXHIBIT 6
The Effects of a Restrictive Monetary Policy

The stabilization effects of restrictive monetary policy depend on the state of the economy when the policy exerts its primary impact. Restrictive monetary policy will reduce aggregate demand. If the restraint takes effect when aggregate demand is strong and the economy is overheated, it will limit or even prevent the occurrence of an inflationary boom (a). In contrast, if the restraint in aggregate demand takes effect when the economy is at full employment, it will disrupt the long-run equilibrium, reduce output, and result in a recession (b).

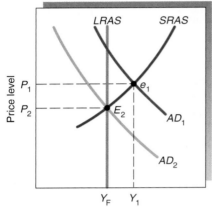

(a) Restrictive policy to control inflation

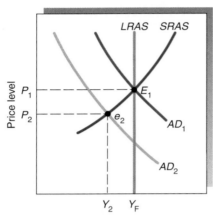

(b) Restrictive policy that causes a recession

will decline from Y_F to Y_2. Under these circumstances, the restrictive policy will cause output to fall below the economy's full-employment capacity and throw the economy into a recession.

Shifts in Monetary Policy and Economic Stability

As with fiscal policy, monetary policy must be properly timed if it is going to exert a stabilizing impact on the economy. Exhibits 4 and 6 highlight this point. When an economy is operating below its long-run capacity, expansionary monetary policy can increase aggregate demand and push the output of the economy to its sustainable potential (part a of Exhibit 4). Similarly, if properly timed, restrictive monetary policy can help control (or prevent) inflation (part a of Exhibit 6).

If it is timed improperly, however, monetary policy can be destabilizing. Expansionary monetary policy will cause inflation if the effects of the policy are felt when the economy is already at or beyond its capacity (part b of Exhibit 4). Similarly, if the effects of a restrictive policy come when an economy is operating at its potential GDP, a recession is the likely outcome (part b of Exhibit 6). Worse still, the impact of a restrictive policy can be disastrous if imposed on an economy that's already in a recession.

Monetary Policy in the Long Run

The Quantity Theory of Money

Since the middle of the eighteenth century, economists have argued that excessive money growth leads to inflation. Nearly a hundred years ago, Englishman Alfred Marshall and American Irving Fisher formalized the **quantity theory of money** in support of this view. ***The quantity theory of money predicts that an increase in the supply of money will cause a proportional increase in the price level.***

Quantity theory of money

A theory that hypothesizes that a change in the money supply will cause a proportional change in the price level because velocity and real output are unaffected by the quantity of money.

The quantity theory of money can be more easily understood once we recognize that there are two ways of viewing GDP. As the *AD–AS* model shows, nominal GDP is the sum of the price, *P*, times the output, *Y*, of each final-product good purchased during the period. In aggregate, *P* represents the economy's price level, while *Y* indicates real income or real GDP. There is also a second way of visualizing GDP. When the existing money stock, *M*, is multiplied by the number of times, *V*, that money is used to buy final products, this, too, yields the economy's nominal GDP. Therefore,

$$PY = GDP = MV$$

The **velocity of money** (*V*) is simply the average number of times a dollar is used to purchase a final product or service during a year. Velocity is equal to nominal GDP divided by the size of the money stock. For example, in 2008, GDP was equal to $14,265 billion, whereas the M1 money supply was $1,423 billion. Therefore, the velocity of the M1 money stock was 10.0 ($14,265 billion divided by $1,423 billion). The velocity of the M2 money stock can be derived in a similar manner. In 2008, the M2 money stock was $7,711 billion. Thus, the velocity of M2 was 1.8 ($14,265 billion divided by $7,711 billion).

The concept of velocity is closely related to the demand for money. When decision makers conduct a specific amount of business with a smaller amount of money, their demand for money balances is reduced. Each dollar, though, is being used more often, so the velocity of the money has increased. Thus, for a given GDP level, when the demand for money declines, the velocity of money increases. Correspondingly, an increase in the demand for money is a reflection of a reduction in velocity.

When considering the behavior of prices, output, money, and velocity over time, we can write the quantity theory equation in terms of growth rates:

Rate of inflation + Growth rate of real output = Growth rate of the money supply + Growth rate of velocity

Economists call the *MV = PY* relationship the **equation of exchange** because it reflects both the monetary and real sides of each final-product exchange. The quantity theory of money, though, assumes that *Y* and *V* are determined by factors other than the amount of money in circulation. Classical economists believed that real output, *Y*, was determined by factors like technology, the size of the economy's resource base, and the skill of its labor force. These factors were thought to be unrelated to changes in the money supply. Likewise, the velocity of money, *V*, was thought to be determined primarily by institutional factors, like the organization of banking and credit, the frequency of income payments, transportation speed, and the communication system.[5] These factors will generally change slowly.

Thus, classical economists thought that, for all practical purposes, both *Y* and *V* were constant (or changed only by small amounts) over periods of two, three, or four years. If both *Y* and *V* are constant, then the *MV = PY* relationship indicates that an increase in the money supply (*M*) will lead to a proportional increase in the price level (*P*). Correspondingly, an increase in the growth rate of the money supply can be expected to cause a similar increase in the rate of inflation. Thus, the quantity theory of money highlights the linkage between monetary growth and inflation.

Long-Run Impact of Monetary Policy: The Modern View

Now let's consider the long-run impact of expansionary monetary policy within the framework of our basic macroeconomic model. We will begin with a simple case. Suppose real GDP is growing at a 3 percent annual rate and that the monetary authorities (the Fed in

Velocity of money

The average number of times a dollar is used to purchase final goods and services during a year. It is equal to GDP divided by the stock of money.

Equation of exchange

MV = PY, where *M* is the money supply, *V* is the velocity of money, *P* is the price level, and *Y* is the output of goods and services produced in an economy.

[5]We previously noted that credit cards often make it possible for people to handle their purchases and payments with smaller money balances. When this happens on a large scale, the velocity of money will increase. This has been observed over the past several decades. The velocity of the M1 money supply has risen from 3.8 in 1960 to 7.0 in 1980 and 10.0 in 2008. No doubt, the increased use of credit cards as a means of making payment has contributed to this substantial increase in the velocity of the M1 money supply.

the case of the United States) are expanding the money supply by 3 percent each year. In addition, let's assume that the velocity of money is constant. This would imply that the 3 percent annual increase in output, or GDP, would lead to a 3 percent annual increase in the demand for money. In this case, the 3 percent monetary growth would be consistent with stable prices (zero inflation). Initially, we will assume that the economy's real interest rate is 4 percent. Because the inflation rate is zero, the nominal rate of interest is also equal to 4 percent. **EXHIBITS 7 and 8** illustrate an economy initially (Period 1) characterized by these conditions.

What will happen if the monetary authorities permanently increase the growth rate of the money supply from 3 percent to 8 percent annually (see part a of Exhibit 7, beginning in Period 2)? In the short run, the expansionary monetary policy will reduce the real interest rate and stimulate aggregate demand (shift it to AD_2 in part b of Exhibit 7), just as we previously explained (in Exhibits 3 and 4). For a time, real output will exceed the economy's potential. However, many resource suppliers will want to modify their long-term agreements as soon as they can in light of the strong demand conditions. Over time, more and more resource suppliers (including workers represented by union officials) will have the opportunity to alter their prior contracts. As this happens, wages and other resource prices will increase. As they do, costs will rise and profit margins will fall back to normal levels. The higher costs will reduce aggregate supply (shift it to AS_2). As the rapid monetary growth continues in subsequent periods (periods 3, 4, and so on), both AD

EXHIBIT 7

The Long-Run Effects of a More Rapid Expansion in the Money Supply on the Goods and Services Market

Here, we illustrate the long-run impact of an increase in the annual growth rate of the money supply from 3 to 8 percent. Initially, prices are stable (P_{100}) when the money supply is expanding by 3 percent annually. The acceleration in the growth rate of the money supply increases aggregate demand (shifts it to AD_2). At first, real output may expand beyond the economy's potential (Y_F). However, abnormally low unemployment and strong demand conditions will create upward pressure on wages and other resource prices, shifting aggregate supply to AS_2. Output will return to its long-run potential and the price level will increase to P_{105} (E_2). If the more rapid monetary growth continues in subsequent periods, AD and AS will continue to shift upward, leading to still higher prices (E_3 and periods beyond). The net result of the process is sustained inflation.

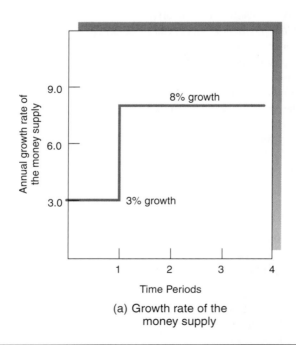

(a) Growth rate of the money supply

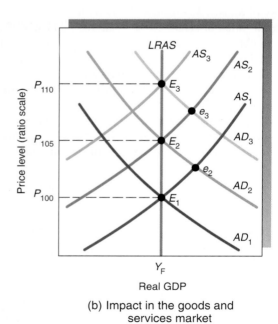

(b) Impact in the goods and services market

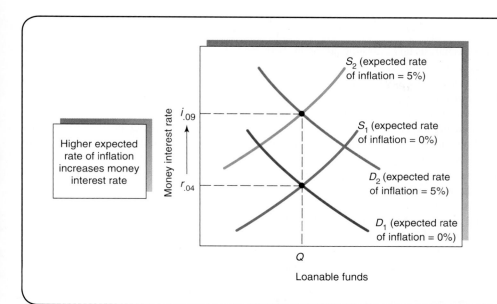

EXHIBIT 8

The Long-Run Effects of More Rapid Expansion in the Money Supply on the Loanable Funds Market

When prices are stable, supply and demand in the loanable funds market are in balance at a real and nominal interest rate of 4 percent. If a more rapid monetary expansion leads to a long-term 5 percent inflation rate, borrowers and lenders will build the higher inflation rate into their decision making. As a result, the nominal interest rate (i) will rise to 9 percent—the 4 percent real rate plus a 5 percent inflationary premium.

and *AS* will shift upward. As shown in Exhibit 7b, the price level will rise to P_{105}, P_{110}, and so on to still higher levels as the money supply continues to grow more rapidly than the monetary growth rate consistent with stable prices. The continuation of the expansionary monetary policy leads to a higher and higher price level—that is, a sustained inflation.

Suppose an inflation rate of 5 percent eventually emerges from the more rapid growth rate of the money supply (8 percent rather than 3 percent). In the long run, more and more people will make decisions based on the persistent 5 percent inflation because it will be what they come to expect. In the resource market, both buyers and sellers will eventually include the 5 percent expected inflation rate into long-term contracts like collective bargaining agreements. Once this happens, resource prices and costs will rise as rapidly as prices in the goods and services market. When the 5 percent long-run rate of inflation is fully anticipated, it will fail to either reduce real wages or improve profit margins. Output will recede to its long-run potential, and unemployment will return to its natural rate.

Exhibit 8 shows the long-run adjustments in the loanable funds market once borrowers and lenders expect the 5 percent inflation rate. When lenders expect a 5 percent annual increase in the price level, a 9 percent interest rate will be necessary to provide them with as much incentive to supply loanable funds as a 4 percent rate did *when stable prices were expected.* Thus, the supply of loanable funds will shift vertically by the 5 percent expected rate of inflation. Simultaneously, borrowers who were willing to pay 4 percent interest on their loans when stable prices were expected will be willing to pay 9 percent when they expect prices to increase by 5 percent annually. The demand for loanable funds will therefore also increase (shift vertically) by the expected inflation rate. Once borrowers and lenders anticipate the higher (5 percent) inflation rate, the equilibrium money interest rate will rise to 9 percent. Of course, the real interest rate is equal to the money interest rate (9 percent) minus the expected rate of inflation (5 percent). In the long run, a 4 percent real interest rate will emerge with inflation, just as it did with stable prices. Therefore, in the long run, expansionary monetary policy will not reduce real interest rates. Instead, it will lead to inflation and higher nominal interest rates.

Real-world observations support the linkage between monetary expansion and high nominal interest rates. During the 1970s, the monetary policy of the United States was highly expansionary, and it led to both inflation and high nominal interest rates. On the other hand, interest rates were lower during the 1960s and 1990s, when monetary policy was less expansionary and the inflation rate lower. The picture is the same internationally. The highest interest rates in the world are found in countries experiencing hyperinflation due to very rapid money supply growth: Argentina and Brazil in the 1980s and Russia in the 1990s, for example. Conversely, the lowest interest rates are found in countries like Switzerland that have followed monetary policies that have kept the inflation rate low.

Money and Inflation

Modern analysis highlights the difference between the short- and long-run effects of monetary policy. In the short run, shifts in monetary policy exert an impact on real output and employment. A shift to a more restrictive policy will tend to throw the economy into a recession, while a shift to a more expansionary monetary policy will expand real output and employment.

However, if the more expansionary policy persists, the long-run impact will be inflation and higher nominal interest rates, without any positive impact on real output and employment. The more rapid the sustained growth rate of the money supply (relative to real output), the higher the expected rate of inflation. Thus, modern analysis indicates that the long-run implications of the earlier quantity theory of money are correct: money growth and inflation are closely linked.

The empirical evidence is highly consistent with this view. **EXHIBIT 9** presents data on the annual growth rate of the money supply (adjusted for the growth rate of the nation's output) and the rate of inflation for ninety-three countries for which data were available during the 1985–2005 period. The results clearly illustrate the link between monetary policy and inflation. Countries with single-digit rates of money growth—for example, Belgium, Central African

EXHIBIT 9

Money and Inflation—An International Comparison, 1985–2005

The relationship between the average annual growth rate of the money supply and the rate of inflation is shown here for the 1985–2005 period. Clearly, there is a close relationship between the two. Higher rates of money growth lead to higher rates of inflation.

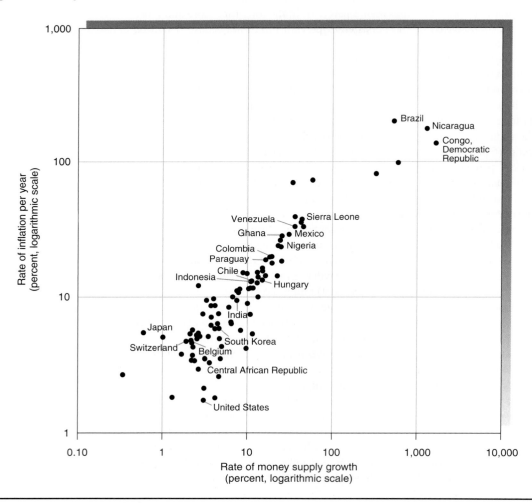

Republic, India, Japan, South Korea, Switzerland, and the United States—also experienced single-digit rates of inflation. Similarly, countries with rates of money growth in the 10 percent to 25 percent range experienced rates of inflation in this same range. The data for Chile, Colombia, Ghana, Indonesia, Hungary, Paraguay, and Nigeria illustrate this point. Countries like Mexico, Sierra Leone, and Venezuela, with money growth rates in the 30 percent to 50 percent range, had inflation rates within this same range. Finally, look at the data for Brazil, the Democratic Republic of Congo, and Nicaragua. The average annual rate of money growth of these countries exceeded 100 percent during 1985–2005. So, too, did their rates of inflation.

When looked at over a lengthy time period, the link between money growth and inflation is one of the most consistent relationships in all of economics. Inflation is a monetary phenomenon. Persistently low rates of money growth lead to low rates of inflation. Similarly, high rates of money growth lead to high rates of inflation.

Time Lags, Monetary Shifts, and Economic Stability

While analyzing how monetary policy works, we glossed over a crucially important issue: the time lag between a change in monetary policy and when the change begins to exert an impact on interest rates, aggregate demand, and eventually output and the price level. While the Fed can shift policy rapidly, it will take time for the change to impact the economy. Economists estimate that it will generally take six to fifteen months for a shift in monetary policy to exert a major impact on aggregate demand and real output. An even longer time lag—eighteen to thirty-six months—will pass before there is a significant impact on the price level and inflation rate. Clearly, proper timing of changes in monetary policy is not an easy task. Moreover, if the changes are improperly timed, monetary policy will become a source of economic instability.

Changes in interest rates play an important role in the transmission of monetary policy. In order to keep things simple, we have proceeded as if there were only a single interest rate in the loanable funds market. In the real world, of course, there are numerous interest rates reflecting loans of differing risks and time lengths. For example, there are short-term interest rates, such as those for federal funds, Treasury bills, and savings deposits. There are also longer-term rates, like those for home mortgages and long-term bonds. Initially, Fed actions will exert their primary impact on short-term interest rates. When the Fed increases the reserves available to banks, short-term interest rates will fall. On the other hand, draining reserves from the banking system will push the short-term rates upward.

The transmission of monetary policy sheds light on why it takes time for monetary policy to work. When the Fed shifts toward monetary expansion and injects additional reserves into the banking system, short-term interest rates will fall. But this reduces the opportunity cost of holding money balances. At the lower interest rate, households and businesses are willing to hold a larger quantity of money, and therefore the velocity of money will decline. As a result, the initial effects of the expansionary monetary policy will often be weak. For a time, total spending (aggregate demand) may not change much because the reduction in velocity is, at least partially, offsetting the increase in the supply of money. Of course, if the more expansionary monetary policy persists, a combination of the lower real interest rates and more readily available credit will eventually stimulate aggregate demand and real output. Still later, the increase in demand will place upward pressure on prices and nominal interest rates. When this happens—and eighteen to thirty-six months may pass before it does— the velocity of money will increase, amplifying the demand stimulus of the monetary expansion. It is at this point that the effects on inflation will be the strongest.

The same forces will also affect the operation of restrictive monetary policy. When the Fed shifts to a more restrictive policy and drains reserves from the banking system, the federal funds and other short-term interest rates will rise. At the higher rates, however, people will want to hold less money, and the velocity of money will increase. For a time, the increase in velocity will at least partially offset the reduction in the supply of money and weaken the initial restrictive effects of the policy. Of course, if the restrictive policy persists, banks will have to cut back on their extension of loans and the higher interest rates will eventually reduce aggregate demand. However, at least a few quarters may pass before the restrictive policy exerts a strong impact on the economy.

Thus, both the transmission path of monetary policy and the empirical evidence indicate that shifts in monetary policy will exert an impact on output and the general level of prices with a time lag. Moreover, these lags will be of variable length, and sometimes they will be quite long. Given our limited forecasting ability, these time lags will make it difficult for policy makers to institute changes in monetary policy in a manner that will promote economic stability.

Rather than shifting back and forth between expansion and restriction in an effort to smooth the ups and downs of the business cycle, many economists believe that the Fed should simply follow a steady and highly predictable path in order to reduce disturbances arising from monetary sources. Given the unpredictable time lags, veering to one direction and then to the other is likely to generate instability rather than reduce it. In some ways, the conduct of monetary policy is a little like riding a bicycle. It is pretty easy when you are on a steady path. But once you veer off track, it is not so easy to steer back to a nice steady course.

Measurement of Monetary Policy

How can you tell whether monetary policy is expansionary or restrictive and to what degree? In the 1960s and 1970s, the growth rate of the M1 money supply was a reasonably accurate monetary policy indicator. If the money supply was increasing at a rate substantially greater than the 3 percent long-term historical growth of real GDP, this was indicative of an excessively expansionary monetary policy that would lead to inflation. On the other hand, when the annual growth rate of M1 fell significantly below the 3 percent long-term growth rate, this implied that monetary policy was restrictive. Moreover, it was also widely perceived that monetary growth at approximately the 3 percent annual rate would lead to price stability.

However, as we discussed in the previous chapter, in the early 1980s, the introduction of interest-earning checking deposits and money market mutual funds changed the nature of the M1 money supply. M1 grew rapidly during the 1980s, but this growth was primarily a reflection of the changing nature of money rather than highly expansionary monetary policy. Through time, other innovations, including no-load mutual bond and equity funds, increased use of credit and debit cards, and various types of online payment and deposit procedures have changed the nature of both the M1 and M2 money supply and reduced their reliability as indicators of monetary policy.

Responding to these measurement problems, the Fed has relied more extensively on its control over short-term interest rates in its conduct of monetary policy during the past two decades. When the Fed wanted to shift to a more expansionary monetary policy, it reduced its target federal funds interest rate and provided the banking system with sufficient reserves to push this rate downward to the desired level. Conversely, when the Fed wanted to shift toward restriction, perhaps because of concern about inflation, it pushed the federal funds rate upward by selling bonds and thereby withdrawing reserves from the banking system. As the result of these changes, movements of short-term interest rates have emerged as a more reliable monetary policy indicator than the money supply figures. This is particularly true for the time frame since the mid-1980s.

Taylor Rule

A rule that indicates the federal funds interest rate that is most consistent with maximum sustainable output and price stability. Because the federal funds interest rate is largely determined by monetary policy, this rule acts as both a guide for monetary policy makers and a benchmark to evaluate their performance.

What Is the Taylor Rule and Why Is It Important?

John Taylor of Stanford University developed an instrument, known as the **Taylor Rule**, which can be used to measure the consistency of monetary policy with price stability and the full employment rate of output. The Taylor Rule provides an estimate for the federal funds interest rate that would be consistent with both of these objectives.[6] The Taylor Rule equation for the target federal funds rate is

$$f = r + p + .5^* (p - p^*) + .5^*(y - y^p)$$

where f is the target federal funds rate, r is the equilibrium real interest rate (assumed to be 2.5 percent), p is the inflation rate, p^* is the desired inflation rate (assumed to be 2%),

[6]See John B. Taylor (1993), "Discretion versus Policy Rules in Practice," *Carnegie-Rochester Conference Series on Public Policy*, vol. 39, pp. 195–214.

y is the output, and *y*^p is the potential output. (*Note:* We will present the Taylor Rule target federal funds rate assuming that the desired rate of inflation is 2 percent. Most economists believe that price indexes slightly overstate the rate of inflation. Thus, the 2 percent figure might be thought of as approximate price stability.)

The general idea of the Taylor Rule is straightforward. The higher the rate of inflation and the larger the current output relative to the potential, the more restrictive the monetary policy needed for the achievement of full employment with price stability—therefore, the higher the federal funds rate that is needed to restrain demand and bring it into line with the maximum output and price stability objectives. On the other hand, the lower the inflation rate (relative to the 2 percent target) and the greater the shortfall of actual GDP relative to the economy's potential, the more the expansionary monetary policy needed for full employment with price stability—therefore, the lower the target federal funds rate needed to achieve the desired objectives.

The Taylor Rule is important because it provides an instrument for both the conduct of monetary policy and evaluation of how well it is being conducted. The rule provides policy makers with a compass for the conduct of monetary policy in a stabilizing manner. If the actual federal funds rate is below the target rate implied by the Taylor Rule, this indicates that monetary policy is overly expansionary, and therefore policy makers should shift toward a more restrictive monetary policy in order to maintain full employment and price stability. On the other hand, when the actual federal funds rate is above the target rate, this signals that monetary policy is too restrictive, and therefore a shift to a more expansionary policy would be appropriate. When the actual and target rates are equal, this indicates that monetary policy is right on course for the maintenance of low inflation and maximum sustainable output and employment.

The Taylor Rule also provides a benchmark for the evaluation of monetary policy. **EXHIBIT 10** shows the actual and target federal funds rate based on the Taylor Rule from 1960 to 2009. The actual and target rates were quite close during the first half of the 1960s, indicating that monetary policy was pretty much on target. However, look at

---

EXHIBIT 10

The Taylor Rule and Monetary Policy, 1960–2009

The actual federal funds interest rate and the appropriate target rate implied by the Taylor Rule are shown here. Note that the actual Fed funds rate tracked the target rate quite closely during most of the 1960s and the 1986–1999 period, indicating that monetary policy was appropriate for the maintenance of full employment and low inflation. In contrast, the actual Fed funds rate was substantially less than the target rate in the inflationary 1970s and during 2002–mid-year 2005. This indicates that monetary policy was too expansionary during these periods.

Source: Federal Reserve Bank of St. Louis.

the relationship between the actual and the target rate during 1968–1979. During this period, monetary policy was constantly shifting back and forth between expansion and restriction. Moreover, the difference between the actual and target rate was substantial, and the actual rate was often well below the target rate. This is indicative of monetary policy that is too expansionary. The high and variable inflation rates of the 1970s confirm this view.

It is interesting to compare and contrast the monetary policy of the past two decades. Note how the actual federal funds rate closely tracked the appropriate rate implied by the Taylor Rule during 1986–1999. Sometimes the actual federal funds rate was a little above the appropriate rate implied by the Taylor Rule, and sometimes it was a little below. But the differences between the actual and appropriate rates were small. This indicates that monetary policy was highly consistent with the objectives of price stability and full employment during this era.

Now look at the deviations between the actual and appropriate federal funds rate during 2000–2008. During this nine-year period, the absolute difference between the actual and target rate averaged 2.0 percentage points, more than double the figure of the previous decade. Except for three quarters, the actual federal funds rate was below the target rate throughout the nine-year period. The Taylor Rule indicates that monetary policy was particularly expansionary from mid-year 2002 through mid-year 2005.

Did Monetary Policy Cause the Crisis of 2008?

The foundation for the Crisis of 2008 was laid during 2002–2006. Between January 2002 and mid-year 2006, housing prices increased by 87 percent. This run-up in housing prices was fueled by several factors. Government regulations imposed on banks and two huge government-sponsored mortgage lenders, Fannie Mae and Freddie Mac, made credit for housing finance both abundantly available and easily accessible. Beginning in the late 1990s, there was a substantial increase in the volume of mortgage loans extended, with little or no down payment to parties borrowing large amounts relative to their income. Moreover, these loans were often bundled together into a relatively new type of asset, mortgage-backed securities that were sold throughout the world. These securities were marketed and widely held by both commercial and investment banks with only small amounts of reserves and capital relative to their mortgage holdings.

Expansionary monetary policy fueled the credit expansion and run-up in housing prices. As Exhibit 10 shows, the Taylor Rule indicates that monetary policy was particularly expansionary from mid-year 2002 through mid-year 2005. The federal funds interest rate was approximately 2 full percentage points lower than the rate consistent with maintenance of full employment and price stability during this period. There were other indicators that monetary policy was excessively expansionary. The foreign exchange value of the dollar was falling. The yield curve—the difference between long- and short-term interest rates—was steep, providing still more evidence that monetary policy was overly expansionary.

EXHIBIT 11 provides additional insight into the linkage between Fed policy and the housing boom and bust. Exhibit 11a shows the path of the federal funds and one-year Treasury bill rate over the past decade. Note how both of these short-term interest rates were held below 2 percent for three years during 2002–2004. These low interest rates and abundant credit increased the demand for housing and thereby helped propel the soaring housing prices. But, just as our analysis predicts, the expansionary monetary policy eventually generated upward pressure on the general level of prices. As Exhibit 11b shows, when the inflation rate began to increase in 2005–2006, the Fed shifted to a more restrictive monetary policy and began pushing interest rates upward. In turn, the higher interest rates increased borrowing costs, weakening the demand for housing. By the second half of 2006, housing prices were leveling off and beginning to fall, mortgage defaults were increasing, and housing foreclosures rising. All of this was well before the recession began in December of 2007.

EXHIBIT 11
Short-Term Interest Rates and Inflation, 1998–2009

Short-term (federal funds and one-year Treasury bill) interest rates are shown in part (a) and the rate of inflation in part (b) for 1998–2009. Rising short-term rates are indicative of monetary restriction, while falling rates imply expansion. Note how the short-term rates were pushed to historic lows during 2002–2004 as housing prices soared, and then rose again in 2005–2006 as the Fed moved toward restriction to fight inflation. The Fed shifted again (toward expansion) in 2007–2008 as the economy plunged into recession.

Source: Board of Governors of the Federal Reserve System and http://www.economagic.com.

The housing bust eventually spread to the rest of the economy and generated trouble for lending institutions holding large quantities of the mortgage-backed securities that tumbled in value as mortgage default rates rose. There were other contributing factors to the Crisis of 2008. The world price of crude oil nearly tripled between the beginning of 2007 and July 2008, pushing the price of gasoline above $4 per gallon in the United States. Stock prices fell by more than 50 percent during the seventeen months following October 2007. The importance of the combination of factors underpinning the 2008 crisis is subject to debate, but inappropriate monetary policy clearly played a role. (See Special Topic 5, "The Crash of 2008: Cause and Aftermath," for additional information on this topic.)

Current Fed Policy and the Future

As the recession lingered and became more severe during the second half of 2008, the Fed shifted to a highly expansionary monetary policy. As we indicated in the previous chapter, the Fed injected a huge quantity of reserves into the banking system, leading to a doubling of the monetary base during the last six months of 2008. This expansionary monetary policy pushed the federal funds and other short-term interest rates to near zero and created a huge overhang of excess reserves in the banking system.

Given the severity of the 2008–2009 recession, the Fed's shift toward expansionary policy was certainly understandable. During the last half of 2008 and the first half of 2009, the M1 and M2 money supply figures expanded at 15 percent and 10 percent, respectively. But even these high rates of monetary growth were far less rapid than the monetary base because banks were maintaining huge excess reserves. Of course, monetary policy works with a lag. It will take some time for the expansionary monetary policy to stimulate demand and economic recovery. However, once the recovery process begins, banks will use more and more of their excess reserves to extend loans and make investments. This will confront the Fed with a dilemma. If the Fed does not shift toward restriction quickly enough, the bank lending of the vast quantity of excess reserves will generate rapid growth of the money supply and inflation. On the other hand, if the Fed moves toward restraint too quickly, it may stifle the recovery and throw the economy back into another recession.

Clearly, monetary policy makers are walking a tight rope in the months immediately ahead. Will they be able to direct the economy back to full employment and price stability? The Fed certainly has the tools to keep the money supply from soaring out of control. It can sell some of the securities it has purchased, which will drain reserves from the banking system. It can also pay banks higher interest rates on their excess reserves, which will encourage them to continue holding large quantities of these reserves rather than extending loans and thereby expanding the money supply.

But the problem is not the Fed's ability to control the money supply but rather its ability to time policy shifts appropriately. Remember, the time lags between when the Fed makes a policy shift and when the shift exerts a major impact on output and the general level of prices are long and variable. These time lags increase the likelihood that errors will be made. Monetary policy has been on a stop–go path for almost a decade now. As the experience of the 1970s indicates, once you are on this course, it is not easy to get back to economic stability. It will be interesting to see how it works out, but the unpredictability of the time lags and the Fed's past record provide reasons for concern.

Looking ahead

As we discussed in this chapter, theory indicates that the impact of monetary policy will be influenced by whether people anticipate its effects. How do people form expectations about the future? The next chapter will consider this important question and analyze its implications in more detail.

KEY POINTS

▼ The quantity of money people want to hold is inversely related to the money interest rate. Higher interest rates make it more costly to hold money instead of interest-earning assets like bonds. The supply of money is vertical because it is determined by the Fed. The money interest rate will gravitate toward the rate at which the quantity of money people want to hold is just equal to the quantity supplied by the Fed.

▼ The impact of a shift in monetary policy is generally transmitted through interest rates, exchange rates, and asset prices.

▼ When instituting a more expansionary monetary policy, the Fed generally increases the reserves available to banks and pushes interest rates downward. In the short run, an *unanticipated* shift to a more expansionary policy will stimulate aggregate demand and thereby increase output and employment.

▼ When instituting a more restrictive monetary policy, the Fed drains reserves from the banking system and pushes interest rates upward. In the short run, an unanticipated shift to a more restrictive monetary policy will increase real interest rates and reduce aggregate demand, output, and employment.

▼ The quantity theory of money postulates that the velocity of money is constant (or approximately so) and that real output is independent of monetary factors. When these assumptions hold, an increase in the stock of money will lead to a proportional increase in the price level.

▼ While monetary policy can influence real output in the short run, in the long run, the primary impact

of monetary policy will be on prices rather than output. Rapid monetary growth will merely lead to inflation.

▼ Shifts in monetary policy exert an impact on output and employment only after time lags that are variable and sometimes lengthy. This will make it difficult for policy makers to make regular changes in monetary policy in a stabilizing manner. Historically, erratic monetary policy has often been a source of economic instability.

▼ The Fed's low interest rate policy of 2002–2004, followed by its shift to a more restrictive policy in 2005–2006, contributed to the boom and bust of housing prices that provided the foundation for the Crisis of 2008.

CRITICAL ANALYSIS QUESTIONS

1. Why do people hold money? How will an increase in the interest rate influence the amount of money that people will want to hold?

*2. How would each of the following influence the quantity of money you would want to hold?
   a. an increase in the interest rate on checking deposits
   b. an increase in the expected rate of inflation
   c. an increase in income
   d. an increase in the differential interest rate between money market mutual funds and checking deposits

*3. What is the opportunity cost of the following?
   a. obtaining a $100,000 house
   b. holding the house for one year
   c. obtaining $1,000
   d. holding the $1,000 in your checking account for one year

4. Historically, shifts toward a more expansionary monetary policy have often been associated with increases in real output. Is this surprising? Why or why not? Would a more expansionary policy increase the long-term growth rate of real GDP? Why or why not?

5. What impact will an unanticipated increase in the money supply have on the real interest rate, real output, and employment in the short run? How will expansionary monetary policy affect these factors in the long run? Explain.

6. How rapidly has the money supply (M1) grown during the past twelve months? How rapidly has M2 grown? Do you think the monetary authorities should increase or decrease the growth rate of the money supply during the next year? Why? (The data necessary to answer this question are available at the Web site of the Federal Reserve Bank of St. Louis, http://www.stls.frb.org.)

*7. If the Fed shifts to a more restrictive monetary policy, it will generally sell some of its current holdings of bonds in the open market. How will this action influence each of the following? Briefly explain each of your answers.
   a. the reserves available to banks
   b. real interest rates
   c. household spending on consumer durables
   d. the exchange rate value of the dollar
   e. net exports
   f. the prices of stocks and real assets like apartment or office buildings
   g. real GDP

8. Did monetary policy help promote economic stability during 1985 through 1999? Has monetary policy exerted a stabilizing impact on the U.S. economy during the past decade? Explain your response to these questions.

9. Political officials often call on the monetary authorities to expand the money supply more rapidly so that interest rates can be reduced. Will expansion-

ary monetary policy reduce interest rates in the short run? Will it do so in the long run?

*10. Many economists believe that there is a "long and variable time lag" between the time a change in monetary policy is instituted and the time its primary impact on output, employment, and prices is felt. If true, how does this long and variable time lag affect the ability of policy makers to use monetary policy as a stabilization tool?

*11. "Historically, when interest rates are high, the inflation rate is high. High interest rates are a major cause of inflation." Evaluate this statement.

12. What is the Taylor Rule? Why is the Taylor Rule important? What did the Taylor Rule indicate about monetary policy during 2002–2006?

13. a. What is the quantity theory of money?
    b. Is the quantity theory of money valid?
    c. Does it explain the impact of shifts in monetary policy on the economy? Why or why not?

14. Did monetary policy contribute to the economic crisis of 2008? Why or why not? How did monetary policy makers respond to this crisis? Has their response created an environment for future stability and growth? Explain.

*Asterisk denotes questions for which answers are given in Appendix B.

Stabilization Policy, Output, and Employment

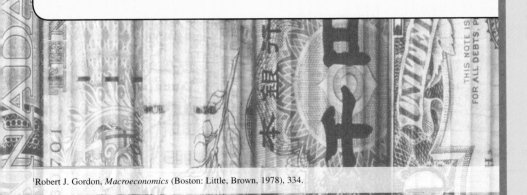

CHAPTER FOCUS

- Can monetary and fiscal policy reduce the ups and downs of the business cycle? Why or why not?

- How are expectations formed? Do expectations influence how macroeconomic policy works?

- What is the Phillips curve? Why were the early views about the Phillips curve wrong?

- Have important areas of agreement emerged from the experience and debate on stabilization policy of the past fifty years? Are there points of continuing disagreement?

- How does the economic instability of recent decades compare with earlier time periods?

Unfortunately, policymakers cannot act as if the economy is an automobile that can quickly be steered back and forth. Rather, the procedure of changing aggregate demand is much closer to that of a captain navigating a giant supertanker. Even if he gives a signal for a hard turn, it takes a mile before he can see a change, and ten miles before the ship makes the turn.

—*Robert J. Gordon*[1]

[1]Robert J. Gordon, *Macroeconomics* (Boston: Little, Brown, 1978), 334.

n previous chapters, we analyzed the impact of both fiscal and monetary policy on output, employment, and prices. We also noted that the initial impact of a policy change is often different than the impact over a more lengthy time period. We now want to take a more comprehensive look at stabilization policy. Can active management of fiscal and/or monetary policy reduce economic instability? This chapter will consider the record and examine both the potential and limitations of stabilization policy in more detail. ■

Economic Fluctuations—The Historical Record

Wide fluctuations in the general level of business activity—income, employment, and the price level—make personal economic planning extremely difficult. Such changes can cause even well devised investment plans to go awry. The tragic stories of unemployed workers begging for food and newly impoverished investors jumping out of windows during the Great Depression vividly portray the enormous personal and social costs of economic instability and the uncertainty that it generates.

Historically, there have been substantial fluctuations in real output. **EXHIBIT 1** illustrates the growth record of real GDP in the United States during the past 100 years. Prior to World War II, double-digit swings in real GDP during a single year were not uncommon. Real GDP rose by more than 10 percent annually during World War I, during an economic boom in 1922, during a mid-1930s recovery, and again during World War II. In contrast,

EXHIBIT 1

Economic Instability: The Record of the Past Century

Prior to the conclusion of World War II, the United States experienced double-digit increases in real GDP in 1918, 1922, 1935–1936, and 1941–1943. In contrast, real output fell by 5 percent or more in 1920–1921, 1930–1932, 1938, and 1946. However, as illustrated here, fluctuations in real GDP have been considerably more moderate since 1950. Most economists believe that more appropriate macroeconomic policy— particularly monetary policy— deserves much of the credit for the increased stability of recent decades.

Sources: *Historical Statistics of the United States*, 224; and Bureau of Economic Analysis, http://www.bea.gov.

output fell at an annual rate of 5 percent or more during the 1920–1921 recession, in the depression years of 1930–1932 and 1938, and again following World War II. Since 1950, economic ups and downs have been much more moderate. Nevertheless, periods of recession and economic boom are still observable.

Can Discretionary Policy Promote Economic Stability?

There is widespread agreement about the goals of macroeconomic policy. Economists of almost all persuasions favor the goals of steady growth, price stability, and full employment (unemployment at the natural rate). However, there are disagreements about how to achieve these objectives. Most of these disagreements focus on the potential and limitations of discretionary macro policy as a stabilization tool.

If monetary and fiscal policies could inject stimulus during economic slowdowns and apply restraint during inflationary booms, this would help reduce the ups and downs of the business cycle. Some macroeconomists, sometimes called **activists**, believe that this is possible. The activists believe that policy makers will be able to manage demand and respond to various disruptions and changing economic conditions in a manner that will promote economic stability. Other economists, called **nonactivists**, argue that the discretionary use of monetary and fiscal policy in response to changing economic conditions is likely to do more harm than good. The nonactivists note that erratic use of macro policy has been a major source of economic instability in the past. Thus, they believe that the economy would be more stable if policy makers merely followed a steady course rather than constantly trying to respond to turns in the economic road.

Both activists and nonactivists recognize that conducting macro policy in a stabilizing manner is not an easy task. Let's take a closer look at some of the complicating factors and available tools that might help improve the effectiveness of stabilization policy.

The Time Lag Problem

If monetary and fiscal policies are going to exert a stabilizing impact, proper timing is crucially important. Three different types of time lags complicate the achievement of proper timing.

First, there is the **recognition lag**, the time period between a change in economic conditions and recognition of the change by policy makers. It generally takes a few months to gather and tabulate reliable information on the recent performance of the economy in order to determine whether it has dipped into a recession or whether the inflation rate has accelerated, and so forth.

Second, even after the need for a policy change is recognized, there is generally an additional time period before the policy change is instituted. Economists refer to this delay as **administrative lag**. In the case of monetary policy, the administrative lag is generally quite short. The Federal Open Market Committee meets every few weeks and is in a position to institute a change in monetary policy quickly. This is a major advantage of monetary policy. For discretionary fiscal policy, the administrative lag is usually more lengthy. Congressional committees must meet. Legislation must be proposed and debated. Congress must act, and the president must consent. Each of these steps typically takes several months. These delays are a major disadvantage that limits the use of discretionary fiscal policy as a stabilization tool.

Finally, there is the **impact lag**, the time period between the implementation of a macro policy change and when the change exerts its primary impact on the economy. Although the impact of a change in tax rates is generally felt quickly, the expansionary effects of an increase in government spending are usually less rapid. It will take time for contractors to submit competitive bids and new contracts to be arranged and signed. Several months may pass before work on a new project actually begins. As we discussed

Activists

Economists who believe that discretionary changes in monetary and fiscal policy can reduce the degree of instability in output and employment.

Nonactivists

Economists who believe that discretionary macro policy adjustments in response to cyclical conditions are likely to increase, rather than reduce, instability. Nonactivists favor steady and predictable policies regardless of business conditions.

Recognition lag

The time period after a policy change is needed from a stabilization standpoint but before the need is recognized by policy makers.

Administrative lag

The time period after the need for a policy change is recognized but before the policy is actually implemented.

Impact lag

The time period after a policy change is implemented but before the change begins to exert its primary effects.

in the previous chapter, the impact lag for monetary policy is variable and often lengthy. Six to eighteen months may pass before a shift in monetary policy exerts much impact on demand, output, and employment. Moreover, the time lag before there is a significant impact on the general level of prices and the rate of inflation is likely to be even longer.

Forecasting Tools and Macro Policy

If a shift in policy is going to exert the desired effect at the proper time, policy makers cannot wait until a problem develops before they act. They need to know what economic conditions will be like six to fifteen months in the future. Policy makers need to know if a recession or an economic boom is around the corner. How can they find out? Forecasting tools can provide them with some information. Let's consider some of the forecasting devices available to policy makers.

Index of Leading Indicators

Index of leading indicators

An index of economic variables that historically has tended to turn down prior to the beginning of a recession and turn up prior to the beginning of a business expansion.

The **index of leading indicators** is the single most widely used and closely watched forecasting tool. The index is a composite statistic based on ten key variables that generally turn down prior to a recession and turn up before the beginning of a business expansion (see Measures of Economic Activity, "Index of Leading Indicators"). The index is published monthly, and a decline for three consecutive months is considered a warning that the economy is about to dip into a recession.

EXHIBIT 2 illustrates the path of the index during the 1959–2009 period. The index has correctly forecast each of the eight recessions since 1959. On five occasions, the downturn occurred eight to ten months prior to a recession, providing policy makers with sufficient lead time to modify policy, particularly monetary policy. In all but one instance, the downturn in the index preceded the recession by an even longer period. For example, it turned down eighteen months prior to the 1990–1991 recession.

A downturn in the index, however, is not always an accurate indicator of the future. On four occasions (1962, 1966, 1984, and 1995), a decline in the index of leading indicators forecast a recession that did not materialize. This has given rise to the quip that the index has accurately forecast twelve of the last eight recessions.

The index of leading indicators turned down five months before the start of the 2008–2009 economic crisis and declined steadily until it reached a low in March 2009. The index rose three consecutive months in April, May, and June of 2009, thereby forecasting a recovery. It will be interesting to see how long it takes for the recovery to emerge.

Computer Forecasting Models

Economists have developed highly complex econometric (statistical) models to improve the accuracy of macroeconomic forecasts. In essence, these models use past data on economic interrelationships to project how currently observed changes will influence the future path of key economic variables, such as real GDP, employment, and the price level. The most elaborate models use hundreds of variables and equations to simulate the future direction of various sectors and the economy's overall output and employment. Powerful high-speed computers are employed to forecast the future direction of the economy and analyze the effects of policy alternatives.

To date, the record of computer forecasting models is mixed. When economic conditions are relatively stable (for example, when the growth of real GDP and the rate of inflation follow a steady trend), the models have generally provided accurate forecasts for both aggregate economic variables and important subcomponents of the economy. Unfortunately, however, they have generally missed the major turns in the economic road. For example, none of the major computer models predicted the recessions of either 1990 or 2001. Neither did they forecast the severity of the downturn in 2008.

EXHIBIT 2
Index of Leading Indicators

The shaded periods represent recessions. The index of leading indicators forecasted each of the eight recessions during the 1959–2009 period. As the arrows show, however, the time lag between when the index turned down and when the economy fell into a recession varied. In addition, on four occasions (1962, 1966, 1984, and 1995), the index forecast a recession that did not occur.

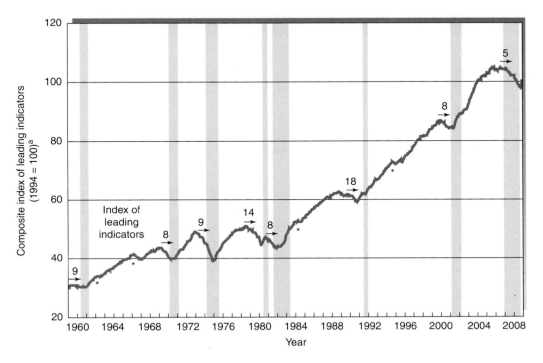

Source: http://www.conference-board.org.
[a]The arrows indicate the number of months that the downturn in the index preceded a recession. An asterisk (*) indicates a false signal of a recession.

Market Signals as Forecasting Tools

Many policy makers have favorite indicators—such as the consumer confidence index or the number of first-time applicants for unemployment benefits—that they believe are particularly good forecasting tools. Information supplied by certain markets can also sound an early warning that a change in policy is needed. For example, because they fluctuate daily and are determined in auction markets, changes in commodity prices often foretell future changes in the general price level. An increase in a broad index of commodity prices implies that money is plentiful (relative to demand). This suggests that the Fed should shift toward a more restrictive policy in order to offset future inflation. In contrast, falling commodity prices indicate that deflation is a potential future danger, in which case the Fed might want to shift toward a more expansionary policy.

Changes in exchange rates are also a source of information about the relative scarcity of money and fear of inflation. Because exchange rates, to a degree, reflect the willingness of foreigners to hold U.S. dollars, a decline in the exchange rate value of the dollar relative to other currencies suggests a fear of higher inflation and a reluctance to hold dollars. This would signal the need to shift to a more restrictive policy. Conversely, an increase in the exchange rate value of the dollar would indicate that the Fed has some leeway to shift to a more expansionary monetary policy. Most policy makers view market signals like commodity prices and exchange rates as supplements to, rather than substitutes for, other forecasting devices.

MEASURES OF ECONOMIC ACTIVITY

The Index of Leading Indicators

History indicates that no single indicator is able to forecast accurately the future direction of the economy. However, several economic variables do tend to reach a high or low prior to the peak of a business expansion or the trough of an economic recession. Such variables are called leading economic indicators.

To provide more reliable information on the future direction of the economy, economists have devised an index of ten such indicators:

1. Length of the average workweek in hours
2. Initial weekly claims for unemployment compensation
3. New orders placed with manufacturers
4. Percentage of companies receiving slower deliveries from suppliers
5. Contracts and orders for new plants and equipment
6. Permits for new housing starts
7. Interest rate spread, ten-year Treasury bonds less fed funds rate
8. Index of consumer expectations
9. Change in the index of stock prices (500 common stocks)
10. Change in the money supply (M2)

The variables included in the index were chosen both because of their tendency to lead (or predict) turns in the business cycle and because they are available frequently and promptly. In some cases, it is easy to see why a change in an economic indicator precedes a change in general economic activity. Consider the indicator of "new orders placed with manufacturers" (measured in constant dollars). An expansion in the volume of orders is generally followed by an expansion in manufacturing output. Similarly, manufacturers will tend to scale back their future production when a decline in new orders signals the probability of weak future demand for their products. The index of leading indicators can be found in *Business Cycle Indicators*, published by the Conference Board, a nonprofit business and research organization and online at http://www.conference-board.org.

Is Accurate Forecasting Feasible?

Many economists maintain that accurate forecasts of turns in the economy are beyond the reach of economics. Two major factors underlie this view. First, turns in the economic road often reflect economic shocks and unforeseen events—for example, an unexpected policy change, discovery of a new resource or technology, abnormal weather, or political upheaval in an important oil-exporting nation. There is no reason to believe that economists or anyone else will be able to predict these changes accurately and consistently. Thus, while economic theory helps to predict the implications of unforeseen events, it cannot foretell what those events will be and when they might occur. Second, the critics of forecasting models argue that the future will differ from the past because people will often make different choices as the result of what they learned from previous events. Therefore, forecasting models based on past relationships—including elaborate computer models—will never be able to generate consistently accurate predictions.

One thing is for sure: Forecasting the future direction of the economy is an imperfect science, and it is likely to remain so in the foreseeable future. But this is not the only deterrent to effective stabilization policy. Policy makers must also deal with expectations. A policy shift may exert a very different impact, depending on whether it is widely expected or catches people by surprise. Expectations may also influence the time lags and potency of alternative policy measures. Given the importance of expectations, we need to analyze how they are formed.

How Are Expectations Formed?

There are two general theories about how expectations are formed. Let's consider both of them.

Adaptive Expectations

The simplest theory concerning the formation of expectations is that people rely on the past to predict future trends. According to this theory, which economists call the **adaptive-expectations hypothesis**, decision makers believe that the best indicator of the future is what has happened in the recent past. For example, individuals would expect the price level to be stable next year if stable prices had been present during the past two or three years. Similarly, if prices had risen at an annual rate of 4 or 5 percent during the past several years, people would expect similar increases next year.

EXHIBIT 3 presents a graphic illustration of the adaptive-expectations hypothesis. In period 1, prices were stable (part a). Therefore, on the basis of the experience of period 1, decision makers assume that prices will be stable in period 2 (part b). Suppose, however, that the actual rate of inflation in period 2 jumps to 4 percent. If the 4 percent inflation rate continues throughout the period (periods may range from six months to two or three years in length), decision makers will change their expectations about the next period. Relying on the experience of period 2, they anticipate 4 percent inflation in period 3. When their expectations turn out to be incorrect (the actual rate of inflation during period 3 is 8 percent), they again alter their expectations accordingly. Then, during period 4, the actual rate of inflation declines to 4 percent, less than the expected rate. In period 5, decision makers adjust their expectations about future inflation downward but only after a time lag.

Of course, we would not expect the precise mechanical link between past occurrences and future expectations outlined in Exhibit 3. Rather than simply using the inflation rate of the immediate past period, people may use something like an average of recent inflation rates when forming their expectations. It is the structure, however, that is important. With adaptive expectations, people expect that the future will be pretty much like the recent past.

Adaptive-expectations hypothesis

The hypothesis that economic decision makers base their future expectations on actual outcomes observed during recent periods. For example, according to this view, the rate of inflation actually experienced during the past two or three years would be the major determinant of the rate of inflation expected for the next year.

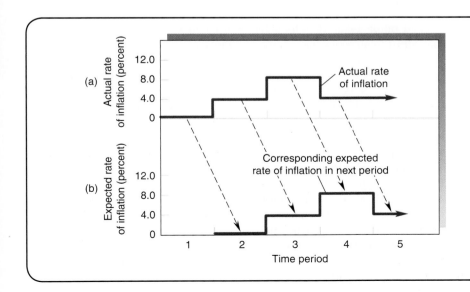

EXHIBIT 3
Adaptive-Expectations Hypothesis

According to the adaptive-expectations hypothesis, the actual occurrence during the most recent period (or set of periods) determines people's future expectations. Thus, the expected future rate of inflation (b) lags behind the actual rate of inflation (a) by one period as expectations are altered over time.

Moreover, when there is a movement upward or downward, there will always be a time lag before people will alter their expectations in light of the changed conditions.

Rational Expectations

Rational-expectations hypothesis

The hypothesis that economic decision makers weigh all available evidence, including information concerning the probable effects of current and future economic policy, when they form their expectations about future economic events (like the probable future inflation rate).

The idea that people form their expectations about the future on the basis of all available information, including knowledge about policy changes and how they affect the economy, is called the **rational-expectations hypothesis**. According to this view, rather than merely assuming that the future will be like the immediate past, people also consider the expected effects of changes in policy. Based on their understanding of economic policy, for example, people may alter their expectations regarding the future rate of inflation when the government runs a larger deficit or expands the supply of money more rapidly.

Perhaps an example will help clarify the rational-expectations hypothesis. Suppose that prices had increased at an annual rate of 3 percent during each of the past three years. In addition, assume that decision makers believe there is a relationship between the growth rate of the money supply and rising prices. They note that the money stock has expanded at a 12 percent annual rate during the last nine months, up from the 4 percent rate of the past several years. According to the rational-expectations hypothesis, people will integrate the shift to the more expansionary monetary policy into their forecast of the future inflation rate. For example, they might project an increase in the inflation rate, perhaps to the 6 to 10 percent range. In other words, based on the more expansionary monetary policy, people will begin to anticipate the higher rate of inflation even before it actually occurs. In contrast, under the adaptive-expectations hypothesis, the more expansionary monetary policy would exert no impact on the expectations of people, at least not until there was an increase in the rate of inflation.

The rational-expectations hypothesis does not assume that forecasts will always be correct. We live in a world of uncertainty. Even rational decision makers will err. But they will not continue to make the same errors. Thus, the rational-expectations hypothesis assumes that the forecasting errors of decision makers will tend to be random. For example, sometimes decision makers may overestimate the increase in the inflation rate caused by monetary expansion, and at other times they may underestimate it. But because they learn from prior experience, people will not continue to make the same types of mistakes year after year.

What Are the Major Differences between the Two Theories?

The adaptive- and rational-expectations theories differ in two major respects: (1) how quickly people adjust to a change and (2) the likelihood of systematic forecasting errors. If the adaptive-expectations theory is correct, people will adjust more slowly. When a more expansionary policy leads to inflation, for example, there will be a significant time lag, perhaps two or three years, before people come to expect the inflation and incorporate it into their decision making. In contrast, the rational-expectations theory implies that people will begin to anticipate more inflation as soon as they observe a move toward a more expansionary policy—perhaps even before there is an actual increase in the rate of inflation. Therefore, the time lag between a shift in policy and a change in expectations will be shorter under rational than under adaptive expectations.

Second, systematic errors will occur under adaptive but not under rational expectations. For example, with adaptive expectations, when the inflation rate is rising, decision makers will systematically tend to underestimate the future rate of inflation. In contrast, when the rate of inflation is falling, individuals will tend systematically to overestimate its future rate. The errors will be random under rational expectations. With rational expectations, people will be as likely to overestimate as to underestimate the inflationary impact of a shift to a more expansionary policy.

OUTSTANDING ECONOMIST

Robert Lucas (1937–)

The 1995 Nobel laureate Robert Lucas is generally given credit for the introduction of the rational-expectations theory into macroeconomics. Lucas's technical work in this area has substantially altered the way economists think about macroeconomic policy. He is a longtime professor of economics at the University of Chicago.

Macro Policy Implications of Adaptive and Rational Expectations

When it comes to setting macro policy, does it make any difference how quickly people alter their expectations and whether errors are random or systematic? The *AD–AS* model can be used to address this question. Suppose that there is a shift to a more expansionary macro policy—an increase in the money growth rate, for example. As part (a) of **EXHIBIT 4** illustrates, the policy shift will stimulate aggregate demand and place upward pressure on the price level (or the inflation rate in the dynamic case). Under adaptive expectations, people will initially fail to anticipate the higher prices. Therefore, as we have previously discussed, output will temporarily increase to Y_2, beyond the economy's long-run potential.

EXHIBIT 4
Expectations and the Short-Run Effects of Demand Stimulus

Because under adaptive expectations people do not anticipate inflation until after it occurs, a shift to a more expansionary policy will increase aggregate demand and lead to a temporary increase in real GDP from Y_F to Y_2, (part a). In contrast, under rational expectations, people quickly anticipate the inflationary impact of demand–stimulus policies and therefore resource prices and production costs rise as rapidly as prices. In this case, both AD and SRAS shift upward leading to an increase in the general level of prices (inflation), but there is no change in real output, even in the short run (part b).

(a) Expansionary policy under adaptive expectations

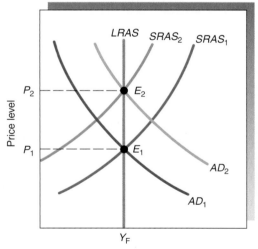

(b) Expansionary policy under rational expectations

Correspondingly, employment will expand and unemployment will recede below the economy's natural rate. When the effects of expansionary policy are unanticipated, both output and employment increase in the short run.

However, the output rate beyond the economy's capacity will be unsustainable even with adaptive expectations. As the expansionary policies persist and the rate of inflation increases, people will eventually begin to anticipate the higher rate of inflation. Once this happens, resource prices will rise as rapidly as product prices, and output will return to its long-run potential (Y_F). As a result, the high level of output and employment will only be temporary.

Part (b) of Exhibit 4 illustrates the impact of expansionary macroeconomic policy under rational expectations. Remember, with rational expectations, decision makers will quickly begin to anticipate the probable effects of the more expansionary policy—stronger demand and a rising rate of inflation, for example—and alter their choices accordingly. Agreements specifying future wage rates and resource prices will quickly make allowance for an expected increase in the price level. These agreements might even incorporate **escalator clauses** providing for automatic increases in nominal wages as the general price level rises. When buyers and sellers in the resource market anticipate fully and adjust rapidly to the effects of the demand–stimulus policies, wage rates and resource prices will rise as rapidly as product prices. Hence, the short-run aggregate supply curve will shift upward (to $SRAS_2$) as rapidly as the aggregate demand curve. Under these circumstances, an expansionary policy that leads to an increase in aggregate demand will generate only a higher general level of prices (the move from E_1 to E_2 in part b of Exhibit 4). There will be no real output increase even in the short run. Thus, the rational-expectations hypothesis implies that when decision makers quickly anticipate the inflationary side effects of an expansionary policy, the policy will fail to expand output even temporarily.

Policy Implications: Short Run versus Long Run

The policy implications of the two theories differ in the short run but not in the long run. In the short run, demand–stimulus policies will expand output and employment under adaptive expectations but not under rational expectations. In the long run, however, the implications of the two theories are identical. Like rational expectations, the adaptive-expectations theory indicates that decision makers will eventually anticipate the inflationary effects of the more expansionary policy. Once this happens, output will recede to the economy's long-run potential. Therefore, both theories imply that the long-run effects of a more expansionary macro policy will be inflation rather than sustainable increases in output. Both also imply that price stability and full-employment output are complementary when considered over lengthy time frames.

The Phillips Curve: The View of the 1960s versus Today

In the late 1950s, British economist A. W. Phillips examined the historical data on the relationship between wage inflation and unemployment in the United Kingdom.[2] As a result, a curve indicating the relationship between the rate of inflation and the rate of unemployment is known as the **Phillips curve**. **EXHIBIT 5** uses a graphic from the 1969 *Economic Report of the President* to illustrate the idea of the Phillips curve. When the unemployment rate was plotted against the rate of inflation in the United States during 1954–1968, the points mapped out a curve indicating that there was an inverse relationship between the rate of inflation and the rate of unemployment. When inflation was high, the unemployment rate tended to be low. Correspondingly, when the inflation rate was low, the unemployment rate tended to be high.

Escalator clause

A contractual agreement that periodically and automatically adjusts money wage rates upward as the price level rises. Such clauses are sometimes referred to as cost-of-living adjustments, or COLAs.

Phillips curve

A curve that illustrates the relationship between the rate of inflation and the rate of unemployment.

[2]A. W. Phillips, "The Relationship between Unemployment and the Rate of Change of Money Wages in the United Kingdom, 1861–1957," *Economica* 25 (1958): 238–99.

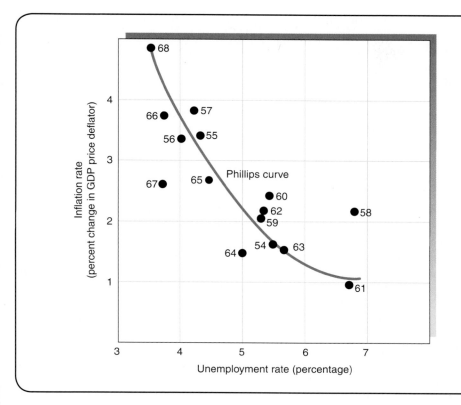

EXHIBIT 5
Early View of the Phillips Curve

The Phillips curve shows the relationship between inflation and unemployment. The dots on this diagram from the 1969 Economic Report of the President represent the inflation rate and unemployment rate for each year between 1954 and 1968. Note that the chart suggests that higher rates of inflation are associated with lower rates of unemployment. Because they failed to recognize the importance of expectations, many economists and policy makers in the 1960s and 1970s thought this relationship was stable. Thus, they believed that expansionary (inflationary) policies could permanently reduce the rate of unemployment. As the record of the 1970s shows, this view is fallacious.

In the 1960s, most macroeconomists ignored the potential impact of expectations. Instead, they believed that there was a direct trade-off between inflation and unemployment—that a lower rate of unemployment could be achieved if we were willing to tolerate a little more inflation.[3] This view provided the foundation for the inflationary policies of the 1970s. As John Maynard Keynes once noted, ideas have consequences, both when they are right and when they are wrong.

Beginning in the latter part of the 1960s, both monetary and fiscal policy became more expansionary. The inflation rate rose to the 3 percent to 6 percent range, but as the higher rates of inflation persisted, the unemployment rate also began to rise. As macroeconomic policy became even more expansionary, the unemployment rate dipped briefly, but it soon returned to exceedingly high levels. By the end of the 1970s, the U.S. economy was characterized by high rates of both inflation and unemployment. The inflation rate in 1979 was 11.3 percent, and in 1980 it jumped to 13.5 percent, about 10 percentage points higher than the rates of the late 1960s. But even these high rates of inflation failed to reduce the unemployment rate. In 1980, the rate of unemployment stood at 7.1 percent, well above the 4.9 percent registered during the recessionary year of 1970.

What went wrong? Given what we know today about expectations, this is now an easy question to answer. As both the adaptive- and rational-expectations theories indicate, the alleged trade-off between inflation and unemployment will dissipate once people anticipate a higher rate of inflation. Put another way, the Phillips curve is not fixed. When the inflation rate increases, people will come to anticipate the higher rate of inflation, and this will cause the Phillips curve to shift upward and to the right. The adaptive-expectations theory implies that there will be a time lag—perhaps one to three years—before people are able to anticipate and adjust fully to a higher rate of inflation. But once the higher inflation rate is anticipated,

---

[3]For example, Nobel prize winners Paul Samuelson and Robert Solow told the American Economic Association in 1959,

"In order to achieve the nonperfectionist's goal of high enough output to give us no more than 3 percent unemployment, the price index might have to rise by as much as 4 to 5 percent per year. That much price rise [inflation] would seem to be the necessary cost of high employment and production in the years immediately ahead."

See Paul A. Samuelson and Robert Solow, "Our Menu of Policy Changes," *American Economic Review* (May 1960).

it will not lead to an expansion in either output or employment. The rational-expectations theory indicates that the adjustment period will be brief. In fact, with rational expectations, there may not be any trade-off between inflation and unemployment, even in the short run.

However, the more important point is that both adaptive and rational expectations imply that people will eventually anticipate the higher rate of inflation and, once this happens, the inflationary policies will fail to expand output and employment. Integration of expectations into the Phillips curve analysis indicates that there is no sustainable trade-off between inflation and unemployment. Expectations undermine the simple Phillips curve analysis of the 1960s.[4]

Expectations and the Modern View of the Phillips Curve

If accurately anticipated by decision makers, even high rates of inflation—rates of 10 or 15 percent, for example—will fail to reduce unemployment below its natural rate.[5] Of course, people won't always correctly anticipate the rate of inflation, particularly if there is an abrupt change in the rate. Within the expectations framework, it is the difference between the actual and expected inflation rate that will influence output and employment. On the one hand, when inflation is greater than anticipated, profit margins will improve, output will expand, and unemployment will fall below its natural rate. On the other hand, when the actual rate of inflation is less than the expected rate, profits will be abnormally low, output will recede, and unemployment will rise above its natural rate.

EXHIBIT 6 recasts the Phillips curve within the expectations framework. When people underestimate the actual rate of inflation, abnormally low unemployment will occur. Conversely, when decision makers expect a higher rate of inflation than what actually occurs—when they overestimate the inflation rate—unemployment will rise above its natural rate. When the actual and expected inflation rates are equal, the economy's output will be at its potential and unemployment at its natural rate.

EXHIBIT 6
Modern Expectational
Phillips Curve

It is the difference between the actual and expected rates of inflation that influences the unemployment rate, not the size of the inflation rate, as the earlier, naive Phillips curve analysis implied. When inflation is greater than anticipated (people underestimate it), unemployment will fall below the natural rate. In contrast, when inflation is less than people anticipate (people overestimate it) unemployment will rise above the natural rate. If the inflation rate is correctly anticipated by decision makers, the natural rate of unemployment will result.

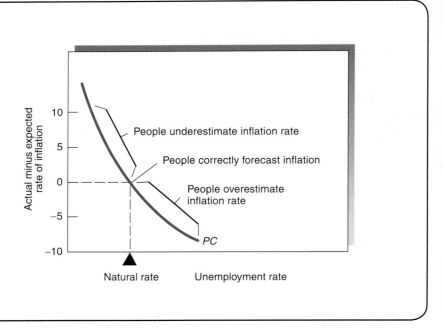

[4]Even during the 1960s, there were some critics of the inflation–unemployment trade-off view. See Edmund S. Phelps, "Phillips Curves, Expectations of Inflation and Optimal Employment over Time," *Economica* 3 (1967): 254–81; and Milton Friedman, "The Role of Monetary Policy," *American Economic Review* (May 1968): 1–17.

[5]Empirically, higher rates of inflation are generally associated with greater variability in the inflation rate. Erratic variability increases economic uncertainty. It is likely to inhibit business activity, reduce the volume of mutually advantageous exchange, and cause the level of employment to fall. Thus, higher, more variable inflation rates may well increase the rate of unemployment.

When the inflation rate is steady, when it is neither rising nor falling, people will come to anticipate the rate accurately. The steady rate will be built into long-term contracts, like collective bargaining agreements, building leases, and bank loans. Under these conditions, profit margins will be normal, and output will move toward the economy's long-run potential. Correspondingly, the actual rate of unemployment will move toward its natural rate—its minimum sustainable rate. In fact, the natural rate of unemployment is sometimes defined as the unemployment rate present when the inflation rate is neither rising nor falling. In contrast with the early Phillips curve view, the modern view indicates that if policy makers want to keep the unemployment rate low, they should follow policies consistent with a low and steady rate of inflation—one that people will be able to forecast accurately.

EXHIBIT 7 presents data on the *change* in the inflation rate (the four-quarter moving average) over the past several decades. The exhibit illustrates the impact of both abrupt changes and low steady rates of inflation. When the change in the inflation rate spikes upward, it means there has been a sharp increase in the rate of inflation during the last twelve months. Conversely, a downward spike means that the inflation rate has fallen sharply. Predictably, these abrupt changes will be difficult for people to forecast accurately. Therefore, the actual rate of inflation is likely to rise above the expected rate when the inflation rate increases abruptly and fall below it when there is an abrupt downturn in the inflation rate.

Thus, one would expect the unemployment rate to fall when there is a sharp upturn in the inflation rate and rise when there is a sharp downturn. As Exhibit 7 shows, this has been the case. Notice how the substantial increases in the rate of inflation during 1973 and 1976–1978 and even the more moderate increases of the 1980s were associated with

EXHIBIT 7
Unemployment and Changes in the Rate of Inflation

Here, we show the relationship between changes in the inflation rate (four-quarter moving average) and the rate of unemployment. Abrupt changes in the inflation rate will be difficult for people to anticipate correctly. Notice how the sharp falls in the inflation rate during 1974, 1980–1981, and 1988–1989 preceded recessions and substantial increases in the unemployment rate. Also notice that the steadier (and lower) inflation rates since the early 1990s have been associated with lower and stabler rates of unemployment.

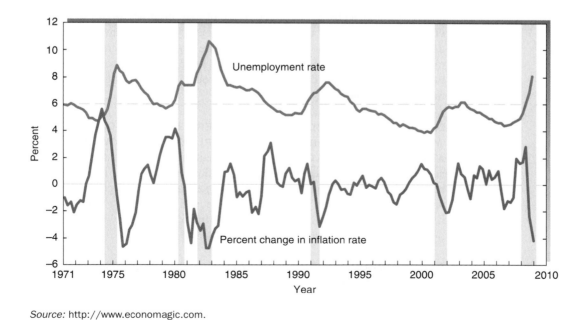

Source: http://www.economagic.com.

downturns in the rate of unemployment. In contrast, the sharp reductions in the rate of inflation during 1974, 1980–1981, and 1989 preceded substantial increases in the rate of unemployment. The economic crisis of 2008–2009 was a little different. In that case, a sharp decline in the inflation rate was associated with a substantial increase in the unemployment rate during the same time period.

Exhibit 7 also shows that when the inflation rate is steadier, the unemployment rate tends to be lower and more stable. Note how, compared to the 1970s, the inflation rate was lower and the swings in the rate were more moderate during 1985–2005. Correspondingly, the rate of unemployment was also lower and more stable during the latter period of greater price stability.

What Have We Learned about Macro Policy?

Macroeconomics is relatively new. Prior to the Great Depression, research on measurement of national income and sources of economic fluctuations was sparse. It was not until the 1960s that policy makers developed much interest in the possible use of fiscal policy as a stabilization tool. Moreover, fifty years ago, neither economists nor policy makers thought that monetary policy exerted much impact on anything other than the general level of prices. While awareness of the potential effects of fiscal and monetary policy increased during 1960–1980, there was little appreciation of the time lags, importance of expectations, and difficulties involved in the effective use of these tools to promote stability.

Macroeconomics has come a long way during the past half century. Real world experience, research, and developments in economic theory have vastly expanded our knowledge of both the potential and limitations of fiscal and monetary policy. Substantial agreement has emerged on a number of key points. Debate continues on several others. As we bring our analysis of economic fluctuations to a close, let's consider both.

Areas of Agreement

1. IT IS DIFFICULT TO TIME CHANGES IN MONETARY AND FISCAL POLICY CORRECTLY, AND THEREFORE CONSTANT POLICY SWINGS ARE LIKELY TO DO MORE DAMAGE THAN GOOD. If it is going to exert a stabilizing impact, a macro policy change must exert stimulus during downturns and restraint during inflationary booms. Automatic stabilizers can help achieve these objectives, but **effective use of discretionary policy is problematic.** Given our limited forecasting abilities and the time lags accompanying changes in monetary and fiscal policy, persistent shifts in policy are likely to be destabilizing. Therefore, policy makers should not be constantly changing policy in response to business cycle conditions. Instead, they should follow a steady course that will reduce instability arising from inappropriate policy.

2. EXPANSIONARY POLICIES THAT GENERATE STRONG DEMAND AND INFLATION WILL NOT REDUCE THE RATE OF UNEMPLOYMENT BELOW THE NATURAL RATE— AT LEAST NOT FOR LONG. Both the integration of expectations into macroeconomic analysis and the experience of the 1970s illustrate that there is no sustainable trade-off between inflation and unemployment. Once people come to expect inflation, the inflation–unemployment trade-off will dissipate. Moreover, excessively expansionary monetary and fiscal policy will lead to high and variable inflation rates that will generate uncertainty and instability, and thereby retard long-run economic growth.

3. PRICE STABILITY IS THE PROPER GOAL OF MONETARY POLICY. Inflation is caused by expansionary monetary policy, and therefore its control is the responsibility of monetary policy makers. When the Fed keeps the inflation rate at a low and therefore easily predictable rate, it lays the groundwork for the smooth operation of markets and long-term healthy growth. In fact, price stability is so important that it is one of our twelve Keys to Prosperity.

Maintenance of price stability is the essence of sound monetary policy; price stability provides the foundation for both economic stability and the efficient operation of markets.

The high standard of living that Americans enjoy is the result of gains from specialization, division of labor, and mass production processes. Price stability and the smooth operation of the pricing system will help individuals more fully realize the potential gains from these sources. In contrast, high and variable rates of inflation create uncertainty, distort relative prices, and reduce the efficiency of a market economy.

If investors and other business decision makers can count on monetary policy makers to maintain price stability, a potential source of uncertainty is reduced. This will encourage investment and other business activities and thereby promote a high level of employment and strong economic growth. When the monetary authorities persistently achieve price stability, they have done their part to establish the environment for long-run prosperity.

Areas of Continued Debate

While general agreement has emerged in some areas, debate continues in others. These unresolved questions add to the excitement of economics. We will mention three key areas of continued debate among macroeconomists.

1. DOES FISCAL POLICY EXERT MUCH IMPACT ON AGGREGATE DEMAND? While most economists do not believe that discretionary fiscal policy can be constantly adjusted in a manner that will promote stability, nonetheless, many believe that budget deficits provide demand stimulus, particularly during a severe recession. Others argue that the secondary effects of higher interest rates and future taxes undermine the potency of fiscal policy.

2. DURING A SEVERE RECESSION, WILL AN INCREASE IN GOVERNMENT SPENDING BE MORE EFFECTIVE THAN A REDUCTION IN TAXES AS A TOOL TO PROMOTE RECOVERY? Most Keynesian economists favor increases in government spending because they fear that a large share of a tax reduction will be saved and therefore not add much stimulus to aggregate demand. Non-Keynesians argue that the demand stimulus effects of spending increases are likely to be timed poorly and that they will generally be driven by special interest politics and therefore likely to flow into projects that are economically inefficient. Moreover, supply-side economists argue that reductions in tax rates will enhance the incentive to work, invest, and employ others, which will help promote recovery.

3. IS ECONOMIC INSTABILITY THE RESULT OF THE NATURAL TENDENCIES OF A MARKET ECONOMY OR THE ERRORS OF POLICY MAKERS? Many economists, particularly Keynesians, believe that market economies are inherently unstable. This view stresses that economic expansions breed optimism, rising asset prices, and strong aggregate demand, which culminate in inflation and an unsustainable economic boom. Similarly, a downturn will tend to feed on itself, leading to pessimism, falling asset prices, and reductions in aggregate demand, which, if not counteracted by macro policy, will end in chronic and prolonged recessions.

Other economists, particularly monetarists, argue that economic fluctuations are largely the result of stop–go monetary policy. They believe that the severe episodes of both inflation and depression have been the result of monetary disturbances. Those who stress policy errors cite the unstable and highly expansionary monetary policy of the 1970s as the primary reason for the inflation and instability of that era. They also point to the 30 percent decline in the money supply between 1929 and 1933 and another decline during 1937–1938 as the primary cause of the Great Depression. (For more information on this topic, see Special Topic 6, Lessons From the Great Depression.)

The crisis of 2008 illustrates the continuing debate. Those who stress the inherent instability of markets point to the excessive leverage of major banks, the fear, and sharp reduction in demand that engulfed the economy during the latter half of 2008 as support

EXHIBIT 8
Reduction in the
Incidence of Recession

*The U.S. economy was in
recession 32.8 percent of the
time during the 1910–1959
period and 22.8 percent of the
time between 1960 and 1982,
but only 6.0 percent of the time
during 1983–2007.*

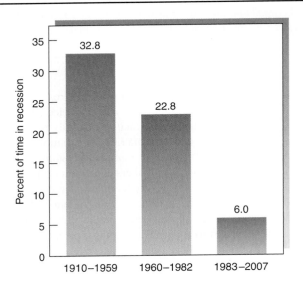

Source: R. E. Lipsey and D. Preston, *Source Book of
Statistics Relating to Construction* (1966); and National
Bureau of Economic Research, http://www.nber.org.

for their view. On the other hand, those who stress the role of policy errors argue that
the primary cause of the crisis was housing regulations that undermined sound lending
practices and the instability of Fed policy during 2002–2006. Of course, the two theories
are not mutually exclusive. Both the nature of markets and policy errors may be important
sources of economic instability.

Perspective on Recent Instability

The crisis of 2008–2009 was probably the most severe since the Great Depression. In
some ways, it was generated by "the perfect storm," a combination of improper monetary
policy, perverse regulation, a long-term increase in household indebtedness, and excessive
leverage by financial institutions. (See Special Topic 5, The Crash of 2008: Cause and
Aftermath, for a detailed analysis of this issue.)

However, while reflecting on the lessons of this crisis, we should not forget that
1983–2007 was the most stable quarter of a century in American history. During this
twenty-five-year period, there were only two downturns, and the economy experienced
only seventeen months of recession. This stability is unprecedented. **EXHIBIT 8** illustrates
this point. From 1910 to 1959, the U.S. economy was in recession 32.8 percent of the
time. Between 1960 and 1982, recession was present 22.8 percent of the time. But, during
1983–2007, the economy was in recession only 6.0 percent of the time.

These figures show that the economic ups and downs of the past fifty years have been
less severe than during earlier periods. Inspection of Exhibit 1 also illustrates this point.
What accounts for the greater stability of recent years? Most economists would credit
monetary policy. Certainly, monetary policy mistakes were made. Both the growth rate of
the money supply and the Taylor Rule indicate that monetary policy was excessively expansionary and characterized by an unnecessary stop–go cycle during 1968–1979. There is also
good reason to believe that monetary instability was a major contributing factor to both the
substantial increase and then the collapse of housing prices that provided the foundation for
the crisis of 2008. However, compared to earlier periods, monetary policy has been more
stable during the past fifty years. This has been particularly true since the Fed, under the
leadership of Paul Volcker, moved to bring the inflation of the 1970s under control. Since
the mid-1980s, the Fed has avoided wide swings in the rate of inflation. In turn, the lower
and more stable rates of inflation have enhanced the overall stability of the U.S. economy.

Looking ahead

As we have stressed, macroeconomics is about economic growth and fluctuations. While recent chapters have focused on fluctuations, the next three chapters will address economic growth. They will explain why income levels and growth rates differ across countries and analyze what policy makers can do to create an environment conducive for growth and prosperity.

KEY POINTS

▼ Historically, the United States has experienced substantial swings in real output. Prior to World War II, year-to-year changes in real GDP of 5 to 10 percent were experienced on several occasions. In recent decades, the fluctuations in real GDP have been more moderate.

▼ If stimulus could be injected during periods of recession and restraint during inflationary booms, macro policy could moderate the ups and downs of the business cycle. Proper timing, however, is difficult to achieve because it takes time to recognize and institute a policy change, and the effects of the change are not immediate.

▼ In order to time a change properly, policy makers need to know where the economy will be six to eighteen months in the future. Forecasting devices such as the index of leading indicators will be helpful, but forecasting is a highly imperfect science.

▼ There are two major theories as to how expectations are formed. According to the adaptive-expectations hypothesis, individuals form their expectations about the future on the basis of data from the recent past. The rational-expectations hypothesis assumes that people use all pertinent information, including data on the conduct of current policy, when forming their expectations about the future.

▼ With adaptive expectations, an unanticipated shift to a more expansionary policy will temporarily stimulate output and employment. In contrast, with rational expectations, expansionary policy may fail to increase output, and, if achieved, any increase in output will be brief. However, both expectations theories indicate that sustained expansionary policies will lead to inflation without permanently increasing output and employment.

▼ The Phillips curve outlines the relationship between inflation and unemployment. In the 1960s, it was widely believed that higher rates of inflation could be used to reduce the unemployment rate. This view provided the foundation for the expansionary policies and inflation of the 1970s. Once expectations are integrated into macro analysis, it is clear that this early view of the Phillips curve is fallacious.

▼ Monetary policy consistent with price stability is a key ingredient of effective stabilization policy. The fluctuations in output and employment have been less severe in recent decades. A more stable monetary policy deserves much of the credit for this increased stability.

CRITICAL ANALYSIS QUESTIONS

1. The chair of the Council of Economic Advisers has requested that you write a short paper explaining how economic policy can be used to stabilize the economy and achieve a high level of economic growth during the next five years. Be sure to make specific proposals. Indicate why your recommendations will work. You may submit your paper to your instructor.

*2. How does economic instability during the past sixty years compare with instability prior to World War II? Is there any evidence that stabilization policy has either increased or decreased economic stability during recent decades?

3. State in your own words the adaptive-expectations hypothesis. How does the theory of rational expectations differ from that of adaptive expectations?

4. What is the index of leading indicators? Why is it useful to macro policy makers?

*5. How would you expect the actual unemployment rate to compare with the natural unemployment rate in the following cases?
   a. Prices are stable and have been stable for the last four years.
   b. The current inflation rate is 3 percent, and this rate was widely anticipated more than a year ago.
   c. Expansionary policies lead to an abrupt increase in the inflation rate from 3 percent to 7 percent.
   d. There is an abrupt reduction in the inflation rate from 7 percent to 2 percent.

6. Compare and contrast the impact of an unexpected shift to a more expansionary monetary policy under rational and adaptive expectations. Are the implications of the two theories different in the short run? Are the long-run implications different? Explain.

*7. What are some of the practical problems that limit the effective use of discretionary monetary and fiscal policy as stabilization tools?

8. Many central banks now indicate that their primary objective is to keep inflation at a persistently low rate. If the rate of inflation is persistently low, will this help reduce the ups and downs of the business cycle? Why or why not?

9. How did integration of expectations into the Phillips curve analysis and rejection of the view that higher inflation will reduce the unemployment rate affect macro policy in the last two decades?

10. Prior to the mid-1970s, many economists thought that inflation would lead to a lower rate of unemployment. Why? How does the modern view of the Phillips curve differ from the earlier view?

*11. Answer the following questions:
   a. What is the most important thing the Fed can do to promote economic stability?
   b. Can expansionary monetary policy reduce interest rates and stimulate a higher growth rate of real output in the long run?
   c. If monetary policy is too expansionary, how will nominal interest rates and the general level of prices be affected?

12. Is a market economy inherently unstable? Historically, have policy errors been the primary source of economic instability? Cite empirical evidence to support your response to each of these questions.

*Asterisk denotes questions for which answers are given in Appendix B.

Creating an Environment for Growth and Prosperity

- Why is economic growth important?

- How does sustained economic growth change income levels and the lives of people?

- What are the major sources of economic growth?

- What institutions and policies will promote growth and prosperity?

Certain fundamental principles— formulating sound monetary and fiscal policies, removing domestic price controls, opening the economy to international market forces, ensuring property rights and private property, creating competition, and reforming and limiting the role of government— are essential for a healthy market economy.

—Economic Report of the President, 1991

Throughout history, most of the world's population has struggled fifty, sixty, and seventy hours per week just to obtain the basic necessities of life—food, clothing, and shelter. During the last two centuries, sustained economic growth has changed that situation for most people in North America, Europe, Oceania, and Japan. Even in these regions, however, rising incomes have not always been the norm. According to Henry Phelps Brown, a twentieth-century British economist and author, the real income of English building-trade workers was virtually unchanged between 1215 and 1798, a period of nearly six centuries.[1] In other parts of Europe, workers experienced a similar stagnation of real earnings throughout much of this period. Low incomes and widespread poverty are still the norm in most countries—particularly those of South and Central America, Africa, and South-Central Asia.

Why do some countries grow and achieve high levels of income while others stagnate? The Keys to Prosperity series has already addressed several dimensions of this issue, but we now want to consider it more directly, and in a more comprehensive manner. ∎

The Importance of Economic Growth

Robert Lucas, the 1995 Nobel laureate, has stated, "Once you start thinking about economic growth, it is hard to think about anything else."[2] Why do Lucas and many other economists place so much emphasis on economic growth? Growth provides the source for higher incomes and living standards. Growth of real output is necessary for the growth of real income. Without growth, higher income levels cannot be achieved.

Economic growth expands the productive capacity of an economy. As **EXHIBIT 1** shows, an expansion in output can be illustrated within the production possibilities analysis framework. For example, if a country experienced economic growth during the first decade of this century, this means that the country would be able to produce a larger quantity of both consumer and capital goods in 2010 than was true in 2000. This growth will shift the economy's production possibilities curve outward (from *AA* to *BB*).

Per capita GDP

Income per person. Increases in income per person are vital for the achievement of higher living standards.

When a nation's real GDP is increasing more rapidly than its population, **per capita GDP**—that is, GDP per person—will also expand. Growth of per capita GDP means more goods and services per person. In most cases, this will mean that the typical person has a higher standard of living—a better diet, improved health and access to medical services, a longer life expectancy, and greater educational opportunity. Studies have also shown that as per capita income increases, people place more emphasis on clean air and water and generally take more time for recreation and leisure. Thus, a higher per capita income means not only more material goods but also a cleaner environment, more leisure time, and the availability of a wide range of goods and services that most would consider an improvement in the quality of life.

The Impact of Sustained Economic Growth

Rule of 70

If a variable grows at a rate of *x* percent per year, 70/*x* will approximate the number of years required for the variable to double.

There is a tendency to think that a 1 or 2 percent difference in growth is of little consequence. When sustained over a lengthy period, however, seemingly small differences in growth can exert a huge impact.

The **rule of 70** provides a simple tool that can help us understand the importance of sustained growth. This rule makes it easy to figure how many years it will take for income to

[1]Henry Phelps Brown with Margaret H. Browne, *A Century of Pay: The Course of Pay and Production in France, Germany, Sweden, the United Kingdom, and the United States of America,* 1860–1960 (London: Macmillan, 1968).

[2]Robert E. Lucas Jr., "On the Mechanics of Economic Development," *Journal of Monetary Economics* 22, no. 1 (1988): 3–42.

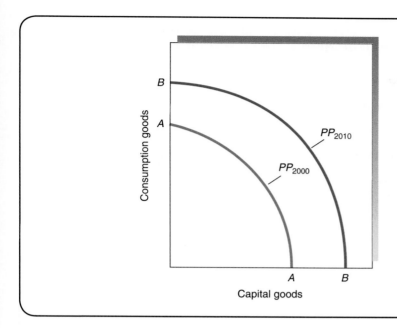

double at various rates of growth. If you divide seventy by a country's average growth rate, it will approximate the number of years required for an income level to double.[3] For example, at an average annual growth rate of 5 percent, it would take fourteen years (70 divided by 5) for the income level to double. If a country's average annual growth rate was 3.5 percent, income would double every twenty years (70 divided by 3.5). At a 1 percent growth rate, it would take 70 years for income to double. (*Note*: The rule of 70 also applies to the rate of return on savings and investments. Clearly, over a long period of time, small differences in rates of return can make a big difference in the accumulated value of your savings or investment.)

EXHIBIT 2 illustrates the impact of differences in growth rates over a lengthy time period, 30 years in this example. Consider four countries with the same initial level of per capita income, $10,000. The exhibit indicates what their incomes will be 30 years later at four different growth rates: 4 percent, 2 percent, 1 percent, and 0 percent. After 30 years, the country growing at an annual rate of 4 percent will have an income of $32,434. The income of the country growing at a 2 percent rate will be only $18,114. A country with a 1 percent rate of growth will achieve only an income of $13,478 after 30 years, while the income of the country with a 0 percent growth rate will still be $10,000. Thus, even though the four countries all had the same initial income, 30 years later the income level of the one with the 4 percent growth rate will be far greater than that of the others.

Differences in sustained growth rates over a few decades will substantially alter the relative incomes of countries. On the one hand, nations that experience sustained periods of rapid economic growth will move up the income ladder swiftly and eventually achieve high-income status. On the other hand, nations that grow slowly or experience declines in real GDP per capita will slide down the economic ladder.

Key Sources of Economic Growth and High Incomes

Why do some countries grow and achieve high income levels whereas others remain poor and less developed? Gains from trade, entrepreneurial discovery, and investment are the major sources of economic growth. Let's take a closer look at each.

---

[3]Sometimes this rule is called the rule of 72, rather than 70. Whereas 70 yields more accurate estimates for growth rates of less than 5 percent, 72 yields slightly more accurate estimates when the annual rate of growth exceeds 5 percent.

EXHIBIT 2

The Impact of Growth Rate Differences over a Thirty-Year Period

Here, we consider the impact of growth over a thirty-year period on four economies with the same initial income level, $10,000. If a country grows 4 percent annually, thirty years later its income will be $32,434, more than 3.2 times the initial figure. In contrast, if a country grows at a 2 percent annual rate, thirty years later its income will be only a little more than half that of the economy that grew more rapidly. The income of a country growing at a 1 percent rate will be even lower, $13,478.

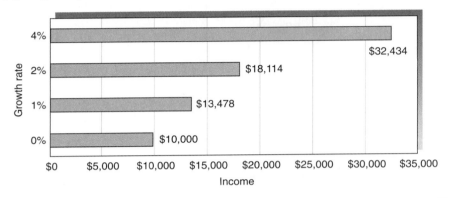

Gains from Trade

As we have stressed throughout this textbook, trade is mutually advantageous. All trading partners potentially gain, and this provides the motivation for the exchange. Trade moves goods, services, and resources from people who value them less to people who value them more. It also helps trading partners achieve larger outputs and income levels as the result of division of labor, specialization, and adoption of methods of mass production. When individuals and businesses specialize in those activities for which they are a low opportunity cost supplier, they will be able to produce more output. Similarly, larger outputs and lower unit cost can often be achieved when a good or service is supplied in large quantities. For example, goods ranging from pencils to automobiles to DVD players can be produced more economically when they are supplied by firms producing them in the millions rather than the thousands.

Henry Ford developed the automobile assembly line shown here. His mass production methods resulted in substantially lower per unit cost. Mass production methods and expansion in the size of the market help us get more from the available resources and achieve higher income levels.

AP Photo/Ford Motor Co.

It is easy to recognize that our living standard would be meager if we could not trade with others, as we all acquire numerous goods through trade that would be costly or virtually impossible for us to produce for ourselves. Suppose that you and others in your neighborhood, city, or even state could not trade with outsiders. Clearly, your living standards would decline sharply because you would derive fewer benefits from specialization and economies that accompany large-scale production methods.

It is difficult to exaggerate the importance of trade in our modern world. When individuals and businesses are permitted to trade over a broader market area, they will be able to produce a larger output and consume a more diverse bundle of goods. Conversely, obstacles that restrict trade, either domestic or international, will reduce output, income, and the general living standard of the populace.

Entrepreneurship, Technology, and the Discovery of Better Ways of Doing Things

The discovery of new products that are highly valued relative to cost and new production methods that reduce costs provide a driving force for economic growth. Sometimes these discoveries reflect **technological advancement**. In other instances, they are the result of innovation; the practical application, extension, and dissemination of new ideas, processes, and technologies. Clearly, the use of brainpower to discover new products and lower cost production processes has substantially enhanced our production possibilities. During the last 250 years, the substitution of power-driven machines for human labor; the development of miracle grains, fertilizer, and new sources of energy; and improvements in transportation and communication have vastly improved living standards. Innovations and advancements in technology continue to affect the availability of goods and services. Just think of the new products introduced during the last fifty years: CD players, high definition televisions, microcomputers, word processors, microwave ovens, video cameras, cell phones, DVD players, heart bypass surgery, hip replacements, LASIK eye surgery, auto air conditioners, and so on. These products have vastly changed the quality of our lives.

New and improved products have replaced older ones and often rendered them obsolete. The automobile replaced the horse and buggy; the word processor replaced the typewriter; the phonograph was replaced by the cassette tape player, which was later largely replaced by CD and now MP3 players. Joseph Schumpeter, the great Austrian economist, referred to this discovery and replacement process as "creative destruction."

But, new and improved products do not just happen. They must be discovered. This highlights the role of the entrepreneur, the decision maker willing to take risks and try out new ideas.[4] Some of the new ideas will be good ones, but many will not. The majority of new businesses fail within the first few years, and relatively few turn into major successes like Microsoft, eBay, or FedEx did.

In order to be successful, an entrepreneur must be good at discovering how to apply scientific knowledge in a practical manner. For example, Henry Ford played only a minor role in the invention and development of the automobile. Nonetheless, he literally "put America on wheels" via his application of specialization and division of labor. Through his innovative assembly line production techniques, he lowered the production cost of automobiles. This cost saving was passed on to consumers in the form of lower prices, making cars affordable to more people. Soon, almost everyone could afford a car, and Ford consequently realized both record sales and profits. More recently, Fred Smith, the president and founder of FedEx, realized that the computer age would generate a strong demand for a rapid delivery system. He figured out how to combine both ground and air transportation into a network delivery system capable of transporting a package virtually overnight anywhere in the world. Without

Technological advancement

The introduction of new techniques or methods that increase output per unit of input.

---

[4]The modern understanding of the importance of entrepreneurship as a source of economic growth is founded on the work of Joseph Schumpeter and Israel Kirzner. See Joseph A. Schumpeter, *Capitalism, Socialism, and Democracy* (New York: Harper, 1942); Israel M. Kirzner, *Competition and Entrepreneurship* (Chicago: University of Chicago Press, 1973); and "Entrepreneurial Discovery and the Competitive Market Process: An Austrian Approach," *Journal of Economic Literature* 35, no. 1 (1997): 60–85.

Entrepreneurial discovery of improved products and lower-cost production methods is a driving force of economic growth. For example, when it was initially developed, the phonograph made recorded music available to millions of listeners. But it was eventually replaced by the CD player and still later by the MP3 player. Economists refer to this replacement of a product by a new and superior one as "creative destruction."

innovators like Ford, Smith, and millions of others operating on a smaller scale, scientific breakthroughs are merely ideas waiting to be discovered and brought to market.

Before a new idea is tried, it is difficult to tell if it is a good one. From the standpoint of economic growth, it is vitally important that entrepreneurs have a strong incentive to try out new ideas, but it is also important that wasteful projects that reduce the value of resources be brought to a halt. In a market economy, profits and losses achieve these objectives. New ideas that increase the value of resources—by creating enough value to consumers to offset the opportunity cost of production—generate economic profits for the entrepreneurs who discover them. In contrast, ideas that drain resources away from other more valuable uses and turn them into something not as valuable to consumers result in losses, which will provide entrepreneurs with a strong incentive to discontinue such projects. Thus, the market process promotes both the discovery of better ways of doing things and the termination of projects that reduce the value of resources.

Investment in Physical and Human Capital

Equipment can have a substantial impact on a person's ability to produce. Even Robinson Crusoe living on an uninhabited island could catch more fish with a net than he could with his hands. Farmers working with modern tractors and plows can cultivate many more acres than could their great-grandparents, who probably worked with hoes. Similarly, education and training that upgrade workers' knowledge and skills can vastly improve their productivity. For example, a cabinetmaker, skilled after years of training and experience, can build cabinets far more rapidly and efficiently than a neophyte.

Investment in both physical capital (machines) and human capital (knowledge and skills) can expand the productive capacity of a worker. In turn, people who produce more goods and services valued by others will tend to have higher incomes.

Other things constant, countries using a larger share of their resources to produce tools, machines, and factories will tend to grow more rapidly. Correspondingly, allocation of more resources to education and training will also enhance economic growth. It is important, however, to recognize that investment is not a "free lunch." When more resources are used to produce machines, factories, and schooling, fewer resources are available to produce current-consumption goods.

EXHIBIT 3
Major Sources of Economic Growth and High Levels of Income

The major sources of growth and high income levels are gains from trade, entrepreneurial discovery, and investment in physical and human capital.

SOURCE OF GROWTH	EXPLANATION
1. Gains from trade	Specialization, division of labor, and economies of scale lead to larger outputs.
2. Entrepreneurship	Innovation, technological improvements, and discovery of better ways of doing things make larger outputs and higher income levels possible.
3. Investment in physical work experience, and human capital	Machines, structures, and tools (physical capital) and education, and training (human capital) make larger outputs possible.

During the 1960s and 1970s, many growth economists stressed the importance of inputs (for example, more capital equipment and more education) as the driving force of economic growth. However, whereas investment is a source of growth, high investment rates do not guarantee rapid growth. The experiences of the centrally planned economies of the former Soviet bloc countries illustrate this point. These economies had both very high rates of capital formation and rapid improvements in schooling levels. Despite their high rates of investment, however, their performance was unimpressive. Slow growth and poor living standards eventually led to their collapse.

EXHIBIT 3 summarizes the three major sources of economic growth and high levels of income. It also summarizes how and why each of the three factors contributes to the growth and income of an economy.

The Institutional Environment

Trade, entrepreneurial discovery, and investment do not take place in a vacuum. They are influenced by a country's **institutions** and policies. How important are the legal, business, political, trade, and social rules and regulations that make up a country's institutional environment? What institutions and policies promise to enhance the performance of an economy? During the last several decades, considerable research has focused on these questions. Building on the work of Peter Bauer and Douglass C. North, modern growth analysis stresses the importance of institutions and policies for the development and efficient use of resources. Daron Acemoglu of MIT, Robert Barro of Harvard University, and Barry Weingast of Stanford University are among the leading contributors to the recent

Institutions

The legal, regulatory, and social constraints that affect the security of property rights and enforcement of contracts. They exert a major impact on transaction costs between parties, particularly when the trading partners do not know each other.

OUTSTANDING ECONOMIST

Douglass C. North (1920–)

The 1993 recipient of the Nobel Prize in Economics, Douglass C. North is best known for his application of both economic theory and statistical analysis to topics in the field of economic history. A professor at Washington University in St. Louis, North's work has shown that the development of both patent laws and the corporation as a legal entity were important sources of economic growth during the seventeenth and eighteenth centuries. His analysis of the link between institutional change and economic progress has played an important role in the development of modern growth theory.

literature in this area.[5] This institutional approach stresses that when nations foster a sound economic environment, people will trade, invest, and engage in entrepreneurial activities in a manner that will stimulate economic growth and make high levels of income possible. In many ways, the modern institutional approach to growth reflects the view of Adam Smith, who also stressed the importance of policies and institutions.

What Institutions and Policies Will Promote Growth?

The growth process reflects a combination of factors, and they are often interrelated. Much as the performance of an athletic team reflects the joint output of the team members, economic growth is jointly determined. And just as one or two weak players can substantially reduce overall team performance, weakness in one or two key areas can substantially harm the overall performance of an economy.

While numerous factors influence growth, a few are vitally important. Let's take a closer look at several factors that are central to the growth process.

Legal System: Secure Property Rights, Rule of Law, and Even-Handed Enforcement of Contracts

As we discussed in Chapter 2, private ownership rights legally protect people against those who would use violence, theft, or fraud to take things that do not belong to them. The important thing about private ownership is the incentive structure that it creates. When labor services, other resources, goods, and assets are privately owned, people will have a strong incentive to engage in productive activities, actions that increase the value of resources. With well-defined and enforced private ownership rights, people get ahead by helping and cooperating with others. Employers, for example, have to provide prospective employees and other resource suppliers with at least as good a deal as they can get elsewhere. To succeed, business owners will have to develop and provide potential customers with goods and services that they value highly (relative to their cost). Entrepreneurs will have a strong incentive to innovate and discover new and better products and production methods. Investors will have a potent incentive to search for and undertake productive projects. The bottom line: When property is owned privately, people are permitted to keep what they earn; this provides them with a powerful stimulus to develop and use resources wisely, innovate and discover better ways of doing things, and invest and conserve for the future. As we just discussed, these are the major ingredients that underlie growth and high income levels.

Throughout history, people have searched for, and established, alternatives to private ownership they thought would be more humanitarian or more productive. These experiences have ranged from unsuccessful to disastrous. To date, there is no record of an institutional arrangement that provides individuals with as much freedom and incentive to use resources productively and efficiently as private ownership.[6]

In contrast, when private ownership rights are insecure or highly restricted, the incentive of entrepreneurs to engage in productive activity is eroded. Citizens will spend more time trying to take the property of others through political and legal plunder and less time

---

[5]For background on this literature, see Peter T. Bauer, *Dissent on Development: Studies and Debates in Development Economics* (Cambridge: Harvard University Press, 1972); Douglass C. North, *Institutions, Institutional Change, and Economic Performance* (Cambridge: Cambridge University Press, 1990); Robert Barro and Xavier Sala-i-Martin, *Economic Growth* (New York: McGraw-Hill, 1995); and Daron Acemoglu, Simon Johnson, and James A. Robinson, "Institutions as a Fundamental Cause of Long-Run Growth," in *Handbook of Economic Growth*, vol.1, Philippe Aghion and Steven Durlauf, eds. (Amsterdam; Elsevier, 2005), 385–472.

[6]For evidence that a legal system that protects property rights, enforces contracts, and relies on rule-of-law principles for the settlement of disputes among parties promotes economic growth, see Stephen Knack and Philip Keefer, "Institutions and Economic Performance: Cross-Country Tests Using Alternative Institutional Measures," *Economics and Politics* 7 (1995): 207–227.

producing and developing resources. When a citizen or investor's assets are at risk of being taken by others because property rights are not enforced, the incentive to invest in building the productive capital assets that help to generate prosperity is diminished. As a result, growth will be retarded, and income will fall well short of its potential.

The security of property rights is often undermined by political instability, civil unrest, and war. Historically, some governments have confiscated the physical and financial assets of their citizens, imposed punitive taxes on them, and used regulations to punish those out of favor with the current political regime. Countries with a history like this will find it difficult to restore confidence and reestablish the security of property rights.

Unfortunately, the political climate of many poor, **less-developed countries** is highly unstable. In some cases, prejudice, injustice, and highly unequal wealth status create a fertile environment for political upheaval. In other instances, political corruption and a history of favoritism to a ruling class provide the seeds for unrest. In recent years, political instability has contributed to the dismal economic performance of several nations, including the Democratic Republic of the Congo, Haiti, Nicaragua, Russia, and Iraq.

Less-developed countries

Countries with low per capita incomes, low levels of education, widespread illiteracy, and widespread use of production methods that are largely obsolete in high income countries. They are sometimes referred to as developing countries.

Competitive Markets

As Adam Smith stressed long ago, when competition is present, even self-interested individuals will tend to promote the general welfare. Conversely, when competition is weakened, business firms have more leeway to raise prices and pursue their own objectives and less incentive to innovate and develop better ways of doing things.

Competition is a disciplining force for both buyers and sellers. In a competitive environment, producers must provide goods at a low cost and serve the interests of consumers; if they don't, other suppliers will. Firms that develop improved products and figure out how to produce them at a low cost will succeed. Sellers that are unwilling or unable to provide consumers with quality goods at competitive prices will be driven from the market. This process leads to improved products and production methods and directs resources toward projects that create more value. It is a powerful stimulus for economic progress. Policies like free entry into businesses and occupations and the freedom to exchange goods and services promote competition and economic progress. In contrast, policies like business subsidies, price controls, and entry restraints stifle competition and hinder economic progress.

Competition is also important in a nation's capital market. If investment is to increase the wealth of a nation, capital must be channeled into productive projects. When the value of the additional output derived from an investment exceeds the cost of the investment, the project will increase the value of the resources, and thereby create wealth. In contrast, if the value of the additional output is less than the cost of the investment, undertaking the project will reduce wealth. Competition provides private investors with a strong incentive to evaluate projects carefully and allocate their funds to projects they expect to yield the highest rates of return. In turn, profitable projects will tend to increase the wealth not only of the investor but also of the nation.

Stable Money and Prices

A stable monetary environment provides the foundation for the efficient operation of a market economy. In contrast, monetary and price instability makes both the price level and relative prices unpredictable, generates uncertainty, and undermines the security of contractual exchanges. When prices increase 20 percent one year, 50 percent the next year, 15 percent the year after that, and so on, the ability of individuals and businesses to develop sensible long-term plans and investment decisions is undermined. Many investors and business decision makers will move their activities to countries with a more stable environment. Foreigners will invest elsewhere, and citizens will often go to great lengths to get their savings (potential funds for investment) out of the country. As a result, the potential gains from capital formation and business activities that might have been realized won't materialize.

Minimal Regulation

As we have stressed, gains from trade and entrepreneurship are important sources of growth and high levels of income. When regulations stifle exchange and limit entry into various businesses and occupations, they retard economic progress. Thus, it is important that such regulations be kept to a minimum.

The proponents of regulations often argue that a proposed regulation will keep the unqualified out of a market, prohibit unfair competition, raise wages, reduce prices, or restrict the layoff of workers. To an economic illiterate, they often look like a "free lunch." Unfortunately, regulations are a blunt instrument and they often have harmful unintended consequences. Restrictions that make it more difficult to lay off an employee will reduce the incentive of employers to hire workers. Regulations designed to keep out unwanted rivals will limit competition and lead to higher prices. Fixing prices below the market level will lead to shortages and deterioration in the quality of a product or service, but fixing prices above market levels will lead to surpluses. The list of unintended side effects of regulations goes on and on.

In addition, when governments become heavily involved in playing favorites by imposing regulations that favor some at the expense of others, they encourage people to spend more time rent seeking—trying to get government favors. Rather than focusing on how to produce better products at a lower cost, businesses will spend more time lobbying government officials. As a result, extensive regulation will tend to distort and corrupt the political process. Even democratic political decision making deteriorates as government officials trade regulatory favors to business and labor interests in exchange for political contributions and other personal favors.

Regulation is a poor substitute for well-defined property rights and voluntary market exchange. Regulatory policies that force traders to pass through various political roadblocks are almost always counterproductive. A country cannot realize its full potential unless restrictions that limit trade and increase the cost of doing business are kept to a minimum.

Many worry that without government regulation of food, safety and other items, people will be harmed by bad products or employers providing unsafe working conditions. However, under a legal system with sound enforcement of liability, individuals and businesses are accountable for their actions that harm others. Those harmed will be in a position to collect for damages in a court of law. Thus, minimal regulations coupled with a good legal system work together to promote prosperity.

The Avoidance of High Tax Rates

High marginal tax rates take a large share of the rewards generated by productive activities, making it less attractive for people to work and undertake profitable business projects. People who are not permitted to keep much of what they earn tend not to earn very much. Some of them, perhaps those with working spouses, will drop out of the labor force to work at home where their labor is not taxed. Others will simply work fewer hours, retire earlier, or take jobs with longer vacations or a more preferred location.

High taxes also reduce economic efficiency. Because they create a large gap between an employer's cost of hiring a worker and the employee's take-home pay, they tend to drive these transactions into the underground economy, or black markets, where the legal structure is less certain and property rights less secure. High tax rates also encourage people to purchase items that are tax deductible even though they are not valued as much as nondeductible goods of similar price. Worse yet, high tax rates can drive a nation's most productive citizens abroad where taxes are lower. All of these things will retard a country's economic growth.

Trade Openness

Like domestic trade, international trade is mutually beneficial. It allows a country's residents to use more of their resources to supply goods that they can produce at a low cost to the world market and use the sale proceeds to purchase goods that are expensive for them to produce domestically. Together, trading partners are able to produce more goods and services and purchase a wider variety of them at cheaper prices. Trade openness and the competition that flows from it will also keep domestic producers on their toes—they will be less likely to gouge consumers with high prices, for example.

In contrast, policies that restrict international trade stifle this process and retard economic progress. Obviously, tariffs (taxes on imported goods) and quotas fall into this category because they limit the ability of domestic citizens to trade with people in other countries. So, too, do trade restrictions that impede international exchanges involving financial and real assets. When a nation's financial markets are integrated with the world, the nation will be able to attract worldwide savings at the lowest possible price (or interest rate). Similarly, its citizens will have access to the most attractive investment opportunities, regardless of where those opportunities are located.

As a result, domestic businesses will be able to acquire financial capital at a lower cost, and domestic investors will be able to earn more attractive returns than would otherwise be the case. The international trade section of this book will analyze these issues in more detail.

The accompanying **Thumbnail Sketch** summarizes the key elements of an institutional and policy environment conducive to growth and prosperity. It also indicates what governments can do to help their citizens achieve higher income levels.

ROLE OF GOVERNMENT

Governments promote economic progress when they protect individuals and their property, enforce contracts impartially, provide access to money of stable value, avoid high taxes and excessive regulation, and foster competitive markets and free international trade.

Other Factors That May Influence Growth and Income

Through the years, economists have developed several theories about why some countries grow and achieve high income levels while others remain poor. Some of these theories have validity; others are either incorrect or incomplete. In this section, we will consider noninstitutional factors that are often thought to influence growth.

1. GROWTH OF THE POPULATION. Thomas Malthus developed one of the earliest theories of economic growth, or more accurately a theory about why growth could not be sustained. Malthus argued that as per person income increased much above the subsistence level, it

THUMBNAIL SKETCH

Institutions, Policies, and Economic Growth

The following institutions and policies provide the foundation for growth and the achievement of high levels of income:

1. Legal system: Private ownership, rule of law, and even-handed enforcement of contracts
2. Competitive markets: Freedom of entry into businesses and occupations
3. Monetary and price stability: Low and predictable rates of inflation
4. Minimal regulation: Avoid regulations that restrict entry and interfere with voluntary exchange
5. Low taxes: Keep tax rates, particularly marginal tax rates, low
6. Trade openness: Avoid tariffs, quotas, and other regulations that restrict residents from trading with people in other countries

would trigger a population boom that would soon drive income back to the level necessary to sustain life. Because population would grow exponentially while the resources required to expand production would only grow linearly, a rapid growth of population would soon eliminate income levels above subsistence.[7] This bleak picture of existence at or near subsistence has caused some to refer to economics as the "dismal science."

Fortunately, history illustrates that this theory is invalid. The theory ignores the role of technological improvements, innovation, and the discovery of better ways of doing things. It also ignores that people have brains and two hands, as well as mouths. Today, some of the most densely populated areas of the world, places like Hong Kong, Singapore, and Japan, also have some of the world's highest per capita incomes.

2. NATURAL RESOURCES. There is a tendency to think that the wealth of nations is largely dependent upon natural resources. Resources clearly give some nations an advantage. For example, oil-rich countries like Saudi Arabia, Bahrain, and the United Arab Emirates have substantially higher per capita incomes than other similar countries with few natural resources. But it is equally clear that resource endowments are not the primary source of cross-country differences in growth and income. Some of the highest-income countries in the world have few natural resources. Other than their harbor, neither Hong Kong nor Singapore has significant natural resources. Likewise, Japan has few natural resources, and it imports almost all of its industrial energy supply. Nonetheless, the growth rates of all three have been among the most rapid in the world since 1960. Conversely, many resource-rich countries such as Nigeria, Venezuela, and Russia have both low income levels and poor records of economic growth.

These observations show that institutions are far more important than natural resources. Countries that follow sound policies are able to import the resources required for growth and prosperity. Without sound institutions and policies, however, resource-rich countries are generally unable to sustain strong growth and achieve high levels of income. Abundant resources can often undermine the incentive to adopt sound institutions. Historically, resource riches have often led to conflict, instability, authoritarian political regimes, and even war. This has given rise to what some refer to as the "resource curse," the view that abundant resources often lead to the adoption of counterproductive policies that undermine the usefulness of the resources.

3. FOREIGN AID. In the 1950s and 1960s, it was widely believed that assistance from high-income developed countries to low-income less-developed countries would provide the latter with the start-up capital needed to ignite the growth process. Given their low incomes, many believed that it would be impossible for poor countries to save enough to finance major investment projects like roads and power-generating plants. Further, projects like these were thought to provide the foundation for economic growth. Thus, if the world's wealthy countries provided aid, it could be channeled into investment that would trigger growth and development.

While the theory sounded reasonable, the experience was dramatically different. The law of unintended consequences helps explain why. By its nature, aid is driven by political considerations rather than market forces. Not surprisingly, the aid was often channeled into projects designed to maintain the grip of the current political leadership, and in some cases, it even ended up in their personal bank accounts. There were also harmful side effects on the development of markets. High-income countries often provided less-developed countries with agricultural products and actually used this aid as a vehicle to dispose of surplus products resulting from their agricultural price support programs. In turn, this aid disrupted markets in less-developed countries and reduced their long-term capabilities of producing food products.

Studies indicate that the aid was largely ineffective and sometimes disastrously so. At the same time, the poor countries that registered the most impressive growth during

[7]Thomas Malthus, *An Essay on the Principle of Population* (London: J. Johnson, 1798).

APPLICATIONS IN ECONOMICS

Poverty, Foreign Aid, and the Quality of Institutions in Africa

More foreign aid has been directed toward Africa than any region of the world. During 1980–2005, the per capita foreign aid to sub-Saharan Africa was 2.8 times the amount directed to Latin America and 6.4 times the figure for Asia. Omitting South Africa and oil-rich Nigeria, foreign aid summed to 12 percent of GDP of sub-Saharan Africa during the past two decades.

The results can only be described as disappointing. **EXHIBIT 4** presents data for the $1 and $2 per day poverty rates for sub-Saharan Africa and the rest of the developing world. (*Note:* The high-income countries are omitted in these calculations.) In Africa, the $1 and $2 poverty rates were virtually unchanged throughout 1985–2005. In contrast, substantial progress was made against poverty in the rest of the world. The $1 poverty rate fell from 30 percent in 1985 to 15 percent in 2005 in developing countries outside of Africa. The percentage point reduction in the $2 poverty rate was similar. In 2005, the extreme poverty rate (less than $1 per day) of Africa was more than three times the rate for the rest of the developing world. Moreover, the number of Africans living in extreme poverty has increased by more than 100 million in the last decade alone.

Why hasn't foreign aid been more effective in Africa? Malaria and human immunodeficiency virus provide part of the explanation, and foreign assistance has funded valuable medical resources for treatment in both of these areas. But counterproductive institutions and policies are a

The one dollar per day poverty rate in Africa is approximately three times that of the rest of the world.

Ton Koene/Visuals Unlimited, Inc./Getty Images

EXHIBIT 4
Poverty Rates in Africa and the Rest of the World, 1985–2005

As Part (a) shows, 47 percentage of the population of sub-Saharan Africa had an income of $1 per day or less in 2005, compared to 15 percentage in the rest of the world. While the $1 per day poverty rate outside of Africa fell from 30 percentage in 1985 to 15 percentage in 2005, the rate was virtually unchanged in Africa during these two decades. As Part (b) shows, the $2 per day poverty rate followed a similar pattern. (Note: The high-income countries of North America and Europe, along with Australia, New Zealand, and Japan, are excluded from these figures.)

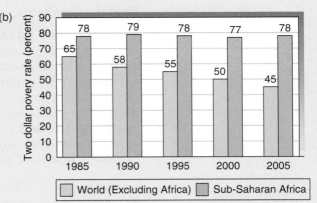

Note: The $1 and $2 per day poverty rates are the percentage of the population living on less than $1 and $2 per day measured in 1985 international prices. These numbers are normalized across countries using the purchasing power parity method.

Source: World Bank, *World Development Indicators, 2008.*

APPLICATIONS IN ECONOMICS

major factor underlying the generally poor results. Almost all foreign aid is either granted to, or channeled through, governments. During 1980–2005, foreign aid covered between 60 and 70 percent of government expenditures in sub-Saharan African countries. This aid often made it possible for governments, including ones that were highly corrupt, to remain in power even though their policies were characterized by uncertain protection of property rights, biased law enforcement, trade restrictions, and regulations that restrict entry into markets and impose heavy costs on business.

The *Economic Freedom of the World* project provides ratings for the legal structure, security of property rights, openness of international trade, and regulation of business for 141 countries. Most sub-Saharan African countries rank in the bottom group in all of these areas.[1]

Think for a moment about how high trade restrictions impact Africa. The countries of sub-Saharan Africa are approximately the geographic size of the typical U.S. state. Before resources and products can cross these national boundaries, they are subject to both taxes and customs clearance delays that often last two or three weeks. This is a costly, time-consuming, and onerous ordeal that exerts a

corrupting influence on both business and government. Most important, it is a major deterrent to gains from specialization, economies of scale, entrepreneurship, and investment. If trade restrictions of this type were present among the states, the United States would also be poor.

The trade restrictions alone would be enough to undermine prosperity, but when coupled with legal systems that fail to enforce contracts and protect property rights, and regulations that restrict entry and drive up the cost of doing business, the results are catastrophic. The United Nations Millennium Development Goals project is planning a four-fold increase in aid to Africa by 2015. Without major changes in institutions and policies, past experience indicates that this aid will be largely ineffective. Foreign aid, even in large doses, will not reduce poverty, at least not by much, unless institutions and policies consistent with economic growth are present.

---

[1]James Gwartney and Robert Lawson, *Economic Freedom of the World: 2008 Annual Report* (Vancouver, Fraser Institute, 2008). See particularly Chapter 2 of this report, "Economic Freedom and Combating World Poverty" by Seth W. Norton and James Gwartney.

1960–1990—like Hong Kong and Singapore—received little foreign aid. Instead, they followed policies supportive of market allocation and had respect for private property. In contrast, the countries that received the most aid recorded unimpressive growth and now have the world's lowest per capita income levels. In most cases, they are also characterized by institutions and policies—for example, investment controls, trade restrictions, and corrupt legal and political systems that undermine economic progress. Unless widespread institutional change is undertaken, the residents of these countries face a very bleak future.[8] (See Applications in Economics: Poverty, Foreign Aid, and the Quality of Institutions in Africa.)

4. CLIMATE AND LOCATION. Jeffery Sachs of Columbia University has been at the forefront of those arguing that tropical climate conditions and location far away from the world's major markets adversely affect growth and income. According to this view, the hot and humid tropical climatic conditions erode the energy level of workers and increase the risk of disabling and life-threatening diseases such as malaria. As a result, worker productivity and the general level of development are retarded in tropical areas. Furthermore, the lengthy travel distance to the world's major markets of Western Europe, North America, and Japan make tropical countries unattractive as a location for productive facilities. This, too, adversely affects their economic prospects.[9]

---

[8]For additional information on the impact of foreign aid on economic growth, see G. Raghuram Rajan and Arvind Subramanian. "Aid and Growth: What Does the Cross-Country Evidence Really Show?" *The Review of Economics and Statistics* 90, no. 4 (November 2008): 643–65; Simeon Djankov, Jose G. Montalvo, and Marta Reynal-Querol, "Does Foreign Aid Help?" *Cato Journal* 26, no. 1 (2006): 1–28; and William Easterly, *The White Man's Burden: Why the West's Efforts to Aid the Rest Have Done So Much Ill and So Little Good* (New York: Penguin, 2006).

[9]For additional information on the impact of climate and location on growth and income, see Jeffrey Sachs, "Tropical Underdevelopment," NBER Working Paper No. 8119 (February 2001); John Gallup, Jeffrey Sachs, and Andrew Mellinger, "Geography and Environment," NBER Working Paper No. w6849 (December 1998); and Jared Diamond, *Guns, Germs, and Steel: The Fates of Human Societies* (New York: W. W. Norton & Company, 1997).

The income levels of tropical countries, with a few exceptions, are generally lower than incomes in more temperate climates. But it is also true that the institutions and policies of most tropical countries are less consistent with the realization of gains from trade, entrepreneurship, and investment. Thus, most economists believe that the generally poorer performance of tropical countries is largely a reflection of their poor institutional quality rather than their climate and location.[10]

Institutions, Policies, and Prosperity

The severity of the 2008–2009 recession has focused the attention of political decision makers on economic fluctuations and actions to combat them. This is an important issue, but so too is economic growth. Moreover, the shape and structure of incentives are central to both a sound stabilization policy and the achievement of growth and high income levels. Unless countries adopt institutions and policies supportive of trade, entrepreneurial discovery, and private investment, they will be unable to sustain long-term growth and achieve high income levels. While other factors such as natural resources, climate, and location exert some influence, institutions and policies are the major source of cross-country differences in growth rates and income levels.

As the noted economist, William Baumol, indicated, the rules of the game make a huge difference; they determine what individuals do with their time, talents, and energy.[11] Baumol noted that the institutional environment may encourage productive, unproductive, or even destructive activities. When institutions and policies provide secure property rights, a fair and balanced judicial system, monetary stability, and effective limits on government's ability to transfer wealth through taxation and regulation, creative individuals are more likely to engage in product development, investment, and other productive activities. However, if the legal and regulatory environment fails to protect property rights and is often used to favor some at the expense of others, the same individuals are instead more likely to engage in attempts to manipulate the political and legal process in order to plunder wealth from others. Rent seeking, lobbying, bribes, and other forms of plunder replace productive activities.

For example, when entrepreneurs know that market forces will be used to allocate goods, a steel entrepreneur will react to more intense competition by trying to find a better way of producing steel (productive entrepreneurship). But when political bailouts are more probable, the steel producer will be more likely to lobby for subsidies, tariff protection, or regulatory favors (unproductive entrepreneurship). In turn, institutions that encourage productive activities and discourage counterproductive ones will lead to more growth and higher incomes.

Looking ahead

This chapter focused on the general characteristics of key institutions and policies that economic analysis indicates will help promote growth. The following chapter will present evidence on cross-country differences in income levels and growth rates and provide empirical evidence on the sources of those differences.

---

[10]For literature on the importance of institutions relative to climate and location, see Daron Acemoglu, Simon Johnson, and James A. Robinson, "The Colonial Origins of Comparative Development: An Empirical Investigation," *American Economic Review* 91 (December 2001): 1369–1401; Robert E. Hall and Charles I. Jones, "Why Do Some Countries Produce So Much More Output per Worker than Others?" *Quarterly Journal of Economics* 114 (February 1999): 83–116; Mancur Olson, "Big Bills Left on the Sidewalk: Why Some Nations Are Rich, and Others Poor," *Journal of Economic Perspectives* 10 (Spring 1996): 3–24; Dani Rodrik, Arvind Subramanian, and Francesco Trebbi, "Institutions Rule: The Primacy of Institutions over Geography and Integration in Economic Development," *Journal of Economic Growth* 9 (June 2004): 131–65; and Jeffrey D. Sachs, "Institutions Don't Rule: Direct Effects of Geography on Per Capita Income," NBER Working Paper no. 9490 (February 2003).

[11]See William Baumol, "Entrepreneurship: Productive, Unproductive and Destructive," *Journal of Political Economy* 98 (October 1990): 893–921; and William J. Baumol, *Entrepreneurship, Management, and the Structure of Payoffs* (Cambridge, MA: MIT Press, 1993).

KEY POINTS

▼ Economic growth increases the production possibilities of an economy. The growth of per capita real GDP means more goods and services per person, which typically leads to higher living standards and improvements in life expectancy, literacy, and health.

▼ Even seemingly small differences in growth rates sustained over two or three decades will substantially alter relative incomes. For example, if Country A and Country B have the same initial income but the growth rate of A is 2 percentage points greater than that of B, after thirty-five years the income level of Country A will be twice that of B.

▼ Economic growth is a complex process. Economists stress the importance of three major sources of economic progress: (1) gains from trade and expansion in the size of the market, (2) discovery of new technologies and innovative applications, and (3) investment in physical and human capital.

▼ The institutional and policy environment exerts a major impact on growth and income. The following institutions and policies provide the foundation for efficient use of resources, economic growth, and the achievement of high levels of income:
  1. legal system that protects property rights and enforces contracts in an even-handed manner
  2. competitive markets
  3. monetary and price stability
  4. minimal regulation
  5. avoidance of high tax rates
  6. openness to international trade

▼ While population growth, natural resources, foreign aid, and climatic conditions can influence growth and income, without sound institutions and policies, these factors will fail to generate long-term sustained growth and prosperity.

CRITICAL ANALYSIS QUESTIONS

1. How does economic growth influence the living standards of people? Does it really make much difference whether an economy grows at 2 percent or 4 percent annually? Discuss.

2. Indicate in your own words why trade, entrepreneurial discovery, and investment are important sources of economic growth and achievement of high income levels.

*3. "Without aid from industrial nations, poor countries are caught in a poverty trap. Because they are poor, they are unable to save and invest; and, lacking investment, they remain poor." Evaluate this view.

4. More than 200 years ago, Adam Smith argued that the wealth of nations depends on gains from (a) specialization and trade, (b) expanding the size of the market, and (c) discovering better (more productive) ways of doing things. Explain why you either agree or disagree with Smith's view.

*5. Why is competition important for the efficient use of resources? What must a firm do in order to compete effectively? Competitive forces often result in firms being driven out of business. How does this "business failure" influence the growth of income?

6. "Regulatory policies that restrict trade and voluntary agreements between parties will retard economic progress." Indicate why you either agree or disagree with this statement.

7. What must an entrepreneur do in order to introduce a new innovative product? What determines whether the new product will be a success or failure? How important is innovation as a source of economic growth? Discuss.

*8. "Because government-operated firms do not have to make a profit, they can usually produce at a lower cost and charge a lower price than privately owned enterprises." Evaluate this view.

9. How does money of stable value influence the volume of trade? When the inflation rate is volatile, how is the volume of trade affected? How will this influence the income levels of people?

10. What impact do natural resources have on economic growth? Will it be possible for a country with few natural resources to grow rapidly? Why or why not?

11. "The institutional environment is the key to economic growth. If a nation creates an environment conducive to economic growth, people will

supply and develop the resources and technology." Evaluate this view. Is the proper economic environment more important than the supply of resources? Why or why not?

*12. The diversity of goods available to consumers today is much greater than in the past. How does this influence consumer welfare? Do the GDP growth figures capture the impact of the increased diversity? Why or why not?

*13. When the government is heavily involved in the regulation of markets, how will this influence the gains from trade? How will it influence the degree of rent seeking by business and labor groups and the campaign contributions available to politicians?

14. Suppose that you have just been appointed to a high-level position in the economic analysis unit of the State Department. The Secretary of State has asked you to prepare a memo describing the key policies and economic arrangements that less-developed countries should follow in order to achieve rapid growth and high income levels. Briefly describe your response. Be sure to indicate why each factor you mention is important if a nation is going to attain a high level of economic progress.

*Asterisk denotes questions for which answers are given in Appendix B.

Institutions, Policies, and Cross-Country Differences in Income and Growth

CHAPTER FOCUS

- How large are the income differences across countries?

- How do growth rates vary across countries? Are the rich countries getting richer while the poor are getting poorer?

- How does the quality of institutions and policies differ across countries?

- What impact do sound institutions and policies have on growth and income?

- How do sound institutions and policies affect investment? Why is this important?

- Why is the legal structure of a country crucially important?

History is overwhelmingly a story of economies that failed to produce a set of economic rules of the game (with enforcement) that induce sustained economic growth. The central issue of economic history and of economic development is to account for the evolution of political and economic institutions that create an economic environment that induces increasing productivity.[1]

—Douglass C. North, 1993 Nobel Laureate

n the last chapter, we explained why the institutions and policies of a country exert a major impact on economic growth. This chapter will investigate this issue empirically. We will begin by looking at the cross-country differences in income levels and growth rates. Then we will turn to the measurement of institutional quality, consider how institutions differ across countries, and analyze how these differences influence economic performance. The chapter concludes with a discussion of the relationship between political decision making and economic institutions and policies. ■

How Large Are the Income Differences across Countries?

When different currencies are used, how can incomes be measured across countries? One possibility would be to use the exchange rate to convert the income figures to a common currency. For example, if the income per person in France was 20,000 euros and the exchange rate was $1.40 = 1 euro, you could multiply the French income in euros by 1.4 to convert it into dollars. In this case, the average French income would be $28,000. However, the exchange rate is influenced by international exchanges of assets like stocks and bonds, and it reflects only goods and services that are traded internationally. Thus, it may not be a good measure of cross-country differences in the cost of purchasing the typical bundle consumed by people in different countries.

Purchasing power parity method (PPP)

Method in which the relative purchasing power of each currency is determined by comparing the amount of each currency required to purchase a common bundle of goods and services in the domestic market. This information is then used to convert the GDP of each nation to a common monetary unit like the U.S. dollar.

Economists generally prefer to use the **purchasing power parity (PPP) method** when comparing incomes across countries. This procedure is very similar to the use of the consumer price index to adjust for differences in the general level of prices across time periods. The cost in domestic currency of purchasing a specific bundle of goods and services that is typically consumed is derived. This bundle would include items like housing, food, electricity, gasoline, automobiles, and other items that are consumed in almost every country. The cost of purchasing this bundle is then used to derive the general level of prices (and the purchasing power of the domestic currency) in each country. Finally, this price index is used to convert the incomes in different countries to a common currency. Most economists believe that the purchasing power parity method results in income comparisons that more accurately reflect real income differences across countries and time periods.

EXHIBIT 1 shows per person GDP for 2007 for various high-, middle-, and low-income countries. The figures were derived by the purchasing power parity method. Take a close look at these income data. The income per person of Norway is $49,359, the highest in the world. The United States was second at $43,055. Hong Kong, Switzerland, Netherlands, Canada, and Ireland all had income levels above $36,000. Incomes in the middle group ranged from South Korea's $23,399 to those of South Africa, Brazil, and Thailand, which were a little less than $10,000. The per person income in Chile, Mexico, and Russia was about $13,000, less than one-third that of the United States. In the lower group, the income level in China was about one-eighth that of the United States, and the figures for India and Indonesia are even lower. The incomes of Sierra Leone, Malawi, and Niger are the lowest in the world. The per person incomes in the United States and Norway are more than fifty times those of the three lowest-income countries.

Some caution is called for regarding the precision of the income figures of Exhibit 1, particularly the size of the differences between high- and low-income countries. Remember, GDP excludes most productive activities within the household because they do not involve a

EXHIBIT 1

The 2007 per Person GDP Levels of Various High-, Middle-, and Low-Income Countries (measured in 2005 PPP U.S. dollars)

High-Income Countries		Middle-Income Countries		Low-Income Countries	
Norway	$49,359	South Korea	$23,399	Ukraine	$6,529
United States	43,055	Hungary	17,894	China	5,084
Hong Kong	39,953	Poland	15,634	Bolivia	3,972
Switzerland	37,581	Russian Federation	13,873	Honduras	3,585
The Netherlands	36,956	Mexico	13,307	Indonesia	3,506
Canada	36,260	Chile	13,108	Philippines	3,217
Ireland	36,118	Malaysia	12,766	India	2,600
United Kingdom	33,717	Argentina	12,502	Nigeria	1,859
Germany	33,181	Turkey	11,825	Bangladesh	1,172
Japan	31,689	South Africa	9,215	Malawi	719
France	31,625	Brazil	9,034	Sierra Leone	641
Italy	28,682	Thailand	7,682	Niger	592

Source: World Bank, *World Development Indicators online* (accessed July 2009).

market exchange. Household production will nearly always be a larger share of total output in low- than high-income countries. For example, families in a low-income country like Nigeria or even Mexico are more likely than their U.S. counterparts to make their own clothing, raise and prepare their own food, provide their own child care services, and even build their own homes. These productive labor services, originating in the household sector, are excluded from GDP. Because of this omission, the per person GDP figures will tend to understate the income levels of less-developed countries (LDCs) relative to their richer counterparts.

However, given the size of the income differences between the high- and low-income countries of Exhibit 1, it is clear that the differences are still huge even after taking the omission of household production into account. Data on other quality of life factors are highly consistent with this view. For example, the residents of countries with higher per person incomes nearly always live longer and have lower illiteracy and infant mortality rates than those living in countries with lower incomes.

How Do Growth Rates Vary across Countries?

Which countries are growing most rapidly? Which are falling behind? **EXHIBIT 2** presents data on the growth of per person GDP for (a) high-growth economies, (b) high-income industrial nations, and (c) the economies with the worst growth records. The left side of Exhibit 2 indicates the ten fastest-growing countries in the world during 1990–2007. All of these countries achieved an average annual growth rate of more than 4 percent over this lengthy time frame. China, Vietnam, Ireland, and South Korea head the list. Except for Ireland, all of the high-growth countries were classified as LDCs a quarter of a century ago.[2] One-third of the world's population live in the two most populated countries, China and India. Both of these countries are included in the high-growth list. Remember,

---

[2]Since 1980, the income levels of two of the high-growth countries, Hong Kong and Singapore, have risen so much that they are no longer classified as less developed.

EXHIBIT 2

The Growth of per Person GDP for High-Growth, High-Income Industrial, and Low-Growth Countries, 1990–2007

High Growth	Growth of per Person GDP, 1990–2007	High-Income Industrial	Growth of per Person GDP, 1990–2007	Low Growth	Growth of per Person GDP, 1990–2007
China	9.4%	Norway	2.6%	Central African Republic	−1.0%
Vietnam	6.1%	United Kingdom	2.1%	Georgia	−1.2%
Ireland	5.1%	The Netherlands	2.1%	Ukraine	−1.2%
South Korea	4.8%	Australia	2.0%	Serbia	−1.5%
Taiwan	4.7%	United States	2.0%	Kyrgyz Republic	−1.6%
Trinidad and Tobago	4.7%	Canada	1.8%	Guinea-Bissau	−2.0%
India	4.6%	Germany	1.5%	Burundi	−2.4%
Chile	4.1%	France	1.4%	Haiti	−2.4%
Sri Lanka	4.1%	Japan	1.2%	Moldova	−2.7%
Singapore	4.1%	Italy	1.1%	Congo, Dem. Rep.	−4.4%
		Switzerland	0.7%		

Source: World Bank, *World Development Indicators online* (accessed July 2009).

---

a 4.0 percent annual growth rate means that per person GDP doubles approximately every seventeen years. Clearly, per person incomes in the high-growth economies have increased sharply during the last couple of decades, and living standards improved dramatically.

Among the high-income industrial economies, growth rates were tightly bunched. Norway had the highest growth rate at 2.6 percent annually, while Switzerland had the lowest at 0.7 percent. Except for these two, the annual growth rates of the nine populous high-income countries averaged between 1.1 percent and 2.1 percent over the seventeen years. Except for Ireland, most of the less populous high-income countries not included in the table also had growth rates between 1 and 2 percent during the period.

Unfortunately, LDCs dominate not only the high-growth list but also the group with the worst economic record (see the right side of Exhibit 2). The income levels of this latter group have not only failed to grow but they have also regressed. The per capita incomes of ten LDCs declined at an annual rate of more than 1 percent during 1990–2007. In the case of the Democratic Republic of the Congo (formerly Zaire), Moldova, Haiti, Burundi, and Guinea-Bissau, per capita income fell 2 percent or more annually during the seventeen years following 1990. This implies that the per person income level in these five countries in 2007 was only about 60 percent the level of 1990.

The growth picture of LDCs is clearly one of diversity. Most of the ten fastest-growing countries in the world since 1990, including two with a third of the world's population (China and India), were LDCs. Income per person in these countries has grown about twice as fast as was true in the high-income industrial countries. These countries have not only closed the gap, but in a few cases, they now have higher income levels than many of their historically wealthier counterparts. At the same time, other LDCs are doing very poorly and falling farther and farther behind. Later in this chapter, we will return to this topic and consider the reasons underlying the differential growth rates among the poor countries of the world.

Economic Freedom as a Measure of Sound Institutions

In the last chapter, we discussed the major sources of economic growth: gains from trade, entrepreneurial discovery, and investment. Realization of gains from these sources is largely dependent upon institutions and policies supportive of voluntary exchange, market allocation, freedom to compete, and protection of people and their property from aggressors. These ingredients comprise the foundation of **economic freedom**.

Economic freedom is complex and multidimensional. Therefore, it is difficult to measure. In the mid-1980s, the Fraser Institute of Vancouver, Canada, began work on a special project designed to measure the consistency of a nation's institutions and policies with economic freedom. Several leading scholars, including Nobel laureates Milton Friedman, Gary Becker, and Douglass C. North, participated in the endeavor. This eventually led to the development of the *Economic Freedom of the World* (EFW) index that is now published annually by a worldwide network of more than seventy institutes.

The EFW index uses forty-two separate components to measure the consistency of a nation's institutions and policies with personal choice, freedom of exchange, and protection of private property. The data for each of the components are placed on a zero to ten scale and used to derive a summary rating, as well as ratings in five major areas.[3] In order to achieve a high EFW rating, a country must provide secure protection of privately owned property, evenhanded enforcement of contracts, and a stable monetary environment. It also must keep taxes low, refrain from creating barriers to both domestic and international trade, and rely more fully on markets rather than governments to allocate goods and resources. In many respects, the EFW index reflects the institutional and policy factors that Chapter 16 indicates are important sources of economic growth.

The EFW data for some countries go back to 1970 and the ratings are available for 122 countries throughout the 1990–2007 period. **EXHIBIT 3** presents data on the ten highest- and ten lowest-rated economies, as well as the ratings of ten other large countries over this seventeen-year period. In order to rank in the top group, a country would have to maintain persistently high ratings. Thus, the countries in the top group might be thought of as those that maintained institutions and policies that were highly consistent with economic freedom.

Among the 122 countries, Hong Kong, Singapore, Switzerland, and the United States headed the list of the most persistently free economies. At the other end of the spectrum, the Democratic Republic of the Congo, Myanmar, Guinea-Bissau, Rwanda, Algeria, and Niger had the least free economies. Among the large economies, Germany, Chile, Japan, and France were more toward the economically free end of the spectrum, whereas Brazil, China, and Argentina were in the less free range.

Economic freedom

Method of organizing economic activity characterized by (1) personal choice, (2) voluntary exchange coordinated by markets, (3) freedom to enter and compete in markets, and (4) protection of people and their property from aggression by others.

Institutions, Policies, and Economic Performance

If institutions and policies are important, the freer economies should outperform those that are less free. When considering the impact of institutions, it is important to focus on long-term growth and income rather than short-term growth, which may reflect mostly the ups and downs of business cycle conditions. Thus, our focus will be on the relationship

---

[3]The five areas are (1) size of government; (2) legal system and protection of property rights; (3) access to sound money; (4) freedom to trade with foreigners; and (5) regulation of credit, labor, and business. To the fullest extent possible, the components of the index are based on objective variables such as government consumption as a share of total consumption, standard deviation of the inflation rate, and mean tariff rate. When it was necessary to use survey data to measure important elements of economic freedom, as was often the case in the legal and regulatory areas, data from outside sources were used in order to minimize value judgments. For additional details, see James Gwartney and Robert Lawson, *Economic Freedom of the World: 2009 Annual Report* (Vancouver: Fraser Institute, 2009) and the Web site http://www.freetheworld.com.

EXHIBIT 3
The Economic Freedom Rating for the Top-, Middle-, and Lowest-Rated
Countries, Average for 1990–2007.

TOP-RATED COUNTRIES			MIDDLE-RATED COUNTRIES			LOWEST-RATED COUNTRIES		
1.	Hong Kong	8.9	12.	Germany	7.6	113.	Central Afr. Rep.	4.7
2.	Singapore	8.7	15.	Chile	7.5	114.	Ukraine	4.7
3.	Switzerland	8.3	20.	Japan	7.3	115.	Congo, Rep. of	4.6
4.	United States	8.3	29.	France	7.1	116.	Zimbabwe	4.5
5.	New Zealand	8.3	43.	South Korea	6.6	117.	Niger	4.5
6.	United Kingdom	8.1	50.	Mexico	6.5	118.	Algeria	4.5
7.	Canada	8.0	55.	Indonesia	6.4	119.	Rwanda	4.2
8.	Ireland	7.9	62.	Argentina	6.2	120.	Guinea-Bissau	4.1
9.	Luxembourg	7.8	79.	China	5.8	121.	Myanmar	4.0
10.	The Netherlands	7.8	101.	Brazil	5.3	122.	Congo, Dem. R.	3.9

Source: James Gwartney and Robert Lawson, *Economic Freedom of the World, 2009 Annual Report* (Vancouver: Fraser Institute, 2009).

Quartile

A quarter (25 percent) of a group. The quartiles are often arrayed on the basis of an indicator like income or degree of economic freedom.

between institutional quality and economic performance over a lengthy time period. We now turn to an examination of this issue.

The 122 countries with economic freedom ratings throughout 1990–2007 were divided into **quartiles**. The thirty countries with the highest average economic freedom rating over the period comprise the top quartile, the thirty with the next highest average ratings make up the next quartile, and so on.

EXHIBIT 4 presents data on the per person income levels of the quartiles, ranged from the least free to the most free. Clearly, the economies with institutions and policies more consistent with economic freedom had substantially higher income levels. The per person income of countries in the freest quartile were more than twice those of the second freest quartile. Correspondingly, the income levels of countries in the second quartile were twice those of the third quartile, which were substantially greater than those of the least economically free quartile. The per person incomes of countries in the freest quartile were more than eight times the income levels of countries in the least free quartile. Clearly, there is a strong positive relationship between economic freedom and income levels.

EXHIBIT 5 uses the quartile analysis to illustrate the relationship between economic freedom and growth. In the freest quartile of economies, per person income grew at an average annual rate of 2.4 percent during the twenty-five year period, compared to 2.3 for the second freest quartile and 2.1 percent for the third quartile. Countries in the least free group grew at an annual rate of only 0.9 percent. Thus, the income levels of countries in the top quartile grew at nearly three times the average rate of those in the bottom quartile.

In summary, the freer economies achieved higher per person income levels and grew more rapidly. Although these data are not adjusted for other factors, such as initial income level, demographic factors, and years of schooling, more comprehensive analysis indicates that even after these factors are taken into consideration, countries with more economic freedom achieve higher income levels and grow more rapidly.[4]

[4]For additional details on how economic freedom affects income levels and growth rates, see Niclas Berggren, "The Benefits of Economic Freedom: A Survey," *Independent Review* 8 (Fall 2003): 193–211; John W. Dawson, "Institutions, Investment, and Growth: New Cross-Country and Panel Data Evidence," *Economic Inquiry* 36 (October 1998): 603–19; and James Gwartney, "Institutions, Economic Freedom, and Cross-Country Differences in Performance," *Southern Economic Journal* 75, no. 4 (April 2009): 937–56.

EXHIBIT 4
Economic Freedom
and Income

The 2007 income per person of countries ordered by economic freedom rating is shown here by quartiles. Note the strong positive linkage. The income per person in countries in the freest quartile was more than eight times the figure for the least free group.

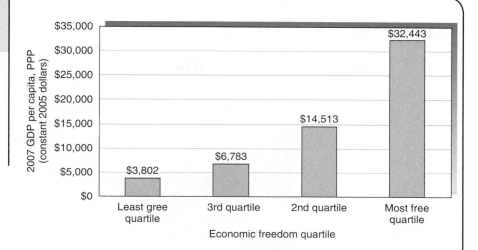

Source: James Gwartney and Robert Lawson, *Economic Freedom of the World, 2009 Annual Report* (Vancouver: Fraser Institute, 2009).

EXHIBIT 5
Economic Freedom and
Growth

The relation between the economic freedom of a country and its growth rate during 1990–2007 is shown here. Countries in the most economically free quartile grew at an annual rate of 2.4 percent compared to 0.9 percent growth for the least free quartile.

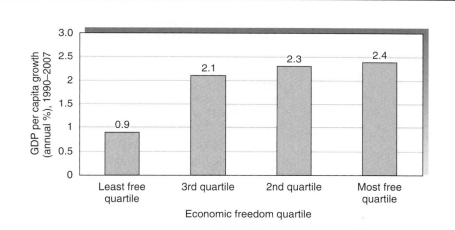

Source: James Gwartney and Robert Lawson, *Economic Freedom of the World, 2009 Annual Report* (Vancouver: Fraser Institute, 2009).

Economic Freedom, Institutions, and Investment

As we discussed in the previous chapter, investment is an important source of economic growth. Other things constant, countries that invest more will tend to grow more rapidly, and, with time, achieve higher levels of income.

When institutions and policies are similar across countries, investment capital should flow into the projects that promise the highest expected rate of return. In poor, less-developed countries, wages are relatively low and capital is in relatively short supply. Therefore, economics indicates that investment should flow into these countries. They promise a higher rate of return on investment than the rate of return expected in rich countries, which are relatively abundant in capital and have high-wage workers. Just as low-wage workers try to migrate to higher wage, more-developed countries, capital should try to migrate to low-wage countries that currently have substantially less capital per worker.

Hong Kong is a modern economic miracle. Its real income per person in 2007 was more than eight times its 1960 figure. It is one of the freest economies in the world.

© Dennis Cox/Almay

But this is not what we observe. Instead, most capital flows into high-wage developed economies that already have an abundance of capital.

How can this puzzling pattern be explained? Cross-country differences in the quality of institutions and policies provide the answer. Investors will be attracted to economies in which markets are open, the regulatory burden is minimal, and the legal system protects the property rights of investors and provides for the evenhanded enforcement of exchange agreements. In contrast, when regulations limit entry and restrict voluntary exchange, taxes are high, protection of property rights is uncertain, and favoritism is often present in the enforcement of contracts, investors will take their funds elsewhere.

EXHIBIT 6 illustrates the impact of institutions and policies on investment during 1980–2000. The top frame of the exhibit shows both total investment and private investment as a share of the economy for three economic freedom rating categories (greater than 7.0, 5–7, and less than 5.0) during the two decades. The investment rate increased with economic freedom. Total investment was 23.1 percent of GDP in the freest group, compared with 19.7 percent for the least free group. However, look at the striking difference in private investment among the three groups. Private investment constituted 18.0 percent of GDP for countries with an EFW rating of 7.0 or more compared to 14.1 percent for the middle group and only 9.6 percent for the least free group. Thus, the private investment rate of the economically free group was nearly twice that for the least free group.

The lower frame of Exhibit 6 shows the data for foreign direct investment (FDI) as a share of GDP. Foreign direct investment is particularly interesting because it is almost entirely private and it reflects the development of real assets, structures, and businesses by foreigners. These investors are clearly free to choose among countries, and therefore their choices are quite sensitive to the quality of the local environment. Note how FDI increases steadily with economic freedom. FDI was 3.8 percent of GDP in the freest group of countries compared to 2.1 percent in the middle group and only 1.4 percent in the least free countries. Thus, measured as a share of GDP, the freest group attracted almost three times as much FDI as the least free group. Again, more detailed analysis indicates that these positive relationships between institutions more consistent with economic freedom and higher investment rates hold after accounting for other major factors.

The investment figures add to the clarity of the relationship between sound institutions and economic performance.[5] Gains from trade, entrepreneurial discovery, and capital

[5]For a more detailed analysis of how economic freedom influences economic performance through investment, See James Gwartney, Randall Holcombe, and Robert Lawson, "Institutions and the Impact of Investment on Growth," *Kyklos* 59 (May 2006): 255–276.

EXHIBIT 6
Economic Freedom and Private Investment

Here, the countries are ordered on the basis of their average EFW rating during 1980–2000 and divided into three groups: rating greater than 7.0, between 5 and 7, and less than 5.0. As shown, investment is positively linked to economic freedom. This is particularly true for private investment. Private investment was 18.0 percent of GDP in the freest group of countries, compared to only 9.6 percent of GDP for the least free group (left panel). As right panel shows, the foreign direct investment rate in the freest group was more than twice the rate for the least free group.

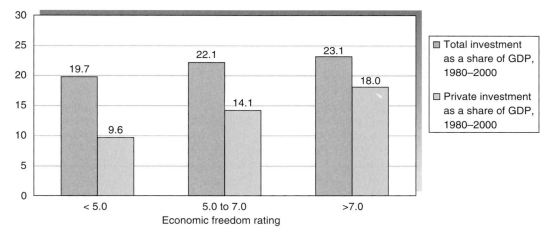

☐ Total investment as a share of GDP, 1980–2000

☐ Private investment as a share of GDP, 1980–2000

Source: James Gwartney, Randall Holcombe, and Robert Lawson, "Institutions and the Impact of Investment on Growth," *Kyklos* 59 (May 2006): 255–76.

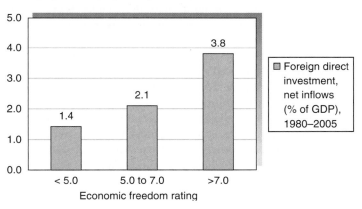

☐ Foreign direct investment, net inflows (% of GDP), 1980–2005

Source: World Bank, *World Development Indicators CD-ROM (2007).*

formation provide the fuel for growth and achievement of high income levels. Realization of gains from these sources will require investment, but when the institutional environment is unattractive, growth is stifled and incomes will stagnate.

The Institutional Environment and the Productivity of Investment

The institutional environment influences not only the level of investment but also the pay-off. When governments fix interest rates and tax some activities heavily while subsidizing others, they undermine the ability of markets to bring savers and investors together and channel funds into wealth-creating projects. Correspondingly, when investment funds are

EXHIBIT 7
Economic Freedom and the Productivity of Investment

The estimated impact of a percentage point increase in investment as a share of GDP on the annual rate of economic growth during 1980–2000 is shown here. In the most economically free countries, a 1 percentage point increase in private investment enhances long-term growth by an estimated 0.33 of a percentage point, compared to only 0.19 of a percentage point in the least free economies. The estimated impact of a percentage point increase in government investment as a share of GDP was even lower, 0.17 of a percentage point.

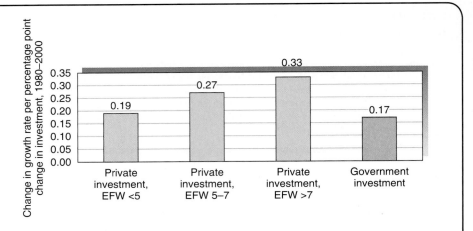

Source: James Gwartney, Randall Holcombe, and Robert Lawson, "Institutions and the Impact of Investment on Growth," *Kyklos* 59 (May 2006): 255–76, Table 2. These estimates above are after adjustments for the impact of the initial (1980) income level, tropical location, coastal location, and the growth of human capital are taken into account.

allocated by governments rather than capital markets, political clout rather than the expected rate of return will determine which projects will be undertaken. The expected result is lower productivity of investment and an increase in the quantity of funds channeled into unprofitable and unproductive projects.

EXHIBIT 7 illustrates the impact on long-term growth of a one percentage point increase in private investment as a share of GDP for the three different levels of economic freedom. In countries with EFW ratings of 7 or more, a one percentage point increase in private investment as a share of GDP was associated with a 0.33 percent increase in growth during the 1980–2000 period. For countries with EFW ratings between 5 and 7, a percentage point increase in investment as a share of GDP enhanced growth by only 0.27 percent, and when EFW was less than 5, a percentage point increase in the investment/GDP ratio increased growth by only 0.19 percent. Thus, the productivity of investment—the impact of a unit change on growth—was approximately 70 percent higher in the more free economies than for the group with the least economic freedom. Interestingly, the estimated productivity of government investment was 0.17, approximately half the productivity of investment in the relatively free economies and even lower than that for private investment in countries with little economic freedom. These figures are after adjustment was made for initial income level, changes in human capital, tropical location, and share of the population residing near an ocean coastline.[6]

Is Institutional Change Possible?

Can less-developed countries escape from poor institutions and harmful policies? There is evidence that a country's history during colonialism leaves a big imprint. Researchers have found that countries with colonial settlers who planned on staying were likely to develop sound institutions and policies. Because of their long-term commitment, they sought to protect individual property rights and limit the power of government. In contrast, colonizers settling in harsh climates and with short-term interests in the extraction of mineral resources were more likely to choose institutions that provided few limitations on the power of government. They were not very interested in individual rights, protection of property, and evenhanded application and enforcement of the law. Even after independence, the colonial institutional influences remained and continued to exert an impact on institutions and policies.

[6]Ibid. Gwartney, Holcombe, and Lawson, "Institutions and the Impact of Investment on Growth."

According to this view, countries like the United States, Canada, Australia, and New Zealand developed sound institutions and policies because their colonizing Europeans planned on staying. They had long-range plans and sought to protect their investments, gains from trade, and returns on new discoveries. Conversely, protective institutions were largely absent in Africa and Latin America, where the European colonizers were primarily interested in resource extraction.[7]

This view implies that history matters. What happened fifty or a hundred years ago continues to shape the institutions and policies of various countries. While no country can entirely escape its past, there are at least three reasons to believe that the opportunity for constructive institutional change is now greater than in the past. First, the colonial era is over. Countries that were previously colonized by European powers are now in a position to make their own institutional and policy choices. Second, the collapse of communism has also expanded the opportunity for institutional change. Much like former colonies, the institutional choices of countries under Soviet domination were also limited. Third, and perhaps most important, substantial reductions in transportation and communication costs have increased the importance of institutions and policies. Lower transportation and communication costs mean that, to a greater extent than in the past, entrepreneurs can choose where to locate a productive facility. This increases the potential gains from trade, including those accompanying the importation of investment and technology from abroad. It also increases the incentive for countries to adopt sound institutions and policies.

Recent Institutional Change and Economic Performance

There is evidence that a number of countries have made substantial changes in their institutions and policies in recent decades. Beginning in the 1960s, both Hong Kong and Singapore began to liberalize their economies and, by the 1970s, both were among the world's freest economies. Their growth rates have been impressive. In 1960, the per capita incomes of both Hong Kong and Singapore were well below those of Latin American countries like Brazil, Argentina, and Venezuela. The figures are now dramatically different. In 2007, the per person incomes of Hong Kong and Singapore were more than twice those of the Latin American countries and even greater than several of the high-income industrial economies of Western Europe.

Other economies have undertaken major reforms during the last three decades. The EFW can be used along with data on institutional reform from the International Monetary Fund to identify the major reformers.[8] **EXHIBIT 8** provides information on both institutional change and its impact. Countries that have achieved and sustained an increase of 2 points or more in their EFW rating following adoption of reforms are included in this exhibit. China and Chile began instituting key reforms in the 1970s. At the time, both were among the least free economies in the world, but the reform process increased their EFW ratings substantially. In turn, their growth rates have been impressive since 1980. China was the world's fastest-growing economy during 1980–2007, and Chile's 3.4 annual growth rate during that period placed it in the top ten (see Exhibit 2). Chile now has the highest per capita income level in South America.

Eight other economies undertook major reforms beginning in the 1980s. Four of these countries (Bangladesh, Botswana, Ghana, and Mauritius) began the reform process with very low incomes, while the other four (Iceland, Ireland, New Zealand, and United Kingdom) started from higher income levels. Since 1990, the per capita income of the 1980s reformers has grown at an average annual rate of 3.0 percent. The growth rates of Ireland, Botswana, and Mauritius have been particularly impressive. During 1995–2007,

---

[7]For additional information on this perspective, see Robert E. Hall and Charles I. Jones, "Why Do Some Countries Produce So Much More Output per Worker than Others?" *Quarterly Journal of Economics* 114 (1999): 83–116; and Daron Acemoglu, Simon Johnson, and James A. Robinson, "The Colonial Origins of Comparative Development: An Empirical Investigation," *American Economic Review* 91 (2001): 1369–1401.

[8]See International Monetary Fund, "Building Institutions," *IMF World Economic Outlook* (September 2005).

EXHIBIT 8
The Growth Rates and Income Levels of Countries with Major Changes in Institutions and Policies since 1975

	Begining Year of Change	Sustained EFW Increase 1970s	2005 EFW Rating	Growth 1980–2007	Growth 1990–2007	Growth 1995–2007	Per Capita GDP, 2007
Countries Beginning Reform during the 1970s							
Chile	1976	3.8	7.8	3.4%	4.1%	3.0%	$13,108
China	1978	2.1	6.3	8.8%	9.4%	8.8%	$5,084
Average		**3.0**	**7.1**	**6.1%**	**6.8%**	**5.9%**	**$9,096**
Countries Beginning Reform during the 1980s							
Bangladesh	1987	2.2	6.0		3.1%	6.5%	$1,172
Botswana	1985	2.3	7.2		3.8%	4.9%	$12,847
Ghana	1985	3.6	6.2		2.3%	2.6%	$1,260
Iceland	1988	3.0	7.8		2.0%	3.2%	$36,118
Ireland	1987	1.6	7.9		5.1%	5.5%	$41,036
Mauritius	1985	2.5	7.5		3.7%	3.7%	$10,668
New Zealand	1985	2.3	8.5		1.9%	1.9%	$25,281
United Kingdom	1980	1.9	8.1		2.1%	2.4%	$33,717
Average		**2.4**	**7.4**		**3.0%**	**3.8%**	**$20,262**
Countries Beginning Reform during the 1990s							
Costa Rica	1991	2.1	7.4			3.0%	$10,239
El Salvador	1994	3.0	7.6			1.3%	$5,481
Estonia	1995	2.3	8.0			7.8%	$19,327
Hungary	1995	2.3	7.5			4.1%	$17,894
India	1990	2.1	6.6			5.2%	$2,600
Israel	1991	3.7	7.1			1.6%	$24,824
Nicaragua	1994	4.2	6.5			2.5%	$2,427
Peru	1993	4.0	7.2			2.8%	$7,400
Poland	1990	2.9	6.9			4.7%	$15,634
Tanzania	1995	2.9	6.3			3.0%	$1,141
Uganda	1995	3.6	6.5			3.6%	$1,000
Zambia	1996	3.4	6.7			2.0%	$1,283
Average		**3.0**	**7.0**			**3.5%**	**$9,104**
Countries that Regressed							
Congo, Republic	1995	−0.5	4.0		−4.4%	0.6%	$3,316
Venezuela	2000	−0.9	4.9		1.1%	1.0%	$11,480
Zimbabwe	1998	−2.6	2.9		−2.7%	−3.4%	$1,813
Average					**−2.0%**	**−0.6%**	**$5,536**

Source: James Gwartney and Robert Lawson, *Economic Freedom of the World: 2007 Annual Report*; International Monetary Fund, *World Economic Outlook*, September 2005, Chapter 3, "Building Institutions"; and World Bank, *World Development Indicators Online*. The International Monetary Fund is the source of the year in which the reforms were initiated. The data for Zimbabwe were only available through 2005.

the eight countries achieved an annual growth rate of 3.8 percent. The recent acceleration in their growth rates is not surprising because it takes time for reforms to acquire credibility and for people to make desired adjustments. Thus, several years may pass before the full positive effects of reforms are registered.

During the 1990s, twelve additional countries instituted major reforms that increased their EFW rating by two or more points. Except for Hungary and Israel, all of the 1990 reformers had very low incomes prior to the institution of reforms. This is a diverse group, including countries from Asia, Latin America, Africa, and Eastern Europe. The average growth record of the twelve was 3.5 percent during 1995–2007. The growth achievements of Estonia, Hungary, India, and Poland were particularly impressive.

Finally, Exhibit 8 also contains information on countries with reductions in EFW of one-half point or more since 1990. Since the mid-1980s, the overall EFW ratings have been increasing, primarily as a result of a more stable monetary policy, lower tax rates, and trade liberalization. Thus, reductions in EFW ratings have been far less common than increases. There were only three countries—the Democratic Republic of the Congo, Venezuela, and Zimbabwe—with rating reductions of half a point or more. Monetary instability, confiscation of property, and violation of rule of law principles played a role in the declining economic freedom rating of these countries. As Exhibit 8 shows, the rating reductions were accompanied by poor economic performance. Both the Democratic Republic of the Congo and Zimbabwe had negative growth rates during 1990–2007. While Venezuela achieved a positive growth of 1.1 percent during 1990–2007, all of this growth occurred during 2006–2007, and it was driven by the soaring world price of oil of that period.

Sustained growth of per capita income of 2 percent or more over a lengthy time period is relatively uncommon. As Exhibit 2 shows, only a few of the high-income industrial economies grew at annual rates of 2 percent or more during 1990–2007. Interestingly, except for New Zealand, which had a growth rate of 1.9 percent, all ten of the countries that made major moves toward reform during the 1970s and 1980s achieved an annual growth rate of more than 2 percent during 1995–2007. While their rates varied substantially, all of the countries moving toward reform achieved a positive growth of income per person. This is strong evidence that changes in institutional quality exert an impact on growth and income.

The Legal System, Growth, and Prosperity

As we have stressed, exchange, entrepreneurial discovery, and investment are the driving forces of economic growth. But a sound legal system is vitally important for the realization of gains from these sources. If the legal system does not provide for the protection of private property and the evenhanded enforcement of contracts, individuals' incentive to develop productive resources and engage in entrepreneurial activities is eroded. Correspondingly, without confidence in an evenhanded legal system, both the risk and cost of transactions will increase. In turn, the higher transaction costs will eliminate mutually advantageous trades and the accompanying gains from division of labor, specialization, and large-scale production methods.

The work of Douglass C. North and Friedrich Hayek explains why the legal system is so important. Our modern living standards are the result of what North calls "depersonalized exchange," that is, trade between parties that do not know each other and will probably never meet. These exchanges are coordinated by what Hayek refers to as the "extension of the market" from the local town or village to the region, nation, and indeed to the far corners of the world. Almost everything that households in North America, Europe, and other parts of the developed world consume is the result of gains from depersonalized exchange and extension of the market. Without these gains, high levels of per capita income and modern living standards would be impossible. But

APPLICATIONS IN ECONOMICS

China: Institutions, Markets, and Growth

Since 1980, China has been the world's fastest-growing economy. How can this be? Isn't China a centrally planned socialist economy? It certainly was for three decades following World War II. However, even though the Communist Party of China remains in charge, the Chinese economy has experienced remarkable change during the past three decades.

Following the 1978 Communist Party Congress, China began introducing institutional reforms that have dramatically changed the structure of the economy. Today, there are essentially two Chinese economies: (1) agriculture, small businesses, and "special economic zones; and (2) state enterprises. The activities in the first category take place within a now relatively free economy, whereas those in the second continue to be owned and operated by various levels of government.

China's liberalization started with the agricultural sector. Following the 1978 Communist Party Congress, collective farms were dismantled and replaced with what the Chinese refer to as a contract responsibility system. Under this system, families are now permitted to lease land from the government for periods of up to fifty years. Except for a modest production quota supplied to the government, farmers are permitted to keep what they produce and/or sell it at market prices. Even though the legal ownership of land remains with the state, the system of long-term leases provides farmers with something akin to a private property right. This is particularly true because renewing the lengthy leases is now virtually automatic. But the land cannot be used as collateral, and this ownership system has led to some corruption and social unrest. Currently, more than 85 percent of the grain output (rice, wheat, and barley) is produced privately and sold at market-determined prices. Restrictions on individual stock breeding, household sideline occupations, the transport of agricultural goods, and trade fairs (marketplaces) have been removed.

Success in China's agriculture led to reforms in other sectors. Restrictions on the operation of small-scale service and retail businesses were relaxed in the 1980s. As a result, private restaurants, stores, and repair shops sprang up and began to compete with state-operated enterprises. By the mid-1980s, Chinese cities were teeming with sidewalk vendors, restaurants, small retail businesses, and hundreds of thousands of individuals providing personal services.

China also established so-called special economic zones. Approximately 30 percent of the people in the Chinese labor force now work in these areas. Regulations are more liberal and taxes lower in the zones. People are permitted to establish businesses, engage in trade with foreigners, maintain bank accounts in foreign currencies, and undertake investment without having to obtain government approval. During recent decades, the zones attracted a large amount of investment from abroad, which has contributed to the growth of the Chinese investment rate. Economic activity in these regions has also made a sizable contribution to the growth of the trade sector.

The Chinese economy has become much more open to international trade in recent decades. In 1980, international trade (the average of imports plus exports) as a share of GDP was 10 percent of the Chinese economy. By 2005, the trade sector had grown to 35 percent of the Chinese economy. By way of comparison, international trade is about 14 percent of the U.S. economy. Even though China is more populous, measured as a share of GDP, China's trade sector is more than double the size of the trade sector of the United States. No doubt, the increased openness and rapid expansion of the trade sector have been major factors contributing to the impressive growth of the Chinese economy.

China's economic freedom rating is still relatively low. In 2007, it ranked eighty-second among the 141 countries of the EFW report. However, its rating has improved substantially since 1980. Moreover, the degree of economic freedom in the special economic zones, which now cover a large share of the economy, is substantially greater than for the country as a whole.

The liberal reforms have surely contributed to China's rapid growth. However, it is possible that some of the growth has been exaggerated. This was the case for the former Soviet Union and the countries of Eastern Europe during the 1970s and 1980s. Because centrally planned economies do not rely on market prices to allocate goods and services, output in the planned sector is generally measured by the physical quantities of goods produced and the value of inputs used. These factors might not reliably reflect the value of what is actually produced. Also, as China has moved away from a command/barter economy in recent years toward greater reliance on markets, some productive activities that were not counted (or were counted only at a depressed level) are now being counted as part of GDP. This will also tend to exaggerate the growth of GDP. Thus, while China's growth is clearly impressive, the figures should be interpreted with a degree of caution.

these gains from depersonalized trade cannot be realized without a legal system that can be counted on to protect property rights and enforce contracts fairly. The failure of a country's legal system to perform these functions places a tight constraint on its prosperity.

The data of the EFW project can be used to investigate this issue. In addition to the overall rating, the EFW project also provides ratings in five major areas, including legal structure and the protection of property rights. The Legal System Area indicates the consistency of a nation's legal structure with protection of property rights, unbiased enforcement of contracts, independence of the judiciary, and rule of law principles.[9]

Among the ninety-nine countries for which data were available throughout the 1980–2000 period, twenty-four countries had an average Legal System Area rating of 7.0 or more. As **EXHIBIT 9** shows, these twenty-four countries had an average per capita GDP in 2007 of $35,810 and an average annual real growth rate of 2.4 percent during the 1980–2007 period. Among these countries with a relatively sound legal system, the lowest 2007 per capita income level was the $17,894 figure of Hungary. All twenty-four of the countries with sound legal systems achieved positive real growth of per capita GDP during 1980–2007. In fact, only one (Switzerland at 1.0) of the twenty-four had an annual growth rate of less than 1.5 percent. Thus, all of the countries with sound legal systems grew and achieved relatively high levels of per capita income.

At the other end of the spectrum, there were twenty-one countries with an average 1980–2000 Legal System Area rating of less than 4.0. Among these countries, the average 2007 per capita GDP was $3,837, about one-ninth the average for the countries with quality legal systems. All of the countries with a low-quality legal system had incomes that were substantially lower than that of the country (Hungary) with the lowest income among the group with better legal systems! The average growth of per capita GDP for the group with poor legal systems was 0.8 percent, 1.6 percentage points below the average for the quality legal system group. Whereas four of these countries had growth rates of more than 2 percent, all of the four were excedingly poor (per capita GDP of $4,007 or less). None of the twenty-one countries with low-quality legal systems were able to achieve both a 2007 per capita income appreciably more than $4,000 and a growth rate of 2.0 percent during 1980–2007.

All of this suggests that it will be virtually impossible for countries with legal systems that fail to protect property rights and enforce contracts to move up to even lower-middle income status. While this is a tragic result, it highlights the importance of the "rules of the game" that protect property rights and support the exchange process. When the rules undermine gains from depersonalized trade, expansion in the size of markets, entrepreneurship, and investment, economic growth is stifled and income levels remain low. Unless they make improvements, countries with poor legal institutions will almost surely remain poor and fall farther and farther behind those with sounder legal environments.[10]

Rich and Poor Nations Revisited

Observing income differences between the wealthy and poor nations, some have argued that the rich are consistently getting richer while the poor are getting poorer. Is this true? Look back at Exhibit 2 as you think about this question. Interestingly, as Exhibit 2 shows,

[9]The components for the Legal System Area rating are from (1) The PRS Group, *International Country Risk Guide* (Syracuse, NY: PRS Group); and (2) the World Economic Forum, *Global Competitiveness Report* (Oxford University Press, annual). The former is a private organization that has provided investors with information about the risk of legal systems in various countries for more than a quarter of a century. The latter is based on a survey of business decision makers in each country on the presence of rule of law principles and even handedness of the court system. The EFW legal system area rating is based on five components from these two sources.

[10]While the variation in economic freedom is much smaller among U.S. states (and Canadian provinces) than is true for countries, there is some variation in the legal, tax, and regulatory policies among states. For evidence on this point, see Amela Karabegovic and Fred McMahon, *Economic Freedom of North America: 2008 Annual Report* (Vancouver: The Fraser Institute, 2008). For evidence that differences in economic freedom among states are large enough to influence economic performance, see Russell Sobel, ed., *Unleashing Capitalism: Why Prosperity Stops at the West Virginia Border and How to Fix It* (Morgantown, WV: Public Policy Foundation of West Virginia, 2007).

EXHIBIT 9
Per Person Income (2005) and Growth Rate (1980–2007) for the Countries with High and Low Ratings in the Legal Structure Area

The Legal System and Income Growth—Countries with Average Rating from 1980–2000 for "Area 2: Legal Structure and Security of Property Rights" Greater than 7.0

The Legal System and Income Growth—Countries with Average Rating from 1980–2000 for "Area 2: Legal Structure and Security of Property Rights" Less than 4.0

Countries with Average Legal Rating > 7.0 from 1980 to 2000	Legal System Rating	GDP per Capita 2007 (PPP 2005US$)	Growth of GDP per Capita from 1980 to 2007 (Percent)	Countries with Average Legal Rating < 4.0 from 1980 to 2000	Legal System Rating	GDP per Capita 2007 (PPP 2005US$)	Growth of GDP per Capita from 1980 to 2007 (Percent)
Switzerland	8.7	$37,581	1.0	Indonesia	3.9	$3,506	3.6
The Netherlands	8.6	$36,956	2.0	Senegal	3.8	$1,573	0.4
United States	8.6	$43,055	2.0	Pakistan	3.7	$2,357	2.6
Austria	8.5	$35,537	1.9	Sri Lanka	3.7	$4,007	3.6
Luxembourg	8.5	$72,783	3.7	Honduras	3.6	$3,585	0.9
New Zealand	8.5	$25,281	1.5	Iran	3.6	$10,346	1.4
Denmark	8.4	$34,905	1.9	Syria	3.6	$4,260	0.9
Finland	8.4	$33,324	2.3	Algeria	3.5	$7,310	0.5
Germany	8.4	$33,181	1.8	Nicaragua	3.5	$2,427	−0.4
Australia	8.3	$32,735	1.9	Peru	3.5	$7,400	0.7
Canada	8.3	$36,260	1.7	Philippines	3.5	$3,217	0.8
Norway	8.3	$49,359	2.4	Colombia	3.4	$8,109	1.7
Iceland	8.1	$36,118	1.9	Uganda	3.4	$1,000	1.9
Sweden	8.1	$34,090	1.9	El Salvador	3.3	$5,481	0.8
Belgium	8.0	$33,399	1.8	Nigeria	3.3	$1,859	0.2
Ireland	7.9	$41,036	4.4	Bangladesh	3.2	$1,172	2.4
Singapore	7.9	$46,939	4.4	Bolivia	3.2	$3,972	0.2
United Kingdom	7.9	$33,717	2.3	Congo, Rep. of	3.2	$3,316	0.5
Japan	7.8	$31,689	2.0	Guatemala	3.0	$4,308	0.4
France	7.5	$31,615	1.6	Haiti	3.0	$1,090	−2.5
Portugal	7.5	$21,169	2.2	Congo, Dem. R.	2.4	$282	−3.6
Hong Kong	7.2	$39,953	4.0	**Average**	**3.4**	**$3,837**	**0.8**
Hungary	7.2	$17,894	1.9				
Taiwan	7.0	$20,868	5.1				
Average	**8.1**	**$35,810**	**2.4**				

countries with a low per capita income in 1990 dominate the list of both countries that have grown most rapidly and those that have regressed and experienced falling incomes since 1990.

How can this pattern be explained? When you think about it, the rapid growth of less-developed countries with a low initial income should not be surprising. When low-income countries establish sound institutions and policies, they actually have an advantage. The low-income economies can copy or emulate ideas and technologies that have been successful in the high-income countries. Further, in a world of diminishing returns, the rate of return on investment in low-income economies with sound institutions will generally be higher than in capital-rich, more advanced economies. Thus, foreign investors will be attracted, and high investment rates will promote more rapid growth. To a degree, the rapid growth in recent decades of economies such as China, South Korea, Botswana, India, Singapore, and Hong Kong reflects these advantages. These countries would not have grown as rapidly if their initial incomes had been higher and they had not been in a position to attract investment and emulate technologies, business procedures, and other ideas from more advanced economies. However, it is also important to note that the high-growth economies of Exhibit 2 had either persistently high economic freedom ratings (Hong Kong and Singapore) or a major improvement in their EFW rating (China, Botswana, Ireland, and India are examples).

However, if a low-income country is going to benefit from borrowing technologies from more advanced economies and an influx of investment capital, it must have sound institutions. As the data of the prior section show, sound legal institutions are particularly important. Access to modern technology is of little value when the institutional and policy environment undermine the potential attractiveness of entrepreneurial activity. This has been the case in many less-developed countries. The ten economies with the worst growth records shown in Exhibit 2 are all among the world's least free economies. Disastrous institutional conditions explain the persistence of both low incomes and poor growth. Many low-income economies continue to perform poorly and even regress because their institutions and policies stifle gains from trade, entrepreneurship, and investment.

Economic Rules and Political Decision Making

A country's economic rules make a huge difference in its economic growth. When the institutions and policies of a country encourage market exchanges, reward the discovery of better ways of doing things, and protect people and their property, investment will be attracted to the nation, and people will engage in productive activities. Rapid growth and movement up the income ladder will result. In contrast, if the rules make unproductive and destructive activities profitable, people will pursue such activities and potentially productive resources will be squandered.

Economics indicates the types of institutions and policies that will lead to wealth creation, growth, and prosperity. However, institutions and policies are an outgrowth of the political process. Unfortunately, there is no assurance that political decision making will lead to sound policies.

Authoritarian political regimes will typically reflect the interests of those holding power and their desire to maintain their control. However, if more rapid growth will help an authoritarian government remain in power, it will be an incentive to move toward sounder policies. In recent decades, Chile, Singapore, South Korea, and Taiwan moved toward economic liberalization even though their political regimes were authoritarian. China's Communist government has also moved in this direction since 1978 even while maintaining a firm grip on the political machinery of the country. But growth may not always be advantageous to those in political control. In addition, history teaches that power corrupts. Even if an authoritarian government adopts some sensible economic policies, there is no assurance that they will persist.

Democracy

A form of political organization in which adult citizens are free to participate in the political process (vote, lobby, and choose among candidates), elections are free and open, and outcomes are decided by majority voting, either directly or by elected representatives.

Won't **democracy** ensure that a government will undertake productive policies? Think about the difference between markets and political democracy as you ponder this question. The two are quite different. Market exchange is based on agreement and mutual gain. When markets are open and property rights are well defined, market activities will persist only when they are mutually advantageous. Most important, the agreement of the market participants provides strong evidence that the activity is productive. In contrast, the majority rules criteria of democracy generate "losers" as well as "winners." And there is no assurance that the gains of the winners will be greater than the costs imposed on the losers. This is particularly true when the primary beneficiaries of the decisions made differ from those who are paying the costs related to those decisions.

As the public choice analysis highlights, there are several circumstances under which there is good reason to expect that the costs imposed on the minority will be greater than, and often substantially greater than, the benefits derived by the political majority. Majoritarian democracy tends to be shortsighted. It is biased toward the adoption of programs that provide immediate, highly visible benefits at the expense of future costs that are difficult to identify. Furthermore, special interests will exert disproportional power at the expense of the ordinary citizen. Political incentives will lead politicians to "trade" favors to interest groups in exchange for political contributions that will help them win the next election. When the government becomes heavily involved in activities that provide favors to some at the expense of others, people will be encouraged to divert resources away from productive activities and toward lobbying, campaign contributions, and other forms of political favor seeking. All of these shortcomings tend to corrupt the political process and lead even democratic governments to adopt counterproductive policies.

Aren't our elected political leaders acting with good intentions and trying to do what is right? No doubt, many of them are. But, as we discussed in Chapter 1, good intentions will not guarantee desirable outcomes. Neither will they provide protection from unsound policies. The doctors of the eighteenth century had good intentions. They thought that leeches would draw various diseases out of the blood stream and lead to recovery. But their good intentions did not protect their patients from the adverse consequences of unsound practices. Neither will good intentions protect ordinary citizens from unsound governmental policies.

Could political institutions be designed in a manner that would make political action more reflective of mutual agreement and provide better protection of economic rights? Clearly, the answer is "yes." Such a design would include (1) checks on the powers of both the executive and simple legislative majorities; (2) constitutional protection of economic rights like ownership of property, freedom to trade and compete, and use of alternative currencies; and (3) political decentralization so that citizens can more easily escape from governmental units that fail to provide an attractive economic environment.[11]

However, merely because it is possible to design a political system reasonably consistent with growth and prosperity does not mean it will happen. Just because we have knowledge about what works does not mean sound policies will flow from the political process. As the chapter-opening quote from Professor North indicates, history is a story about countries that fail to adopt and enforce a set of economic rules that generate sustained economic growth. Achievement and maintenance of political power often conflict with sound economics.

Furthermore, the political process will be influenced by the current severe economic recession. In 2008–2009, the U.S. economy was characterized by rising mortgage default rates, troubles in the banking and finance sectors, heavy household indebtedness, huge federal budget deficits, and a severe recession. To a large degree, this crisis was the result

[11]The framers of the U.S. Constitution recognized the danger of unlimited government. They sought to limit federal actions to those areas of widespread agreement through the establishment of two legislative bodies based on different criteria; separation of powers among the executive, legislative, and judicial branches; and the listing of the specific powers of the central government (the enumerated powers of Article I, Section 8). All other powers were left to the states and the people (Tenth Amendment). Thus, decentralization of government was also an integral part of the structural design. The U.S. Constitution also provides some protection for both trade and private ownership. Taxes on exports and state legislation "impairing the obligation of contracts" (Article I, Section 10) were prohibited. The Fifth Amendment specifies that private property shall not be "taken for public use without just compensation." With the passage of time, however, the economic protections built into the U.S. Constitution have been eroded by court decisions. This is particularly true for the enumerated powers section.

of government regulations that mandated an expansion of mortgage loans to subprime borrowers and central bank policies that created a boom and bust in the housing industry. See Special Topic 5, "The Crisis of 2008: Causes and Lessons to Be Learned" for a comprehensive analysis of this issue. The financial crisis has spread around the world, and countries with large trade sectors have been particularly hard hit. How will the response to this crisis affect the quality of institutions? Will the United States and other countries move toward institutions and policies more consistent with long-term growth and prosperity, or will there be a move in the opposite direction? The answer to this question will determine the primary cost of this crisis.

The ingredients of sound institutions and policies in the decades ahead are the same as they have been in decades past: well-defined property rights, rule of law, monetary and price stability, open markets, low taxes, control of government spending, and neutral treatment of both people and enterprises. The shape of the twenty-first century may well depend on the general understanding of this issue. This is an exciting time to be studying economics.

Looking ahead

As we have already discussed, international trade is an important source of growth and prosperity. The following chapter will provide a more detailed analysis of this issue.

KEY POINTS

▼ Purchasing power parity comparisons indicate that the per person income in wealthy countries such as Norway and the United States is about fifty times the income level of the world's poorest countries. While these figures may result in some overstatement because GDP excludes production within the household sector, it is clear that the income differences between high- and low-income countries are huge.

▼ The world's fastest-growing economies were almost all low-income, less-developed countries a couple of decades ago. China and India, with a third of the world's population, are included in the fast-growing group of LDCs. But there is also a large number of LDCs that have experienced falling incomes in recent decades.

▼ The *Economic Freedom of the World* (EFW) index is designed to measure the consistency of a nation's institutions and policies with personal choice, voluntary exchange, open markets, and protection of property rights. In order to score high on this index, countries must rely on markets, refrain from regulations that restrain trade, keep taxes low, and provide access to sound money and a legal system

that protects privately owned property and enforces contracts in an evenhanded manner.

▼ Countries with institutions and policies consistent with economic freedom have achieved higher income levels and grown more rapidly than those that are less free. The 2007 per capita income in the persistently free quartile of countries was more than eight times the figure for the least free quartile.

▼ Even though wages are lower and capital less abundant in low-income countries, both private investment rates and the productivity of investment are low in countries with less economic freedom.

▼ Countries that have substantially improved the quality of their institutions in recent decades have registered impressive growth rates. Ireland, Botswana, Chile, Estonia, and even China are examples. In contrast, countries such as Zimbabwe and Venezuela that have moved toward policies that conflict with economic freedom have performed poorly.

▼ A legal structure that protects property rights and enforces contracts in an evenhanded manner is vitally important. Without such a legal system, people will not be able to derive the benefits of depersonalized trade with people living in distant locations. Without the gains from a vast network of depersonalized exchanges coordinated by markets, high income levels and living standards will be unattainable.

▼ Economic institutions and policies will reflect political choices. The political environment often conflicts with the adoption of sound economic policy. Even democratic politics will sometimes lead to the adoption of policies that reduce growth and prosperity.

CRITICAL ANALYSIS QUESTIONS

1. Indicate five countries with a high income per capita. Why do you think the income is so high in these countries? How many of your high-income countries also ranked among the fastest-growing countries in the world since 1990?

2. Indicate five of the fastest-growing economies in the world since 1990. Why do you think these economies have grown so rapidly?

3. "The rich countries are getting richer, while the poor are getting poorer." Evaluate this statement.

4. What is economic freedom? Indicate some of the ways in which institutions and policies in economies that are more free differ from those that are less free.

5. Indicate five of the world's economies that are most free. How do the income levels and growth rates of freer economies compare with those that are less free?

6. What are the major sources of economic growth? Why do some countries grow and achieve high income levels while others stagnate in poverty? What do you think can be done to change this situation?

7. Does the legal system of a country influence its economic performance? From an economic viewpoint, what are the key characteristics of a sound legal system?

*8. If there were no high-income developed countries like those of Western Europe, North America, and Japan, would less-developed countries like Hong Kong, Singapore, South Korea, China, and India have been able to grow so rapidly in recent decades? Explain.

*9. What conditions must be present for a country to achieve a high score on the *Economic Freedom of the World* index?

10. Do we count on majority rule to protect civil liberties such as the right to free speech, freedom of the press, the right to assembly, and religious freedom? Should we count on majority rule to protect economic rights like the freedom to trade, the freedom to compete in the business or occupation of one's choice, and the protection against the taking of one's property by others, including the government? Discuss both of these questions.

*11. Does a country have to be democratic in order to achieve economic freedom? If a country is democratic, will it necessarily be economically free? Why or why not?

12. Why are income levels in the United States so high? Is the United States prosperous because it is democratic? Discuss.

*13. Firms can choose where to establish a production facility. What are some of the major factors that will influence whether a firm will invest and produce in a country?

*14. Even though workers in low-wage countries often seek to emigrate to higher-wage countries, the flow of investment toward low-wage countries is small. Why is this so?

*15. Why will political decentralization make it more difficult for governments to levy taxes and spend the revenues on things that provide citizens with little value relative to cost?

*Asterisk denotes questions for which answers are given in Appendix B.

ADDENDUM

Economic Freedom and Quality of Life

This chapter illustrated that countries with better institutions and policies had higher investment rates, grew more rapidly, and achieved higher levels of income per person. What about other indicators of quality of life? Here, we will divide the 122 countries for which the economic freedom data were available throughout 1990–2007 into quartiles, arrayed from least free to most free and present data on their relationship to several quality of life indicators. No doubt, many of these relationships will reflect the indirect impact of institutions working through income rather than a direct causal link. In other cases, the observed relationships may reflect the fact that some of the variables that influence economic freedom may also influence political factors like the impartiality of the legal system. Nonetheless, it is interesting to view the relationship between economic freedom and alternative measures of economic well-being.

The following graphics illustrate this point.

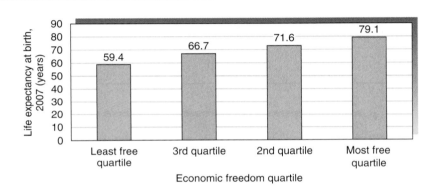

Source: *Economic Freedom of the World: 2009 Annual Report* and World Bank, *World Development Indicators, CD-ROM, 2009.*

EXHIBIT A-1
Life Expectancy at Birth

The life expectancy at birth of people living in the most-free quartile of countries was 79.1 compared to 59.4 in the least-free quartile. The two middle quartiles fell between these extremes. Thus, people in the most-free economies had twenty additional years of life compared to those in the least free economies.

Source: *Economic Freedom of the World: 2009 Annual Report* and World Bank, *World Development Indicators, CD-ROM, 2009.*

EXHIBIT A-2
Infant Mortality Rate, 2007

The infant mortality rate declined as economic freedom increased. The infant mortality rate in the leastfree economies was more then ten times higher than for the most-free.

EXHIBIT A-3
Improved Water Source

*The access to sanitary water in-
creased with economic freedom.*

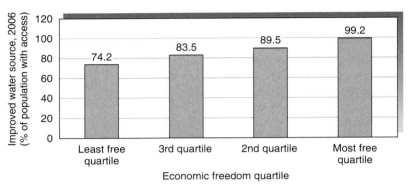

Source: Economic Freedom of the World: 2009 Annual Report and World Bank, World
Development Indicators, CD-ROM, 2009.

EXHIBIT A-4
Environmental Quality,
2007/2008

*Studies have shown that the
quality of the environment is
strongly linked to income. Thus,
the positive relationship observed
here is largely a reflection of the
higher incomes achieved by the
more free economies.*

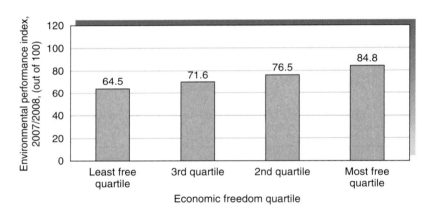

The Environmental Performance Index (EPI) is an initiative of the Yale Center for
Environmental Law and Policy (YCELP) and the Center for International Earth Science
Information Network (CIESIN) of Columbia University, in collaboration with the World
Economic Forum and the Joint Research Centre of the European Commission (2008).

Source: 2008 Environmental Performance Index, http://epi.yale.edu,
Accessed: 9 June 2008.

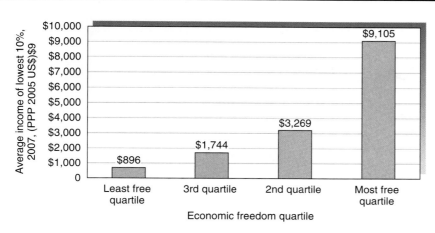

Source: *Economic Freedom of the World: 2009 Annual Report* and World Bank, *World Development Indicators, CD-ROM, 2009.*

EXHIBIT A-5
Income of Lowest 10%

The annual income of the poorest 10 percent of the population increased with economic freedom. In nations of the top quartile, the average income of the poorest 10 percent of the population is $9,105 compared with $896 for those in the bottom quartile.

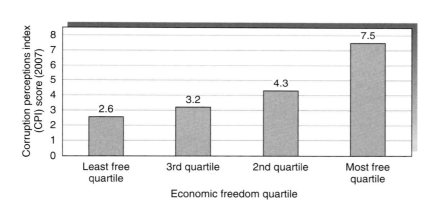

2007 Corruption Perceptions Index (CPI) Score - relates to perceptions of the degree of corruption as seen by business people and country analysts and ranges between 10 (highly clean) and 0 (highly corrupt).

Source: Transparency International, http://www.transparency.org/policy_research/surveys_indices/cpi/2007.

EXHIBIT A-6
Political Corruption

The incidence of political corruption was lower in the more free economies. These numbers are a reflection of the higher quality legal systems of the freer economies.

Economic Freedom Index

8.9–8.0	Most Free
7.9–7.5	
7.4–7.0	
6.9–6.5	
6.4–6.0	
5.9–5.5	
Less than 5.5	Least Free
Indicates data unavailable to rate these countries	

EXHIBIT A-7
The Most Recent Economic Freedom Ratings

Institutions and policies generally change slowly, and it takes time for changes to exert much impact on income. Thus, we have generally focused on the quality of institutions and policies over a lengthy time frame such as 1980–2007. However, the recent data are also of interest. The above map and the following chart provide the 2007 economic freedom ratings for the 141 countries now included in the Economic Freedom of the World Project.

8.97	1	Ho
8.66	2	Si
8.30	3	Ne
8.19	4	Sw
8.14	5	Ch
8.06	6	Ur
7.98	7	Ire
7.91	8	Ca
7.89	9	Au
7.89	9	Un
7.81	11	Es

7.74	12	Denmark	7.54	23	Malta
7.67	13	Austria	7.53	24	Iceland
7.65	14	Luxembourg	7.53	24	Norway
7.65	14	Panama	7.52	26	Slovak Rep
7.62	16	Finland	7.50	27	Germany
7.62	16	Mauritius	7.48	28	El Salvador
7.62	16	Taiwan	7.48	28	Honduras
7.58	19	Unit. Arab Em.	7.46	30	Japan
7.56	20	Bahrain	7.46	30	Kuwait
7.56	20	Costa Rica	7.45	32	Korea, South
7.56	20	The Netherlands	7.43	33	France

7.40	34	Jordan
7.38	35	Lithuania
7.36	36	Cyprus
7.36	36	Oman
7.33	38	Hungary
7.32	39	Spain
7.28	40	Sweden
7.26	41	Peru
7.25	42	Georgia
7.25	42	Guatemala
7.22	44	Latvia
7.19	45	Jamaica
7.19	45	Portugal
7.18	47	Belgium
7.17	48	Armenia
7.13	49	Zambia
7.12	50	Botswana
7.12	50	Kazakhstan
7.11	52	Greece
7.10	53	Bahamas
7.09	54	Czech Rep.
7.09	54	Kenya
7.07	56	Trinidad & Tob.
7.06	57	Albania
7.06	57	South Africa
7.04	59	Thailand
6.96	60	Nicaragua
6.95	61	Italy
6.95	61	Uruguay
6.91	63	Mongolia
6.90	64	Slovenia
6.90	64	Uganda
6.88	66	Malaysia
6.87	67	Belize
6.85	68	Mexico
6.83	69	Namibia
6.83	69	Philippines
6.80	71	Ghana
6.80	71	Kyrgyz Republic
6.79	73	Romania
6.78	74	Poland
6.75	75	Barbados
6.74	76	Bulgaria
6.71	77	Pap. New Guinea
6.69	78	Israel
6.68	79	Egypt
6.64	80	Fiji
6.58	81	Montenegro
6.54	82	China
6.50	83	Russia
6.47	84	Serbia
6.46	85	Azerbaijan
6.45	86	India
6.44	87	Haiti
6.42	88	Turkey

6.40	89	Macedonia
6.39	90	Tunisia
6.38	91	Paraguay
6.36	92	Lesotho
6.35	93	Indonesia
6.34	94	Moldova
6.33	95	Croatia
6.32	96	Tanzania
6.31	97	Nigeria
6.29	98	Madagascar
6.28	99	Mali
6.27	100	Dominican Rep.
6.22	101	Vietnam
6.20	102	Rwanda
6.18	103	Bolivia
6.16	104	Morocco
6.10	105	Argentina
6.10	105	Bosnia and Herzegovina
6.10	105	Sri Lanka
6.09	108	Cote d'Ivoire
6.05	109	Mauritania
6.01	110	Pakistan
6.00	111	Brazil
5.99	112	Iran
5.98	113	Guyana
5.97	114	Sierra Leone
5.93	115	Bangladesh
5.93	115	Malawi
5.90	117	Togo
5.89	118	Benin
5.87	119	Burkina Faso
5.83	120	Ecuador
5.81	121	Colombia
5.80	122	Gabon
5.79	123	Cameroon
5.76	124	Syria
5.74	125	Mozambique
5.72	126	Senegal
5.71	127	Ethiopia
5.68	128	Ukraine
5.58	129	Nepal
5.54	130	Burundi
5.34	131	Algeria
5.11	132	Niger
5.09	133	Chad
5.00	134	Congo, Dem. R.
4.84	135	Guinea-Bissau
4.79	136	Central Afr. Rep.
4.44	137	Congo, Rep. of
4.33	138	Venezuela
4.04	139	Angola
3.69	140	Myanmar
2.89	141	Zimbabwe

International Economics

The volume of international trade has grown dramatically in recent decades. Although the same general principles apply to both domestic and international trade, the latter also involves the exchange of one currency for another. Thus, this part will analyze the impact of both international trade and the operation of the foreign exchange market.

The world is becoming a global village

Gaining from International Trade

The evidence is overwhelmingly persuasive that the massive increase in world competition—a consequence of broadening trade flows—has fostered markedly higher standards of living for almost all countries who have participated in cross-border trade. I include most especially the United States.

—Alan Greenspan[1]

CHAPTER FOCUS

- How has the volume of international trade changed in recent decades?

- Under what conditions can a nation gain from international trade?

- What effects do trade restrictions have on an economy?

- How have open economies performed relative to those that are more closed?

- What accounts for the political popularity of trade restraints?

- Do trade restrictions create jobs? Does trade with low-wage countries depress wage rates in high-wage countries like the United States?

[1]Alan Greenspan, speech before the Alliance for the Commonwealth Conference on International Business (Massachusetts, June 2, 1999).

W e live in a shrinking world. The breakfast of many Americans includes bananas from Honduras, coffee from Brazil, or hot chocolate made from Nigerian cocoa beans. Americans often drive a car produced by a Japanese or European manufacturer that consumes gasoline refined from petroleum extracted in Saudi Arabia or Venezuela. Similarly, many Americans work for companies that sell a substantial number of their products to foreigners.

Spurred by cost reductions in transportation and communications, the volume of international trade has grown rapidly in recent decades. It may surprise some people that most international trade is not between the governments of different nations but rather between people and firms located in different countries. Why do people engage in international trade? The expectation of gain provides the answer. Domestic producers are often able to sell their products to foreigners at attractive prices, and domestic consumers sometimes find that the best deals are available from foreign suppliers. Like other voluntary exchanges, international trade occurs because both the buyer and the seller expect to gain and generally do. If both parties did not expect to gain, they would not agree to the exchange. ■

The Trade Sector of the United States

As **EXHIBIT 1** illustrates, the size of the trade sector of the United States has grown rapidly during the last several decades. In 1960, total exports of goods and services accounted for 3.6 percent of the U.S. economy, whereas imports summed to 4.1 percent. By 1980, both exports and imports were approximately 6 percent of the economy. In 2008, exports accounted for 13.0 percent of total output, while imports summed to 17.7 percent. Thus, U.S. international trade (exports + imports) in goods and services has more than doubled as a share of the economy since 1980 and more than tripled since 1960.

Who are the major trading partners of Americans? **EXHIBIT 2** shows the share of U.S. trade (exports + imports) with each of its ten leading trading partners. These ten countries account for approximately two-thirds of the total volume of U.S. trade. Canada, China, Mexico, and Japan are the four largest trading partners of Americans. Nearly half of all U.S. trade is with these four countries. The United States also conducts a substantial volume of trade with the nations of the European Union, particularly Germany, the United Kingdom, and France.

What are the leading imports and exports of the United States? Capital goods like automobiles, computers, semiconductors, telecommunications equipment, and industrial machines are bought and sold in worldwide markets. The United States both imports and exports substantial quantities of these goods. Civilian aircraft, electrical equipment, chemicals, and plastics are also among the leading products the United States exports. Crude oil, textiles, toys, sporting goods, and pharmaceuticals are major products it imports.

Clearly, the impact of international trade differs across industries. In some industries, domestic producers find it very difficult to compete with their rivals abroad. For example, over 95 percent of the shoes purchased by Americans and the majority of the radio and television sets, watches, and motorcycles are produced abroad. A high percentage of the clothing and textile products, paper, cut diamonds, and DVD players consumed in the United States are also imported. In contrast, a large proportion of the aircraft, power-generating equipment, scientific instruments, construction equipment, and fertilizers produced in the United States are exported to purchasers abroad.

EXHIBIT 1

The Growth of the Trade Sector in the United States: 1960–2008

During the past several decades, international trade has persistently risen as a share of GDP. Imports of goods and services as a share of GDP rose from 4 percent in 1960 to 6 percent in 1980 and almost 18 percent in 2008. Similarly, exports increased from 4 percent of GDP in 1960 to 6 percent in 1980 and 13 percent in 2008.

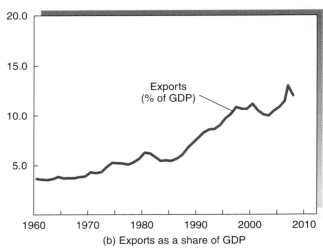

(a) Imports as a share of GDP

(b) Exports as a share of GDP

Source: http://www.economagic.com. The figures are based on data for real imports, exports, and GDP.

EXHIBIT 2

The 2008 Leading Trading Partners of the United States

Canada, China, Mexico, and Japan are the leading trading partners of the United States. Approximately one-half of all U.S. trade involves imports from or exports to these four countries.

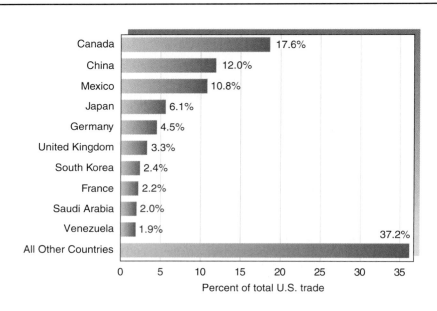

Source: http://www.census.gov.

Gains from Specialization and Trade

Like domestic trade, international trade promotes growth and prosperity. We are now ready to analyze this topic in detail. The law of **comparative advantage** explains why a group of individuals, regions, or nations can gain from specialization and exchange. International trade leads to mutual gains because it allows residents of different countries to: (1) specialize in the production of those things they do best, and (2) import goods foreign producers are willing to supply at a lower cost than domestic producers. Resources and labor-force skills differ substantially across countries, and these differences influence costs. A good that is quite costly to produce in one country might be produced at a lower cost in another. For example, the warm, moist climates of Brazil, Colombia, and Guatemala make it more economical to produce coffee. Countries such as Saudi Arabia and Venezuela with rich oil fields can produce petroleum cheaply. Countries with an abundance of fertile land, such as Canada and Australia, are able to produce products such as wheat, feed grains, and beef at a low cost. In contrast, land is scarce in Japan, a nation with a highly skilled labor force. The Japanese, therefore, specialize in manufacturing, using their comparative advantage to produce cameras, automobiles, and electronic products for export. With international trade, the residents of different countries can gain by specializing in the production of goods they can produce economically. They can then sell those goods in the world market and use the proceeds to import other goods that are expensive to produce domestically.

The failure to comprehend the principle of mutual gains from trade is often a source of "fuzzy" economic thinking. Because of this, we will take the time to illustrate the principle in detail. To keep things simple, let's consider a case involving only two countries, the United States and Japan, and two products, food and clothing. Furthermore, let's assume that labor is the only resource used to produce these products. In addition, because we want to illustrate that gains from trade are nearly always possible, we are going to assume that Japan has an **absolute advantage**—that the Japanese workers are more efficient than the Americans—at producing both food and clothing. **EXHIBIT 3** illustrates this situation. Perhaps due to their prior experience or higher skill levels, Japanese workers can produce three units of food per day, compared with only two units per day for U.S. workers.

Comparative advantage

The ability to produce a good at a lower opportunity cost than others can produce it. Relative costs determine comparative advantage.

Absolute advantage

A situation in which a nation, as the result of its previous experience and/or natural endowments, can produce more of a good (with the same amount of resources) than another nation.

EXHIBIT 3
Gains from Specialization and Trade

Columns 1 and 2 indicate the daily output of either food or clothing of each worker in the United States and Japan. If the United States moves three workers from the clothing industry to the food industry, it can produce six more units of food and three fewer units of clothing. Similarly, if Japan moves one worker from food to clothing, clothing output will increase by nine units, while food output will decline by three units. With this reallocation of labor, the United States and Japan are able to increase their aggregate output of both food (three additional units) and clothing (six additional units).

COUNTRY	OUTPUT PER WORKER DAY		POTENTIAL CHANGE IN OUTPUT[a]	
	FOOD (1)	CLOTHING (2)	FOOD (3)	CLOTHING (4)
United States	2	1	+6	−3
Japan	3	9	−3	+9
Change in Total Output			+3	+6

[a]Change in output if the United States shifts three workers from the clothing to the food industry and if Japan shifts one worker from the food to the clothing industry.

Similarly, Japanese workers are able to produce nine units of clothing per day, compared with one unit of clothing per day for U.S. workers.

Can two countries gain from trade if one of them can produce both goods with fewer resources? The answer is "Yes." As long as the *relative* production costs of the two goods differ between Japan and the United States, gains from trade will be possible. Consider what would happen if the United States shifted three workers from the clothing industry to the food industry. This reallocation of labor would allow the United States to expand its food output by six units (two units per worker), while clothing output would decline by three units (one unit per worker). Suppose Japan reallocates labor in the opposite direction. When Japan moves one worker from the food industry to the clothing industry, Japanese clothing production expands by nine units, while food output declines by three units. The exhibit shows that this reallocation of labor *within* the two countries has increased their joint output by three units of food and six units of clothing.

The source of this increase in output is straightforward: Aggregate output expands because the reallocation of labor permits each country to specialize more fully in the production of the goods it can produce at a *relatively* low cost. Our old friend, the opportunity-cost concept, reveals the low-cost producer of each good. If Japanese workers produce one additional unit of food, they sacrifice the production of three units of clothing. Therefore, in Japan the opportunity cost of one unit of food is three units of clothing. Conversely, one unit of food in the United States can be produced at an opportunity cost of only a half-unit of clothing. American workers are therefore the low-opportunity-cost producers of food, even though they cannot produce as much food per day as the Japanese workers. Simultaneously, Japan is the low-opportunity-cost producer of clothing. The opportunity cost of producing a unit of clothing in Japan is only a third of a unit of food, compared with two units of food in the United States. The reallocation of labor illustrated in Exhibit 3 expanded joint output because it moved resources in both countries toward areas where they had a comparative advantage.

To reiterate: As long as the relative costs of producing the two goods differ in the two countries, gains from specialization and trade will be possible. Both countries will find it cheaper to trade for goods they can produce only at a high opportunity cost. For example, both countries will gain if the United States trades food to Japan for clothing at a trading ratio greater than one unit of food to one half-unit of clothing (the U.S. opportunity cost of food) but less than one unit of food to three units of clothing (the Japanese opportunity cost of food). Any trading ratio between these two extremes will permit the United States to acquire clothing more cheaply than it could be produced within the country and simultaneously permit Japan to acquire food more cheaply than it could be produced domestically.

How Trade Expands Consumption Possibilities

Because trade permits nations to expand their joint output, it also allows each nation to expand its consumption possibilities. The production possibilities concept can be used to illustrate this point. Suppose that there were 200 million workers in the United States and 50 million in Japan. Given these figures and the productivity of workers indicated in Exhibit 3, **EXHIBIT 4** presents the production possibilities curves for the two countries. If the United States used all of its 200 million workers in the food industry, it could produce 400 million units of food per day—two units per worker—and zero units of clothing (*N*). Alternatively, if the United States used all its workers to produce clothing, daily output would be 200 million units of clothing and no food (*M*). Intermediate output combinations along the production possibilities line (*MN*) between these two extreme points also could be achievable. For example, the United States could produce 150 million units of clothing and 100 million units of food (US_1).

Part (b) of Exhibit 4 illustrates the production possibilities of the 50 million Japanese workers. Japan could produce 450 million units of clothing and no food (*R*), 150 million units of food and no clothing (*S*), or various intermediate combinations, like 225 million units of clothing and 75 million units of food (J_1). The slope of the production possibilities

---

EXHIBIT 4

The Production Possibilities of the United States and Japan before
Specialization and Trade

Here, we illustrate the daily production possibilities of a U.S. labor force with 200 million workers and a Japanese labor force with 50 million workers, given the cost of producing food and clothing presented in Exhibit 3. In the absence of trade, consumption possibilities will be restricted to points such as US_1 in the United States and J_1 in Japan along the production possibilities curve of each country.

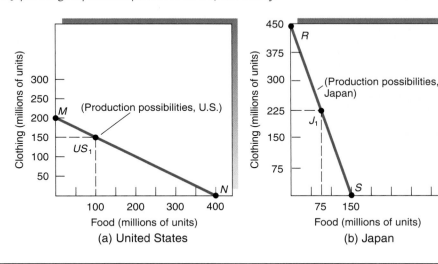

(a) United States   (b) Japan

---

constraint reflects the opportunity cost of food relative to clothing. Because Japan is the high-opportunity-cost producer of food, its production possibilities constraint is steeper than the constraint for the United States.

In the absence of trade, the consumption of each country is constrained by its production possibilities. Trade, however, expands the consumption possibilities of both. As we previously said, both countries can gain from specialization if the United States trades food to Japan at a price greater than one unit of food equals one half-unit of clothing but less than one unit of food equals three units of clothing. Suppose that they agree on an intermediate price of one unit of food equals one unit of clothing. As part (a) of **EXHIBIT 5** shows, when the United States specializes in the production of food (where it has a comparative advantage) and trades food for clothing (at the price ratio where one unit of food equals one unit of clothing), it can consume along the line *ON*. If the United States insisted on self-sufficiency, it would be restricted to consumption possibilities like US_1 (100 million units of food and 150 million units of clothing) along its production possibilities constraint of *MN*. With trade, however, the United States can achieve a combination

---

ECONOMICS *at The Movies*

Cast Away (2000)

In *Cast Away*, Tom Hanks is stranded alone on an island for four years. Hanks must be self-sufficient and produce everything he consumes. Because he's unable to specialize and trade with others, his standard of living while on the island is clearly meager.

EXHIBIT 5
Consumption Possibilities with Trade

The consumption possibilities of a country can be expanded with specialization and trade. If the United States can trade one unit of clothing for one unit of food, it can specialize in the production of food and consume along the ON line (rather than its original production possibilities constraint, MN). Similarly, when Japan is able to trade one unit of clothing for one unit of food, it can specialize in the production of clothing and consume any combination along the line RT. For example, with specialization and trade, the United States can increase its consumption from US₁ to US₂, gaining 50 million units of clothing and 100 million units of food. Simultaneously, Japan can increase consumption from J₁ to J₂, a gain of 125 million units of food and 25 million units of clothing.

(a) United States

(b) Japan

like US_2 (200 million units of food and 200 million units of clothing) along the line *ON*. Trade permits the United States to expand its consumption of both goods.

Simultaneously, Japan is able to expand its consumption of both goods when it is able to trade clothing for food at the one-to-one price ratio. As part (b) of Exhibit 5 illustrates, Japan can specialize in the production of clothing and consume along the constraint *RT* when it can trade one unit of clothing for one unit of food. Without trade, consumption in Japan would be limited to points like J_1 (75 million units of food and 225 million units of clothing) along the line *RS*. With trade, however, it is able to consume combinations like J_2 (200 million units of food and 250 million units of clothing) along the constraint *RT*.

Look what happens when Japan specializes in clothing and the United States specializes in food. Japan can produce 450 million units of clothing, export 200 million to the United States (for 200 million units of food), and still have 250 million units of clothing remaining for domestic consumption. Simultaneously, the United States can produce 400 million units of food, export 200 million to Japan (for 200 million units of clothing), and still have 200 million units of food left for domestic consumption. Again, after specialization and trade, the United States is able to consume at the point of US_2 and Japan at point J_2, consumption levels that would be unattainable without trade. Specialization and exchange permit the two countries to expand their joint output, and, as a result, both countries can increase their consumption of both commodities.

The implications of the law of comparative advantage are clear: trade between nations will lead to an expansion in total output and mutual gain for each trading partner when each country specializes in the production of goods it can produce at a relatively low cost and uses the proceeds to buy goods that it could produce only at a high cost. It is comparative advantage that matters. As long as there is some variation in the relative opportunity cost of goods across countries, each country will always have a comparative advantage in the production of some goods.

Some Real-World Considerations

To keep things simple, we ignored the potential importance of transportation costs, which, of course, reduce the potential gains from trade. Sometimes transportation and other transaction costs, both real and artificially imposed, exceed the potential for mutual gain. In this case, exchange does not occur.

We also assumed that the cost of producing each good was constant in each country. This is seldom the case. Beyond some level of production, the opportunity cost of producing a good will often increase as a country produces more and more of it. Rising marginal costs as the output of a good expands will limit the degree to which a country will specialize in the production of a good. This situation would be depicted by a production possibilities curve that was convex, or bowed out from the origin. In a case like this, there will still be gains from trade, but generally such a situation won't lead to one country completely specializing in the production of the good.

INTERNATIONAL TRADE

When people are permitted to engage freely in international trade, they are able to achieve higher income levels and living standards than would otherwise be possible.

Like trade within a country, trade between people living in different nations is mutually beneficial. As we just explained, the trading partners will be able to produce a larger joint output and consume a larger, more diverse bundle of goods when they each specialize in areas where they have a comparative advantage. Open markets also lead to gains from other sources. We will briefly discuss three of them.

1. MORE GAINS FROM LARGE-SCALE PRODUCTION. International trade makes it possible for both domestic producers and consumers to derive larger gains from the lower per-unit costs that often accompany large-scale production, marketing, and distribution activities. When economies of scale are important in an industry, successful domestic firms will be able to produce larger outputs and achieve lower unit costs than they would if they were unable to sell their products internationally. This is particularly important for firms located in small countries. For example, textile manufacturers in Malaysia, Taiwan, and South Korea would face much higher per-unit costs if they could not sell abroad because the domestic markets of these countries are too small to support large-scale production. There simply aren't enough buyers. However, if the firms can access the world market, where there are many more buyers, they can operate on a large scale and compete quite effectively.

Domestic consumers also benefit because international trade often makes it possible for them to acquire goods at lower prices from large-scale producers in other countries. The aircraft industry vividly illustrates this point. Given the huge design and engineering costs it takes to produce a single jet, no firm would be able to produce them economically if it weren't able to sell them abroad. Because of international trade, however, consumers around the world are able to purchase planes economically from large-scale producers like Boeing, which is based in the United States.

2. GAINS FROM MORE COMPETITIVE MARKETS. International trade promotes competition and encourages production efficiency and innovation. Competition from abroad keeps domestic producers on their toes and gives them a strong incentive to improve the quality of their products.

International trade also allows technologies and innovative ideas developed in one country to be disseminated to others. In many cases, local entrepreneurs will emulate production procedures and products that have been successful in other places and even further improve or adapt them for local markets. Dynamic competition of this type is an important source of growth and prosperity, particularly for less-developed countries.

3. MORE PRESSURE TO ADOPT SOUND INSTITUTIONS. Not only do firms in open economies face more intense competition, so, too, do their governments. The gains from trade and the prosperity that results from free trade motivate political officials to establish sound institutions and adopt constructive policies. If they do not, both labor and capital will move toward more favorable environments. For example, neither domestic nor foreign investors will want to put their funds in countries characterized by hostile business conditions, monetary instability, legal uncertainty, high taxes, and inferior public services. When labor and capital are free to move elsewhere, implementing government policies that penalize success and undermine productive activities becomes more costly. This aspect of free trade is generally overlooked, but it may well be one of its most beneficial attributes.[2]

Supply, Demand, and International Trade

Like other things, international trade can be analyzed within the supply and demand framework. An analysis of supply and demand in international markets can show us how trade influences prices and output in domestic markets.

EXHIBIT 6
Producer Benefits from Exports

The price of soybeans and other internationally traded commodities is determined by the forces of supply and demand in the world market (b). If U.S. soybean producers are prohibited from selling to foreigners, the domestic price will be P_n (a). Free trade permits the U.S. soybean producers to sell Q_p units at the higher world price (P_w). The quantity $Q_p - Q_c$ is the amount U.S. producers export. Compared with the no-trade situation, the producers' gain from the higher price ($P_w bcP_n$) exceeds the cost imposed on domestic consumers ($P_w acP_n$) by the triangle abc.

(a) U.S. market for soybeans

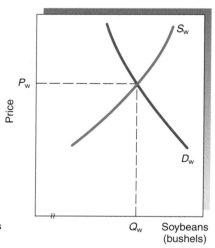

(b) World market for soybeans

---

[2]For evidence that trade openness helps improve the institutional quality of a country, see International Monetary Fund, "Building Institutions," *IMF World Economic Outlook* (September 2005).

Consider the market for a good that U.S. producers are able to supply at a low cost. Using soybeans as an example, **EXHIBIT 6** illustrates the relationship between the domestic and world markets. The price of soybeans is determined by the forces of supply and demand in the world market. In an open economy, domestic producers are free to sell and domestic consumers are free to buy the product at the world market price (P_w). At this price, U.S. producers will supply Q_p, and U.S. consumers will purchase Q_c. Reflecting their low cost (comparative advantage), U.S. soybean producers will export $Q_p - Q_c$ units at the world market price.

Let's compare this open-economy outcome with the outcome that would occur in the absence of trade. If U.S. producers were not allowed to export soybeans, the domestic price would be determined by the domestic supply (S_d) and demand (D_d) only. A lower "no-trade" price (P_n) would emerge.

Who are the winners and losers as the result of free trade in soybeans? Clearly, soybean producers gain. Free trade allows domestic producers to sell a larger quantity (Q_p rather than Q_n). As a result, the net revenues of soybean producers will rise by $P_w bc P_n$. In contrast, domestic consumers of soybeans will have to pay a higher price under free trade. Soybean consumers will lose (1) because they have to pay P_w rather than P_n for the Q_c units they purchase, and (2) because they lose the consumer surplus on the $Q_n - Q_c$ units now purchased at the higher price. Thus, free trade imposes a net cost of $P_w ac P_n$ on consumers. As you can see in Exhibit 6, however, the gains of soybean producers outweigh the losses to the consumers by the triangle *abc*. In other words, free trade leads to a net welfare gain.

This exporting example makes it seem like free trade benefits producers relative to consumers, but this ignores the secondary effects: If foreigners do not sell goods to Americans, they will not have the purchasing power necessary to purchase goods from Americans. U.S. imports—the purchase of goods from low-cost foreign producers—provide foreigners with the dollar purchasing power necessary to buy U.S. exports. In turn, the lower prices in the import-competitive markets will benefit the U.S. consumers who appeared at first glance to be harmed by the higher prices (compared with the no-trade situation) in export markets.

Using shoes as an example, **EXHIBIT 7** illustrates the situation when the United States is a net importer. In the absence of trade, the price of shoes in the domestic market would be P_n, the intersection of the domestic supply and demand curves. However, the world

---

EXHIBIT 7
Consumer Benefits from Imports

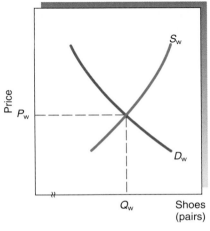

(a) U.S. market for shoes   (b) World market for shoes

In the absence of trade, the domestic price of shoes would be P_n. Because many foreign producers have a comparative advantage in the production of shoes, international trade leads to lower prices. At the world price P_w, U.S. consumers will demand Q_c units, of which $Q_c - Q_p$ are imported. Compared with the no-trade situation, consumers gain $P_n abP_w$, while domestic producers lose $P_n acP_w$. A net gain of abc results.

price of shoes is P_w. In an open economy, many U.S. consumers would take advantage of the low shoe prices available from foreign producers. At the lower world price, U.S. consumers would purchase Q_c units of shoes, importing $Q_c - Q_p$ from foreign producers.

Compared with the no-trade situation, free trade in shoes results in lower prices and greater domestic consumption. The lower prices lead to a net consumer gain of $P_n abP_w$. Domestic producers lose $P_n acP_w$ in the form of lower sales prices and reductions in output. However, the net gain of the shoe consumers exceeds the net loss of producers by abc.

International competition will direct resources toward their area of comparative advantage. If domestic producers have a comparative advantage in the production of a good, they will be able to compete effectively in the world market and profit from the export of goods to foreigners. In turn, the exports will generate the purchasing power necessary to buy goods that foreigners can supply more economically.

The Economics of Trade Restrictions

Despite the potential benefits of free trade, almost all nations have erected trade barriers. Tariffs, quotas, and exchange rate controls are the most commonly used trade-restricting devices. Let's consider how various types of trade restrictions affect the economy.

Economics of Tariffs

Tariff

A tax levied on goods imported into a country.

A **tariff** is nothing more than a tax on imports from foreign countries. As **EXHIBIT 8** shows, average tariff rates of between 30 percent and 50 percent of product value were often levied on products imported to the United States prior to 1945. The notorious Smoot-Hawley Tariff Act of 1930 pushed the average tariff rate upward to 60 percent. Many economists believe that this legislation contributed significantly to the length and severity of the Great Depression. During the past sixty years, however, tariff rates in the United States have declined substantially. In 2008, the average tariff rate on imported goods was only 4.0 percent.

EXHIBIT 9 shows the impact of a tariff on automobiles. In the absence of a tariff, the world market price of P_w would prevail in the domestic market. At that price, U.S. consumers purchase Q_1 units. Domestic producers supply Q_{d1}, while foreigners supply $Q_1 - Q_{d1}$ units to the U.S. market. When the United States levies a tariff, t, on automobiles,

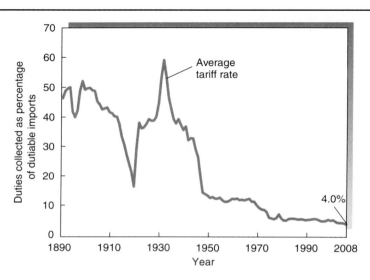

EXHIBIT 8
How High Are U.S. Tariffs?

Tariff rates in the United States spiked up sharply in the early 1930s, then declined during the period from 1935 to 1950. After rising slightly during the late 1950s, they have trended downward since 1960. In 2008, the average tariff rate on merchandise imports was 4.0 percent.

Source: http://dataweb.usitc.gov/scripts/AVE.PDF.

EXHIBIT 9
The Impact of a Tariff

Here, we illustrate the impact of a tariff on automobiles. In the absence of the tariff, the world price of automobiles is P_w. U.S. consumers purchase Q_1 units (Q_{d_1} from domestic producers plus $Q_1 - Q_{d_1}$ from foreign producers). The tariff makes it more costly for Americans to purchase automobiles from foreigners. Imports decline and the domestic price increases. Higher prices reduce consumer surplus by the areas $S + U + T + V$. Producers gain the area S, and the tariff generates T tax revenues for the government. The areas U and V are deadweight losses. Consumers lose the surplus associated with these two areas, but producers and the government don't gain it.

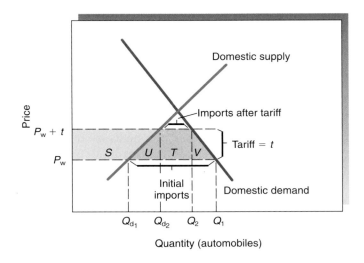

Americans can no longer buy cars at the world price. U.S. consumers now have to pay $P_w + t$ to purchase an automobile from foreigners. At that price, domestic consumers demand Q_2 units (Q_{d2} supplied by domestic producers and $Q_2 - Q_{d2}$ supplied by foreigners). The tariff results in a higher domestic price and lower level of domestic consumption.

The tariff benefits domestic producers and the government at the expense of consumers. Because domestic producers don't have to pay the tariff, they will expand their output in response to the higher (protected) market price. In effect, the tariff acts as a subsidy to domestic producers. Domestic producers gain the area S (Exhibit 9) in the form of additional net revenues. The tariff raises revenues equal to the area T for the government. The areas U and V represent costs imposed on consumers and resource suppliers that do not benefit the government. Simply put, U and V represent *deadweight losses*: consumer and producer surpluses that could have been gained if the tariff hadn't been imposed.

As a result of the tariff, resources that could have been used to produce other U.S. goods more efficiently (compared with producing them abroad) are diverted to automobile production. Ultimately, we end up producing fewer products in areas where we have a comparative advantage and more products in areas where we are a high-cost producer. Because of this, potential gains from specialization and trade will go unrealized. In addition, most nations, including the United States, impose higher tariffs on some goods than others. This encourages producers in specific industries to lobby for higher tariffs on goods they produce. This diverts resources away from production and toward plunder, which also reduces the overall size of the economic pie.

The Economics of Quotas

An **import quota**, like a tariff, is designed to restrict foreign goods and protect domestic industries. A quota places a ceiling on the amount of a product that can be imported during a given period (typically a year). The United States imposes quotas on several products,

Import quota

A specific limit or maximum quantity (or value) of a good permitted to be imported into a country during a given period.

including brooms, shoes, sugar, dairy products, and peanuts. For example, since 1953, the United States has imposed an annual peanut quota that in 2009 limited imports to 118.5 million pounds, about four-tenths of a pound per American. Like tariffs, the primary purpose of quotas is to protect domestic industries from foreign competition.

Using peanuts as an example, **EXHIBIT 10** illustrates the impact of a quota. If there were no trade restraints, the domestic price of peanuts would be equal to the world market price (P_w). Under those circumstances, Americans would purchase Q_1 units. At the price P_w, domestic producers would supply Q_{d1}, and the amount $Q_1 - Q_{d1}$ would be imported from foreign producers.

Now consider what happens when a quota limits imports to $Q_2 - Q_{d2}$, a quantity well below the free-trade level of imports. Because the quota reduces the foreign supply of peanuts to the domestic market, the price of the quota-protected product increases (to P_2). At the higher price, U.S. consumers will reduce their purchases to Q_2, and domestic producers will happily expand their production to Q_{d2}. With regard to the welfare of consumers, the impact of a quota is similar to that of a tariff. Consumers lose the area $S + U + T + V$ in the form of higher prices and the loss of consumer surplus. Similarly, domestic producers gain the area S, while the areas U and V represent deadweight losses in the form of reductions in consumer surplus, gains that buyers would have derived in the absence of the quota.

While the adverse impact of a quota on consumer welfare is similar to that of a tariff, there is a big difference with regard to the area T. Under a tariff, the U.S. government would collect revenues equal to T, representing the tariff rate multiplied by

EXHIBIT 10
The Impact of a Quota

Here, we illustrate the impact of a quota, such as the one the United States imposes on peanuts. The world market price of peanuts is P_w. If there were no trade restraints, the domestic price would also be P_w, and the domestic consumption would be Q_1. Domestic producers would supply Q_{d1} units, while $Q_1 - Q_{d1}$ would be imported. A quota limiting imports to $Q_2 - Q_{d2}$ would push up the domestic price to P_2. At the higher price, the amount supplied by domestic producers increases to Q_{d2}. Consumers lose the sum of the area $S + U + T + V$, while domestic producers gain the area S. In contrast with tariffs, quotas generate no revenue for the government. The area T goes to foreign producers, who are granted permission to sell in the U.S. market.

the number of units imported. With a quota, however, these revenues will go to foreign producers, who are granted licenses (quotas) to sell various amounts in the U.S. market. Clearly, this right to sell at a premium price (because the domestic price exceeds the world market price) is extremely valuable. Thus, foreign producers will compete for the permits. They will hire lobbyists, make political contributions, and engage in other rent-seeking activities in an effort to secure the right to sell at a premium price in the U.S. market.

In many ways, quotas are more harmful than tariffs. With a quota, foreign producers are prohibited from selling additional units regardless of how much lower their costs are relative to those of domestic producers. In contrast to a tariff, a quota brings in no revenue for the government. While a tariff transfers revenue from U.S. consumers to the Treasury, quotas transfer these revenues to foreign producers. Rewarding domestic producers with higher prices and foreign producers with valuable import permits will create *two* interest groups with a strong incentive to lobby for a quota. As a result, lifting the quota will often be more difficult than lowering a tariff would be.

In addition to tariffs and quotas, governments sometimes use regulations and political pressure to restrain foreign competition. For example, the United States prohibits foreign airlines from competing in the domestic air travel market. Japanese regulations make it illegal for domestic automobile dealers to sell both foreign and domestically produced vehicles; this makes it more difficult for foreign manufacturers to establish the dealer networks they need to penetrate the Japanese market effectively. Like tariffs and quotas, regulatory barriers such as these reduce the supply to domestic markets and the gains from potential trades. Overall output is reduced, and domestic producers benefit at the expense of domestic consumers.

Exchange Rate Controls as a Trade Restriction

Some countries fix the exchange rate value of their currency above the market rate and impose restrictions on exchange rate transactions.[3] At the official (artificially high) exchange rate, the country's export goods will be extremely expensive to foreigners. As a result, foreigners will purchase goods elsewhere, and the country's exports will be small. In turn, the low level of exports will make it extremely difficult for domestic residents to obtain the foreign currency they need to purchase imports. Exchange rate controls both reduce the volume of trade and lead to black-market currency exchanges. Indeed, a large black-market premium indicates that the country's exchange rate policy is substantially limiting the ability of its citizens to trade with foreigners. While exchange rate controls have declined in popularity, they are still an important trade barrier in countries such as Myanmar and Zimbabwe.

Why Do Nations Adopt Trade Restrictions?

As social philosopher Henry George noted over a century ago, trade restraints act like blockades. Why would political officials want to erect blockades against their own people? As we consider this question, we will take a look at three arguments often raised by the proponents of trade restrictions: the national-defense, infant-industry, and antidumping arguments. Finally, we will look at the politics of trade restrictions and analyze how the nature of the restraints influences their political popularity.

Protective tariffs are as much applications of force as are blockading squadrons, and their objective is the same—to prevent trade. The difference between the two is that blockading squadrons are a means whereby nations seek to prevent their enemies from trading; protective tariffs are a means whereby nations attempt to prevent their own people from trading.

—Henry George[4]

---

[3]The most common exchange rate restriction is that individuals are required to obtain approval from the government before they engage in transactions involving foreign currency.

[4]Henry George, *Protection or Free Trade* (Washington, DC: U.S. Government Printing Office, 1886), 37.

The National-Defense Argument

According to the national-defense argument, certain industries—aircraft, petroleum, and weapons, for example—are vital to a nation's defense. Therefore, these industries and their inputs should be protected from foreign competitors so that a domestic supply of necessary materials would be available in case of an international conflict. Would we want to be entirely dependent upon Arabian or Russian petroleum? Would complete dependence on French aircraft be wise? Many Americans would answer "no," even if it meant imposing trade restrictions that would lead to higher prices on products they buy.

Although the national-defense argument has some validity, it is often abused. Relatively few industries are truly vital to our national defense. If a resource is important for national defense, often it would make more sense to stockpile the resource during peacetime rather than follow protectionist policies to preserve a domestic industry. Furthermore, fostering an economy robust enough to produce the mass quantity of goods necessary to sustain a war effort in the first place is, itself, part of a strong defense.

The Infant-Industry Argument

Infant-industry advocates believe that new domestic industries should be protected from foreign competition for a period of time so that they will have a chance to develop. As the new industry matures, it will be able to stand on its own feet and compete effectively with foreign producers, at which time the protection can be removed.

The infant-industry argument has a long and often notorious history. Alexander Hamilton used it to argue for the protection of early U.S. manufacturing. The major problem with the argument is that the protection, once granted, will be difficult to remove. For example, a century ago, this argument was used to gain tariff protection for the newly emerging steel industry in the United States. Over time, the steel industry developed and became very powerful, both politically and economically. Despite its maturity, the tariffs remained. To this day, legislation continues to provide the steel industry with various protections that limit competition from abroad.

APPLICATIONS IN ECONOMICS

Do More Open Economies Perform Better?

Economic theory indicates that more open economies will perform better than those with sizable trade restrictions. Is this really true? In order to address this question, a measure of trade openness—the freedom of individuals to engage in voluntary exchange across national boundaries—is needed. Economist Charles Skipton developed a trade openness index (TOI) for eighty-one countries during the 1980–2002 period.[1] To achieve a high rating on the zero-to-ten TOI scale (with ten indicating more openness to free trade), a country had to maintain low tariff rates, a freely convertible currency (no exchange rate controls), and refrain from imposing quotas and other regulations reducing the size of its trade sector.

EXHIBIT 11 shows the countries with the ten highest and ten lowest trade openness ratings. The ratings reflect the *average* degree of openness for the entire 1980–2002 period. This is important because the gains from increased openness can only be realized over time. Expanding the openness of trade is a long-term growth strategy, not a short-term "quick fix." In other words' Hong Kong, Singapore, Bahrain, Belgium, and Malaysia head the list of the most open of the eighty-one economies. By way of comparison, the United States ranked sixteenth. At the other end of the spectrum, the TOI indicates that Bangladesh, Iran, Burundi, Sierra Leone, and Algeria were the least open economies during the period.

[1]Charles Skipton, "The Measurement of Trade Openness" (Ph.D. Diss., Florida State University, 2003).

APPLICATIONS IN ECONOMICS

EXHIBIT 11
Trade Openness, Income, and Growth

	TOI	2005 GDP per Capita (2000 Dollars)	Growth Rate, 1980–2005
Ten Most Open Economies			
Hong Kong	10.0	$30,989	3.9
Singapore	9.9	26,390	4.3
Bahrain	8.6	19,112	1.0
Belgium	8.6	28,575	1.7
Malaysia	8.6	9,681	3.6
Luxembourg	8.5	53,583	3.7
Netherlands	8.4	29,078	1.6
Taiwan	8.4	20,868	5.1
Ireland	8.1	34,256	4.5
Australia	7.9	29,981	1.9
Average	**8.7**	**$28,251**	**3.1**
Ten Least Open Economies			
India	4.3	$3,072	4.0
Tanzania	4.1	662	2.3
Egypt	4.1	3,858	2.5
Pakistan	3.9	2,109	2.4
Syria	3.8	3,388	0.6
Algeria	3.4	6,283	0.5
Sierra Leone	3.4	717	−1.1
Burundi	3.0	622	−1.0
Iran	2.9	7,089	1.1
Bangladesh	2.5	1,827	2.2
Average	**3.5**	**$2,963**	**1.4**

Source: The trade openness index data are from Charles Skipton, "The Measurement of Trade Openness" (Ph.D. diss., Florida State University, 2003), Table 4.6. The initial calculations were through 1999, but they were updated through 2002 by Skipton. The per capita GDP and growth rates are from the World Bank, *World Development Indicators*, CD-ROM, 2007. The per capita income figures were derived by the purchasing power parity method.

As Exhibit 11 shows, the 2005 average GDP per person of $28,251 of the ten most open economies was nearly ten times the comparable figure for the ten least open economies. Moreover, the more open economies also grew more rapidly. During 1980–2005, real GDP per person in the ten most open economies expanded at an annual rate of 3.1 percent, compared with 1.4 percent in the ten least open economies. Of course, the data of Exhibit 11 do not take into account other cross-country differences that theory indicates will influence growth. However, Skipton found that even after the differences in countries' inflation rates, legal structures, and similar factors were taken into account, trade openness continued to have a strong positive impact on both per capita GDP and growth rates.[2]

---

[2]For additional information on the relationship between international trade and economic growth, see Jeffrey A. Frankel and David Romer, "Does Trade Cause Growth?" *American Economic Review* (June 1999): 379–99; and Jeffrey D. Sachs and Andrew Warner, "Economic Reform and the Process of Global Integration," *Brookings Papers on Economic Activity,* no. 1 (1995): 1–95.

The Antidumping Argument

Dumping involves the sale of goods by a foreign firm at a price below cost or below the price charged in the firm's home-base market. Dumping is illegal and if a domestic industry is harmed, current law provides relief in the form of antidumping duties (tariffs imposed against violators). In addition, under the Byrd Amendment enacted in 2000, the revenues collected from the antidumping duties are transferred to the firms and unions lodging antidumping complaints, further increasing their incentive to levy such charges.[5]

Proponents of the antidumping argument argue that foreign producers will temporarily cut prices, drive domestic firms out of the market, and then use their monopoly position to gouge consumers. However, there is reason to question the effectiveness of this strategy. After all, the high prices would soon attract competitors, including other foreign suppliers.

Antidumping cases nearly always involve considerable ambiguity. The prices charged in the home market generally vary, and the production costs of the firms charged with dumping are not directly observable. This makes it difficult to tell whether a dumping violation has really occurred. Furthermore, aggressive price competition is an integral part of the competitive process. When demand is weak and inventories are large, firms will lower the prices of their products below their average total cost of production. Domestic firms are permitted to engage in this practice, and consumers benefit from it. Why shouldn't foreign firms be allowed to do the same?

One thing is for sure: Antidumping legislation gives politicians another way to channel highly visible benefits to powerful business and labor interests—another open invitation for rent seeking. The dumping charges are adjudicated by political officials in the International Trade Commission and the Department of Commerce. Consequently, it's naive to believe that political considerations won't be an important element underlying the charges that are levied and how they are resolved. Unsurprisingly, the number of claimants bringing charges of dumping has increased substantially over the past few decades.

Protectionism is a politician's delight because it delivers visible benefits to the protected parties while imposing the costs as a hidden tax on the public.

—Murray L. Weidenbaum[6]

Special Interests and the Politics of Trade Restrictions

Regardless of the arguments made by the proponents of trade restrictions, in truth, the restrictions are primarily special-interest related. (See the quotation from Weidenbaum.) ***Trade restrictions typically provide highly visible, concentrated benefits for a small group of people, while imposing on the general citizenry costs that are widely dispersed and difficult to identify.*** As we discussed in Chapter 6, the political process handles such issues poorly. It often leads to their adoption, even when they lower income levels and living standards.

The politics of trade restrictions are straightforward and play out over and over again. Well-organized business and labor interests gain substantially from restrictions that limit competition from abroad. Because their personal gain is large, they will feel strongly about the issue and generally vote for or against candidates on the basis of their positions on trade restrictions. Most important, the special-interest groups will be an attractive source of political contributions. When it comes to consumers, however, even if the total cost of the restrictions is quite large, it will be spread thinly among them; most consumers will be unaware that they are paying slightly higher prices for various goods because of the restrictions.

As you can see, courting special-interest groups helps politicians solicit campaign contributions and generate votes on the one hand. On the other hand, little political gain

---

[5]In effect, the Byrd Amendment provides subsidies to firms and unions willing to lend their support to antidumping charges and places them at a competitive advantage relative to those who fail to support the petitions. Thus, it encourages the filing of antidumping charges. In August 2004, the World Trade Organization ruled that the Byrd Amendment was a violation of international trade rules and authorized Japan, Europe, Korea, and several other countries to levy specific levels of retaliation duties against U.S. products.

[6]Murray L. Weidenbaum, personal correspondence with the authors. Weidenbaum is a former chairman of the President's Council of Economic Advisers and former director of the Center for the Study of American Business of Washington University.

can be derived from poorly organized and largely uninformed consumers. Given this incentive structure, the adoption of trade restrictions is not surprising.

The U.S. tariff code itself is a reflection of the politics of trade restrictions. It is both lengthy (the schedule fills 3,091 pages) and highly complex. This makes it difficult for even a well-educated citizen to figure out how it works. High tariffs are imposed on some products (for example, apparel, tobacco, and footwear), whereas low tariffs are imposed on others. Highly restrictive quotas limit the import of a few commodities, most notably agricultural products. Even though this complex system of targeted trade restrictions is costly to administer, it is no accident. It reflects the rent seeking of special-interest groups and the political contributions and other side payments the system generates for politicians.

Trade Barriers and Popular Trade Fallacies

Fallacies abound in the area of international trade. Why? Failure to consider the secondary effects of international trade is part of the answer. Key elements of international trade are closely linked; you cannot change one element without changing the other. For example, you cannot reduce imports without simultaneously reducing the demand for exports. The political incentive structure is also a contributing factor. As business, labor, and political leaders seek to gain from trade restrictions, they will often use half-truths and wrong-headed ideas to achieve their political objectives. Two of the most popular trade fallacies involve the effects of imports on employment and the impact of trade with low-wage countries. Let's take a closer look at both.

TRADE FALLACY 1: TRADE RESTRICTIONS THAT LIMIT IMPORTS SAVE JOBS AND EXPAND EMPLOYMENT. Like most fallacies, this one has just enough truth to give it some credibility. When tariffs, quotas, and other trade barriers limit imports, they are likely to foster employment in the industries shielded from competition. But this is only half of the story: Simultaneously, jobs in other domestic sectors will be destroyed. Here's how: When trade barriers reduce the amount of goods Americans buy from foreigners, sales to foreigners will also fall. This is because our imports provide foreigners with the dollars they need to buy our exports. Because foreigners cut back on the items they would normally buy from us, other U.S. sectors will suffer job losses because they're selling less.

Furthermore, when trade restrictions are imposed on a resource domestic producers use as an input, they will have to pay a higher price for it than their foreign rivals. This will increase their costs and make it more difficult for them to compete internationally. As a result, they will have to lay off some of their employees. The import quotas imposed on steel during 2002–2003 vividly illustrate this point. The quotas helped the domestic steel industry, but they virtually wiped out the domestic industry producing steel barrels, a product the United States had exported prior to the quota being imposed. The quota also increased costs and reduced the competitiveness of industries that were major users of steel, like the automobile- and appliance-manufacturing industries. Employment in those industries fell as well. The same phenomenon occurred after the United States imposed sugar quotas. The import quotas pushed domestic sugar prices to two or three times the world price. As a result, several large candy makers relocated abroad so that they could buy sugar at the lower world price. Again, the jobs lost in U.S. industries using sugar were offset by any increase in employment by U.S. sugar producers.

On balance, there is no reason to expect that trade restrictions will either create or destroy jobs. Instead, they will reshuffle them. The restrictions artificially direct workers and other resources toward the production of things that we do poorly, as shown by our inability to compete effectively in the world market. Simultaneously, employment will decline in areas where American firms would be able to compete successfully in the world market if it were not for the side effects of the restrictions. In other words, more Americans will be employed producing things we do poorly and fewer will be employed producing things we do well. As a result, our overall income level will be lower than it would have been otherwise.

Unfortunately, the jobs "saved" by the import quotas are more visible than those destroyed in other sectors. This increases the political popularity of trade restraints and perpetuates the fallacy that the restraints increase employment. But it does not change the reality of the situation. As Exhibit 1 shows, imports increased from 6 percent of GDP in 1980 to 18 percent in 2008. If the growth of imports destroys jobs, as the proponents of trade restrictions argue, the rapid import growth should have adversely affected U.S. employment. But this was not the case. On the contrary, civilian employment in the United States rose from 99 million in 1980 to 119 million in 1990 and 145 million in 2008. Far from retarding employment, the unprecedented growth of imports during the last two decades was associated with unprecedented employment growth.

TRADE FALLACY 2: FREE TRADE WITH LOW-WAGE COUNTRIES LIKE MEXICO AND CHINA WILL REDUCE THE WAGES OF AMERICANS. Many Americans believe that without trade restrictions, their wages will fall to the wage levels of workers in poor countries. How can Americans compete with workers in countries like Mexico and China who are willing to work for $1 or less per hour? This fallacy stems from a misunderstanding of both the source of high wages and the law of comparative advantage. Workers in the United States generally are well educated, possess high skill levels, and work with large amounts of capital equipment. These factors contribute to their high productivity, which is the source of their high wages. Similarly, in countries like Mexico and China, wages are low precisely because productivity is low. Workers are generally less skilled in these countries, and there is less capital equipment to make them more productive.

The key thing to remember, though, is that gains from trade emanate from comparative advantage, not absolute advantage (see Exhibits 3, 4, and 5). The United States cannot produce *everything* more cheaply than Mexico or China merely because U.S. employees are more productive and work with more capital. Neither can Mexico and China produce *everything* more cheaply merely because their wage rates are low compared with the United Sates.

As long as there are differences between countries when it comes to their comparative advantages, gains from trade will be possible, no matter what the wages of the employees in the two countries are. Trade reflects relative advantage, not wage levels. We can illustrate this point using trade between individuals. No one argues that trade between doctors and lawn service workers, for example, will cause the wages of doctors to fall. Because of their different skills and costs of providing alternative goods, both high-wage doctors and low-wage lawn care workers can gain from trade. The same is also true for trade between rich and poor nations.

If foreigners (including low-wage foreigners) have a comparative advantage and can sell us a product for less than we ourselves can produce it, we can gain by buying it. This will give us more resources to invest in and produce other things. Perhaps an extreme example will illustrate this point. Suppose a foreign producer is willing to supply us automobiles free of charge (perhaps because its employees were willing to work for nothing). Would it make sense to impose tariffs or quotas to keep the automobiles from coming into the country? Of course not. Resources that were previously used to produce automobiles would then be freed up to produce other goods, and the real income and availability of goods would expand. It makes no more sense to erect trade barriers to keep out cheap foreign goods than it would to keep out the free autos.

The Changing Nature of Global Trade

Since World War II, there has been a gradual reduction in tariff rates and other trade barriers. Liberalized trade policies and lower transportation and communication costs have propelled the growth of international trade. The growth of trade—some might say the globalization of the economy—has also resulted in a changing institutional environment. This section will focus on the institutions of international trade and the prospects for future trade liberalization.

GATT and the WTO

Following World War II, the major industrial nations of the world established the **General Agreement on Tariffs and Trade (GATT)**. For almost five decades, GATT played a central role in reducing tariffs and relaxing quotas. The average tariff rates of GATT members fell from approximately 40 percent in 1947 to about 3.0 percent in 2009, for example.

Following 1993, GATT was given a new name: the **World Trade Organization (WTO)**. This organization of 153 countries is now responsible for monitoring and enforcing the trade agreements developed through GATT. The WTO gives member nations a forum for development of trade rules and the settlement of disputes among members.

NAFTA and Other Regional Trade Agreements

Canada has been a major trading partner of the United States for many decades. In contrast, U.S. trade with Mexico was small prior to the 1990s. Historically, Mexico has been a relatively closed economy. This began to change in the mid-1980s, when Mexico began cutting its tariff rates and unilaterally removing other trade barriers. In 1988, the United States and Canada negotiated a trade agreement designed to reduce barriers limiting both trade and the flow of capital between the two countries. A few years later, the United States, Canada, and Mexico finalized the **North American Free Trade Agreement (NAFTA)**, which took effect in 1994. As the result of NAFTA, the tariffs of most goods moving among the three countries have now been eliminated. In addition to its participation in NAFTA, Mexico has also adopted a free-trade agreement with the European Union. During the last two decades, Mexico has moved from one of the world's more protectionist countries to one of its more open economies.

As **EXHIBIT 12** shows, U.S. trade with both Mexico and Canada has grown rapidly in recent years. Measured as a share of GDP, trade with Mexico jumped from 1.4 percent in 1990 to 3.1 percent in 2008. During the same period, trade with Canada rose from 3.8 percent of GDP to 5.2 percent. This growth of trade, particularly with Mexico, has not been without controversy. Business and labor groups often blame employment contractions and plant closings on competition with Mexican firms. The news media generally give such stories ample exposure. However, there is no evidence that increased trade with Mexico has adversely affected the U.S. economy. The growth rate of the United States was strong and the unemployment rate relatively low during the period following the passage of NAFTA. Clearly, the dire predictions about the "jobs going to Mexico" were not realized.

The Future of Free Trade

For several decades following World War II, the United States and most other high-income countries were leaders among those pursuing and promoting more liberal trade policies. In contrast, India, China, and most of the less-developed economies of Africa and Latin America imposed sizable trade restraints, and they were reluctant to relax them.

Since 1980, the situation has changed dramatically. Observing the success of open economies like Hong Kong and Singapore, many less-developed countries unilaterally reduced many of their trade restrictions during the last two decades. On average, the tariff rates of less-developed countries are now less than half their levels in the early 1980s. Exchange rate controls are becoming increasingly rare, and capital market controls are much less restrictive than they were a decade ago. Today, many leaders in less-developed

General Agreement on Tariffs and Trade (GATT)

An organization formed after World War II to set the rules for the conduct of international trade and reduce trade barriers among nations.

World Trade Organization (WTO)

The new name given to GATT in 1994; the WTO is currently responsible for monitoring and enforcing multilateral trade agreements among its 153 member countries.

North American Free Trade Agreement (NAFTA)

A comprehensive trade agreement between the United States, Mexico, and Canada that went into effect in 1994.

EXHIBIT 12
U.S. Trade with Canada and Mexico, 1980–2008

Measured as a share of GDP, U.S. trade with both Canada and Mexico has increased sharply as a result of NAFTA during the last fifteen years.

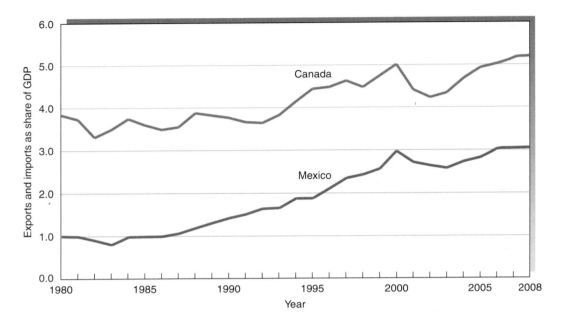

Source: *Statistical Abstract of the United States* (various years) and http://www.bea.gov.

countries recognize that free trade is the surest route to higher income levels and improved living standards. These countries are often the fiercest advocates of trade liberalization.

By contrast, the United States, Japan, and European Union nations have agricultural price support programs contrary to free trade. It will take considerable effort to reduce, let alone remove, the price supports and subsidies to agriculture interests. To date, these countries have been unwilling to do so, and their resistance has become a major stumbling block on the road to trade liberalization. Furthermore, protectionist proponents—particularly those in high-income countries like the United States—have successfully lobbied to impose labor and environmental regulations that block trade liberalization. Meanwhile, the Internet and other technological changes continue to reduce transport and communications costs and thereby encourage the movement of goods, ideas, and people across national boundaries. All of this promises to enliven trade issues in the years ahead.

Looking ahead

There are many similarities between domestic trade and trade across national boundaries, but there is also a major difference: International trade generally involves exchanging foreign currencies. For students studying macroeconomics, we will now turn to this issue.

KEY POINTS

▼ The volume of international trade has grown rapidly in recent decades. In the United States, international trade (imports plus exports) summed to 31 percent of GDP in 2008, compared with 12 percent in 1980 and 6 percent in 1960.

▼ Comparative advantage rather than absolute advantage is the source of gains from trade. As long as relative production costs of goods differ, trading partners will be able to gain from trade. Specialization and trade make it possible for trading partners to produce a larger joint output and expand their consumption possibilities.

▼ International specialization and trade result in lower prices for imported products and higher domestic prices for exported products. However, the net effect is an expansion in the aggregate output and consumption possibilities of trading nations.

▼ Import restrictions, such as tariffs and quotas, reduce the supply of foreign goods to domestic markets. This causes the domestic price to rise. Essentially, the restrictions are a subsidy to producers (and workers) in protected industries at the expense of (1) consumers and (2) producers (and workers) in export industries. Jobs protected by import restrictions are offset by jobs destroyed in export-related industries.

▼ Trade restrictions generally provide concentrated benefits to the producers in industries they're designed to protect. The costs are spread thinly among consumers in the form of higher prices. Even though the impact of trade restrictions on the economy as a whole is harmful, they generate benefits for interest groups that politicians can then tap for campaign contributions and other side payments.

▼ Persistently open economies have grown more rapidly and achieved higher per capita income levels than economies more closed to international trade.

CRITICAL ANALYSIS QUESTIONS

1. Why do American households and businesses buy things from foreigners? What are the characteristics of the items we buy from foreigners? What are the characteristics of the things we sell to foreigners?

*2. "Trade restrictions limiting the sale of cheap foreign goods in the United States are necessary to protect the prosperity of Americans." Evaluate this statement made by an American politician.

3. Suppose as the result of the Civil War that the United States had been divided into two countries and that, through the years, high trade barriers had grown up between the two. How might the standard of living in the "divided" United States have been affected? Explain.

*4. Can both of the following statements be true? Why or why not?
   a. "Tariffs and import quotas promote economic inefficiency and reduce the real income of a nation. Economic analysis suggests that nations can gain by eliminating trade restrictions."
   b. "Economic analysis suggests that there is good reason to expect that trade restrictions will exist in the real world."

5. "The average American is hurt by imports and helped by exports." Do you agree or disagree with this statement?

*6. "An increased scarcity of a product benefits producers and harms consumers. In effect, tariffs and other trade restrictions increase the domestic scarcity of products by reducing the supply from abroad. Such policies benefit domestic producers of the restricted product at the expense of domestic consumers." Evaluate this statement.

7. Suppose that a very high tariff was placed on steel imported into the United States. How would that affect employment in the U.S. auto industry? (*Hint:* Think about how higher steel prices will impact the cost of producing automobiles.)

*8. "Getting more Americans to realize that it pays to make things in the United States is the heart of the competitiveness issue." (This is a quote from an American business magazine.)
   a. Would Americans be better off if more of them paid higher prices in order to "buy American" rather than purchase from foreigners? Would U.S. employment be higher? Explain.

b. Would Californians be better off if they bought goods produced only in California? Would the employment in California be higher? Explain.

9. How do tariffs and quotas differ? Can you think of any reason why foreign producers might prefer a quota rather than a tariff? Explain your answer.

*10. It is often alleged that Japanese producers receive subsidies from their government permitting them to sell their products at a low price in the U.S. market. Do you think we should erect trade barriers to keep out cheap Japanese goods if the source of their low price is a government subsidy? Why or why not?

11. In recent years, the European Union has virtually eliminated trade restrictions among its members, and most members now use a common currency. What impact have these changes had on European economies?

*12. Does international trade cost Americans jobs? Does interstate trade cost your state jobs? What is the major effect of international and interstate trade?

13. "The United States is suffering from an excess of imports. Cheap foreign products are driving American firms out of business and leaving the U.S. economy in shambles." Evaluate this view.

*14. The United States uses an import quota to maintain the domestic price of sugar well above the world price. Analyze the impact of the quota. Use supply and demand analysis to illustrate your answer. To whom do the gains and losses of this policy accrue? How does the quota affect the efficiency of resource allocation in the United States? Why do you think Congress is supportive of this policy?

15. As U.S. trade with low-wage countries like Mexico increases, will wages in the United States be pushed down? Why or why not? Are low-wage workers in the United States hurt when there is more trade with Mexico? Discuss.

*16. "Tariffs not only reduce the volume of imports, they also reduce the volume of exports." Is this statement true or false? Explain your answer.

17. "Physical obstacles like bad roads and stormy weather increase transaction costs and thereby reduce the volume of trade. Tariffs, quotas, exchange rate controls, and other human-made trade restrictions have similar effects." Evaluate this statement. Is it true? Why or why not?

*Asterisk denotes questions for which answers are given in Appendix B.

International Finance and the Foreign Exchange Market

CHAPTER FOCUS

- What determines the exchange rate value of the dollar relative to other currencies? Why do exchange rates change?

- What are the alternative types of exchange rate systems? Which types work well and which will lead to financial problems?

- What information is included in the balance-of-payments accounts of a nation? Will the balance-of-payments accounts of a country always be in balance?

- Will a healthy economy run a balance-of-trade surplus? Does a balance-of-trade deficit indicate that a nation is in financial trouble?

Currencies, like tomatoes and football tickets, have a price at which they are bought and sold. An exchange rate is the price of one currency in terms of another.

—*Gary Smith*[1]

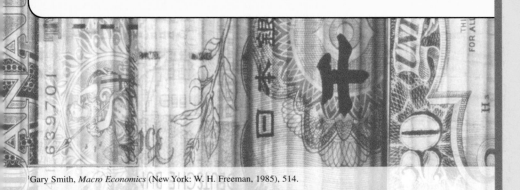

[1]Gary Smith, *Macro Economics* (New York: W. H. Freeman, 1985), 514.

T rade across national boundaries is complicated by the fact that nations generally use different currencies to buy and sell goods in their respective domestic markets. The British use pounds; the Japanese, yen; the Mexicans, pesos; sixteen European countries, the euro; and so on. Therefore, when a good or service is purchased from a seller in another country, it is generally necessary for someone to convert one currency to another.

As we previously discussed, the forces of supply and demand will determine the exchange rate value of currencies in the absence of government intervention. This chapter will focus more directly on the foreign exchange market. We will consider how exchange rates both exert an impact on and are influenced by the flow of trade and the flow of capital across national boundaries. We will also analyze alternative exchange rate regimes and consider some of the recent changes in the structure of currency markets around the world. ■

Foreign Exchange Market

Foreign exchange market

The market in which the currencies of different countries are bought and sold.

When trading parties live in different countries, an exchange will often involve a currency transaction. Currency transactions take place in the **foreign exchange market**, the market where currencies of different countries are bought and sold. Suppose that you own a sporting goods shop in the United States and are preparing to place an order for athletic shoes. You can purchase them from either a domestic or foreign manufacturer. If you decide to purchase the shoes from a British firm, either you will have to change dollars into pounds at a bank and send them to the British producer or the British manufacturer will have to go to a bank and change your dollar check into pounds. In either case, purchasing the British shoes will involve an exchange of dollars for pounds.

Suppose the British producer has offered to supply the shoes for 30 pounds per pair. How can you determine whether this price is high or low? To compare the price of the British-supplied shoes with the price of those produced domestically, you must know the **exchange rate** between the dollar and the pound. *The exchange rate is one of the most important prices because it enables consumers in one country to translate the prices of foreign goods into units of their own currency. Specifically, the dollar price of a foreign good is determined by multiplying the foreign product price by the exchange rate (the dollar price per unit of the foreign currency).* For example, if it takes $1.80 to obtain 1 pound, then the British shoes priced at 30 pounds would cost $54 (thirty times the $1.80 price of the pound).

Exchange rate

The domestic price of one unit of foreign currency. For example, if it takes $1.80 to purchase one English pound, the dollar–pound exchange rate is 1.80.

Suppose the exchange rate is $1.80 = 1 pound and that you decide to buy 200 pairs of athletic shoes from the British manufacturer at 30 pounds ($54) per pair. You will need 6,000 pounds in order to pay the British manufacturer. If you contact an American bank that handles foreign exchange transactions and write the bank a check for $10,800 (the $1.80 exchange rate multiplied by 6,000), it will supply the 6,000 pounds. The bank will typically charge a small fee for handling the transaction.

Where does the American bank get the pounds? The bank obtains the pounds from British importers who want dollars to buy things from Americans. Note that the U.S. demand for foreign currencies (such as the pound) is generated by the demand of Americans for things purchased from foreigners. In contrast, the supply of foreign currencies in exchange for dollars reflects the demand of foreigners for things bought from Americans.

EXHIBIT 1 presents data on the exchange rate—the cents required to purchase a European euro, Japanese yen, British pound, and Canadian dollar—from 1990 to 2009.

EXHIBIT 1
Foreign Exchange Rates, 1990–2009

U.S. CENTS PER UNIT OF FOREIGN CURRENCY

YEAR	EURO	JAPANESE YEN	BRITISH POUND	CANADIAN DOLLAR	INDEX OF EXCHANGE RATE VALUE OF THE DOLLAR[a]
1990	—	0.691	178.49	85.7	71.4
1992	—	0.789	176.42	82.7	76.9
1994	—	0.979	153.21	73.2	90.9
1996	—	0.919	156.16	73.3	97.5
1998	—	0.764	165.71	67.4	115.9
2000	92.3	0.927	151.59	67.3	119.4
2001	89.6	0.823	144.01	64.6	125.9
2002	94.5	0.798	150.24	63.7	126.7
2003	113.2	0.863	163.48	71.4	119.1
2004	124.4	0.925	183.26	76.8	113.6
2005	124.4	0.908	181.98	89.2	110.7
2006	125.6	0.859	184.29	88.2	108.5
2007	137.1	0.849	200.17	93.1	103.4
2008	147.0	0.967	185.22	93.7	99.8
2009	141.9	0.964	165.24	86.2	105.3

[a]Note: 2009 figures are as of July 1, 2009.

Source: http://www.economagic.com

Under the flexible rate system present in most industrial countries, the exchange rate between currencies changes from day to day and even from hour to hour. The exchange rate figures for years prior to 2009 are the average for the year. The 2009 figures are for exchange rates as of July 1, 2009.

An **appreciation** in the value of a nation's currency means that fewer units of the currency are now required to purchase one unit of a foreign currency. For example, as Exhibit 1 shows, it took 165.24 cents to purchase a British pound in 2009, down from 185.22 cents in 2008. Thus, the dollar appreciated against the pound during this period. As the result of this appreciation, goods purchased from British suppliers became less expensive to Americans.[2] At the same time, the prices of American goods to British consumers moved in the opposite direction. An appreciation of the U.S. dollar relative to the British pound is the same thing as a depreciation in the British pound relative to the dollar.

When a **depreciation** occurs, it will take more units of the domestic currency to purchase a unit of foreign currency. During the 2002–2008 period, the dollar depreciated against all of the major currencies (see Exhibit 1). In 2008, it took 185.22 cents to purchase a British pound, up from 144.01 in 2001. Similarly, it took 147.0 cents to purchase a euro in 2008, up from only 89.6 in 2001. The number of cents required to purchase a Canadian dollar and Japanese yen also increased during this time frame. As the number of cents required to purchase a unit of foreign currency increases, the dollar depreciates, and foreign goods become more expensive for Americans.

Exhibit 1 also provides an index of the foreign exchange value of the dollar against twenty-six major currencies. This broad index provides evidence on what is happening to the dollar's general exchange rate value.[3] An increase in the index implies an appreciation

Appreciation

An increase in the value of the domestic currency relative to foreign currencies. An appreciation makes foreign goods cheaper for domestic residents.

Depreciation

A reduction in the value of the domestic currency relative to foreign currencies. A depreciation makes foreign goods more expensive for domestic residents.

---

[2]Because an appreciation means a lower price of foreign currencies, some may think it looks like a depreciation. Just remember that a lower price of the foreign currency means that one's domestic currency will buy more units of the foreign currency and thus more goods and services from foreigners.

[3]In the construction of this index, the exchange rate of each currency relative to the dollar is weighted according to the proportion of U.S. trade with the country. For example, the index weights the U.S. dollar–Japanese yen exchange rate more heavily than the U.S. dollar–Swiss franc exchange rate because the volume of U.S. trade with Japan exceeds the volume of trade with Switzerland.

in the dollar, whereas a decline is indicative of a depreciation. Between 1996 and 2002, the dollar appreciated by approximately 30 percent against these twenty-six currencies. Between 2002 and 2008, however, the index indicates that the dollar depreciated by approximately 21 percent (down to 99.8 from 126.7) relative to this broad bundle of currencies. The dollar appreciated again during the first half of 2009. Frequently, people will use the terms "strong" and "weak" when referring to the exchange rate value of a currency. A currency is said to be strong when it has been appreciating in value, whereas a weak currency is one that has been depreciating on the foreign exchange market.

Flexible exchange rates

Exchange rates that are determined by the market forces of supply and demand. They are sometimes called floating exchange rates.

A pure **flexible exchange rate** system is one in which market forces alone determine the foreign exchange value of the currency. The exchange rate system in effect since 1973 might best be described as a managed flexible rate regime. It is flexible because all the major industrial countries allow the exchange rate value of their currencies to float. But the system is also "managed" because the major industrial nations have from time to time attempted to alter supply and demand in the foreign exchange market by buying and selling various currencies. Compared with the total size of this market, however, these transactions have generally been small. Thus, the exchange rate value of major currencies like the U.S. dollar, British pound, Japanese yen, and the European euro is determined primarily by market forces. Several countries link their currency to major currencies like the U.S. dollar or European euro. As we proceed, we will investigate alternative methods of linking currencies and analyze the operation of different regimes.

Determinants of the Exchange Rate

To simplify our explanation of how the exchange rate is determined, let's assume that the United States and Great Britain are the only two countries in the world. When Americans buy and sell with each other, they use dollars. Therefore, American sellers will want to be paid in dollars. Similarly, when the British buy and sell with each other, they use pounds. As a result, British sellers will want to be paid in pounds.

In our two-country world, the demand for pounds in the exchange rate market originates from the purchases by Americans of British goods, services, and assets (both real and financial). For example, when U.S. residents purchase men's suits from a British manufacturer; travel in the United Kingdom; or purchase the stocks, bonds, or physical assets of British business firms, they demand pounds from (and supply dollars to) the foreign exchange market to pay for these items.

Correspondingly, the supply of foreign exchange (pounds in our two-country case) originates from sales by Americans to foreigners. When Americans sell goods, services, or assets to the British, for example, the British buyers will supply pounds (and demand dollars) in the exchange rate market in order to acquire the dollars to pay for the items purchased from Americans.[4]

EXHIBIT 2 illustrates the supply and demand curves of Americans for foreign exchange—British pounds in our two-country case. The demand for pounds is downward sloping because a lower dollar price of the pound—meaning a dollar will buy more pounds—makes British goods cheaper for American importers. The goods produced by one country are generally good substitutes for the goods of another country. This means that when foreign (British) goods become cheaper, Americans will increase their expenditures on imports (and therefore the quantity of pounds demanded will increase). Thus, as the dollar price of the pound declines, Americans will both buy more of the lower-priced (in dollars) British goods and demand more pounds, which are required for the purchases.

Similarly, the supply curve for pounds is dependent upon the sales by Americans to the British (i.e., the purchase of American goods by the British). An increase in the dollar

---

[4]We analyze the foreign exchange market in terms of the demand for and supply of foreign currencies. Alternatively, this analysis could be done in terms of the supply of and demand for dollars. Because one currency is traded for another, the same actions that generate a demand for foreign exchange simultaneously generate a supply of dollars. Correspondingly, the same exchanges that create a supply of foreign currencies simultaneously generate a demand for dollars in the foreign exchange market.

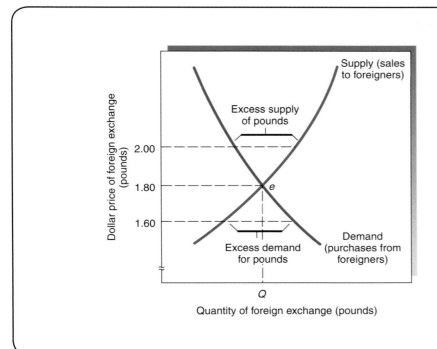

The dollar price of the pound is measured on the vertical axis. The horizontal axis indicates the flow of pounds to the foreign exchange market. The equilibrium exchange rate is $1.80 = 1 pound. At the equilibrium price, the quantity of pounds demanded just equals the quantity supplied. On the one hand, a higher dollar price per pound ($2.00 = 1 pound) will lead to an excess supply of pounds, causing the dollar price of the pound to fall. On the other hand, a lower dollar price per pound ($1.60 = 1 pound) will result in an excess demand for pounds, causing the pound to appreciate.

price of the pound means that a pound will purchase more dollars and more goods priced in dollars. Thus, the price (in pounds) of American goods, services, and assets to British purchasers declines as the dollar price of the pound increases. As this happens, the British will purchase more from Americans and therefore supply more pounds to the foreign exchange market. Thus, the supply curve for pounds will slope upward to the right.

As Exhibit 2 shows, equilibrium is present at the dollar price of the pound that brings the quantity demanded and quantity supplied of pounds into balance, $1.80 in this case. *The market-clearing price of $1.80 per pound not only equalizes demand and supply in the foreign exchange market but also equalizes (1) the value of U.S. purchases of items supplied by the British with (2) the value of items sold by U.S. residents to the British.* Demand and supply in the currency market are simply the mirror images of these two factors.

What would happen if the price of the pound were above equilibrium—$2.00 = 1 pound, for example? At the higher dollar price of the pound, British goods would be more expensive for Americans. Americans would cut back on their purchases of shoes, glassware, textile products, financial assets, and other items supplied by the British, and the quantity of pounds demanded by Americans would therefore decline. Simultaneously, the higher dollar price of the pound would make U.S. exports cheaper for the British. For example, an $18,000 American automobile would cost British consumers 10,000 pounds when 1 pound trades for $1.80, but it would cost only 9,000 pounds when 1 pound exchanges for $2.00. If the dollar price of the pound were $2.00, the British would supply more pounds to the foreign exchange market than Americans would demand. As you can see in Exhibit 2, this excess supply of pounds would cause the dollar price of the pound to decline until equilibrium is restored at the $1.80 = 1 pound price.

At a below-equilibrium price, such as $1.60 = 1 pound, an opposite set of forces would be present. The lower dollar price of the pound would make British goods cheaper for Americans and American goods more expensive for the British. At the $1.60 price for a pound, the purchases of Americans from the British would exceed their sales to them, leading to an excess demand for pounds. In turn, the excess demand would cause the dollar price of the pound to rise until equilibrium was restored at $1.80 = 1 pound.

The implications of the analysis are general. In our multicountry and multicurrency world, the demand for foreign currencies in exchange for dollars reflects the purchases by

Americans of goods, services, and assets from foreigners. The supply of foreign currencies in exchange for dollars reflects the sales by Americans of goods, services, and assets to foreigners. The equilibrium exchange rate will bring the quantity of foreign exchange demanded by Americans into balance with the quantity supplied by foreigners. It will also bring the purchases by Americans from foreigners into balance with the sales by Americans to foreigners.

Why Do Exchange Rates Change?

When exchange rates are free to fluctuate, the market value of a nation's currency will appreciate and depreciate in response to changing market conditions. Any change that alters the quantity of goods, services, or assets bought from foreigners relative to the quantity sold to them will alter the exchange rate. Let's consider the major factors that will alter the foreign exchange value of a nation's currency.

Changes in Income

An increase in domestic income will encourage the nation's residents to spend a portion of their additional income on imports. When the income of a nation grows rapidly, the nation's imports tend to rise rapidly as well. As **EXHIBIT 3** illustrates, an increase in imports also increases the demand for foreign exchange (the pound in our two-country case). As the demand for pounds increases, the dollar price of the pound rises (from $1.80 to $2.00). This depreciation of the dollar reduces the incentive of Americans to import British goods and services, while increasing the incentive of the British to purchase U.S. exports. These two forces will restore equilibrium in the foreign exchange market at a new, higher dollar price of the pound.

Just the opposite takes place when the income of a trading partner (Great Britain in our example) increases. Rapid growth of income abroad will lead to an increase in U.S. exports, causing the supply of foreign exchange (and demand for dollars) to increase. This will cause the dollar to appreciate—the dollar price of the pound will fall, in other words.

What will happen if both countries are growing? Other things constant, it is the relative growth rate that matters. A country that grows more rapidly than its trading partners will increase its imports relative to its exports, which will cause the exchange rate value of its currency to fall. Conversely, sluggish growth of a country's income relative to its trading partners will lead to a

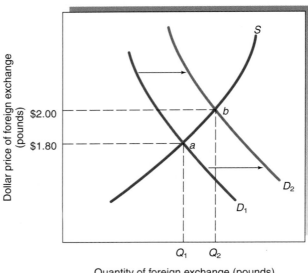

EXHIBIT 3
The Growth of U.S.
Income and Imports

Other things constant, if incomes grow in the United States, U.S. imports will grow. The increase in the imports will increase the demand for pounds, causing the dollar price of the pound to rise (from $1.80 to $2.00).

decline in imports relative to exports, which will cause the exchange rate value of its currency to rise. Granted, it seems paradoxical that sluggish growth relative to one's trading partners will cause a country's currency to appreciate, but that's in fact what happens.

Differences in Rates of Inflation

Other things constant, domestic inflation will cause the value of a nation's currency to depreciate, whereas deflation will cause its currency to appreciate. Suppose prices in the United States rise by 50 percent while our trading partners are experiencing stable prices. The domestic inflation will cause U.S. consumers to increase their demand for imported goods (and foreign currency). In turn, the inflated domestic prices will cause foreigners to reduce their purchases of U.S. goods, thereby reducing the supply of foreign currency to the exchange market. As **EXHIBIT 4** illustrates, the exchange rate will adjust to this set of circumstances. In our two-country example, the dollar will depreciate relative to the pound.

Exchange rate adjustments permit nations with even high rates of inflation to engage in trade with countries experiencing relatively stable prices.[5] A depreciation in a nation's currency in the foreign exchange market compensates for the nation's inflation rate. For example, if inflation increases the price level in the United States by 50 percent and the value of the dollar in exchange for the pound depreciates (such that the value of the foreign currency increases 50 percent), then the prices of American goods measured in pounds are unchanged to British consumers. Thus, when the exchange rate value of the dollar changes from $1.80 = 1$ pound to $2.70 = 1$ pound, the depreciation in the dollar restores the original prices of U.S. goods to British consumers even though the price level in the United States has increased by 50 percent.

On the one hand, when domestic prices are increasing more rapidly than those of one's trading partners, the value of the domestic currency will tend to depreciate in the foreign exchange market. On the other hand, if a nation's inflation rate is lower than that of its trading partners, then its currency will tend to appreciate.

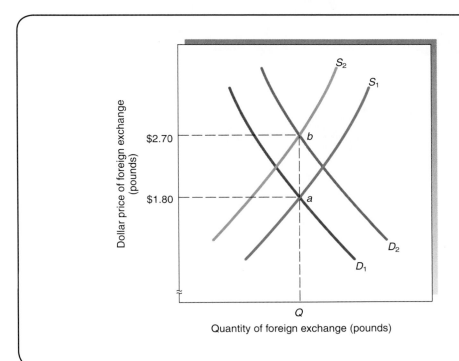

EXHIBIT 4
Inflation with Flexible Exchange Rates

If prices were stable in Britain while the price level increased 50 percent in the United States, the U.S. demand for British products (and pounds) would increase, whereas U.S. exports to Britain would decline, causing the supply of pounds to fall. These forces would cause the dollar to depreciate relative to the pound.

[5]However, high rates of inflation are likely to cause greater variability in the foreign exchange value of a currency across time periods. In turn, this increased variability of the exchange rate will generate uncertainty and reduce the volume of international trade—particularly transactions involving a time dimension. Thus, exchange rate instability is generally harmful to the health of an economy.

American consumer purchases an auto from a Japanese manufacturer.

American vacationer buys a ticket on British Airways.

Foreign student pays tuition to Harvard.

Foreign investor purchases a bond from a U.S. corporation.

How will each of these transactions influence the demand for and supply of foreign currencies in exchange for the dollar?

Changes in Interest Rates

Financial investments will be quite sensitive to changes in real interest rates—that is, interest rates adjusted for the expected rate of inflation. International loanable funds will tend to move toward areas where the expected real rate of return (after compensation for differences in risk) is highest. ***Thus, increases in real interest rates relative to a nation's trading partners will tend to cause that nation's currency to appreciate.*** For example, if real interest rates rise in the United States relative to Britain, British citizens will demand dollars (and supply their currency, pounds) in the foreign exchange market to purchase the high-yield American assets. The increase in demand for the dollar and supply of pounds will then cause the dollar to appreciate relative to the British pound.

In contrast, when real interest rates in other countries increase relative to rates in the United States, short-term financial investors will move to take advantage of the higher yields abroad. As investment funds move from the United States to other countries, there will be an increase in the demand for foreign currencies and an increase in the supply of dollars in the foreign exchange market. A depreciation in the dollar relative to the currencies of the countries with the higher real interest rates will be the result.

Changes in the Business and Investment Climate

The inflow and outflow of capital will also be influenced by the quality of the business and investment environment. The monetary, legal, regulatory, and tax climates are particularly important here. Countries that follow a monetary policy consistent with price stability, protect property rights, keep taxes low, and treat people impartially will tend to attract capital. In turn, the inflow of capital will strengthen the demand for the domestic currency and thereby cause it to appreciate. In contrast, when investors are concerned about the stability of the monetary climate, fairness of the legal system, high taxes, and excessive regulation, many will choose to do business elsewhere. As they do so, an outflow of capital and depreciation in the foreign exchange value of the domestic currency will result. Thus, other things constant, the foreign exchange value of a nation's currency will tend to appreciate when its policy environment is improving, while it will tend to depreciate if investors believe that the policy climate is deteriorating.

The accompanying Thumbnail Sketch summarizes the major forces that cause a nation's currency to appreciate or depreciate when exchange rates are determined by market forces.

THUMBNAIL SKETCH

What Factors Cause a Nation's Currency to Appreciate or Depreciate?

These Factors Will Cause a Nation's Currency to Appreciate:
1. Slow growth of income (relative to one's trading partners) that causes imports to lag behind exports
2. A rate of inflation that is lower than that of one's trading partners
3. Domestic real interest rates that are higher than real interest rates abroad
4. A shift toward sound policies that attract an inflow of capital

These Factors Will Cause a Nation's Currency to Depreciate:
1. Rapid growth of income (relative to one's trading partners) that stimulates imports relative to exports
2. A rate of inflation that is higher than that of one's trading partners
3. Domestic real interest rates that are lower than real interest rates abroad
4. Movement toward unsound policies that cause an outflow of capital

International Finance and Alternative Exchange Rate Regimes

There are three major types of exchange rate regimes: (1) flexible rates; (2) fixed rate, unified currency; and (3) pegged exchange rates. So far, we have focused on the operation of a flexible rate regime. We now consider the other two.

Fixed Rate, Unified Currency System

Obviously, the fifty states of the United States have a unified currency, the dollar. In addition, the U.S. dollar has been the official currency of Panama for almost a century. Ecuador adopted the U.S. dollar as its official currency in 2000, and El Salvador did so in 2001. The currency of Hong Kong is also closely linked to the U.S. dollar. Hong Kong has a **currency board** that has the power to create currency only in exchange for a specific quantity of U.S. dollars (7.7 HK dollars = 1 U.S. dollar).[6] Countries that adopt the currency board approach do not conduct monetary policy. Instead, they merely accept the monetary policy of the nation to which their currency is tied—the U.S. policy in the case of Hong Kong. Thus, the United States, Panama, Ecuador, El Salvador, and Hong Kong have a unified currency regime.

Sixteen countries of the European Union—Austria, Belgium, Cyprus, Finland, France, Germany, Greece, Ireland, Italy, Luxembourg, Malta, Netherlands, Portugal, Slovakia, Slovenia, and Spain—have also established a unified currency regime. The official currency in each of these countries is the euro. Several other European countries, including Estonia, Bulgaria, Latvia, Lithuania, Bosnia, and Herzegovina use a currency board to link their domestic currency to the euro. Thus, the euro is a unified currency in all of these countries. In turn, the foreign exchange value of the euro relative to other currencies, such as the dollar, the British pound, and the Japanese yen, is determined by market forces (flexible exchange rates).

The distinguishing characteristic of a fixed rate, unified currency regime is the presence of only one central bank with the power to expand and contract the supply of money. For the dollar, that central bank is the Federal Reserve System; for the euro, it is the European Central Bank. Those linking their currency at a fixed rate to the dollar or the euro do not conduct monetary policy; they merely accept the monetary policy of the central bank for their currency. For example, the former central banks of the countries now using the euro no longer have the power to create money. In essence, they are now branches of the European Central Bank, much like the regional and district Federal Reserve banks are branches of the Fed. Similarly, currency boards do not create additional currency. They merely agree to exchange their domestic currency for the currency to which it is linked at a fixed rate.

A pure gold standard system, in which each country agrees to exchange units of its domestic currency for gold at a designated price and fully backs its domestic money supply with gold, is also a fixed rate, unified system. In this case, the world supply of gold (rather than a central bank) determines the total supply of money. If a country's purchases from foreigners exceeded its sales to them, its supply of gold would fall, which would reduce the domestic supply of money. This would put downward pressure on the domestic price level and bring the payments to and receipts from foreigners back into balance. Things would change in the opposite direction if a country was selling more to foreigners than it was purchasing from them. In this case, the excess of sales relative to purchases would lead to an inflow of gold, expansion in the domestic money supply, and higher domestic prices. International financial arrangements approximated those of a

---

Currency board

An entity that (1) issues a currency with a fixed designated value relative to a widely accepted currency (for example, the U.S. dollar), (2) promises to continue to redeem the issued currency at the fixed rate, and (3) maintains bonds and other liquid assets denominated in the other currency that provide 100 percent backing for all currency issued.

---

[6]A currency board like that of Hong Kong does two things. First, it issues domestic currency at a fixed rate in exchange for a designated foreign currency. Second, the foreign currency is then invested in bonds denominated in that currency. This means that the money issued by the currency board is backed 100 percent by the foreign currency. Therefore, the holders of the money issued by the currency board know that it will always have sufficient funds to exchange the domestic currency for the foreign one at the fixed rate. In essence, the country with a currency board accepts the monetary policy of the nation to which its currency is tied.

gold standard during the period between the U.S. Civil War and the establishment of the Federal Reserve System in 1913.

Between 1944 and 1971, most of the world operated under a system of **fixed exchange rates**, where each nation fixed the price of its currency relative to others. In essence, this was a quasi-unified system. It was unified in the sense that the value of one currency was fixed relative to others over lengthy time periods. But it was not a fully unified system because each country continued to exercise control over its monetary policy. Nations maintained reserves with the **International Monetary Fund**, which could be drawn on when payments to foreigners exceeded receipts from them. This provided each with some leeway in the conduct of monetary policy. However, countries running persistent payment deficits would eventually deplete their reserves. This constrained the country's monetary independence and provided its policy makers with an incentive to keep its monetary policy approximately in line with that of its trading partners. Under this fixed exchange rate regime, nations often imposed tariffs, quotas, and other trade barriers in an effort to keep their payments and receipts in balance at the fixed rate. Various restrictions on the convertibility of currencies were also common. These problems eventually led to the demise of the system.

Pegged Exchange Rate Regime

A **pegged exchange rate system** is one in which a country commits itself to the maintenance of a specific exchange rate (or exchange-rate range) relative to another currency (like the U.S. dollar) or a bundle of currencies. In contrast with the currency board approach, however, countries adopting the pegged exchange rate continue to conduct monetary policy. Thus, an excess of purchases from foreigners relative to sales to them does not automatically force the country to reduce its domestic money supply.

However, maintaining the pegged rate will restrict the independence of monetary policy. A country can either (1) follow an independent monetary policy and allow its exchange rate to fluctuate or (2) tie its monetary policy to maintain the fixed exchange rate. It cannot, however, maintain the convertibility of its currency at the fixed exchange rate while following a monetary policy more expansionary than the country to which its currency is tied. Attempts to do so will lead to a financial crisis—a situation in which falling foreign currency reserves eventually force the country to forgo the pegged exchange rate.

This is precisely what happened in Mexico during 1989–1994. Mexico promised to exchange the peso for the dollar at a pegged rate, but it also expanded its domestic money supply much more rapidly than the United States. In the early 1990s, this led to a higher rate of inflation in Mexico than in the United States. Responding to the different inflation rates, more and more people shifted away from the Mexican peso and toward the dollar. By December 1994, Mexico's foreign exchange reserves were virtually depleted. As a result, it could no longer maintain the fixed exchange rate with the dollar. Mexico devalued its currency, triggering a crisis that affected several other countries following similar policies.

In 1997–1998, much the same thing happened in Brazil, Thailand, and Indonesia. Like Mexico, these countries sought to maintain fixed exchange rates (or rates within a narrow band), while following monetary and fiscal policies that were inconsistent with the fixed rate. As their reserves declined, they were forced to abandon their exchange rate pegs. This was extremely disruptive to these economies. Imports suddenly became much more expensive and therefore less affordable. Businesses (including banks) that had borrowed money in dollars (or some other foreign currency) were unable to repay their loans as the result of the sharp decline in the exchange rate value of the domestic currency. In turn, these disruptions led to severe economic declines.

Both economic theory and real-world experience indicate that either a purely flexible exchange rate regime or a fixed rate, unified regime with a single central bank will work reasonably well. In contrast, a pegged exchange rate regime is something like a time bomb. Pushed by political considerations, monetary policy makers in most countries are unable to follow a course consistent with the maintenance of pegged rates. Failure to do so, however, eventually leads to abandonment of the peg and a financial crisis.

Fixed exchange rate

An exchange rate that is set at a determined amount by government policy.

International Monetary Fund (IMF)

An international banking organization, currently with more than 180 member nations, designed to oversee the operation of the international monetary system. Although it does not control the world supply of money, it does hold currency reserves for member nations and makes currency loans to national central banks.

Pegged exchange rate system

A commitment to use monetary and fiscal policy to maintain the exchange rate value of the domestic currency at a fixed rate or within a narrow band relative to another currency (or bundle of currencies).

Balance of Payments

Just as countries calculate their gross domestic product (GDP) so that they have a general idea of their domestic level of production, most countries also calculate their balance of international payments in order to keep track of transactions across national boundaries. The **balance of payments** summarizes the transactions of the country's citizens, businesses, and governments with foreigners. Balance-of-payments accounts are kept according to the principles of basic bookkeeping. Any transaction that creates a demand for foreign currency (and a supply of the domestic currency) in the foreign exchange market is recorded as a debit, or minus, item. Imports are an example of a debit item. Transactions that create a supply of foreign currency (and demand for the domestic currency) on the foreign exchange market are recorded as a credit, or plus, item. Exports are an example of a credit item. *Because the foreign exchange market will bring quantity demanded and quantity supplied into balance, it will also bring the total debits and total credits into balance.*

EXHIBIT 5 summarizes the balance-of-payments accounts of the United States for 2008. As the exhibit shows, the transactions can be grouped into one of three basic categories: the current account, capital account, or the official reserve account. Let's take a look at each of these major categories.

Current-Account Transactions

Current-account transactions involve only current exchanges of goods and services and current income flows (and gifts). They do not involve changes in the ownership of either real or financial assets. **Current-account** transactions are dominated by the trade in goods and services. The export and import of merchandise goods are the largest components in the current account. When U.S. producers export their products, foreigners will supply their currency in exchange for dollars in order to pay for the U.S.-produced goods. Because U.S. exports generate a supply of foreign exchange and demand for dollars in the foreign exchange market, they are a credit (plus) item. In contrast, when Americans import goods, they will demand foreign currencies and supply dollars in the foreign exchange market. Thus, imports are a debit (minus) item.

In 2008, the United States exported $1,277.0 billion of merchandise goods compared with imports of $2,117.2 billion. The difference between the value of a country's merchandise exports and the value of its merchandise imports is known as the **balance of merchandise trade** (or *balance of trade*). If the value of a country's merchandise exports falls short of the value of its merchandise imports, it is said to have a balance-of-trade deficit. In contrast, the situation in which a nation exports more than it imports is referred to as a trade surplus. In 2008, the United States ran a merchandise-trade deficit of $840.2 billion (line 3 of Exhibit 5).

The export and import of services are also sizable. Service trade involves the exchange of items like insurance, transportation, banking services, and items supplied to foreign tourists. Like the export of merchandise goods, service exports generate a supply of foreign exchange and demand for dollars. For example, a Mexican business that is insured by an American company will supply pesos and demand dollars to pay its premiums for the service. Thus, service exports are recorded as credits in the balance-of-payments accounts of exporting nations. Conversely, the import of services from foreigners generates a demand for foreign currency and a supply of dollars in the exchange market. Therefore, service imports are a debit item.

As Exhibit 5 illustrates, in 2008, U.S. service exports were $549.6 billion, compared with service imports of $405.3 billion. Thus, the United States ran a $144.3 billion surplus on its service trade transactions (line 6 of Exhibit 5). When we add the balance of service exports and imports to the balance of merchandise trade, we obtain the **balance on goods and services**. In 2008, the United States ran a $695.9 billion deficit (the sum of the $840.2

Balance of payments

A summary of all economic transactions between a country and all other countries for a specific time period, usually a year. The balance-of-payments account reflects all payments and liabilities to foreigners (debits) and all payments and obligations received from foreigners (credits).

Current account

The record of all transactions with foreign nations that involve the exchange of merchandise goods and services, current income derived from investments, and unilateral gifts.

Balance of merchandise trade

The difference between the value of merchandise exports and the value of merchandise imports for a nation. It is also called simply the *balance of trade* or *net exports*. The balance of merchandise trade is only one component of a nation's total balance of payments and its current account.

Balance on goods and services

The exports of goods (merchandise) and services of a nation minus its imports of goods and services.

EXHIBIT 5
U.S. Balance of Payments, 2008 (in Billions of Dollars)

		DEBITS	CREDITS	BALANCE
CURRENT ACCOUNT				
1	U.S. merchandise exports		1277.0	
2	U.S. merchandise imports	−2117.2		
3	Balance of merchandise trade (1 + 2)			−840.2
4	U.S. service exports		549.6	
5	U.S. service imports	−405.3		
6	Balance on service trade (4+5)			144.3
7	Balance on goods and services (3+6)			
8	Income receipts of Americans from abroad		764.6	−695.9
9	Income receipts of Foreigners in the United States	−646.4		
10	Net income receipts			118.2
11	Net unilateral transfers			−128.4
12	Balance on current account (7 + 10 + 11)			−706.1
CAPITAL ACCOUNT				
13	Foreign investment in the United States (capital inflow)		389.6	
14	U.S. investment abroad (capital outflow)	−271.3		
15	Net Other Currency Transactions[a]		105.6	
16	Balance on capital account (13 + 14 + 15)			223.9
OFFICIAL RESERVE TRANSACTIONS				
17	U.S. official reserve assets	−4.8		
18	Foreign official assets in the U.S.		487.0	
19	Balance, Official Reserve Account (17 + 18)			482.2
20	Total (12 + 16 + 19)			0.0

[a]Statistical discrepancy is included in this figure.

Source: http://www.bea.gov.

billion merchandise-trade deficit and the $144.3 billion service surplus) in the goods and services account.

Two other relatively small items are also included in current-account transactions: (1) net income from investments and (2) unilateral transfers. Americans have made substantial investments in stocks, bonds, and real assets in other countries. As these investments abroad generate income, dollars will flow from foreigners to Americans. This flow of income to Americans will supply foreign currency (and create a demand for dollars) in the foreign exchange market. Thus, the net income to Americans is entered as a credit in the U.S. current account. Correspondingly, foreigners earn income from their investments in the United States. This net income to foreigners is recorded as a debit in the U.S. current account because the supply of dollars to the foreign exchange market creates a demand for foreign exchange.

As Exhibit 5 shows, in 2008, Americans earned $764.6 billion from investments abroad, whereas foreigners earned $646.4 billion from their investments in the United States. On balance, Americans earned $118.2 billion more on their investments abroad than foreigners earned on their investments in the United States. This $118.2 billion net inflow of investment income reduced the size of the deficit on current-account transactions.

Gifts to foreigners, like U.S. aid to a foreign government or private gifts from U.S. residents to their relatives abroad, generate a demand for foreign currencies and supply of dollars in the foreign exchange market. Thus, they are a debit item. Correspondingly, gifts to Americans from foreigners are a credit item. Because the U.S. government and private U.S. citizens gave $128.4 billion more to foreigners than we received from them, this net unilateral transfer was entered as a debit item on the current account in 2008.

Balance on Current Account

Balance on current account

The import–export balance of goods and services, plus net investment income earned abroad, plus net private and government transfers. If the value of the nation's export-type items exceeds (is less than) the value of the nation's import-type items plus net unilateral transfers to foreigners, a current-account surplus (deficit) is present.

The difference between (1) the value of a country's current exports (both goods and services) and earnings from its investments abroad and (2) the value of its current imports (again, both goods and services) and the earnings of foreigners on their domestic assets (plus net unilateral transfers to foreigners) is known as the **balance on current account**. The current-account balance provides a summary of all current-account transactions. As with the balance of trade, when the value of the current-account debit items (import-type transactions) exceeds the value of the credit items (export-type transactions), we say that the country is running a current-account deficit. Alternatively, if the credit items are greater than the debit items, the country is running a current-account surplus. In 2008, the United States ran a current-account deficit of $706.1 billion.

Because trade in goods and services dominates current-account transactions, the trade- and current-account balances are closely related. Countries with large trade deficits (surpluses) almost always run substantial current-account deficits (surpluses).

Capital-Account Transactions

Capital account

The record of transactions with foreigners that involve either (1) the exchange of ownership rights to real or financial assets or (2) the extension of loans.

In contrast with current-account transactions, **capital-account** transactions focus on changes in the ownership of real and financial assets. These transactions are composed of (1) direct investments by Americans in real assets abroad (or by foreigners in the United States) and (2) loans to and from foreigners. When foreigners make investments in the United States—for example, by purchasing stocks, bonds, or real assets from Americans—their actions will supply foreign currency and generate a demand for dollars in the foreign exchange market. Thus, these capital inflow transactions are a credit.

Conversely, capital outflow transactions are recorded as debits. For example, if a U.S. investor purchases a shoe factory in Mexico, the Mexican seller will want to be paid in pesos. The U.S. investor will supply dollars (and demand pesos) on the foreign exchange

"If other countries are treating us fairly, our exports to them should be approximately equal to our imports from them."

Politicians like to bash countries like Japan and China that export much more to us than they import from us. Some have even called for trade restraints to limit imports from these countries until our exports to and imports from them are brought into balance. This view is based on a misconception about bilateral trade balances. Flexible exchange rates will bring total purchases from foreigners into balance with total sales to them. However, there is no reason to expect that imports and exports with any specific country will be in balance.

Consider the trade "deficits" and "surpluses" of a doctor who likes to golf. The doctor can be expected to run a trade deficit with sporting goods stores, golf caddies, and course operators. Why? These suppliers sell items that the golfer–doctor purchases in sizable quantities. The doctor, on the other hand, probably sells few items the sporting goods store purchases. Similarly, the doctor can be expected to run trade surpluses with medical insurers, elderly patients, and those with chronic illnesses. These trading partners are major purchasers of the services provided by the doctor, although the doctor might purchase very little from them.

The same principles are at work across nations. A nation will tend to run trade deficits with countries that are low-cost suppliers of items it imports and trade surpluses with countries that buy a lot of the things it exports. Japan is a major importer of resources like oil and a major exporter of high-tech manufacturing goods. Americans import a lot of the latter, but they export very little of the former. Similarly, China is a low-cost producer of labor-intensive items like toys and textile products, items that are costly for a high-wage country like the United States to produce domestically. On the other hand, the United States is a low-cost producer of high-tech products and grains like wheat and corn that are purchased only in small quantities by poor countries like China. The bottom line is this: Japan and China are low-cost producers of many items that we import, and the United States is not a major exporter of items imported intensively by Japan and China. Thus, our bilateral trade deficits with them are perfectly understandable.

In recent years, the United States has run trade surpluses with the Netherlands, Australia, Belgium, Luxembourg, Brazil, and the United Kingdom. Do these bilateral trade surpluses indicate that the United States treats these countries unfairly? Of course not. The surpluses merely reflect that these countries import substantial amounts of items supplied economically by U.S. producers and export only small amounts of items imported intensively by Americans. It may be good politics to bash those with whom we run bilateral trade deficits, but the argument is nonetheless based on a fallacious view of trade balances between countries.

---

market. Because U.S. citizens will demand foreign currency (and supply dollars) when they invest in stocks, bonds, and real assets abroad, these transactions enter into the balance-of-payments accounts as a debit. In 2008, foreign investments in the United States (capital inflow) summed to $389.6 billion, while U.S. investments abroad (capital outflow) totaled $271.3 billion. In 2008, there was also a net capital inflow of $105.6 billion from other currency transactions including financial derivatives and changes in U.S. currency abroad. Because the capital inflow exceeded the outflow, the United States ran a $223.9 billion capital-account surplus in 2008.

Official Reserve Account

As we noted earlier, the current exchange rate regime is not a pure flexible rate system. Countries with pegged exchange rates will often engage in official reserve transactions in an effort to maintain their pegged rate. These transactions are debited and credited in a country's **official reserve account**. Even countries with flexible exchange rates may engage in official reserve transactions in order to influence their exchange rate. When a nation's currency is appreciating rapidly, a country may try to slow the appreciation by purchasing foreign financial assets. Conversely, when a currency is depreciating, the country may attempt to halt the depreciation by using some of its foreign currency reserves to purchase the domestic currency in the foreign exchange market. Because

Official reserve account
The record of transactions among central banks.

of the credibility and widespread use of the U.S. dollar, these official reserve transactions often involve assets denominated in dollars, particularly bonds issued by the U.S. Treasury.

The official reserve transactions are usually small relative to the size of the foreign exchange market, but they were sizable in 2008. As the financial crisis unfolded during the year, foreign central banks purchased $487.0 billion of dollar assets, mostly Treasury bonds. The U.S. purchases of foreign reserves were small, only $4.8 billion. Thus, the United States ran a surplus of $482.2 billion on official reserve transactions in 2008.

What impact do these purchases of U.S. Treasury bonds by foreign central banks have on the U.S. economy? Their impact is much like that of other capital inflows. These foreign purchases, like other capital inflows, will increase the demand for the dollar in the foreign exchange market, causing the foreign exchange value of the dollar to be higher than would otherwise be the case. They will also lead to lower domestic interest rates. Domestic interest rates will fall because the capital inflow will raise the supply of loanable funds. There is a positive side to these official reserve purchases of the dollar. If foreign central banks did not have confidence in both the economy and the monetary policy of the United States, they would not want to purchase and hold U.S. financial assets.

The Balance of Payments Must Balance

The sum of the debit and credit items of the balance-of-payments accounts must balance. Thus, the following identity must hold:

Current-Account Balance + Capital-Account Balance + Official Reserve-Account Balance = 0

However, the specific components of the accounts need not balance. For example, the debit and credit items of the current account need not be equal. Specific components may run either a surplus or a deficit. Nevertheless, because the balance of payments as a whole must balance, a deficit in one area implies an offsetting surplus in other areas. Similarly, even though market forces will bring about an overall balance, there is no reason to expect that the trade flows between any two countries will be in balance. See the accompanying Myths of Economics box feature on this topic.

If a nation is experiencing a current-account deficit, it must experience an offsetting surplus on the sum of its capital-account and official reserve-account balances. This has been the case for the United States in recent years.

In 2008, the United States ran a $706.1 billion current-account deficit and a $223.9 billion capital-account surplus. The difference between these two figures—a $482.2 billion deficit—was exactly offset by a $482.2 billion surplus in the official reserve account. Thus, the deficits and surpluses of the current-, capital-, and official reserve accounts summed to zero as is shown in Exhibit 5 (line 20).

Under a pure flexible rate system, official reserve transactions would be zero. Under these conditions, a capital-account surplus (inflow of capital) would mean that the current account must have a deficit. Similarly, a capital-account deficit (outflow of capital) would mean that the current account must have a surplus.

With flexible exchange rates, changes in the net inflow of capital will influence the current-account balance. If a nation is experiencing an increase in net foreign investment, perhaps as the result of attractive investment opportunities, this increase in the capital-account surplus (inflow of capital) will enlarge the current-account deficit. In contrast, capital flight (outflow of capital) will move the current account toward a surplus.

Are Trade Deficits Bad and Trade Surpluses Good?

The word "deficit" suggests things like excessive spending relative to income, bank overdrafts, indebtedness, and a future day of reckoning. Thus, there is an understandable tendency to believe that trade deficits must be bad and surpluses good. However, factors that often lead to trade deficits provide reason for caution. A trade deficit is present when a nation's imports exceed its exports. Many times, this occurs because a nation is growing more rapidly than its trading partners. Rapid domestic growth stimulates imports, while slow growth abroad weakens demand for a nation's exports. This combination often causes a trade deficit. Trade deficits can also result because an economy offers more attractive investment opportunities than are available elsewhere. The attractive investment environment will lead to an inflow of capital, which will cause the nation's currency to appreciate. In turn, the currency appreciation will stimulate imports relative to exports and thereby shift the trade balance toward a deficit. In essence, trade (and current-account) deficits are the flip side of capital inflows. Thus, rapid economic growth and an attractive investment environment—both of which are generally associated with a strong economy—are major causes of trade (and current-account) deficits.

EXHIBIT 6 presents data on the foreign exchange value of the dollar, current-account balance, and inflow of capital for the United States over the last three decades. (*Note:* While the data in the middle frame are for the current-account balance, the trade balance figures would be virtually identical because trade in goods and services is the dominant component of the current account.) The link between the inflow of capital and the current-account deficit is clearly visible. As the middle and lower panels illustrate, the two are almost mirror images. When net foreign investment increases, the current-account (trade) balance shifts toward a deficit. Correspondingly, when net foreign investment shrinks, so, too, does the current-account deficit. This is the expected outcome under a flexible rate system. With flexible rates, the overall payments to and receipts from foreigners must balance. Thus, a deficit in one area is not an isolated event. If a nation runs a current-account (trade) deficit, it must also run a capital-account (plus official reserve account) surplus of equal magnitude.

Prior to 1981, net foreign investment in the United States was relatively small, and so too was the current-account deficit. However, as the U.S. economy grew briskly following the 1982 recession, net foreign investment (bottom panel) in the United States increased sharply. Simultaneously, the U.S. dollar appreciated and the current-account deficit widened. As the U.S. economy slowed during the late 1980s and the recession of the early 1990s, net capital inflow fell to a trickle, and the current account actually registered a small surplus in 1991. But as the U.S. economy recovered from the 1990 recession and grew rapidly during the 1990s, once again net foreign investment increased substantially, the U.S. dollar appreciated, and the current account moved toward a large deficit.

As during the expansions of the 1980s and 1990s, there was also an inflow of capital and a substantial increase in the U.S. current-account deficit during the expansion that began in 2002. However, there was also an important difference. While the dollar appreciated during the two earlier recoveries, it depreciated during the most recent expansion. Furthermore, as Exhibit 5 shows, approximately half of the inflow of capital reflects dollar purchases by foreign central banks. In many cases, these purchases were motivated

EXHIBIT 6
The Exchange Rate, Current-Account Balance, and Net Foreign Investment

Here, we show the relationship between the exchange rate, the current-account deficit, and net foreign investment (capital inflow). The shaded areas represent recessions.

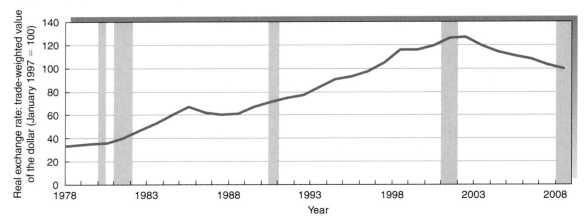

(a) Exchange-rate value of the dollar (compared with 26 currencies)

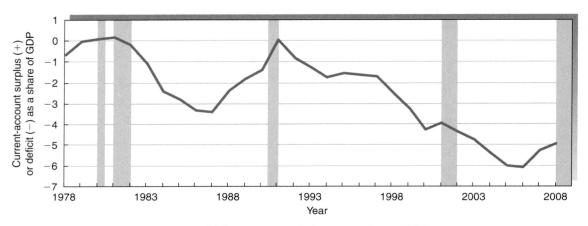

(b) Current-account balance as a share of GDP

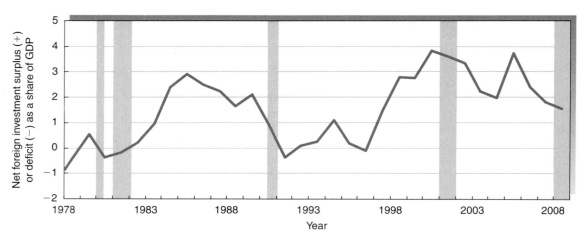

(c) Net foreign investment as a share of GDP

Note: Data are given in billions of dollars.

Source: http://www.economagic.com.

by foreigners' desire to slow the depreciation of the dollar (and the appreciation of their domestic currency). As we noted in Exhibit 1, during 2002–2008, the dollar depreciated by 21 percent against an index of twenty-six currencies, and the depreciations relative to the euro, pound, and yen were even greater. Had it not been for the sizable purchases of U.S. Treasury bonds by foreign central banks in recent years, the depreciation of the dollar would surely have been larger.

Can a country continue to run current-account (and trade) deficits? Perhaps surprisingly, the answer is "yes." Trade deficits are primarily a reflection of the inflow of capital. The inflow can and will continue as long as investors find the U.S. economy an attractive place in which to invest. Foreigners will be happy to supply investment capital to the U.S. economy as long as they can earn competitive returns. And there is no reason why this cannot continue indefinitely. The historical evidence is consistent with this view. The United States experienced trade deficits and capital inflows year after year from 1820 to 1870. During that period, investment opportunities in the New World were more attractive than those in Europe, so Europeans were quite willing to continue financing undertakings in the New World.

When considering the significance of the U.S. trade deficit, one should keep two points in mind. First, no legal entity is responsible for the trade deficit. It reflects an aggregation of the voluntary choices of businesses and individuals.[7] Thus, it is not like a business loss or even the budget deficit of a government. Second, to a large degree, the inflow of capital reflects the confidence of investors in both the U.S. economy and the monetary policy of the United States. If either should become less attractive in the future, the situation would change. For example, if the United States becomes a high-tax country or if large budget deficits were financed with monetary expansion and inflation, the inflow of capital would decline and so would the current-account deficit.

The Future

The shape of financial and exchange rate regimes is likely to change substantially in the years ahead. Several of the emerging market economies of southern and Eastern Europe have linked their currency to the euro through currency boards. Others are likely to follow. It appears that the euro will emerge as the dominant currency throughout Europe. The euro has gained substantial credibility in recent years and has already emerged as a major competitor with the dollar for use as a reserve currency.

It would not be surprising to see a similar consolidation toward a single currency in Central and South America. Brazil, Mexico, and several other countries in the Americas may well seek currency stability through some form of linkage with the dollar. A substantial share of international trade is also conducted in Japanese yen. In the future, the dollar, euro, and yen, perhaps along with two or three other currencies, may well emerge as the dominant currencies used throughout the world for domestic and international trade. These developments make this an exciting time to follow international finance.

[7]As the late Herbert Stein, a former chair of the President's Council of Economic Advisers, once put it: "The trade deficit does not belong to any individual or institution. It is a pure-statistical aggregate, like the number of eggs laid in the U.S. or the number of bald-headed men living here." See Herbert Stein, "Leave the Trade Deficit Alone," *The Wall Street Journal* (March 11, 1987).

KEY POINTS

▼ Because countries generally use different currencies, international trade usually involves the conversion of one currency to another. The currencies of different countries are bought and sold in the foreign exchange market. The exchange rate is the price of one national currency in terms of another.

▼ The dollar demand for foreign exchange arises from the purchase (import) of goods, services, and assets by Americans from foreigners. The supply of foreign currency in exchange for dollars arises from the sale (export) of goods, services, and assets by Americans to foreigners. The equilibrium exchange rate will bring these two forces into balance.

▼ With flexible exchange rates, the following will cause a nation's currency to appreciate: (1) rapid growth of income abroad (and/or slow domestic growth), (2) low inflation (relative to one's trading partners), (3) rising domestic real interest rates (and/or falling rates abroad), and (4) improvement in the business and investment environment. The reverse of these conditions will cause a nation's currency to depreciate.

▼ There are three major types of exchange rate regimes: (1) flexible rates; (2) fixed rate, unified currency; and (3) pegged exchange rates. Both flexible rate and fixed rate, unified currency systems

work quite well. Pegged rate systems, however, often lead to problems because they require that the nation follow a monetary policy consistent with maintaining the pegged rate. Political pressure often makes this difficult to do.

▼ The balance-of-payments accounts provide a summary of transactions with foreigners. There are three major balance-of-payments components: (1) the current account, (2) capital account, and (3) the official reserve account. The balances of these three components must sum to zero, but the individual components of the accounts need not be in balance.

▼ Under a pure flexible rate system, there will be no official reserve-account transactions. Under these circumstances, the current and capital accounts must balance. Therefore, an inflow of capital will shift the current account toward a deficit, while an outflow of capital will move the current account toward a surplus.

▼ Trade deficits are not necessarily bad. Countries that grow rapidly and follow policies that investors find attractive will tend to experience an inflow of capital and a trade deficit.

▼ There is no reason to expect that bilateral trade between countries will balance.

CRITICAL ANALYSIS QUESTIONS

*1. If the dollar depreciates relative to the Japanese yen, how will this affect the dollar price of a Japanese camera produced by Nikon, for example? How will this change influence the quantity of Nikon cameras purchased by Americans?

2. How will the purchases of items from foreigners compare with the sales of items to foreigners when the foreign exchange market is in equilibrium? Explain.

3. Will a flexible exchange rate bring the imports of goods and services into balance with the exports of goods and services? Why or why not?

*4. The accompanying chart indicates an actual newspaper quotation of the exchange rate of various currencies. On February 2, did the dollar appreciate or depreciate against the British pound? How did it fare against the Canadian dollar?

	U.S. Dollar Equivalent	
	February 1	February 2
British pound	1.755	1.746
Canadian dollar	0.6765	0.6775

*5. Suppose the exchange rate between the United States and Mexico freely fluctuates in the open market. Indicate whether each of the following would cause the dollar to appreciate or depreciate relative to the peso.

 a. an increase in the quantity of drilling equipment purchased in the United States by Pemex, the Mexican oil company, as a result of a Mexican oil discovery

 b. an increase in the U.S. purchase of crude oil from Mexico as a result of the development of Mexican oil fields

 c. higher real interest rates in Mexico, inducing U.S. citizens to move their financial investments from U.S. to Mexican banks

 d. lower real interest rates in the United States, inducing Mexican investors to borrow dollars and then exchange them for pesos

 e. inflation in the United States and stable prices in Mexico

 f. an increase in the inflation rate from 2 percent to 10 percent in both the United States and Mexico

 g. an economic boom in Mexico, inducing Mexicans to buy more U.S.-made automobiles, trucks, electric appliances, and manufacturing equipment

 h. attractive investment opportunities in Mexico, inducing U.S. investors to buy stock in Mexican firms

6. Explain why the current-account balance and capital-account balance must sum to zero under a pure flexible rate system.

7. Rapidly growing strong economies often experience trade deficits, whereas economies with sluggish growth often have trade surpluses. Can you explain this puzzle?

*8. In recent years, a substantial share of the domestic capital formation in the United States has been financed by foreign investors. Is this dependence on foreign capital dangerous? What would happen if the inflow of foreign capital came to a halt?

*9. Suppose that the United States were running a current-account deficit. How would each of the following changes influence the size of the current-account deficit?

 a. a recession in the United States

 b. a decline in the attractiveness of investment opportunities in the United States

 c. an improvement in investment opportunities abroad

10. If taxes imposed on personal and corporate income increased substantially in the United States and the monetary policy of the United States was less stable and more inflationary than other countries, how would these policies affect the trade deficit? Why?

*11. If foreigners have confidence in the U.S. economy and therefore move to expand their investments in the United States, how will the U.S. current-account balance be affected? How will the exchange-rate value of the dollar be affected?

12. Is a trade surplus indicative of a strong, healthy economy? Why or why not?

*13. "Changes in exchange rates will automatically direct a country to a current-account balance under a flexible exchange rate system." Is this statement true or false?

*14. Several members of Congress have been highly critical of Japan and China because U.S. imports from these countries have persistently been substantially greater than our exports to them.

 a. Under a flexible exchange rate system, is there any reason to expect that the imports from a given country will tend to equal the exports to that country?

 b. Can you think of any reason why the United States might persistently run a trade deficit with these countries?

*15. In recent years, the central banks of both Japan and China have purchased large amounts of U.S. Treasury bonds. These purchases increase the exchange rate value of the dollar relative to the Japanese yen and Chinese yuan. Are these purchases harmful to the U.S. economy? Why or why not?

*Asterisk denotes questions for which answers are given in Appendix B.

Applying the Basics: Special Topics in Economics

Economics has a lot to say about current issues and real-world events. What impact will the Internet have on your life? Why does the current Social Security system face problems, and what might be done to minimize them? Is ownership of stock risky? What caused the economic crisis of 2008 and what are the important lessons we need to learn from it? What might be done to improve the quality of health care and education? How can we best protect the environment? This section will focus on these topics and several other current issues.

Government Spending and Taxation

[A] wise and frugal government, which shall restrain men from injuring one another, shall leave them otherwise free to regulate their own pursuits of industry and improvement, and shall not take from the mouth of labor the bread it has earned. This is the sum of good government....

—Thomas Jefferson[1]

FOCUS

- How has government spending per person changed historically in the United States?

- How has the composition of government spending changed in recent decades?

- How is the federal response to the financial crisis affecting spending and taxes?

- Do taxes measure the cost of government?

- Do the rich pay their fair share of taxes? Do they pay less now than they did a couple of decades ago?

- How does the size of government in the United States compare with other countries?

- How does the size of government affect prosperity and economic growth?

[1] Thomas Jefferson, First Inaugural Address (March 4, 1801).

n chapters 5 and 6, we analyzed the economic role of government and the operation of the political process. We learned that whereas the political process and markets are alternative ways of organizing the economy, a sound legal system, secure property rights, and stable monetary regime are vitally important for the efficient operation of markets. We also noted that there may be advantages of using government to provide certain classes of goods that are difficult to supply efficiently through markets. However, as public-choice analysis indicates, the political process is not a corrective device. Even democratic representative government will often lead to the adoption of counterproductive programs. This feature will take a closer look at government in the United States and will provide some additional details with regard to the characteristics of both its spending and taxation. ◼

Government Expenditures

As we noted in Chapter 6, total government spending (federal, state, and local) sums to over one-third of the U.S. economy. Government spending on the purchase of goods and services, including the payments made to employees, accounts for nearly 20 percent of the total economy, while spending on transfer payments sums to nearly 16 percent of total income. Moreover, government spending has risen rapidly during the last eighty years. Measured as a share of the economy, government spending rose from less than 10 percent in 1929 to over 35 percent in 2008. Based on current budget projections, the government's recent stimulus efforts will result in federal spending increasing by an additional 7.1 percent of GDP in 2009, pushing government spending up to approximately 40 percent of the U.S. economy.

Approximately three-fifths of the spending by government now takes place at the federal level. Federal expenditures on just four things, (1) income transfers (including Social Security and other income security programs), (2) health care, (3) national defense, and (4) net interest on the national debt, accounted for 87 percent of federal spending in 2008. (See Chapter 6, Exhibit 2.) This means that expenditures on everything else—the federal courts, national parks, highways, education, job training, agriculture, energy, natural resources, federal law enforcement, and numerous other programs—were less than 13 percent of the federal budget. Major spending categories at the state and local level include education, public welfare and health, transportation and highways, utilities, and law enforcement.

Government Spending per Person, 1792–2008

Article 1, Section 8, of the U.S. Constitution outlined a limited set of functions that the federal government was authorized to perform. These included the authority to raise up an army and navy, establish a system of weights and measures, issue patents and copyrights, operate the Post Office, and regulate the value of money that it issued. Beyond this, the federal government was not authorized to do much else. The founders of the United States were skeptical of governmental powers, and they sought to limit those powers, particularly those at the federal level. (See the quotation by Thomas Jefferson at the beginning of this feature.)

During the United States' first 125 years, the constitutional limitations worked pretty much as planned; the economic role of the federal government was quite limited, and its expenditures were modest. In the nineteenth century, except during times of war, most government expenditures were undertaken at the state and local level. The federal government spent funds on national defense and transportation (roads and canals), but not much else.

EXHIBIT 1 presents data on real federal spending per person (measured in terms of the purchasing power of the dollar in 2000). Just prior to the Civil War, real federal expenditures were $50 per person, not much different than the $40 figure of 1800. Federal spending per person rose sharply during the Civil War, but it soon receded and remained in a range between $90 and $150 throughout the 1870–1916 period. Thus, prior to World War I, federal expenditures per person were low and the growth of government was modest.

Beginning with the World War I spending of 1917, however, the situation changed dramatically. Federal spending remained well above the prewar levels during the 1920s and rose rapidly during the 1930s. It soared during World War II, and after receding at the end of the war, federal spending continued to grow rapidly throughout the 1950–1990 period. After a brief reduction during the 1990s, per capita real federal spending is once again on the upswing. Whereas per capita federal spending fell by 4.6 percent during the 1990s, it has increased by 25 percent during 2000–2008. In 2008, it amounted to $7,883, roughly seventy times the $112 figure of 1916. The additional government expenditures came with a cost. On average, Americans paid more federal taxes in one week during 2008 than during the entire year in 1916, and based on current budget projections, the federal tax burden will continue to grow in 2009 and beyond.

Not only has federal spending grown rapidly, there has also been a dramatic shift in the composition of that spending. Since 1960, spending on defense has fallen as both a share of the budget and as a share of the economy, while expenditures on health care, transfer payments, and subsidies have soared.

EXHIBIT 1
Real Federal Expenditure per Capita: 1792–2008

Real federal spending per person (measured in 2000 dollars) was generally less than $50 prior to the Civil War, and it ranged from $90 to $150 throughout the 1870–1916 period. However, beginning with the spending buildup for World War I in 1917, real federal spending per person soared, reaching $7,883 in 2008—over seventy times the level of 1916.

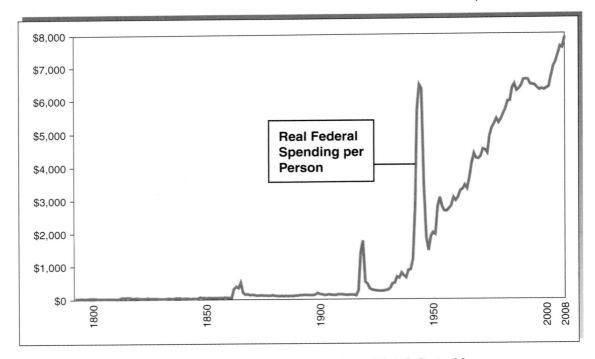

Real Federal Spending per Person

Sources: U.S. Census Bureau, *Historical Statistics of the United States* (Washington, DC: U.S. Dept. of Commerce, U.S. Bureau of the Census, 1975); and *Economic Report of the President* (Washington, DC: U.S. Government Printing Office, 2009).

As **EXHIBIT 2** illustrates, defense expenditures constituted more than half (52.2 percent) of federal spending in 1960. By 2000, defense spending was only 16.5 percent of the federal budget. Largely because of the wars in Iraq and Afghanistan, defense spending has risen since 2000 to 21.0 percent of the federal budget. In contrast, government expenditures on income transfers (including Social Security and other income-transfer programs) and health care (primarily Medicare and Medicaid) rose from 21.5 percent of the federal budget in 1960 to 57.7 percent in 2008.

Thus, there has been a dramatic change in the composition of federal spending during the last four decades. In contrast with earlier times, national defense is no longer the primary focus of the federal government. In essence, the federal government has become an entity that taxes working-age Americans in order to provide income transfers and healthcare benefits primarily for senior citizens. Furthermore, spending on the elderly is almost certain to increase as the baby boomers retire throughout the next decade. Also, over the next decade, interest payments on the rapidly rising federal debt are projected to grow from their current level of 8.5 percent of the federal budget to over 14 percent by 2019.

Taxes and the Finance of Government

Government expenditures must be financed through taxes, user charges, or borrowing.[2] Borrowing is simply another name for future taxes that will have to be levied to pay the

---

EXHIBIT 2

The Changing Composition of Federal Spending

In 2008, national defense expenditures accounted for 21.0 percent of the federal budget, down from 52.2 percent in 1960. In contrast, spending on income transfers and health care rose from 21.5 percent of the federal budget in 1960 to 57.7 percent in 2008.

(a) Defense expenditures

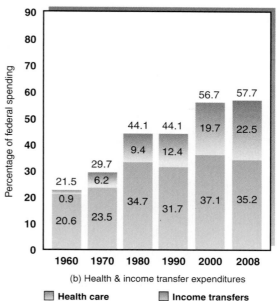

(b) Health & income transfer expenditures

■ Health care   ■ Income transfers

Source: Economic Report of the President (Washington, DC: U.S. Government Printing Office, 2009).

---

[2] In addition to user charges, taxes, and borrowing, the operations of government might be financed by printing money. But this is also a type of tax (it is sometimes called an "inflation tax") on those who hold money balances.

I'm proud to be paying taxes in the United States. The only thing is—I could be just as proud for half the money.

—Comedian Arthur Godfrey

interest on the borrowed funds. Thus, it affects the timing but not the level of taxes. In the United States, taxes are by far the largest source of government revenue. The power to tax sets governments apart from private businesses. Of course, a private business can put whatever price tag it wishes on its products; but no private business can force you to buy its products. With its power to tax, a government can force citizens to pay, whether or not they receive something of value in return. As government expenditures have increased, so, too, have taxes. Taxes now take approximately one-third of the income generated by Americans.

Types of Taxes

EXHIBIT 3 indicates the major revenue sources for the federal and state and local levels of government. At the federal level, the personal income tax accounts for almost half of all revenue. Although income from all sources is covered by the income tax, only earnings derived from labor are subject to the payroll tax. Payroll taxes on the earnings of employees and self-employed workers finance Social Security, Medicare, and unemployment compensation benefits. The payroll tax accounts for almost 36 percent of federal revenue. The remaining sources of revenue, including the corporate income tax, excise taxes, and customs duties, account for a little less than 20 percent of federal revenue.

Both sales and income taxes are important sources of revenue for state governments. A sales tax is levied by forty-five of the fifty states (Alaska, Delaware, Montana, New Hampshire, and Oregon are the exceptions). State and local governments derive about 15 percent of their revenue from this source. Personal income taxes are imposed by forty-one states (Alaska, Florida, Nevada, New Hampshire, South Dakota, Tennessee, Texas,

---

EXHIBIT 3
Sources of Government Revenue

Almost half of federal revenues are derived from the personal income tax. The payroll tax is another major source of federal revenue. The major revenue sources of state and local governments are sales and excise taxes, personal income taxes, user charges, grants from the federal government, and property taxes.

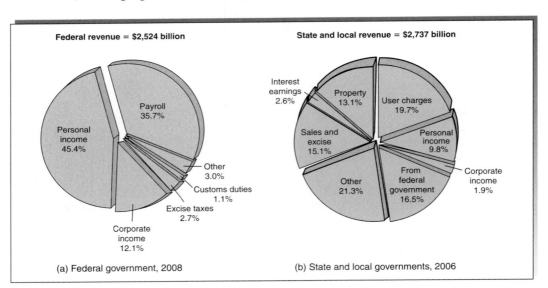

(a) Federal government, 2008

(b) State and local governments, 2006

Sources: Economic Report of the President (Washington, DC: Government Printing Office, 2009); and *State and Local Government Finances* (2006), http://www.census.gov.

Washington, and Wyoming are the exceptions), and they provide approximately 10 percent of state and local government revenue.[3] Property taxes (levied mostly at the local level), grants from the federal government, and user charges (prices for government services) also provide substantial revenues for state and local governments.

Taxes and the Cost of Government

There are no free lunches. Regardless of how they are financed, activities undertaken by the government are costly. When governments purchase resources and other goods and services to provide rockets, education, highways, health care, and other goods, the resources used by the government will be unavailable to produce goods and services in the private sector. As a result, private-sector output will be lower. This reduction in private-sector output is an opportunity cost of government. Furthermore, this cost will be present whether government activities are financed by taxes or borrowing.

Moreover, a tax dollar extracted from an individual or a business ends up costing the private economy much more than just one dollar. There are two main reasons why this is the case. *First, the collection of taxes is costly.* The administration, enforcement, and compliance of tax legislation requires a sizable volume of resources, including the labor services of many highly skilled experts. The IRS itself employs 115,000 people. In addition, an army of bookkeepers, tax accountants, and lawyers is involved in the collection process. According to the Office of Management and Budget, each year individuals and businesses spend more than 6.6 billion hours (the equivalent of 3.3 million full-time year-round workers) keeping records, filling out forms, and learning the tax rules and other elements of the tax-compliance process.[4] More than half of U.S. families now retain tax-preparation firms like H&R Block and Jackson Hewitt to help them file the required forms and comply with the complex rules. Businesses spend roughly $5 billion each year in tax-consulting fees to the four largest accounting firms, to say nothing of the fees paid to other accounting, law, and consulting firms. In total, the resources involved amount to between 3 percent and 4 percent of national income (or 12 to 15 percent of the revenues collected). If these resources were not tied up with the tax-collection process, they could be employed producing goods and services for consumption.

Second, taxes impose an additional burden on the economy because they eliminate some productive exchanges (and cause people to undertake some counterproductive activities). As we noted in Chapter 4, economists refer to this as an excess burden (or deadweight loss) because it imposes a burden over and above the tax revenue transferred to the government. It results because taxes distort incentives. When buyers pay more and sellers receive less due to the payment of a tax, trade and the production of output become less attractive and decline. Individuals will spend less time on productive (but taxed) market activities and more time on tax avoidance and untaxed activities, such as leisure. Research indicates that these deadweight losses add between 9 percent and 16 percent to the cost of taxation.[5] This means that $1 in taxes paid to the government imposes a cost of somewhere between $1.20 and $1.30 on the economy. Thus, the cost of a $100 million government program financed with taxes is really somewhere between $120 million and $130 million. As a result, the government's supply of goods and services generally costs the economy a good bit more than either the size of the tax bill or the level of government spending implies.

When the burden of taxation is considered, it is also important to recognize that all taxes are paid by people. Politicians often speak of imposing taxes on "business" as if part of the tax burden could be transferred from individuals to a nonperson (business). This is

---

[3] New Hampshire and Tennessee have limited income taxes that only tax income derived from dividend and interest (so wage income is not subject to the personal income tax).

[4] Office of Management and Budget, *Information Collection Budget of the United States Government* and Tax Foundation *Special Brief,* by Arthur Hall (March 1996).

[5] The classic article on this topic is Edgar K. Browning, "The Marginal Cost of Public Funds," *Journal of Political Economy* 84, no. 2 (April 1976): 283–98.

not the case. Business taxes, like all other taxes, are paid by individuals. A corporation or business firm might write the check to the government, but it merely collects the money from someone else—from its customers in the form of higher prices, its employees in the form of lower wages, or its stockholders in the form of lower dividends—and transfers the money to the government.

How Has the Structure of the Personal Income Tax Changed?

The personal income tax is the largest single source of revenue for the federal government. The rate structure of the income tax is progressive; taxpayers with larger incomes face higher tax rates. However, the structure of the rates has changed substantially since 1960. In the early 1960s, there were twenty-four marginal tax brackets ranging from a low of 20 percent to a high of 91 percent. The Kennedy–Johnson tax cut reduced the lowest marginal rate to 14 percent and the top rate to 70 percent. The rate reductions during the Reagan years cut the top marginal rate initially to 50 percent in 1981 and later to approximately 30 percent during the period 1986–1988. During the 1990s, the top rate was increased to 39.6 percent, but the tax reductions during the administration of George W. Bush rolled back the top rate to 35 percent. These cuts are scheduled to expire at the end of 2010, which means that the top rate will return to 39.6 percent beginning in 2011.

Thus, since the late 1980s, Americans with the highest incomes have paid sharply lower top marginal tax rates—rates in the 30 to 40 percent range, compared to top rates of 91 percent in the early 1960s and 70 percent prior to 1981. These reductions in the top rate make it tempting to jump to the conclusion that high-income Americans are now getting a free ride—that they now shoulder a smaller share of the personal income tax burden than in the past. But such a conclusion would be fallacious.

EXHIBIT 4 presents the Internal Revenue Service data on the share of the personal income tax paid by various classes of high-income taxpayers, as well as those in the bottom half of the income distribution, for the years 1963, 1980, 1990, and 2006. These data show that the share of the personal income tax paid by high-income Americans has increased substantially since 1963, and the increase has been particularly sharp since 1980. For example, the top 1 percent of earners paid 39.9 percent of the personal income tax in

EXHIBIT 4
Share of Federal Income Taxes Paid by Various Groups, 1963–2006

Even though marginal tax rates have been reduced substantially during the last four decades, upper-income Americans pay a much larger share of the federal income tax today than was previously the case. In 2006, the richest 1 percent of Americans paid 39.9 percent of the federal income tax, up from 18.3 percent in 1963 and 19.1 percent in 1980. The richest 5 percent of Americans paid over half of the personal income tax, whereas the entire bottom half of the income distribution (the bottom 50 percent) paid only 3.0 percent of the total.

INCOME GROUP	SHARE OF TOTAL FEDERAL PERSONAL INCOME TAX PAID			
	1963	1980	1990	2006
Top 1%	18.3%	19.1%	25.1%	39.9%
Top 5%	35.6%	36.8%	43.6%	60.1%
Top 10%	47.0%	49.3%	55.4%	70.8%
Top 25%	68.8%	73.0%	77.0%	86.3%
Top 50%	89.6%	93.0%	94.2%	97.0%
Bottom 50%	10.4%	7.1%	5.8%	3.0%

Source: Internal Revenue Service (also available online at the Tax Foundation's Web site: http://www.taxfoundation.org/).

2006, up from 19.1 percent in 1980 and 18.3 percent in 1963. The top 10 percent of income recipients paid 70.8 percent of the personal income tax in 2006, compared to 49.3 percent in 1980 and 47 percent in 1963. At the same time, the share of the personal income tax paid by the bottom half of the income recipients has steadily fallen from 10.4 percent of the total in 1963 to 7.1 percent in 1980 and 3.0 percent in 2006.

What is going on here? How can one explain the fact that high-income Americans are now paying more of the personal income tax even though their rates are now sharply lower than those in effect prior to 1981? Two major factors provide the answer. First, when marginal rates are cut by a similar percentage, the "incentive effects" are much greater in the top tax brackets. For example, when the top rate was cut from 91 percent to 70 percent during the Kennedy–Johnson years, high-income taxpayers in this bracket got to keep $30 out of every $100 of additional earnings after the tax cut, compared to only $9 before the rates were reduced. Thus, their incentive to earn additional income increased by a whopping 233 percent (30 minus 9 divided by 9)! Conversely, the rate reduction in the lowest tax bracket from 20 percent to 14 percent meant that the low-income taxpayers in this bracket now got to keep $86 of each additional hundred dollars that they earned compared to $80 prior to the tax cut. Their incentive to earn increased by a modest 7.5 percent (86 minus 80 divided by 80). Because the rate reductions increased the incentive to earn by much larger amounts in the top tax (and therefore highest income) brackets, the income base on which high-income Americans were taxed expanded substantially as their rates were reduced. As a result, the tax revenues collected from them declined only modestly. In the very highest brackets, the rate reductions actually increased the revenues collected from high-income Americans. (See Laffer curve analysis of Chapter 4.) In contrast, the incentive effects were much weaker in the lower tax brackets and, as a result, rate reductions led to approximately proportional reductions in revenues collected from low- and middle-income taxpayers. This combination of incentive effects shifts the share of taxes paid toward those with higher incomes, the pattern observed in Exhibit 4.

Second, both the standard deduction and personal exemption have been increased substantially during the last couple of decades. This means that Americans are now able to earn more income before they face any tax liability. In 2006, for example, 32 percent (approximately 43 million returns) of those filing an income tax return either had zero tax liability or actually received funds from the IRS as the result of the **Earned Income Tax Credit**. This change in the structure of the personal income tax explains why people in the bottom half of income now pay such a small percentage of the personal income tax: 3.0 percent in 2006 compared to 10.4 percent in 1963.[6]

Income Levels and Overall Tax Payments

In addition to the personal income tax, the federal government also derives sizable revenues from payroll, corporate income, and excise taxes. How is the overall burden of federal taxes allocated among the various income groups? **EXHIBIT 5** presents Congressional Budget Office estimates for the average amount of federal taxes paid in 2005 according to income. On average, the top quintile (20 percent) of earners are estimated to pay 25.5 percent of their income in federal taxes. The average federal tax rate for the quintile with the next-highest level of income falls to 17.4 percent, and the average tax rate continues to fall as income declines. The average tax rate of the bottom quintile is 4.3 percent, about one-sixth of the average rate for the top quintile of earners. Clearly, the federal tax system is highly progressive, meaning that it takes a larger share of the income of those with higher incomes than from those with lower income levels.

Earned Income Tax Credit

A provision of the tax code that provides a credit or rebate to people with low earnings (income from work activities). The credit is eventually phased out if the recipient's earnings increase.

[6] The data of Exhibit 4 consider only the tax liability of taxpayers. They do not reflect the payments from IRS to taxpayers as the result of the Earned Income Tax Credit, which was established in the mid-1980s. If these payments to taxpayers were taken into consideration, the net taxes paid by the bottom half of income recipients would have been less than 1 percent. Thus, the data of Exhibit 4 actually understate the reduction in the net share of taxes paid by the bottom half of income recipients during the last two decades.

EXHIBIT 5

Total Federal Taxes as a
Share of Income, 2005

Federal taxes are highly progressive. In 2005, federal taxes took 25.5 percent of the income generated by the top quintile (20 percent) of earners, compared to 14.2 percent from the middle-income quintile and 4.3 percent from the lowest quintile of earners.

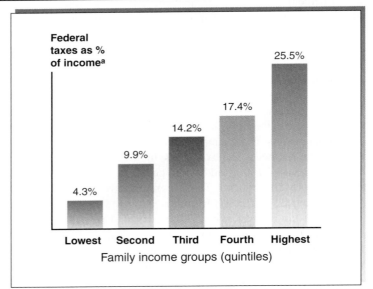

Source: Congressional Budget Office, *Historical Effective Federal Tax Rates: 1979–2005* (December 2007).
[a]Total federal taxes include income, payroll, and excise taxes.

Does the Growth of Income Benefit the Federal Government?

The federal personal income tax brackets are indexed for inflation. Therefore, the tax brackets are widened as inflation increases the nominal incomes of individuals and families. However, no adjustment is made for increases in real incomes. Under a progressive tax system, a larger and larger share of income will be taxed at higher rates as real incomes rise. As a result, the growth of real income will automatically increase federal revenues more than proportionally. Thus, if tax rates are unchanged, the progressive tax structure means that the federal government takes a larger share of income as the economy grows. Some economists, particularly those with a public-choice perspective, believe that this "automatic" increase in revenues will tend to reduce the efficiency of government spending. According to this view, elected political officials would be more likely to make sound expenditure decisions if they were forced to vote for higher taxes in order to expand government as a share of the economy.

Size of Government: The United States versus Other Countries

There is substantial variation in the size of government across countries. As **EXHIBIT 6** illustrates, the relative size of government in most other high-income industrial countries is greater than that of the United States. In 2007, government spending summed to over 50 percent of the economy in Sweden, France, and Denmark. Government spending in Belgium, Italy, and Austria hovered at around 48 percent of the economy. Compared to the United States, government was also larger in the United Kingdom and Germany, but somewhat smaller in Ireland and Australia. Government spending as a share of the economy in Japan and New Zealand was similar to that of the United States, about 37 percent. Interestingly, the size of government was substantially smaller in South Korea, Singapore, Thailand, and Hong Kong—four Asian nations that have achieved rapid growth and substantial increases in living standards during the last four decades.

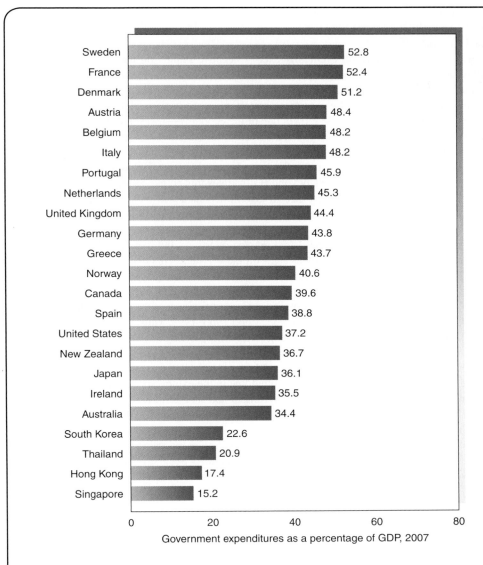

Source: International Monetary Fund, *Government Finance Statistics Yearbook* (2008). (The data for Belgium, Japan, and Hong Kong are for 2006, and South Korea for 2005.)

How Does the Size of Government Affect Economic Growth?

Throughout this text, we have analyzed how governments influence the efficiency of resource use and the growth of income. It is clear that a legal environment that protects people and their property and provides for the impartial enforcement of contracts is vitally important. So, too, is a monetary and regulatory environment that provides the foundation for the smooth operation of markets. As we discussed in Chapter 5, there are also a few goods—economists call them public goods—that may be difficult to provide through markets. National defense, roads, and flood-control projects provide examples. Because they generate joint benefits and it is difficult to limit their availability to paying customers, sometimes they can be provided more efficiently through government. But public goods are rare and the market can often devise reasonably efficient methods of dealing with them. If resources are going to be allocated efficiently, government spending on provision of public goods will generally be only a small share of the economy.

As governments expand beyond these core functions, however, the beneficial effects wane and eventually become negative as government moves into areas ill-suited for political action and in which the political process works poorly. Thus, expansion of government activities beyond a certain point will eventually exert a negative impact on the economy. **EXHIBIT 7** illustrates the implications with regard to the expected relationship between the size of government and economic growth, *assuming that governments undertake activities based on their rate of return.* As the size of government, measured on the horizontal axis, expands from zero (complete anarchy), initially the growth rate of the economy—measured on the vertical axis—increases. The *A* to *B* range of the curve illustrates this situation. As government continues to grow as a share of the economy, expenditures are channeled into less-productive (and later counterproductive) activities, causing the rate of economic growth to diminish and eventually to decline. The range of the curve beyond B illustrates this point.[7] Thus, our analysis indicates that there is a set of activities and size of government that will maximize economic growth. Expansion of government beyond (and outside of) these functions will retard growth.

How large is the growth-maximizing size of government? Do large governments actually retard economic growth? These are complex questions, but they have been addressed by several researchers. **EXHIBIT 8** sheds light on these issues. This exhibit presents data on the relationship between size of government (*x*-axis) and economic growth (*y*-axis) for the twenty-three long-standing members of the Organization for Economic Cooperation and Development (OECD). The exhibit contains four dots (observations) for each of the twenty-three countries—one for each of the four decades during the period 1960–1999. Thus, there are ninety-two total dots. Each dot represents a country's total government spending as a share of GDP *at the beginning of the decade* and its accompanying growth of real GDP *during that decade*. Government expenditures ranged from a low of about 15 percent of GDP in some countries to a high of more than 60 percent in others. As the plotted line in the exhibit shows, there is an observable negative relationship between size of government and long-term real GDP growth. Countries with higher levels of government spending grew less rapidly. The line drawn through the points of Exhibit 8 indicates that a 10-percentage-point increase in government expenditures as a share of GDP leads to approximately a 1-percentage-point reduction in economic growth.[8]

Time series data for specific countries have also been used to investigate the link between size of government and growth. Edgar Peden estimates that for the United States, the "maximum productivity growth occurs when government expenditures represent

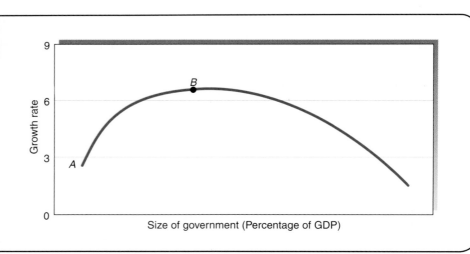

EXHIBIT 7
Economic Growth Curve and Government Size

If a government undertakes activities in the order of their productivity, its expenditures will promote economic growth (the growth rate will move from A to B). Additional expenditures, however, will eventually retard growth (the growth rate will move along the curve to the right of B).

---

[7] In the real world, governments may not undertake activities based on their rate of return and comparative advantage. Many governments that are small relative to the size of the economy fail to focus on the core activities that are likely to enhance economic growth. Thus, one would expect that the relationship between size of government and economic growth will be a loose one.

[8] For additional information on the relationship between size of government and growth, see James Gwartney, Robert Lawson, and Randall Holcombe, "The Scope of Government and the Wealth of Nations," *The Cato Journal* (Fall 1998): 163–90.

EXHIBIT 8

Government Spending and Economic Growth among the Twenty-Three OECD Countries: 1960–1999

Here, we show the relationship between size of government and the growth of real GDP for the twenty-three longtime OECD members during each decade since 1960. The data indicate that a 10 percent increase in government expenditures as a share of GDP reduces the annual rate of growth by approximately 1 percent. The data also imply that the size of government in these countries is beyond the range that maximizes economic growth.

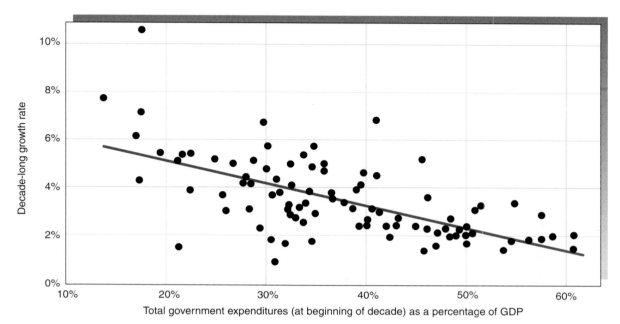

Total government expenditures (at beginning of decade) as a percentage of GDP

Sources: OECD, *OECD Economic Outlook* (various issues); and the World Bank, *World Development Indicators*, CD-ROM, 2001.

about 20% of GDP." Gerald Scully estimates that the growth-maximizing size of government (combined federal, state, and local) is between 21.5 percent and 22.9 percent of the economy. Although the methodology of these studies differs, they do have one thing in common: They indicate that in the ranges observed, high levels of government spending tend to retard economic growth.[9] They also indicate that the size and scope of most governments around the world are larger than the size that would maximize the income growth of their citizens. Moreover, the estimates imply that the recent expansion in the size of the government sector in the United States is likely to reduce the future growth of income.

The Future

The federal government has responded to the financial crisis and recession of 2008–2009 with a huge increase in both expenditures and borrowing. In fiscal year 2009, the federal deficit comprised 12 percent of GDP. A whopping 48 percent of this spending was financed through borrowing. Measured as a share of the economy, the spending levels and budget deficits are projected only slightly lower in fiscal year 2010. These deficit levels are similar to those of World War II, and they clearly are not sustainable. Nonetheless, they are already pushing the national debt up rapidly and are sure to result in higher federal interest payments in the years ahead. All of this could not have come at a worse time. As we noted earlier, a major share of government spending in the United States is now directed

[9] See Edgar Peden, "Productivity in the United States and Its Relationship to Government Activity: An Analysis of 57 Years, 1929–1986," *Public Choice* 69 (1991): 153–73; and Gerald Scully, *What Is the Optimal Size of Government in the United States?* (Dallas, TX: National Center for Policy Analysis, 1994).

toward the elderly. As the baby boomers begin moving into the retirement phase of life, the already large federal spending on Social Security and Medicare is going to balloon. This combination of higher interest payments on the debt and soaring expenditures on senior citizen programs will make it very difficult to control the growth of government during the next decade.

KEY POINTS

▼ During the first 125 years of U.S. history, federal expenditures per person were small and grew at a relatively slow rate. But the size and nature of government has changed dramatically during the past 100 years. Today, the real (adjusted for inflation) spending per person of the federal government is roughly seventy times the level of 1916.

▼ During the last four decades, the composition of federal spending has shifted away from national defense and toward spending on income transfers and health care.

▼ As the size of government has grown, taxes have increased. Taxes impose a burden on the economy over and above the revenue transferred to the government because of (1) the administration and compliance costs and (2) the deadweight losses that accompany taxation.

▼ Overall, the federal tax system of the United States is highly progressive. Taxes as a percentage of income are approximately six times greater for the

top quintile (20 percent) of families than for the bottom quintile.

▼ The size of government of the United States is smaller than that of the major Western European countries, but larger than for a number of high-growth Asian economies.

▼ When governments focus on the core activities of providing (1) a legal and enforcement structure that protects people and their property from aggression by others and (2) a limited set of public goods, they promote economic growth. However, when governments grow beyond this size, expanding into activities for which they are ill-suited, they deter growth.

▼ The huge deficits and growth of the national debt during 2009 and 2010 will lead to higher future interest payments. This factor, along with soaring spending on Social Security and Medicare as the baby boomers retire, will make it difficult to control the growth of government in the decade immediately ahead.

CRITICAL ANALYSIS QUESTIONS

*1. How do taxes influence the efficiency of resource use? How much does it cost for the government to raise an additional dollar (or $1 billion) of tax revenue?

2. During the last four decades, a smaller share of the federal budget has been allocated to national defense and a larger share to income transfers and health care. Does economics indicate that this change will help Americans achieve higher living standards?

3. Because the structure of the personal income tax is progressive, a larger share of income is taxed at higher rates as income grows. Therefore, economic growth automatically results in higher taxes unless offsetting legislative action is taken. Do you think this is an attractive feature of the current tax system? Why or why not?

4. Compared with the situation prior to 1981, the marginal tax rates imposed on individuals and

families with high incomes are now lower. What was the top marginal personal income tax rate in 1980? What is the top rate now? Are you in favor of or opposed to the lower marginal rates? Why?

*5. As the result of changes during the last two decades, the bottom half of income recipients now pay little or no personal income tax. Rather than paying taxes, many of them now receive payments back from the IRS as the result of the Earned Income Tax Credit and Child Tax Credit programs. Do you think the increase in the number of people who pay no taxes will affect the efficiency of the political process? Why or why not?

6. How have the size and functions of government changed during the last two centuries? Did the framers of the U.S. Constitution seek to limit the size of the federal government? If so, how?

*Asterisk denotes questions for which answers are given in Appendix B.

The Internet: How Is It Changing the Economy?

FOCUS

- Why is the development of the Internet an important economic phenomenon?

- How is the Internet changing product markets?

- What is the effect of the Internet on the labor market?

The Internet is kind of like a gold rush where there really is gold.

—Bill Gates[1]

[1]Bill Gates, *Microsoft Magazine* (January/February 1996).

The Internet is a gigantic library, super shopping mall, and extensive transportation system all wrapped into one. Far more documents can be obtained over the Internet than from even the largest brick-and-mortar library facility. Although a large mall can provide you with access to hundreds of shops in a given locality, the Internet provides access to millions of businesses located around the world. And for only a small fee, you can open your own shop in the world's super mall.

Music, movies, software, and financial services can be transported almost instantaneously over the Internet, something unheard of just a couple of decades ago. For example, online sales of goods and services such as airline tickets, computers, and books totaled $228 billion in 2008. This figure is expected to rise to $319 billion, or nearly 10 percent of all projected retail sales, by 2013.[2] The Web is also influencing labor markets by changing how people find new jobs as well as how labor services are provided. ■

Use of the Internet

As **EXHIBIT 1** shows, the number of Web sites on the Internet has exploded in the past decade. In 1992, there were only 16,000 Web sites, but by 2008, there were more than 100 million sites. This tremendous growth in the number of Web sites has been matched by a dramatic rise in the number of Internet users. By July 2009, nearly three-quarters of the U.S. population, or 227 million people, were using the Internet. The typical user employs the Internet intensively. The average user spends more than seven hours a week surfing the Web and visits twenty-nine different Web sites per week.[3]

As **EXHIBIT 2** demonstrates, the use of the Internet has become a worldwide phenomenon. More than two-fifths of Internet users reside in Asia, compared with one-quarter in Europe and one-sixth in North America. Residents of Latin America, Oceania/Australia, the Middle East, and Africa account for a relatively small portion of the total users.

Economic Gains from the Internet

Why is the development of the Internet an important economic phenomenon? There are good reasons to believe that the Internet has improved productivity and efficiency—that it has helped us generate more value from available resources. There are three major sources of economic gains from the Internet.

1. GAINS FROM BROADER AND MORE COMPETITIVE MARKETS. As we have previously discussed, gains from trade and competition are important sources of growth and prosperity. The Internet promotes the realization of gains from both. The cost of establishing an Internet firm is low, often only a few hundred dollars. The costs of identifying potential suppliers via the Internet are also low, and with the development of more efficient search devices, they are declining. Via the Internet, firms are able to compete over a

---

[2]Jeffrey Grau, "Retail E-Commerce Forecast: Cautious Optimism," *eMarketer Research Report* (New York: eMarketer, Inc., June 2009).

[3]The current number of Internet users as well as usage patterns can be obtained from http://www.nielsen.com/.

EXHIBIT 1
Number of Web Sites, 1992–2008

The number of Web sites rose dramatically between 1992 and 2008. By 2006, there were over 100 million Web sites.

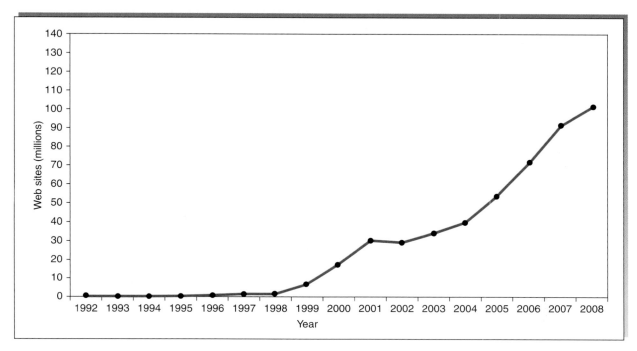

Source: http://www.zooknic.com

EXHIBIT 2
The Geographic Distribution of Internet Use, 2008

Nearly two-fifths of Internet users live in Asia. About one-quarter reside in Europe, and another sixth are in North America.

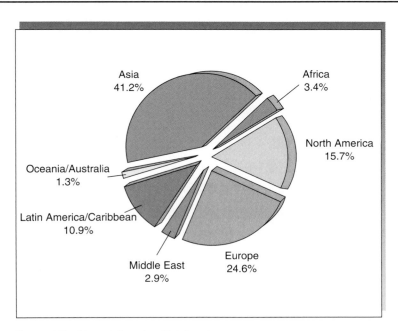

Source: http://www.internetworldstats.com

much larger geographic area than they could a decade ago, and buyers are better able to purchase from sellers who are located far away. A case in point: A farm family in Kansas was able to start a successful business selling tumbleweeds to New York restaurants wanting Southwestern décor. Markets are becoming more competitive and the location of both buyers and sellers less relevant. This is particularly true for goods that can be transported economically, either through the Internet or by other means of transportation.

2. GAINS FROM LOWER TRANSACTION COSTS. Transaction costs are an obstacle to the realization of gains from trade. The Internet, however, often reduces the cost of transactions, including the cost of information. Think about, for example, the software you are able to download and the time and money it saves you from having to go to a store to buy it. The U.S. economy has already reaped substantial gains from these lower transaction costs. But as use of the Internet increases, there is reason to believe that the future gains will be even greater.

3. GAINS FROM NETWORKING. Like the telephone of an earlier era, the Internet is a networking system. Telephones were not very valuable when only a few people had one, but their value increased dramatically as more and more people acquired them. The Internet has this same characteristic. The value of the system to current users increases as more and more people join the network. Growth of the network will make it more likely that Internet sellers will be offering products you want to buy and that potential Internet buyers will be searching for goods you are willing to sell.

Key Sectors of Internet Growth

EXHIBIT 3 shows that the Internet is now extensively used in several consumer product markets. The percentage of sales conducted online is about one-fifth or more in retail markets such as travel, books, and computer hardware and software. The rapid rise in the importance of the Internet in these markets is the result of the relatively low transportation costs for these items as well as the availability of information about these standardized products online. A much smaller percentage of the sales of automobiles and auto parts, electronics and appliances, food, apparel, and sporting goods is conducted online. The

EXHIBIT 3
Online Market
Penetration, 2007

The percentage of sales conducted online is about one-fifth or more in the travel, books, and computer hardware and software markets. The market share for online firms in the automobile, food, apparel, sporting goods, and electronics and appliances markets is much smaller.

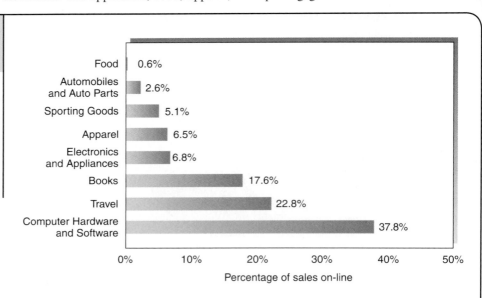

Sources: U.S. Census Bureau, *E-Stats* (May 28, 2009), http://www.census.gov/estats: U.S Census Bureau, *Statistical Abstract of the United States: 2009*, 128th ed. (Washington, DC: Author, 2008); http://www.census.gov/statab/www/, Table 1009.

low market penetration for online firms in the food market is partly because customers can't observe the condition of these items. Similarly, the sale of clothing over the Internet is hampered by the fact that one can't examine the fit of clothing online.

The Internet is also quickly transforming how banking is conducted. The number of households engaged in online banking has been rapidly increasing. In 2007, about 39 percent of American adults paid their bills online.[4]

The Web has revolutionized the market for used consumer durables. The Web site eBay has made it much easier for people to buy or sell used goods. Sales are conducted by an online auction process, and eBay earns money by charging a commission for each sale completed. Prior to purchasing an item on eBay, prospective buyers can examine earlier customers' ratings of a given seller. The ease with which trades can be conducted on the eBay Web site enabled the company to grow to 88 million active users in the second quarter of 2009. Unlike most Internet firms, eBay has been profitable since its inception.[5]

How the Internet Improves Consumer Markets

The Internet helps create value in final product markets by either reducing sellers' costs or improving the matches between sellers and consumers.[6] First, several factors help online retail firms achieve lower costs. Their handling costs will often be lower because it will not be necessary for the firms to unpack products or put them on display. Losses due to shoplifting, which often are about 3 percent of sales, are eliminated. Web-based firms are generally able to use low-cost warehouses rather than expensive stores in urban or suburban areas. Online retailers often have lower sales commissions on their products than traditional brick-and-mortar firms do.

Second, the Internet can improve matches between sellers and consumers by making information about goods easier to get. The Internet is an excellent source of information for consumers about available goods and services because an individual can get very specific information about a product or service at a low cost any time of day or night. Web shoppers can obtain information from online versions of product catalogs, product reviews, and price comparisons. Sites like Amazon.com and eopinions.com also allow users to rate how well they like different products and provide product recommendations to customers based on their past purchases. Web shoppers can get product samples of books, music, and software, which can help them better decide whether to purchase products.

The Web can also make it easier for consumers to obtain access to hard-to-find goods, particularly specialty products and goods with unique characteristics. For example, it is very expensive for a chain such as The Gap to maintain a large inventory of its products at many different locations. As a consequence, each Gap store branch has only a limited inventory of different styles and sizes of jeans. This results in some consumers having to make compromises on the jeans they purchase. Online firms, however, can take advantage of economies of scale of centralized inventories and stock a much wider variety of products. This enables Web-based firms to provide a better match to customers' preferences.

Dell Computers provides the best example of the effect of product customization. Prior to Dell, the typical personal computer manufacturer forecasted demand for various computer models and then produced these computers in batches. The computers were then distributed to wholesalers and retail stores. Changes in inventories and prices were used to create a balance between supply and demand. Dell's primary business model is different.[7]

[4]U.S. Census Bureau, *Statistical Abstract of the United States: 2009,* 128th ed. (Washington, DC: Author, 2008); http://www.census.gov/statab/www/, Table 1122.

[5]http://www.ebay.com/.

[6]For an overview of the effect of the Internet on product markets, see Severin Borenstein and Garth Saloner, "Economics and Electronic Commerce," *Journal of Economic Perspectives* (Winter 2001): 3–12. This section is partly derived from this article.

[7]In 2007, Dell announced that it began selling some preconfigured desktop models through Wal-Mart. However, the Wal-Mart sales are only a small portion of its overall sales.

Online, Dell customers can customize their computer purchases on several dimensions such as the processor, memory, hard drive size, monitor, and so on. After the order is placed, the computer is made and then shipped directly to the customer. As a result, Dell does not need to manufacture all possible configurations of its computers and therefore is able to achieve lower costs.

A major problem, of course, with purchasing goods online is that consumers can't touch, taste, smell, or try on the goods before purchasing them. A potential solution is hybrid stores that act as a showroom for a broad range of products. These stores display only a few of each product available for sale. Shoppers can examine the products and then place their order either in the store or later at home online.

Will Internet firms eventually dominate product markets? It depends on whether they are an efficient method of supplying goods and services. When Internet firms have lower costs or provide consumers with other benefits (for example, broader selection, faster delivery, or greater customization), they will be able to compete effectively. With time, they may even dominate some sectors of the economy. In contrast, when traditional retailers have lower costs and provide consumers with other benefits (immediate access to goods, inspection of the items, and/or local service contacts, for example), they will survive and prosper. In a market economy, consumers are the ultimate judges. Their choices will determine which firms, be they traditional or online, will expand and prosper and which will be driven from the market.

How the Internet Improves Business Efficiency

The ability of the Internet to improve matches between buyers and sellers also applies to business-to-business transactions. In fact, a higher volume of business-to-business transactions is being conducted on the Web than business-to-consumer transactions. In 2007, over 90 percent of all e-commerce was business-to-business sales.[8]

Some online firms serve as intermediaries between companies. For example, some Web sites auction off goods as diverse as steel and advertising space. Other online companies have set up exchanges for a wide variety of goods. One such exchange is Covisint, which was started by Chrysler, Ford, and General Motors to handle their transactions with parts suppliers. It has since expanded to work with over 45,000 organizations in the automotive, health care, public sector, and financial services industries.[9]

These intermediaries can take the form of exchanges, online auctions, and brokers. They can often reduce the buyer's search costs and facilitate one-stop shopping and thereby reduce the need for costly contacts with multiple suppliers.

Many companies are also increasingly conducting "reverse auctions" online. Vendors that supply inputs bid on the prices they will charge the companies conducting the auctions. In other words, instead of bidding to buy products online, vendors are bidding to sell their products online (which is why they are called "reverse" auctions). Sun Microsystems' Web site, for example, allows programmers and other vendors to bid on contracts to solve Sun clients' software problems.

The Internet can also lower sales costs between companies. For example, switching to an electronic version of the purchasing process from a paper one can substantially reduce the cost of buying goods and services. The cost of completing a paper transaction has been estimated to be roughly $50 per transaction. In addition, improved information from a firm's suppliers about the availability of their products can enable the firm to lower its inventory of inputs and thus its costs. In addition, the Web can be used to take advantage of differences in time zones. For example, software projects can often be transferred over

[8]U.S. Census Bureau, *E-Stats* (May 28, 2009), http://www.census.gov/estats.
[9] http://www.covisint.com/.

the Internet from programmers in the United States to their counterparts in India at the end of the workday. Via the Web, radiologists in India examine emergency medical scans overnight so that U.S. radiologists can get some sleep. Being able to outsource work anywhere around the world is also cost-effective for firms.

Labor Markets and the Internet: Faster and Better Employee–Employer Matches[10]

The explosive growth of the Internet has changed how people search for jobs and firms hire workers. There are now more than 3,000 job search sites. Monster.com, the leading job-posting site, indicated that over seventy-five million individuals have an account, and it is one of the top twenty visited sites on the Internet. Currently, the Internet is used in 38 percent of all job searches by unemployed workers. About two-thirds of job seekers with Internet access use it in their job search. Today, more people use the Internet to look for jobs than search methods such as contacting friends or relatives and using private employment agencies.[11]

Job-posting Web sites have several advantages over traditional newspaper help-wanted ads. They contain more job openings and are easier to search. The job openings can be more current because employers can post ads immediately as well as edit them after their initial posting. Online jobs sites also permit individuals to advertise their skills to potential employers. Lastly, the cost to advertise a job opening is lower. The cost of a thirty-day advertisement on Monster.com is less than 5 percent of the cost of a job advertisement in one issue of the Sunday *New York Times*.

Job-posting software on sites can also help match job seekers with employers. Software can compare the résumés of job seekers with descriptions of open positions. If an appropriate match occurs, then both the employer and the job seeker can be notified. Some Web programs advise applicants of new employment opportunities based on the job openings they have applied for in the past. Employers can also screen candidates by administering personality and skills tests over the Internet.

Because matches between employers and prospective employees can be made more quickly, it's possible that the Internet has the potential to reduce frictional unemployment in the economy. Moreover, online screening of candidates can lead to better matches, and better matches lead to higher productivity for firms.

The Internet's effect on employee turnover is less clear, however. On the one hand, better and faster matches can be made, as we have pointed out. On the other hand, because the Internet enables employed workers to search for a new position easily, turnover may increase. In fact, 14 percent of the employed indicate that they use the Internet to search for potential new job opportunities.[12]

The Delivery of Labor Services and the Training of Employees

The Internet has changed how workers provide labor services to employers. Remote access to documents and e-mail will permit some workers to provide part or all of their work at home or other locations. In 2002, about 21 million workers reported working at home at least one day per month.[13] By 2008, this figure had risen to 39 million workers.[14] Less

[10]This section draws on David H. Autor, "Wiring the Labor Market," *Journal of Economic Perspectives* (Winter 2001): 25–40.

[11]Betsey Stevenson, "The Internet and Job Search," in David Autor, ed., *Labor Market Intermediation* (Chicago, IL: University of Chicago Press, forthcoming).

[12]Ibid.

[13] WorldatWork, "Telework Trendlines for 2006" (Scottsdale, AZ: WorldatWork, February 2007).

[14]WorldatWork, "Telework Trendlines 2009" (Scottsdale, AZ: WorldatWork, February 2009).

time is spent going to and from a workplace, leaving more time for work activities that add economic value.

The Internet has also changed how workers obtain their skills. Students, of course, can now go to school and get their degrees online. Many employers provide formal and informal training for their workers online. This training plays an important role in workers' earnings. The online delivery of skills training has the potential to reduce the cost and increase the convenience of getting such training.

Concluding Thought

The Internet is an important technological change—perhaps as important as the development of electricity, the railroad, or the automobile. There are reasons to believe that it will improve economic efficiency and help us achieve higher living standards. It has increased the interaction of people around the world. It may even change lifestyles and alter cultural values. It will be exciting to follow these developments in the decades ahead.

KEY POINTS

▼ The use of the Internet has grown dramatically in the past decade and is now a worldwide phenomenon.

▼ The Internet tends to improve productivity and the efficiency of resource use because it (1) increases the breadth and competitiveness of markets, (2) lowers transaction costs, and (3) becomes more valuable as additional users and Web sites are added.

▼ The Internet can improve the operation of product markets by reducing costs and improving the matches between buyers and sellers. The Internet can reduce both distribution and production costs. Matches are improved through better information about available goods, greater access to goods, and increased customization.

▼ The volume of business-to-business sales being conducted on the Internet is even greater than the volume of retail-to-consumer sales. The Internet is making inputs cheaper and input markets more competitive and is helping streamline production processes.

▼ The Internet has become an integral part of the job search process. Quicker and improved matches between employers and employees have the potential to reduce unemployment. The Internet also makes it possible for many employees to work at home and other locations and get training online.

CRITICAL ANALYSIS QUESTIONS

1. What effect does the Internet have on the efficiency of markets? Explain. How is the Internet likely to influence productivity and the growth of output in the years immediately ahead?

*2. The share of airline tickets bought over the Internet has grown rapidly, whereas the percentage of groceries purchased online remains minuscule. What factors likely explain this difference?

3. Indicate how the production, marketing, and distribution of each of the following are likely to be influenced by the development of the Internet: (a) popular music, (b) movies, (c) automobiles, (d) commercial employment agencies, (e) physician services, and (f) health care. Briefly explain your response.

*Asterisk denotes questions for which answers are given in Appendix B.

The Economics of Social Security

FOCUS

- Why is Social Security headed for problems?

- Will the Social Security Trust Fund lighten the tax burden of future generations?

- Does Social Security transfer income from the rich to the poor? How does it impact the economic status of blacks, Hispanics, and those with fewer years of life expectancy?

- How will Social Security work in the twenty-first century?

Persons who now receive payments get much more than the actuarial value of the taxes that they paid and that were paid on their behalf. Young persons who now pay Social Security taxes are being promised much less than the actuarial value of the taxes that they will pay and that will be paid on their behalf.

—*Milton and Rose Friedman*[1]

[1]Milton Friedman and Rose Friedman, *Free to Choose* (New York: Harcourt Brace Jovanovich, 1980), 104.

The Social Security program in the United States is officially known as Old Age and Survivors Insurance (OASI). It is designed to provide the elderly with a flow of income during retirement. In spite of its official title, Social Security is not based on principles of insurance. Private insurance and pension programs invest the current payments of customers in buildings, farms, or other real assets. Alternatively, they buy stocks and bonds that finance the development of real assets. These real assets generate income that allows the pension fund (or insurance company) to fulfill its future obligations to its customers.

Social Security does not follow this saving-and-investment model. Instead, it taxes current workers and uses the revenues to finance benefits for existing retirees. There is no buildup of productive assets that the federal government can use to fund the future benefits promised today's workers. When current workers retire, their promised Social Security benefits will have to come from taxes levied on future generations. *In essence, Social Security is an intergenerational income-transfer program*. The system is based on "pay as you go" rather than the savings and investment principle.

The Social Security retirement program is financed by a flat rate payroll tax of 10.6 percent applicable to employee earnings up to a cutoff level. In 2009, the earnings cutoff was $106,800. Thus, employees earning $106,800 or more paid $11,321 in Social Security taxes to finance the OASI retirement program.[2] The income cutoff is adjusted upward each year by the growth rate of nominal wages. Whereas the payroll tax is divided equally between employee and employer, it is clearly part of the employees' compensation package, and most economists believe that the burden of this tax falls primarily on the employee. The formula used to determine retirement benefits favors those with lower earnings during their working years. However, as we will discuss later, the redistributive effects toward those with lower incomes are more apparent than real.

When the program began in 1935, not many people lived past age sixty-five, and the nation had lots of workers and few eligible retirees. As **EXHIBIT 1** illustrates, there were 16.5 workers for every Social Security beneficiary in 1950. That ratio has declined sharply through the years. As a result, higher and higher taxes per worker have been required just to maintain a constant level of benefits. There are currently 3.2 workers per Social Security retiree. By 2030, however, that figure will decline to only 2.2.

When there were many workers per beneficiary, it was possible to provide retirees with generous benefits while maintaining a relatively low rate of taxation. Many of those who retired in the 1960s and 1970s received real benefits of three or four times the amount they paid into the system, far better than they could have done had they invested the funds privately. The era of high returns, however, is now over. The program has matured, and the number of workers per beneficiary has declined. Payroll taxes have risen greatly over the decades, and still higher taxes will be necessary merely to fund currently promised benefits.

Studies indicate that those now age forty and younger can expect to earn a real rate of return of about 2 percent on their Social Security tax dollars, substantially less than what they could earn from personal

---

[2]Additional payroll taxes are levied for the finance of disability programs (1.8 percent) and Medicare (2.9 percent). Thus, the total payroll tax sums to 15.3 percent, but only revenues from the 10.6 percent rate are used for the finance of benefits to retirees and surviving dependents. (*Note:* The earnings cutoff does not apply to the Medicare portion of the payroll tax.)

investments. Thus, Social Security has been a good deal for current and past retirees. It is not, however, a very good deal for today's middle-aged and younger workers. ■

Why Is Social Security Headed for Problems?

The flow of funds into and out of a pay-as-you-go retirement system is sensitive to demographic conditions. Since 1990, the Social Security system has enjoyed a period of highly favorable demographics. The U.S. birthrate was low during the Great Depression and World War II. People born in this era have moved into the retirement phase of life during the past fifteen years. Because the 1930–1945 generation was relatively small, the retirement payments to it were also small. The birthrate rose sharply during the two decades following World War II. These baby boomers are now in their prime working years, and their large numbers are expanding the flow of revenues into the Social Security retirement system.

However, as **EXHIBIT 2** shows, the situation will change dramatically when the baby boomers begin to retire around 2010. Their retirement, combined with rising life expectancies, will lead to a rapid increase in senior citizens in the years immediately ahead. The number of people age sixty-five years and over will soar from 40 million in 2010 to 71 million in 2030. As a result, the number of workers per Social Security retiree will fall from today's 3.2 to only 2.2 in 2030.

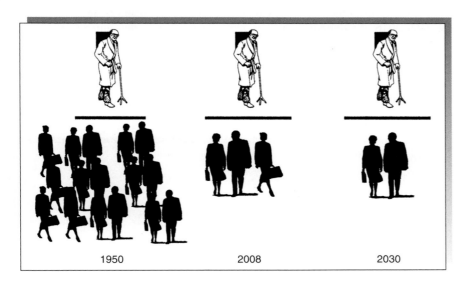

EXHIBIT 1
Workers per Social Security Beneficiary

In 1950, there were 16.5 workers per Social Security beneficiary. By 2008, the figure had fallen to just 3.2. By 2030, there will be only 2.2 workers per retiree. As the worker/beneficiary ratio falls under a pay-as-you-go system, either taxes must be increased or benefits reduced (or both).

1950	2008	2030

Source: 2009 Annual Report of the Board of Trustees of the Federal Old Age and Survivors Insurance and Disability Insurance Trust Funds (Washington, DC: Government Printing Office, 2009), p. 51.

EXHIBIT 2

U.S. Population Age Sixty-Five and Over, 1980–2008, and Projections to 2030

As shown here, the growth rate of the elderly population will accelerate rapidly as the baby boomers move into the retirement phase of life during the years following 2010. This will place strong pressure on both the Social Security and Medicare programs.

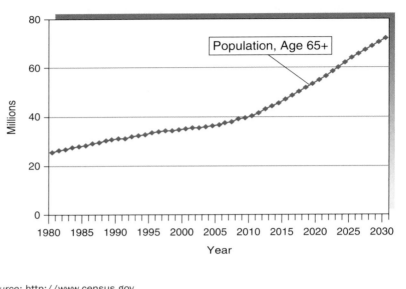

Source: http://www.census.gov.

EXHIBIT 3 illustrates the impact of this change on the pay-as-you-go Social Security system. Currently, the funds flowing into the system (pushed up by the large baby boom generation) exceed the expenditures on benefits to retirees (pulled down by the small Great Depression/World War II generation). But the retirement of the baby boomers around 2010 will begin pushing the expenditures of the system upward at a rapid rate. The current surplus of revenues from the payroll tax relative to retirement benefits will dissipate around 2016. After 2016, the deficits will grow larger and larger as the number of beneficiaries relative to workers continues to grow in the decades ahead.

The revenues derived from the payroll tax have exceeded the benefits paid to retirees since the mid-1980s. Presently, about 90 percent of the tax revenues flowing into the

EXHIBIT 3

The Forthcoming Deficit between Payroll Tax Revenues and Benefit Expenditures

Given current payroll taxes and retirement benefit levels, the system will run larger and larger deficits during the 2016–2030 period and beyond.

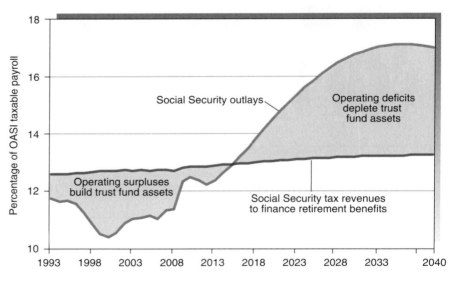

Source: Social Security Administration 2007 OASDI Annual Trustees Report, http://www.ssa.gov.

system are required for payments to the beneficiaries. The system is currently generating a surplus—about $60 billion per year. However, the surpluses will continue for only a few more years.

Under current law, the surpluses are channeled into the Social Security Trust Fund (SSTF). The fund uses the revenue to buy special nonmarketable bonds from the U.S. Treasury. By 2016, the SSTF is expected to grow to $3.7 trillion; however, the deficits of the system will draw down these funds and are projected to deplete them by 2037.

Will the Trust Fund Make It Easier to Deal with the Retirement of the Baby Boomers?

Perhaps surprising to some, the SSTF will not reduce the burden accompanying the retirement of the baby boomers. Unlike the bonds, stocks, and physical assets of a private pension fund or insurance company, the SSTF bonds will not generate a stream of future income for the federal government. Neither are they a "pot of money" set aside for the payment of future benefits. Instead, the trust fund bonds are an IOU from one government agency, the Treasury, to another, the Social Security Administration. The federal government is both the payee and recipient of the interest and principal represented by the SSTF bonds. *No matter how many bonds are in the trust fund, their net asset value to the federal government is zero!*

Thus, the number of IOUs in the trust fund is largely irrelevant.[3] The size of the trust fund could be doubled or tripled, but that would not give the federal government any additional funds for the payment of benefits. Correspondingly, the trust fund could be abolished and the government would not be relieved of any of its existing obligations or commitments. In order to redeem the bonds and thereby provide the Social Security system with funds to cover future deficits, the federal government will have to raise taxes, cut other expenditures, or borrow from the public. Neither the presence nor the absence of the trust fund will alter these options.

As we indicated in Chapter 6, politicians have an incentive both to spend on programs providing highly visible benefits and conceal the burden of taxes. The SSTF has helped them do this. The Social Security surplus was transferred to the general Treasury, and the funds were used to finance current government spending. During the last two decades, the government has spent all of the surplus and even borrowed beyond these amounts. Thus, even while spending the funds on current programs, Congress and several presidents have projected the view that funds were being set aside for the future retirement of the baby boomers. Given the structure of political incentives, none of this should be surprising.

The Real Problem Created by the Current System

The real problem faced by the pay-as-you-go Social Security system will arise around 2016 when the revenues from the payroll tax will begin to fall short of the benefits promised to retirees. At that time, the current Social Security surpluses will be transformed into deficits that will become larger and larger throughout the 2020s and 2030s. Under current law, revenues will be sufficient to pay only about three-quarters of promised benefits by 2030, and less in later years.

---

[3]Of course, the SSTF bonds represent funds borrowed by the Treasury from the Social Security system. This increases the legitimacy of claims on these funds by future Social Security recipients. It also indicates that the trust fund is similar to what is called budget authority, which provides the legal permission for the government to spend funds on an item.

There are only four ways to cover future shortfalls: (1) cut benefits, (2) increase taxes, (3) cut spending in other areas, or (4) borrow. None of these options is attractive, and, regardless of how the gap is filled, a slowdown in the rate of economic growth is likely to occur. If benefits are reduced, current beneficiaries and people near retirement will—quite correctly—feel that a commitment made to them has been broken. It will also be difficult to cover the shortfall with higher taxes. Once the baby boom generation retires, approximately a 50 percent increase in the payroll tax or a 30 percent increase in the personal income tax will be needed to cover Social Security deficits. Tax increases of this magnitude will exert a negative impact on the economy. Neither will it be easy to cut expenditures in other areas of the federal budget. Defense spending was cut substantially as a share of the economy during the 1990s. Furthermore, the growth of the elderly population will also place huge upward pressure on spending for Medicare, another major federal program. Finally, borrowing to cover the shortfall will place upward pressure on interest rates and necessitate higher future taxes merely to cover the interest obligations. Thus, borrowing would merely delay the problem.

Not even robust economic growth would eliminate the future shortfall. Retirement benefits are indexed to average growth in nominal wages. If higher productivity enables *real* (inflation-adjusted) wages to rise quickly, so will Social Security benefits. For example, if inflation is zero and real wages start growing at 2 percent a year instead of their previous level of 1 percent, the formula used to calculate Social Security benefits will also begin to push those benefits up more rapidly. Higher economic growth may temporarily improve Social Security's finances, but under current law the improvement will not last.[4]

Does Social Security Help the Poor?

Social Security has gained many supporters because of the belief that it redistributes wealth from the rich to the poor. The system is financed with a flat tax rate up to the cutoff limit, but the formula used to calculate benefits disproportionately favors workers with low lifetime earnings.[5] However, other aspects of the system tend to favor those with higher incomes. First, workers with more education and high earnings tend to live longer than those with less education and lower earnings. As **EXHIBIT 4** shows, the age-adjusted mortality rate of people with less than a high school education is 8 to 10 percent higher than the average for all Americans. As years of schooling increase, mortality rates fall. The age-adjusted mortality rate of college graduates is 21 percent below the average for all Americans, whereas the rate for people with advanced degrees is 32 percent below the average. Given the strong correlation between education and earnings, the age-adjusted mortality figures indicate that, on average, Americans with higher earnings live longer than their counterparts with less education and lower earnings. As a result, high-wage workers will, on average, draw Social Security benefits for a longer period of time than low-wage workers. Correspondingly, low-wage workers are far more likely to pay thousands of dollars in Social Security taxes and then die before, or soon after, becoming eligible for retirement benefits.

Second, low-wage workers generally begin full-time work at a younger age. Many work full time and pay Social Security taxes for years, while future high-wage workers are still in college and graduate school. Low-wage workers generally pay more into the system earlier, and therefore forgo more interest, than high-wage workers.

---

[4]See Garth Davis, "Faster Economic Growth Will Not Solve the Social Security Crisis," Heritage Center for Data Analysis (February 3, 2000).

[5]Retirement benefits are based on the best thirty-five years of earnings from a worker's career. Benefits are calculated by taking 90 percent of the first $8,928 a year of earnings, 32 percent of earnings between $8,928 and $53,796, and just 15 percent of earnings above $53,796 up to the earnings cutoff of $106,800. Therefore, as base earnings rise, benefits fall as a percentage of average earnings (and payroll taxes paid) during one's lifetime. For example, the retirement benefits of people with base annual earnings of $10,000 sum to 84 percent of their average working year earnings. In contrast, the retirement benefits of those with base earnings of $60,000 are only 39 percent of their average pre-retirement earnings. These figures are based on the formula for 2009. The figures are adjusted each year for the growth of nominal wages.

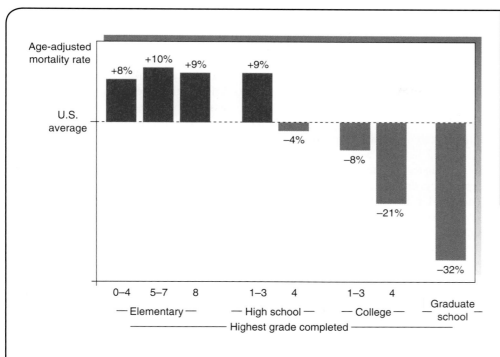

EXHIBIT 4
Mortality Rates by
Level of Education

As shown here, the age-adjusted mortality rates are lower for those with more education. Because of the close link between education and income, people with higher incomes tend to live longer and, therefore, draw Social Security benefits for a lengthier time period than those with less education and income.

Source: Center for Data Analysis, Heritage Foundation.

Third, labor participation tends to fall as spousal earnings increase. As a result, couples with a high-wage worker are more likely to gain from Social Security's spousal benefit provision, which provides the nonworking spouse with benefits equal to 50 percent of those the working spouse receives.

Two recent studies taking these and other related factors into consideration suggest that Social Security may actually transfer wealth from low-wage to high-wage workers. A study using data from the Social Security Administration and the Health and Retirement Study found that when Social Security benefits are assessed for family units rather than for individuals, the progressivity of the system disappears. Another study adjusted for differences in mortality rates, patterns of lifetime income, and other factors. It found that if a 2 percent real interest rate (discount rate) is used to evaluate the pattern of taxes paid and benefits received, the redistributive effects of Social Security are essentially neutral. However, at a more realistic 4 percent real interest rate, Social Security actually favors higher-income households.[6]

Social Security and the Treatment of Blacks and Working Married Women

When Social Security was established in 1935, the population was growing rapidly, only a few Americans lived to age sixty-five, and the labor force participation rate of married women was very low. Social Security was designed for this world. But today's world is dramatically different. Several aspects of the system now seem outdated, arbitrary, and in some cases, unfair. Let's consider a couple of these factors.

---

[6]See Alan Gustman and Thomas Steinmeier, "How Effective Is Redistribution under the Social Security Benefit Formula?" *Journal of Public Economics* 82 (October 2001): 1–28; and Julia Lynn Coronado, Don Fullerton, and Thomas Glass, "Long Run Effects of Social Security Reform Proposals on Lifetime Progressivity," in Martin Feldstein and Jeffrey B. Liebman, eds., *The Distributional Aspects of Social Security and Social Security Reform* (Chicago: University of Chicago Press, 2002).

Social Security Adversely Affects Blacks and Other Groups with Below-Average Life Expectancy

Currently, the average retiree reaching age sixty-five can expect to spend eighteen years receiving Social Security benefits, after more than forty years of paying into the system. But what about those who do not make it into their eighties or even to the normal retirement age of sixty-five? Unlike private financial assets, Social Security benefits cannot be passed on to heirs. Thus, those who die before age sixty-five or soon thereafter receive little or nothing from their payroll tax payments.

Social Security was not set up to transfer income from some ethnic groups to others, but under its current structure, it nonetheless does so. Because of their shorter life expectancy, the Social Security system adversely affects the economic welfare of blacks. Compared with whites and Hispanics, blacks are far more likely to pay a lifetime of payroll taxes and then die without receiving much in the way of benefits. Thus, the system works to their disadvantage. In contrast, Social Security is particularly favorable to Hispanics because of their above-average life expectancy and the progressive nature of the benefit formula. As a result, Hispanics derive a higher return than whites and substantially higher than blacks.[7]

EXHIBIT 5 presents the expected real returns for those born in 1975, according to gender, marital status, and ethnicity.[8] Single black males born in 1975 can expect to derive a real annual return of *negative* 1.3 percent on their Social Security tax payments, compared

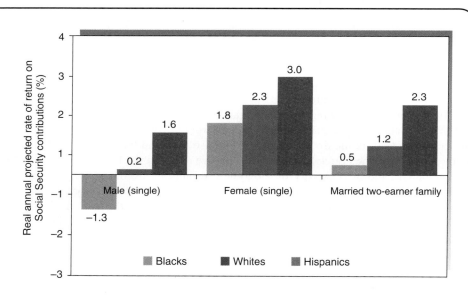

EXHIBIT 5
Rates of Return by Gender, Marital Status, and Ethnicity

The earnings of blacks are lower than whites, but blacks have a shorter life expectancy. The latter effect dominates, and therefore blacks derive a lower rate of return from Social Security than whites. In contrast, Hispanics have both lower earnings and a little longer life expectancy than whites. Thus, their returns from Social Security are higher than whites, and substantially higher than blacks.

Source: Center for Data Analysis, Heritage Foundation.

[7]For additional details on the redistributive effects of Social Security across ethnic groups, see William W. Beach and Gareth Davis, "More for Your Money: Improving Social Security's Rate of Return," in David C. John, ed., *Improving Retirement Security: A Handbook for Reformers* (Washington, DC: Heritage Foundation, 2000), 25–64; and Martin Feldstein and Jeffrey Liebman, "The Distributional Effects of an Investment-Based Social Security System," in Martin Feldstein and Jeffrey B. Liebman, eds., *The Distributional Aspects of Social Security and Social Security Reform* (Chicago: University of Chicago Press, 2002).

[8]It is common to calculate a rate of return on financial investments by comparing initial investments with the stream of projected future income (or benefits). Social Security is not like a regular financial investment because there is no accumulation of assets and no legal right to benefits. Nonetheless, a rate of return can be calculated by comparing the payroll taxes a worker pays with the future benefits he or she is promised. The rate-of-return figures of Exhibit 5 were derived in this manner. They assume that the current tax level and promised future benefits will be maintained. However, as we noted, projections indicate that current tax rates will cover only about three-fourths of promised benefits by 2030. Thus, higher taxes will be required to maintain the promised benefit levels. In turn, the higher taxes will lower rates of return. Therefore, the figures of Exhibit 5 probably overstate the rates of return for the various groups.

with returns of 0.2 percent for single white males and 1.6 percent for single Hispanic males. Similarly, a two-earner black couple born in 1975 can expect a real return of 0.5 percent, compared with returns of 1.2 percent and 2.3 percent for white and Hispanic couples born during the same year. A similar pattern exists when comparisons are made for those born in other years.

The Social Security retirement system also works to the disadvantage of those with life-shortening diseases. People with diabetes, heart disease, AIDS, and other diseases often spend decades paying 10.6 percent of their earnings into the system, only to die with loved ones unable to receive benefits from the Social Security taxes they have paid. (People with life-shortening diseases may receive disability insurance, but if they die before retirement they collect nothing from their payments into the retirement system.)

Discrimination against Married Women in the Workforce

When Social Security was established, relatively few married women worked outside the home. Therefore, individuals were permitted to receive benefits based on either their own earnings or 50 percent of the benefits earned by their spouse, whichever is greater. This provision imposes a heavy penalty on married women in the workforce. In the case of many working married women, the benefits based on the earnings of their spouses are approximately equal to, or in some cases greater than, benefits based on their own earnings. Thus, the payroll tax takes a big chunk of their earnings without providing them with any significant additional benefits.

Is the Structure of Social Security Suitable for the Twenty-First Century?

When the number of retirees grows more rapidly than the number of workers, pay-as-you-go financing does not work well. The return retirees can expect from their tax payments into the system will be low. As we mentioned, today's typical worker can expect a return of only 2.0 percent from the taxes paid into the Social Security system. By way of comparison, stock market investments have averaged a real return of approximately 7 percent annually for more than a century. Furthermore, when regular investments are made into a diverse holding of stocks, the variation in the return has been relatively low.[9] Mutual funds now make it feasible for even a small novice investor to invest in a diverse stock portfolio while still keeping administrative costs low. (See Special Topic 4, feature on the stock market.)

As a result of the changing demographics, the Social Security and Medicare programs now confront huge **unfunded liabilities**, shortfalls between promised future benefits and the revenues that can be expected at current tax rates. The trustees of these two programs project that the unfunded liability of Social Security is $8 trillion, whereas that of Medicare is estimated to be $38 trillion.[10] The sum of these figures is more than three times the current size of the U.S. economy. Predictably, deteriorating financial conditions will lead politicians to look for ways of dealing with this situation. Thus, a combination of factors—low returns from Social Security, a structure that seems outdated, and deteriorating financial conditions—may virtually force Congress to seriously consider modifications in the future.

Unfunded liability

A shortfall of tax revenues at current rates relative to promised benefits for a program. Without an increase in tax rates, the promised benefits cannot be funded fully.

---

[9]See Liqun Liu, Andrew J. Rettenmaier, and Zijun Wang, "Social Security and Stock Market Risk," *NCPA Policy Report No. 244*, National Center for Policy Analysis (July 23, 2001).

[10]See *2009 Annual Report of the Boards of Trustees of the Federal Hospital Insurance and Federal Supplementary Medical Insurance Trust Fund*, 201–202, http://www.cms.hhs.gov/ReportsTrustFunds/.

THE WIZARD OF ID

Personal retirement account (PRAs)

An account that is owned personally by an individual in his or her name. The funds in the account could be passed along to heirs.

From an economic viewpoint, the most viable option would be some form of **personal retirement accounts (PRAs)** that would incorporate savings and investment into the financing of retirement. In varying degrees, several countries have already moved in this direction. Beginning in the early 1980s, Chile shifted to a retirement system based on saving and investing through PRAs rather than pay as you go. The Chilean plan was so successful that other Latin American countries, including Mexico, Bolivia, Columbia, and Peru, adopted similar plans in the 1990s. High-income countries have also moved in this direction. In 1986, the United Kingdom began allowing workers to channel 4.6 percentage points of their payroll tax into PRAs in exchange for acceptance of a lower level of benefits from the pay-as-you-go system. The PRA option is currently chosen by nearly three-fourths of British workers. Other countries that now permit at least some substitution of PRAs for payroll taxes and pay-as-you-go benefits include the Netherlands, Australia, Sweden, and Germany.

Ownership rights exert a powerful impact on incentives. Personal retirement accounts would provide workers with a property right to the funds contributed into their accounts. The funds paid into a PRA could be passed along to heirs. In contrast with higher taxes, payments into a personally owned investment account that would enhance one's retirement income would not exert a harmful impact on the incentive to work and earn. Furthermore, PRAs would encourage saving and investment, which would help to promote economic growth. They would also reduce the dependency of senior citizens on political officials. There are numerous ways to structure personal retirement accounts. Several plans have already been put forth, and others are sure to arise in the future.

Political debate about the structure of Social Security and how to plan for retirement will continue in the years ahead. This debate is particularly important for younger people because the way it is handled will exert a major impact on their future tax liability and the quality of their life during retirement.

KEY POINTS

▼ Social Security does not follow the saving-and-investment model. Most of the taxes paid into the system are used to finance the benefits of current retirees.

▼ Although the current tax revenues exceed the payments to retirees, this will change dramatically as the baby boomers begin to move into the retirement phase of life. Beginning around 2016, the system's current surplus will shift to a deficit, which will persist for several decades.

▼ The current surplus of the Social Security system is used to purchase U.S. Treasury bonds. Because the federal government is the payee and the recipient of these bonds, their net asset value to the federal government is zero. They will not reduce the level of future taxes needed to cover the Social Security deficit when the baby boomers begin to retire.

▼ The major problem resulting from the current pay-as-you-go system is that large tax increases, spending cuts, and/or additional borrowing will be required to cover the Social Security deficits following the retirement of the baby boom generation.

▼ Whereas the Social Security benefit formula favors those with lower lifetime earnings, low-wage workers have a lower life expectancy, begin work at a younger age, and gain less from the spousal benefit provisions of the current system. These latter factors largely, if not entirely, offset the egalitarian effects of the benefit formula.

▼ Because of their shorter life expectancy, blacks derive a lower rate of return from Social Security than whites and a substantially lower return than Hispanics.

▼ The demographics of the twenty-first century reduce the attractiveness of pay-as-you-go Social Security. Various plans that would place more emphasis on saving and investment are likely to be considered in the future.

CRITICAL ANALYSIS QUESTIONS

1. Is the Social Security system based on the same principles as private insurance? Why or why not?

*2. Why does the Social Security system face a crisis? Are there real assets in the Social Security Trust Fund that can be used to pay future benefits? Will the trust fund help to avert higher future taxes and/or benefit reductions when the baby boomers retire? Why or why not?

3. Do you think workers should be permitted to invest all or part of their Social Security taxes into a personal retirement account? Why or why not?

4. How does Social Security affect the economic well-being of blacks relative to whites and Hispanics? Explain.

5. Does the current Social Security system promote income equality? Why or why not?

6. The Social Security payroll tax is split equally between the employee and the employer. Would it make any difference if the entire tax was imposed on employees? Would employees be helped if all the tax was imposed on employers? (*Hint:* You may want to consult Chapter 4, section on tax incidence.)

*Asterisk denotes questions for which answers are given in Appendix B.

The Stock Market:
Its Function, Performance
and Potential as an
Investment Opportunity

*Though the stock market functions
as a voting machine in the short
run, it acts as a weighing machine
in the long run.*

—Ben Graham,[1]
Securities Analyst

FOCUS

- **What is the economic function of the stock market?**

- **What determines the price of a stock? Can experts forecast the future direction of stock prices?**

- **Can an ordinary investor profit from stock market investments? If so, how and under what circumstances?**

- **How has the stock market been affected by the recent financial crisis? Is now a good time to invest in the stock market?**

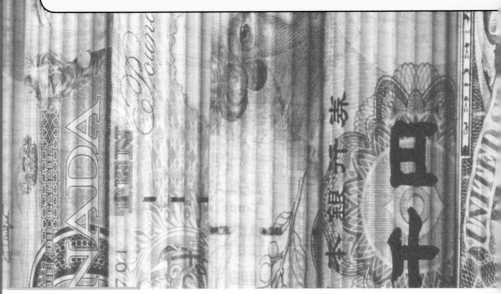

[1]As quoted by Warren Buffett in Carol Loomis, "Warren Buffett on the Stock Market," *Fortune* (December 10, 2001), 80–87.

The market for corporate shares is called the stock market. The stock market makes it possible for investors, including small investors, to share in the profits (and the risks) of large businesses. About one-half of all households now own stock, either directly or indirectly through shares in an equity mutual fund. In recent years, changes in stock prices have often been front-page news. This feature will focus on the economic functions of the stock market and analyze its potential as an investment tool through which people can build their wealth. ■

The Economic Functions of the Stock Market

The stock market performs several important functions in a modern economy. Let's consider three of the most important.

1. THE STOCK MARKET PROVIDES INVESTORS, INCLUDING THOSE WHO ARE NOT INTERESTED IN PARTICIPATING DIRECTLY IN THE OPERATION OF THE FIRM, WITH AN OPPORTUNITY TO OWN A FRACTIONAL SHARE OF THE FIRM'S FUTURE PROFITS. As a firm earns profits, its shareholders may gain as the result of both dividend payments and increases in the market value of the stock. Ownership of stock is risky. There is no guarantee that any firm will be profitable in the future. But the shareholders' potential losses are limited to the amount of their initial investment. Beyond this point, shareholders are not responsible for the debts of the corporations that they own.

2. NEW STOCK ISSUES ARE OFTEN AN EXCELLENT WAY FOR FIRMS TO OBTAIN FUNDS FOR GROWTH AND PRODUCT DEVELOPMENT. Essentially, there are three ways for a firm to obtain additional financing. It can use retained earnings (profits earned but not paid out to stockholders), it can borrow money, or it can sell stock. When borrowing, the firm promises to repay the lender a specific amount, including principal and interest. Conversely, new stock issues provide the firm with additional financing, and the owner of the stock acquires an ownership right to a fraction of the future revenues generated by the firm.

Newly issued stocks are sold to the public through specialized firms. A firm that issues new stock sells it in the **primary market**. When news reports tell us about how stock prices are changing, they are referring to **secondary markets**, in which previously issued stocks are traded. Secondary markets make it easy to buy and sell listed stock. This is important to the primary market. The initial buyers want to know that their stock will be easy to sell later. Entry is more attractive when exit will be easy. This will help the corporation issuing new stock to sell it for a higher price.

A stock exchange is a secondary market. It is a place where stockbrokers come to arrange trades for buyers and sellers. The largest and best-known stock market is the New York Stock Exchange, in which more than 2,800 stocks are traded. There are other such markets in the United States, as well as in London, Tokyo, Hong Kong, and other trading centers around the world.

3. STOCK PRICES PROVIDE INFORMATION ABOUT THE QUALITY OF BUSINESS DECISIONS. Changing stock prices reward good decisions and penalize bad ones. It pays for a stockholder, especially a large one, to be alert to whether the firm's decisions are good or bad. Those who spot a corporation's problems early can sell part or all of their stock in that firm before others notice and lower the price by selling their own stock. Similarly, those who first notice decisions that will be profitable can gain by increasing

Primary market

The market in which financial institutions aid in the sale of new securities.

Secondary market

The market in which financial institutions aid in the buying and selling of existing securities.

467

their holdings of the stock. Stockholder alertness benefits the corporation, too. The firm's board of directors can utilize the price changes resulting from investor vigilance to reward good management decisions. They often do so by tying the compensation of the top corporate officers to stock performance. How? Rather than paying these officers entirely in the form of salaries, a board of directors can integrate **stock options** into the compensation package of top executives. On the one hand, when good decisions drive the stock price up, the executives' options will be very valuable. On the other hand, if bad decisions cause the stock price to fall, then the options will have little or no value.

Stock options

The option to buy a specified number of shares of the firm's stock at a designated price. The designated price is generally set so that the options will be quite valuable if the firm's shares increase in price but of little value if their price falls. Thus, when used to compensate top managers, stock options provide a strong incentive to follow policies that will increase the value of the firm.

Stock Market Performance: The Historical Record

Even after considering the recent decline in the stock market, on the whole investors in American stocks have done exceedingly well. Furthermore, this has been true over a lengthy period of time. During the last two centuries, after adjustment for inflation, corporate stocks have yielded a real return of approximately 7 percent per year, compared with a real return of about 3 percent for bonds. The historic returns derived from savings accounts and money market mutual funds are even lower. A 7 percent real return may not sound particularly good, but when it is compounded, it means that the real value of your investment will double every ten years. In contrast, it will take twenty-three years to double your money at a 3 percent interest return.[2]

The Standard and Poor's 500 Index (S&P 500) is one measure of the performance of the broad stock market. This index factors in the value of dividends as if they were reinvested in the market. Thus, it provides a measure of the rate of return received by investors in the form of both dividends and changes in share prices. **EXHIBIT 1** presents data on the real rate of return earned by stockholders each year since 1950 as measured by the changes in the S&P 500 during the year. The compound annual nominal rate of return of the S&P 500 was 10.2 percent during the fifty-eight-year period. Even after adjustment for inflation, the real compound annual return was 6.5 percent for the entire period. The returns during the 1980s and 1990s were even higher. Since 2000, however, the returns have not been as high, and during 2008 alone investors experienced a negative 37 percent return.

Exhibit 1 highlights one of the risks that accompanies the ownership of stock: The returns and therefore the value of the stock can be quite volatile. The broad stock market, as measured by the S&P 500, provided double-digit returns during thirty-five of the fifty-eight years between 1950 and 2008, but the returns were negative during fourteen of those years. Stock market investors can never be sure what return they will earn or what the value of their stock holdings will be at a specified time in the future.

But this volatility is a big reason that stocks yield a significantly higher return than savings accounts, money market certificates, and corporate or government bonds, all of which guarantee you a given nominal return in the future. Because most people value the additional certainty in the yields that bonds and savings accounts provide over stocks, the average return on stocks has to be higher to attract investors away from financial assets with more predictable returns.

Given the rather large decline in the stock market since October 2007, some might think that the stock market is no longer a good investment. However, even if one would have started a regular monthly investment program at just about the worst possible time in the history of the U.S. stock market—just prior to the crash of 1929 and the Great Depression of the 1930s in which the value of stocks declined by almost 90 percent—one would still have earned a better return within four years than a person who had invested

---

[2]You can approximate the number of years it will take to double your funds at alternative interest rates by simply dividing the yield into 70. This is sometimes referred to as the rule of 70.

EXHIBIT 1
Annual Return for Stocks, 1950–2008

During the past fifty-eight years, the broad S&P 500 indicates that stock investors earned a 10.2 percent compound annual rate of return. Double-digit returns were earned in thirty-five of the fifty-eight years, whereas returns were negative during only fourteen of the years.

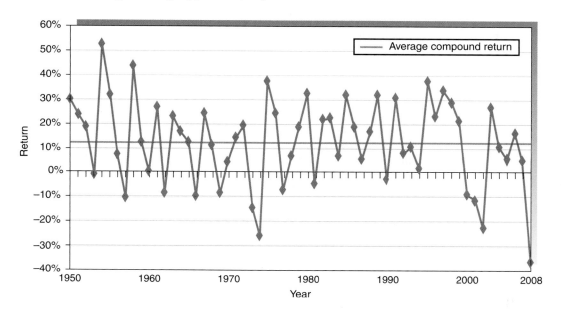

Source: Global Financial Data, http://www.globalfindata.com; and Standard & Poor's, http://www.standardandpoors.com.

in U.S. Treasury bills and would have ended up with a 13 percent nominal return (or an 11 percent real return) over the next thirty years. In fact, with stock prices now lower than they were a few years ago, this actually may be particularly good time to begin investing in the stock market.

The Interest Rate, the Value of Future Income, and Stock Prices

The present value of the firm's expected future net earnings (profit) underlies today's price of a firm's stock. What those future profits are worth to an investor today depends on three things: (1) the expected size of future net earnings, (2) when these earnings will be achieved, and (3) how much the investor discounts the future income. The last depends on the interest rate. As we noted in an earlier chapter, the present-value procedure can be used to determine the current value of any future income (or cost) stream. If *D* represents dividends (and gains from a higher stock price) earned in various years in the future (indicated by the subscripts) and *i* represents the discount or interest rate, the present value of the future income stream is:

$$PV = \frac{D_1}{(1 + i)} + \frac{D_2}{(1 + i)^2} + \cdots + \frac{D_3}{(1 + i)^3}$$

As this formula shows, a higher interest rate will reduce the present value of future revenues (returns), including those derived from stocks. This is true even if the size of the future returns is not affected by changes in the interest rate.

Stock analysts often stress that lower interest rates are good for the stock market. This should not be surprising because the lower rates of interest will increase the value of future income (and capital gains). For a specific annual income stream in perpetuity, the present value is equal simply to R/i, where R is the annual revenue stream and i is the interest rate. Thus, for example, when the interest rate is 12.5 percent, the discounted value of $10 of future income to be received each year in perpetuity is $80 ($10 divided by 0.125), eight times the stream of earnings. But when the interest rate is 5 percent, the discounted value of this same income stream is $200 ($10 divided by 0.05), or twenty times the stream of earnings. Therefore, if the $10 represented the expected future income stream from a share of stock, the present value of the income stream would be higher when the interest rate was lower. Other things being constant, lower interest rates will increase the value of future income and thereby increase the market value of stocks.

How can one tell whether stock prices are high or low? The answer to that question depends on both the interest rate and expectations about the future income generated by the stock (or bundle of stocks). The price/earnings (P/E) ratio provides information on the price of a stock relative to its current earnings. It is interesting to look at the historical path of the P/E ratio and observe how it has responded to changes in interest rates and business-cycle conditions. Of course, the latter is likely to influence the future earnings prospects of business firms.

EXHIBIT 2 presents data on the P/E ratio over the 1950–2008 period for the stocks included in the S&P 500. The P/E ratio average during this lengthy period was 17. From the early 1950s through the mid-1990s, the P/E ratio ranged from a low of 8 to a high of 24. During the 1960s, the economy grew rapidly and both the inflation and interest rates

---

EXHIBIT 2
Price/Earnings Ratio, 1950–2008

Since 1950, the average price/earnings ratio of the S&P 500 has been around 17. This ratio was between 8 and 24 throughout the 1951–1997 period. It was persistently near the lower end of this range (between 8 and 10) during the 1970s. It rose during the period 1985–1997 and eventually soared above 30 during the period 1998–2002. A combination of stock price declines and higher earnings as the economy recovered from the 2001 recession caused the price/earnings ratio to recede, but it soared to over 30 in 2008, primarily because of a sharp decline in earnings during the financial crisis.

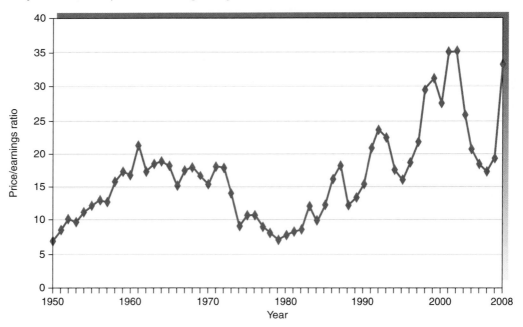

Source: Standard & Poor's, http://www.standardandpoor's.com.

were relatively low. Throughout most of that period, the P/E ratio was near 20. The 1970s was a period of both high inflation and high interest rates. As we just indicated, high interest rates will reduce the value of future income. Reflecting this factor, the P/E ratio during the 1970s was near 10 throughout the decade, considerably lower than during the 1960s.

As the economy grew rapidly, and both the inflation rate and interest rates declined and remained at a low level during the 1984–1997 period, the P/E ratio rose sharply. By the mid-1990s, it had risen to the 20 to 25 range, quite high by historical standards. But the stock market continued to boom, and by 1999 the P/E ratio had risen to an extremely high level, 31.7. By the late 1990s, there was considerable talk of a "stock market bubble," high stock prices that could not be maintained because they were out of line with the future earning prospects of business firms. The bubble burst and stock prices fell sharply. As a result, the S&P 500 lost nearly 50 percent of its value during 2000–2002 (see Exhibit 1). As the economy recovered from the recession of 2001, corporate earnings picked up and the P/E ratio receded. By 2005–2006, the P/E ratio had returned closer to its historical average, but once again rose above 30 in 2008. This increase was primarily the result of sharp reductions in earnings and the marking down of bad assets during the 2008 financial crisis.

The Random Walk Theory of the Stock Market

Most economists adhere to the **random walk theory** of stock prices. According to this theory, current stock prices already reflect all available information that is known or can be predicted with any degree of accuracy, including information about the future state of corporate earnings, interest rates, the health of the economy, and other factors that influence stock prices. In other words, current stock prices will already reflect the best information currently available. In the future, the direction of stock prices will be driven by surprise occurrences—things that differ from what people are currently anticipating. By their very nature, these factors are unpredictable. If they were predictable, they would already be reflected in current stock prices.

The random walk theory applies to the price of a specific stock as well as to the market as a whole. The prices of specific stocks will reflect their future earnings prospects. The stock prices of firms with attractive future profit potential will be high relative to their current earnings. Consequently, their current prices will already reflect their attractive future earnings prospects. The opposite will be true for firms with poor future prospects. Although numerous factors affect the future price of any specific stock, changes in the current price will be driven by changes that differ from current expectations. Thus, because the future prices of both specific stocks and the market as a whole are driven by unexpected and unpredictable factors, no one can consistently forecast their future path with any degree of accuracy.

Random walk theory

The theory that current stock prices already reflect known information about the future. Therefore, the future movement of stock prices will be determined by surprise occurrences. This will cause them to change in a random fashion.

How the Ordinary Investor Can Beat the Experts

Historically, ordinary Americans have often refrained from investing in the stock market because of the risks involved. But there are ways this risk can be reduced, particularly for long-term investments. The value of any specific stock can rise or fall by a huge amount within a relatively short time period. But the risk accompanying these movements can be reduced by holding a diverse **portfolio**, a collection of stocks characterized by relatively small holdings of a large number of companies in different markets and industries. **Equity mutual funds** make this possible. They provide the ordinary investor with a low-cost method of owning a diverse bundle of stocks. An equity mutual fund is a corporation that buys and holds shares of stock in many firms. This diversification puts the law of large

Portfolio

All the stocks, bonds, or other securities held by an individual or corporation for investment purposes.

Equity mutual fund

A corporation that pools the funds of investors, including small investors, and uses them to purchase a bundle of stocks.

numbers to work for you. Whereas some of the investments in a diversified portfolio will do poorly, others will do extremely well. The performance of the latter will offset that of the former, and the rate of return will converge toward the average. Remember, the average real return of equities has been substantially higher than for bonds, savings accounts, and other readily accessible methods of saving.

As **EXHIBIT 3** shows, there was a huge increase in the quantity of funds flowing into mutual funds during the 1990s. The value of mutual fund investments increased from $246 billion in 1990 to approximately $4 trillion in 1999–2000. Although equity mutual fund investments declined as stock prices fell during 2000–2002, they rebounded and had soared to $6.5 trillion by 2007 before falling over 43 percent to a value of $3.7 trillion in 2008. They now account for about 30 percent of all publicly traded U.S. stocks.

EXHIBIT 3
Value of Equity Mutual Funds

The amount of money that people put into U.S. equity mutual funds, in order to hold shares in the ownership of stocks, rose dramatically in the 1990s. Purchasing shares in a mutual fund is a simple way for an individual to buy and hold an interest in a large variety of stocks with one purchase. Due to the recent financial crisis, the value of equity mutual funds fell by 43 percent from 2007 to 2008.

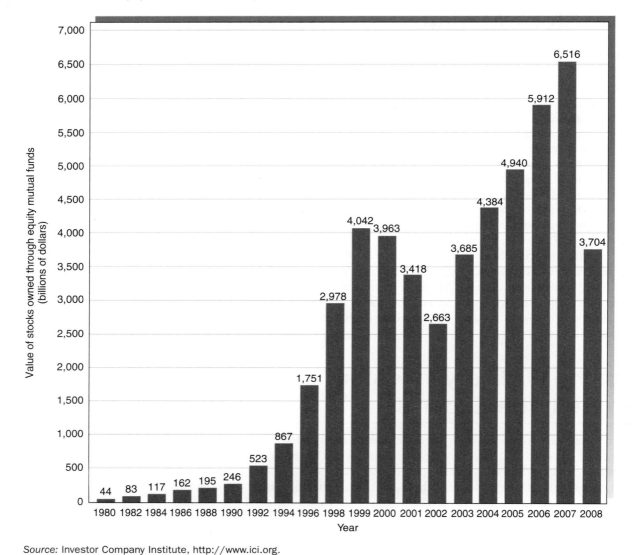

Source: Investor Company Institute, http://www.ici.org.

A second source of risk facing the stock market investor is the possibility that nearly all stocks in the market can rise or fall together when expectations about the entire economy change. This has happened on several occasions. For example, on October 19, 1987, the stocks listed in the Dow Jones Industrial Average lost more than 22 percent of their value in just one trading day. The high-tech stocks listed on the NASDAQ exchange lost about 70 percent of their value during 2000 and 2001; and most recently the S&P 500 lost about 57 percent of its value between October 2007 and March 2009. However, the risks accompanying such short-term movements can be substantially reduced if an investor either continually adds to or holds a diverse portfolio of stocks over a lengthy period of time, say, thirty or thirty-five years.

EXHIBIT 4 illustrates this point. This exhibit shows the highest and lowest real returns (the returns adjusted for inflation) earned from stock market investments for periods of varying lengths between the years 1871 and 2008. The exhibit assumes that the investor paid a fixed amount annually into a mutual fund that mirrored the S&P 500, a basket of stocks thought to represent the market as a whole. Clearly, huge swings are possible when stocks are held for only a short time period. During the 1871–2008 period, the single-year returns of the S&P 500 ranged from 47.2 percent to –40.8 percent. Even over a five-year period, the compound annual returns ranged from 29.8 percent to –16.7 percent. Note that the "best returns" and "worst returns" converged as the length of the investment period increased. When a thirty-five-year period was considered, the compound annual return for the best thirty-five years between 1871 and 2008 was 9.5 percent, compared with 2.7 percent for the worst thirty-five years.[3] Thus, the annual real return of stocks during the worst-case scenario was about the same as the real return for bonds. Furthermore, the

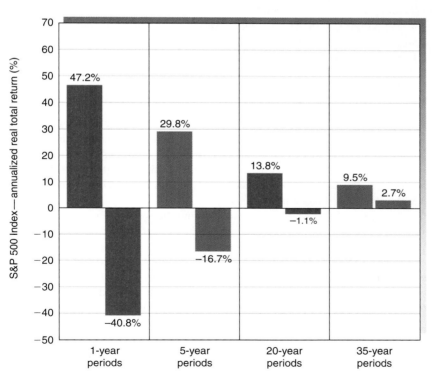

EXHIBIT 4
Stocks Are Less Risky When Held for a Lengthy Time Period

This exhibit shows the best and the worst annualized real performance for each investment period from 1871 to 2008. It shows that there is less risk of a low or negative return when an investment in a portfolio of stocks (S&P 500) is held for a longer period of time.

Source: Liqun Liu, Andrew J. Rettenmaier, and Zijun Wang, "Social Security and Market Risk," National Center for Policy Analysis Working Paper Number 244 (July 2001). The returns are based on the assumption that an individual invests a fixed amount for each year in the investment period. Data updated through 2008.

[3]Based on Liqun Liu, Andrew J. Rettenmaier, and Zijun Wang, "Social Security and Market Risk," *National Center for Policy Analysis Working Paper Number 244* (July 2001). Data updated through 2008.

Are stocks riskier than bonds? If held for only a short time— five years, for example—stocks are riskier. However, when held over lengthy periods, such as twenty or thirty years, historically the rate of return on stocks has been both higher and less variable than that of bonds. What does this imply for people in their twenties and thirties who are saving for their retire- ment? Where should they put their funds?

© Zephyr Picture/Index Stock Imagery

annual real rate of return from the stock investments during the period was 7 percent— more than twice the comparable rate for bonds.

The bottom line is this: When held over a lengthy period, a diverse portfolio of stocks has yielded a high rate of return, and the variation in that return has been low. Thus, for the long-term investor, such as a person saving for his or her retirement years, a diverse portfolio of stocks is not particularly risky.

The Advantages of Indexed Mutual Funds

When purchasing a mutual fund, the investor can choose either a managed or an indexed fund. A **managed equity mutual fund** is one in which an "expert," generally supported by a research staff, tries to pick and choose the stock holdings of the fund in a manner that will maximize its rate of return. In contrast, an **indexed equity mutual fund** merely holds stocks in the same proportion as they exist in a broad stock market index like the S&P 500 or the Dow Jones Industrials.

In the case of indexed funds, neither comprehensive research nor extensive stock trading is needed because the fund merely seeks to mirror the index and earn the rate of return of the broad market that it represents. Thus, because they do not spend much on either research or stock trading, the operating costs of indexed funds are substantially lower than they are for managed funds. Therefore, they are able to charge lower fees, which means that a larger share of the investor's money flows directly into the purchase of stock.

As a result, the average rate of return yielded by a broad indexed fund beats the return of almost all managed mutual funds when comparisons are made over periods of time such as a decade. This is not surprising because, as the random walk theory indicates, not even the experts will be able to forecast consistently the future direction of stock prices with any degree of accuracy. Over the typical ten-year period, the S&P 500 has yielded a higher return than 85 percent of actively managed funds. And over twenty-year periods, mutual funds indexed to the S&P 500 have generally outperformed about 98 percent of actively managed funds.[4] Thus, the odds are very low, about 1 in 50, that you or anyone else will

Managed equity mutual fund

An equity mutual fund that has a portfolio manager who decides what stocks will be held in the fund and when they will be bought or sold. A research staff generally provides support for the fund manager.

Indexed equity mutual fund

An equity mutual fund that holds a portfolio of stocks that matches their share (or weight) in a broad stock mar- ket index such as the S&P 500. The overhead of these funds is usually quite low because their expenses on stock trading and research are low.

[4]See Jeremy J. Siegel, *Stocks for the Long Run*, 3rd ed. (New York: McGraw-Hill, 2002), 342–43.

be able to select an actively managed fund that will do better than the market average *over the long run.*

Should You Invest in a Fund Because of Its Past Performance?

People marketing mutual funds often encourage customers to invest in mutual funds that have yielded high rates of return in the past. This sounds like a good strategy, but history indicates that it is not. Mutual funds with outstanding records over a five- or ten-year period often perform poorly in the future. On average, the top funds during the 1970s underperformed during the 1980s. For example, the top fund (Twentieth Century Growth) during the 1970s fell to 176th place in the 1980s. The second-place fund in the 1970s (Templeton Growth) fell to 126th place in the 1980s. The fund "44 Wall Street" was in fourth place in the 1970s, but fell to 309th place in the 1980s.

The same pattern has presented itself in recent years. The top twenty managed equity funds of the 1980s outperformed the S&P 500 by 3.9 percent per year over the course of the decade. But if investors entering the market in 1990 thought they would beat the market by choosing the "hot" funds of the 1980s, they would have been disappointed. The top twenty funds of the 1980s underperformed the S&P 500 by 1.2 percent per year during the 1990s. The "hot" funds in the late 1990s ended up in similar shape. For example, during the period 1998–1999, the top-performing managed fund in the marketplace was Van Wagoner's Emerging Growth fund. During this time, the Emerging Growth fund yielded an astonishing 105.52 percent average annual return. But over the two-year period 2000–2001, the fund ranked 1,106th, earning an average annual return of *minus* 43.54 percent.[5]

Why is past performance such an unreliable indicator? Two factors provide insight on the answer to this question. First, some of the mutual funds with above-average returns during a period were merely lucky. After all, if you flip a coin 100 times, you will not always get 50 heads and 50 tails. Sometimes, the coin will come up heads maybe 60 times out of 100. But this does not mean you can expect 60 heads during the next sequence of 100. So it is with stock market mutual funds. Given that there are a large number of funds, some of them will have above-average performance for a time period. But this does not mean that the above-average performance can be expected in the future.

Second, a strategy that works well in one environment, inflationary conditions, for example, is often disastrous when conditions change. For example, mutual funds with substantial holdings of gold-mining companies did exceedingly well during the inflationary 1970s. But their performance was disastrous during the 1980s and 1990s as the inflation was brought under control. Similarly, some mutual funds that performed well during the bull market of the 1990s were among the worst performers during the bear market that began in 2000.

Virtually none of the experts are able to "beat the market average" consistently over lengthy time periods and changing market conditions. Thus, broad market indexes outperform the stock pickers in the long run. This is something you will not often hear from brokerage firms and other experts trying to sell their services to you. But knowing this will make you a smarter investor.

---

[5]Burton G. Malkiel, *A Random Walk Down Wall Street: The Time Tested Strategy for Successful Investing* (New York: W.W. Norton & Company, 2003), 189–90.

KEY POINTS

▼ The stock market makes it possible for investors without either specialized business skills or the time to become involved in the operation of a business firm to share in the risks and opportunities that accompany the ownership of corporate businesses.

▼ During the last two centuries, after adjustment for inflation, corporate stocks have yielded a real return of approximately 7 percent per year, compared with a real return of about 3 percent for bonds and even lower yields for savings accounts and money market mutual funds.

▼ Most economists adhere to the random walk theory of stock prices. According to this theory, current stock prices already reflect all information about factors influencing stock prices that is known or can be forecast with any degree of accuracy. Thus, the future direction of stock prices will be driven by surprise occurrences and, as a result, no one will be able to forecast future stock prices with any degree of accuracy.

▼ Buying and selling individual stocks without specialized knowledge for a quick profit is very risky. But holding a diverse portfolio of unrelated stocks and holding them for long periods of time greatly reduces the risk of investing in the stock market.

▼ An equity mutual fund that is tied to a broad stock market index like the S&P 500 provides an attractive method for long-term investors to obtain relatively high yields with minimal risk. Indexed mutual funds have substantially lower operating costs than managed funds because they engage in less trading and have no need for either a market expert or research staff.

▼ The recent financial crisis has resulted in a substantial decline in stock prices. The S&P 500 lost about 57 percent of its value between October 2007 and March 2009. However, based on historical evidence, this does not necessarily imply that now is a bad time to invest in the stock market.

CRITICAL ANALYSIS QUESTIONS

*1. A friend just inherited $50,000. She informs you of her investment plans and asks for your advice. "I want to put it into the stock market and use it for my retirement in thirty years. What do you think is the best plan that will provide high returns at a relatively low risk?" What answer would you give? Explain.

2. Suppose that more expansionary monetary policy leads to inflation and higher nominal interest rates. How is this likely to affect the value of stocks? Explain.

*3. Microsoft stock rose from less than $10 in 1995 to more than $100 per share in 2000. Microsoft has made sizable profits but never paid a dividend. Why were people willing to pay such a high price knowing that they might not get dividends for many years?

4. If an investment adviser gives you some hot new stock tip, is it likely to be a "sure thing"? Why or why not? If you have a stockbroker and purchase the stocks promoted by the broker, are you likely to earn a high return on your stock investments? Why or why not?

*5. The stocks of some corporations that have never made a profit, especially those in high-technology industries, have risen in price. What causes investors to be willing to buy these stocks?

6. What is an indexed equity mutual fund? What is a managed equity mutual fund? How will the administrative costs of the two differ?

7. What is the random walk theory of stock prices? What does it indicate about the ability of "experts" to forecast accurately the future direction of stock prices?

8. Congress is currently considering legislation that would increase both the tax on dividends and the tax on capital gains derived from the appreciation of assets. How would an increase in the tax rate applied to dividends and capital gains income affect stock prices? Why?

9. Are stocks a risky investment? How can one reduce the risk accompanying stock market investments?

*Asterisk denotes questions for which answers are given in Appendix B.

The Crisis of 2008: Causes and Lessons for the Future

FOCUS

- Why did housing prices rise rapidly during 2001–2005 and then fall in the years immediately following? Did regulation play a role? Did monetary policy contribute to the housing boom and bust?

- What caused the economic Crisis of 2008?

- What lessons should we learn from the Crisis of 2008?

U.S. housing policies are the root cause of the current financial crisis. Other players—"greedy" investment bankers; foolish investors; imprudent bankers; incompetent rating agencies; irresponsible housing speculators; shortsighted homeowners; and predatory mortgage brokers, lenders, and borrowers—all played a part, but they were only following the economic incentives that government policy laid out for them.

—Peter J. Wallison[1]

[1]Peter J. Wallison, "Cause and Effect: Government Policies and the Financial Crisis," AEI Financial Services Outlook, http://www.aei.org/publication29015.

he headlines of 2008 were dominated by falling housing prices, rising default and foreclosure rates, failure of large investment banks, and huge bailouts arranged by both the Federal Reserve and the U.S. Treasury. The Crisis of 2008 substantially reduced the wealth of most Americans and generated widespread concern about the future of the U.S. economy. This crisis and the response to it will probably be the most important macroeconomic event of our lives. Thus, it is vitally important for each of us to understand what happened, why things went wrong, and the lessons that need to be learned from the experience.

Let's take a closer look at the key events leading up to the crisis and the underlying factors that generated the collapse. ■

Key Events Leading Up to the Crisis

The housing boom and bust during the first seven years of this century are central to understanding the economic events of 2008. As **EXHIBIT 1** shows, housing prices were relatively stable during the 1990s, but they began to increase rapidly toward the end of the decade. By 2002, housing prices were booming. Between January 2002 and mid-year 2006, housing prices increased by a whopping 87 percent. This translates to an annual growth rate of approximately 13 percent. But the housing boom began to wane in 2006. Housing prices leveled off, and by the end of 2006, they were falling. The boom had turned to a bust, and the housing price decline continued throughout 2007 and 2008. By year-end 2008, housing prices were approximately 30 percent below their 2006 peak.

EXHIBIT 1
Annual Change in the Price of Existing Houses, 1987–2008

Housing prices increased slowly during the 1990s, but they began rising more rapidly toward the end of the decade. Between January 2002 and mid-year 2006, housing prices increased by a whopping 87 percent. But the boom turned to a bust during the second half of 2006, and the housing price decline continued throughout 2007–2008.

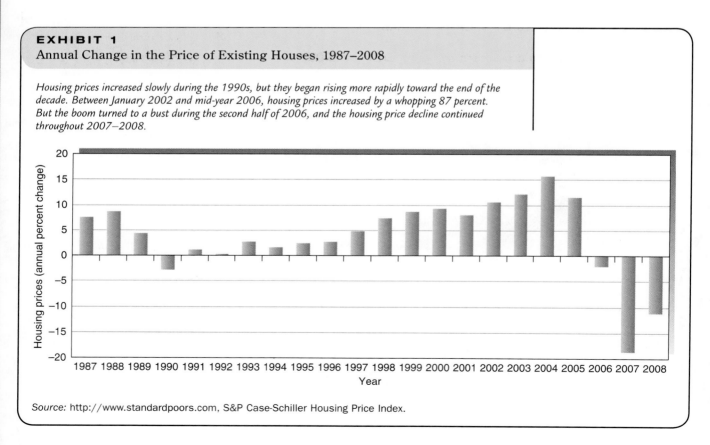

Source: http://www.standardpoors.com, S&P Case-Schiller Housing Price Index.

EXHIBIT 2a a presents data on the **mortgage default rate** from 1979 through 2008. (*Note:* The default rate is also known as the serious delinquency rate.) As these figures illustrate, the default rate fluctuated, within a narrow range, around 2 percent prior to 2006. It increased only slightly during the recessions of 1982, 1990, and 2001.

However, even though the economy was relatively strong and unemployment low, the default rate began to increase sharply during the second half of 2006. By the fourth quarter of 2007, it had already risen to 3.6 percent, up from 2.0 percent in the second quarter of 2006. The increase continued and the default rate reached 5.2 percent in 2008.

As Exhibit 2b illustrates, the pattern of the mortgage **foreclosure rate** was similar. It fluctuated between 0.2 and 0.5 during 1978–2005. The recessions of 1982–1983, 1990, and 2001 exerted little impact on the foreclosure rate. However, like the mortgage default rate, the foreclosure rate started to increase during the second half of 2006, and it tripled over the next two years.

During 2008, housing prices were falling, default rates were increasing, and the confidence of both consumers and investors was deteriorating. These conditions were reinforced by sharply rising prices of crude oil, which pushed gasoline prices to more than $4 per gallon during the first half of the year. Against this background, the stock market

Mortgage default rate

The percentage of home mortgages on which the borrower is late by ninety days or more with the payments on the loan or it is in the foreclosure process. This rate is sometimes referred to as the serious delinquency rate.

Foreclosure rate

The percentage of home mortgages on which the lender has started the process of taking ownership of the property because the borrower has failed to make the monthly payments.

EXHIBIT 2
Mortgage Default and Housing Foreclosure Rates, 1979–2008

As frame (a) shows, the mortgage default rate fluctuated within a narrow range around 2 percent for more than two decades prior to 2006. It increased only slightly during the recessions of 1982, 1990, and 2001 but started to increase in the second half of 2006 and soared to more than 5 percent in 2008. As frame (b) shows, the foreclosure rate followed a similar pattern. It ranged between 0.2 and 0.5 percent prior to 2006, before soaring to 1.2 percent in 2008.

(a) Mortgage default rate

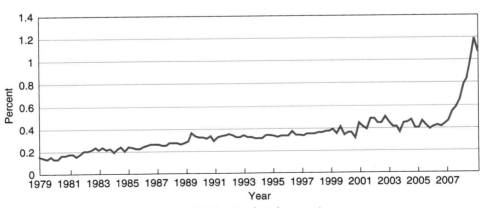

(b) Housing foreclosure rate

Source: http://mbaa.org, *National Delinquency Survey.*

EXHIBIT 3

Changes in Stock Prices, 1996–2009

Stock prices as measured by the Standard and Poors 500 are shown here. Note how stock prices fell by approximately 55 percent between October 2007 and March 2009. This collapse eroded the wealth and endangered the retirement savings of many Americans.

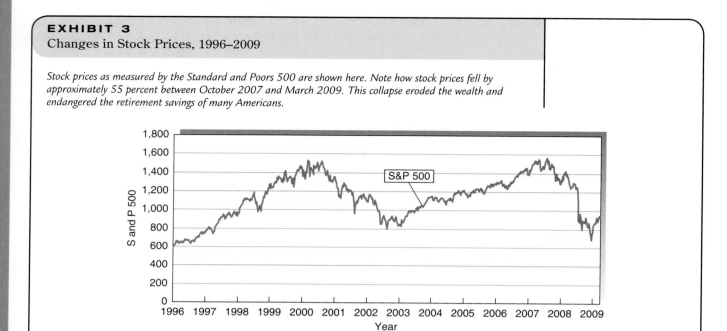

Source: http://www.standardpoors.com.

took a huge tumble. As **EXHIBIT 3** shows, the S&P 500 index of stock prices fell by 55 percent between October 2007 and March 2009. This collapse eroded the wealth and endangered the retirement savings of many Americans.

What Caused the Crisis of 2008?

Why did housing prices rise rapidly, then level off, and eventually collapse? Why did the mortgage default and housing foreclosure rates increase rapidly well before the start of the recession, which did not begin until December 2007? Why are the recent default and foreclosure rates so much higher than the rates of earlier years, including those of prior recessions? Why did large, and seemingly strong, investment banks like Bear Stearns and Lehman Brothers run into financial troubles so quickly? Four factors combine to provide the answers to all of these questions.[2]

FACTOR 1: CHANGE IN MORTGAGE LENDING STANDARDS

The lending standards for home mortgage loans changed substantially beginning in the mid-1990s. The looser lending standards did not just happen. They were the result of federal policy designed to promote more home ownership among households with incomes below the median. Home ownership is a worthy goal, but it was not pursued directly through transparent budget allocations and subsidies to homebuyers. Instead, the federal government imposed a complex set of regulations and regulatory mandates that forced various lending institutions to extend more loans to low- and moderate-income households. To meet these mandates, lenders had to lower their standards. By the early years of the twenty-first century, it was possible to borrow more (relative to your income) and purchase a house or condo with a lower down payment than was the case a decade earlier.

[2]For additional details on the Crisis of 2008, see Thomas Sowell, *The Housing Boom and Bust* (New York: Basic Books, 2009); Stan J. Liebowitz, "Anatomy of a Train Wreck: Causes of the Mortgage Meltdown," Ch. 13 in Randall G. Holcombe and Benjamin Powell, eds, *Housing America: Building Out of a Crisis* (New Brunswick, NJ: Transaction Publishers, 2009); Peter J. Wallison, "Cause and Effect: Government Policies and the Financial Crisis," *AEI Financial Services Outlook.* http://www.aei.org/publication29015; and Lawrence H. White, "How Did We Get Into This Financial Mess?" (Cato Institute: Briefing Paper 110, November 18, 2008) available at http://www.cato.org/pub_display.php?pub_id=9788.

The Federal National Mortgage Association and Federal Home Loan Mortgage Corporation, commonly known as Fannie Mae and Freddie Mac, played a central role in this relaxation of mortgage lending standards. These two entities were created by Congress to help provide liquidity in secondary mortgage markets. Fannie Mae, established by the federal government in 1938, was spun off as a "government-sponsored enterprise" (GSE) in 1968. Freddie Mac was created in 1970 as another GSE to provide competition for Fannie Mae.

Fannie Mae and Freddie Mac were privately owned (for profit) businesses, but, because of their federal sponsorship, it was widely perceived that the government would back their bonds if they ever ran into financial trouble. As a result, Fannie and Freddie were able to borrow funds at 50–75 **basis points** cheaper than private lenders. This gave them a competitive advantage, and they were highly profitable for many years. However, the GSE structure also meant that they were asked to serve two masters: their stockholders, who were interested in profitability, and Congress and federal regulators, who predictably were more interested in political objectives.

As a result of their GSE structure, Fannie Mae and Freddie Mac were highly political. The top management of Fannie and Freddie provided key congressional leaders with large political contributions and often hired away congressional staffers into high-paying jobs lobbying their former bosses. Between the 2000 and 2008 election cycles, high-level managers and other employees of Fannie Mae and Freddie Mac contributed more than $14.6 million to the campaign funds of dozens of senators and representatives, most of whom were on congressional committees important for the protection of their privileged status.

The lobbying activities of Fannie Mae and Freddie Mac were legendary. Between 1998 and 2008, Fannie spent $79.5 million and Freddie spent $94.9 million on congressional lobbying, placing them among the biggest spenders on these activities. They also set up "partnership offices" in the districts and states of important legislators, often hiring the relatives of these lawmakers to staff these local offices.[3] The politicians, for their part, and the regulators who answered to them fashioned rules that made very high profits possible for the GSEs, at least in the short run. Although it was a relationship that reflected political favoritism (some would say corruption), members of Congress, particularly those involved in banking regulation, were highly supportive of the arrangement.

Fannie Mae and Freddie Mac did not originate mortgages. Instead, they purchased the mortgages originated by banks, mortgage brokers, and other lenders. Propelled by their cheaper access to funds, Fannie Mae and Freddie Mac grew rapidly during the 1990s. As **EXHIBIT 4** shows, the share of all mortgages held by Fannie Mae and Freddie Mac jumped from 25 percent in 1990 to 45 percent in 2001. Their share has fluctuated around 40 percent since 2001. Their dominance of the **secondary mortgage market** was even greater. During the decade prior to their insolvency and takeover by the federal government during the summer of 2008, Fannie Mae and Freddie Mac purchased about 90 percent of the mortgages sold in the secondary market. Because of this dominance, their lending practices exerted a huge impact on the standards accepted by mortgage originators.

Responding to earlier congressional legislation, the Department of Housing and Urban Development (HUD) imposed regulations designed to make housing more affordable. The HUD mandates, adopted in 1995, required Fannie Mae and Freddie Mac to extend a larger share of their loans to low- and moderate-income households. For example, under the HUD mandates, 40 percent of new loans financed by Fannie Mae and Freddie Mac in 1996 had to go to borrowers with incomes below the median. This mandated share was steadily increased to 50 percent in 2000 and 56 percent in 2008. Similar increases were mandated for borrowers with incomes of less than 60 percent of the median. Moreover, in 1999, HUD guidelines required Fannie Mae and Freddie Mac to accept smaller down payments and extend larger loans relative to income.

Basis points

One one-hundredth of a percentage point. Thus, 100 basis points are equivalent to one percentage point.

Secondary mortgage market

A market in which mortgages originated by a lender are sold to another financial institution. In recent years, the major buyers in this market have been Fannie Mae, Freddie Mac, and large investment banks.

---

[3]For additional details, see Peter J. Wallison and Charles W. Calomiris, "The Destruction of Fannie Mae and Freddie Mac," American Enterprise Institute, online (posted Tuesday, September 30, 2008). Also see Common Cause, "Ask Yourself Why . . . They Didn't See This Coming" (September 24, 2008), available at http://www.commoncause.org/site/pp.asp?c=dkLNK1MQIwG&b=4542875; and Center for Responsive Politics, "Lobbying: Top Spenders" (2008), available at http://www.opensecrets.org/lobby/top.php?indexType=s.

EXHIBIT 4

The Share of Total Outstanding Mortgages Held by Fannie Mae and Freddie Mac, 1990–2008

Fannie Mae and Freddie Mac dominated the mortgage market for many years. Because of their government sponsorship, they were able to obtain funds cheaper than private firms. They held 45 percent of all mortgages in 2001, up from 25 percent in 1990. During 2001–2008, their share fluctuated around 40 percent. Their dominance of the secondary market, where loans are purchased from originators, is even greater. In July 2008, they were declared insolvent and taken over by the U.S. Treasury.

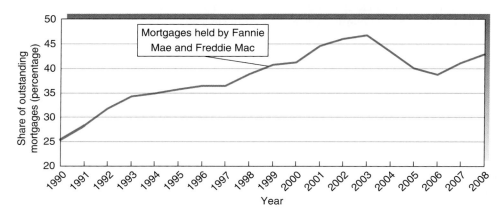

Source: Office of Federal Housing Enterprise Oversight, http://www.ofheo.gov.

Subprime loan

A loan made to a borrower with blemished credit or one who provides only limited documentation of income, employment history, and other indicators of creditworthiness.

FICO score

A credit score measuring a borrower's likely ability to repay a loan. A person's FICO score will range between 300 and 850. A score of 700 or more indicates that the borrower's credit standing is good. FICO is an acronym for the Fair Isaac Corporation, the creators of the FICO score.

Alt-A loans

Loans extended with little documentation and/or verification of the borrowers' income, employment, and other indicators of their ability to repay. Because of this poor documentation, these loans are risky.

The policies of Fannie Mae and Freddie Mac exerted an enormous impact on the actions of banks and other mortgage lenders. Recognizing that riskier loans could be passed on to Fannie and Freddie, mortgage originators had less incentive to scrutinize the creditworthiness of borrowers and more incentive to reduce the required down payment, in order to sell more mortgages. After all, when the mortgages were soon sold to Fannie or Freddie, the risk was transferred to them also. The bottom line: required down payments were reduced and the accepted credit standards lowered.

Modifications to the Community Reinvestment Act (CRA) in 1995 also loosened mortgage-lending standards. These changes required banks to meet numeric goals based on the low-income and minority population of their service areas when extending mortgage loans. In order to meet these requirements, many banks, especially those in urban areas, were forced to reduce their lending standards and extend more loans to borrowers who did not meet the conventional credit criteria.

The lower standards resulting from the GSE and CRA regulations reduced lending standards across the board. Lenders could hardly offer low down payment loans and larger mortgages relative to housing value on **subprime loans**, without offering similar terms to prime borrowers. As the regulations tightened, the share of loans extended to subprime borrowers steadily increased. **EXHIBIT 5** illustrates this point. Measured as a share of mortgages originated during the year, subprime mortgages rose from 4.5 percent in 1994 to 13.2 percent in 2000 and 20 percent in 2005 and 2006. (*Note:* Bank examiners consider a loan to be subprime if the borrower's **FICO score** is less than 660.) When the **Alt-A loans**, those extended without full documentation, were added to the subprime, a third of the mortgages extended in 2005–2006 were to borrowers with either poor or highly questionable credit records. At the same time, conventional loans for which borrowers were required to make at least a 20 percent down payment fell from two-thirds of the total in the early 1990s to only one-third in 2005–2006.

The shift from conventional loans to "creative finance" and "flexible standards," as the regulators called the new criteria, is highly important because the foreclosure rates for subprime loans ranges from seven to ten times the rate for conventional loans to prime borrowers. Predictably, the growing share of loans to those with weaker credit would lead to higher default and foreclosure rates.

FACTOR 2: PROLONGED LOW-INTEREST RATE POLICY OF THE FED DURING 2002–2004

Following the high and variable inflation rates of the 1970s, Federal Reserve policy focused on keeping the inflation rate low and stable. By the mid-1980s, the inflation rate had been reduced to 3 percent. Throughout 1985–1999, the Fed kept the inflation rate low and avoided abrupt year-to-year changes. In turn, the relative price stability reduced uncertainty and created an environment for both strong growth and economic stability. During this era, it was widely believed that price stability was the only objective that could be achieved with monetary policy, and if this objective was achieved, the monetary policy makers had done their job well.

However, as the lessons of this period began to dissipate, Fed policy makers, including Chairman Alan Greenspan, began to focus more on control of real variables such as employment and real GDP. Since 1999, the Fed has followed a stop–go policy. Monetary policy was expansionary just before Y2K, restrictive prior to the recession of 2001, and then highly expansionary during the recovery from that recession. As **EXHIBIT 6** shows, the Fed kept short-term interest rates at historic lows throughout 2002–2004. These extremely low short-term rates increased the demand for interest-sensitive goods like automobiles and housing.

The Fed's artificially low short-term rates substantially increased the attractiveness of **adjustable rate mortgages (ARM)** to both borrowers and lenders. As **EXHIBIT 7** shows, adjustable rate mortgages jumped from 10 percent of the total outstanding mortgages in 2000 to 21 percent in 2005. The low initial interest rates on adjustable rate mortgages made it possible for homebuyers to afford the monthly payments for larger, more expensive homes. This easy credit provided fuel for the housing boom. But the low rates and ARM loans also meant that as short-term interest rates increased from their historic low levels, home buyers would face a higher monthly payment two or three years in the future. Unsurprisingly, this is precisely what happened.

Adjustable rate mortgage (ARM)

A home loan in which the interest rate, and thus the monthly payment, is tied to a short-term rate like the one-year Treasury bill rate. Typically, the mortgage interest rate will be two or three percentage points above the related short-term rate. It will be reset at various time intervals (e.g., annually), and thus the interest rate and monthly payment will vary over the life of the loan.

EXHIBIT 5:

Subprime and Alt-A Mortgages as a Share of the Total, 1994–2007

Both subprime and Alt-A mortgages reflect loans to borrowers with a weak credit history. Note how the share of loans to borrowers in these two categories jumped from roughly 10 percent in 2001–2003 to 33 percent in 2005–2006.

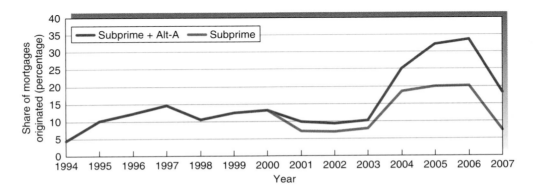

Source: The data for 1994–2000 are from Edward M. Gramlich, Financial Services Roundtable Annual Housing Policy Meeting, Chicago, Illinois (21 May 2004), http://www.federalreserve.gov/boarddocs/speeches/2004/20040521/default.htm. The data for 2001–2007 are from the Joint Center for Housing Studies of Harvard University, The State of the Nation's Housing 2008, http://www.jchs.harvard.edu/son/index.htm.

EXHIBIT 6
Fed Policy and Short-Term Interest Rates, 1995–2009

Here we show the federal funds and one-year Treasury bill interest rates. These short-term rates are reflective of monetary policy. Note how the Fed pushed these rates to historic lows (less than 2 percent) throughout 2002–2004 but then increased them substantially during 2005–2006. The low rates provided fuel for the housing price boom, but the rising rates led to higher interest rates and monthly payments on ARM loans, which helped push the mortgage default and foreclosure rates upward beginning in the second half of 2006.

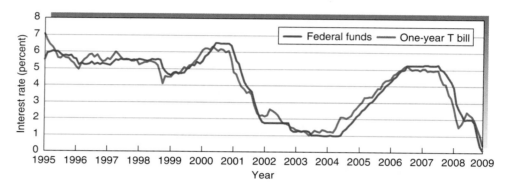

Sources: http://www.federalreserve.gov and http://www.economagic.com.

EXHIBIT 7
Adjustable Rate Mortgages (ARMs) as a Share of Total Outstanding Mortgages, 1990–2008

The interest rate and monthly payment on ARMs are tied to a short-term interest rate (e.g., the one-year Treasury bill rate). The Fed's low-interest rate policy of 2002–2004 increased the attractiveness of ARMs. Note how ARM loans increased as a share of total mortgages from 10 percent in 2000 to 21 percent in 2005.

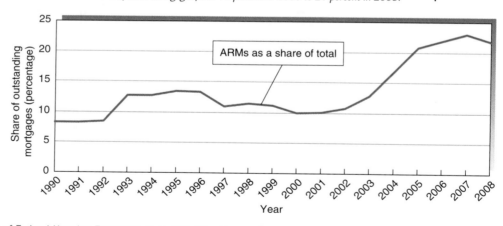

Source: Office of Federal Housing Enterprise Oversight, http://www.ofheo.gov.

By 2005, the expansionary monetary policy of 2002–2004 was clearly placing upward pressure on the general level of prices. The Fed responded with a shift to a more restrictive monetary policy, which pushed interest rates upward (see Exhibit 6). Many who purchased houses with little or no down payment and adjustable rate loans when interest rates were low during 2002–2004 faced substantially higher monthly payments as interest rates rose and the monthly payments on their ARM loans were reset during 2006 and 2007. These owners had virtually no equity in their homes. Therefore, when housing prices leveled off and began to decline during the second half of 2006, the default and foreclosure rates on these loans began to rise almost immediately (see Exhibits 1 and 2). Owners with little or no initial equity simply walked away as their outstanding loan exceeded the value of their house.

Essentially, the small down payment and ARMs combination made it possible for homebuyers to gamble with someone else's money. If housing prices rose, buyers could reap a sizable capital gain without risking much of their own investment capital. Based on the rising housing prices of 2000–2005, many of these homebuyers expected to sell the house for a profit and move on in a couple of years. There were even television programs and investment seminars pushing this strategy as the route to riches.

EXHIBIT 8 shows the foreclosure rates for fixed interest rate and ARM loans for both subprime and prime loans. Compared to their prime borrower counterparts, the foreclosure rate for subprime borrowers was approximately ten times higher for fixed rate mortgages and seven times higher for adjustable rate mortgages. These huge differentials explain why the increasing share of loans to subprime borrowers substantially increased the default and foreclosure rates.

As Exhibit 8 shows, there was no upward trend in the foreclosure rate on fixed interest rate loans for either prime or subprime borrowers during 2000–2008. On the other hand, the foreclosure rate on ARMs soared for both prime and subprime loans during 2006–2008. In fact, the percentage increase in foreclosures on ARM loans was higher for

EXHIBIT 8
The Foreclosure Rate of Fixed and Adjustable Rate Mortgages for Subprime and Prime Borrowers, 1998–2007

The foreclosure rates on fixed and adjustable interest rate mortgages are shown here for both subprime (frame a) and prime (frame b) borrowers. Note how the foreclosure rate was generally seven to ten times higher for subprime loans than for those to prime borrowers. As housing prices leveled off and declined in 2006–2008, the foreclosure rate on fixed interest rate mortgages did not change much. In contrast, the foreclosure rate for ARM loans soared beginning in the second half of 2006, and this was true for ARM loans to both subprime and prime borrowers. Clearly, the increasing share of both subprime and ARM loans during 2000–2005 contributed to the boom and bust of the housing market.

(a) Subprime loans

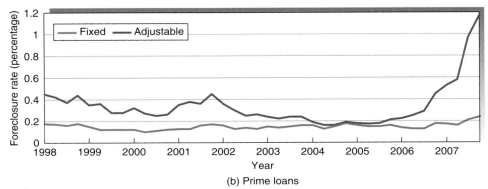

(b) Prime loans

Source: Stan J. Liebowitz, "Anatomy of a Train Wreck: Causes of the Mortgage Meltdown," Ch. 13 in Randall G. Holcombe and Benjamin Powell, eds, *Housing America: Building Out of a Crisis* (New Brunswick, NJ: Transaction Publishers, 2009, forthcoming). We would like to thank Professor Liebowitz for making this data available to us.

prime than subprime borrowers. This is highly revealing. It illustrates that both prime and subprime borrowers played the low down payment, mortgage casino game.

The crisis is often referred to as the "subprime mortgage crisis." This is true, but it is only part of the story. It was also an ARM loan crisis. Fed policy encouraging ARM loans, the increasing proportion of these loans as a share of the total, and their higher default and foreclosure rates also contributed substantially to the housing boom and bust. The combination of the mortgage lending regulations and the Fed's artificially low interest rate policies encouraged decision makers to borrow more money and make additional investments in everything from housing to factories. Unfortunately, from an economic standpoint, these are investments that should have never been undertaken, something economists call **malinvestment**. To get the U.S. economy back on track, these malinvestments must be cleansed from the system. As the severe contraction of the construction industry illustrates, this is a costly and painful process.

FACTOR 3: THE INCREASED DEBT/CAPITAL RATIO OF INVESTMENT BANKS

A rule change adopted by the Securities and Exchange Commission (SEC) in April 2004 made it possible for **investment banks** to increase the leverage of their investment capital, which eventually led to their collapse. A firm's **leverage ratio** is simply the ratio of its investment holdings (including loans) relative to its capital. Thus, if a firm had investment funds that were twelve times the size of its equity capital, its leverage ratio would be 12 to 1. Prior to the SEC rule change, this was approximately the leverage ratio of both investment and commercial banks.

Essentially, the SEC applied regulations known as Basel I to investment banking. These regulations, which have been adopted by most of the industrial countries, require banks to maintain at least 8 percent capital against assets like loans to commercial businesses. This implies a leverage ratio of approximately 12 to 1. However, the Basil regulations provide more favorable treatment of residential loans. The capital requirement for residential mortgage loans is only 4 percent, which implies a 25 to 1 leverage ratio. Even more important, the capital requirement for low-risk securities is still lower at 1.6 percent. This means that the permissible leverage ratio for low-risk securities could be as high as 60 to 1.

Key investment banking leaders, including Henry Paulson who was CEO of Goldman Sachs at the time, urged the SEC to apply the higher leverage ratio to investment banks. Ironically, Paulson later became Secretary of the Treasury and was in charge of the federal "bailout" of the banks that got into trouble because of the excessive leveraging of their capital.

Following the rule change, large investment banks, like Lehman Brothers, Goldman Sachs, and Bear Stearns, expanded their mortgage financing activities. They bundled large holdings of mortgages together and issued securities for their finance. Because of the diversity of the mortgage portfolio, investment in the underlying securities was thought to involve minimal risk. **Security-rating** firms provided the **mortgage-backed securities** with a AAA rating, which made it possible for the investment banks to leverage them up to 60 to 1 against their capital.

The mortgage-backed securities, financed with short-term leverage lending, were highly lucrative. The large number of mortgages packaged together provided lenders with diversity and protection against abnormally high default rates in specific regions and loan categories. But it did not shield them from an overall increase in mortgage default rates. As default rates increased sharply in 2006 and 2007, it became apparent that the mortgage-backed securities were far more risky than had been previously thought. When the risk of these mortgages became more apparent, the value of the mortgage-backed securities plummeted because it was difficult to know their true value. As the value of the mortgage-backed securities collapsed, the highly leveraged investment banks faced massive short-term debt obligations with little reserves on which to draw. This is why the investment banks collapsed so quickly. In fact, when the Fed financed the acquisition of Bear Stearns by JP Morgan Chase, the leverage ratio of Bear Stearns was an astounding 33 to 1, about two and a half times the historical level associated with prudent banking practices.

Why didn't key Wall Street decision makers see the looming danger? No doubt, they were influenced by the low and relatively stable default rates over the past several decades

Malinvestment

Malinvestment is misguided (or excess) investment caused when the Fed holds interest rates artificially low, encouraging too much borrowing. The new bank credit is invested in capital projects that cost more than the value they create. At some point, a correction must occur to cleanse these uneconomical investments from the system.

Investment bank

An institution that acts as an underwriter for securities issued by other corporations or lenders. Unlike traditional banks, investment banks do not accept deposits from, or provide loans to, individuals.

Leverage ratios

The ratio of loans and other investments to the firm's capital assets.

Security rating

A rating indicating the risk of default of the security. A rating of AAA indicates that the risk of default is low.

Mortgage-backed securities

Securities issued for the financing of large pools of mortgages. The promised returns to the security holders are derived from the mortgage interest payments.

(see Exhibit 2). Even during serious recessions like those of 1974–1975 and 1982–1983, the mortgage default rates were only a little more than 2 percent, less than half the rates of 2008. But one would still have thought that analysts at investment companies and security-rating firms would have warned that the low historical rates were for periods when down payments were larger, borrowing was more restricted relative to income, and fewer loans were made to subprime borrowers. A few analysts did provide warnings, but their views were ignored by high-level superiors.

However, the incentive structure also helps explain why highly intelligent people failed to see the oncoming danger. The bonuses of most Wall Street executives are closely tied to short-term profitability, and the mortgage-backed securities were highly profitable when housing prices were rising and interest rates were low. If a personal bonus of a million dollars or more is at stake this year, one is likely to be far less sensitive to the long-term dangers.

The incentive structure accompanying the regulation and rating of securities also played an important role. Only three firms—Moody's, Standard and Poors, and Fitch—are legally authorized to rate securities. These rating agencies are paid by the firm requesting the rating. A Triple-A rating was exceedingly important. It made higher leveraging possible, but, even more important, the Triple-A rating made it possible to sell the mortgage-backed securities to institutional investors, retirement plans, and investors around the world looking for relatively safe investments. The rating agencies were paid attractive fees for their ratings, and Triple-A approval would mean more business for the rating agencies as well as the investment banks. Clearly, this incentive structure is not one that encourages careful scrutiny and hard-nosed evaluation of the quality of the underlying mortgage bundle. Paradoxically, the shortsighted and counterproductive incentive structures that characterize some of Wall Street's best-known firms contributed to their collapse.

FACTOR 4: HIGH DEBT/INCOME RATIO OF HOUSEHOLDS

During the past two decades, household debt has grown to unprecedented levels. As **EXHIBIT 9** shows, household debt as a share of disposable (after-tax) income ranged from 40 percent to 65 percent during 1953–1984. However, since the mid-1980s, the debt-to-income ratio of households climbed at an alarming rate. It reached 135 percent in 2007, more than twice the level of the mid-1980s. Unsurprisingly, more debt means that a larger share of household income is required just to meet the interest payments. Today, interest payments consume nearly 15 percent of the after-tax income of American households, up from about 10 percent in the early 1980s.

Interest payments on home mortgages and home equity loans are tax deductible, but household interest on other forms of debt is not. This incentive structure encourages households to concentrate their debt into loans against their housing. But a large debt against one's housing will mean that housing will be the hardest hit by unexpected events that force major adjustments. This is precisely what occurred in 2006–2008. The rising interest rates and mere leveling off of housing prices soon led to an increase in mortgage defaults and foreclosures, because households were heavily indebted and a huge share of that indebtedness was in the form of mortgages against their housing. As the economy weakened, of course, this situation quickly worsened. Thus, the high level of household indebtedness also contributed to the Crisis of 2008.

Housing, Mortgage Defaults, and the Crisis of 2008

The combination of the HUD regulations, low down payment requirements, and the Fed's low interest policy of 2002–2004 resulted in the rapid growth of both subprime and ARM loans during the first five years of this century. As is often the case with policy changes, the initial effects were positive—strong demand for housing, rising housing prices, and a construction boom. But the long-term effects were disastrous. The increasing share of subprime loans began to push default rates upward. Similarly, the low short-term interest rates that made adjustable rate mortgages attractive during 2004 soon reversed and led to higher

EXHIBIT 9
Household Debt to Disposable Personal Income Ratio, 1953–2008

Between 1953 and 1984, household debt as a share of disposable (after-tax) income ranged from 40 percent to 65 percent. However, since the mid-1980s, this debt-to-income ratio has increased dramatically. By 2007, it soared to 135 percent, more than twice the level of the mid-1980s.

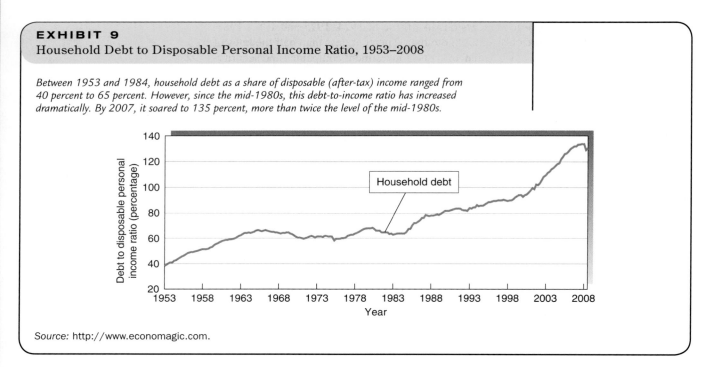

Source: http://www.economagic.com.

monthly payments as the interest rates on ARM loans were reset in the years immediately ahead. As these two factors converged in the latter half of 2006, they generated falling housing prices and soaring mortgage default and foreclosure rates. The housing and lending crisis soon spread to other sectors and economies around the world. Moreover, the Triple-A rated mortgage-backed securities were marketed throughout the world, and, as their value plunged with rising default rates, turmoil was created in global financial markets.

It is important to note that both the mortgage default and foreclosure rates soared well before the recession began in December 2007. This illustrates that the housing crisis was not caused by the recession. Instead, it was the other way around.

Lessons from the Crisis

The Crisis of 2008 has numerous villains, including greedy lenders, incompetent rating agencies, speculative homebuyers, and unethical investment managers. All played a role. But it is also important to note that to a large degree, the major players were doing pretty much what the politicians and regulators wanted them to do: extending more credit to promote home ownership.

What are the key lessons to be learned from this crisis? Reflection on this question requires that we think seriously about incentives, accountability, and the unintended side effects of policy. In this regard, the following three factors are important.

1. REGULATION IS A TWO-EDGED SWORD: IT CAN HAVE ADVERSE AS WELL AS POSITIVE RESULTS. Regulations that undermined sound lending standards were a central cause of the Crisis of 2008. Using HUD and the Community Reinvestment Act, the regulators mandated and pressured Fannie Mae, Freddie Mac, and commercial banks to extend loans with little or no down payment, make large loans relative to income, accept poorly documented loan applications, and make more "interest only" and variable rate mortgages. The stated objective of the regulators, and the politicians who empowered them, was the promotion of home ownership, particularly among low- and moderate-income households. Nonetheless, their actions undermined sound lending practices and forced lenders to make imprudent loans.

In the aftermath of the Crisis of 2008, many policy makers are calling for new regulations that will prevent the next crisis. As this debate goes forward, the regulatory involvement in the current crisis needs to be kept in mind. History illustrates that regulation is not a cure all. Regulatory agencies will be characterized by "tunnel vision." They will focus on their narrow objectives (e.g., promoting home ownership), and they will largely ignore the secondary effects of their actions. Regulators have a poor record with regard to foreseeing future problems. Mortgage lending and banking are two of the most heavily regulated sectors of our economy, but none of their regulators foresaw the forthcoming problems. With time, a sweetheart relationship will nearly always develop between the regulators and those whom they regulate. All of these factors should cause one to pause before believing that a new regulatory apparatus will head off the next crisis.

2. MONETARY POLICY NEEDS TO FOCUS ON MONETARY AND PRICE STABILITY. This is what the Fed did during the 1985–1999 era. But during the past decade, it has followed a stop–go path. When monetary policy makers attempt to manipulate real output and employment through persistent shifts in monetary policy, their actions will generate instability rather than stability.

During the crisis, it appeared that the Fed was an extension of the Treasury. It was heavily involved in subsidizing merger deals, providing aid to nonbanking institutions, and engaging in actions that favored some business firms relative to others. Some now want to give the Fed more regulatory powers. The experience of other countries indicates that this would be a mistake. Central banks that are more dependent on political officials are more prone to financing government programs with money creation and inflation. Moreover, loading the Fed down with other regulatory functions will detract from its primary mission: achievement of price stability.

3. INSTITUTIONAL REFORMS THAT RESTORE SOUND LENDING PRACTICES, STRENGTHEN THE PROPERTY RIGHTS OF SHAREHOLDERS, AND PROVIDE CORPORATE MANAGERS WITH A STRONGER INCENTIVE TO PURSUE LONG-TERM SUCCESS WOULD HELP PROMOTE RECOVERY AND FUTURE PROSPERITY. To a large degree, the Crisis of 2008 reflects what happens when policies confront people with perverse incentives. Constructive reforms need to focus on getting the incentives right. Consider the following questions. Would the mortgage market work better if loan originators were held responsible for defaults on loans they originated, even if they sold them to another party? Does it really make sense to encourage households to concentrate all of their debt against their house, as current tax policy does? Should shareholders have more control over the salaries and bonuses of high-level corporate executives? Should high-level corporate managers be provided with a stronger incentive to pursue the long-term success of their company? Should compensation in the form of stock options require that the options must be held at least five years (rather than the current one year) in order to qualify for the lower capital gains tax rate? Incentives related to all of these questions played a role in the Crisis of 2008. Although the precise response is not obvious, the crisis suggests that review of current policies in these and other areas would be wise.

Will we address the right issues and adopt constructive changes as a result of the crisis? It is too early to provide a definitive response to this question. But it is already clear that there is a major stumbling block: politicians in both major parties are reluctant to face up to their own involvement in creating the crisis. Instead, the political incentives will encourage them to blame others and deny the adverse consequences of their policies.

KEY POINTS

▼ After soaring during the previous five years, housing prices began to decline during the second half of 2006, and mortgage defaults and housing foreclosures started to increase. As the housing bust spread to other sectors, stock prices plunged, major investment banks experienced financial troubles, unemployment increased sharply, and by 2008 the economy was in a severe recession.

▼ Fannie Mae and Freddie Mac grew rapidly during the 1990s. Their government sponsorship made it possible for them to obtain funds cheaper than private rivals. Because of their dominance of the secondary market, in which mortgages are purchased from originators, their lending standards exerted a huge impact on the mortgage market.

▼ Beginning in the mid-1990s, mandates imposed on Fannie Mae and Freddie Mac, along with regulations imposed on banks, forced lenders to reduce their lending standards, extend more mortgages to subprime borrowers, and reduce down payment requirements. The share of mortgages extended to subprime borrowers (including Alt-A loans) rose from 10 percent in 2001–2003 to 33 percent in 2005–2006. This is highly important because the foreclosure rate on subprime loans is seven to ten times higher than for loans to prime borrowers.

▼ The historically low interest rate policies of the Fed during 2002–2004 increased the demand for housing and the attractiveness of adjustable rate mortgages. This provided fuel for the soaring housing prices. ARM loans increased from 10 percent of total mortgages in 2000 to 21 percent in 2005. As Fed policy pushed interest rates up in 2005–2006 and ARM loans were reset, the default and foreclosure rates on these loans soared for prime as well as subprime borrowers.

▼ As a result of regulations adopted in April 2004, investment banks were allowed to leverage their capital by as much as 60 to 1 when financing mortgages with Triple-A rated securities. The rating agencies provided the Triple-A ratings, and the mortgage-backed securities were sold around the world. As the mortgage default rates rose in 2007–2008, Fannie Mae, Freddie Mac, and the major investment banks holding large quantities of these securities quickly fell into financial troubles, and several collapsed.

▼ The ratio of household debt to personal income increased steadily during 1985–2007, reaching a historic high at the end of that period.

▼ Low down payment requirements, the growth of subprime and ARM loans, the Fed's easy credit policy, highly leveraged mortgage-backed securities, and heavy borrowing by households fueled the run-up in housing prices. With time, however, this was a disastrous combination that provided the ingredients for the recession and Crisis of 2008.

▼ The Crisis of 2008 reflects the unintended consequences of regulatory and monetary policy and what happens when the incentive structure is polluted by unsound institutions and policies.

CRITICAL ANALYSIS QUESTIONS

1. Why did housing prices rise rapidly during 2002–2005? Why did the mortgage default rate increase so sharply during 2006 and 2007 even before the current recession began?

2. What happened to the credit standards (e.g., minimum down payment, mortgage loan relative to the value of the house, and creditworthiness of the borrower) between 1995 and 2005? Why did the credit standards change? How did this influence the housing price bubble and later the default and foreclosure rates?

*3. If owners have little or no equity in their houses, how will this influence the likelihood that they will default on their mortgage? Why?

4. When did mortgage default and housing foreclosure rates begin to rise rapidly? When did the economy go into the current recession? Was there a causal relationship between the two? Discuss.

*5. When mortgage originators sell mortgages to Fannie Mae, Freddie Mac, and investment banks the originators have no additional liability for possible default by the borrower. How will this arrangement influence the incentive of the originators to scrutinize the creditworthiness of the borrower? Would the incentive structure be different if the originator planned to hold the mortgage until it was paid off? Why or why not?

6. Some charge that the Crisis of 2008 was caused by the "greed" of Wall Street firms and other bankers. Do you agree with this view? Do you think there was more greed on Wall Street in the first five years of this century than during the 1980s and 1990s? Why or why not?

*Asterisk denotes questions for which answers are given in Appendix B.

Lessons from the Great Depression

FOCUS

- What caused the Great Depression? Was it the stock market crash of 1929?

- Why was the Great Depression so long and severe?

- Did the New Deal policies end the Great Depression?

- Did monetary and fiscal policy help promote recovery from the Great Depression?

- Does the Great Depression reflect a failure of markets or a failure of government?

We now know, as a few knew then, that the depression was not produced by a failure of private enterprise, but rather by a failure of government in an area in which the government had from the first been assigned responsibility.

—Milton and Rose Friedman[1]

[1]Milton and Rose Friedman, *Free to Choose* (New York: Harcourt Brace Jovanovich, 1980), p. 71.

Т he Great Depression is perhaps the most catastrophic economic event in American history. It is also one of the most misunderstood. Misconceptions abound with regard to what actually happened. The Great Depression is a tragic story about economic illiteracy and the adverse impact of unsound policies. People who do not learn from the lessons of history are prone to repeat them. If we want to avoid similar experiences in the future, understanding of this experience and the forces underlying it is vitally important.

The Economic Record of the Great Depression

EXHIBIT 1 presents data on the change in real GDP and the rate of unemployment during 1929–1940. As part (a) illustrates, real GDP fell by 8.6 percent in 1930, 6.5 percent in 1931, and a whopping 13.1 percent in 1932. By 1933, real GDP was nearly a third less than that

EXHIBIT 1
Real GDP and the Rate of Unemployment, 1929–1940

The change in real GDP (part a) and rate of unemployment (part b) figures during the Great Depression are shown here. These data illustrate both the severity and length of the economic contraction. For four successive years (1930–1933), real output fell. Unemployment soared to nearly one-quarter of the workforce in 1932 and 1933. Although real output expanded and the rate of unemployment declined during 1934–1937, the economy again fell into the depths of a depression in 1938. In 1939, a decade after the economic plunge started, 17.2 percent of the labor force was still unemployed and real GDP was virtually unchanged from the level of 1929.

(a) Change in real GDP

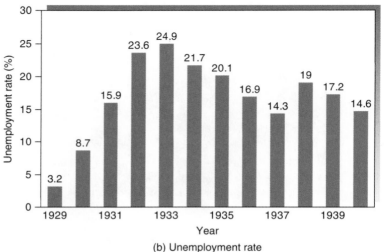

(b) Unemployment rate

Sources: Real GDP growth rates for are from http://www.bea.gov The unemployment data is from the BLS at http://www.bls.gov.

The Great Depression was a pro-longed period of falling incomes, high unemployment, and difficult living conditions. The downturn that started in 1929 was different from others in American history. Why?

in 1929. There was a temporary rebound during 1934–1936, but growth slowed in 1937 and real GDP fell once again in 1938. In 1939, a full decade after the disastrous downturn started, the real GDP of the United States was virtually the same as it had been in 1929.

While output was declining during the depression era, unemployment was soaring. As Exhibit 1, part (b), shows, the rate of unemployment rose from 3.2 percent in 1929 to 8.7 percent in 1930 and 15.9 percent in 1931. During 1932 and 1933, the unemployment rate soared to nearly one-quarter of the labor force. Even though real GDP grew substantially during 1934 and 1935, the unemployment rate remained above 20 percent during both of those years. After declining to 14.3 percent in 1937, the rate of unemployment rose to 19.0 percent during the downturn of 1938, and it was still 17.2 percent in 1939, a full decade after the catastrophic era began. The unemployment rate was 14 percent or more throughout the ten years from 1931 through 1940. By way of comparison, the unemployment rate has averaged less than 6 percent during the past quarter of a century, and it has never reached 11 percent since the Great Depression. Moreover, the statistics conceal the hardship and suffering accompanying the economic disaster. It was an era of farm foreclosures, bank failures, soup kitchens, unemployment lines, and even a sharply declining birthrate. America would never quite be the same after the 1930s.

Was the Great Depression Caused by the 1929 Stock Market Crash?

The prices of stock shares rose sharply during the 1920s. But this is not surprising because the 1920s were a remarkable decade of innovation, technological advancement, and economic growth. The production of automobiles increased more than tenfold during the 1920s. Households with electricity, telephones, and indoor plumbing spread rapidly throughout the economy. The radio was invented and developed, and it provided an amazing new vehicle for communication. Air conditioning received a boost from its use in "movie houses," as theaters were called at the time. There is good reason why the decade was known as the "roaring twenties." Perhaps more than any other era, the lives of ordinary Americans were transformed during the 1920s. To a large degree, the stock market was merely registering the remarkable growth and development of the decade.[2]

Generations of students have been told that the Great Depression was caused by the stock market crash of October 1929. Is this really true? Let's take a look at the figures.

---

[2] Popular writers often argue that speculators drove the stock market to unsustainable highs in the late 1920s, but this view is an exaggeration. The price/earnings ratio for the Dow was 19 just prior to the crash. This places it at the upper range of normal but not at an unprecedented high. On October 9, 1929, *The Wall Street Journal* reported that railroad stocks were selling at 11.9 times earnings, which would place their P/E ratio toward the lower range of normal. RCA was the hot "high-tech" company of the era, and it earned $6.15 per share in 1927 and $15.98 per share in 1928. It traded at a high in 1928 of $420. This would imply a P/E ratio of 26, not unreasonable for a growth stock with outstanding future earning prospects.

EXHIBIT 2
The Stock Market
(Dow Jones Industrial
Average), 1928–1940

The figures for the Dow Jones Industrial Average are shown here. Clearly, stock prices plunged in September–October 1929, but note how they recovered during the five months from mid-November 1929 through mid-April of 1930. However, this recovery reversed as the Smoot-Hawley tariff bill was debated, passed, and eventually signed into law on June 17, 1930. As part (b) shows, the Dow continued to fall throughout 1931 and 1932 and never reached 200 throughout the remainder of the decade.

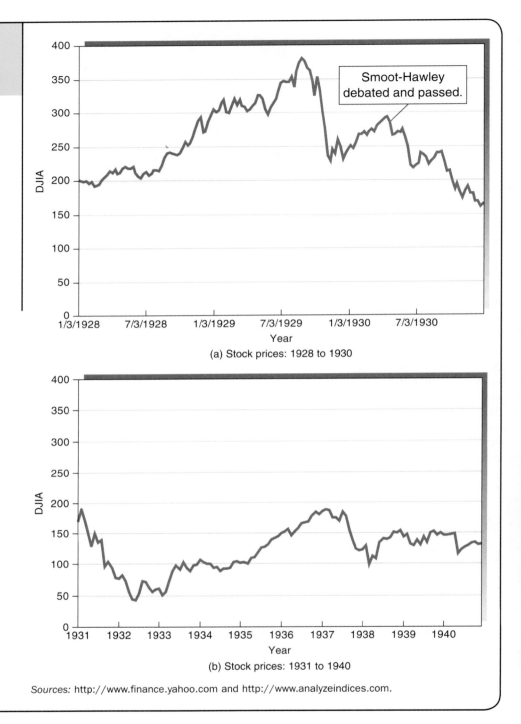

(a) Stock prices: 1928 to 1930

(b) Stock prices: 1931 to 1940

Sources: http://www.finance.yahoo.com and http://www.analyzeindices.com.

As **EXHIBIT 2**, part (a), shows, the Dow Jones Industrial Average opened in 1929 at 300, rose to a high of 381 on September 3, 1929, but gradually receded to 327 on Tuesday, October 22. A major sell-off started the following day, and the Dow began to plunge. By October 29, which is known as Black Tuesday, the Dow closed at 230. Thus, in exactly one week, the stock market lost nearly one-third of its value. A couple of weeks later on November 13, the Dow fell to an even lower level, closing at 199.

However, it is interesting to see what happened during the next five months. From mid-November 1929 through mid-April 1930, the Dow Jones Industrials increased every month, and by mid-April the index had risen to 294, regaining virtually all of the losses experienced during the late October crash. This raises an interesting question: If the

October crash caused the Great Depression, how can one explain that the stock market had regained most of those losses by April 1930?

But from mid-April throughout the rest of 1930, stock prices moved steadily downward and closed the year at 165. Apparently something happened during May–June 1930, which caused the stock market to head downward. We will return to this issue in a moment. Exhibit 2, part (b), presents data for the Dow Jones Industrials for 1931–1940. The index continued to fall in 1931–1932 and rebounded strongly in 1933 but then fluctuated between 100 and 200 for the remainder of the decade. Note the Dow stood at 131 at year-end 1940, even lower than the closing figure for 1930.

There have been several downturns in stock prices of the magnitude experienced during 1929, both before and after the Great Depression, and none of them resulted in anything like the prolonged unemployment and lengthy contraction of the 1930s. For example, the stock market price declines immediately prior to and during the recessions of 1973–1975 and 1982–1983 were as large as those of the 1929 crash, approximately 50 percent. But both of these recessions were over in about eighteen months. Moreover, in 1987, the Dow Industrials fell from 2640 on October 2 to 1740 on October 19, a decline of 34 percent. Whereas the collapse of stock prices in 1987 was similar to the October 1929 crash, that is where the similarity ends. The 1987 crash did not lead to economic disaster. In fact, it was not even followed by a recession.

Of course, the 1929 decline in stock prices reduced wealth and thereby contributed to the reduction in aggregate demand and real output. But stock prices have fallen by 50 percent or more during other recessions, and the economy nonetheless moved toward a recovery within a year or two at the most. Thus, although the decline in stock prices may well have triggered the initial economic decline, the length and severity of the Great Depression were the result of other factors. We will now consider this issue in more detail.

Why was the Great Depression so Lengthy and Severe?

The length and severity of the Great Depression were the result of bad policies. There were four major policy mistakes that caused the initial downturn to worsen and the depressed conditions to continue on and on. Let's take a closer look at each of them.

1. A SHARP REDUCTION IN THE SUPPLY OF MONEY DURING 1930–1933 AND AGAIN IN 1937–1938 REDUCED AGGREGATE DEMAND AND REAL OUTPUT. The supply of money expanded slowly but steadily throughout the 1920s. From 1921 through 1929, the money stock increased at an annual rate of 2.7 percent, approximately the economy's long-term real rate of growth. There was even a slight downward trend in the general level of prices during the decade.

In spite of this price stability, the Fed increased the discount rate, the rate it charges banks for short-term loans, four times between January 1928 and August 1929. During this twenty-month period, the discount rate was pushed from 3.5 percent to 6 percent. After the October stock market crash, the Fed aggressively sold government bonds, which drained reserves from the banking system and reduced the money supply. As **EXHIBIT 3**, part (a), shows, the money supply fell by 3.9 percent during 1930, by 15.3 percent in 1931, and by 8.9 percent in 1932. As banks failed and the money supply collapsed, the Fed did not inject new reserves into the system. Neither did it act as a lender of last resort. The quantity of money at year-end 1933 was 33 percent less than that in 1929.

Predictably, this huge monetary contraction placed downward pressure on prices. As Exhibit 3, part (b), illustrates, the general level of prices fell by 2.3 percent in 1930, 9.0 percent in 1931, and 9.9 percent in 1932.

Economic activity takes place over time. The deflation during 1929–1933 meant that many people who bought businesses and farms in the late 1920s were unable to pay for

EXHIBIT 3

The M1 Money Supply and the Change in the General Level of Prices, 1925–1940

Note how the M1 money supply fell sharply during 1930–1933, rose during 1934–1937 but dipped again in 1938 (part a). The general level of prices followed the same pattern (part b). The sharp reduction in the supply of money and deflation during 1930–1933 changed the terms of loans, investments, and other economic activities that take place across time periods. This was a major factor underlying the initial plunge into the Great Depression. Further, the monetary contraction of 1938 stifled the recovery and contributed to still another downturn.

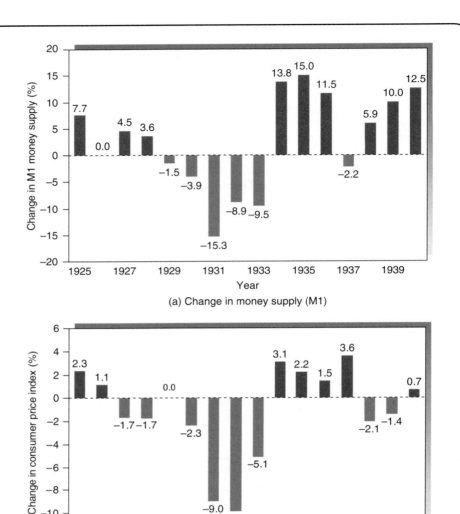

(a) Change in money supply (M1)

(b) Change in CPI

Sources: Change in the money supply is from December to December. The data are from Milton Friedman, and Anna J. Schwartz, A *Monetary History of the United States, 1867–1960* (Princeton: Princeton University Press, 1963); for CPI data: http://www.bls.gov.

them as the prices of their output fell during the 1930s. In essence, the monetary contraction caused unexpected changes in economic conditions. As a result, many people who undertook investments and borrowed funds suffered losses and were unable to fulfill their contracts. As the gains from trade dissipated and aggregate demand plunged, so, too, did output and employment. By 1933, real GDP was 29 percent lower than the 1929 level, and the unemployment rate had soared to nearly 25 percent.

During 1934–1937, the Fed reversed itself and expanded the supply of money. The monetary expansion halted the deflation, and the general level of prices increased. So, too, did the level of economic activity. Real GDP expanded and the unemployment rate fell during 1934–1937. But the Fed doubled the reserve requirements between August 1936 to May 1937, leading to another decline in the money supply and the general level of prices. This caused the economy to falter again and pushed the unemployment rate to almost 20 percent in 1938.

Sound monetary policy is about price stability—following a monetary policy that keeps the inflation rate low and steady. The Federal Reserve totally failed the American people during the 1930s. The severe monetary contraction led to near double-digit deflation. This was followed by a shift to monetary expansion, which generated inflation, but the Fed soon shifted again toward contraction, which caused still more deflation. Essentially, the monetary instability of the 1930s generated uncertainty and undermined the exchange process.[3]

2. THE SMOOT–HAWLEY TRADE BILL OF 1930 INCREASED TARIFFS AND LED TO A HUGE REDUCTION IN THE VOLUME OF INTERNATIONAL TRADE.
Signed into law on June 17, 1930, the Smoot–Hawley trade bill increased tariffs by more than 50 percent on approximately 3,200 imported products. Many of these tariff increases were in dollars per unit, so the subsequent deflation pushed them still higher relative to the price of the product.

Senator Reed Smoot and Congressman Willis Hawley (shown here) spearheaded legislation passed in June 1930 that increased tariff rates by an average of more than 50 percent. They thought their bill would "save jobs" and promote prosperity. Instead, it did the opposite, as other nations retaliated with higher tariffs on American products and world trade fell substantially.

National Photo Company Collection at the Library of Congress

Like their protectionist counterparts today, President Herbert Hoover, Senator Reed Smoot, and Congressman Willis Hawley argued that the trade restrictions would "save jobs." As Congressman Hawley put it, "I want to see American workers employed producing American goods for American consumption."[4] The proponents of the Smoot–Hawley legislation also believed the higher tariffs would bring in additional revenue for the federal government.

More than 100 years prior to the Great Depression, Adam Smith and David Ricardo explained how nations gained when they specialized in the production of goods they could supply at a low cost while trading for those they could produce only at a high cost. Trade makes it possible for both trading partners to generate a larger output and achieve a higher living standard. Moreover, a nation cannot reduce its imports without simultaneously reducing its exports. If foreigners sell less to Americans, then they will earn fewer of the dollars needed to buy from Americans. Thus, a reduction in imports will also lead to a reduction in exports. Jobs created in import competing industries will be offset by jobs lost in exporting industries. There will be no net expansion in employment. The view that import restrictions will generate a net creation of jobs is fallacious.

Having read both Smith and Ricardo, the economists of 1930 were well aware of the benefits derived from international trade and the harm generated by trade restrictions. More than a thousand of them signed an open letter to President Hoover warning of the harmful effects of Smoot–Hawley and pleading with him not to sign the legislation. He rejected their pleas, but history confirmed the validity of their warnings.

The higher tariffs did not generate additional revenue, and they certainly did not save jobs. The import restrictions harmed foreign suppliers, and predictably they retaliated. Sixty countries responded with higher tariffs on American products. By 1932, the volume of U.S. trade had fallen to less than half its earlier level. As a result, the federal government actually derived less revenue at the higher tariff rates. Tariff revenues fell from $602 million in 1929 to $328 million in 1932. Similarly, output and employment declined and the unemployment rate soared. The unemployment rate was 7.8 percent when Smoot–Hawley was passed, but it ballooned to 23.6 percent of the labor force just two years later. Moreover, the "trade war" helped spread the recessionary conditions throughout the world.

There was substantial opposition to the Smoot–Hawley bill and the Senate vote was close (44–42). Last minute changes in the rate schedules were made in order to gain the final votes needed for passage. Some businesses, seeking to gain advantage at the expense of consumers and foreign rivals, lobbied hard for the legislation. But, like the economists, other business leaders recognized that trade restrictions would harm rather than help the economy.

[3]For a comprehensive analysis of monetary policy during the Great Depression, see the chapter on the Great Contraction in Milton Friedman and Anna Schwartz, *A Monetary History of the United States, 1867–1960* (New York: National Bureau of Economic Research, 1963; ninth paperback printing by Princeton University Press, 1993): 411–15.

[4]Frank Whitson Fetter, "Congressional Tariff Theory," *American Economic Review* 23, no. 3 (September 1933): 413–27.

As we previously discussed, stock prices had increased for five straight months following the November 1929 lows, and by mid-April of 1930, the Dow Jones Industrials had returned to the level just prior to the October 1929 crash (see Exhibit 2). But as the Smoot–Hawley bill moved through Congress and its prospects for passage improved, stock prices moved steadily downward. In fact, the reduction in stock prices following the debate and passage of Smoot–Hawley was even greater than that of the 1929 October crash. By year-end 1930, recovery was nowhere in sight, and the Dow Jones Industrial index had fallen to 165, down from 294 in mid-April.

The combination of highly restrictive monetary policy and the Smoot–Hawley trade restrictions were enough to push the economy over the cliff, but Congress and the president were not through.

3. A LARGE TAX INCREASE IN THE MIDST OF A SEVERE RECESSION MADE A BAD SITUATION WORSE. Prior to the Keynesian revolution, the dominant view was that the federal budget should be balanced. Reflecting the ongoing economic downturn, the federal budget ran a deficit in 1931, and an even larger deficit was shaping up for 1932. Assisted by the newly elected Democratic majority in the House of Representatives, the Republican Hoover administration passed the largest peacetime tax rate increase in the history of the United States. As **EXHIBIT 4** indicates, the lowest marginal tax rate on personal income was raised from 1.5 percent to 4 percent in 1932. At the top of the income scale, the highest marginal tax rate was raised from 25 percent to 63 percent. Essentially, personal income tax rates were increased at all levels by approximately 150 percent in one year! This huge tax increase reduced both the after-tax income of households and the incentive to earn and invest.

Fiscal policy analysis indicates that a tax increase of this magnitude in the midst of a severe downturn will be disastrous. Review of Exhibit 1 shows that this was indeed the case. In 1932, real output fell by 13 percent, the largest single-year decline during the Great Depression era. Unemployment rose from 15.9 percent in 1931 to 23.6 percent in 1932.

In 1936, the Roosevelt administration increased taxes again, pushing the top marginal rate to 79 percent. Thus, during the latter half of the 1930s, high earners were permitted to keep only 21 cents of each additional dollar they earned. Moreover, the 1936 tax legislation also imposed a special tax on the retained earnings of corporations, a major source of funds for business investment. These 1936 tax increases further reduced both income levels and the incentive to earn and invest, prolonging the Great Depression and increasing its severity.

EXHIBIT 4
Marginal Income Tax Rates, 1925–1940

The lowest and highest marginal tax rates imposed on personal income are shown here for the period prior to, and during, the Great Depression. Note how the top marginal rate was increased from 25 percent in 1931 to 63 percent in 1932. Real GDP fell by 13.3 percent in 1932, and the unemployment rate soared to nearly a quarter of the labor force (see Exhibit 1). In 1935, the top rate was pushed still higher to 79 percent.

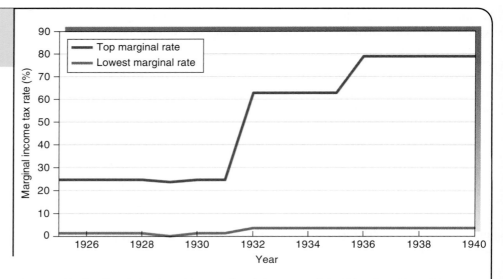

Sources: The Tax Foundation, http://www.taxfoundation.org; and the IRS at http://www.irs.gov.

4. PRICE CONTROLS, ANTICOMPETITIVE POLICIES, AND CONSTANT STRUCTURAL CHANGES DURING THE ROOSEVELT ADMINISTRATION GENERATED UNCERTAINTY AND UNDERMINED MARKETS.

President Roosevelt was elected in 1932, and many history books still credit his New Deal policies with bringing the Great Depression to an end. Numerous policy changes were instituted during the Roosevelt years, and some of them were helpful. In 1933, President Roosevelt

The Agricultural Adjustment Act of 1933 sought to increase the prices of farm products by reducing their supply. Under this Act, six million baby pigs were slaughtered in 1933. Did this help bring the Great Depression to an end?

re-valued the price of gold from $20 per ounce to $35 per ounce, and this contributed to the expansion in the money supply during the years immediately following. The Roosevelt administration also passed the Federal Deposit Insurance program, which provided depositors with protection against bank failures and reduced the occurrence of "bank runs."

However, it is equally clear that many of the major initiatives of the Roosevelt administration were counterproductive and prolonged the Great Depression. Roosevelt perceived that falling prices were a problem, but he failed to recognize that this was because of the monetary contraction. Instead, he tried to keep product prices high by reducing their supply. Under the Agricultural Adjustment Act (AAA) passed in 1933, farmers were paid to plow under portions of their cotton, corn, wheat, and other crops. Potato farmers were paid to spray their potatoes with dye so that they would be unfit for human consumption. Healthy cattle, sheep, and pigs were slaughtered and buried in mass graves in order to keep them off the market. In 1933 alone, six million baby pigs were killed under the Roosevelt agricultural policy. The Supreme Court declared the AAA unconstitutional in 1936, but not before it had kept millions of dollars of agricultural products from American consumers.

The National Industrial Recovery Act (NIRA) was another New Deal effort to keep prices high. Under this legislation passed in June 1933, more than 500 industries ranging from automobiles and steel to dog food and dry cleaners were organized into **cartels**. Business representatives from each industry were invited to Washington to work with NIRA officials to set production quotas, prices, wages, working hours, distribution methods, and other mandates for their industry. Once approved by a majority of the firms, the regulations were legally binding, and they applied to all businesses in the industry, regardless of whether they approved or participated in their development. Firms that did not comply were fined and, in some cases, owners were even thrown in jail. A tax was levied on all firms in these industries in order to cover the administrative cost of the Act. Prior to the NIRA, collusive behavior of this type would have been prosecuted as a violation of antitrust laws, but with the NIRA, the government itself provided the organizational structure for the cartels and prosecuted firms that dared to reduce prices or failed to comply with other regulations. Clearly, the NIRA reduced competition, promoted monopoly pricing, and undermined the market process.

EXHIBIT 5 tracks industrial output prior to, and during, the NIRA's existence. Interestingly, a recovery had started during the first half of 1933. Industrial output increased sharply and factory employment expanded by 25 percent during the four months before the NIRA took affect. But, as the Act was implemented in July 1933, industrial output began to decline precipitously. By the end of 1933, output had fallen by more than 25 percent from its mid-summer high. There were some ups and downs during the next year, but industrial output never returned to its pre-NIRA level until after the Supreme Court in a 9-0 vote declared the Act unconstitutional in May 1935.[5]

The AAA and NIRA were just part of the persistent policy change during the Roosevelt years. The Wagner Act took labor law out of the courts and assigned it to a new regulatory commission, the National Labor Relations Board. Pro-union appointments to

Cartel

An organization of sellers designed to coordinate supply and price decisions so that the joint profits of the members will be maximized. A cartel will seek to create a monopoly in the market for its product.

---

[5]For additional details on the impact of the NRA, see Chapter 4 of the recent book by historian Burton Folsom, *New Deal or Raw Deal* (New York: Simon & Schuster, 2008).

EXHIBIT 5
The NIRA and Industrial Production, 1932–1936

The change in industrial production prior to and following the passage of the National Industrial Recovery Act (NIRA) is shown here. Note how industrial output increased sharply during April–July 1933. However, when the implementation of the NIRA began in July, industrial output fell by more than 25 percent over the next six months. It never reached the June 1933 level again until after the Act was declared unconstitutional in May 1935.

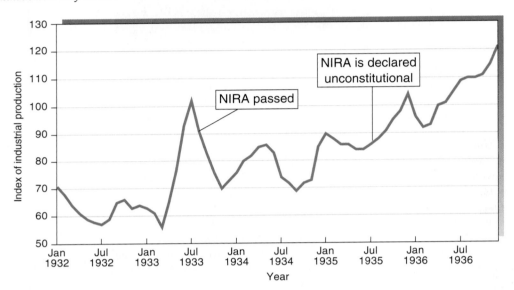

Source: Historical Statistics of the United States. The base period (equal to 100) was the average of the monthly figures during 1923–1925.

this new board dramatically changed collective bargaining and led to a sharp increase in unionization. The Works Progress Administration (WPA) and Civilian Conservation Corps (CCC) vastly expanded government employment. The Davis–Bacon Act required government contractors to employ higher wage union workers, which, in effect, reduced the employment opportunities of minorities and those with fewer skills. Unprecedented high marginal tax rates, establishment of a minimum wage, pay-as-you-go Social Security, and several other programs changed the structure of the U.S. economy.

This persistent introduction of massive new programs and regulations created what Robert Higgs calls "regime uncertainty," the situation in which people are reluctant to undertake business ventures and investments because the government is constantly changing the "rules."[6] Against this background, business planning was undermined and private investment came to a virtual standstill. Roosevelt's Treasury Secretary Henry Morgenthau tried to get the president to make a public statement to reassure investors and the business community. He was unsuccessful. Lammont duPont highlighted the uncertainty generated by the constant whirlwind of New Deal policy changes when he stated:

> *Uncertainty rules the tax situation, the labor situation, the monetary situation, and practically every legal condition under which industry must operate. Are taxes to go higher, lower or stay where they are? We don't know. Is labor to be union or non-union? Are we to have inflation or deflation, more government spending or less? Are new restrictions to be placed on capital, new limits on profits? It is impossible to even guess at the answers.*[7]

[6]Robert Higgs, "Regime Uncertainty: Why the Great Depression Lasted So Long and Why Prosperity Resumed After the War," *The Independent Review* 1, no. 4 (Spring 1997).

[7]Quoted in Herman E. Krooss, *Executive Opinion: What Business Leaders Said and Thought on Economic Issues, 1920s–1960s* (Garden City, NY: Doubleday and Co., 1970), 200.

Did the New Deal policies bring the Great Depression to an end?[8] Through the years, many students have been taught that this was the case. It is difficult to see how anyone could objectively review the data and accept this proposition. Prior to the Great Depression, recessions lasted only one or two years, three years at the most, and recovery pushed income to new highs. The Great Depression was different. In 1933, the monetary contraction was reversed, and there was evidence of a private sector recovery. But the NIRA, AAA, and 1936 tax increases dampened productive activity, and the second monetary contraction pushed the economy into another recession within the depression. In 1938, per capita real GDP of the United States was still below the level of 1929, and the rate of unemployment was 19 percent. In 1939, seven years after the beginning of the New Deal, 17 percent of the labor force was still unemployed. The Great Depression was eventually diminished by the increase in demand for military goods of the English and Russians and our own military buildup prior to World War II.[9]

Fiscal Policy During the Great Depression

What happened to fiscal policy during the Great Depression? This was, of course, prior to the Keynesian revolution, and the view that the government should balance its budget, except perhaps during wartime, was widely accepted. **EXHIBIT 6**, part (a), presents the data for government spending as a share of GDP. The size of the government was much smaller as a share of the economy during this era. Total government spending (federal, state, and local) increased from 8 percent of GDP in 1929 to 16 percent in 1933. To a large degree, however, this increase reflected the maintenance of nominal government expenditures during a period of deflation and declining GDP. After 1933, total government spending as a share of GDP remained in the 15 percent to 16 percent range for the rest of the decade, except during 1937, when the ratio fell to 13 percent.

Exhibit 6, part (b), provides the figures for the federal deficit. The budget was in surplus during both 1929 and 1930. After that, the deficit was generally around 2 percent of GDP, except during 1934 and 1936, and in 1937 when a small surplus was present. Measured as a share of the economy, the increases in government spending and federal deficits during the 1930s were relatively small. Thus, there is little reason to believe that fiscal policy exerted much impact on the economy. Certainly, there is no reason to believe that spending increases and budget deficits were a significant source of fiscal stimulus during the era.

Lessons from the Great Depression

The Great Depression provides several lessons that can help us avoid severe downturns in the future. First, the Great Depression clearly indicates that a prolonged period of monetary contraction will undermine time–dimension economic activity and exert disastrous effects

[8]For additional details on the Great Depression, see Gene Smiley, *Rethinking the Great Depression* (Ivan R. Dee, Chicago, IL 2002); Robert J. Samuelson, "Great Depression," in *The Fortune Encyclopedia of Economics*, ed., David R. Henderson (New York: Warner Books, 1993), available online at http://www.econlib.org; Burton Folsom, *New Deal or Raw Deal?* (New York: Simon & Schuster, 2008); and Amity Shlaes, *The Forgotten Man: A New History of the Great Depression* (New York: HarperCollins Publishers, 2007).

[9]Many argue that the spending increases and large budget deficits of World War II provided sufficient demand stimulus to direct the economy back to full employment and solid growth. Robert Higgs challenges this view. Higgs notes that with 12 million young Americans drafted during the war, this would obviously reduce the unemployment rate to a low level. However, the growth of real GDP is more debatable because almost half of measured output was government spending, and it was added to GDP at cost. Moreover, the income of households was overstated because many goods they would have purchased were unavailable as a result of the price controls. The sharp decline in GDP following the war and the lifting of price controls also imply that the growth of GDP during the war was overstated. Thus, Higgs does not believe that real recovery from the Great Depression occurred until 1946. See Robert Higgs, "Depression, War, and Cold War: Studies in Political Economy" (New York: Oxford University Press), 2006.

EXHIBIT 6

Government Expenditures and Federal Budget Deficits as a Share of GDP, 1929–1940

Measured as a share of the economy, government spending increased during the 1930s, and the federal government generally ran a budget deficit. However, given the depth of the economic decline, the deficits were too small to provide much fiscal stimulus during this era.

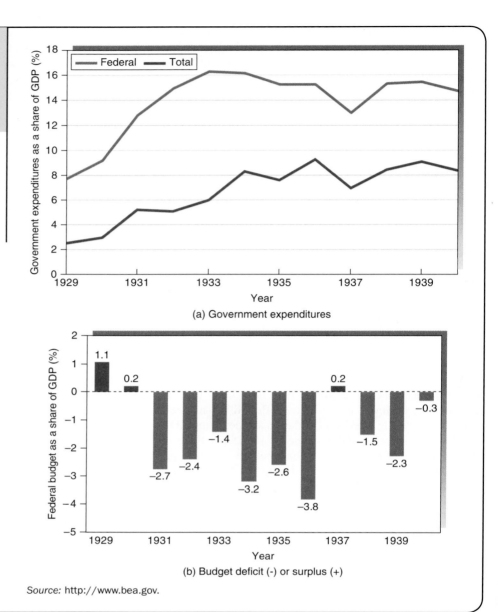

(a) Government expenditures

(b) Budget deficit (-) or surplus (+)

Source: http://www.bea.gov.

on the economy. We seemed to have learned this lesson well. As the severity of the 2008 downturn increased, the Fed injected abundant reserves into the banking system and shifted to a highly expansionary monetary policy. However, it is also true that Fed policy during 2002–2006 contributed to the housing boom and bust and, thereby, the Crisis of 2008. Monetary and price stability is crucially important for the smooth operation of markets. The Great Depression, along with experience since that era, vividly illustrates the importance of monetary stability.

Second, the Great Depression illustrates the fallacy of the "trade restrictions will promote domestic industry" argument. Policies that reduce imports will simultaneously reduce exports. Foreigners will not have the dollars to purchase as much from us if they sell less to us. Trade restrictions will not save jobs. Instead, they will shift employment from sectors in which we are a low-cost producer to those in which we are a high-cost producer. The results are fewer gains from trade, a smaller output, and lower income levels. Both economic theory and the experience of the Smoot–Hawley trade restrictions are consistent with this view.

Third, raising taxes in the midst of a severe recession is a bad idea. Pushing taxes to exceedingly high rates is a recipe for disaster. All of the major macroeconomic theories—Keynesian, new classical, and supply side—indicate that tax increases will be counterproductive during a severe downturn. The experience with the tax increases during the Great Depression ref-enforces these views.

Fourth, the political incentive structure during a severe downturn is likely to encourage politicians to "do something." Even bad policies are likely to be popular, at least for a while. A better strategy would be the oath of the medical profession, "do no harm." The constant policy changes under both Hoover and Roosevelt created uncertainty and froze private sector investment and business activity. Everyone waited to see what the next new policy regime would be; and, as they did so, the depressed conditions were prolonged.

The experience of the 1930s highlights the importance of economic literacy. The decade-long catastrophic decline did not have to happen. It was the result of wrong-headed policies based on the economic illiteracy of both voters and policy makers.

Finally, as we noted in Chapter 1, good intentions are no substitute for sound policy. The Great Depression vividly illustrates this point. There is every reason to believe that Presidents Hoover and Roosevelt, Senator Smoot, Congressman Hawley, other members of Congress, and the monetary policy makers of the 1930s had good intentions. But, it is equally clear that their actions tragically turned what would have been a normal business cycle downturn into a decade of hardship and suffering. The good intentions of political decision makers do not protect the general citizenry from the adverse consequences of unsound policies. This was true during the Great Depression, and it is still true today. If we do not learn from the adverse experiences of history, we are likely to repeat them.

KEY POINTS

▼ The Great Depression was a severe economic plunge that resulted in unemployment rates of nearly 25 percent during 1932–1933 and rates of more than 14 percent for an entire decade. It was the longest, most severe period of depressed economic conditions in American history.

▼ Contrary to a popular view, the Great Depression was not caused by the 1929 stock market crash. We have had similar reductions in stock prices to those of 1929, both before and after the Great Depression, without experiencing prolonged depressed conditions like those of the 1930s.

▼ There were four major reasons why the Great Depression was long and severe:

1. Monetary instability:The money supply contracted by 33 percent between 1929 and 1933, and it took another tumble during 1937–1938.

2. Smoot-Hawley trade bill: This 1930 legislation increased tariffs by more than 50 percent and led to a sharp reduction in world trade.

3. 1932 tax increase: This huge tax increase reduced demand and undermined the incentive to invest and produce.

4. Structural policy changes: Persistent major changes, particulary during the Roosevelt years, generated uncertainty and undermined investment and business planning.

▼ The budget deficits and increases in government spending were too small to exert much impact on total demand and the level of economic activity during the 1930s.

▼ The Great Depression highlights the importance of monetary stability; free trade; avoidance of high tax rates; and avoidance of price controls, entry restraints, and persistent policy changes that generate uncertainty and undermine the security of property rights. Perhaps most important, the Great Depression vividly illustrates that good intentions are not a substitute for sound economic policy.

CRITICAL ANALYSIS QUESTIONS

1. "The Great Depression was caused by the 1929 stock market crash. The 1929 collapse of stock prices was the most severe in U.S. history, and therefore it is not surprising that it caused a prolonged period of economic hardship." Evaluate this statement.

2. Do the length and severity of the Great Depression reflect a defect in the operation of markets? Do they reflect a failure of government policy? Discuss.

3. "Franklin Roosevelt is recognized as one of our greatest presidents because his New Deal policies brought the Great Depression to an end." Evaluate this statement.

4. Could the United States ever experience another Great Depression? Why or why not?

*5. "I'm for international trade, but not when it takes jobs from Americans. If the American worker can produce the product, Americans should not buy it from foreigners." Do you agree with this statement? Why or why not?

6. What are the most important lessons Americans should learn from the Great Depression? Do you think we have learned them? Why or why not?

*Asterisk denotes questions for which answers are given in Appendix B.

Lessons from the Japanese Experience

FOCUS

- What were the underlying factors of the Japanese economic crisis of the 1990s? Were they similar to the 2008 U.S. crisis?

- How did policy makers in Japan respond to the crisis? Were their actions effective?

- What are the similarities and differences between the Japanese crisis of the 1990s and current conditions in the United States?

- What are the important lessons of the Japanese experience for the United States?

The causes of the Japanese asset bubble and American housing bubble are eerily similar.

—Anthony Randazzo, Michael Flynn, and Adam B. Summers[1]

[1]Anthony Randazzo, Michael Flynn and Adam B. Summers, "Avoiding an American 'Lost Decade': Lessons from Japan's Bubble and Recession," Reason Foundation Policy Study. No. 373 (2009), http://reason.org/files/091666ffae05 7ae322adac5dc0f65caa.pdf.

During the latter half of the 1980s, stock market and commercial real estate prices soared in Japan, much like housing prices soared in the United States during 2001–2005. Moreover, the Japanese asset price bubble turned to a bust in 1990–1991. Similarly, the housing price boom in the United States turned to a bust beginning in the second half of 2006. The plunging asset prices in Japan during the early 1990s generated a flood of loan defaults that created huge problems for the banking and financial sectors. The collapse of housing prices created the same result in the United States during 2008–2009. The Japanese financial problems generated uncertainty and a sharp downturn in the growth of real GDP during 1992–1993, and the economic growth of Japan has been sluggish ever since. The United States has already experienced a severe downturn in 2008–2009, but we do not know what lies ahead. Given the similarity of the Japanese experience during 1985–1993 with that of the United States during 2001–2009, it will be interesting to take a closer look at the Japanese experience and consider the lessons that can be drawn from it. This special topic will focus on that issue. ■

The Boom and Bust of Japanese Asset Prices: 1985–1992

The growth rate of the Japanese economy during 1960–1990 was stunning. During that thirty-year period, the real GDP of Japan grew at an annual rate of 6.2 percent. Some of this remarkable growth was the result of what is sometimes called the "catch-up phenomenon," the ability of lower income countries to grow rapidly because they can emulate the successful practices and technology of their higher income counterparts. By 1990, this growth had propelled Japan to a per capita income similar to that of the high-income countries of Western Europe and about 80 percent the level of the United States. Within a relatively short time frame, Japan had moved from a poor country recovering from the devastation of World War II to one of the world's most prosperous nations.

By the latter half of the 1980s, the strong growth and rising incomes had created a wave of optimism about the future of the Japanese economy. This generated a strong demand for both commercial real estate and shares of business firms in Japan. The Bank of Japan reduced its discount rate from 5 percent in January 1986 to 2.5 percent in February 1987. This reduced the cost of buying and holding both real estate and business assets. Fueled by persistently strong growth, optimism, and easy credit, asset prices in Japan soared. By the late 1980s, Japanese investors anticipated that real estate and stock prices would continue to rise, just as many American homebuyers thought that housing prices would keep going up during the early part of the twenty-first century. Moreover, Japanese banks and other lenders also expected the rising prices to continue. Therefore, they were willing to extend loans to borrowers, including many who had very little equity in the purchased asset.

Japanese real estate and stock prices soared during the 1980s, just as housing prices soared in the United States during 2001–2005. But the bubble burst in 1990. **EXHIBIT 1** illustrates the boom and bust in the Japanese stock market. These data are for the Nikkei 225, the Japanese equivalent of the Standard and Poor's 500 index in the United States. Note how the Nikkei index soared from 13,024 in January 1986 to 38,916 at year-end 1989, an increase of nearly 200 percent over a four-year period.

EXHIBIT 1

Japanese Stock Market (Nikkei 225), 1984–2008

The stock prices of Japanese firms tripled during 1986–1989, and the Nikkei 225 soared to nearly 39,000 at year-end 1989. During the first nine months of 1990, however, the Nikkei 225 fell by 46 percent, and it never recovered from this plunge during the rest of the decade. By January 2002, it had fallen below 10,000, approximately one-quarter the level achieved in 1989. At year-end 2008, the index stood at 8860.

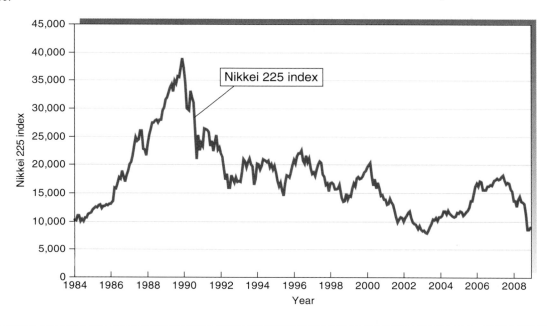

But there was a dramatic change in 1990. By September of 1990, the Nikkei 225 had fallen to 20,984, down 46 percent from the beginning of the year. The index fluctuated in the 22,000–26,000 range during 1991, but it plunged once again to 15,010 in July 1992. Over the next eight years, it was mostly in the 13,000–20,000 range.

The boom–bust pattern of real estate prices was similar. When the prices of both stock and real estate assets collapsed, they took down not only the asset purchasers but also the highly leveraged banking and financial institutions that funded their loans. The asset bust soon spread to the rest of the economy and led to a sharp downturn in economic growth.

As **EXHIBIT 2**, part (a), shows, the growth rate of real GDP fell from the 5 percent range the Japanese had come to expect to 3.3 percent in 1991 and less than 1 percent during 1992–1993. Moreover, during the decade that followed, Japanese real growth averaged only 1 percent, far below the expectations of the late 1980s. Today, that downturn and the persistently weak growth are often referred to as Japan's "lost decade."

Exhibit 2, part (b), presents data on the Japanese unemployment rate. Historically, the unemployment rate in Japan has been low, and it continued at a relatively low rate even during the initial phase of the downturn. During the early 1990s, Japan's rate of unemployment was only 2 percent. The rate trended upward during the decade, reaching 5 percent in 2001. But even this higher rate is well below the figures of most other high-income market economies.

Japan's low unemployment rate reflects a less dynamic business environment and lower labor mobility. For example, the start-up and business failure rates in Japan have been about half those of the United States over the past several decades. Further, the

EXHIBIT 2

Japanese Real GDP and Rate of Unemployment, 1987–2008

The growth of real GDP in Japan averaged 5 percent annually during the 1980s but only 1 percent during 1992–2001, and growth has been only slightly higher during the past seven years (part a). The Japanese unemployment rate is quite low, but there has been an upward trend since 1992 (part b).

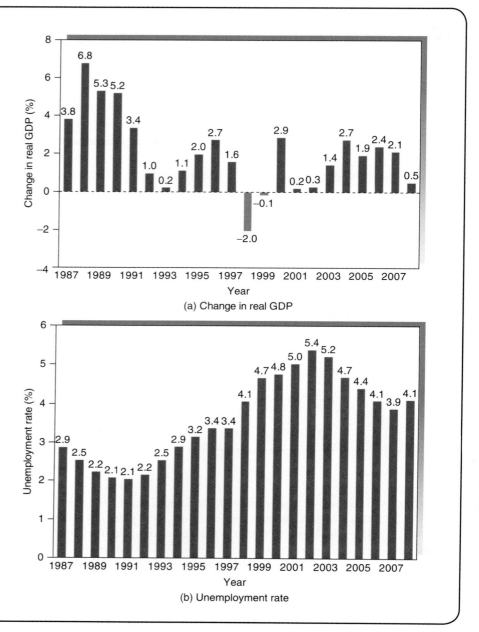

(a) Change in real GDP

(b) Unemployment rate

Japanese labor market is characterized by lifetime employment contracts, a promise by the employer to retain the employee until age 55. In order to make this system viable, the Japanese government has often propped up struggling businesses rather than allowing them to fail. This results in less shifting of employees among employers and a lower rate of unemployment. But it also slows the shift of resources from low to high productivity areas.

Japanese Policy Responses during the 1990s

As growth remained low in the aftermath of the collapse of asset prices, Japan searched for a way to jump-start its economy. We will now take a closer look at its conduct of fiscal and monetary policy during this era.

Fiscal Policy

During the 1990s, Japan adopted at least seven different stimulus packages designed to increase aggregate demand and enhance economic growth. Government spending on infrastructure—roads, bridges, and airports—was increased substantially. Taxes were cut in both 1994 and 1998, but both of these tax cuts were temporary, weakening their impact on aggregate demand. These fiscal policy changes were financed with budget deficits and increased borrowing.

EXHIBIT 3 presents data on the Japanese fiscal record: both government spending and the budget deficit as a share of the economy. As part (a) shows, government expenditures comprised a little more than 30 percent of GDP during the late 1980s and early 1990s. By 1999–2002, government spending had risen to nearly 40 percent of GDP. Thus, government spending rose by approximately 7 percent of GDP during the 1990s.

The increased spending was financed with borrowing. As Exhibit 3, part (b), illustrates, the budget deficits rose throughout the 1990s. At the beginning of the decade, the Japanese government was running a budget surplus, but it soon dissipated, and budget

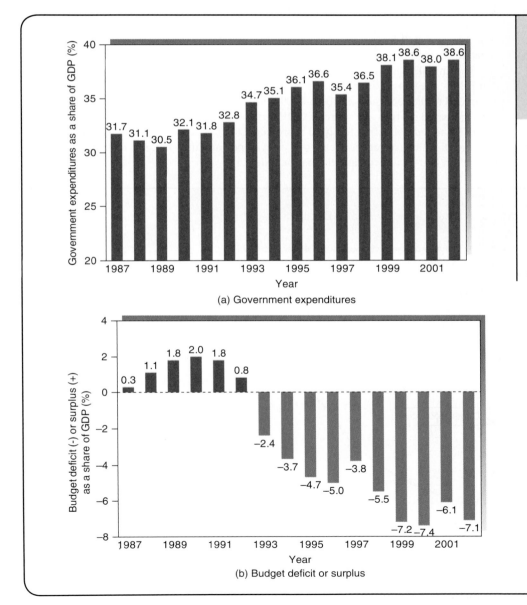

EXHIBIT 3

Japanese Government Expenditures and Budget Deficits as a Share of GDP, 1987–2002

As part (a) shows, government spending increased from a little more than 30 percent of GDP in 1987–1991 to nearly 40 percent of GDP during 1999–2002. As part (b) shows, this increase in government spending was largely financed through borrowing. Japan began running budget deficits in 1993, and they became larger and larger during the decade that followed.

(a) Government expenditures

(b) Budget deficit or surplus

deficits in the range of 4–5 percent of GDP were present during 1994–1997. The deficits were still larger—between 6 percent and 8 percent of GDP—during 1999–2002. By way of comparison, the budget deficits of the United States were generally only 1 or 2 percent during the Great Depression (see Exhibit 6, Special Topic 6). Many economists, particularly Keynesians, argue that the Great Depression deficits were not very effective because they were too small. This argument is less applicable in the case of Japan, because the Japanese budget deficits were large.

Persistently large budget deficits will increase government debt as a share of the economy. As **EXHIBIT 4** shows, this was indeed the case in Japan. Measured as a share of GDP, the net debt of the Japanese central government rose from 14 percent in 1992 to 60 percent in 2000 and 88 percent in 2008. Thus, the data indicate that fiscal policy was highly expansionary in Japan during the decade following the asset price meltdown. Government spending was increased substantially as a share of the economy, and virtually all of this increase was financed through debt.

As our analysis of fiscal policy explained, there are alternative views regarding the stimulus effects of fiscal policy. Keynesians argue that expansionary fiscal policy will stimulate aggregate demand and real output, particularly during a period of economic weakness. In contrast, other economists argue that the spending increases will generate secondary effects—higher interest rates, increased future taxes, and changes in the structure of demand—that will lead to offsetting reductions in private sector spending. The experience of Japan during the 1990s would appear to be more consistent with the latter view.

The initial evidence indicates that the fiscal policy response of the United States will follow the same pattern as that of Japan. Both the Bush and Obama administrations responded to the recession of 2008–2009 with fiscal stimulus programs. Federal expenditures increased sharply as a share of GDP, and the 2009 budget deficit soared to 10 percent of GDP. The federal deficit for 2010 is projected to be 8 percent of GDP. These deficits are far larger than any of recent decades. (For evidence on this point, see Exhibit 1 of Special Topic 8 on budget deficits and the national debt.)

EXHIBIT 4
Net Debt of Japanese Central Government as a Share of GDP, 1987–2008

Measured as a share of GDP, the net debt of the Japanese central government was 14 percent in 1992, but it rose to 60 percent in 2000 and 88 percent in 2008.

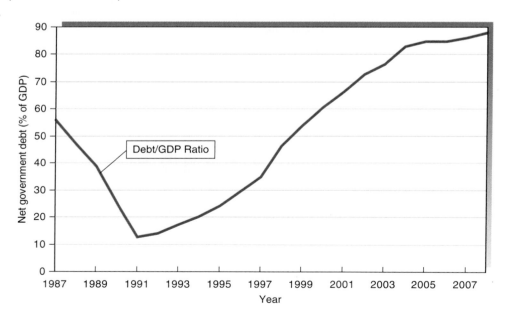

Monetary Policy

EXHIBIT 5 provides evidence on the direction of Japanese monetary policy during the past two decades. As part (a) shows, the broad M2 measure of the money supply increased at double-digit rates during the late 1980s. This monetary expansion pushed interest rates to low levels and, as we mentioned earlier, contributed to the rising asset prices of the late 1980s. However, monetary growth has been restrictive since 1990. The M2 money supply expanded at an average annual rate of only 2.5 percent during 1991–2002.[2]

Exhibit 5, part (b), provides data on the Japanese inflation rate. These figures also indicate that monetary policy was highly restrictive during the 1990s. The Japanese

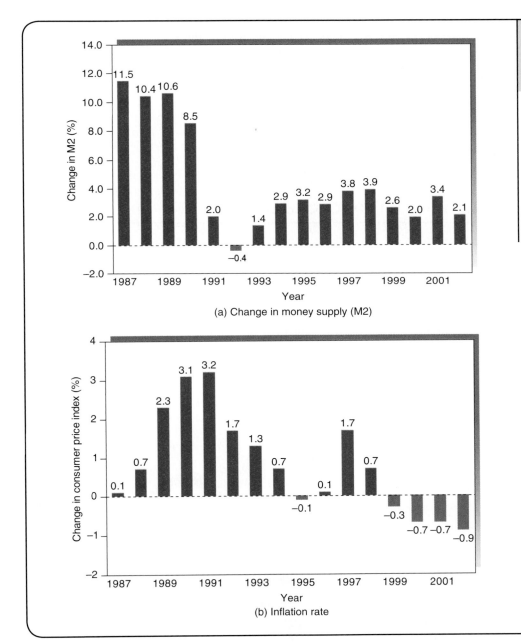

EXHIBIT 5

Japanese Monetary Policy and Inflation, 1987–2002

The broad measure of the money supply (M2) increased at double-digit rates during the late 1980s, but it grew at an average rate of only 2.5 percent during 1991–2002 (part a). The inflation rate has been quite low, and the general level of prices actually fell during five of the eight years between 1995 and 2002 (part b).

(a) Change in money supply (M2)

(b) Inflation rate

[2]The growth rate of the M1 money supply was a little higher—7.8 percent during the 1990s. During the decade, many Japanese transferred funds from their bank savings accounts into government postal deposit accounts for safety reasons. The postal accounts are included in M1, but the bank savings deposits are not. Thus, these transfers inflated the growth rate of the M1 money supply. The postal deposits are used almost exclusively to purchase government bonds. Thus, they did not provide financial capital for the private sector.

inflation rate was exceedingly low throughout the decade. Moreover, the general level of prices actually fell during five of the eight years between 1995 and 2002.

Why was Japan's monetary policy so restrictive during the 1990s at a time when fiscal policy makers were obviously trying to stimulate the economy? Historically, many have thought that low interest rates were indicative of an expansionary monetary policy, but this is not always true. Nominal interest rates are influenced by the expected rate of inflation. When people expect deflation—a decline in the general level of prices—nominal interest rates will be low. They might even approach zero. But far from indicating that monetary policy is expansionary, under these circumstances, the low interest rates are indicative of highly restrictive monetary policy and the expectation of future deflation. Japanese policy makers may have been misled into thinking that their low nominal interest rates were reflective of expansionary rather than highly restrictive monetary policy.

Monetary policy makers in the United States made this error during the 1930s. Many thought that the low interest rates of the Great Depression were reflective of an expansionary monetary policy. However, this was not the case, and the 33 percent reduction in the money supply between 1929 and 1933 vividly illustrates this point. The same thing may have happened in Japan during the 1990s.

The Aging Population of Japan in the 1990s and the United States Today

The age composition of a nation's population influences productivity and income. The labor force of high-income countries like Japan and the United States is highly educated and skilled. But, even well-educated younger workers lack experience. Therefore, their productivity and earnings tend to be below average during this phase of life. As workers acquire additional experience and move into the prime age categories, usually age 35–59, their productivity will increase and reach a peak. However, as they grow older and move into the retirement phase of life, productivity and earnings will again fall below average.

As the share of a nation's population age sixty-five years and older expands, there are two major reasons why this will slow economic growth. First, productivity will slow

The elderly population of Japan rose sharply during the "lost decade" of the 1990s.

Imagewerks (RF)/Getty Images

because the rising share of the elderly will pull down the average productivity of the adult population. Second, a larger elderly population will mean more expenditures for retirement benefits and health care. In high-income countries, a substantial share of these expenditures is generally handled through government. Therefore, increased spending in these categories will mean higher taxes on current workers, which will also act as a drag on economic growth.

EXHIBIT 6 provides data on the share of the population age sixty-five years and older in Japan during 1990–2010 and the projections for the United States during 2010–2030. Note how the elderly population of Japan rose sharply from 12 percent of the total in 1990 to 17.3 percent in 2000 and 23.1 percent in 2010. Thus, the share of the Japanese population age 65 and over almost doubled during the two decades following 1990. During the next two decades, the elderly population of the United States will increase from 13 percent to 19.3 percent of the total, approximately a 50 percent increase. Thus, the pattern in the United States during the next two decades will be the same as that for Japan

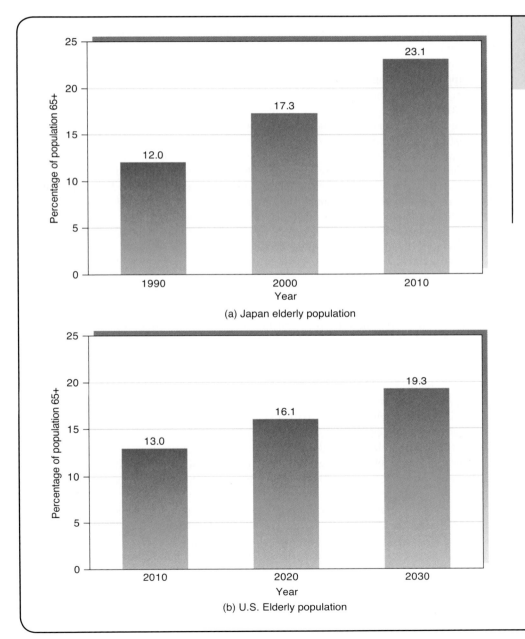

(a) Japan elderly population

(b) U.S. Elderly population

EXHIBIT 6
The Aging of the Japanese and U.S. Populations

As part (a) shows, the share of the Japanese population age 65 and over rose sharply during 1990–2010. Part (b) illustrates that there will be a similar trend in the United States during 2010–2030, although the growth of the elderly population will be a little slower in the United States.

during 1990–2010, although the growth of the elderly population in the United States will be somewhat less rapid.

These demographic changes have adversely affected the growth of the Japanese economy since 1990, although it is difficult to quantify their precise importance. Predictably, they will also slow the growth of productivity and income in the United States in the years immediately ahead.

Lessons from the Japanese Experience

There are a number of similarities between conditions in Japan in the early 1990s and those of the United States today. In both cases, an asset price boom followed by a bust led to an unexpected reduction in wealth, a surge in bad loans, troubles in the banking and financial sector, and widespread pessimism about the future. The fiscal policy response of both has been similar: increased government spending, large budget deficits, and a surge in government debt as a share of the economy. The demographics are also similar: the elderly population increased substantially in Japan during the 1990s, and the same thing will happen in the United States in the decade ahead.

Does this mean that the United States is in for a "lost decade" much like Japan during the 1990s? Not necessarily. Clearly, there is one huge difference in the policy response between the two. Whereas the monetary policy of Japan was restrictive during the 1990s, that has not been the case in the United States. In fact, the Federal Reserve has injected a huge quantity of reserves into the banking system, and monetary policy in the United States has been far more expansionary than that of Japan during the 1990s. If monetary policy exerts a strong impact on the economy, this could mean that the U.S. experience in the decade ahead will be substantially different from that of Japan during the 1990s.

There are other differences that could also be important. The economy is more dynamic and labor markets more flexible in the United States than in Japan. This could hasten the adjustment process from the dislocations resulting from the crisis. On the other hand, the saving rate of Japan is considerably higher than in the United States. This could make it more difficult for the United States to finance a huge run-up in government debt than was true for Japan.

The Japanese experience should provide some caution for Americans in at least three important areas. First, the run-up in housing prices generated malinvestment and excess capacity. It will take time to correct these conditions. Asset prices did not rebound quickly in Japan during the 1990s, and neither are they likely to do so in the United States in the years immediately ahead. Second, fiscal stimulus is unlikely to generate a quick and sustainable recovery, even in a low interest rate environment. The Japanese budget deficits were large, but they still did not exert a strong impact on aggregate demand and real output. Third, although the more expansionary monetary policy of the United States may well promote a stronger recovery, there are also dangers that it will lead to future economic instability somewhat like that of the 1970s. The monetary policy lags are long and variable. Therefore, monetary policy makers are likely to either turn toward restriction too quickly and thereby throw the economy back into recession or stay with the expansionary policy too long and generate future inflation.

Economics is an imprecise science and, to a large degree, the "experiments" of economists are limited to those that emerge from real world change. The years immediately ahead will provide some experiments that will expand our knowledge of macroeconomics and the impact of alternative policies. This is an exciting time to study economics.

KEY POINTS

▼ In the late 1980s, real estate and stock prices in Japan soared, much like housing prices in the United States during 2001–2005. But like the housing boom in the United States, Japan's stock and real estate price boom was followed by a bust in the early 1990s. This price collapse led to a surge in loan defaults, troubles in the banking sector, and a sharp slowdown in the growth of the Japanese economy in the early 1990s. The sluggishness persisted, and the 1990s are now known as Japan's "lost decade."

▼ Japan responded to the economic downturn with several "stimulus programs" that substantially increased spending on roads, bridges, and other infrastructure. Government spending rose from a little more than 30 percent of GDP in the early 1990s to nearly 40 percent of GDP in the latter part of the decade. This increased spending was financed through large budget deficits. Even though fiscal policy was highly expansionary, the Japanese economy continued to stagnate.

▼ In contrast with fiscal policy, the monetary policy of Japan was restrictive during the 1990s. The broad M2 money supply expanded at an annual rate of only 2.5 percent during 1991–2002. The general level of prices changed little during the 1990s, and deflation was present during five of the eight years between 1995 and 2002.

▼ The share of the population age 65 and over in Japan nearly doubled during 1990–2010. The United States will experience a similar change in the composition of the population during the next two decades. This will tend to reduce productivity and lead to higher taxes on current workers for the finance of retirement benefits and health care for the elderly. This slowed economic growth in Japan during the 1990s, and it is likely to do so in the United States in the decade ahead.

▼ There are many similarities between the Japanese economic crisis of 1990 and the 2008 crisis of the United States. Some of the policy responses are also quite similar. But there is one huge difference: whereas monetary policy was restrictive in Japan, it has been highly expansionary in the United States. If monetary policy exerts a strong impact on the economy, the U.S. experience in the decade ahead will differ from that of Japan during the 1990s.

▼ Even if the expansionary monetary policy does lead to a robust recovery in the United States, the long and variable monetary policy lags will make it difficult for the Fed to both promote recovery and then shift back to restraint in a manner that will lead to stability in the decade ahead. We are in the midst of a very interesting "experiment" in macroeconomics.

CRITICAL ANALYSIS QUESTIONS

1. How was the economic experience of Japan prior to and after 1990 similar to that of the United States prior to and after 2008?

*2. Describe the fiscal policy of Japan during the 1990s. Did the Japanese fiscal policy help promote recovery? Why or why not?

3. How did the policy response in the United States following the sharp reductions in housing and stock prices in 2008 differ from that of Japan following the collapse of asset prices in 1990? How were the policy responses similar?

*4. What happened to the share of the Japanese population age 65 and over during the 1990s? How did this change affect economic growth? What are the implications of this for the United States? Why?

5. What are the most important lessons Americans can learn from the Japanese experience of the 1990s?

6. What does the Japanese experience of the 1990s indicate with regard to the return of housing and stock prices to their pre-crisis levels? Why might the future pattern in the United States differ from that of Japan during the 1990s?

*Asterisk denotes questions for which answers are given in Appendix B.

The Federal Budget and the National Debt

FOCUS

- **What is the national debt and how large is it?**

- **How are future generations affected by debt financing?**

- **Are budget deficits the result of the political incentive structure?**

- **Is the federal debt approaching dangerous levels?**

istorically, attitudes toward government debt have undergone dramatic swings. Prior to the 1960s, there was a political consensus that budget deficits were irresponsible and therefore should be

The attractiveness of financing spending by debt issue to the elected politicians should be obvious. Borrowing allows spending to be made that will yield immediate political payoffs without the incurring of any immediate political cost.

—James Buchanan[1]

[1]James Buchanan, *The Deficit and American Democracy* (Memphis: P. K. Steidman Foundation, 1984).

avoided, except perhaps during wartime emergencies. The rise of Keynesian economics altered this view. During the 1960–1980 Keynesian era, deficits were perceived as an important policy tool that could be used to stimulate growth and help promote stability. But large budget deficits during the 1980s and since 2001 have again generated concern about the impact of government debt. This feature will analyze both the economics and politics of debt financing.■

Deficits, Surpluses, and the National Debt

National debt

The sum of the indebtedness of the federal government in the form of outstanding interest-earning bonds. It reflects the cumulative impact of budget deficits and surpluses.

When the federal government uses debt rather than taxes and user charges to pay for its expenditures, the U.S. Treasury fills this gap by borrowing in the loanable funds market. When borrowing funds, the Treasury generally issues interest-bearing bonds. These bonds compose the national debt. In effect, the **national debt** consists of loans various parties have extended to the general fund of the U.S. Treasury.

The federal budget exerts a direct impact on the national debt. The budget deficit or surplus is a "flow" concept (like water running into or out of a bathtub), whereas the national debt is a "stock" figure (like the amount of water in the tub at a point in time). A budget deficit increases the size of the national debt by the amount of the deficit. Conversely, a budget surplus allows the federal government to pay off bondholders and thereby reduce the size of the national debt. In essence, the national debt represents the cumulative effect of all the prior budget deficits and surpluses.

The creditworthiness of an organization is dependent upon the size of its debt relative to its income base. Therefore, when analyzing the significance of budget deficits, surpluses, and the national debt, it makes sense to consider their size relative to the entire economy.

EXHIBIT 1 presents data for the 1960–2010 period for both the federal budget deficit and the national debt as a percentage of GDP. Because the defense effort of World War II was largely financed with debt rather than taxes, the national debt was quite large during the period immediately following the war. But the budget deficits were small—less than 1 percent—as a share of GDP during the 1950s and 1960s. Historically, real output in the United States has grown at an annual rate of approximately 3 percent. When the budget deficit as a percentage of GDP is less than the growth of real output, the federal debt will decline relative to the size of the economy. This is precisely what happened for a quarter of a century following World War II. Budget deficits were present (see Exhibit 1, part a), and they pushed up the nominal national debt. But the economy grew even more rapidly. As a result, the national debt as a share of GDP fell from 56 percent in 1960 to 32 percent in 1974 (see Exhibit 1, part b).

From the mid-1970s to the mid-1990s, federal deficits were both large and continuous. As Exhibit 1, part (a), shows, budget deficits averaged nearly 4 percent of GDP during 1974–1995. These large deficits pushed the national debt up from 32 percent of GDP in 1974 to 67 percent in 1995. As the economy grew rapidly in the 1990s, the budget deficits were eventually transformed into surpluses, leading to a temporary reduction in the national debt.

However, during the last decade, the budget deficits have been large and the federal debt has grown rapidly, particularly during the financial crisis and recession of 2008–2009. As Exhibit 1, part (b), shows, the federal debt to GDP ratio rose from 58 percent in 2000 to 70 percent in 2008 and then soared to 98 percent in 2010. Measured as a share of the economy, the federal debt is now higher than at any time since the years immediately following World War II.

EXHIBIT 1

Budget Deficits, Surpluses, and the National Debt as a Percentage
of GDP, 1960–2010

*Between World War II and 1973, federal budget deficits were small as a share of GDP (see part a).
During this period, the national debt declined as a proportion of GDP (part b). During 1974–1995, the
budget deficits were quite large, causing the national debt to increase as a percentage of GDP. After falling
during 1996–2001, the national debt increased during 2002–2007, and it soared during the recession
of 2008–2009. The federal debt to GDP ratio now stands at the highest level since the years immediately
following World War II.*

(a) Federal budget deficit or surplus as a percentage of GDP

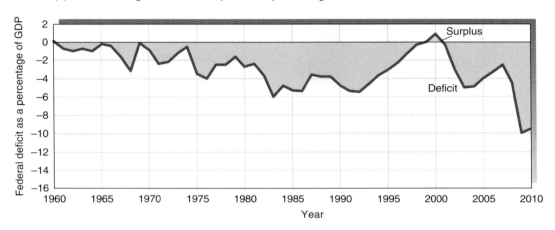

(b) Gross and net federal debt as a percentage of GDP

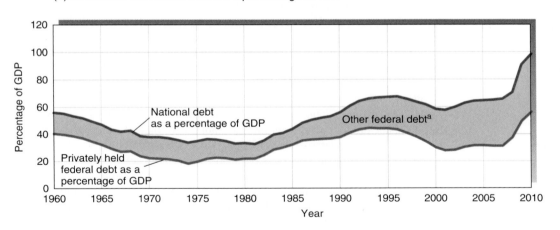

[a]Federal debt held by U.S. government agencies and Federal Reserve banks.
Source: http://www.whitehouse.gov/omb. The figures for 2009 and 2010 are estimated.

Who Owns the National Debt?

As **EXHIBIT 2** illustrates, nearly two-fifths (38.6 percent) of the national debt is held by
agencies of the federal government. For example, Social Security Trust Funds are often
used to purchase U.S. bonds. When the debt is owned by a government agency, it is little
more than an accounting transaction indicating that one government agency (for example,
the Social Security Administration) is making a loan to another (the U.S. Treasury). Even the
interest payments in this case represent little more than an internal government transfer.

EXHIBIT 2
Who Owns the National Debt?

Of the $11.13 trillion national debt (as of March 31, 2009), a little less than half is held by government agencies (primarily the Social Security Trust Fund) and Federal Reserve banks. Of the $6.34 trillion federal debt held privately, a little more than half is held by foreign investors.

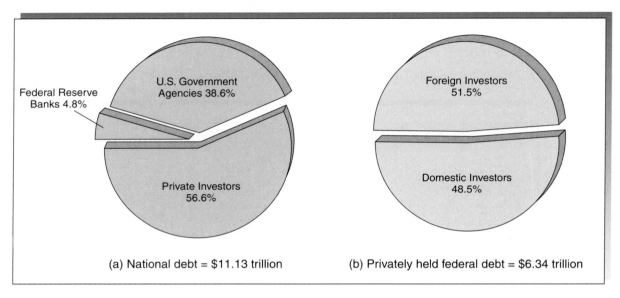

(a) National debt = $11.13 trillion   (b) Privately held federal debt = $6.34 trillion

Source: http://www.fms.treas.gov/bulletin/index.html

Another 4.8 percent of the public debt is held by the Federal Reserve System. When the Fed purchases U.S. securities, it creates money. The bonds held by the Fed, therefore, are indicative of prior government expenditures that have been paid for with "printing-press" money—money created by the central bank. As in the case of the securities held by government agencies, the interest on the bonds held by the Fed is returned to the Treasury after the Fed has covered its costs of operation. The U.S. Treasury both pays and receives almost all of the interest, approximately $32 billion in 2008, on the bonds held by the Federal Reserve. Thus, the bonds held by the Fed, like those held by U.S. government agencies, do not create a net interest liability for the U.S. Treasury.

Privately held government debt

The portion of the national debt owed to domestic and foreign investors. It does not include bonds held by agencies of the federal government or the Federal Reserve.

In contrast, **privately held government debt** imposes a net interest burden on the federal government. In the case of the privately held debt—that is, the bonds held by individuals, insurance companies, mutual funds, and other investors—the federal government will have to impose taxes to meet the future interest payments on these bonds. Therefore, it is important to distinguish between (1) the total national debt and (2) the privately held government debt. Only the latter imposes a net interest obligation on the federal government. As of March 31, 2009, the privately held portion of the national debt was $6.34 trillion, slightly more than half of the $11.13 trillion national debt. Thus, the total national debt vastly overstates the net debt obligations of the federal government.

Slightly more than half of the privately held debt is owned by foreign investors. This portion is sometimes referred to as **external debt**. We will take a closer look at the foreign ownership of Treasury bonds a little later in this feature.

External debt

The portion of the national debt owed to foreign investors.

Part (b) of Exhibit 1 presents data on the size of the privately held federal debt for the 1960–2008 period. Measured as a share of GDP, the general pattern of the privately held debt has been similar to that for the national debt as a whole. Like the total debt, the privately held debt has soared during the past couple of years. Driven by the huge deficits of 2008–2009, the privately held debt rose from 37 percent of GDP in 2008 to 49 percent in 2009 and 56 percent in 2010. Clearly, these trends are not sustainable. As we proceed, we will consider their potential impact on the economy.

How Does Debt Financing Influence Future Generations?

The impact of the national debt on future generations has been a point of controversy for decades.[2] Opponents of debt financing often charge that we are mortgaging the future of our children and grandchildren—that debt financing permits us to consume today, then send the bill to future generations. In the 1960s and 1970s, the overwhelming bulk of the national debt was held by domestic investors. During this era, Keynesians argued that there was little reason for concern because "We owe it to ourselves." Today, new classical economists take the position that debt affects the timing, but not the magnitude, of taxes. Like Keynesians, the new classical economists do not believe that debt financing exerts much impact on the welfare of future generations. Who is right?

When analyzing the issue of debt financing, it is important to keep two points in mind. First, in the case of domestically held debt, our children and grandchildren will indeed pay the taxes to service the debt, but they will also receive the interest payments. Admittedly, those paying the taxes and receiving the interest payments will not always be the same people. Some will gain and others will lose. But both those who gain and those who lose will be members of the future generation.

Second, debt financing of a government activity cannot push the opportunity cost of the resources used by the government onto future generations. If current GDP is $14 trillion and the federal government spends $4 trillion on goods and services, then only $10 trillion will be available for consumption and investment by domestic businesses, state and local governments, and individuals. This will be true regardless of whether the federal government finances its expenditures with taxes or debt. When the government builds a highway, constructs an antimissile defense system, or provides police protection, it draws resources with alternative uses away from the private sector. This cost is incurred in the present; it cannot be avoided through debt financing.

If the opportunity cost of resources occurs during the current period, does this mean that the welfare of future generations is unaffected by debt financing? Not necessarily. Debt financing influences future generations primarily through its potential impact on saving and capital formation. If lots of factories, machines, houses, technical knowledge, and other productive assets are available to future generations, then their productive potential will be high. Alternatively, if the next generation inherits fewer productive assets, then its productive capability will be less. Thus, the true measure of how government debt influences future generations involves knowledge of its impact on capital formation.

The impact of budget deficits on capital formation is a complex issue. Holding government expenditures constant, how will the substitution of debt financing for current taxation influence capital formation? As our discussion of fiscal policy models implies, economists differ in their response to this question. We will consider two major theories: the traditional view that budget deficits reduce future capital stock and the opposing new classical view that such deficits exert no significant future impact.

Traditional View: Budget Deficits Reduce the Future Capital Stock

Most economists embrace the traditional view that budget deficits will retard private investment and thereby reduce the welfare of future generations. Suppose that the government substitutes borrowing for current taxation. For example, consider what would happen if the government cut the current taxes of each household by $1,000 and borrowed the funds to replace the lost revenues. As a result, the after-tax income of each household increases by $1,000. Of course, the households may save some of the $1,000 addition to

[2]See Richard H. Fink and Jack High, eds., *A Nation in Debt: Economists Debate the Federal Budget Deficit* (Frederick, MD: University Publications of America, 1987), for an excellent set of readings summarizing this debate.

their disposable income, but they are also likely to spend some of it on consumption goods, according to the traditional view. If they do not save all of the $1,000, the additional government borrowing will increase the demand for loanable funds relative to the supply and thereby push real interest rates upward.[3] In turn, the higher real interest rates will retard private investment, which will reduce the physical capital available to future generations. To the extent future generations work with less capital (fewer productivity-enhancing tools and machines), their productivity and wages will be lower than would have been the case had the budget deficits not crowded out private investment.

In addition, the higher interest rates will attract foreign investors. But investments in the United States will require dollars. As foreigners increase their investments in the United States, they will demand dollars in the foreign exchange market. This strong demand will cause the dollar to appreciate relative to other currencies. In turn, the appreciation in the exchange rate value of the dollar will make U.S. exports more expensive to foreigners and foreign goods cheaper for Americans. These relative price changes will retard exports and stimulate imports. Predictably, net exports will decline.

The inflow of capital from abroad will dampen both the increase in interest rates and the reduction in domestic investment. However, it will also increase the asset holdings of foreigners in the United States. The returns to these assets will generate income for foreigners rather than Americans. Therefore, compared to the situation in which government was financed with current taxation, future generations of Americans will inherit both a smaller stock of physical capital and less income from that capital (because the share owned by foreigners has increased). Succeeding generations will be less well off as a result.

In summary, the traditional view argues that the substitution of debt financing for current taxation will increase current consumption, push up real interest rates, and retard private investment. In addition, the higher real interest rates will lead to an increase in net foreign investment, appreciation in the exchange rate value of the dollar, and a decline in net exports (imports will increase relative to exports). According to the traditional view, budget deficits will retard the growth rate of capital formation, particularly that owned by Americans, and reduce national income and future living standards of Americans.

New Classical View: Budget Deficits Exert Little Impact on Future Capital Stock

Not all economists accept the traditional view of budget deficits. An alternative theory, most closely associated with Robert Barro of Harvard University, encompasses the new classical perspective of fiscal policy.[4] This new classical view stresses that additional debt implies an equivalent amount of future taxes. If, as the new classical model assumes, individuals fully anticipate the added future tax liability accompanying the debt, current consumption will be unaffected when governments substitute debt for taxes. According to this view, when future taxes (debt) are substituted for current taxes, people will save the reduction in current taxes so that they will have the required income to pay the higher future taxes implied by the additional debt. Continuing with our previous example, the new classical theory implies that households receiving a $1,000 reduction in current taxes financed by issuing bonds (that imply higher future taxes) will save all the $1,000 increase in their current disposable income. This increase in saving, triggered by the anticipation of the higher future taxes, allows the additional government debt to be financed without an increase in the real rate of interest. Because there is no increase in interest rates, private investment is unaffected. Neither is there an influx of foreign capital. Under these circumstances, the substitution of debt for taxes exerts little or no impact on either capital formation or the welfare of future generations.

---

[3]Alternatively, one could approach this topic from the viewpoint of how households value the government bonds relative to the future tax liability implied by the bonds. If bondholders recognize the asset value of the government bonds and taxpayers fail to recognize fully the accompanying tax liability, then the general populace will have an exaggerated view of its true wealth position. Wealth is an important determinant of consumption. When people think they are wealthier, they will consume more and save less than they would if they had fully recognized their future tax liability. Of course, the increase in consumption and reduction in savings would place upward pressure on the real rate of interest. This is simply an alternative way of viewing the substitution of government debt for current taxation.

[4]See Robert Barro, "Are Government Bonds Net Wealth?" *Journal of Political Economy* 82 (November–December 1974): 1095–1117; and "The Ricardian Approach to Budget Deficits," *Journal of Economic Perspectives* 2 (Spring 1989).

Empirical Evidence on the Impact of the Deficit

What does the empirical evidence indicate with regard to the validity of the two theories? Empirical studies have found little, if any, relationship between year-to-year changes in the budget deficit and real interest rates. New classical economists argue that these findings are supportive of their theory. However, the experience of the last decade provides support for the traditional theory. As budget deficits rose during 2001–2010, Americans increased their current consumption expenditures and substantially reduced their domestically financed capital formation. Simultaneously, there was an inflow of net foreign investment and a reduction in net exports (imports increased relative to exports). This pattern is consistent with the traditional theory. Thus, the empirical evidence with regard to the impact of budget deficits is mixed. This is an important area of continuing research.

Government Debt: A Cross-Country Comparison

How does the net government debt of the United States compare with other major industrial nations? **EXHIBIT 3** provides the answer. Among these countries, the net public debt/GDP ratio in 2009 was lowest for Australia. The debt/GDP ratio of the United States was

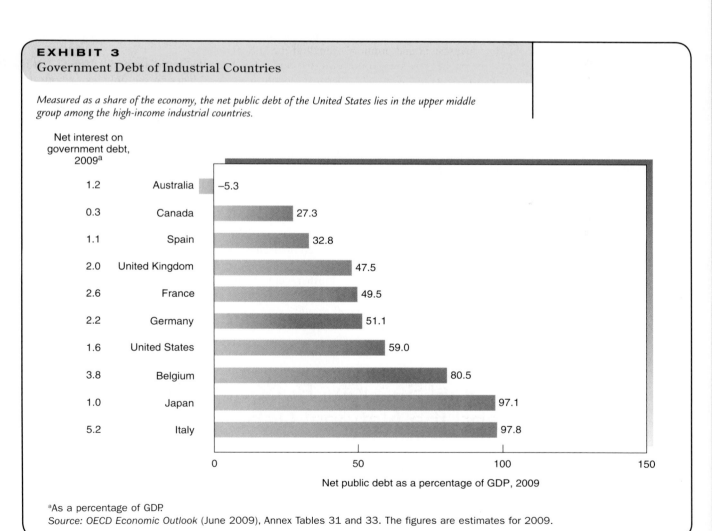

EXHIBIT 3
Government Debt of Industrial Countries

Measured as a share of the economy, the net public debt of the United States lies in the upper middle group among the high-income industrial countries.

Net interest on government debt, 2009[a]

	Country	Net public debt as a percentage of GDP, 2009
1.2	Australia	−5.3
0.3	Canada	27.3
1.1	Spain	32.8
2.0	United Kingdom	47.5
2.6	France	49.5
2.2	Germany	51.1
1.6	United States	59.0
3.8	Belgium	80.5
1.0	Japan	97.1
5.2	Italy	97.8

[a]As a percentage of GDP.
Source: OECD Economic Outlook (June 2009), Annex Tables 31 and 33. The figures are estimates for 2009.

higher by about 10 percentage points than the figures for the United Kingdom, Germany, and France. The debt ratio was highest in Belgium, Japan, and Italy. Thus, the net debt/GDP ratio of the United States places it in the upper middle group among the high-income industrial economies.

A large outstanding debt generally means higher taxes for the financing of the interest payments. This was the case in both Belgium and Italy, in which interest payments as a share of the economy were approximately twice the level of the United States. In Japan, however, the interest payments were a relatively small share of GDP, even though the outstanding government debt was large. This occurred because the domestic saving rate of Japan has been exceedingly high, and this has kept domestic interest rates low in recent years.

Is the Foreign Holding of Federal Debt Dangerous?

Foreign ownership of the federal debt has increased sharply in recent years. Foreigners now hold $3.3 trillion of U.S. Treasury bonds. This is 52 percent of the outstanding privately held debt, up from only 24 percent in 1995. Foreign central banks, particularly those of China, Japan, and Taiwan, account for approximately two-thirds of the foreign holdings.[5]

To a degree, the foreign ownership of Treasury bonds reflects the increasingly global nature of financial markets. The purchase of Treasury bonds by foreigners indicates that they are willing to finance federal debt at lower interest rates than domestic lenders. When foreigners buy U.S. bonds, the supply of loanable funds will increase, which will place downward pressure on domestic interest rates. In turn, the lower interest rates will stimulate investment and promote growth of the U.S. economy.

For the past several decades, the dollar has been the world's premier currency. It is readily accepted worldwide because people have confidence in the policies of both the Federal Reserve and the U.S. government. Central banks and currency boards throughout the world hold U.S. Treasury bonds because they enhance the credibility of their domestic currency. In addition, many internationally traded goods like oil are often bought and sold in dollars even when Americans are not involved in the transactions.

What would happen if foreigners lost confidence in the dollar and the policies of the U.S. government? If the United States follows sensible monetary, financial, and regulatory policies, this is unlikely to happen. But investors and world traders have alternatives. In the years immediately ahead, the euro may challenge the dollar as the world's premier currency. Between 2002 and 2009, the euro appreciated by about 50 percent against the dollar. Bulgaria, Estonia, Latvia, Lithuania, and Bosnia and Herzegovina recently established currency boards, and all of them tied their currency to the euro. If confidence in the euro continues to grow, a larger share of future international trade may be conducted in euros and a smaller share in dollars. Further, central banks with large holdings of U.S. Treasury bonds—China and Japan, for example—might decide to shift some of these holdings to bonds in euros. These changes would cause the foreign exchange value of the dollar to depreciate and domestic interest rates in the United States to rise. If the changes took place abruptly, they could exert a sizable negative impact on the U.S. economy.

Social Security, Budget Deficits, and the National Debt

As conventionally measured, the budget deficit includes the revenues and expenditures of government trust funds, including the Social Security Trust Fund. Under legislation adopted in 1983, Social Security payroll tax rates were set at levels designed to generate

[5]The figures presented here are from http://www.economagic.com and http://www.gpoaccess.gov/usbudget/fy10/pdf/spec.pdf.

surpluses for the years prior to the retirement of the baby boom generation. Currently, the revenues flowing into the Social Security system are about $60 billion more than the benefits paid out (or $160 billion if interest on the Social Security trust fund bonds is included). Thus, the inclusion of Social Security in the budget calculation makes the deficit appear smaller than would otherwise be the case.

This is important because the current Social Security surplus will swing to a deficit once the baby boomers start retiring, beginning around 2010. As this happens, rather than reducing the federal government's overall budget deficit, the Social Security system will add to it. This will make it even more difficult for the federal government to balance its budget.

Interestingly, the "implicit debt" accompanying the Social Security and Medicare programs is far greater than the national debt. At current tax rates, the revenues flowing into the Social Security system are sufficient to cover only about 70 percent of the promised benefits. Thus, 30 percent of the promised Social Security benefits are unfunded. They cannot be paid without an increase in taxes (or additional borrowing). These unfunded Social Security benefits amount to about $8 trillion. The situation is even worse for Medicare. At current rates, Medicare taxes will fall short of the promised future benefits by an estimated $38 trillion.[6] Thus, the implicit debt (promised benefits that exceed revenues generated at current tax rates) of the Social Security and Medicare programs is four or five times the national debt.

Like the official federal debt, these unfunded liabilities will mean either higher taxes or broken promises in the future. This is a point that is often overlooked in discussions about the size of the national debt.

The Political Economy of Debt Financing

As we noted earlier, prior to 1960, almost everyone—including the leading figures of both political parties—thought the federal government should balance its budget. In essence, there was widespread implicit agreement, something like a Constitutional rule, that the federal budget should be balanced. Against this political background, both deficits and surpluses were small relative to the size of the economy during times of peace.

The Keynesian revolution changed all of this. Rather than balancing the budget, Keynesians argued that the budget should be shifted toward deficit when stimulus was needed and toward surplus when there was concern about inflation. In essence, the Keynesian revolution released political decision makers from the discipline imposed by a balanced budget. Freed from this constraint, politicians persistently spent more than they were willing to tax.[7] Since 1960, there have been only two brief periods of budget surplus, one in 1969 and the other in 1998–2001.

From a public choice viewpoint, the political attractiveness of spending compared to taxation is not surprising. Politicians have a strong incentive to spend money on programs that benefit the voters of their district and special interest groups that will help them win reelection. In contrast, they do not like to levy taxes because they impose a visible cost on voters. Borrowing provides politicians with an attractive alternative. Because they push the taxes into the future, deficits impose a less visible cost than current taxation. Thus, borrowing allows politicians to supply voters with immediate benefits without having to impose a parallel visible cost in the form of higher taxes or user charges.

The same is true for unfunded promises like those of Social Security and Medicare. Like borrowing, this technique makes it possible for politicians to take credit for the

---

[6]See *2009 Annual Report of the Boards of Trustees of the Federal Hospital Insurance and Federal Supplementary Medical Insurance Trust Fund*, pp. 201–202, http://www.cms.hhs.gov/ReportsTrustFunds/.

[7]See James M. Buchanan and Richard Wagner, *Democracy in Deficit: The Political Legacy of Lord Keynes* (New York: Academic Press, 1977), for a detailed account of the changes wrought by the Keynesian Revolution.

promised benefits now without having to levy the equivalent amount of taxes. Thus, the political popularity of both debt financing and unfunded promised benefits is a reflection of the political incentive structure—the desire of elected officials to spend and their reluctance to tax. Unless the incentive structure is changed—for example, by requiring a two-thirds or three-fourths majority to approve spending measures or additional borrowing—debt financing can be expected to continue.

Politics, Demographics, Federal Debt, and the Dangers Ahead

Both the budget deficit and federal debt soared during the financial crisis of 2008–2009. The federal government borrowed nearly $1.5 trillion during 2009, and it is expected to borrow more than $1 trillion in 2010. As we noted earlier, these huge deficits have pushed the federal debt and the privately held debt to their highest levels since the years immediately following World War II (see Exhibit 1). Moreover, unfavorable demographics will soon make the situation worse. During the past quarter of a century, the Social Security program has been running a surplus, but that will soon reverse because the baby boomers are now moving into the retirement phase of life. As a result, federal expenditures on Social Security and Medicare are sure to soar during the next decade. Projections indicate that the federal government's net debt will rise to 80 percent of GDP by 2019, and many think this forecast is optimistic.

What will happen if the federal government does not bring its finances under control? As the size of a nation's debt gets larger and larger relative to income, there will be repercussions in credit markets. Extension of loans to the government of a country with a large debt/GDP ratio is risky. As a result, the highly indebted government will have to pay higher interest rates. This happened in Ireland in 1986 and Belgium in 1994. Of course, the higher interest rates will increase the interest cost on the outstanding debt, which will make it still more difficult to control the budget deficit.

When a country's outstanding debt is high, substantial tax receipts will be required to pay the interest on the debt. As it becomes more difficult to service the debt with taxes, governments will be tempted to use money creation to reduce the debt. However, if lenders even sense that will happen, there will be a run on the currency, inflation will soar, the foreign exchange value of the currency will plunge, and these factors will lead to a financial and economic crisis.

This has occurred in other countries that have failed to control government finances, and the United States is not immune to the laws of economics. Even though both politics and demographics will be placing upward pressure on government spending and budget deficits in the years immediately ahead, control in these areas is vitally important. The future prosperity of Americans is dependent on it.

KEY POINTS

▼ The national debt is the sum of the outstanding bonds of the U.S. Treasury. Budget deficits increase the national debt, whereas surpluses reduce it. The national debt reflects the cumulative effect of all prior budget deficits and surpluses.

▼ A little less than half of the national debt is owned by U.S. government agencies and the Federal Reserve. For this portion of the debt, the government

both pays and receives the interest (except for the expenses of the Fed). Only the privately held federal debt—the portion of the national debt owned by domestic and foreign investors—generates a net interest obligation for the government.

▼ Budget deficits affect future generations through their impact on capital formation. According to the traditional view, the substitution of debt financing for taxes will increase real interest rates and reduce the rate of capital formation—particularly capital owned by Americans. Thus, the traditional view indicates that future generations are adversely affected.

▼ In contrast with the traditional view, the new classical theory argues that people will increase their saving in anticipation of the higher future taxes implied by additional debt. In the new classical model, the substitution of debt for taxes leaves interest rates, consumption, and investment unaffected.

▼ Currently, inclusion of Social Security in the budget calculations makes the deficit appear smaller than would be true if these funds were omitted.

▼ Politicians find debt financing attractive because it allows them to spend without levying the equivalent

amount of taxes. Thus, political considerations make it difficult to achieve balanced budgets. This factor, along with increased spending on Social Security and Medicare as the baby boomers begin retiring in the years following 2010, will make it particularly difficult to control debt financing in the decade ahead.

▼ Measured as a share of GDP, the net outstanding debt of the United States falls in the upper middle group among high-income industrial countries. But the federal debt to GDP ratio has soared during 2008–2010, and it now stands at the highest levels since the years immediately following World War II. If the upward trend in this ratio is not halted, it will lead to serious economic problems in the future.

CRITICAL ANALYSIS QUESTIONS

*1. Does the national debt have to be paid off at some time in the future? What will happen if it is not?

2. What is the difference between the national debt and privately held federal debt? Why is the distinction between the two important?

*3. When government bonds are held by foreigners, the interest income from the bonds goes to foreigners rather than to Americans. Would Americans be better off if we prohibited the sale of bonds to foreigners?

4. How does the Social Security system currently influence the size of the budget deficit? How will it influence the deficit a decade from now? Is this a cause for concern? Why or why not?

*5. Would you predict that government expenditures would be higher or lower if taxes (or user charges) were required for the finance of all expenditures? Why? Do you think the government would spend

funds more or less efficiently if it could not issue debt? Explain.

6. How does foreign ownership of Treasury bonds influence the incentive of U.S. policy makers to follow sound policies? Is this good or bad? Explain.

*7. Does an increase in the national debt increase the supply of money (M1)? Can the money supply increase when the U.S. Treasury is running a budget surplus?

8. "Given the incentive of elected political officials to spend and their reluctance to tax, two-thirds approval of the House and Senate should be required for both spending measures and increases in government debt." Do you think this is a good idea? Why or why not?

*Asterisk denotes questions for which answers are given in Appendix B.

General Business and Economics Indicators for the United States

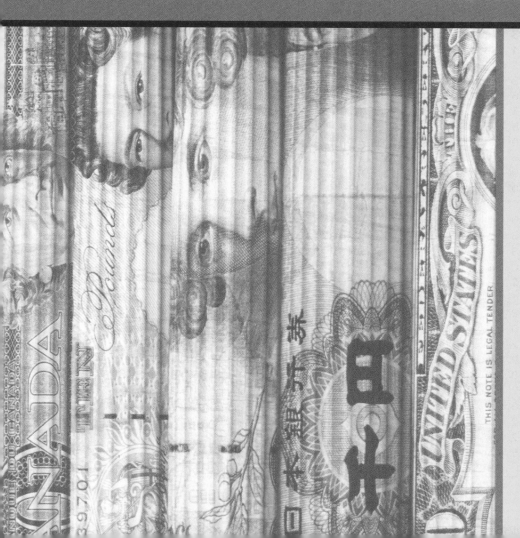

SECTION 1
Gross Domestic Product and its Components

Year	Personal Consumption Expenditures (Billions)	Gross Private Domestic Investment (Billions)	Government Consumption and Gross Investment (Billions)	Net Exports (Billions)	Gross Domestic Product (Billions)	Real GDP 2005 Prices	Real GDP Annual Real Rate (Percent)	Real GDP per Capita
1960	$331.8	$78.9	$111.5	$4.2	$526.4	$2,830.9	2.5	$15,612
1961	342.2	78.2	119.5	4.9	544.8	2,896.9	2.3	15,716
1962	363.3	88.1	130.1	4.1	585.7	3,072.4	6.1	16,415
1963	382.7	93.8	136.4	4.9	617.8	3,206.7	4.4	16,888
1964	411.5	102.1	143.2	6.9	663.6	3,392.3	5.8	17,625
1965	443.8	118.2	151.4	5.6	719.1	3,610.1	6.4	18,523
1966	480.9	131.3	171.6	3.9	787.7	3,845.3	6.5	19,504
1967	507.8	128.6	192.5	3.6	832.4	3,942.5	2.5	19,778
1968	558.0	141.2	209.3	1.4	909.8	4,133.4	4.8	20,526
1969	605.1	156.4	221.4	1.4	984.4	4,261.8	3.1	20,951
1970	648.3	152.4	233.7	4.0	1,038.3	4,269.9	0.2	20,746
1971	701.6	178.2	246.4	0.6	1,126.8	4,413.3	3.4	21,175
1972	770.2	207.6	263.4	−3.4	1,237.9	4,647.7	5.3	22,059
1973	852.0	244.5	281.7	4.1	1,382.3	4,917.0	5.8	23,107
1974	932.9	249.4	317.9	−0.8	1,499.5	4,889.9	−0.6	22,781
1975	1,033.8	230.2	357.7	16.0	1,637.7	4,879.5	−0.2	22,517
1976	1,151.3	292.0	383.0	−1.6	1,824.6	5,141.3	5.4	23,488
1977	1,277.8	361.3	414.1	−23.1	2,030.1	5,377.7	4.6	24,327
1978	1,427.6	438.0	453.6	−25.4	2,293.8	5,677.6	5.6	25,411
1979	1,591.2	492.9	500.7	−22.5	2,562.2	5,855.0	3.1	25,925
1980	1,755.8	479.3	566.1	−13.1	2,788.1	5,839.0	−0.3	25,569
1981	1,939.5	572.4	627.5	−12.5	3,126.8	5,987.2	2.5	25,953
1982	2,075.5	517.2	680.4	−20.0	3,253.2	5,870.9	−1.9	25,208
1983	2,288.6	564.3	733.4	−51.7	3,534.6	6,136.2	4.5	26,110
1984	2,501.1	735.6	796.9	−102.7	3,930.9	6,577.1	7.2	27,742
1985	2,717.6	736.2	878.9	−115.2	4,217.5	6,849.3	4.1	28,632
1986	2,896.7	746.5	949.3	−132.5	4,460.1	7,086.5	3.5	29,357
1987	3,097.0	785.0	999.4	−145.0	4,736.4	7,313.3	3.2	30,079
1988	3,350.1	821.6	1,038.9	−110.1	5,100.4	7,613.9	4.1	31,037
1989	3,594.5	874.9	1,100.6	−87.9	5,482.1	7,885.9	3.6	31,835
1990	3,835.5	861.0	1,181.7	−77.6	5,800.5	8,033.9	1.9	32,070
1991	3,980.1	802.9	1,236.1	−27.0	5,992.1	8,015.1	−0.2	31,593
1992	4,236.9	864.8	1,273.5	−32.8	6,342.3	8,287.1	3.4	32,213
1993	4,483.6	953.3	1,294.8	−64.4	6,667.4	8,523.4	2.9	32,646
1994	4,750.8	1,097.3	1,329.8	−92.7	7,085.2	8,870.7	4.1	33,550
1995	4,987.3	1,144.0	1,374.0	−90.7	7,414.7	9,093.7	2.5	34,112
1996	5,273.6	1,240.2	1,421.0	−96.3	7,838.5	9,433.9	3.7	34,977
1997	5,570.6	1,388.7	1,474.4	−101.4	8,332.4	9,854.3	4.5	36,102
1998	5,918.5	1,510.8	1,526.1	−161.8	8,793.5	10,283.5	4.4	37,238
1999	6,342.8	1,641.5	1,631.3	−262.1	9,353.5	10,779.8	4.8	38,592
2000	6,830.4	1,772.2	1,731.0	−382.1	9,951.5	11,226.0	4.1	39,750
2001	7,148.8	1,661.9	1,846.4	−371.0	10,286.2	11,347.2	1.1	39,774
2002	7,439.2	1,647.0	1,983.3	−427.2	10,642.3	11,553.0	1.8	40,107
2003	7,804.0	1,729.7	2,112.6	−504.1	11,142.1	11,840.7	2.5	40,728
2004	8,285.1	1,968.6	2,232.8	−618.7	11,867.8	12,263.8	3.6	41,806
2005	8,819.0	2,172.2	2,369.9	−722.7	12,638.4	12,638.4	3.1	42,692
2006	9,322.7	2,327.2	2,518.4	−769.3	13,398.9	12,976.2	2.7	43,425
2007	9,826.4	2,288.5	2,676.5	−713.8	14,077.6	13,254.1	2.1	43,926
2008	10,129.9	2,136.1	2,883.2	−707.8	14,441.4	13,312.2	0.4	43,714

Source: http://www.bea.gov.

SECTION 2
Prices and Inflation

YEAR	GDP DEFLATOR		CONSUMER PRICE INDEX	
	INDEX (2005 = 100)	ANNUAL PERCENTAGE CHANGE	INDEX (1982–84 = 100)	PERCENTAGE CHANGE
1960	18.6	1.4	29.6	1.0
1961	18.8	1.1	29.9	1.1
1962	19.1	1.4	30.3	1.2
1963	19.3	1.1	30.6	1.2
1964	19.6	1.6	31.0	1.3
1965	19.9	1.8	31.5	1.6
1966	20.5	2.8	32.5	3.0
1967	21.1	3.1	33.4	2.8
1968	22.0	4.3	34.8	4.3
1969	23.1	4.9	36.7	5.5
1970	24.3	5.3	38.8	5.8
1971	25.5	5.0	40.5	4.3
1972	26.6	4.3	41.8	3.3
1973	28.1	5.5	44.4	6.2
1974	30.7	9.0	49.3	11.1
1975	33.6	9.5	53.8	9.1
1976	35.5	5.7	56.9	5.7
1977	37.8	6.4	60.6	6.5
1978	40.4	7.0	65.2	7.6
1979	43.8	8.3	72.6	11.3
1980	47.8	9.1	82.4	13.5
1981	52.3	9.4	90.9	10.3
1982	55.5	6.1	96.5	6.1
1983	57.7	3.9	99.6	3.2
1984	59.8	3.8	103.9	4.3
1985	61.6	3.0	107.6	3.5
1986	63.0	2.2	109.6	1.9
1987	64.8	2.8	113.6	3.7
1988	67.0	3.4	118.3	4.1
1989	69.5	3.8	124.0	4.8
1990	72.2	3.9	130.7	5.4
1991	74.8	3.5	136.2	4.2
1992	76.5	2.4	140.3	3.0
1993	78.2	2.2	144.5	3.0
1994	79.9	2.1	148.2	2.6
1995	81.5	2.1	152.4	2.8
1996	83.1	1.9	156.9	2.9
1997	84.6	1.8	160.5	2.3
1998	85.5	1.1	163.0	1.6
1999	86.8	1.5	166.6	2.2
2000	88.6	2.2	172.2	3.4
2001	90.7	2.3	177.1	2.8
2002	92.1	1.6	179.9	1.6
2003	94.1	2.2	184.0	2.3
2004	96.8	2.8	188.9	2.7
2005	100.0	3.3	195.3	3.4
2006	103.3	3.3	201.6	3.2
2007	106.2	2.9	207.3	2.8
2008	108.5	2.1	215.3	3.8

Sources: http://www.bea.gov and http://www.bls.gov.

SECTION 3
Population and Employment

| Year | Civilian Noninstitutional Population Age 16+ (Millions) | Civilian Labor Force (Millions) | Civilian Labor Force Participation Rate (Percent) | Civilian Employment/ Population Ratio (Percent) | Unemployment Rates | | | |
					All Workers	Both Sexes, Age 16 to 19	Men Age 20+	Women Age 20+
1960	117.2	69.6	59.4	56.1	5.5	14.7	4.7	5.1
1961	118.8	70.5	59.3	55.4	6.7	16.8	5.7	6.3
1962	120.2	70.6	58.8	55.5	5.5	14.7	4.6	5.4
1963	122.4	71.8	58.7	55.4	5.7	17.2	4.5	5.4
1964	124.5	73.1	58.7	55.7	5.2	16.2	3.9	5.2
1965	126.5	74.5	58.9	56.2	4.5	14.8	3.2	4.5
1966	128.1	75.8	59.2	56.9	3.8	12.8	2.5	3.8
1967	129.9	77.3	59.6	57.3	3.8	12.9	2.3	4.2
1968	132.0	78.7	59.6	57.5	3.6	12.7	2.2	3.8
1969	134.3	80.7	60.1	58.0	3.5	12.2	2.1	3.7
1970	137.1	82.8	60.4	57.4	4.9	15.3	3.5	4.8
1971	140.2	84.4	60.2	56.6	5.9	16.9	4.4	5.7
1972	144.1	87.0	60.4	57.0	5.6	16.2	4.0	5.4
1973	147.1	89.4	60.8	57.8	4.9	14.5	3.3	4.9
1974	150.1	91.9	61.3	57.8	5.6	16.0	3.8	5.5
1975	153.2	93.8	61.2	56.1	8.5	19.9	6.8	8.0
1976	156.2	96.2	61.6	56.8	7.7	19.0	5.9	7.4
1977	159.0	99.0	62.3	57.9	7.1	17.8	5.2	7.0
1978	161.9	102.3	63.2	59.3	6.1	16.4	4.3	6.0
1979	164.9	105.0	63.7	59.9	5.8	16.1	4.2	5.7
1980	167.7	106.9	63.8	59.2	7.1	17.8	5.9	6.4
1981	170.1	108.7	63.9	59.0	7.6	19.6	6.3	6.8
1982	172.3	110.2	64.0	57.8	9.7	23.2	8.8	8.3
1983	174.2	111.6	64.0	57.9	9.6	22.4	8.9	8.1
1984	176.4	113.5	64.4	59.5	7.5	18.9	6.6	6.8
1985	178.2	115.5	64.8	60.1	7.2	18.6	6.2	6.6
1986	180.6	117.8	65.3	60.7	7.0	18.3	6.1	6.2
1987	182.8	119.9	65.6	61.5	6.2	16.9	5.4	5.4
1988	184.6	121.7	65.9	62.3	5.5	15.3	4.8	4.9
1989	186.4	123.9	66.5	63.0	5.3	15.0	4.5	4.7
1990	189.2	125.8	66.5	62.8	5.6	15.5	5.0	4.9
1991	190.9	126.3	66.2	61.7	6.8	18.7	6.4	5.7
1992	192.8	128.1	66.4	61.5	7.5	20.1	7.1	6.3
1993	194.8	129.2	66.3	61.7	6.9	19.0	6.4	5.9
1994	196.8	131.1	66.6	62.5	6.1	17.6	5.4	5.4
1995	198.6	132.3	66.6	62.9	5.6	17.3	4.8	4.9
1996	200.6	133.9	66.8	63.2	5.4	16.7	4.6	4.8
1997	203.1	136.3	67.1	63.8	4.9	16.0	4.2	4.4
1998	205.2	137.7	67.1	64.1	4.5	14.6	3.7	4.1
1999	207.8	139.4	67.1	64.3	4.2	13.9	3.5	3.8
2000	212.6	142.6	67.1	64.4	4.0	13.1	3.4	3.6
2001	215.1	143.7	66.8	63.7	4.7	14.7	4.2	4.1
2002	217.6	144.9	66.6	62.7	5.8	16.5	5.2	5.1
2003	221.2	146.5	66.2	62.3	6.0	17.5	5.4	5.1
2004	223.4	147.4	66.0	62.3	5.5	17.0	4.9	4.9
2005	226.1	149.3	66.0	62.7	5.1	16.6	4.5	4.6
2006	228.8	151.4	66.2	63.1	4.6	15.4	4.1	4.1
2007	231.9	153.1	66.0	63.0	4.6	15.7	4.1	4.0
2008	233.8	154.3	66.0	62.2	5.8	18.7	5.2	4.9

Source: http://www.bls.gov.

SECTION 4
Federal Budget National Debt

Year	M1 (Billions)	Annual Change (Percent)	M2 (Billions)	Annual Change (Percent)	Aaa Bonds (Percent)	Federal Budget Fiscal Year Outlays (Billions)	Federal Budget Fiscal Year Receipts (Billions)	National Debt[1] Surplus/ Deficit (Billions)	National Debt[1] Billions of Dollars	National Debt[1] Percent of GDP
1960	$ 140.3	−0.1	$304.3	3.8	4.4	$ 92.2	$ 92.5	0.3	$ 210.3	40.5%
1961	143.1	2.0	324.8	6.7	4.4	97.7	94.4	(3.3)	211.1	39.8%
1962	146.5	2.4	350.1	7.8	4.3	106.8	99.7	(7.1)	218.3	38.5%
1963	151.0	3.1	379.6	8.4	4.3	111.3	106.6	(4.8)	222.0	37.0%
1964	156.8	3.8	409.3	7.8	4.4	118.5	112.6	(5.9)	222.1	34.6%
1965	163.4	4.3	442.5	8.1	4.5	118.2	116.8	(1.4)	221.7	32.2%
1966	171.0	4.6	471.4	6.5	5.1	134.5	130.8	(3.7)	221.5	29.3%
1967	177.7	3.9	503.6	6.8	5.5	157.5	148.8	(8.6)	219.9	27.1%
1968	190.1	7.0	545.3	8.3	6.2	178.1	153.0	(25.2)	237.3	27.3%
1969	201.4	6.0	578.7	6.1	7.0	183.6	186.9	3.2	224.0	23.6%
1970	209.1	3.8	601.5	3.9	8.0	195.6	192.8	(2.8)	225.5	22.3%
1971	223.1	6.7	674.4	12.1	7.4	210.2	187.1	(23.0)	237.5	22.0%
1972	239.0	7.1	758.2	12.4	7.2	230.7	207.3	(23.4)	251.0	21.3%
1973	256.3	7.2	831.8	9.7	7.4	245.7	230.8	(14.9)	265.7	20.3%
1974	269.1	5.0	880.6	5.9	8.6	269.4	263.2	(6.1)	263.1	18.3%
1975	281.3	4.5	963.5	9.4	8.8	332.3	279.1	(53.2)	309.7	19.8%
1976	297.2	5.6	1,086.5	12.8	8.4	371.8	298.1	(73.7)	382.7	22.0%
1977	319.9	7.6	1,221.2	12.4	8.0	409.2	355.6	(53.7)	444.1	22.5%
1978	346.2	8.2	1,322.2	8.3	8.7	458.7	399.6	(59.2)	491.6	22.2%
1979	372.6	7.6	1,425.7	7.8	9.6	504.0	463.3	(40.7)	524.7	21.0%
1980	395.7	6.2	1,540.2	8.0	11.9	590.9	517.1	(73.8)	591.1	21.7%
1981	425.0	7.4	1,679.3	9.0	14.2	678.2	599.3	(79.0)	664.9	21.7%
1982	453.0	6.6	1,832.6	9.1	13.8	745.7	617.8	(128.0)	790.1	24.5%
1983	503.2	11.1	2,056.9	12.2	12.0	808.4	600.6	(207.8)	981.7	28.5%
1984	538.6	7.1	2,221.2	8.0	12.7	851.9	666.5	(185.4)	1,151.9	29.9%
1985	587.0	9.0	2,419.0	8.9	11.4	946.4	734.1	(212.3)	1,337.5	32.2%
1986	666.3	13.5	2,615.7	8.1	9.0	990.4	769.2	(221.2)	1,549.8	35.2%
1987	743.6	11.6	2,785.8	6.5	9.4	1,004.1	854.4	(149.7)	1,677.7	36.0%
1988	774.8	4.2	2,936.2	5.4	9.7	1,064.5	909.3	(155.2)	1,822.4	36.4%
1989	782.2	1.0	3,059.7	4.2	9.3	1,143.8	991.2	(152.6)	1,970.6	36.5%
1990	810.6	3.6	3,227.4	5.5	9.3	1,253.1	1,032.1	(221.0)	2,177.1	37.9%
1991	859.0	6.0	3,347.0	3.7	8.8	1,324.3	1,055.1	(269.2)	2,430.4	41.0%
1992	965.9	12.4	3,409.3	1.9	8.1	1,381.6	1,091.3	(290.3)	2,703.3	43.3%
1993	1,078.4	11.7	3,445.6	1.1	7.2	1,409.5	1,154.5	(255.1)	2,922.7	44.4%
1994	1,145.2	6.2	3,493.1	1.4	8.0	1,461.9	1,258.7	(203.2)	3,077.9	44.2%
1995	1,143.0	−0.2	3,565.9	2.1	7.6	1,515.9	1,351.9	(164.0)	3,230.3	44.1%
1996	1,106.9	−3.2	3,738.8	4.8	7.4	1,560.6	1,453.2	(107.4)	3,343.1	43.4%
1997	1,070.2	−3.3	3,924.1	5.0	7.3	1,601.3	1,579.4	(21.9)	3,347.8	40.9%
1998	1,080.6	1.0	4,205.8	7.2	6.5	1,652.7	1,722.0	69.3	3,262.9	37.8%
1999	1,102.3	2.0	4,515.6	7.4	7.0	1,702.0	1,827.6	125.6	3,135.7	34.4%
2000	1,103.6	0.1	4,784.5	6.0	7.6	1,789.2	2,025.5	236.2	2,898.4	29.9%
2001	1,140.3	3.3	5,201.5	8.7	7.1	1,863.2	1,991.4	128.2	2,785.5	27.7%
2002	1,196.3	4.9	5,598.9	7.6	6.5	2,011.2	1,853.4	(157.8)	2,936.2	28.3%
2003	1,273.5	6.5	5,984.8	6.9	5.7	2,160.1	1,782.5	(377.6)	3,257.3	30.2%
2004	1,344.4	5.6	6,262.7	4.6	5.6	2,293.0	1,880.3	(412.7)	3,595.2	31.3%
2005	1,371.7	2.0	6,527.3	4.2	5.2	2,472.2	2,153.9	(318.3)	3,855.9	31.5%
2006	1,374.4	0.2	6,855.1	5.0	5.6	2,655.4	2,407.3	(248.2)	4,060.0	31.2%
2007	1,373.2	−0.1	7,249.7	5.8	5.6	2,728.9	2,568.2	(160.7)	4,255.5	31.2%
2008	1,429.0	4.1	7,747.8	6.9	5.6	2,982.9	2,524.3	(458.6)	5,311.6	37.3%

Sources: http://www.economagic.com and http://www.whitehouse.gov/omb/.

[1]National debt is debt held by private investors.

SECTION 5
Size of Government as a Share of GDP

SIZE OF GOVERNMENT AS A PERCENT OF GDP[1]

YEAR	EXPENDITURES (% OF GDP)	REVENUES (% OF GDP)	PURCHASES OF GOODS AND SERVICES (% OF GDP)	NON-DEFENSE PURCHASES OF GOODS AND SERVICES (% OF GDP)	TRANSFER PAYMENTS TO PERSONS (% OF GDP)
1960	23.3%	25.5%	21.2%	11.1%	5.3%
1961	24.3%	25.5%	21.9%	11.6%	5.8%
1962	24.4%	25.7%	22.2%	11.8%	5.6%
1963	24.5%	26.3%	22.1%	12.2%	5.5%
1964	24.0%	25.1%	21.6%	12.5%	5.3%
1965	23.7%	25.1%	21.1%	12.6%	5.3%
1966	24.5%	25.7%	21.8%	12.7%	5.3%
1967	26.4%	26.1%	23.1%	13.1%	6.0%
1968	27.1%	27.7%	23.0%	13.2%	6.4%
1969	27.1%	28.8%	22.5%	13.4%	6.5%
1970	28.4%	27.6%	22.5%	14.1%	7.4%
1971	28.9%	26.9%	21.9%	14.4%	8.1%
1972	28.7%	28.0%	21.3%	14.3%	8.3%
1973	27.9%	28.2%	20.4%	14.0%	8.3%
1974	29.1%	28.8%	21.2%	14.8%	9.0%
1975	31.0%	27.0%	21.8%	15.5%	10.3%
1976	30.1%	27.7%	21.0%	14.9%	10.0%
1977	29.4%	27.9%	20.4%	14.4%	9.5%
1978	28.5%	28.1%	19.8%	14.1%	9.1%
1979	28.3%	28.4%	19.5%	13.9%	9.1%
1980	30.2%	28.6%	20.3%	14.3%	10.0%
1981	30.8%	29.3%	20.1%	13.8%	10.0%
1982	33.0%	28.8%	20.9%	14.0%	10.8%
1983	33.0%	28.3%	20.7%	13.7%	10.7%
1984	31.9%	28.3%	20.3%	13.1%	9.9%
1985	32.4%	28.8%	20.8%	13.5%	9.9%
1986	32.7%	28.9%	21.3%	13.9%	9.9%
1987	32.4%	29.6%	21.1%	13.7%	9.7%
1988	31.7%	29.4%	20.4%	13.4%	9.6%
1989	31.6%	29.7%	20.0%	13.4%	9.7%
1990	32.3%	29.4%	20.3%	13.9%	10.1%
1991	33.0%	29.3%	20.6%	14.2%	10.4%
1992	33.8%	29.1%	20.1%	14.1%	11.8%
1993	33.3%	29.2%	19.4%	13.9%	12.0%
1994	32.4%	29.5%	18.7%	13.7%	11.8%
1995	32.5%	29.9%	18.5%	13.8%	11.9%
1996	32.0%	30.4%	18.1%	13.6%	11.9%
1997	31.0%	30.7%	17.7%	13.5%	11.5%
1998	30.1%	31.0%	17.4%	13.4%	11.1%
1999	29.5%	31.0%	17.4%	13.6%	10.9%
2000	29.2%	31.5%	17.4%	13.7%	10.8%
2001	30.1%	30.3%	18.0%	14.1%	11.4%
2002	30.8%	27.9%	18.6%	14.5%	12.0%
2003	31.0%	27.3%	19.0%	14.5%	12.2%
2004	30.8%	27.5%	18.8%	14.2%	12.1%
2005	31.0%	29.0%	18.8%	14.1%	12.1%
2006	31.0%	29.8%	18.8%	14.1%	12.2%
2007	31.4%	29.9%	19.0%	14.3%	12.4%
2008	32.8%	28.1%	20.0%	14.9%	13.2%

Source: http://www.bea.gov.

[1]There are some differences across reporting agencies with regard to accounting procedures and the treatment of government enterprises. This results in some differences in statistical measures of the size of government.

SECTION 6
Share (Percentage) of Federal Income Taxes Paid by Income Groupings

YEAR	TOP 1%	TOP 5%	TOP 10%	NEXT 40%	BOTTOM 50%
1980	19.1	36.8	49.3	43.7	7.0
1981	17.6	35.1	48.0	44.6	7.5
1982	19.0	36.1	48.6	44.1	7.3
1983	20.3	37.3	49.7	43.1	7.2
1984	21.1	38.0	50.6	42.1	7.4
1985	21.8	38.8	51.5	41.4	7.2
1986	25.7	42.6	54.7	38.9	6.5
1987	24.8	43.3	55.6	38.3	6.1
1988	27.6	45.6	57.3	37.0	5.7
1989	25.2	43.9	55.8	38.4	5.8
1990	25.1	43.6	55.4	38.8	5.8
1991	24.8	43.4	55.8	38.7	5.5
1992	27.5	45.9	58.0	36.9	5.1
1993	29.0	47.4	59.2	36.0	4.8
1994	28.9	47.5	59.4	35.8	4.8
1995	30.3	48.9	60.7	34.6	4.6
1996	32.3	51.0	62.5	33.2	4.3
1997	33.2	51.9	63.2	32.5	4.3
1998	34.8	53.8	65.0	30.8	4.2
1999	36.2	55.5	66.5	29.5	4.0
2000	37.4	56.5	67.3	28.8	3.9
2001	33.9	53.3	64.9	31.1	4.0
2002	33.7	53.8	65.7	30.8	3.5
2003	34.3	54.4	65.8	30.7	3.5
2004	36.9	57.1	68.2	28.5	3.3
2005	39.4	59.7	70.3	26.6	3.1
2006	39.9	60.1	70.8	26.2	3.0
2007	40.4	60.6	71.2	25.9	2.9

Source: Internal Revenue Service.

Answers to Selected Critical Analysis Questions

CHAPTER 1: THE ECONOMIC APPROACH

2. Production of scarce goods always involves a cost; there are no free lunches. When the government provides goods without charge to consumers, other citizens (taxpayers) will bear the cost of their provision. Thus, provision by the government affects how the costs will be covered, not whether they are incurred.

4. For most taxpayers, the change will reduce the after-tax cost of raising children. Other things being constant, one would predict an increase in the birthrate.

5. False. Intentions do not change the effect of the policy. If the policy runs counter to sound economics, it will lead to a counterproductive outcome even if that was not the intention of the policy. Bad policies are often advocated by people with good intentions.

7. Raising the price of new cars by requiring safety devices, which customers would not have purchased if given the choice, slows the rate of sales for new cars. Thus, the older, less safe cars are driven longer, partially offsetting the safety advantage provided by the newer, safer cars. Also, drivers act a bit differently—they may take more risks—when they believe the safety devices will provide protection should they have an accident. In fact, economist Gordon Tullock says that the greatest safety device of all might be a dagger built into the center of the steering wheel, pointed directly at the driver's chest!

8. Money has nothing to do with whether an individual is economizing. Any time a person chooses, in an attempt to achieve a goal, he or she is economizing.

9. Positive economics can help one better understand the likely effects of alternative policies. This will help one choose alternatives that are less likely to lead to disappointing results.

10. Association is not causation. It is likely that a large lead, near the end of the game, caused the third team to play more, rather than the third team causing the lead.

14. This is a question that highlights the importance of marginal analysis. In responding to the question, think about the following. After pollution has already been reduced substantially, how much will it cost to reduce it still more? If the quality of air and water were already high, how much gain would result from still less pollution?

CHAPTER 2: SOME TOOLS OF THE ECONOMIST

2. This is an opportunity cost question. Even though the productivity of brush painters has changed only slightly, rising productivity in other areas has led to higher wages in other occupations, thereby increasing the opportunity cost of being a house painter. Because people would not supply house painting services unless they were able to meet their opportunity costs, higher wages are necessary to attract house painters from competitive (alternative) lines of work.

4. The statement reflects the view that "exchange is a zero sum game." This view is false. No private business can force customers to buy. Consumers purchase various goods and services from businesses because they gain by doing so. If they did not gain, they would not continue to purchase items from a business. Similarly, the business firms also gain from their production and sale activities. Mutual gain provides the foundation for voluntary exchange, including that between business firms and their customers.

8. Yes. This question highlights the incentive of individuals to conserve for the future when they have private ownership rights. The market value of the land will increase in anticipation of the future harvest as the trees grow and the expected day of harvest grows closer. Thus, with transferable private property, the tree farmer will be able to capture the value added by his planting and holding the trees for a few years, even if the actual harvest does not take place until well after his death.

9. In general, it sanctions all forms of competition except for the use of violence (or the threat of violence), theft, or fraud.

11. If consumer demand for beef fell, the profitability of cattle herding would fall as well. Many cattle farmers would let their cattle herds dwindle and quit keeping cattle altogether. The result would be a smaller population of cattle, not a larger one. Because cattle are privately owned, an increase in their value in human consumption results in more cattle being kept, whereas a decrease would result in fewer cattle. To "save the cows," you should eat more beef!

12. Those who get tickets at the lower price gain, whereas those who are prevented from offering a higher price to ticket holders may not get a ticket even though both the prospective buyer and some ticket holders would have gained from the exchange at the higher price. Ticket holders may simply break the law or may sell at the regulated price only to buyers willing to provide them with other favors. Price controls, if they are effective, always reduce the gains from trade.

17. The opportunity cost of those individuals will rise, and they will likely consume less leisure.

CHAPTER 3: SUPPLY, DEMAND, AND THE MARKET PROCESS

1. Choices (a) and (b) would increase the demand for beef; (c) and (d) would affect primarily the supply of beef, rather than the demand; (e) leads to a change in quantity demanded, not a change in demand.

4. Prices reflect marginal value, not total value. The marginal value of a good is the maximum amount a consumer would be willing to pay for a specific unit. The height of the demand curve reflects the value that consumers place on each unit. The total value is the total benefit consumers derive from all units consumed. The area under the demand curve for the number of units consumed reflects the total value. Water provides an example of a good with high total value but low marginal value. With regard to the last question, are there more nurses or professional wrestlers?

8. Neither markets nor the political process leaves the determination of winners and losers to chance. Under market organization, business winners and losers are determined by the decentralized choices of millions of consumers who use their dollar votes to reward firms that provide preferred goods at a low cost and penalize others who fail to do so. Under political decision making, the winners and losers are determined by political officials who use taxes, subsidies, regulations, and mandates to favor some businesses and penalize others.

10. **a.** Profitable production increases the value of resources owned by people and leads to mutual gain for resource suppliers, consumers, and entrepreneurs. **b.** Losses reduce the value of resources, which reduces the well-being of at least some people. There is no conflict.

12. The supply curve is constructed under the assumption that other things are held constant. A reduction in the supply of oranges such as would occur under adverse weather conditions would lead to both a higher price and smaller total quantity supplied. This is perfectly consistent with economic theory.

14. Questions for thought: What happened to the cost of producing calculators during the period? How would this affect the supply curve and price of the calculators?

17. Business firms do have a strong incentive to serve the interest of consumers, but this is not what motivates them. Instead, they are motivated by self-interest and the pursuit of income, but they must provide consumers with a quality product if they

are going to be successful. Good intentions are not required for people to engage in actions that are helpful to others.

CHAPTER 4: SUPPLY AND DEMAND: APPLICATIONS AND EXTENSIONS

1. An increase in demand for housing will also increase the demand for the resources required for its production, including the services of carpenters, plumbers, and electricians. This will lead to higher wages and an increase in employment for people in these groups.

4. Agreement of both buyer and seller is required for an exchange. Price ceilings push prices below equilibrium and thereby reduce the quantity sellers are willing to offer. Price floors push prices above equilibrium and thereby reduce the quantity consumers wish to buy. Both decrease the actual quantity traded in the market.

6. **a.** Decreases; **b.** Increases; **c.** Decreases; **d.** Increases

11. The deadweight loss is the loss of the potential gains of buyers and sellers emanating from trades that are squeezed out by the tax. It is an excess burden because even though the exchanges that are squeezed out by the tax impose a cost on buyers and sellers, they do not generate tax revenue (because the trades do not take place).

14. The employment level of low-skilled workers with large families would decline. Some would attempt to conceal the presence of their large family in order to get a job.

16. No. As the tax rate approaches the revenue maximum point, the higher rates substantially reduce the number of trades that take place. This is why the higher rates do not raise much additional revenue. As rates increase toward the revenue maximum point, the lost gains from trade are large and the additions to revenue are small. Thus, rates in this range are highly inefficient.

17. **a.** The quantity of cigarettes sold legally will decline sharply. The evidence is consistent with this view. After the tax hike was instituted, the number of cigarette-tax stamps issued by the city of New York fell by approximately 50 percent.

   b. Because the quantity of cigarettes sold legally in New York City will decline sharply, the revenues raised from the tax may actually decline.

   c. Internet purchases will increase. Approximately 80 percent of the cigarettes sold through the Internet are from Indian reservations, which are exempt from state sales tax.

   d. The incidence of smoking by New Yorkers may not decline very much because there are good substitutes available for cigarettes purchased in New York City, namely cigarettes purchased through the Internet or in states with a lower cigarette tax. Thus, the cost of smoking for New Yorkers may not rise very much. Predictably, the tax will lead to a sharp increase in both the legal purchase and illegal smuggling of cigarettes into New York City from localities (such as Virginia and North Carolina) that impose a much lower tax on cigarettes.

CHAPTER 5: DIFFICULT CASES FOR THE MARKET AND THE ROLE OF GOVERNMENT

1. When payment is not demanded for services, potential customers have a strong incentive to attempt a "free ride." However, when the number of nonpaying customers becomes such that the sales revenues of sellers are diminished (and in some cases eliminated), the sellers' incentive to supply the good is thereby reduced (or eliminated).

4. The antimissile system is a public good for the residents of Washington, D.C. Strictly speaking, none of the other items is a public good because each could be provided to some consumers (paying customers, for example) without being provided to others.

9. By reducing output below the efficient level, sellers of toasters would no longer produce or exchange some units of the good, despite the fact that the consumers value the marginal units more than it costs to produce them.

11. A public good reflects the characteristics of the good, not the sector in which it is provided. Elementary education is not a public good because it is relatively easy to exclude nonpaying customers and establish a one-to-one link between payment for and receipt of the good.

14. A government intervention would be efficient if the benefits from the intervention exceeded the cost of the intervention. All opportunity costs (such as tax money required, resources utilized, and deadweight losses) would need to be considered in the comparison. A government intervention would be considered inefficient if the costs exceeded the benefits.

CHAPTER 6: THE ECONOMICS OF COLLECTIVE DECISION MAKING

2. Corporate officers, although they surely care about the next few months and the profits during that time, also care about the value of the firm and its stock price. If the stock price rises sufficiently in the next few months—as it will if investors believe that current investments in future-oriented projects (planting new trees, for example) are sound—then the officers will find their jobs secure even if current profits do not look good. Rights to the profits from those (future) trees are salable now in the form of the corporation's stock. There is no such mechanism to make the distant fruits of today's investments available to the political entrepreneurs who might otherwise fight for the future-oriented project. Only if the project appeals to today's voters, and only if they are willing to pay today for tomorrow's benefits, will the program be a political success. In any case, the wealth of the political official is not directly enhanced by his or her successful fight for the project.

4. The problem is not so much that the "wrong guys" won the last election as it is the incentive structure confronted by political decision makers. Even if the "right people" were elected, they would be unlikely to improve the efficiency of government, at least not very much, given the strong incentive to support special interest and shortsighted policies and the weak incentives for operational efficiency when decisions are made by the political process.

6. True. Because each individual computer customer both decides the issue (what computer, if any, will be purchased) and bears the consequences of a mistaken choice, each has a strong incentive to acquire information needed to make a wise choice. In contrast, each voter recognizes that one vote, even if mistaken, will not decide the congressional election. Thus, a voter has little incentive to search for information to make a better-informed choice.

8. It is difficult for the voter to know what a candidate will do once elected, and the rationally ignorant voter is usually unwilling to spend the time and effort required to understand issues because the probability that any single vote will decide the issue is exceedingly small. Special-interest voters, in contrast, will know which candidate has promised them the most on their issue. Also, the candidate who is both competent and prepared to ignore special interests will have a hard time getting these facts to voters without financial support from special-interest groups.

Each voter has an incentive to be a "free rider" on the "good government" issue. Interestingly, controlling government on behalf of society as a whole is a public good. As in the case of other public goods, there is a tendency for too little of it to be supplied.

10. No. The government is merely an alternative form of organization. Government organization does not permit us to escape either scarcity or competition. It merely affects the nature of the competition. Political competition (for example, voting, lobbying, political contributions, and politically determined budgets) replaces market competition. Neither is there any reason to believe that government organization modifies the importance of personal self-interest.

12. When the welfare of a special-interest group conflicts with that of a widely dispersed, unorganized majority, the legislative political process can reasonably be expected to work to the benefit of the special interest.

16. The presence of the sugar price supports and highly restrictive import quotas reflect the special-interest nature of the issue. Even though there are far more sugar consumers than growers, politicians apparently gain more by supporting the sugar growers and soliciting their political contributions than by representing the interests of consumers. Government action in this area has almost certainly reduced the income levels and living standards of Americans.

CHAPTER 7: TAKING THE NATION'S ECONOMIC PULSE

1. Choices (a), (c), (f), (g), and (h) will exert no effect on GDP; (b) and (d) will increase GDP by the amount of the expenditure; and (e) will increase GDP by $250 (the commission on the transaction).

3. Because the furniture was produced last year, the sale does not affect GDP this year. It reduces inventory investment by $100,000 and increases consumption by $100,000, leaving GDP unchanged.

5. The reliability of GDP comparisons over long periods of time is reduced because the leisure and human costs may change substantially between the two years, and because the types of goods available for consumption during the two years may be vastly different.

7. $8.10

9. a. $1,000; **b.** $600; **c.** $200; **d.** 0; **e.** $20,000

11. a. False. Inventory investment indicates whether the holdings of unsold goods are rising or falling. A negative inventory investment merely indicates that there was a reduction in the size of inventories during the period. **b.** False. If gross investment is less than the depreciation of capital goods during the period, net investment would be negative. Net investment in the United States was negative for several years during the Great Depression of the 1930s. **c.** Not necessarily. Rather, it may be the result of an increase in prices, population, or hours worked.

12. Neither the receipts nor the expenditures on payouts would count toward GDP because they are merely transfers—they do not involve production. However, expenditures on operations, administration, and government-provided goods and services from lottery proceeds would add to GDP.

14. a. 0; **b.** 0; **c.** $300; **d.** $500; **e.** $300; **f.** 0; **g.** 0; **h.** 0

16. a. $2,506.7 billion; **b.** $3,776.4 billion; **c.** 54.0; **d.** $5,803.8 billion; **e.** 108.6; **f.** $9,817 billion; and **g.** $11,654.4 billion

CHAPTER 8: ECONOMIC FLUCTUATIONS, UNEMPLOYMENT, AND INFLATION

2. Job seekers do not know which employers will offer them the more attractive jobs. They find out by searching. Job search is "profitable" and consistent with economic efficiency as long as the marginal gain from search exceeds the marginal cost of searching. The job search process will lead to a better match between the skills of employees and the requirements of the available jobs.

3. Individuals (e) and (f) would be classified as employed; (a), (b), and (c) would be classified as unemployed; (d) is not in the labor force.

6. When the actual unemployment rate is equal to the natural rate of unemployment, cyclical unemployment is absent and potential GDP is at its sustainable rate.

7. a. 60 percent; **b.** 8.3 percent; **c.** 55 percent

8. No. It means that there were no jobs available at wage rates acceptable to the potential workers who were unemployed. Thus, they continued to search for more attractive opportunities.

10. a. $646,552; $925,926; $581,395; $417,537; $400,000; **b.** 1940; **c.** The real salary rose because the price level fell between 1920 and 1940.

13. The wages people earn are also prices (prices for labor services) and, like other prices, they usually rise as the general level of prices increases. The statement ignores this factor. It implicitly assumes that money wages are unaffected by inflation—that they would have increased by the same amount (6 percent) even if prices would have been stable. Generally, this will not be the case.

CHAPTER 9: AN INTRODUCTION TO BASIC MACROECONOMIC MARKETS

4. If the inflation rate unexpectedly falls from 3 percent to zero, the real wages of union members will rise. If other unions have similar contracts, the unemployment rate will increase because employment costs have risen relative to product prices. Profit margins will be cut, and producers will respond by reducing output and laying off workers. In contrast, if the inflation rate rises to 8 percent, profit margins will improve, producers will expand their output, and the unemployment rate will decline.

6. An increase in the real interest rate will make it more attractive for foreigners to purchase bonds and make other investments in the United States. As a result, there will be an increase in the inflow of capital from abroad.

8. When the price level is higher than decision makers had anticipated, real wages will be lower and the level of employment higher than would have been the case if the price level had been anticipated accurately. Profit margins will increase; the actual rate of unemployment will fall below the natural rate. The high current rate of output will not be sustainable because real wages will rise as there is opportunity to renegotiate existing contracts.

10. They are all equal.

12. $10,000; $20,000

13. Inversely; an increase in interest rates is the same thing as a reduction in bond prices.

16. a. 5,700; **b.** No, because the actual price level will be 110, higher than what was anticipated. **c.** Actual unemployment will be less than the natural rate because the unexpected high level of prices will improve profit margins, reduce real wage rates, and cause the firms to expand output in the short run.

CHAPTER 10: DYNAMIC CHANGE, ECONOMIC FLUCTUATIONS, AND THE AD-AS MODEL

1. Choice (a) would decrease *AD*; (b), (c), and (d) would increase it; and (e) would leave it unchanged. For the "why" part of the question, see the *Factors That Shift Aggregate Demand* section at the beginning of the chapter.

2. Choices (a), (b), (c), and (d) will reduce *SRAS*; (e) will increase it.

6. At the lower-than-expected inflation rate, *real wages* (and costs) will increase relative to product prices. This will squeeze profit margins and lead to reductions in output and employment, causing the unemployment rate to rise.

8. Tightness in resource markets will result in rising resource prices relative to product prices, causing the *SRAS* to shift to the left. Profit margins will decline, output rates will fall, and long-run equilibrium will be restored at a higher price level. The above-normal output cannot be maintained because it reflects input prices that people would not have agreed to and output decisions they would not have chosen if they had anticipated the current price level (and rate of inflation). Once they have a chance to correct these mistakes, they do so; output returns to the economy's long-run potential.

10. The increase in demand for exports will increase aggregate demand. In the short run, this unanticipated expansion in demand will tend to increase output and employment while exerting modest upward pressure on the price level. In the long run, the primary impact will be a higher price level, with no change in output and employment.

13. The assets destroyed (such as World Trade Center and a portion of the Pentagon) by the attack reduced the productive assets of the United States and thereby adversely affected potential real output. However, these assets were a relatively small share, less than 0.01 percent, of U.S. capital assets. Thus, the direct effect on potential output was small. But there were also indirect effects, such as increased expenditures on national defense and domestic security. The opportunity cost of these indirect effects reduced the future potential output of *consumer* goods and thereby adversely affected the future living standard of Americans. These indirect effects may well be larger than the effect of the assets destroyed.

CHAPTER 11: FISCAL POLICY, HISTORICAL PERSPECTIVE, AND THE KEYNESIAN VIEW

3. The multiplier principle is the concept that a change in one of the components of aggregate demand—investment, for example—will lead to a far greater change in the equilibrium level of income. Because the multiplier equals $1/(1-MPC)$, its size is determined by the marginal propensity to consume. The multiplier makes stabilizing the economy more difficult, because relatively small changes in aggregate demand have a much greater effect on equilibrium income.

6. Either an increase in government expenditures or a reduction in taxes should be employed to shift the budget toward a larger deficit (or smaller surplus).

8. Automatic stabilizers are built-in features (unemployment compensation, corporate profit tax, progressive income tax) that tend automatically to promote a budget deficit during a recession and a budget surplus (or smaller deficit) during an inflationary boom. Automatic stabilizers have the major advantage of providing needed restraint, or stimuli, without congressional approval—which, in turn, minimizes the problem of proper timing.

10. This statement depicts the views of many economists three decades ago. Today, most economists recognize that it is naive. Given our limited ability to forecast

future economic conditions accurately, timing fiscal policy is more difficult than was previously thought. Political considerations—remember, the government is merely an alternative form of social organization, not a corrective device—reduce the likelihood that fiscal policy will be used as a stabilization tool. Changes in interest rates and private spending may offset fiscal actions and thereby reduce the potency of fiscal policy. All factors considered, it is clear that the use of fiscal policy to stabilize the economy is both difficult and complex.

CHAPTER 12: FISCAL POLICY, INCENTIVES, AND SECONDARY EFFECTS

2. The crowding-out effect is the theory that budget deficits will lead to higher real interest rates, which retard private spending. The crowding-out effect indicates that fiscal policy will not be nearly as potent as the simple Keynesian model implies. The new classical theory indicates that anticipation of higher future taxes (rather than higher interest rates) will reduce private spending when government expenditures are financed by debt.

10. In the Keynesian model, investment is determined by factors other than the interest rate. Thus, budget deficits would not exert much effect on capital formation. In the crowding-out model, capital formation would be reduced because the budget deficits would lead to higher interest rates, which would crowd out private investment. In the new classical model, households will save more, and, as a result, budget deficits could be financed without either an increase in the interest rate or a reduction in capital formation.

13. Yes. Only the lower rates would increase the incentive to earn marginal income and thereby stimulate aggregate supply.

15. No. If it takes more workers to generate a specific amount of energy with wind power, this implies that wind power is a more costly method of generating energy than either coal or natural gas. Thus, the implications of the statement are exactly the opposite of what the wind energy proponents imply.

CHAPTER 13: MONEY AND THE BANKING SYSTEM

1. A liquid asset is one that can easily and quickly be transformed into money without experiencing a loss of its market value. Assets such as high-grade bonds and stocks are highly liquid. In contrast, illiquid assets cannot be easily and quickly converted to cash without some loss of their value. Real estate, a family-owned business, business equipment, and artistic works are examples of illiquid assets.

3. Money is valuable because of its scarcity relative to the availability of goods and services. The use of money facilitates (reduces the cost of) exchange transactions. Money also serves as a store of value and a unit of account. Doubling the supply of money while holding output constant would simply cause its purchasing power to fall without enhancing the services that it performs. In fact, fluctuations in the money supply generally create uncertainty about the future value of money and thereby reduce its ability to serve as a reliable store of value, accurate unit of account, and medium of exchange for time-dimension contracting.

6. **a.** There is no change; currency held by the public increases, but checking deposits decrease by an equal amount. **b.** Bank reserves decrease by $100. **c.** Excess reserves decrease by $100, minus $100 multiplied by the required reserve ratio.

8. Answers (b), (e), and (f) will reduce the money supply; (a) and (c) will increase it. If the Treasury's deposits (or the deposits of people who receive portions of the

Treasury's spending) are considered part of the money supply, then (d) will leave the money supply unchanged.

10. Whereas the transformation of deposits into currency does not directly affect the money supply, it does reduce the excess reserves of banks. The reduction in excess reserves will cause banks to reduce their outstanding loans and thereby shrink the money supply. Therefore, an increase in the holding of currency relative to deposits will tend to reduce the supply of money.

12. There are two major reasons. First, the money supply can be altered quietly via open market operations, whereas a reserve requirement change focuses attention on Fed policy. Second, open market operations are a fine-tuning method, whereas a reserve requirement change is a blunt instrument. Generally, the Fed prefers quiet, marginal changes to headline-grabbing, blunt changes that are more likely to disrupt markets.

13. a. False; statements of this type often use "money" when they are really speaking about wealth (or income).

    b. False; the checking deposit also counts as money. In addition, the deposit increases the reserves of the receiving bank and thereby places it in a position to extend additional loans that would increase the money supply.

    c. False; only an increase in the availability of goods and services valued by people will improve Americans' standard of living. Without an additional supply of goods and services, more money will simply lead to a higher price level.

16. a. Money supply increases by $100,000; **b.** $80,000; **c.** $500,000; **d.** no; there will be some leakage in the form of additional currency holdings by the public and additional excess reserve holdings by banks.

18. a. Money supply will increase by $2 billion; **b.** $1.8 billion; **c.** $20 billion.

CHAPTER 14: MODERN MACROECONOMICS AND MONETARY POLICY

2. Choices (a) and (c) would increase your incentive to hold money deposits; (b) and (d) would reduce your incentive to hold money.

3. a. The cost of obtaining the house is $100,000.

    b. The cost of holding it is the interest forgone on the $100,000 sales value of the house.

    c. The cost of obtaining $1,000 is the amount of goods one must give up in order to acquire the $1,000. For example, if a pound of sugar sells for 50 cents, the cost of obtaining $1,000 in terms of sugar is 2,000 pounds.

    d. As in the case of the house, the cost of holding $1,000 is the interest forgone.

7. a. Bank reserves will decline; **b.** Real interest rates will rise; **c.** Spending on consumer durables will fall; **d.** The dollar will appreciate because the higher interest rates will attract bond purchases by foreigners; **e.** Exports will decline because the appreciation of the dollar will make U.S. goods more expensive for foreigners; **f.** The higher real interest rates will tend to reduce real asset prices; **g.** Real GDP will fall.

10. If the time lag is long and variable (rather than short and highly predictable), it is less likely that policy makers will be able to time changes in monetary policy so that they will exert a countercyclical effect on the economy. The policy makers will be more likely to make mistakes and thereby exert a destabilizing influence.

11. Association does not reveal causation. Decision makers, including borrowers and lenders, will eventually anticipate a high rate of inflation and adjust their choices accordingly. As the expected rate of inflation increases, the demand for loanable funds will increase and the supply will decrease. This will lead to higher nominal interest rates. Thus, economic theory indicates that the causation tends to run the opposite direction from that indicated by the statement.

CHAPTER 15: STABILIZATION POLICY, OUTPUT, AND EMPLOYMENT

2. Compared with earlier periods, the United States has experienced less economic instability since 1960. This has been particularly true during the past twenty-five years. An increase in the stability of monetary policy deserves much of the credit for the more stable economic conditions of recent decades.

5. For (a) and (b), the actual and natural rates of unemployment will be equal. For (c), the actual rate will be less than the natural rate. For (d), the actual rate will exceed the natural rate.

7. Here are three practical problems that limit the effectiveness of discretionary macro policy as a stabilization tool: (1) inability to forecast the future direction of the economy with a high degree of accuracy, (2) lengthy and uncertain time lags between when a policy change is instituted and when the primary effects are felt, and (3) political factors that make it difficult to alter fiscal policy quickly.

11. a. Keep the inflation rate at a low and highly predictable level; **b.** No; **c.** Both nominal interest rates and the general level of prices will rise.

CHAPTER 16: CREATING AN ENVIRONMENT FOR GROWTH AND PROSPERITY

3. If poor countries follow sound policies and provide an attractive economic environment, foreigners will be willing to supply investment funds. Propelled by foreign investment, some poor countries have achieved exceedingly high rates of both investment and growth during recent decades.

5. Competition is important because it encourages producers to supply goods that consumers value highly relative to cost, and to do so efficiently. Firms that fail to do so will be unable to compete effectively, and eventually they will be driven out of business. In turn, this will release the resources for use in the production of other things that are more highly valued.

8. When considering the answer to this question, think about the following: Is there an opportunity cost of the capital used by government firms? Do government firms have a strong incentive to keep costs low? Are government firms innovative?

12. The increase in diversity provides consumers with more options and thereby improves their welfare. For the most part, the GDP figures fail to capture the impact of this factor.

13. Regulations such as price ceilings, price floors, and mandated product characteristics will generally reduce the volume of gains from trade. Simultaneously, they will encourage rent-seeking activities, which will increase the contributions available to political officials.

CHAPTER 17: INSTITUTIONS, POLICIES, AND CROSS-COUNTRY DIFFERENCES IN INCOME AND GROWTH

8. It is hard to see how the less-developed economies could have grown so rapidly without borrowing technologies and ideas from the high-income countries. The high-income countries also provided both investment capital and markets for the sale of products for the LDCs. Historical growth records buttress this view. The per capita incomes of several economies, including Hong Kong, Singapore, South Korea, and China, have grown at annual rates of 5 percent or more over periods of twenty-five years or more. Prior to 1960, no country was able to achieve long-term growth at anywhere near such a rate. By way of comparison, per capita income in the United Kingdom and the United States grew at an annual rate of approximately 1 percent during the nineteenth century when countries with significantly higher incomes were absent.

9. In order to make a high score on the EFW index, a country must rely extensively on markets, protect property rights and enforce the law in an even-handed manner, provide for monetary/price stability, refrain from policies that restrict trade, and keep taxes low.

11. A country does not have to be democratic in order to be economically free. Hong Kong illustrates this point. Neither does democracy guarantee economic freedom. India was democratic, but it was one of the world's least free economies prior to 1990.

13. Quality of the legal system: Does it protect property rights and enforce contracts fairly; tax rates; freedom to trade with others; onerous regulations, to list a few of the factors.

14. Poor economic institutions and policies provide the primary reason.

15. Because citizens can move elsewhere at a low cost. When significant numbers vote with their feet by leaving an area, the tax base will erode and this confronts politicians with an incentive to change their ways.

CHAPTER 18: GAINING FROM INTERNATIONAL TRADE

2. Availability of goods and services, not jobs, is the source of economic prosperity. When a good can be purchased cheaper abroad than it can be produced at home, a nation can expand the quantity of goods and services available for consumption by specializing in the production of those goods for which it is a low-cost producer and trading them for the cheap (relative to domestic costs) foreign goods. Trade restrictions limiting the ability of Americans to purchase low-cost goods from foreigners stifle this process and thereby reduce the living standard of Americans.

4. Statements (a) and (b) are not in conflict. Because trade restrictions are typically a special-interest issue, political entrepreneurs can often gain by supporting them even when they promote economic inefficiency.

6. True. The primary effect of trade restrictions is an increase in domestic scarcity. This has distributional consequences, but it is clear that, as a whole, a nation will be harmed by the increased domestic scarcity that accompanies the trade restraints.

8. **a.** No. Americans would be poorer if we used more of our resources to produce things for which we are a high-opportunity-cost producer and less of our resources to produce things for which we are a low-opportunity-cost producer. Employment might either increase or decrease, but the key point is that it is the value of goods produced, not employment, that generates income and provides for the wealth of a nation. The answer to (b) is the same as (a).

10. In thinking about this issue, consider the following points. Suppose that the Japanese were willing to give products such as automobiles, electronic goods, and clothing to us free of charge. Would we be worse off if we accepted the gifts? Should we try to keep the free goods out? What is the source of real income—jobs or goods and services? If the gifts make us better off, doesn't it follow that partial gifts would also make us better off?

12. Although trade reduces employment in import-competing industries, it expands employment in export industries. On balance, there is no reason to believe that trade

either promotes or destroys jobs. The major effect of trade is to permit individuals, states, regions, and nations to generate a larger output by specializing in the things they do well and trading for those things that they would produce only at a high cost. A higher real income is the result.

14. The quota reduces the supply of sugar to the domestic market and drives up the domestic price of sugar. Domestic producers benefit from the higher prices at the expense of domestic consumers (see Exhibit 9). Studies indicate that the quota expanded the gross income of the 11,000 domestic sugar farmers by approximately $130,000 per farm in the mid-1980s, at the expense (in the form of higher prices of sugar and sugar products) of approximately $6 per year to the average domestic consumer. Because the program channels resources away from products for which the United States has a comparative advantage, it reduces the productive capacity of the United States. Both the special-interest nature of the issue and rent-seeking theory explain the political attractiveness of the program.

16. True. If country A imposes a tariff, other countries will sell less to A and therefore acquire less purchasing power in terms of A's currency. Thus, they will have to reduce their purchases of A's export goods.

CHAPTER 19: INTERNATIONAL FINANCE AND THE FOREIGN EXCHANGE MARKET

1. The Japanese cameras will become more expensive, and the quantity purchased by Americans will decline.

4. On February 2, the dollar appreciated against the British pound and depreciated against the Canadian dollar.

5. Scenarios (a) and (g) would cause the dollar to appreciate; (b), (c), (d), (e), and (h) would cause the dollar to depreciate; (f) would leave the exchange rate unchanged.

8. Some people fear that foreign investment makes the United States vulnerable because foreigners might decide to sell their assets and leave suddenly. When you consider this argument, it is important to recognize that foreign and domestic investors are influenced by pretty much the same considerations. Anything that would cause foreigners to withdraw funds would also cause domestic investors to do likewise. In fact, the vulnerability runs the other way. If foreign investors were to leave, the assets financed by their funds would remain. Thus, they would be in a weak position to impose harm on the U.S. economy.

9. Each of the changes would reduce the size of the current-account deficit.

11. The current-account balance will move toward a larger deficit (or smaller surplus), and the dollar will appreciate.

13. False. Flexible exchange rates bring the sum of the current and capital accounts into balance, but they do not necessarily lead to balance for either component.

14. a. No. The exchange rate will bring the overall purchases and sales into balance, but there is no reason to expect the imports and exports to any given country to be in balance.

    b. The United States imports large quantities of goods Japan and China produce at a low cost (for example, electronic products, and labor intensive goods like toys and textiles), but it is not a major exporter of goods purchased intensively by these countries (natural resources, building materials, and inexpensive consumer items).

15. These purchases increase the foreign exchange value of the dollar, which makes imports cheaper relative to exports and thereby enlarges the trade deficit. Politicians often charge that this reduces output and employment. However, the bond purchases are an inflow of capital that will also result in lower U.S. interest rates, which will

tend to stimulate output and employment. Thus, there is little reason to believe that the net effect will be either substantial or harmful.

CHAPTER 20: CONSUMER CHOICE AND ELASTICITY

1. Revenue will rise (fall) if students who enroll pay more (less) extra revenue than is lost due to lower enrollment. Revenue will remain the same if those who enroll pay just enough more to offset the loss from reduced enrollment. A price elasticity of −1.2 implies that raising tuition rates would reduce tuition revenue.

2. If your opportunity cost of time is more than $10, it will make sense to take the plane. Thus, Mary will take the plane and Michele the bus.

3. It is likely that the income effect of cigarette price changes is much larger for low-income smokers than for high-income smokers, perhaps because expenditures on cigarettes are a larger proportion of the household budget for those with lower incomes. Thus, the income effect will be larger for this group.

6. Both income and time constrain our ability to consume. Because, in a wealthier society, time becomes more binding and income less binding, time-saving actions will be more common in a wealthier society. As we engage in time-saving actions (fast food, automatic appliances, air travel, and so on) in order to shift the time restraint outward, our lives become more hectic.

9. All three statements are true.

10. The answer to the first question is "No." Even for things we like, we will experience diminishing returns. Eventually, the cost of additional units of pizza will exceed their benefits. And, in answer to the second question, perfection in any activity is generally not worth the cost. For example, reading every page of this text three, four, or five times may improve your grade, but it may not be worth it. One function of a text is to structure the material (highlighted points, layout of graphs, and so on) so that the reader will be able to learn quickly (at a lower cost).

11. Carole

12. **a.** −1.59; elastic

   b. −1.54; elastic

CHAPTER 21: COSTS AND THE SUPPLY OF GOODS

1. The economic profit of a firm is its total revenue minus the opportunity cost of all resources used in the production process. Accounting profit often excludes the opportunity cost of certain resources—particularly the equity capital of the firm and any labor services provided by an owner-manager. Zero economic profit means that the resources owned by the firm are earning their opportunity cost—that is, the rate of return is as high as the highest valued alternative forgone. Thus, the firm would not gain by pursuing other lines of business.

2. **a.** The amount paid for the course is a sunk cost. It is not directly relevant to whether one should attend the lectures. **b.** There is an opportunity cost of one's house even if it is paid for. **c.** The decline in the price of the stock is a sunk cost and therefore it is not directly relevant to whether or not to sell at this time. **d.** There is an opportunity cost of public education even if it is provided free to the consumer.

5. True. If it could produce the output at a lower cost, its profit would be greater.

7. At low output, the firm's plant (a fixed cost) is underutilized, implying a high average cost. As output rises toward the designed output level, average cost falls, but then rises as the designed or optimal output for that size plant is surpassed and diminishing returns set in.

11. Because owners receive profits, clearly profit maximization is in their interest. Managers, if they are not owners, have no property right to profit and therefore no direct interest in profit maximization. Because a solid record of profitability tends to increase the market value (salary) of corporate managers, they do have an indirect incentive to pursue profits. However, corporate managers may also be interested in gaining power, having nice offices, hiring friends, expanding sales, and other activities, which may conflict with profitability. Thus, owners need to provide incentives for managers to seek profits and to monitor the results.

12. **a.** The interest payments; **b.** The interest income forgone. The tax structure encourages debt rather than equity financing because the firm's tax liability is inversely related to its debt/equity ratio.

14. Check list. Did your marginal cost curve cross the *ATC* and *AVC* curves at their low points? Does the vertical distance between the *ATC* and *AVC* curves get smaller and smaller as output increases? If not, redraw the three curves correctly. See Exhibit 6b.

17. $2,500: the $2,000 decline in market value during the year plus $500 of potential interest on funds that could be obtained if the machine were sold new. Costs associated with the decline in the value of the machine last year are sunk costs.

18. Because they believe they will be able to restructure the firm and provide better management so that the firm will have positive net earnings in the future. If the firm is purchased at a low enough price, this will allow the new owners to cover the opportunity cost of their investment and still earn an economic profit. Alternatively, they may expect to sell off the firm's assets, receiving more net revenue than the cost of purchasing the firm.

CHAPTER 22: PRICE TAKERS AND THE COMPETITIVE PROCESS

1. In a highly competitive industry such as agriculture, lower resource prices might improve the rate of profit in the short run, but in the long run, competition will drive prices down until economic profit is eliminated. Thus, lower resource prices will do little to improve the long-run profitability in such industries.

2. The market price will decline because the profits will attract new firms (and capital investment) into the market and supply will increase, driving down the price until the profits are eliminated.

5. **a.** Increase; **b.** Increase; **c.** Increase: firms will earn economic profit; **d.** Rise (compared with its initial level) if coffee is an increasing-cost industry, but return to initial price if it is a constant-cost industry; **e.** Increase even more than it did in the short run; **f.** Economic profit will return to zero.

6. **a.** Decline; **b.** Increase; **c.** Decline; **d.** Decline

9. Competition virtually forces firms to operate efficiently and produce goods and services that consumers value highly relative to cost. Firms that fail to do so will find it difficult to compete and eventually losses will drive them from the market.

11. **a.** The reduction in supply led to higher prices. **b.** Because demand is inelastic, the total revenue from sales increased. **c.** Overall, the profitability of farming increased, although some of the producers that were hardest hit by the drought experienced losses because of their sharp reduction in output.

15. **b.** Six or seven tons—$250 profit; **c.** seven or eight tons—$600 profit; **d.** five or six tons—$50 loss. Because the firm can cover its variable cost, it should stay in business if it believes that the low ($450) price is temporary.

CHAPTER 23: PRICE-SEARCHER MARKETS WITH LOW ENTRY BARRIERS

3. The amount of variety is determined by the willingness of consumers to pay for variety relative to the cost of providing it. If consumers value variety highly and the added costs of producing different styles, designs, and sizes is low, there will be a lot of variety. Alternatively, if consumers desire similar products, or if variation can be produced only at a high cost, little variety will be present. Apparently, consumers place a substantial value (relative to cost) on variety in napkins but not in toothpicks.

4. The tax would increase the price of lower quality (and lower priced) automobiles by a larger percentage than higher quality automobiles. Consumers would substitute away from the lower quality autos after their relative price had increased. This substitution would increase the average quality of automobiles sold. Because the funds from the tax would be rebated to citizens through the lottery, one would expect this substitution effect to dominate any possible income effect.

7. No. A firm that maximizes *total* revenue would expand output as long as marginal revenue is positive. When marginal costs are positive, the revenue-maximizing price would be lower (and the output greater) than the price that would maximize the firm's profits.

8. In any of these cases, the answer is competition. To survive, a given type and size of firm must be able to produce at a low cost. Those firms with high per-unit cost will be driven from the market.

10. Building the new resort is more risky (and less attractive) because if the market analysis is incorrect, and demand is insufficient, it probably will be difficult to find other uses for the newly built resort. If the airline proves unprofitable, however, the capital (airplanes) should be extremely mobile. However, the resort would have one offsetting advantage: If demand were stronger than expected, and profits larger, it would take competitors longer to enter the market (build a new resort), and they would be more reluctant to make the more permanent investment.

12. In a competitive setting, only the big firms will survive if economies of scale are important. When economies of scale are unimportant, small firms will be able to compete effectively.

14. Competition provides the answer. If McDonald's fails to provide an attractively priced, tasty sandwich with a smile, people will turn to Burger King, Wendy's, Dairy Queen, and other rivals. If Wal-Mart does not provide convenience and value, people will turn to Kmart, Target, and other retailers. Similarly, as recent experience has shown, even a firm as large as General Motors will lose customers to Ford, Honda, Toyota, Chrysler, Volkswagen, and other automobile manufacturers if it fails to please the customer as much as rival suppliers do.

17. **a.** Total revenue: $0; $8,000; $14,000; $18,000; $20,000; $20,000; Total cost: $0; $5,000; $10,000; $15,000; $20,000; $25,000; Economic profit: $0; $3,000; $4,000; $3,000; $0; $5,000 (loss).

   b. Marginal revenue: $8,000; $6,000; $4,000; $2,000; $0; Marginal cost: $5,000; $5,000; $5,000; $5,000; $5,000.

   c. Profit-maximizing price: $7,000.

   d. Rod will sell two boats at the profit-maximizing price of $7,000.

   e. Rod's economic profits will be $4,000 per week. Sales volume will be 2.

   f. Yes, boats 1 and 2 are the only boats for which marginal revenue is higher than marginal cost.

g. Because of the existence of economic profit, more boat dealers will open up in the area. This will result in more competition and lower prices. The entry will continue until boat dealers' economic profits fall to zero.

h. When demand is elastic, lowering price increases total revenue; thus, Rod's demand is elastic between the prices of $9,000 and $5,000. When demand is unitary elastic, lowering price leaves revenue unchanged; thus, Rod's demand is unitary elastic between the prices of $5,000 and $4,000. One could also assume that Rod's demand would eventually become inelastic below a price of $4,000 because the elasticity of demand keeps falling as one moves down along a demand curve. When this happens, Rod's total revenue will begin to fall as he continues to lower price. For example, at a price of $3,000, Rod may sell six boats per week, resulting in only $18,000 in revenue, which is less than the revenue Rod receives at a price of $4,000.

CHAPTER 24: PRICE-SEARCHER MARKETS WITH HIGH ENTRY BARRIERS

1. The statement is true. Profits cannot exist in the long run without barriers to entry because without barriers new entrants seeking the profits would increase supply, drive down price, and eliminate the profits. But barriers to entry are no guarantee of profits. Sufficient demand is also a necessary condition.

3. No; No; No.

8. Because use of product variation and quality improvements to obtain a larger share of the market will be more difficult to monitor and control than a simple price reduction.

11. Reductions in the cost of transportation generally increase competition because they force firms to compete with distant rivals and permit consumers to choose among a wider range of suppliers. As a result, the U.S. economy today is generally more competitive, in the rivalry sense, than it was hundred years ago.

12. The stock price, when the uncle bought the stock, no doubt reflected the well-known profits of Microsoft. The previous owners of the stock surely would not have sold it at a price that failed to reflect its high expected rate of future profit. Thus, there is no reason to believe that the stock purchase will earn a high rate of return for the uncle.

13. a. $15, profit = $110,000; **b.** $10.

CHAPTER 25: THE SUPPLY OF AND DEMAND FOR PRODUCTIVE RESOURCES

3. a. Five; **b.** $350; **c.** Four. The firm will operate in the short run, but it will go out of business in the long run unless the market prices rise.

4. Yes. General increases in the productivity of the labor force will cause a general increase in wages. The higher general wage rates will increase the opportunity cost of barbering and cause the supply of barbers to decline. The reduction in the supply of barbers will place upward pressure on the wages of barbers, even if technological change and worker productivity have changed little in barbering.

6. The job opportunities outside of teaching are more attractive for people with math and science training than for those with English and history degrees. Therefore, the same salary that attracts a substantial number of English and history teachers will be insufficient to attract the required number of math and science teachers.

8. No. The dressmaker needs to employ more capital and less labor because the marginal dollar expenditures on the former are currently increasing output by a larger amount than the latter.

10. Other things being constant, a lengthy training requirement to perform in an occupation reduces supply and places upward pressure on the earnings level. However, resource prices, including those for labor services, are determined by both demand and supply. When demand is weak, earnings will be low, even though a considerable amount of education may be necessary to perform in the occupation. For example, the earnings of people with degrees in English literature and world history are generally low, even though most people in these fields have a great deal of education.

12. **a.** MP 14; 12; 11; 9; 7; 5; 4. TR 70; 130; 185; 230; 265; 290; 310. MRP 70; 60; 55; 45; 35; 25; 20. **b.** 4; **c.** Employment would decline to 3.

CHAPTER 26: EARNINGS, PRODUCTIVITY, AND THE JOB MARKET

2. U.S. workers are more productive. By investing in human capital, the laborers are somewhat responsible, but the superior tools and physical capital that are available to U.S. workers also contribute to their higher wages.

6. Although this statement, often made by politicians, sounds true, in fact, it is false. Output of goods and services valued by consumers, not jobs, is the key to economic progress and a high standard of living. Real income cannot be high unless real output is high. If job creation were the key to economic progress, it would be easy to create millions of jobs. For example, we could prohibit the use of farm machinery. Such a prohibition would create millions of jobs in agriculture. However, it would also reduce output and our standard of living.

8. The opportunity cost of leisure (nonwork) for higher wage workers is greater than it is for lower wage workers.

9. False. Several additional factors, including differences in preferences (which would influence time worked, the trade-off between money wage and working conditions, and evaluation of alternative jobs), differences in jobs, and imperfect labor mobility, would result in variations in earnings.

10. Scenarios (a), (b), (e), and (f) will generally increase hourly earnings; (c) and (d) will generally reduce hourly earnings.

11. Hourly wages will be highest in B because the higher wages will be necessary to compensate workers in B for the uncertainty and loss of income during layoffs. Annual earnings will be higher in A in order to compensate workers in A for the additional hours they will work during the year.

CHAPTER 27: INVESTMENT, THE CAPITAL MARKET, AND THE WEALTH OF NATIONS

1. All the changes would increase interest rates in the United States.

4. No. The average outstanding balance during the year is only about half of $1,000. Therefore, the $200 interest charge translates to almost a 40 percent annual rate of interest.

6. *Hints:* Which has been considered to be more risky—purchasing a bond or a stock? How does risk influence the expected rate of return?

8. 6 percent.

10. **a.** Mike; **b.** Yes, people who save a lot are able to get a higher interest rate on their savings as the result of people with a high rate of time preference; **c.** Yes, people who want to borrow money will be able to do so at a lower rate when there are more people (like Alicia) who want to save a lot.

11. They are helped. This question is a lot like prior questions involving Alicia and Mike. Potential gains from trade are present. If obstacles do not restrain trade, the low-income countries will be able to attract savings (from countries with a high saving rate) at a lower interest rate than would exist in the absence of trade. Similarly, people in the high-income countries will be able to earn a higher return than would otherwise be possible. Each can gain because of the existence of the other.

12. **a.** Approximately $1.277 million; **b.** Yes; **c.** The lottery earnings are less liquid. Because there is not a well-organized market transforming lottery earnings into present income, the transaction costs of finding a "buyer" (at a price equal to the present value of the earnings) for the lottery earnings "rights" may be higher than for the bond, if one wants to sell in the future.

14. No. The present value of the $500 annual additions to earnings during the next ten years is less than the cost of the schooling.

16. Consider the following when answering this question: Whose money is being invested by each of the two entities? If a private investment project goes bad, who is hurt? If a private project is successful, who reaps the gain? Answer the same two questions for political officials.

CHAPTER 28: INCOME INEQUALITY AND POVERTY

2. Differences in family size, age of potential workers, nonmoney "income," taxes, and cost-of-living among areas reduce the effectiveness of annual money income as a measure of economic status. In general, high-income families are larger, are more likely to be headed by a prime-age worker, have less nonmoney income (including leisure), pay more taxes, and reside in higher-cost-of-living areas (particularly large cities). Thus, money income comparison between high- and low-income groups often overstates the economic status of the former relative to the latter.

4. If there were no intergenerational mobility, the diagonal numbers would all be 100 percent. If there were complete equality of opportunity and outcomes, the numbers in each column and row would be 20 percent.

6. No. The increase in marginal tax rates will reduce the incentive of the poor to earn income. Therefore, their income will rise by $1,000 minus the reduction in their personal earnings due to the disincentive effects of the higher marginal tax rates.

7. 67 percent

SPECIAL TOPIC 1: GOVERNMENT SPENDING AND TAXATION

1. Taxes reduce economic efficiency because they eliminate some exchanges and thereby reduce the gains from these transactions. Because of (a) the deadweight losses accompanying the elimination of exchanges and (b) the cost of collecting taxes, the costs of additional tax revenue will be greater than the revenue transferred to the government. Studies indicate that it costs between $1.20 and $1.30 for each dollar of tax revenue raised by the government.

5. As we discussed in Chapter 6, the political process works better when there is a close relationship between who pays for and who benefits from government programs. An

increase in the number of people who pay no income taxes is likely to weaken this relationship. Whereas those with low incomes pay payroll taxes, the revenues from this tax are earmarked for the finance of the Social Security and Medicare programs. Thus, expansions in government are financed primarily by the personal income tax. In the future, exemption of large numbers of people from this tax is likely to make it more difficult to control the growth of government. If you do not have to help pay for more government spending, why would you oppose it?

SPECIAL TOPIC 2: THE INTERNET: HOW IS I.T CHANGING THE ECONOMY?

2. Airline tickets can be "transported" electronically; groceries cannot. Customers can observe the ticket information online, but they cannot observe the condition of fruits, vegetables, and other grocery products via the Internet.

SPECIAL TOPIC 3: THE ECONOMICS OF SOCIAL SECURITY

2. The pay-as-you-go Social Security system will face a crisis sometime around 2018, when the inflow of tax revenue will be insufficient to cover the promised benefits. Although the Social Security Trust Fund has bonds, they are merely an IOU from the Treasury to the Social Security Administration. To redeem these bonds and provide additional funds to finance Social Security benefits, the federal government will have to raise taxes (or pay the interest on additional Treasury bonds it sells), or cut other expenditures, or both. Thus, the presence of the SSTF bonds does not do much to alleviate the crisis.

SPECIAL TOPIC 4: THE STOCK MARKET: ITS FUNCTION, PERFORMANCE, AND POTENTIAL AS AN INVESTMENT OPPORTUNITY

1. History shows that in the U.S. stock market, fairly high returns can be gained at a relatively low risk by people who hold a diverse portfolio of stocks in unrelated industries for a period of twenty years or more. An indexed equity mutual fund is an option that would allow a person to purchase a diverse portfolio while keeping commission costs low.

3. The expectation of high profits in the future drove up the price of the stock, despite the lack of a dividend payment in the first years of the firm. Investors are equally happy with high dividends or the equivalent in rising stock value due to the firm's retaining its profits for further investment.

5. Investors are buying such a stock for its rising value (price), which reflects expected future earnings and dividends.

SPECIAL TOPIC 5: THE CRISIS OF 2008: CAUSES AND LESSONS FOR THE FUTURE

3. The less equity the owner has in his or her house, the more likely he or she will default. This is particularly true in the United States because most home mortgages here are nonrecourse loans: the owner is not responsible for the debt beyond turning the property over to the lender in case of default. The lender has no legal claim on assets of the borrower beyond the asset that was mortgaged. Thus, when the value of a house falls below the outstanding loan, the borrower will often gain by simply abandoning the property. This is precisely what many have done in recent years.

5. The incentive to evaluate the borrower's creditworthiness carefully is reduced. If the mortgage originator had to keep the loan until it was repaid, there would be greater incentive for the lender to evaluate the creditworthiness of the borrower more diligently.

SPECIAL TOPIC 6: LESSONS FROM THE GREAT DEPRESSION

5. The statement reflects a failure to recognize the secondary effects of limiting imports. If we buy less from foreigners, they will have fewer dollars that are required for the purchase of our exports. Therefore, a reduction in imports will also reduce exports and there is no reason to expect any net increase in employment. Instead, trade restraints lead to less output and lower incomes.

SPECIAL TOPIC 7: LESSONS FROM THE JAPANESE EXPERIENCE

2. The growth of government spending as a share of GDP and the large and increasing budget deficits in the 1990s indicate that Japan's fiscal policy was expansionary. It failed to stimulate aggregate demand and recovery.

4. The population in Japan of people aged sixty five years and over increased from 12.0 percent of the total in 1990 to 17.3 percent in 2000. This tended to slow economic growth. The United States will experience a similar trend during 2010–2020, and it too will tend to slow the growth of the U.S. economy.

SPECIAL TOPIC 8: THE FEDERAL BUDGET AND THE NATIONAL DEBT

1. No. Both private corporations and governments can, and often do, have continual debt outstanding. Borrowers can continue to finance and refinance debt as long as lenders have confidence in their ability to pay. This will generally be the case as long as the interest liability is small relative to income (or the potential tax base).

3. No. Remember, trade is a positive-sum game. Bonds are sold to foreigners because they are offering a better deal (acceptance of a lower interest rate) than is available elsewhere. Prohibiting the sale of bonds to foreigners would result in higher real interest rates and less investment, both of which would adversely affect Americans.

5. Lower; voters do not enjoy paying taxes and, therefore, voter dissatisfaction places a restraint on higher taxes, which would also restrain expenditures if the budget had to be balanced. More efficiently, the restraint of tax increases would tighten the budget constraint and make the reality of opportunity cost more visible to both voters and politicians.

7. No. Yes.

SPECIAL TOPIC 9: THE ECONOMICS OF HEALTH CARE

2. Health insurance benefits are a component of the employee's compensation package. Unless the employer values the services of the employee by an amount greater than or equal to the total cost of the employee's compensation, the worker will not be hired. Thus, like other components of the compensation package, health insurance benefits are earned by employees.

4. Medicare and Medicaid increased both total health care spending and the share of that spending paid by a third party. Both of these factors increased the demand for and prices of medical services, thereby making them more expensive for people who do not qualify for these programs.

6. Personal choices exert a major impact on health care expenditures. Individuals who smoke, consume alcohol, and eat excessively; fail to exercise and control their weight; use recreational drugs; and engage in other risky behavior will have higher health care cost. Under systems in which all are charged the same premium, the incentive to adopt a healthy lifestyle is reduced. Persons who make choices that promote good health are forced to subsidize those who do not. This perverse incentive structure also pushes health care costs upward.

8. The incentive to purchase insurance when you are healthy will be reduced.

SPECIAL TOPIC 10: SCHOOL CHOICE: CAN IT IMPROVE THE QUALITY OF EDUCATION IN AMERICA?

2. The incentive is weak to keep costs low because the suppliers (public schools) don't face competition from rivals. Because consumers cannot take their funding and go elsewhere, they are in a weak position to discipline the district schools that are not doing a good job. Furthermore, a lower quality of service can often be used as an argument for more government funding. Economics indicates that an absence of competitive forces will lead to higher costs and lower quality of the product or service supplied. There is no reason to expect that education will be an exception.

SPECIAL TOPIC 11: IS DISCRIMINATION RESPONSIBLE FOR THE EARNINGS DIFFERENCES BETWEEN MEN AND WOMEN?

2. a. The average years of work experience of women relative to men would decline because many of the women entering the labor force would have little prior work experience.

b. The average hours of work of women would also decline because many of the married women would be looking for part-time employment and hours that were complementary with their historic household responsibilities.

c. The increased labor force participation of married women would cause the female/male earnings ratio to fall.

4. Not necessarily. Compared with married men, single men tend to be younger, have fewer dependents, be more likely to drop out of the labor force, and be less likely to receive earnings-enhancing assistance from another person. All these factors will reduce their earnings relative to married men.

SPECIAL TOPIC 12: DO LABOR UNIONS INCREASE THE WAGES OF WORKERS?

1. If the union is able to raise the wages of the farm workers: (a) the cost of Florida oranges will rise, causing supply to decline and price to rise in the long run; (b) profits of the Florida orange growers will decline in the short run, but in the long run they will return to the normal rate; (c) mechanization will be encouraged; and (d) the employment of fruit pickers will decline—particularly in the long run.

3. If only part of an industry is unionized, if the union pushes up the wages of the unionized firms, this will increase their cost and make it difficult for them to compete effectively with their nonunion rivals. Thus, the union will be unable to increase wages much without experiencing a substantial reduction in the employment of its members.

5. False. Competition constrains both employers and employees. Employers must compete with other employers for labor services. To gain the labor services of an employee, an employer must offer a compensation package superior to one that the employee can get elsewhere. If the employer does not offer a superior package, the employee will work for a rival employer or choose self-employment. Similarly, employees must compete with other employees. Therefore, their ability to demand whatever wage they would like is also restrained. Thus, competition prevents both the payment of low (below-market) wages by employers and the imposition of high (above-market) wages by employees.

6. Not necessarily. Adjustment must be made for differences in (a) the productivity characteristics of the union and nonunion workers and (b) the types of jobs they occupy (for example, work environment, job security, likelihood of layoff, and so on). Adjustment for these factors may either increase or reduce the $1.50 differential.

7. Remember, union members compete with other workers, including less-skilled workers. An increase in the minimum wage makes unskilled, low-wage workers more expensive. A higher minimum wage increases the demand for high-skilled employees who are good substitutes for the low-skilled workers. Union members are overrepresented among the high-skilled group helped by an increase in the minimum wage. Therefore, although union leaders will generally pitch their support for a higher minimum wage in terms of a desire that all workers be paid a "decent wage," the effect of the legislation on union members suggests that self-interest rather than altruism underlies their support for the legislation.

SPECIAL TOPIC 13: ARE WE RUNNING OUT OF RESOURCES?

2. When demand expands in resource markets, prices send signals and provide the incentives that will reduce future demand relative to supply. These forces will avoid lasting shortages.

5. If any resource, including water, is bought and sold, then market signals will automatically be provided to signal the desires of users to have, and the abilities of suppliers to supply, more. A market provides productive incentive to all concerned. Users conserve more when a market price rises, suppliers provide more, and there is greater incentive to develop and use substitutes for the higher priced resource. If markets are not used to allocate a resource, these benefits will be lost.

SPECIAL TOPIC 14: DIFFICULT ENVIRONMENTAL CASES AND THE ROLE OF GOVERNMENT

1. The ITQ would allow fishers to fish at their own speed without fear of losing their quota to others.

3. The cost of stopping the buildup would be very large. Avoiding the buildup would be very costly. That large opportunity cost could accomplish instead much else that would help future generations. The forecasted risks are only speculatively the result of the buildup and would occur mostly far in the future. And a warmer world has advantages as well as disadvantages.

4. In a market with strong property rights in place, a polluter would have to be concerned about harming others and being sued by them for damages. Without strong property rights in place, regulation might help. Or it might not. In any case, regulators need information available only in a market to judge how tightly to regulate if the regulator is seeking efficiency.

Glossary

Absolute advantage A situation in which a nation, as the result of its previous experience and/or natural endowments, can produce more of a good (with the same amount of resources) than another nation.

Accounting profits The sales revenues minus the expenses of a firm over a designated time period, usually one year. Accounting profits typically make allowances for changes in the firm's inventories and depreciation of its assets. No allowance is made, however, for the opportunity cost of the equity capital of the firm's owners, or other implicit costs.

Activists Economists who believe that discretionary changes in monetary and fiscal policy can reduce the degree of instability in output and employment.

Adaptive-expectations hypothesis The hypothesis that economic decision makers base their future expectations on actual outcomes observed during recent periods. For example, according to this view, the rate of inflation actually experienced during the past two or three years would be the major determinant of the rate of inflation expected for the next year.

Adjustable rate mortgage (ARM) A home loan in which the interest rate, and thus the monthly payment, is tied to a short-term rate like the one-year Treasury bill rate. Typically, the mortgage interest rate will be two or three percentage points above the related short-term rate. It will be reset at various time intervals (e.g., annually), and thus the interest rate and monthly payment will vary over the life of the loan.

Administrative lag The time period after the need for a policy change is recognized but before the policy is actually implemented.

Aggregate demand curve A downward-sloping curve showing the relationship between the price level and the quantity of domestically produced goods and services all households, business firms, governments, and foreigners (net exports) are willing to purchase.

Aggregate supply curve The curve showing the relationship between a nation's price level and the quantity of goods supplied by its producers. In the short run, it is an upward-sloping curve, but in the long run the aggregate supply curve is vertical.

Alt-A loans Loans extended with little documentation and/or verification of the borrowers' income, employment, and other indicators of their ability to repay. Because of this poor documentation, these loans are risky.

Anticipated change A change that is foreseen by decision makers in time for them to make adjustments.

Anticipated inflation An increase in the general level of prices that was expected by most decision makers.

Appreciation An increase in the value of the domestic currency relative to foreign currencies. An appreciation makes foreign goods cheaper for domestic residents.

Automatic stabilizers Built-in features that tend automatically to promote a budget deficit during a recession and a budget surplus during an inflationary boom, even without a change in policy.

Autonomous expenditures Expenditures that do not vary with the level of income. They are determined by factors such as business expectations and economic policy.

Average fixed cost Total fixed cost divided by the number of units produced. It always declines as output increases.

Average product The total product (output) divided by the number of units of the variable input required to produce that output level.

Average tax rate (ATR) Tax liability divided by taxable income. It is the percentage of income paid in taxes.

Average total cost Total cost divided by the number of units produced. It is sometimes called per-unit cost.

Average variable cost The total variable cost divided by the number of units produced.

Balance of merchandise trade The difference between the value of merchandise exports and the value of merchandise imports for a nation. It is also called simply the balance of trade or net exports. The balance of merchandise trade is only one component of a nation's total balance of payments and its current account.

Balance of payments A summary of all economic transactions between a country and all other countries for a specific time period, usually a year. The balance-of-payments account reflects all payments and liabilities to foreigners (debits) and all payments and obligations received from foreigners (credits).

Balance on current account The import–export balance of goods and services, plus net investment income earned abroad, plus net private and government transfers. If the value of the nation's export-type items exceeds (is less than) the value of the nation's import-type items plus net unilateral transfers to foreigners, a current-account surplus (deficit) is present.

Balance on goods and services The exports of goods (merchandise) and services of a nation minus its imports of goods and services.

Balanced budget A situation in which current government revenue from taxes, fees, and other sources is just equal to current government expenditures.

Bank reserves Vault cash plus deposits of banks with Federal Reserve banks.

Barriers to entry Obstacles that limit the freedom of potential rivals to enter and compete in an industry or market.

Basis points One one-hundredth of a percentage point. Thus, 100 basis points are equivalent to one percentage point.

Black market A market that operates outside the legal system in which either illegal goods are sold or legal goods are sold at illegal prices or terms.

Budget constraint The constraint that separates the bundles of goods that the consumer can purchase from those that cannot be purchased, given a limited income and the prices of the products.

Budget deficit A situation in which total government spending exceeds total government revenue during a specific time period, usually one one year.

Budget surplus A situation in which total government spending is less than total government revenue during a time period, usually a year.

Business cycle Fluctuations in the general level of economic activity as measured by variables such as the rate of unemployment and changes in real GDP.

Capital Human-made resources (such as tools, equipment, and structures) used to produce other goods and services. They enhance our ability to produce in the future.

Capital account The record of transactions with foreigners that involve either (1) the exchange of ownership rights to real or financial assets or (2) the extension of loans.

Capitalism An economic system in which productive resources are owned privately and goods and resources are allocated through market prices.

Cartel An organization of sellers designed to coordinate supply and price decisions so that the joint profits of the members will be maximized. A cartel will seek to create a monopoly in the market for its product.

Central bank An institution that regulates the banking system and controls the supply of a country's money.

Ceteris paribus A Latin term meaning "other things constant" that is used when the effect of one change is being described, recognizing that if other things changed, they also could affect the result. Economists often describe the effects of one change, knowing that in the real world, other things might change and also exert an effect.

Choice The act of selecting among alternatives.

Civilian labor force The number of people sixteen years of age and over who are either employed or unemployed. To be classified as unemployed, a person must be looking for a job.

Collective decision making The method of organization that relies on public-sector decision making (voting, political bargaining, lobbying, and so on) to resolve basic economic questions.

Collusion Agreement among firms to avoid various competitive practices, particularly price reductions. It may involve either formal agreements or merely tacit recognition that competitive practices will be self-defeating in the long run. Tacit collusion is difficult to detect. In the United States, antitrust laws prohibit collusion and conspiracies to restrain trade.

Commercial banks Financial institutions that offer a wide range of services (for example, checking accounts, savings accounts, and loans) to their customers. Commercial banks are owned by stockholders and seek to operate at a profit.

Comparative advantage The ability to produce a good at a lower opportunity cost than others can produce it. Relative costs determine comparative advantage.

Competition as a dynamic process Rivalry or competitiveness between or among parties (for example, producers or input suppliers) to deliver a better deal to buyers in terms of quality, price, and product information.

Competitive price-searcher market A market in which the firms have a downward-sloping demand curve, and entry into and exit from the market are relatively easy.

Complements Products that are usually consumed jointly (for example, bread and butter, hot dogs and hot dog buns). A decrease in the price of one will cause an increase in demand for the other.

Constant returns to scale Unit costs that are constant as the scale of the firm is altered. Neither economics nor diseconomies of scale are present.

Constant-cost industry An industry for which factor prices and costs of production remain constant as market output is expanded. The long-run market supply curve is therefore horizontal in these industries.

Consumer price index (CPI) An indicator of the general level of prices. It attempts to compare the cost of purchasing the market basket bought by a typical consumer during a specific period with the cost of purchasing the same market basket during an earlier period.

Consumer surplus The difference between the maximum price consumers are willing to pay and the price they actually pay. It is the net gain derived by the buyers of the good.

Consumption function The relationship between disposable income and consumption. When disposable income increases, current consumption expenditures rise, but by less than the increase in income.

Consumption opportunity constraint The constraint that separates consumption bundles that are attainable from those that are unattainable. In a money–income economy, this is usually a budget constraint.

Contestable market A market in which the costs of entry and exit are low, so a firm risks little by entering. Efficient production and zero economic profits should prevail in a contestable market.

Corporation A business firm owned by shareholders who possess ownership rights to the firm's profits, but whose liability is limited to the amount of their investment in the firm.

Countercyclical policy A policy that tends to move the economy in an opposite direction from the forces of the business cycle. Such a policy would stimulate demand during the contraction phase of the business cycle and restrain demand during the expansion phase.

Creative destruction The replacement of old products and production methods by innovative new ones that consumers judge to be superior. The process generates economic growth and higher living standards.

Credit Funds acquired by borrowing.

Credit unions Financial cooperative organizations of individuals with a common affiliation (such as an employer or a labor union). They accept deposits, including checkable deposits, pay interest (or dividends) on them out of earnings, and lend funds primarily to members.

Crowding-out effect A reduction in private spending as a result of higher interest rates generated by budget deficits that are financed by borrowing in the private loanable funds market.

Currency Medium of exchange made of metal or paper.

Currency board An entity that (1) issues a currency with a fixed designated value relative to a widely accepted currency (for example, the U.S. dollar), (2) promises to continue to redeem the issued currency at the fixed rate, and (3) maintains bonds and other liquid assets denominated in the other currency that provide 100 percent backing for all currency issued.

Current account   The record of all transactions with foreign nations that involve the exchange of merchandise goods and services, current income derived from investments, and unilateral gifts.

Cyclical unemployment   Unemployment due to recessionary business conditions and inadequate labor demand.

Deadweight loss   The loss of gains from trade to buyers and sellers that occurs when a tax is imposed. The deadweight loss imposes a burden on both buyers and sellers over and above the actual payment of the tax.

Decreasing-cost industry   An industry for which costs of production decline as the industry expands. The market supply is therefore inversely related to price. Such industries are atypical.

Demand deposits   Non–interest-earning checking deposits that can be either withdrawn or made payable on demand to a third party. Like currency, these deposits are widely used as a means of payment.

Demand for money   A curve that indicates the relationship between the interest rate and the quantity of money people want to hold. Because higher interest rates increase the opportunity cost of holding money, the quantity of money demanded will be inversely related to the interest rate.

Democracy   A form of political organization in which adult citizens are free to participate in the political process (vote, lobby, and choose among candidates), elections are free and open, and outcomes are decided by majority voting, either directly or by elected representatives.

Deposit expansion multiplier   The multiple by which an increase in reserves will increase the money supply. It is inversely related to the required reserve ratio.

Depository institutions   Businesses that accept checking and savings deposits and use a portion of them to extend loans and make investments. Banks, savings and loan associations, and credit unions are examples.

Depreciation   The estimated amount of physical capital (for example, machines and buildings) that is worn out or used up producing goods during a period.

Depreciation   A reduction in the value of a currency relative to foreign currencies. A depreciation reduces the purchasing power of the currency over foreign goods.

Depression   A prolonged and very severe recession.

Derived demand   The demand for a resource; it stems from the demand for the final good the resource helps produce.

Differentiated products   Products distinguished from similar products by characteristics like quality, design, location, and method of promotion.

Discount rate   The interest rate the Federal Reserve charges banking institutions for short-term loans.

Discounting   The procedure used to calculate the present value of future income, which is inversely related to both the interest rate and the amount of time that passes before the funds are received.

Discretionary fiscal policy   A change, in laws or appropriation levels, that alters government revenues and/or expenditures.

Division of labor   A method that breaks down the production of a product into a series of specific tasks, each performed by a different worker.

Dumping   Selling a good in a foreign country at a lower price than it's sold for in the domestic market.

Earmarking   The direction of budgeted funds to specific projects, programs, and locations. The technique is costly but provides major benefits to business firms and other concentrated constituent groups, and to the districts where the spending takes place. The benefits are often targeted to those willing to make substantial campaign contributions.

Earned Income Tax Credit   A feature of the personal income tax system that provides supplementary payments to workers with low incomes.

Earned Income Tax Credit   A provision of the tax code that provides a credit or rebate to people with low earnings (income from work activities). The credit is eventually phased out if the recipient's earnings increase.

Economic efficiency   A situation that occurs when (1) all activities generating more benefit than cost are undertaken, and (2) no activities are undertaken for which the cost exceeds the benefit.

Economic freedom   Method of organizing economic activity characterized by (1) personal choice, (2) voluntary exchange coordinated by markets, (3) freedom to enter and compete in markets, and (4) protection of people and their property from aggression by others.

Economic profit   The difference between the firm's total revenues and its total costs, including both the explicit and implicit cost components.

Economic theory   A set of definitions, postulates, and principles assembled in a manner that makes clear the "cause-and-effect" relationships.

Economies of sale   Reductions in the firm's per-unit costs associated with the use of large plants to produce a large volume of output.

Economizing behavior   Choosing the option that offers the greatest benefit at the least possible cost.

Employment/population ratio   The number of people sixteen years of age and over employed as civilians divided by the total civilian population sixteen years of age and over. The ratio is expressed as a percentage.

Entrepreneur   A person who introduces new products or improved technologies and decides which projects to undertake. A successful entrepreneur's actions will increase the value of resources and expand the size of the economic pie.

Equation of exchange $MV = PY$, where M is the money supply, V is the velocity of money, P is the price level, and Y is the output of goods and services produced in an economy.

Equilibrium   A state in which the conflicting forces of supply and demand are in balance. When a market is in equilibrium, the decisions of consumers and producers are brought into harmony with one another, and the quantity supplied will equal the quantity demanded.

Equity mutual fund   A corporation that pools the funds of investors, including small investors, and uses them to purchase a bundle of stocks.

Escalator clause   A contractual agreement that periodically and automatically adjusts money wage rates upward as the price level rises. Such clauses are sometimes referred to as cost-of-living adjustments, or COLAs.

Excess burden of taxation   Another term for deadweight loss. It reflects losses that occur when beneficial activities are forgone because they are taxed.

Excess reserves   Actual reserves that exceed the legal requirement.

Exchange rate   The price of one unit of foreign currency in terms of the domestic currency. For example, if it takes $1.50 to purchase an English pound, the dollar–pound exchange rate is 1.50.

Expansionary fiscal policy   An increase in government expenditures and/or a reduction in tax rates, such that the expected size of the budget deficit expands.

Expansionary monetary policy   A shift in monetary policy designed to stimulate aggregate demand. Injection of additional bank reserves, lower short-term interest rates, and an acceleration in the growth rate of the money supply are indicators of a more expansionary monetary policy.

Expenditure multiplier   The ratio of the change in equilibrium output to the independent change in investment, consumption, or government spending that brings about the change. Numerically, the multiplier is equal to 1 *divided by* (1 − MPC) when the price level is constant.

Explicit costs   Payments by a firm to purchase the services of productive resources.

Exports   Goods and services produced domestically but sold to foreigners.

External benefits   Spillover effects that generate benefits for nonconsenting third parties.

External costs   Spillover effects that reduce the well-being of nonconsenting third parties.

Externalities   Spillover effects of an activity that influence the well-being of nonconsenting third parties.

External debt   The portion of the national debt owed to foreign investors.

Fallacy of composition   Erroneous view that what is true for the individual (or the part) will also be true for the group (or the whole).

Federal Deposit Insurance Corporation (FDIC)   A federally chartered corporation that insures the deposits held by commercial banks, savings and loans, and credit unions.

Federal funds market   A loanable funds market in which banks seeking additional reserves borrow short-term funds (generally for seven days or less) from banks with excess reserves. The interest rate in this market is called the federal funds rate.

Federal Open Market Committee (FOMC)   A committee of the Federal Reserve system that establishes Fed policy with regard to the buying and selling of government securities—the primary mechanism used to control the money supply. It is composed of the seven members of the Board of Governors and the twelve district bank presidents of the Fed.

Federal Reserve System   The central bank of the United States; it carries out banking regulatory policies and is responsible for the conduct of monetary policy.

Fiat money   Money that has neither intrinsic value nor the backing of a commodity with intrinsic value; paper currency is an example.

FICO score   A mathematically determined score measuring a borrower's likely ability to repay a loan, similar to a credit score. The FICO score takes into account a borrower's payment history, current level of indebtedness, types of credit used and length of credit history, and new credit. A person's FICO score will range between 300 and 850. A score of 700 or more indicates that the borrower's credit standing is good and therefore the risk of providing them with credit would be low. FICO is an acronym for the Fair Isaac Corporation, the creators of the FICO score.

Final market goods and services   Goods and services purchased by their ultimate user.

Fiscal policy   The use of government taxation and expenditure policies for the purpose of achieving macroeconomic goals.

Fixed exchange rate   An exchange rate that is set at a determined amount by government policy.

Flexible exchange rates   Exchange rates that are determined by the market forces of supply and demand. They are sometimes called floating exchange rates.

Foreclosure rate   The percentage of home mortgages on which the lender has started the process of taking ownership of the property because the borrower has failed to make the monthly payments.

Foreign exchange market   The market in which the currencies of different countries are bought and sold.

Fractional reserve banking   A system that permits banks to hold reserves of less than 100 percent against their deposits.

Franchise   A right or license granted to an individual to market a company's goods or services or use its brand name. The individual firms are independently owned but must meet certain conditions to continue to use the name.

Free rider   A person who receives the benefit of a good without paying for it. Because it is often virtually impossible to restrict the consumption of public goods to those who pay, these goods are subject to free-rider problems.

Frictional unemployment   Unemployment due to constant changes in the economy that prevent qualified unemployed workers from being immediately matched up with existing job openings. It results from imperfect information and search activities related to suitably matching employees with employers.

Full employment   The level of employment that results from the efficient use of the labor force taking into account the normal (natural) rate of unemployment due to information costs, dynamic changes, and the structural conditions of the economy. For the United States, full employment is thought to exist when approximately 95 percent of the labor force is employed.

Game theory   A tool used to analyze the strategic choices made by competitors in a conflict situation like the decisions made by firms in an oligopoly.

GDP deflator   A price index that reveals the cost during the current period of purchasing the items included in GDP relative to the cost during a base year (currently 2000). Unlike the consumer price index (CPI), the GDP deflator also measures the prices of capital goods and other goods and services purchased by businesses and governments. Because of this, it is thought to be a more accurate measure of changes in the general level of prices than the CPI.

General Agreement on Tariffs and Trade (GATT)   An organization formed after World War II to set the rules for the conduct of international trade and reduce trade barriers among nations.

Going out of business   The sale of a firm's assets and its permanent exit from the market. By going out of business, a firm is able to avoid its fixed costs, which would continue during a shutdown.

Goods and services market   A highly aggregated market encompassing the flow of all final-user goods and services. The market counts all items that enter into GDP. Thus, real output in this market is equal to real GDP.

Gross domestic product (GDP)   The market value of all final goods and services produced within a country during a specific period.

Gross national product (GNP)   The total market value of all final goods and services produced by the citizens of a country. It is equal to GDP minus the net income of foreigners.

Human resources   The abilities, skills, and health of human beings that contribute to the production of both current and future output. Investment in training and education can increase the supply of human resources.

Health savings accounts   Special savings accounts that individuals and families can use for the payment of medical bills and the purchase of a catastrophic (high deductible) health insurance plan.

Impact lag   The time period after a policy change is implemented but before the change begins to exert its primary effects.

Implicit costs   The opportunity costs associated with a firm's use of resources that it owns. These costs do not involve a direct money payment. Examples include wage income and interest forgone by the owner of a firm who also provides labor services and equity capital to the firm.

Implicit marginal tax rate   The amount of additional (marginal) earnings that must be paid explicitly in taxes or implicitly in the form of lower income supplements. The marginal tax rate establishes the fraction of an additional dollar earned that an individual is permitted to keep, so it is an important determinant of the incentive to work and earn.

Import quota   A specific limit or maximum quantity (or value) of a good permitted to be imported into a country during a given period.

Imports   Goods and services produced by foreigners but purchased by domestic consumers, businesses, and governments.

Income effect   That part of an increase (decrease) in amount consumed that is the result of the consumer's real income being expanded (contracted) by a reduction (rise) in the price of a good.

Income elasticity   The percentage change in the quantity of a product demanded divided by the percentage change in consumer income that caused the change in quantity demanded. It measures the responsiveness of the demand for a good to a consumer's change in income.

Income mobility   Movement of individuals and families either up or down income distribution rankings when comparisons are made at two different points in time. When substantial income mobility is present, a person's current position in the rankings will not be a very good indicator of what his or her position will be a few years in the future.

Increasing-cost industry   An industry for which costs of production rise as output is expanded. In these industries, even in the long run, higher market prices will be needed to induce firms to expand total output. As a result, the long-run market supply curve in these industries will slope upward to the right.

Index of leading indicators   An index of economic variables that historically has tended to turn down prior to the beginning of a recession and turn up prior to the beginning of a business expansion.

Indexed equity mutual fund   An equity mutual fund that holds a portfolio of stocks that matches their share (or weight) in a broad stock market index such as the S&P 500. The overhead of these funds is usually quite low because their expenses on stock trading and research are low.

Indifference curve   A curve, convex from below, that separates the consumption bundles that are more preferred by an individual from those that are less preferred. The points on the curve represent combinations of goods that are equally preferred by the individual.

Indirect business taxes   Taxes that increase a business firm's costs of production and, therefore, the prices charged to consumers. Examples are sales, excise, and property taxes.

Inferior good   A good that has a negative income elasticity, so that, as consumer income rises, the demand for the good falls.

Inflation   An increase in the general level of prices of goods and services. The purchasing power of the monetary unit, such as the dollar, declines when inflation is present.

Inflationary premium   A component of the money interest rate that reflects compensation to the lender for the expected decrease, due to inflation, in the purchasing power of the principal and interest during the course of the loan. It is determined by the expected rate of future inflation.

Innovation   The successful introduction and adoption of a new product or process; the economic application of inventions and marketing techniques.

Institutions   The legal, regulatory, and social constraints that affect the security of property rights and enforcement of contracts. They exert a major impact on transaction costs between parties, particularly when the trading partners do not know each other.

Intermediate goods   Goods purchased for resale or for use in producing another good or service.

International Monetary Fund (IMF)   An international banking organization, currently with more than 180 member nations, designed to oversee the operation of the international monetary system. Although it does not control the world supply of money, it does hold currency reserves for member nations and makes currency loans to national central banks.

Invention   The creation of a new product or process, often facilitated by the knowledge of engineering and science.

Inventory investment   Changes in the stock of unsold goods and raw materials held during a period.

Investment   The purchase, construction, or development of capital resources, including both nonhuman capital and human capital. Investments increase the supply of capital.

Investment bank   An institution that acts as an underwriter for securities issued by other corporations or lenders. Unlike traditional banks, investment banks do not accept deposits from, or provide loans to, individuals.

Investment in human capital   Expenditures on training, education, skill development, and health designed to increase human capital and people's productivity.

Invisible hand principle   The tendency of market prices to direct individuals pursuing their own interests to engage in activities promoting the economic well-being of society.

Labor force participation rate   The number of people in the civilian labor force sixteen years of age or over who are either employed or actively seeking employment as a percentage of the total civilian population sixteen years of age and over.

Labor union   A collective organization of employees who bargain as a unit with employers.

Laffer curve   A curve illustrating the relationship between the tax rate and tax revenues. Tax revenues will be low at both very high and very low tax rates. When tax rates are quite high, lowering them can increase tax revenue.

Law of comparative advantage   A principle that states that individuals, firms, regions, or nations can gain by specializing in the production of goods that they produce cheaply (at a low opportunity cost) and exchanging them for goods they cannot produce cheaply (at a high opportunity cost).

Law of demand   A principle that states there is an inverse relationship between the price of a good and the quantity of it buyers are willing to purchase. As the price of a good increases, consumers will wish to purchase less of it. As the price decreases, consumers will wish to purchase more of it.

Law of diminishing marginal utility   The basic economic principle that as the consumption of a product increases, the marginal utility derived from consuming more of it (per unit of time) will eventually decline.

Law of diminishing returns   The postulate that as more and more units of a variable resource are combined with a fixed amount of other resources, using additional units of the variable resource will eventually increase output only at a decreasing rate. Once diminishing returns are reached, it will take successively larger amounts of the variable factor to expand output by one unit.

Law of supply   A principle that states there is a direct relationship between the price of a good and the quantity of it producers are willing to supply. As the price of a good increases, producers will wish to supply more of it. As the price decreases, producers will wish to supply less.

Less-developed countries   Countries with low per capita incomes, low levels of education, widespread illiteracy, and widespread use of production methods that are largely obsolete in high income countries. They are sometimes referred to as developing countries.

Leverage ratios   The ratio of loans and other investments to the firm's capital assets.

Licensing   A requirement that one obtain permission from the government in order to perform certain business activities or work in various occupations.

Liquid asset   An asset that can be easily and quickly converted to money without loss of value.

Loanable funds market   A general term used to describe the market that coordinates the borrowing and lending decisions of business firms and households. Commercial banks, savings and loan associations, the stock and bond markets, and insurance companies are important financial institutions in this market.

Logrolling   The exchange between politicians of political support on one issue for political support on another.

Long run (in production)   A time period long enough to allow the firm to vary all of its factors of production.

Loss   A deficit of sales revenue relative to the opportunity cost of production. Losses are a penalty imposed on those who produce goods even though they are valued less than the resources required for their production.

M1 (money supply)   The sum of (1) currency in circulation (including coins), (2) checkable deposits maintained in depository institutions, and (3) traveler's checks.

M2 (money supply)   Equal to M1 plus (1) savings deposits, (2) time-deposits (accounts of less than $100,000) held in depository institutions, and (3) money market mutual fund shares.

Macroeconomics   The branch of economics that focuses on how human behavior affects outcomes in highly aggregated markets, such as the markets for labor or consumer products.

Malinvestment   Malinvestment is misguided (or excess) investment caused when the Fed holds interest rates artificially low, encouraging too much borrowing. The new bank credit is invested in capital projects that cost more than the value they create. At some point, a correction must occur to cleanse these uneconomical investments from the system.

Managed equity mutual fund   An equity mutual fund that has a portfolio manager who decides what stocks will be held in the fund and when they will be bought or sold. A research staff generally provides support for the fund manager.

Marginal   Term used to describe the effects of a change in the current situation. For example, a producer's marginal cost is the cost of producing an additional unit of a product, given the producer's current facility and production rate.

Marginal benefit   The maximum price a consumer will be willing to pay for an additional unit of a product. It is the dollar value of the consumer's marginal utility from the additional unit, and therefore it falls as consumption increases.

Marginal cost   The change in total cost required to produce an additional unit of output.

Marginal product (MP)   The change in total output that results from the employment of one additional unit of a resource.

Marginal propensity to consume (MPC)   Additional current consumption divided by additional current disposable income.

Marginal rate of substitution   The change in the consumption level of one good that is just sufficient to offset a unit change in the consumption of another good without causing a shift to another indifference curve. At any point on an indifference curve, it will be equal to the slope of the curve at that point.

Marginal revenue (MR)   The change in a firm's total revenue that results from the production and sale of one additional unit of output.

Marginal revenue product (MRP)   The change in the total revenue of a firm that results from the employment of one additional unit of a resource. The marginal revenue product of an input is equal to its marginal product multiplied by the marginal revenue of the good or service produced.

Marginal tax rate (MTR)   The additional tax liability a person faces divided by his or her additional taxable income. It is the percentage of an extra dollar of income earned that must be paid in taxes. It is the marginal tax rate that is relevant in personal decision making.

Marginal utility The additional utility, or satisfaction, derived from consuming an additional unit of a good.

Market An abstract concept encompassing the forces of supply and demand, and the interaction of buyers and sellers with the potential for exchange to occur.

Market organization A method of organization in which private parties make their own plans and decisions with the guidance of unregulated market prices. The basic economic questions of consumption, production, and distribution are answered through these decentralized decisions.

Market power The ability of a firm that is not a pure monopolist to earn persistently large profits, indicating that it has some monopoly power. Because the firm has few (or weak) competitors, it has a degree of freedom from vigorous competition.

Means-tested income transfers Transfers that are limited to people or families with an income below a certain cutoff point. Eligibility is thus dependent upon low-income status.

Medium of exchange An asset that is used to buy and sell goods or services.

Microeconomics The branch of economics that focuses on how human behavior affects the conduct of affairs within narrowly defined units, such as individual households or business firms.

Middleman A person who buys and sells goods or services or arranges trades. A middleman reduces transaction costs.

Minimum wage Legislation requiring that workers be paid at least the stated minimum hourly rate of pay.

Monetarists A group of economists who believe that (1) monetary instability is the major cause of fluctuations in real GDP and (2) rapid growth of the money supply is the major cause of inflation.

Monetary base The sum of currency in circulation plus bank reserves (vault cash and reserves with the Fed). It reflects the purchases of financial assets and extension of loans by the Fed.

Monetary policy The deliberate control of the money supply, and, in some cases, credit conditions, for the purpose of achieving macroeconomic goals.

Money interest rate The percentage of the amount borrowed that must be paid to the lender in addition to the repayment of the principal. The money interest rate overstates the real cost of borrowing during an inflationary period. When inflation is anticipated, an inflationary premium will be incorporated into this rate. The money interest rate is often called the nominal interest rate.

Money market mutual funds Interest-earning accounts that pool depositors' funds and invest them in highly liquid short-term securities. Because these securities can be quickly converted to cash, depositors are permitted to write checks (which reduce their share holdings) against their accounts.

Money rate of interest The rate of interest in monetary terms that borrowers pay for borrowed funds. During periods when borrowers and lenders expect inflation, the money rate of interest exceeds the real rate of interest.

Money supply The supply of currency, checking account funds, and traveler's checks. These items are counted as money because they are used as the means of payment for purchases.

Monopolistic competition A term often used by economists to describe markets characterized by a large number of sellers that supply differentiated products to a market with low barriers to entry. Essentially, it is an alternative term for a competitive price-searcher market.

Monopoly A market structure characterized by (1) a single seller of a well-defined product for which there are no good substitutes and (2) high barriers to the entry of any other firms into the market for that product.

Mortgage default rate The percentage of home mortgages on which the borrower is late by ninety days or more with the payments on the loan or it is in the foreclosure process. This rate is sometimes referred to as the serious delinquency rate.

Mortgage-backed securities Securities issued for the financing of large pools of mortgages. The promised returns to the security holders are derived from the mortgage interest payments.

Multiplier principle Concept that an increase in spending on a project will generate income for the resource suppliers, who will then increase their consumption spending. In turn, their additional consumption will generate income for others and lead to still more consumption. As this process goes through successive rounds, total income will expand by a multiple of the initial increase in spending.

National debt The sum of the indebtedness of the federal government in the form of outstanding interest-earning bonds. It reflects the cumulative impact of budget deficits and surpluses.

National income The total income earned by a country's nationals (citizens) during a period. It is the sum of employee compensation, self-employment income, rents, interest, and corporate profits.

Natural monopoly A market situation in which the average costs of production continually decline with increased output. In a natural monopoly, the average costs of production will be lowest when a single, large firm produces the entire output demanded by the marketplace.

Natural rate of unemployment The "normal" unemployment rate due to frictional and structural conditions in labor markets. It is the unemployment rate that occurs when the economy is operating at a sustainable rate of output. The current natural rate of unemployment in the United States is thought to be approximately 5 percent.

Net exports Exports minus imports.

Net income of foreigners The income that foreigners earn by contributing labor and capital resources to the production of goods within the borders of a country minus the income the nationals of the country earn abroad.

New classical economists Economists who believe that there are strong forces pushing a market economy toward full-employment equilibrium and that macroeconomic policy is an ineffective tool with which to reduce economic instability.

Nominal GDP GDP expressed at current prices. It is often called money GDP.

Nominal values Values expressed in current dollars.

Nonactivists Economists who believe that discretionary macro policy adjustments in response to cyclical conditions are likely to increase, rather than reduce, instability. Nonactivists favor steady and predictable policies regardless of business conditions.

Nonhuman resources   The durable, nonhuman inputs used to produce both current and future output. Machines, buildings, land, and raw materials are examples. Investment can increase the supply of nonhuman resources. Economists often use the term physical capital when referring to nonhuman resources.

Nonrenewable resources   Those that are not created or renewed naturally at a significant rate.

Normal good   A good that has a positive income elasticity, so that, as consumer income rises, demand for the good rises, too.

Normal profit rate   Zero economic profit, providing just the competitive rate of return on the capital (and labor) of owners. An above-normal profit will draw more entry into the market, whereas a below-normal profit will lead to an exit of investors and capital.

Normative economics   Judgments about "what ought to be" in economic matters. Normative economic views cannot be proven false because they are based on value judgments.

North American Free Trade Agreement (NAFTA)   A comprehensive trade agreement between the United States, Mexico, and Canada that went into effect in 1994.

Objective   A fact based on observable phenomena that is not influenced by differences in personal opinion.

Official reserve account   The record of transactions among central banks.

Oligopoly   A market situation in which a small number of sellers constitutes the entire industry. It is competition among the few.

Open market operations   The buying and selling of U.S. government securities and other financial assets in the open market by the Federal Reserve.

Opportunity cost of production   The total economic cost of producing a good or service. The cost component includes the opportunity cost of all resources, including those owned by the firm. The opportunity cost is equal to the value of the production of other goods sacrificed as the result of producing the good.

Opportunity cost of equity capital   The rate of return that must be earned by investors to induce them to supply financial capital to the firm.

Opportunity cost   The highest valued alternative that must be sacrificed as a result of choosing an option.

Other checkable deposits   Interest-earning deposits that are also available for checking.

Paradox of thrift   The idea that when many households simultaneously try to increase their saving, actual saving may fail to increase because the reduction in consumption and aggregate demand will reduce income and employment.

Partnership   A business firm owned by two or more individuals who possess ownership rights to the firm's profits and are personally liable for the debts of the firm.

Pegged exchange rate system   A commitment to use monetary and fiscal policy to maintain the exchange rate value of the domestic currency at a fixed rate or within a narrow band relative to another currency (or bundle of currencies).

Per capita GDP   Income per person. Increases in income per person are vital for the achievement of higher living standards.

Personal consumption   Household spending on consumer goods and services during the current period. Consumption is a flow concept.

Personal retirement account   An account that is owned personally by an individual in his or her name. The funds in the account could be passed along to heirs.

Phillips curve   A curve that illustrates the relationship between the rate of inflation and the rate of unemployment.

Pork-barrel legislation   A package of spending projects benefiting local areas financed through the federal government. The costs of the projects typically exceed the benefits in total, but the projects are intensely desired by the residents of a particular district who get the benefits without having to pay much of the costs.

Portfolio   All the stocks, bonds, or other securities held by an individual or corporation for investment purposes.

Positive economics   The scientific study of "what is" among economic relationships.

Positive rate of time preference   The desire of consumers for goods now rather than in the future.

Potential deposit expansion multiplier   The maximum potential increase in the money supply as a ratio of the new reserves injected into the banking system. It is equal to the inverse of the required reserve ratio.

Potential output   The level of output that can be achieved and sustained in the future, given the size of the labor force, its expected productivity, and the natural rate of unemployment consistent with the efficient operation of the labor market. Actual output can differ from the economy's potential output.

Poverty threshold income level   The level of money income below which a family is considered to be poor. It differs according to family characteristics (e.g., number of family members) and is adjusted when consumer prices change.

Present value (PV)   The current worth of future income after it is discounted to reflect the fact that revenues in the future are valued less highly than revenues now.

Price ceiling   A legally established maximum price sellers can charge for a good or resource.

Price controls   Government-mandated prices that are generally imposed in the form of maximum or minimum legal prices.

Price discrimination   A practice whereby a seller charges different consumers different prices for the same product or service.

Price elasticity of demand   The percentage change in the quantity of a product demanded divided by the percentage change in the price that caused the change in quantity. The price elasticity of demand indicates how responsive consumers are to a change in a product's price.

Price elasticity of supply   The percentage change in quantity supplied, divided by the percentage change in the price that caused the change in quantity supplied.

Price floor   A legally established minimum price buyers must pay for a good or resource.

Price searchers   Firms that face a downward-sloping demand curve for their product. The amount the firm is able to sell is inversely related to the price it charges.

Price takers   Sellers who must take the market price in order to sell their product. Because each price taker's output is small relative to the total market, price takers can sell all their output at the market price, but they are unable to sell any of their output at a price higher than the market price.

Primary market   The market in which financial institutions aid in the sale of new securities.

Principal–agent problem   The incentive problem that occurs when the purchaser of services (the principal) lacks full information about the circumstances faced by the seller (the agent) and cannot know how well the agent performs the purchased services. The agent may to some extent work toward objectives other than those sought by the principal paying for the service.

Private investment The flow of private-sector expenditures on durable assets (fixed investment) plus the addition to inventories (inventory investment) during a period. These expenditures enhance our ability to provide consumer benefits in the future.

Privately held government debt The portion of the national debt owed to domestic and foreign investors. It does not include bonds held by agencies of the federal government or the Federal Reserve.

Private-property rights Property rights that are exclusively held by an owner and protected against invasion by others. Private property can be transferred, sold, or mortgaged at the owner's discretion.

Producer surplus The difference between the price suppliers actually receive and the minimum price they would be willing to accept. It measures the net gains to producers and resource suppliers from market exchange. It is not the same as profit.

Production possibilities curve A curve that outlines all possible combinations of total output that could be produced, assuming (1) a fixed amount of productive resources, (2) a given amount of technical knowledge, and (3) full and efficient use of those resources. The slope of the curve indicates the amount of one product that must be given up to produce more of the other.

Productivity The average output produced per worker during a specific time period. It is usually measured in terms of output per hour worked.

Profit An excess of sales revenue relative to the opportunity cost of production. The cost component includes the opportunity cost of all resources, including those owned by the firm. Therefore, profit accrues only when the value of the good produced is greater than the value of the resources used for its production.

Progressive tax A tax in which the average tax rate rises with income. People with higher incomes will pay a higher percentage of their income in taxes.

Property rights The rights to use, control, and obtain the benefits from a good or resource.

Proportional tax A tax in which the average tax rate is the same at all income levels. Everyone pays the same percentage of income in taxes.

Proprietorship A business firm owned by an individual who possesses the ownership right to the firm's profits and is personally liable for the firm's debts.

Proved reserves Specific mineral deposits that have been shown by scientific examination and cost calculation to be extractable and deliverable to the market for use, with current technology and expected market conditions.

Public goods Goods for which rivalry among consumers is absent and exclusion of nonpaying customers is difficult.

Public-choice analysis The study of decision making as it affects the formation and operation of collective organizations, like governments. In general, the principles and methodology of economics are applied to political science topics.

Purchasing power parity method Method in which the relative purchasing power of each currency is determined by comparing the amount of each currency required to purchase a common bundle of goods and services in the domestic market. This information is then used to convert the GDP of each nation to a common monetary unit like the U.S. dollar.

Pure competition A market structure characterized by a large number of small firms producing an identical product in an industry (market area) that permits complete freedom of entry and exit. Also called price-taker markets.

Quantity theory of money A theory that hypothesizes that a change in the money supply will cause a proportional change in the price level because velocity and real output are unaffected by the quantity of money.

Quartile A quarter (25 percent) of a group. The quartiles are often arrayed on the basis of an indicator like income or degree of economic freedom.

Random walk theory The theory that current stock prices already reflect known information about the future. Therefore, the future movement of stock prices will be determined by surprise occurrences. This will cause them to change in a random fashion.

Rational ignorance effect Because it is highly unlikely that an individual vote will decide the outcome of an election, a rational individual has little or no incentive to search for and acquire the information needed to cast an informed vote.

Rational-expectations hypothesis The hypothesis that economic decision makers weigh all available evidence, including information concerning the probable effects of current and future economic policy, when they form their expectations about future economic events (like the probable future inflation rate).

Rationing Allocating a limited supply of a good or resource among people who would like to have more of it. When price performs the rationing function, the good or resource is allocated to those willing to give up the most "other things" in order to get it.

Real GDP GDP adjusted for changes in the price level.

Real interest rate The interest rate adjusted for expected inflation: it indicates the real cost to the borrower (and yield to the lender) in terms of goods and services.

Real rate of interest The money rate of interest minus the expected rate of inflation. The real rate of interest indicates the interest premium in terms of real goods and services that one must pay for earlier availability.

Real values Values that have been adjusted for the effects of inflation.

Recession A downturn in economic activity characterized by declining real GDP and rising unemployment. In an effort to be more precise, many economists define a recession as two consecutive quarters in which there is a decline in real GDP.

Recognition lag The time period after a policy change is needed from a stabilization standpoint but before the need is recognized by policy makers.

Regressive tax A tax in which the average tax rate falls with income. People with higher incomes will pay a lower percentage of their income in taxes.

Renewable resources Those that are renewed in nature, like water flows, or grown, like timber.

Rent seeking Actions by individuals and groups designed to restructure public policy in a manner that will either directly or indirectly redistribute more income to themselves or the projects they promote.

Repeat-purchase item   An item purchased often by the same buyer.

Required reserve ratio   The ratio of reserves relative to a specified liability category (for example, checkable deposits) that banks are required to maintain.

Required reserves   The minimum amount of reserves that a bank is required by law to keep on hand to back up its deposits. If reserve requirements were 15 percent, banks would be required to keep $150,000 in reserves against each $1 million of deposits.

Residual claimants   Individuals who personally receive the excess, if any, of revenues over costs. Residual claimants gain if the firm's costs are reduced or revenues increase.

Resource   An input used to produce economic goods. Land, labor, skills, natural resources, and capital are examples. Throughout history, people have struggled to transform available, but limited, resources into things they would like to have—economic goods.

Resource market   A highly aggregated market encompassing all resources (labor, physical capital, land, and entrepreneurship) contributing to the production of current output. The labor market is the largest component of this market.

Resource markets   Markets in which business firms demand factors of production (for example, labor, capital, and natural resources) from household suppliers. The resources are then used to produce goods and services. These markets are sometimes called factor markets or input markets.

Resource mobility   The ease with which factors of production are able to move among alternative uses. Resources that can easily be transferred to a different use or location are said to be highly mobile. Resources with few alternative uses are immobile.

Restrictive fiscal policy   A reduction in government expenditures and/or an increase in tax rates such that the expected size of the budget deficit declines (or the budget surplus increases).

Restrictive monetary policy   A shift in monetary policy designed to reduce aggregate demand and put downward pressure on the general level of prices (or the rate of inflation). A reduction in bank reserves, higher short-term interest rates, and a reduction in the growth rate of the money supply are indicators of a more restrictive monetary policy.

Ricardian equivalence   The view that a tax reduction financed with government debt will exert no effect on current consumption and aggregate demand because people will fully recognize the higher future taxes implied by the additional debt.

Right-to-work laws   Laws that prohibit union shops, the requirement that employees must join a union as a condition of employment. Each state has the option to adopt (or reject) right-to-work legislation.

Rule of 70   If a variable grows at a rate of x percent per year, $70/x$ will approximate the number of years required for the variable to double.

Samaritan's dilemma   The dilemma that occurs when assisting low-income citizens with transfers reduces the opportunity cost of choices that lead to poverty. Providing income transfers to the poor and discouraging behavior that leads to poverty are conflicting goals.

Saving   The portion of after-tax income that is not spent on consumption. Saving is a "flow" concept.

Savings and loan associations   Financial institutions that accept deposits in exchange for shares that pay dividends. Historically, these funds were channeled into residential mortgage loans, but today they offer essentially the same services as a commercial bank.

Scarcity   Fundamental concept of economics that indicates that there is less of a good freely available from nature than people would like.

Scientific thinking   Developing a theory from basic principles and testing it against events in the real world. Good theories are consistent with and help explain real world events. Theories that are inconsistent with the real world are invalid and must be rejected.

Secondary effects   The indirect impact of an event or policy that may not be easily and immediately observable. In the area of policy, these effects are often both unintended and overlooked.

Secondary market   The market in which financial institutions aid in the buying and selling of existing securities.

Secondary mortgage market   A market in which mortgages originated by a lender are sold to another financial institution. In recent years, the major buyers in this market have been Fannie Mae, Freddie Mac, and large investment banks.

Security rating   A rating indicating the risk of default of the security. A rating of AAA indicates that the risk of default by the borrower is low.

Shirking   Working at less than the expected rate of productivity, which reduces output. Shirking is more likely when workers are not monitored, so that the cost of lower output falls on others.

Short run (in production)   A time period so short that a firm is unable to vary some of its factors of production. The firm's plant size typically cannot be altered in the short run.

Shortage   A condition in which the amount of a good offered for sale by producers is less than the amount demanded by buyers at the existing price. An increase in price would eliminate the shortage.

Shortsightedness effect   The misallocation of resources that results because public-sector action is biased (1) in favor of proposals yielding clearly defined current benefits in exchange for difficult-to-identify future costs and (2) against proposals with clearly identifiable current costs that yield less concrete and less obvious future benefits.

Shutdown   A temporary halt in the operation of a firm. Because the firm anticipates operating in the future, it does not sell its assets and go out of business. The firm's variable cost is eliminated by the shutdown, but its fixed costs continue.

Socialism   A system of economic organization in which (1) the ownership and control of the basic means of production rest with the state, and (2) resource allocation is determined by centralized planning rather than market forces.

Special-interest issue   An issue that generates substantial individual benefits to a small minority while imposing a small individual cost on many other citizens. In total, the net cost to the majority might either exceed or fall short of the net benefits to the special-interest group.

Stock options The option to buy a specified number of shares of the firm's stock at a designated price. The designated price is generally set so that the options will be quite valuable if the firm's shares increase in price but of little value if their price falls. Thus, when used to compensate top managers, stock options provide a strong incentive to follow policies that will increase the value of the firm.

Store of value An asset that will allow people to transfer purchasing power from one period to the next.

Strike An action of unionized employees in which they (1) discontinue working for the employer and (2) take steps to prevent other potential workers from offering their services to the employer.

Structural unemployment Unemployment due to the structural characteristics of the economy that make it difficult for job seekers to find employment and for employers to hire workers. Although job openings are available, they generally require skills many unemployed workers do not have.

Subjective An opinion based on personal preferences and value judgments.

Subprime loan A loan made to a borrower with blemished credit or one who provides only limited documentation of income, employment history, and other indicators of creditworthiness.

Subsidy A payment the government makes to either the buyer or seller, usually on a per-unit basis, when a good or service is purchased or sold.

Substitutes Products that serve similar purposes. An increase in the price of one will cause an increase in demand for the other (examples are hamburgers and tacos, butter and margarine, Microsoft Xbox and Sony PlayStation, Chevrolets and Fords).

Substitution effect That part of an increase (decrease) in amount consumed that is the result of a good being cheaper (more expensive) in relation to other goods because of a reduction (increase) in price.

Sunk costs Costs that have already been incurred as a result of past decisions. They are sometimes referred to as historical costs.

Supply shock An unexpected event that temporarily increases or decreases aggregate supply.

Supply-side economists Economists who believe that changes in marginal tax rates exert important effects on aggregate supply.

Surplus A condition in which the amount of a good offered for sale by producers is greater than the amount that buyers will purchase at the existing price. A decline in price would eliminate the surplus.

Tariff A tax levied on goods imported into a country.

Tax base The level or quantity of an economic activity that is taxed. Higher tax rates reduce the level of the tax base because they make the activity less attractive.

Tax incidence The way the burden of a tax is distributed among economic units (consumers, producers, employees, employers, and so on). The actual tax burden does not always fall on those who are statutorily assigned to pay the tax.

Tax rate The per-unit amount of the tax or the percentage rate at which the economic activity is taxed.

Taylor Rule A rule that indicates the federal funds interest rate that is most consistent with maximum sustainable output and price stability. Because the federal funds interest rate is largely determined by monetary policy, this rule acts as both a guide for monetary policy makers and a benchmark to evaluate their performance.

Team production A production process in which employees work together under the supervision of the owner or the owner's representative.

Technological advancement The introduction of new techniques or methods that increase output per unit of input.

Technology The technological knowledge available in an economy at any given time. The level of technology determines the amount of output we can generate with our limited resources.

Term Auction Facility (TAF) Newly established procedure used by the Fed to auction credit for an 84-day period to depository institutions willing to bid the highest interest rates for the funds.

Total cost The costs, both explicit and implicit, of all the resources used by the firm. Total cost includes a normal rate of return for the firm's equity capital.

Total fixed cost The sum of the costs that do not vary with output. They will be incurred as long as a firm continues in business and the assets have alternative uses.

Total product The total output of a good that is associated with each alternative utilization rate of a variable input.

Total variable cost The sum of those costs that rise as output increases. Examples of variable costs are wages paid to workers and payments for raw materials.

Trade deficit The situation when a country's imports of goods and services are greater than its exports.

Trade surplus The situation when a country's exports of goods and services are greater than its imports.

Transaction costs The time, effort, and other resources needed to search out, negotiate, and complete an exchange.

Transfer payments Payments to individuals or institutions that are not linked to the current supply of a good or service by the recipient.

Unanticipated change A change that decision makers could not reasonably foresee. The choices they made prior to the change did not take it into account.

Unanticipated inflation An increase in the general level of prices that was not expected by most decision makers.

Underground economy Unreported barter and cash transactions that take place outside recorded market channels. Some are otherwise legal activities undertaken to evade taxes. Others involve illegal activities, such as trafficking drugs and prostitution.

Unemployed The term used to describe a person not currently employed who is either (1) actively seeking employment or (2) waiting to begin or return to a job.

Unemployment rate The percentage of people in the labor force who are unemployed. Mathematically, it is equal to the number of people unemployed divided by the number of people in the labor force.

Unfunded liability A shortfall of tax revenues at current rates relative to promised benefits for a program. Without an increase in tax rates, the promised benefits cannot be funded fully.

Unit of account A unit of measurement used by people to post prices and keep track of revenues and costs.

User charges Payments users (consumers) are required to make if they want to receive certain services provided by the government.

Utility The subjective benefit or satisfaction a person expects from a choice or course of action.

Value marginal product (VMP) The marginal product of a resource multiplied by the selling price of the product it helps produce. For a price-taker firm, marginal revenue product (MRP) will be equal to the value marginal product (VMP).

Velocity of money The average number of times a dollar is used to purchase final goods and services during a year. It is equal to GDP divided by the stock of money.

World Trade Organization (WTO) The new name given to GATT in 1994; the WTO is currently responsible for monitoring and enforcing multilateral trade agreements among its 153 member countries.

Index

The Evolution of

1776

Adam Smith (1723–1790)

Smith's book *An Inquiry into the Nature and Causes of the Wealth of Nations* provided the first comprehensive analysis of wealth and prosperity and introduced "the invisible hand" principle. It also explained that the wealth of a nation was determined by its production of goods and services, not by its gold and silver.

© Hulton-Deutsch Collection / Corbis

1817

David Ricardo (1772–1823)

In his book *On the Principles of Political Economy and Taxation*, Ricardo developed the law of comparative advantage and used it to explain why trade leads to mutual gains.

© Bettmann / Corbis

1871

William Stanley Jevons (1835–1882)

Along with Carl Menger and Leon Walras, Jevons (in *The Theory of Political Economy*) introduced (1) the idea that the value of goods is determined subjectively rather than by the labor required for production, and (2) the law of diminishing marginal utility. Independently, the same concepts were developed by Menger in *Grundsätze* (1871) and Walras in *Elements of Pure Economics* (1874). These two concepts are still an integral part of modern analysis.

1890

Alfred Marshall (1842–1924)

In his book *The Principles of Economics*, Marshall introduced and developed many of the key concepts of modern microeconomics, including concepts like supply and demand, equilibrium, short run and long run, elasticity, and consumer and producer surplus. The book went through eight editions between 1890 and 1920.

Economics as a Science

© Bettmann / Corbis

John Maynard Keynes (1883–1946)

In his book *The General Theory of Employment, Interest, and Money,* Keynes developed the framework for modern macroeconomics. He also developed an explanation for the widespread unemployment of the Great Depression, and he elevated the importance of fiscal policy.

© Hulton-Deutsch Collection / Corbis

Friedrich von Hayek (1899–1992)

In two vitally important publications, *The Road to Serfdom* (1944) and "The Use of Knowledge in Society," an article in the *American Economic Review* in 1945, Hayek explained the role of knowledge in economics, enhanced our understanding of the market process, and highlighted the fatal defects of centrally planned economies.

© Bettmann / Corbis

Milton Friedman (1912–2006)

Friedman's work elevated the importance of monetary policy and convinced many that monetary instability was the major cause of both business fluctuations and inflation. His book *A Monetary History of the United States, 1867-1960* (with Anna Schwartz) was a particularly important publication.

© Ralf-Finn Hestoft / Corbis

Robert Lucas (1937–)

The role people's expectations play in the macroeconomy dramatically altered prior economic analysis. Although several economists made major contributions in this area, Lucas is generally recognized as the leading contributor.

Global Economic Crisis

Impact on Economics

SOUTH-WESTERN
CENGAGE Learning™

Australia • Brazil • Japan • Korea • Mexico • Singapore • Spain • United Kingdom • United States

Building Up to the Current Crisis

Learning Objectives.

By the end of this chapter, you will be able to:

- Explain the important financial market regulation that came out of the Great Depression of the 1930s.

- Describe why the rise of American consumerism took place after World War II.

- Elaborate on why the Savings and Loan crisis took place.

- Describe why there was a drive for mortgage-backed securities during the first decade of the 21st century.

- Delineate how all of these historical events have led up to the current financial crisis.

In January 2007, everything seemed to be going right for the U.S. economy and, by extension, U.S. financial markets. On January 24, 2007, the Dow Jones Industrial Index ended the day at 12,621. This was the first time ever the Dow had climbed above 12,600[1]. As stock prices continued to increase, the Federal Reserve worried that the U.S. economy might be growing too quickly. The Federal Reserve had raised its target for the Fed Funds Rate from 5.25 percent to 5.50 percent six months earlier, in the hopes of cooling a red hot U.S. economy. Even with the higher interest rates, the economy was growing at faster than 4 percent a year, a rate many economists believed was unsustainable for an economy the size of the United States.

By the fall of 2008, things had changed drastically. By November 12, 2008, the Dow had fallen to 8,282, a 41 percent drop from its high of 14,164 on October 9, 2007. The Federal Reserve had cut its target for the Fed Funds rate to a mere 1 percent, in a desperate attempt to keep the economy from sliding into a deep recession.

What on earth happened? How could such a highly successful economy like that of the United States in January 2007 find itself on the brink of a severe recession a mere few months later? At this point, we must ask ourselves: Where is the U.S. economy headed? As the old saying goes, "If you want to know where you are going, you have to understand where you have been." To learn why the current financial crisis occurred and where the global economy is headed, we need to determine how we got here. In fact, to fully grasp how we got to where we are, we have to travel back over seventy years to the

---

1 See http://www.mdleasing.com/djia.htm.

Great Depression of the 1930s. As the American society was coming to grips with the economic catastrophe of the Great Depression, there was a call for greater regulation of our financial markets. Many of these regulations are still in place, and understanding them helps to frame the structure of the current financial crisis.

From the economic despair of the Great Depression, we moved to the post–World War II economic expansion with its boom in the housing market. One of the main players in this post-war housing boom is the Federal National Mortgage Association and later the Federal Home Loan Mortgage Corporation, or as they are better known, Fannie Mae and Freddie Mac, respectfully. The financial troubles of Fannie and Freddie are a centerpiece of the current financial crisis.

The current financial crisis is not the first crisis to have centered on the American mortgage market. Over twenty years ago, the Savings & Loan crisis also focused on entities that lent money to households to buy their homes. The outfall from the Savings & Loan crisis sets the groundwork for the current global financial crisis. While our current crisis has roots dating back over seven decades ago with the Great Depression of the 1930s, the picture is by no means complete. Updates on this discussion can be found on the web page that accompanies this booklet.

THE EARLY CALL FOR REGULATION OF FINANCIAL MARKETS: THE 1930S

From Flappers to Breadlines

The 1920s was a glamorous decade. The "Roaring '20s," as they were called, saw the rise of American consumerism, with American households buying a wide range of goods and services from new automobiles and household appliances to radios and other electrical devices. Americans were able to buy these consumer goods thanks, in great part, to the booming stock market of the times. The New York Times index of 25 industrial stocks was at 110 in 1924[2]; by June 1929, it had risen to 338, and by September 1929, it stood at 452. Thus, someone buying the index in 1924 would have seen his or her investment grow by over 400 percent by September 1929.[3] The flappers with their trendy dresses, flashy zoot suits, and dancing the Charleston all night long epitomized the carefree decade. However, the good times could not last forever. By the end of the decade, the party that had been the Roaring '20s would collapse into the Great Depression of the 1930s.

---

2 Gary Walton and Hugh Rockoff, "History of the American Economy," South-Western College Publishing, 2004.

3 Charles Kindlegerger, *The World in Depression, 1929–1939*, Berkeley: University of California Press, 1973.

The Depression witnessed the once vibrant American economy seemingly imploding overnight. As the previously dynamic and ever-expanding economy contracted, unemployment across the economy increased dramatically. No sector of the economy seemed to be spared of the growing massive unemployment of the 1930s. The unemployment of unskilled workers, skilled craftsmen, farmers, businesspeople, and even executives increased rapidly. The unemployment rate that stood at only 4 percent for much of the 1920s increased to 25 percent by 1932.

The carefree dancing flappers of the 1920s were replaced with long breadlines and soup kitchens feeding the growing masses of unemployed of the 1930s. The once booming stock market seemed to evaporate and take the rest of the economy with it. The fall in the stock market was so dramatic that stocks lost 40 percent of their value in just two months. The stock market crash caused increased uncertainty over future income and employment translated into a reduction of household spending on durable goods such as automobiles and radios. [4]

The Call for Reform

As the economy contracted and unemployment rose, there were cries from the American people for their elected leaders to "do something" about the economic crisis. The election of President Franklin Delano Roosevelt in 1932 marked a dramatic change in how the federal government would approach the crisis. Roosevelt and his fellow Democrats believed that the Depression and the resulting rise in unemployment was due to the rampant speculation in the stock market and financial markets in general.

Even before Roosevelt was sworn in, Senator Ferdinand Pecora had begun hearings to examine the role the financial markets played in triggering the Depression. The Pecora Hearings, as they became known, resulted in sweeping new regulations of the financial markets. Within weeks of taking office, the Roosevelt Administration called for a bank holiday that would close all of the commercial banks in the country for seven days; passed and signed the Securities Act of 1933; and, perhaps most importantly, passed the Glass-Steagall Act or Banking Act of 1933.

The Glass-Steagall Act accomplished three key things:

- It separated commercial banks (i.e., those entities that take deposits and make loans) from investment banks (i.e., those entities involved with underwriting and selling stocks and bonds).

- It created bank deposit insurance.

- It gave the Federal Reserve the power to limit the interest rates commercial banks could pay on deposits.

The Glass-Steagall Act's separation of commercial and investment banking was based on the premise that if commercial banks were allowed to be involved in the selling of

---

4 Christina Romer, "The Great Crash and the Onset of the Depression," *Quarterly Journal of Economics,* August 1990, Vol. 105, no. 3.

stocks and bonds, a conflict of interest could exist and ultimately make commercial banks less safe.

The creation of deposit insurance was also designed to make commercial banks more stable. With the advent of government deposit insurance, depositors at insured banks could be confident that their savings were secure. Even if an insured bank failed, the government's deposit insurance would be there to ensure that savers would not lose their money. However, in order to make certain that banks were not taking on too much risk, government deposit insurance prompted the need for government regulation or oversight of the banking system.

In addition, Regulation Q of the Glass-Steagall Act was enacted to give the Federal Reserve the power to limit interest rates paid on deposits and to make the banking system more stable by limiting the amount of competition between banks. The drafters of the bill feared that if commercial banks competed for deposits, they would ultimately engage in destructive competitive behavior. Thus, to limit the amount of competition, banks were not allowed to pay interest on demand deposits (checking accounts) and had a cap on what interest rates they could pay on savings accounts.

As time went by, other legislation was passed that increased and expanded the government regulation of U.S. financial markets. The Securities Act of 1933 and the Securities Exchange Act of 1934 created the Securities and Exchange Commission, or the SEC, which is still today the main regulator of the bond and stock markets. In 1938, Congress created the Federal National Mortgage Association, or Fannie Mae, to help stabilize the home mortgage market. See the boxed feature for details.

Fannie Mae & Freddie Mac:
Government Entities to "Semi-Private" Financial Intermediaries

A mortgage loan uses real estate as collateral for the loan. Collateral is the pledge of an asset to ensure repayment by the borrower. Collateral serves as protection for the lender in case of default or nonpayment by the borrower. If a person borrows money and pledges something as collateral and does not repay as promised, the lenders allowed to take the collateral in lieu of the payment. So, a home mortgage loan, or what we will simply refer to as a home mortgage, is when the borrower pledges a house as collateral on a loan. A first mortgage is when a lender agrees to loan money to a family or an individual so that they can purchase a house.

Until the 20th century, mortgages were usually short term, lasting only about five to seven years. During those years, the borrower would have to pay interest on the money borrowed and repay the entire amount at the end of the period. Thus, at the end of the mortgage, the borrower would have to try to find someone or some entity to lend them the money again.

During the Great Depression, many people lost their jobs and could not afford to make their monthly mortgage payment, leaving the borrower to foreclose on them and have the family evicted from their home. With the federal government creation of the Federal National Mortgage Association (i.e., Fannie Mae), borrowers were encouraged to lend money to families over a period of 30 years. Over these 30 years, both interest and the loan principle would be paid. At the end of the 30-year mortgage, the borrower would own the home outright.

To entice lenders to loan money for home mortgages, Fannie Mae would agree to buy certain "qualified" mortgages from banks. Fannie Mae would then either hold the mortgages or sell them to interested investors. In doing so, Fannie Mae would free up funds for the lender to loan on new mortgages.

Due to budget constraints, President Johnson privatized Fannie Mae in 1968. In order to ensure that Fannie Mae did not have a monopoly in the mortgage securitizing business, the federal government created the Federal Home Loan Mortgage Corporation (i.e., Freddie Mac) in 1970.

Since both of these entities were created by the Federal government, many in the financial markets believed that Fannie and Freddie enjoyed a government guarantee against failure. Because of this "implied" government guarantee, Fannie and Freddie could borrow money at very low interest rates in financial markets.

The financial market regulation that came out of the Great Depression seemed to work very well. As the U.S. economy recovered from the Depression, financial markets remained stable and the number of banking failures dropped significantly. During World War II, the U.S. financial markets allowed the government to issue war bonds to finance the wars in Europe and the Pacific.

BUILDING THE AMERICAN DREAM: U.S. HOUSING BOOM IN POST-WAR AMERICA

Pent Up Consumption During World War II

The Second World War was a very hard time for American consumers. While household income increased, household spending decreased significantly. This reduction in household spending was in part necessary, as scarce consumer goods were diverted for the war effort. Many consumer goods, including sugar, meat, gasoline, tires, and even clothes, were rationed during the war. To buy these rationed goods, a family would need not only cash but a government-issued ration coupon. Even having a ration coupon did not guarantee that a consumer could find the good available for sale on store shelves. Shortages of popular goods, especially sugar, were commonplace during the war.

While consumer goods were scarce during the war, one thing was not in short supply: jobs. Workers were needed to build the tanks, ships, and arms that were critical to the war effort. The production of many consumer goods was suspended so that resources could be used for the war effort. For example, there were no new automobiles built in the United States between the end of 1942 and 1946, since the factories that built automobiles were converted into plants for making tanks, aircraft, artillery, etc., for the war. Similarly, no new farm tractors were built during the war, as those factories were

5

likewise converted for the war effort. But these factories needed workers to produce war-related products. Because many young males had joined the military to fight in the war, workers were in short supply. For the first time in U.S. history, large numbers of women entered the labor force.

As employment increased during the war, American households saw their incomes increase. However, with the war rationing in effect, households had very few things on which to spend this new income. Instead, scores of Americans saved their money during the War, waiting and hoping for a better future.

Unleashing American Spending

The end of the Second World War saw a return of American consumerism in grand style. The long years of economic hardship of the Great Depression were behind them, as were the days of sacrifice during World War II. The American consumer had pent up spending power that was being unleashed. For military personnel who were returning from fighting the war overseas as well as those who had "fought the war on the home front," the end of the war created an opportunity to capture the "American Dream." A big part of that post-war "American Dream" was home ownership. In 1940, just 44 percent of families owned their own home; by the end of the 1950s, three out of five families owned their home (according to a U.S. Census). This remarkable increase in homeownership was due, in great part, to the expansion of the Savings and Loan industry.

Savings and Loans are depository institutions that take deposits, mostly from households, and make loans mostly to consumers; these loans are often home mortgages. While the Savings and Loan industry has a long history in the United States going back to the 19th century (the forerunners were called Building & Loans), a number of Savings and Loans failed during the depression. As a result, in 1932, Congress passed the Federal Home Loan Bank Act of 1932, which created the Federal Home Loan Bank Board to lend money to Savings and Loans that found themselves short of funds. In 1934, Congress created the Federal Savings and Loan Insurance Corporation (FSLIC), which would offer government deposit insurance to savers at Savings and Loans.[5]

Expansion of the Savings and Loan Industry

During the post–World War II era, the Savings and Loan industry thrived. The first decade after the Second World War saw the Savings & Loan industry grow at its fastest rate ever. The expansion of American suburbs during the late 1940s and 1950s increased the demand for home mortgages that the Savings and Loans were prepared to offer. In addition, the Savings and Loan trade association worked with the managers of the S&Ls

5 David Mason, "From Building and Loans to Bail-outs," Cambridge University Press, 2004.

showing them how to advertise their services and focus on providing a high level of consumer service. As a result, the size and reach of the Savings and Loan industry expanded greatly.

Government regulation of the Savings and Loan industry also played a large role in the industry's expansion. Thanks to Regulation Q, which the Savings and Loans became subject to in 1966, the Savings and Loans faced a cap on their cost of funds. At the same time, government regulations were changing, making it easier for the Savings and Loans to offer even more mortgages and grow even more quickly. These were very successful times for the Savings and Loans. Managers of the Savings and Loans lived by the "3-6-3 Rule," that is, pay 3 percent on deposits, lend the money at 6 percent on mortgages, and be on the golf course by 3:00 pm.

The "3-6-3 Rule" illustrates why the Savings and Loans were so profitable. When a depository institution pays 3 percent for deposits and lends the money out at 6 percent, the difference between the two is what economists call the "interest rate spread." For the Savings and Loans, the 3 percentage point interest rate spread is how they paid their expenses and generated a profit. During the decades after the Second World War, the Savings and Loans were very profitable indeed. These profits allowed existing Savings and Loans to expand and drew in a large number of new S&Ls. By 1965, the Savings and Loan industry held 26 percent of all consumer savings and provided 46 percent of the single-family mortgages in the United States. Unfortunately, the good times would not last forever.

The Savings & Loan Crisis of the 1980s

Inflation and Interest Rates

During the 1970s, the U.S. economy suffered from increased rates of inflation. Inflation is defined as the continuous increase in the general level of prices. A high rate of inflation mean the cost of living for households increases and the cost of operations for firms increase. In addition, as the rate of inflation increases, market interest rates also increase.

To see why this happens, think about how you would feel if you were a lender of money and prices increased. Suppose I ask you to lend me $2 so that I can buy a bottle of diet Coke from a vending machine and agree to repay you tomorrow. . Essentially you are lending me enough resources, the two dollars, to purchase an entire bottle of diet Coke. Now assume the person who refills the vending machine changes the price of a bottle of diet Coke from $2 to $3. Tomorrow comes and I give you $2. You say, "Wait a minute-- I gave you enough resources to buy an entire bottle of diet Coke, and yet you pay me back with resources that can now only buy two-thirds of a bottle of diet Coke!"
Notice what happened: When prices increase, or there is inflation, lenders get paid back in money that simply no longer buys as much. As a result, if lenders think there is going to be inflation, they are going to demand to be compensated for the difference and thus demand a higher interest rate before they will lend their money.

This is what happened during the 1970s. As the inflation rate in the United States increased, market interest rates also increased. Thus, interest rates on Treasury bills, corporate bonds, and other types of debt increased higher and higher as U.S. inflation got worse and worse.

The Problem of Disintermediation

One set of interest rates that did not increase during the 1970s was that paid by the Savings and Loans. Remember that during this time, the Savings and Loans were subject to Regulation Q, the law that stated the maximum interest rate that could be paid on deposits. Thus, while the market interest rates on regular passbook savings accounts could be no higher than 5.5 percent, the yield on a 1-year Treasury bill was over 12 percent by February 1980. As a result of these interest rate differences, savers started to pull their money out of the Savings and Loans in favor of higher paying money market mutual funds. The process of funds moving from one financial intermediary to another is what economists call disintermediation.

To combat disintermediation, the Savings and Loans looked for ways around Regulation Q. One "invention" was the creation of NOW, or negotiable orders of withdrawal. NOW accounts were essentially demand deposits that paid a market rate of interest. Initially the NOW accounts were of questionable legality, since they were violating the premise of Regulation Q that prohibited the paying of interest on demand deposits or checking accounts. But the operators of Savings and Loans thought they had little choice but to offer the NOW accounts. If they did not offer NOW accounts, they would see more and more deposits leave their institutions. If the disintermediation were allowed to go on unchecked, it would lead to a collapse of the Savings and Loan industry, since a depository institution with no deposits simply can not function. Clearly, something needed to change.

DIDMCA: The Solution that Did Not Work

The Savings and Loan industry turned to Washington for help with disintermediation. In response to the growing financial market difficulties, after much debate, Congress passed, and President Carter signed, the Depository Institutions Deregulation and Monetary Control Act (DIDMCA) in 1980. The DIDMCA was the Carter Administration's attempt to bring about some type of financial market reform. Four years earlier, Carter had campaigned on the promise that his administration would bring about such reform, but by 1980, little to nothing had changed in terms of financial market regulation. DIDMCA was about to change all of that.

Two of DIDMCA's major reforms were that it set up for the complete repeal of Regulation Q over six years and it would make it legal for Savings & Loans to offer NOW accounts in order to fend off the disintermediation immediately. While DIDMCA allowed the Savings and Loans to compete with the money market mutual funds for deposits, it created a whole new set of problems. Savings and Loans generated most of their income off the 30-year fixed interest rate mortgages that they had written in the past. The vast majority of these mortgages paid the Savings and Loan a 6 to 8 percent annual rate of interest. When the Savings and Loans were paying 3 to 5.5 percent on deposits, they enjoyed a positive interest rate spread. With the passage of DIDMCA, the Savings and Loans would now be paying upwards of 14 percent on their NOW accounts. That meant that the Savings and Loans would be paying 14 percent for funds while earning only 6 to 8 percent on funds. Thus, the Savings and loans were suffering from a negative interest rate spread.

Garn-St. Germain: Making a Bad Problem Worse

To get relief from their negative interest rate spread, the Savings and Loans returned to Congress in 1981 and 1982 seeking help. In response to the industry's cry for help, Congress passed the Garn-St. Germain Depository Institutions Act of 1982. Garn-St. Germain allowed the Savings and Loans to diversify their lending away from traditional 30-year fixed rate home loans and into shorter term, more profitable business loans. The Act allowed the Savings and Loans to hold up to 40 percent of their assets in commercial mortgages and up to 11 percent of their assets in secured or unsecured commercial loans. In addition, many states, including California and Texas, significantly reduced the amount of regulations on their respective state-chartered Savings and Loans.

As a result of these reduced regulations and a desire to diversify their loan portfolios, the Savings and Loans set off a business lending spree. The Savings and Loans wrote a dizzying array of commercial real estate loans, include loans for high-rise office buildings, massive suburban shopping mall developments, and retail strip mall developments. In addition, many Savings and Loans started lending money for alternative energy development such as windmill farms in the Texas panhandle. One issue with this new lending is that many Savings and Loan lenders had little to no experience in making such loans. As a result, many loans were written where risk was mispriced. Numerous office buildings were built that simply were not needed. Many shopping centers never found enough tenants because they knew shopping centers were not needed. For example, by 1986, nearly one-third of the office space in Houston, Texas, sat unoccupied. As these spaces went unrented, the real estate developers who built these buildings could not pay the loans they had taken out from the Savings and Loans.

The Zombie Savings and Loans

By the late 1980s, the Savings and Loan industry was riddled with insolvent institutions. These institutions had written so many bad loans that they simply did not have enough assets to make good on all of their deposits. These insolvent institutions, sometimes called "Zombie institutions" because they were financially "dead," should have been closed down by their regulators. These regulators, which included the Federal Home Loan Bank and FSLIC, instead chose to suspend the regulatory rules and allowed these Zombie institutions to continue to function. This suspension of the regulatory rules, called "Capital Forbearance," allowed the Zombie institutions to continue in operation and make more and more risky loans.

As the Zombie institutions were allowed to continue in operation, many of the Zombies "infected" the healthy, well run institutions. A Zombie institution would compete with a healthy institution for a loan customer by offering the customer a loan on very favorable terms with a low interest rate and/or easy repayment terms. To compete, the healthy institution would have to offer the loan customer similar terms or face being locked out of the market. Thus, the healthy institution would have to behave like the Zombie institution and essentially "become" a Zombie institution.

One question that has been raised is: why did the regulators allow the Zombie institutions to continue in operation? One answer to this question is that the regulators simply did not have the resources to close all of the Zombie institutions. Closing all of the Zombie institutions would have required perhaps hundreds of billions of dollars to pay insured depositors. Since the regulators did have the resources to close all of these Zombie institutions, they allowed them to continue in operation.

A second potential explanation to why the regulators allowed the Zombie institutions to continue in operation was the political power some of the savings and loan operators wielded. See the box below for one of the more infamous examples of political influence in the savings and loan crisis.

Charles Keating and the Keating 5

One reason many of the Savings and Loan regulators practiced capital forbearance was the political influence of the Savings and Loan operators. An example of this is what became known as the Keating 5. An Arizona real estate developer by the name of Charles Keating was allowed to buy a Savings and Loan in California called Lincoln Savings and Loan. When Lincoln Savings and Loan started to suffer from disintermediation, Keating promised depositors that he could offer them a "special account" that would pay an interest rate much above what money market mutual funds would pay.

Many of Lincoln's depositors were elderly, and they questioned Keating as to the safety of the "special accounts." Keating reassured his elderly customers that the special accounts were fully insured by the federal government. In fact, they were not. The special accounts were actual shares in his real estate development in Arizona.

The regulators of Lincoln Savings and Loan at the Federal Home Bank Board became concerned about the growing riskiness of Lincoln. But Charles Keating did not want the regulators to interfere in his operations. Keating had made large campaign contributions to five key U.S. Senators. Keating now called on these five Senators to intervene with the regulators on his behalf. The five Senators basically did what Keating requested. As a result, Keating was allowed to continue to operate Lincoln Savings and Loan as he saw fit.

In 1989, Lincoln Savings and Loan failed, costing taxpayers $1.3 billion, and more importantly, more than 22,000 depositors/bondholders at Lincoln Savings and Loan lost their savings since they were not in government-insured accounts. Charles Keating eventually was convicted of bank fraud and served four and a half years in prison. What happened to those five Senators known as the Keating 5? Basically, nothing. All were allowed to continue serving in the U.S.

Senate, and two of the Keating 5 went on to run for President of the United States despite their questionable ethical dealings with Charles Keating.

As the 1980s moved on, the Savings and Loan problem grew significantly. In 1988, the FSLIC had closed over 200 Savings and Loans that were insolvent. The problem, however, was that by the end of 1988, over 500 insolvent Savings and Loans continued to operate. Clearly, the current system had failed.

In August 1989, President George H. Bush signed the Financial Institutions Reform Recovery and Enforcement Act. FIRREA was the first dramatic step to resolve the Savings and Loan crisis. Among other things, FIRREA forced the absorption of the FSLIC into the FDIC. In addition, the Federal Home Loan Banks' independence was stripped away and it was taken over by the Office of Thrift Supervision within the Treasury Department. Perhaps most importantly, FIRREA created the Resolution Trust Corporation (RTC), which was to close the insolvent Savings and Loans and sell off their assets.

The once proud Savings and Loan industry that had helped to build the American suburbs after the Second World War was now a mere shadow of itself. The inability or unwillingness of the Savings and Loan operators to measure the riskiness of their loans problem greatly contributed to the industry's demise. The regulators such as the Federal Home Loan Bank and FSLIC arguably did not do their job correctly, and these entities were either stripped of their powers or completely eliminated.

THE SEEKING OF RETURN: 2002–2006

One of the lessons learned from the Savings and Loan crisis is that depository institutions that rely on the interest rate spread between what they earn on long-term loans and what they pay on short-term deposits can suffer greatly when market interest rates increase. The Savings and Loans suffered from negative interest rate spreads throughout the late 1970s and early 1980s, and these negative spreads triggered a series of chain reactions that ultimately led to the current financial crisis.

Banks and Fee Income

In an attempt to avoid a repeat of the Savings and Loan crisis, commercial banks in the United States during the 1990s and throughout the first decade of the 21st century attempted to end their reliance on interest rate spreads. Instead of depending on the spread as a source of profits, commercial banks envisioned themselves as providers of financial services who earned fees for their services. Since fee income was independent of changes in market interest rates, commercial banks saw it as a much more stable source of income and profits.

Commercial banks looked in a variety of places to generate fees. They charged fees for use of ATMs (automated teller machines), for use of the bank lobby, and for printing checks, and they looked at offering new services where they could generate new fees. One expanding market that caught the banks' attention was the home mortgage market. Traditionally, when a depository institution wrote a home mortgage loan, the depository institution would hold the mortgage, collect payment, or service the mortgage for 30 years until the household borrower paid off the mortgage. However, in their desire to earn fees, commercial banks were turning more and more to the securitization of home mortgages.

Securitization

Securitization is the pooling or combining of loans, such as mortgages, into one big bundle. This bundle is then used to create a new financial instrument or bond whose cash flows are the original loans in the pool. For example, the securitization of home mortgages entails the purchase of a large number of home mortgages and the creation of a mortgage-backed security, or MBS. The mortgaged-backed securities are paid the cash flow received from the households as they make their mortgage payments.

Securitization takes place with other loans in addition to home mortgages. Commercial mortgages are also securitized into their own version of securitized securities called Commercial Mortgaged-Backed Assets. Student Loans are also securitized. If you have borrowed money for a student loan, once you signed your promise to repay the loan, the bank or financial institution that lent you the money took your student loan, bundled it with other student loans, and created an Asset-Backed Security, or ABS. In 2006, $79 billion of new student-loan-backed ABS were issued, with the total market size estimated to exceed $350 billion in 2007.

Fannie Mae and Freddie Mac: Their Great Demise

Fannie Mae and Freddie Mac were originally created by Congress to provide liquidity to the mortgage market, and they were very successful. They did so by buying "qualified" mortgages and securitizing them, or bundling them and selling the bundles to investors. The two "government-sponsored entities," or GSEs, came to dominate the mortgage market. Together they hold or guarantee over $5 trillion in mortgages. By comparison, the entire U.S. economy is just over $13 trillion and the total entire outstanding mortgages in the United States amount to $12 trillion.

However, in 2007 and 2008, both Fannie Mae and Freddie Mac ran into a great deal of financial trouble. Both Fannie and Freddie had purchased mortgages without carefully examining the default risks associated with those mortgages. As a result, in 2008, the federal government had to take over both Fannie and Freddie to keep them from failing.

When a commercial bank writes a loan that will be bundled up or securitized, the bank earns a fee from the entity that does the bundling. The "bundler" or securitizer may be an investment bank, a Government-Sponsored Entity (such as Fannie Mae, Freddie Mac, or Sallie Mae--for student loans), or a Special Investment Vehicle, which is created by commercial banks. The bundler then sells the newly created asset, such as a mortgage-backed security, to an institutional investor, such as an insurance company, pension fund, or an endowment.

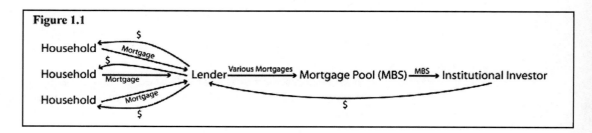

Figure 1.1

Over time, the market for mortgage-backed securities increased. The loan originators, oftentimes commercial banks, liked the process of making mortgage loans and earning a fee and then servicing the mortgage and earning more fees. They could generate fee income and move the long-term mortgages off their balance sheet, so they no longer had to worry about interest rate spreads. The process was appealing too because it enabled the mortgage bundlers to charge a fee for bundling the mortgages together and then selling them to institutional investors.

As time went on, new inventions in the mortgage market came about. One issue that arose was that not all institutional investors had the same desire for risk. Some institutional investors didn't want any risk of default. That is, they wanted to be sure that they received the payments they were expecting. At the same time, other institutional investors were more willing to take on some risk, as long as they were compensated for this increased risk by being paid a higher interest rate.

To meet the differing needs of these institutional investors, the bundlers of Mortgage-Backed Securities decided to slice the MBSs into different pieces. The first slice would be paid first, as the households made their mortgage payments. The next slice would be paid after the first slice was paid, if there was still money left over, meaning if there were only a few or no defaults. Each of the remaining slices would then be paid in descending order. These slices of the MBSs are called *tranches*, from the French word *tranch*, which means slice.

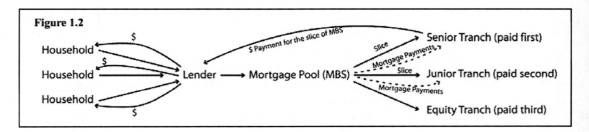

Figure 1.2

In reality, there could be more than just three tranches, but the logic remains the same: the senior tranche gets paid first and so on down the line. Some of the lower tranches, the last to be paid and thus the most risky, the lenders (including commercial banks) held onto the mortgages since they could be very difficult to sell to institutional investors. But, as long as there are no defaults on mortgages, all of the tranches get paid.

Historically, home mortgage defaults were very low, only around 2 percent, so the buyers of the Mortgage-Backed Assets felt fairly safe that they would receive their payments as promised. Thus, the securitized mortgage market grew.

Falling Market Interest Rates

In 2001, in a response to a slowing U.S. economy, the Federal Reserve set out to lower interest rates to stimulate the economy. The collapse of the dot.com boom in 2001 had brought about a significant reduction in the amount of household and business spending. To encourage more borrowing and spending by households and firms, the Federal Reserve cut interest rates throughout 2001, 2002, and 2003. By 2003, market interest rates in the United States were the lowest they had been in forty years.

In response to these falling market interest rates, institutional investors' interest rates in the home mortgage market increased significantly. While other market interest rates had dropped significantly due to the Federal Reserve's actions, the interest rates on home mortgages, and thus the return on mortgage-backed securities, had not fallen as much. Thus, there was a growing interest by institutional investors to buy these mortgage-backed securities.

The mortgage lenders, including commercial banks, were desperate to the meet the growing demand for mortgage-backed assets. But in order to create more mortgage-backed assets, these lenders needed to write more and more mortgages. The problem these lenders faced was that in order to write more mortgages, they would need to go beyond "traditional" borrowers. That is, the lenders needed to lower their lending standards so that more people could qualify for mortgages.

Traditionally, if a family wanted to borrow money to buy a house, they needed to have 20 percent of the purchase price in cash. The family could then borrow the remaining 80 percent of the purchase price of the house via a mortgage. But, as the demand for mortgage-backed assets increased, mortgage lenders began writing "zero-down" mortgages where the borrower puts no money down and borrows 100 percent of the purchase price.

One potential problem with "zero-down" mortgages is that they can result in much higher default rates. In the traditional 20-percent down mortgage, the borrower has some of their own money in the house, or as the saying goes, they have "their skin in the game." If times become financially difficult for the borrower, they would work hard to stay current on their mortgage payments, since defaulting on the mortgage or being foreclosed on would cause the borrower to lose the money they had used to purchase the house. However, with zero-down mortgages, the borrower doesn't have any "skin in the game" or any financial interest in the house. Under this setting, if financial times become difficult, the borrower is much more likely to simply walk away from the house and have the lender foreclose on the house.

Thus, the advent of the zero-down mortgage greatly increased the probability of default by the borrowers. The problem is, many in the financial markets ignored these increasing risks in the mortgage market. Instead, they continued to believe that mortgage default rates would stay exactly as they always had been. In other words, there was a major mispricing of risk occurring in the U.S. mortgage markets.

Heads I Win, Tales the Government Loses

As depository institutions such as Savings and Loans or commercial banks take on more risk, either through writing risky loans or holding risky assets, depositors usually "punish" this behavior by withdrawing their deposits. Depositors do this because if the depository institution fails due to too many of its risky assets failing to pay out as planned, the depositor will lose all of the money they have on deposit. In these cases, the depositors essentially "watch over" the depository institution and help to ensure that Savings and Loans or commercial banks do not engage in excessive risky behavior.

However, deposit insurance changes all of this. With government-sponsored deposit insurance, the depositor knows that even if the depository institution fails, the depositor will not lose any of their money. If the institution fails, all the depositor has to do is go to the government to get a check equal to the amount of the government insurance.

On the other hand, if the depository institution engages in holding risk assets and these risky assets pay off, the institution can "share" these high payoffs with the depositor in the form of higher interest rates on deposits. This is what economists call the "moral hazard" of deposit insurance. A moral hazard is the existence of a contract that can alter behavior by changing incentives.

With the creation of government deposit insurance, the incentives and behavior of depositors change. Depositors no longer "watch over" depository institutions to "keep them safe" and instead have an incentive to push lenders to hold very risky assets. If those risky assets pay off as planned, the depositor benefits, as the institution shares with them the high returns generated by the risky assets. Conversely, if the risky assets fail to pay off as planned and the depository institution fails, the depositor turns to the government to be made whole again. From the point of view of the depositor, government-sponsored deposit insurance creates a situation where the depositor can say "head I win, tails the government loses."

BRINGING IT ALL TOGETHER

The current financial crisis that centers on the home mortgage markets has its roots in the evolution of the U.S. financial markets. Many economists argue that the deposit insurance that was created during the Great Depression of the 1930s may have contributed to the excessive risk taking and the mispricing of risk in the home mortgage market during the first decade of the 21st century. What contributed to this mispricing of risk in the home mortgage market was the rapid expansion of the securitizing of home mortgages, which was an outcome of the Savings and Loan crisis of the 1980s. But this securitization would not have been possible without the rapid expansion of the U.S. housing market in the decades following the Second World War.

But the synopsis of the current financial crisis is not complete. In the next chapter, we will examine in more depth the issues of the current crisis. Updates on the current status of the crisis can be found on the web page www.cengage.com/gec that accompanies this booklet. It will be very interesting and informative to watch this crisis unfold.

The Current Crisis

Chapter Outline

Learning Goals

After reading this chapter, you should be able to answer these questions:
1. Why is there so much uncertainty in financial markets?
2. In what ways is the current financial crisis not limited to just the United States?
3. What issues surround the Wall Street bailout package?
4. What challenges does President Obama face during his first term?

Economic slowdowns and recessions occur for a variety of reasons. Sometimes the economy slows when the central bank raises interest rates to counteract inflation. At other times, the rate of economic growth slows due to a natural disaster or a disruption in the flow of goods and services. The economic recession that began in the United States in December 2007 was triggered by a global financial crisis. Problems in the U.S. home mortgage market set off this widespread financial meltdown. In this chapter, we will examine the current global financial crisis, explain what caused it, and offer potential solutions to resolve it.

As discussed in the previous chapter, the causes of the current financial crisis go back decades. However, the specific events that led to the current financial downturn began in the summer of 2007. One recurring theme in this chapter will be the destructive role that uncertainty has played in pushing the United States into this quagmire. We will see how an entire Wall Street industry, investment banking, has been crippled by it. As policymakers continue to struggle with solutions, we will explore how their past rescue attempts have not worked as planned. Finally, we will look at the economic problems that face the Obama Administration.

The story of the current financial crisis is far from over. Updates to this compelling economic story can be found on the website www.cengage.com/gec that accompanies this chapter.

THE SUMMER OF 2007: THE CRISIS BEGINS

Summer is usually a very slow time for media events in the United States: in Washington, D.C., congress members are on their summer recess; in New York, many people who work in financial markets flee the city for long vacations; and in Europe, financial market activity slows as Europeans take advantage of month-long vacations. But during the late summer of 2007, Washington, New York, and the European financial centers were all a buzz with rumors of what appeared to be a brewing financial storm.

In July 2007, two hedge funds run by investment bank Bear Stearns collapsed, causing an estimated $1.5 billion loss to its investors.[1] The two funds—the High-Grade Structured Credit Strategies Fund and the High-Grade Structured Credit Strategies Enhanced Leveraged Fund—had borrowed huge sums of money to buy a large number of mortgage-backed securities.

In May 2007, as the first wave of mortgage defaults began to be felt, these two funds reported losses much larger than had been anticipated. As a result of these losses and growing uncertainty concerning the future value of the funds under its management, Bear Stearns announced that it would no longer allow investors to withdraw money from these two funds. Commercial banks and investment banks that had loaned money to these funds now demanded more cash as collateral on those loans. Bear Stearns announced on June 26 that it was going to lend the High-Grade Structured Credit Strategies Fund, the more conservative of the two funds, $1.6 billion in an attempt to increase investor confidence. But it was already too late. The market value of the mortgage-backed securities held by these two funds fell so dramatically that by mid-July both funds were essentially worthless.

At the end of July, Federal Reserve Chairman Ben Bernanke told Congress that the losses associated with problems in the mortgage market were "significant" and could approach $100 billion. But, Bernanke said he and the Federal Reserve (the Fed) would remain "alert" and would notify Congress if the problems in the mortgage market posed a threat to the overall economy. Mr. Bernanke did not view the mortgage crisis to be a threat to the overall U.S. economy at that time. Unfortunately for Mr. Bernanke and the Fed, the problems had only begun.

In August 2007, Countrywide Financial Corporation, the largest mortgage lender in the United States, was forced to borrow more than $11 billion from over 40 different

---

1 See Gretchen Morgenson, "Bear Stearns Says Battered Hedge Funds Are Worth Little," *The New York Times*, July 18, 2007.

creditors due to losses on mortgages it had written. Countrywide played a very important role in the U.S. mortgage market. It consistently wrote about 17 percent of all new U.S. mortgages each year; in 2007, it wrote over $400 billion of new mortgages and was servicing about 9 million loans with an estimated value of about $1.5 trillion. The financial troubles at a giant such as Countrywide sent shock waves through the financial markets. People wondered "if Countrywide and Bear Stearns can get into such deep financial troubles, who could be next?"

Who Has What Risk?

One major issue in the current financial crisis is a lack of clarity about *who* has *how much* risk exposure to *what* risk. In a "traditional" mortgage market, the risks are clear: a bank lends money to a household so that the family can purchase a house. The bank holds the mortgage and thus has default risk: the family, for whatever reason, may not be able to make their mortgage payments as promised.

However, with the creation of mortgage-backed securities and payment tranches called **collateralized debt obligations (CDOs)**, it is much more difficult to discern who is holding what portion of what mortgage. Thus, the owner of a CDO might own little slivers of thousands of different mortgages. Determining which of those mortgages is going bad at any point in time is practically impossible. Likewise, during times of financial distress, the value of CDOs can be very difficult to measure because the value of the underlying mortgages or slices of mortgages is unclear. During "good times," holders of CDOs can determine CDO value by looking at the market price of similarly traded CDOs. But when the markets are gripped by uncertainty, as they have been since the summer of 2007, it can become difficult if not impossible to place a market value on those CDOs.

Financial market participants, including bank depositors, hate such uncertainty. People and firms deposit money at commercial banks because they view those banks as safe. However, when those banks have assets, such as CDOs, that are difficult to price, depositors can become worried about their bank's safety. When depositors lose confidence in their bank's security, they can, in mass, attempt to withdrawal their funds all at once. This is called a **bank run**.

In August 2007, the commercial bank division of Countrywide Financial Corporation, called Countrywide Bank, suffered from just such a bank run. Depositors at Countrywide Bank in California feared that since the biggest U.S. mortgage company was in financial trouble that its commercial bank night run out of money.[2] Depositors lined up outside the bank and jammed its phone lines seeking to withdraw their money. Even though all deposits were insured by the FDIC up to $100,000 per account, depositors still wanted to pull their money out of Countrywide Bank "just in case." The uncertainty from the mortgage market and CDOs had now spilled over into the commercial banking market and negatively impacted the expectations and outlook of average depositors.

---

2 See E. Scott Reckard and Annette Haddad "A Rush to Pull out Money," *Los Angeles Times*, August 17, 2007.

The Crisis Goes Global

This inability to correctly price CDOs was also felt around the world. In August 2007, BNP Paribas, the largest bank in France and one of the largest in Europe, ran headlong into the American mortgage crisis. On August 9, BNP Paribas was forced to halt withdrawals from two of its funds because it could not "fairly value" the CDOs it held. BNP said in an August 9 statement:

"The complete evaporation of liquidity in certain market segments of the US securitisation market has made it impossible to value certain assets fairly regardless of their quality or credit rating. The situation is such that it is no longer possible to value fairly the underlying US ABS (Asset Backed Securities) assets …"[3]

The asset-backed securities to which the statement refers are CDOs and mortgaged-backed securities. Because BNP Paribas could not determine the value of these assets, it could not calculate the balance of any individual investor. Thus, it would not allow investors to sell their shares or halt withdrawals. This was very similar to the problem faced by the two American Bear Stearns' hedge funds three months earlier.

Later in August, German bank Landesbank Sachsen Girzentrale ran into financial trouble due to its exposure to the American mortgage market. Sachsen LB, as it was known, first received a $23 billion loan from a group of regional savings banks in Germany, but even that was not enough. Sachsen LB was sold to a larger rival Landesbank by the end of August.

In September 2008, Northern Rock, the United Kingdom's fifth-largest home lender, suffered a bank run. Northern Rock had borrowed money in the short-term global financial markets, called **money markets**, and then loaned that money out to UK home buyers. Consequently, Northern Rock had relatively fewer depositors than would a traditional commercial bank or an American savings & loan.[4] But, since Northern Rock had been considered stable and reliable, it had been able to borrow money in the money markets at a relatively low interest rate and relend those funds at a higher interest rate in the UK mortgage market. In addition, to support its rate of return on assets, Northern Rock had purchased U.S.-based CDOs.

By the fall of 2008, with CDOs more difficult to price and money market participants no longer willing to lend to any bank that might have exposure to the U.S. mortgage crisis, Northern Rock found it increasingly difficult to borrow money in the money markets. But Northern Rock needed these money market loans in order to have enough cash to meet its depositors' needs. Unable to secure needed funds from the money markets, Northern Rock turned to the UK government for assistance.

3 See http://www.bnpparibas.com/en/news/press-releases.

4 Northern Rock at the time had loans and other assets on its balance sheet of £113bn. The value of deposits placed with it by retail customers was £24bn. See http://news.bbc.co.uk/2/hi/business/6994099.stm.

On September 13, the Bank of England agreed to be the lender of last resort to Northern Rock, but it was already too late. Over the next two days, depositors lined up outside Northern Rock branches and inundated its web site, attempting to withdraw their savings. This lack of confidence in Northern Rock was simply devastating. Even though the Bank of England agreed to guarantee Northern Rock funds, depositors and financial markets had lost confidence in the institution, and its fate was sealed. Northern Rock was eventually taken over by the UK government on February 22, 2008.

The Collapse and Bailout of Wall Street

As the year 2007 drew to a close, it seemed that the fallout from the U.S. mortgage and global financial crisis might not dramatically impact the rest of the U.S. economy. The U.S. stock market was doing well in the fall of 2007, having reached a record high of 14,164 on October 9, 2007. But things were about to take a drastic turn for the worse. In December, President Bush announced a plan to help Americans who were about to lose their homes due to higher market interest rates. In presenting the housing rescue plan, President Bush described the housing downturn as a "serious challenge," but he stated: "The economy is strong, flexible and dynamic enough to weather this storm."[5] So, perhaps the worst of the financial crisis was past. Nothing could have been further from the truth.

Monday, January 21, 2008, was the Martin Luther King, Jr. holiday, which meant U.S. financial markets were closed for the day. But the financial markets across the globe were open, and investors began to panic over the growing problems in the U.S. mortgage market. Stock markets in Asia, Europe, and Latin America fell between 4 and 7 percent during the day's trading. Seemingly in response to the global stock market slide, the Federal Reserve's policymaking group, the Federal Open Market Committee, took the historically unprecedented move of holding an emergency meeting on a Monday night. They decided to drastically cut their interest rate target by 0.75 percent, where most recent changes in interest rates had been by 0.25 percent. This surprise move was thus three times the regular size interest rate change, plus it took place in an emergency meeting. One economic pundit described the Fed's move as a "once in a generation event."[6] Clearly, policymakers were worried that something had gone horribly wrong with financial markets and, by extension, the U.S. economy.

As winter gave way to spring, the problems in the financial markets seemed to get worse. In March 2008, the Federal Reserve announced its biggest move to date: it would make $200 billion of loans available to banks and other financial institutions.[7] The Fed was forced into making these funds available because banks were no longer willing to lend money to one another. Due to the uncertainty in financial markets, banks could not be sure of which other banks were connected to the growing U.S. mortgage crisis. Since banks could not evaluate the creditworthiness of other banks, they simply refused to lend money to one another.

5 See http://news.bbc.co.uk/2/hi/business/7129990.stm.

6 See Michael M. Grynbaum and John Holusha, "Fed Cuts Rates 0.75% and Stocks Swing," *The New York Times*, January 22, 2008.

7 See http://news.bbc.co.uk/2/hi/business/7284101.stm.

The lack of bank-to-bank lending caused major problems for other financial markets and the overall economy. If banks are unable to obtain funds from other banks, they will also be unlikely to lend money to nonbank business firms. If businesses are unable to secure loans, they cannot buy much-needed equipment or raw materials nor pay their workers. Thus, banks' refusal to lend to one another can trigger a chain reaction that can cause the entire economy to slow down. This is exactly what was happening in the spring of 2008.

Bear Stearns, JPMorgan Chase, and the Fed

The Fed's emergency lending did not resolve the problem. In March, financial market participants started to lose confidence in Bear Stearns, at the time the fifth-largest investment bank in the country. Investment banks, like commercial banks, depend on their customers' confidence for survival. For 85 years, Bear Stearns' customers had confidence in the big investment bank; it had survived the Great Depression, World War II, and the aftermath of the September 11 terrorist attacks. But it would not survive the current global financial crisis.

Bear Stearns' problems grew to a crisis level in the early days of March, and rumors of its financial distress quickly spread across Wall Street.[8] Only a year earlier, Bear Stearns had been riding a financial high with its stock trading at over $160 a share. But then came the sub-prime mortgage crisis and the failure of two of Bear Stearns' hedge funds. By March 12, the stock price had fallen to only $30 a share, and Bear Stearns' executives took to the airwaves trying in vain to convince the global financial markets that the firm was solvent. This public relations push failed. Bear Stearns needed to borrow huge amounts of money in order to keep up with investors' withdrawals. The bank's executives reportedly called officials at the Fed late in the day of March 13 and asked them to arrange a bailout of the 85-year-old company.

The Fed and Bear Stearns' officials decided to see if JPMorgan Chase would be willing to help the struggling investment bank. JPMorgan Chase had numerous business relationships with Bear Stearns and had much to lose if Bear Stearns failed. But JPMorgan Chase was reluctant to lend money without some type of guarantee of repayment from the Federal Reserve should Bear Stearns eventually fail. The Fed agreed to guarantee the loan from JPMorgan Chase to Bear Stearns, but it was already too little, too late. The financial markets had lost confidence in Bear Stearns. Virtually no one was willing to enter into trades or conduct business with Bear.

Clearly, the Fed-arranged loan was not enough to save Bear Stearns. Over the March 15–16 weekend, the Fed and Bear Stearns' executives worked around the clock to find a buyer for the beleaguered investment bank. Finally, on Sunday March 16, armed with $30 billion of Federal Reserve guarantees of Bear Stearns assets, JPMorgan Chase agreed to buy Bear Stearns at the stunning price of only $2 per share. That price represented a 93 percent discount off the price of a share of Bear Stearns stock on the close of trading on the previous Friday. But the directors of Bear Stearns had little

8 See Matthew Goldstein, "Bear Stearns' Big Bailout," *BusinessWeek*, March 14, 2008.

choice. It was either agree to the purchase by JPMorgan Chase at $2 share or face bankruptcy Monday morning at which point the shares would be essentially worthless.

A major uproar from Bear Stearns' employees, who owned one-third of the firm, as well as Bear Stearns' bondholders who would essentially be wiped out by the buyout, forced JPMorgan Chase to raise its offer to $10 per share a week later. Also, sensing a growing rage in Washington at the potential cost to taxpayers of the Fed's guarantee, JPMorgan Chase agreed that it would absorb the first $1 billion loss on Bear Stearns' assets with the Federal Reserve covering the remaining loss.

The Federal Reserve's quasi-bailout of Bear Stearns raised alarm across U.S. financial markets. Questions were being asked from one end of the country to the other: How sick was Wall Street? Who else would the Fed bail out—either indirectly like Bear Stearns or more directly?

Government Takeover of Fannie Mae and Freddie Mac

By the fall of 2008, the two mortgage market giants, Fannie Mae and Freddie Mac, were in deep financial trouble. Although both Fannie and Freddie had been created by the federal government, they were now publically traded corporations. Fannie Mae and Freddie Mac bought mortgages from lenders, repackaged some of these mortgages, and resold them to investors while holding on to other mortgages.

In order to finance this purchasing of mortgages, Fannie and Freddie issued their own bonds that were sold to a wide variety of investors around the world. Because Fannie and Freddie were both formerly part of the U.S. government, many in the financial markets believed that there was an implied government guarantee behind the bonds they issued. That is, people in financial markets believed that if Fannie and Freddie got into financial difficulty and could not repay their debt, the U.S. federal government would step in and make good on those promises to repay. With this "implicit" government guarantee, Fannie and Freddie could borrow money at a very low interest rate. They used these funds to buy mortgages, repackage them, and sell them for a price that resulted in very sizeable profits.

Although the vast majority of Fannie Mae and Freddie Mac mortgages were being repaid as planned, a small portion of them had fallen into default. What made this a significant problem is that both Fannie and Freddie held only a small amount of reserve cash in case of defaults. In other words, if the default rates on their mortgages increased even slightly, both entities would be near financial collapse.

In an attempt to reassure financial markets, Treasury Secretary Henry Paulson took the unusual step of holding a press conference on a Sunday. Standing on the front steps of the Treasury Building in Washington on July 13, Paulson proclaimed that the Treasury would stand behind both Fannie Mae and Freddie Mac.[9] This highly unusual press conference was held right before the financial markets in Asia opened and was designed

9 See "The Muddle-through Approach," *The Economist*, July 14, 2008.

to calm fears in Asia over the future of Fannie and Freddie. It was also less than a week after bank regulators had taken over the mortgage lender IndyMac Bancorp, which was the largest bank failure to date in American history. Thus, Secretary Paulson was trying to calm some pretty jittery nerves with his announcement.

Even the Treasury's backing was not enough. In fact, some economists argue[10] that the plan actually backfired. When it became clear that the federal government was taking a larger operational role and part ownership in Fannie and Freddie, no investors were willing to buy shares in Fannie and Freddie. The reason was straightforward: the bailout would essentially make the federal government the "senior" stockholder in both, meaning the government would be paid dividends before private shareholders and would have more say in running Fannie and Freddie than would private shareholders. Thus, investors basically refused to buy the shares of either Fannie or Freddie. The Treasury's plan to stand behind Fannie and Freddie was failing.

In addition, the financial markets simply did not have confidence in the financial viability of Fannie Mae and Freddie Mac. This was a major problem for the two mortgage market giants since they had issued $1.6 trillion of debt, the proceeds of which they had used to buy up mortgages. Without the confidence of financial markets, Fannie and Freddie would have a difficult time issuing new debt and thus could not continue to buy new mortgages. Unable to sell newly written mortgages to Fannie and Freddie, mortgage lenders would simply stop writing new mortgages. This would cause an already troubled housing market to spin even more out of control, and the ripple effects would be felt across the entire economy.

With the failure of the July 13 rescue plan, Secretary Paulson held yet another unprecedented Sunday news conference on September 7. This time, Paulson announced that the Treasury had placed both Fannie Mae and Freddie Mac into **conservatorship**. This basically meant that the Treasury Department, and by extension the U.S. federal government and U.S. taxpayers, were taking over Fannie and Freddie. This represented the largest involvement of the federal government in U.S. financial markets since the Great Depression of the 1930s, but it wouldn't be the last federal move. In fact, it would be the start of what news reports would call "10 days that reshaped U.S. finance."[11]

The Bailout of AIG

American International Group (AIG) is one of the world's largest insurance companies. In addition to offering traditional insurance products such as life insurance and automobile insurance, AIG was one of the biggest sellers of credit default swaps. Credit default swaps essentially provide insurance against the default of a financial asset that is tied to corporate debt or a mortgage-backed security. Since credit default swaps are a type of insurance, an insurance giant such as AIG would naturally sell them.

However, as the number of mortgages in default rose through 2007 and 2008, AIG had to pay out more on credit default swaps than it had anticipated. These huge unexpected

10 See http://freakonomics.blogs.nytimes.com/2008/09/18/diamond-and-kashyap-on-the-recent-financial-upheavals.

11 See http://online.wsj.com/article/SB122156561931242905.html.

payouts put a great deal of pressure on AIG, even though its other insurance businesses were doing fine. Things got so bad for AIG that on Monday, September 15, its credit rating was downgraded, which meant that AIG would have to come up with $14.5 billion in cash for collateral on its outstanding debt. While AIG had enough assets that it could sell to raise the $14.5 billion, it could not raise cash fast enough for the financial markets. After having been turned down by a wide variety of banks for an emergency short-term "bridge" loan, AIG turned to the U.S. government for help.

If AIG could not raise the collateral on its outstanding debt, the ripple effect through the U.S. financial markets would be severe. Many financial institutions around the world held debt issued by AIG; a collapse of the insurance giant would badly damage these financial institutions. To prevent such a financial meltdown, the Treasury Department and the Federal Reserve agreed to an $85 billion bailout for AIG. In return for this infusion of cash, the U.S. government would essentially take over the insurance giant. What made this government takeover of AIG even more unusual is that insurance companies such as AIG are not regulated by the federal government; instead, they are regulated by state governments. But the Treasury and the Federal Reserve decided AIG was "too big to fail." The government takeover of AIG represented the end of a 10-day period that saw major changes in U.S. financial markets. From September 6 to September 16, the following events occurred:

- The federal government seized control of Fannie Mae and Freddie Mac.

- Lehman Brothers, a 158-year-old major investment bank, filed for bankruptcy after the Treasury Department refused to help.

- Merrill Lynch, with 60,000 employees and on the verge of collapse, was purchased by Bank of America.

- The federal government took control of AIG.

The day after the AIG takeover—Wednesday, September 16, 2008—the U.S. stock market fell dramatically, with the Dow plummeting more than 446 points. This stock sell-off was due in part to an announcement by Washington Mutual, a major mortgage lender, that it had put itself up for sale due to staggering losses brought on by the troubled U.S. mortgage market. The two remaining investment banks, Goldman Sachs and Morgan Stanley, likewise appeared to be in significant financial trouble. Less than a week later, Goldman Sachs and Morgan Stanley announced that they would seek to become commercial banks and subject themselves to Federal Reserve oversight and regulation. With this move by Goldman Sachs and Morgan Stanley, the financial district in New York saw the end of the investment banking industry as an independent, stand-alone market on Wall Street. All of the major investment banks had failed, been merged into a commercial bank, or evolved into a commercial bank.

The $700 Billion Grasp for a Solution

With no investment banks left standing, Fannie Mae, Freddie Mac, and AIG under government control, banks unwilling to lend to one another, and mortgage default rates increasing, President Bush decided to deliver an address to the nation. On the evening of September 24, 2008, President Bush in a nationally televised speech tried to address the financial crisis by calling on Congress to swiftly pass a $700 billion bailout package for the U.S. financial markets. According to President Bush:

"Financial assets related to home mortgages have lost value during the house decline, and the banks holding these assets have restricted credit. As a result, our entire economy is in danger."

The initial $700 billion bailout bill included very few details on how or when the money would be spent. Under the original three-page plan drafted by the Treasury Department, Secretary Paulson would be given complete discretion over the funds. Paulson could use the money in any way he saw fit, and his use of the money could not be questioned by Congress, the administration, or any court. Thus, Paulson wanted complete control to give $700 billion to anyone he thought needed it in any manner he thought necessary.

Needless to say, many in Congress had serious reservations about the bailout package. To make things even more politically charged, Democrat Speaker of the House of Representatives Nancy Pelosi took to the House floor immediately before a vote on the bailout package and gave a very partisan speech. She blamed the entire financial crisis on Republicans:

"Seven hundred billion dollars, a staggering number, but only a part of the cost of the failed Bush economic policies to our country, policies that were built on budget recklessness. ... For too long this government in 8 years has followed a right-wing ideology ..."

Many Republican House members who planned to vote for the bailout bill on bipartisan terms were greatly put off by Pelosi's partisan speech. Without the Republican votes, the bill could not pass. Speaker Pelosi did little to nothing to calm the angered Republicans, and the bailout bill was rejected by a vote of 228 to 205. The stock market responded negatively to the inability of the politicians in Washington to pass a bailout bill: the Dow plunged 777 points, or 7 percent, in one day. A new bill was quickly introduced and passed by the Senate on October 1 and by the House on October 3. President Bush took the unusual step of signing the bill only two hours later. The $700 billion bailout, officially known as the Emergency Economic Stabilization Act of 2008, gave the Treasury secretary power to purchase any assets from any firm at any price. The $700 billion would be released in stages: $250 billion immediately upon passage, another $100 billion upon White House certification that the funds were necessary, and the remaining $350 billion when the Treasury secretary requested it from Congress.

With the passage of the bailout plan, the Treasury Department established **the Troubled Asset Relief Program (TARP)**, which would be administered through the newly created Office of Financial Stability. The initial purpose of TARP was to buy the difficult-to-price mortgage-backed securities that commercial banks and investment banks held. One of the hardest questions the Treasury Department faced was what price TARP should pay for the mortgage-backed assets it was about to buy from commercial banks and investment banks. This was, perhaps, the most complex finance question to be answered in over 50 years.

To answer this extremely important question, Secretary Paulson, the former CEO of investment bank Goldman Sachs, picked a 35-year-old former underling at Goldman Sachs named Neel Kashkari. In picking Kashkari to run TARP, Paulson passed over many more experienced financial experts such as former Federal Reserve Chairman Paul Volcker. Instead of seeking an experienced hand to run TARP, Paulson picked someone with only a few years of financial market experience.

Kashkari and TARP quickly found that pricing and buying the "troubled" mortgaged-backed securities was in fact very difficult to do. So instead, they decided to do something completely different: buy shares of the troubled financial institutions. In buying shares in these troubled institutions, a process called **recapitalization**, the Treasury hoped that commercial banks would start lending again. There was, of course, no guarantee that they would do so. When the government bought the shares of these banks, or recapitalized them, the banks had complete discretion over what they would do with these new funds. Instead of lending the new funds to customers, the banks could simply hold onto the new funds, pay dividends to their stockholders,[12] buy up other banks,[13] or even pay expenses including executive salaries.

Not surprisingly, a number of prominent economists raised questions about the effectiveness of the TARP program. University of Chicago economist Dr. Luigi Zingales wrote a brief article that circulated widely on the Internet, aptly named "Why Paulson Is Wrong."[14] Dr. Zingales argued that Paulson and the Treasury were going about the bailout with a failed approach. Fellow Chicago economists Anil Kashyap and Doug Diamond similarly raised troubling questions about the wisdom of the TARP.[15] Nobel Prize winner Joseph Stiglitz wrote an article very critical of the conflicts of interest in TARP and argued that the program only addressed some issues of the financial crisis.[16] Criticism of the TARP came from both liberal and conservative economists, and over 100 of them signed a letter of protest.[17]

Finally, on November 12, 2008, Secretary Paulson announced that the TARP would no longer be used to buy troubled assets from financial institutions. Instead, it will be used to offer financial assistance to banks and other firms that issue student, auto, and credit card loans.[18]

From Banks to Autos

As Paulson, Kashkari, and TARP struggled with how to best provide assistance to financial markets, the U.S. auto industry turned to the federal government for financial help. On November 18, the chief executives from the three major American automobile producers asked Congress for $25 billion in emergency loans. In testifying before Congress, Chrysler CEO Robert Nardelli, General Motors CEO Richard Wagoner, Jr.,

---

12 See Binyamin Applebaum, "Banks Continue to Continue Paying Dividends," *Washington Post*, October 30, 2008.

13 See Peter Whoriskey and Zachary A. Goldfarb, "Banks Weighing Other Uses for Bailout Money," *Washington Post*, October 28, 2008.

14 See http://faculty.chicagogsb.edu/luigi.zingales/Why_Paulson_is_wrong.pdf.

15 See http://freakonomics.blogs.nytimes.com/2008/09/18/diamond-and-kashyap-on-the-recent-financial-upheavals/.

16 See Joseph Stiglitz "Henry Paulson's Shell Game," *The Nation*, September 26, 2008.

17 See http://freakonomics.blogs.nytimes.com/2008/09/23/economists-on-the-bailout/.

18 See Peter Whoriskey, David Cho, and Binyamin Applebaum, "Treasury Redefines Its Rescue Program," *Washington Post*, November 12, 2008.

and Ford CEO Alan Mulally all claimed that due to the global financial crisis their companies needed emergency loans from the federal government or else they faced an almost immediate collapse.

A collapse of the U.S. auto industry could significantly impact the entire American economy. Ford, GM, and Chrysler, or The Big 3 as they are known, are the largest purchasers of U.S.-made steel, aluminum, iron, copper, plastics, rubber, and electronic computer chips. The Big 3 employ over 240,000 workers and have suppliers in every one of the 50 states. Thus, the executives argued, a collapse of the Big 3 automakers would dramatically affect the entire country in "days if not hours."

But members of Congress were skeptical about another taxpayer-funded bailout. Since the specific operation of TARP was so vague and had been so ineffective, many in Congress wanted to know, specifically, how the Big 3 would use the taxpayer money. The auto executives could not answer that question. They essentially had no specific plan on how they would use the $25 billion and could only give vague answers as to how they would split the money among the three.

Members of Congress were also upset when they learned that, shortly after receiving a government bailout, the executives at insurance giant AIG had spent $440,000 on a luxury retreat, essentially paid for by the American taxpayers. Likewise, when Congress heard that the executives of the automobile industry had flown to Washington each on their own private corporate jet to ask for taxpayer money, one member of Congress snorted:

"There's a delicious irony in seeing private luxury jets flying into D.C. and people coming off of them with tin cups in their hands … it's almost like seeing guys show up in the soup kitchen in high hat and tuxedo."

Not surprisingly, Congress voted down the auto industry bailout a few days later. Perhaps having learned their lesson, the auto executives returned to Washington two weeks later in automobiles they actually made and with a broad outline of how they would use the government funds.

The auto industry's new plea for help came after quarterly reports indicated the worst sales volume in over 25 years. The executives argued that if they did not get emergency funding within weeks, GM and Chrysler would face dire financial consequences.

PRESIDENT OBAMA'S ECONOMIC CHALLENGES

Upon being sworn in as the 44th president of the United States, Barack Obama will face some daunting economic challenges. Chief among these challenges is how he and his administration will deal with the current global financial crisis. As we have described, one of the main causes of this global downturn is the U.S. home mortgage market. The Obama Administration must find a way to stabilize the mortgage market and that, most likely, will require the stabilization of house prices.

In order to stabilize house prices, the new administration must find a way to deal with borrowers that can no longer afford to make their monthly mortgage payments. Some of these mortgage borrowers undoubtedly are caught up in circumstances beyond their control. Perhaps members of these families have lost their jobs as the economy has slowed. Others may have been duped into mortgages with low initial teaser rates that they did not understand. One could argue that the federal government should assist these types of borrowers.

Clearly, not all mortgage borrowers were innocent victims. Some borrowers sought to make "a quick buck" by purchasing a house and **flipping** the house or selling it at a much higher price in a few months. These borrowers were speculating on the mortgage market, and they lost that speculation. Offering government assistance to these types of borrowers would create what economists call a **moral hazard**.

A moral hazard exists when the creation of a financial contract alters behavior by changing incentives. If the government were to bail out real estate speculators, the government would be sending a clear signal to speculators: *go ahead, undertake risky behavior, because if your bets don't pay off, the government will be there to bail you out.* In such situations, a government bailout would be a type of financial contract that would negatively alter behavior in that it would encourage risky speculation.

Some speculation in markets is fine and even desirable. However, speculators need to suffer losses if they turn out to be wrong. If this is not done, it will encourage an excessive amount of speculation or risky behavior. Therefore, the Obama Administration has to be careful in crafting a program to stabilize house prices: it cannot and should not bail out all home buyers who cannot afford to make their mortgage payments. Arguably, the Obama Administration must find a way to delineate between those home buyers who were caught in a situation that was not of their own making and those that speculated on the housing market and perhaps should have known better.

In addition, the Obama Administration needs to find some way to get banks to start lending and increasing the flow of funds within financial markets. As described above, financial markets depend crucially on trust. If financial market participants do not trust one another, they will not lend to one another nor engage in any other type of financial transaction. The return of trust in financial markets, arguably, depends on transparency or openness. Financial markets need to be able to evaluate the riskiness of various borrowers and entities. As we have seen, the inability to correctly price mortgage-backed securities created major problems in the financial markets. Also, the lack of confidence or trust is what brought on bank runs and created the inability of long-standing firms to borrow money in financial markets.

The Obama Administration must decide what other steps will need to be taken to push the U.S. economy out of its current slowdown. Should the federal government do more to create jobs for the unemployed? As the unemployment rate increases to over 6 percent and the likelihood that firms will be able to borrow money to hire new workers remains slim, where will these unemployed people find work? Also, how will any increase in government spending be paid for? Given that the U.S. government budget deficit is already one of the largest in history, how will any new government programs be funded?

Finally, the Obama Administration will have to reconsider the extent of financial market regulation in the future. While our financial markets have changed dramatically over the past 50 years, the regulation of our markets, both domestically and internationally, has not kept pace. As new financial instruments such as mortgage-backed securities and markets that trade them are created, decisions must be made on who will regulate these markets and what form the regulations should take.

How his administration deals with these and other economic questions will have a significant impact on the success or failure of the Obama presidency. Updates on the current financial crisis and the economic challenges facing the Obama Administration can be found on the website www.cengage.com/gec that accompanies these booklets.

Discussion Questions

1. Assume that you have been appointed as an economic advisor to President Obama. What advice would you give him in terms of how to address the current financial crisis? What should he focus on first and why? Will he be able to get Congress and the American people to go along with what you suggest?

2. What steps could have been taken to prevent this crisis? How can similar crises be avoided in the future?

Key Terms

collateralized debt obligations (CDOs)
bank run
money markets
conservatorship
Troubled Asset Relief Program (TARP)
recapitalization
flipping
moral hazard